THE SEX OFFENDER
CORRECTIONS, TREATMENT
AND LEGAL PRACTICE

Edited by
Barbara K. Schwartz, Ph.D.
and
Henry R. Cellini, Ph.D.

CIVIC RESEARCH INSTITUTE, INC.
Kingston, New Jersey 08528

Printed in the United States of America

Library of Congress Cataloging in Publication Data
The sex offender: Corrections, treatment and legal
practice/Barbara K. Schwartz, Henry R. Cellini

ISBN 1-887554-00-9

Library of Congress Catalog Card Number 95-70893

Second Printing April 1996

Acknowledgments

The editors are grateful to many individuals who throughout the years have shared the journey in search of answers to the many issues surrounding the treatment of sex offenders. Our deepest gratitude goes to the authors of the individual chapters. Our thanks to the National Institute of Corrections and the National Academy of Corrections for sponsoring the initial work. Special thanks to John Moore who fought for the resources and commitment and continues to be a source of support. Thanks to the Safer Society, which has been there from the earliest days with research and resources, and especially to Fay Honey Knopp who has been supportive friend to many sex offender treatment specialists. Grateful acknowledgment to our publisher, Arthur Rosenfeld, and our editor, Marsha Leest. We also thank those who offered personal support, including the Justice Resource Institute of Boston, Greg Canfield, MSW, Susan Wayne, MSW, co-workers at the Massachusetts Treatment Center, and John Kilburn, office manager of the Training and Research Institute. Finally, we thank our families, including Ed, Ben, Betsy, cats and dogs.

Dedicated to Fay Honey Knopp

"Never doubt that a small group of thoughtful committed citizens can change the world; indeed, it's the the the only thing that ever has."—Margaret Mead

Publisher's Note: *The Sex Offender: Corrections, Treatment and Legal Practice* grew out of an earlier work prepared by the Editors for the U.S. Department of Justice in 1988, *A Practitioners' Guide to the Treatment of the Incarcerated Male Sex Offender*. The new work contains substantial additional and updated material. Entirely new are chapters 1, 2, 4, 5, 6, 7, 12, 16, 17, 18, 20, 23, and 30. Substantially revised and updated are chapters 3, 8, 14, 22, 24, 25, 26, 27, 28, and 29. The remaining chapters, 9, 10, 11, 13, 15, 19 and 21 are reprinted from the earlier work.

Preface

According to the ancient Greek myth, when Hercules was dying, he gave his arrows to the skilled archer, Philoctetes, who joined the Greeks against Troy. However, Philoctetes was accidentally wounded by one of the arrows. The wound became infected and began to fester. It gave off such an offensive odor that Philoctetes' shipmates left him behind on the island of Lemnos when they went to do battle in Troy. An oracle had prophesied that only Hercules' arrows could slay Paris, the Prince of Troy, and only Philoctetes had those arrows. The warriors were forced to return to Lemnos to get him. Indeed, as had been forecast, Paris was killed by one of his arrows.

Perhaps this myth teaches modern society that it should not abandon even those it deems the most offensive. Surely the Greek warriors felt justified in abandoning their comrade rather than taking the time and effort to treat him. After all, his condition was repugnant. But abandoning Philoctetes meant losing the war. The warriors could only triumph if they embraced their comrade regardless of his condition.

This book, which is the next step in a process that began in the early 1980s when the National Institute of Corrections first decided to develop a course in treating sex offenders, points out ways we might be able to reclaim some of those that our society might choose to abandon simply because they are viewed as too horrible to live among us. Inevitably, a society that creates a class that "deserves" to be abandoned begins to scorn anyone who is affiliated with that class. The class begins to grow. Then, other groups begin affiliating their particular enemies with this group. The despised class grows even larger. This phenomenon can be seen clearly in anti-gay legislation that has sought to link gays and lesbians with sadists and child molesters. Such a linkage is ludicrous. Ultimately, the quality of our society may well be judged on its treatment of our outcasts.

Recently, the field of sex offender treatment has advanced at a phenomenal rate. This book updates the available material and presents a new treatment model. Initially, sex offender treatment programs relied heavily on the cognitive-behavioral approach. The new model emphasizes an integrative approach that treats sexual deviance from a holistic paradigm. The techniques are not merely added onto each other. Instead, they are integrated together to form a program that focuses on all facets of the problem, from the offender's inner functioning to the different aspects of the criminal justice system.

This volume is intended for therapists, prison and community corrections administrators, probation and parole officers, correctional officers, child protective workers, police, prosecutors, defense attorneys, prison chaplains, and sex offenders who are in treatment and their friends and families. These members of the system all must cooperate in order to address the tragic problem of sexual abuse in this country. We can only combat this problem through education and a coordinated effort.

About the Authors

John Bergman, M.A., R.D.T.

Mr. Bergman received his early education in London. He received his master of arts in theater from Humboldt State College. He was an adjunct member of the faculty at the University of Iowa. Mr. Bergman is the founder of Geese Theater. His work in producing plays for prisoners led to the development of a specialized treatment for sex offenders. He is the director of the British touring company and is affiliated with the Vermont Department of Corrections and the Justice Resource Institute's program at the Massachusetts Treatment Center. He is a registered drama therapist and has consulted internationally on the use of drama therapy with sex offenders and correctional ethics.

Henry R. Cellini, Ph.D.

Dr. Cellini received his degrees in psychology with an emphasis on counseling from Southern Illinois University. He has served on the faculty of the University of New Mexico, Department of Counselor Education and Department of Continuing Education. He has been the director of Mental Health Services at the Penitentiary of New Mexico and chief psychologist for the New Mexico Department of Corrections. He has worked with female offenders at Dwight Correctional Center, Dwight, Illinois. While on loan to the National Academy of Corrections, he developed the first courses on the treatment of sex offenders. Currently he is the president of TriCorp, a consulting firm that provides training and publications on drugs, gangs, violence, and sex assault throughout the country. His publications include *Alcohol, Tobacco and Other Drugs of Abuse* and a chapter in the American Correctional Association's *Managing Delinquency Programs that Work*.

Fred Cohen, D.J.P.

Mr. Cohen received his undergraduate degree at Temple University and his law degree from the Yale Law School. He has been a professor of law at the University of Texas, New York University, University of Iowa, University of Arizona, and University of Puerto Rico. He is currently a professor at the School of Criminal Justice at the State University of New York in Albany. He is the editor-in-chief of the *Criminal Law Bulletin*, and co-editor of the *Correctional Law Report* and the *Community Corrections Report*. He lectures frequently at the National Academy of Corrections on laws related to sex offenders.

Georgia F. Cummings, B.S.

Ms. Cummings received her Bachelor of Science in Criminology and Corrections from Florida State University. She began her career as a probation and parole officer in Vermont. She has been affiliated with the Vermont Sex

Offender Treatment Program since its inception. Currently, she is the Coordinator of Sex Offender Treatment Services for the Vermont Center for Prevention and Treatment of Sexual Abuse. She consults nationally with the National Institute of Corrections and the American Probation and Parole Association.

Michael Dougher, Ph.D.

Dr. Dougher received his degrees from the University of Illinois at Chicago. He founded and directed one of the first behaviorally-based, outpatient treatment programs for sex offenders sponsored by the University of New Mexico, where is he chairman of the psychology department. He has been a consultant on behavioral treatment to the New Mexico Department of Corrections Sex Offender Treatment Program and has served on the faculty of the National Academy of Corrections.

Randy Green, Ph.D.

Dr. Green received degrees from Miami University of Ohio and from the Western Conservative Baptist Seminary in Portland, Ohio. He is the former director of the Sex Offender Program in the Forensic Services Unit at the Oregon State Hospital. He has taught classes in the treatment of sex offenders at the National Academy of Corrections. He is currently affiliated with the Mid-Valley Center for Clinical and Consulting Services Corporation in Salem, Oregon.

William B. Land, M.D.

Dr. Land received his B.A. from Brown University and his M.D. from Northwestern University Medical School. He completed his residency in psychiatry at Massachusetts Mental Health Center and was chief resident in psychopharmocology. In 1992 he received the Gaughan Fellowship for study in forensic psychiatry. Dr. Land is a diplomat on the American Board of Psychiatry and Neurology. He is currently a clinical instructor in psychiatry at Harvard Medical School, a psychopharmacology consultant at Bridgewater State Hospital and Noddles Island Health Center, consulting psychiatrist for the Massachusetts Treatment Program and the Massachusetts Rehabilitation Commission, and supervisor for the Department of psychiatry at Beth Israel Hospital. Dr. Land has written and lectured widely on a variety of topics and his article in this volume received an honorable mention in the American Academy of Forensic Sciences' Competition for Forensic Psychiatry Fellows.

D. R. Laws, Ph.D.

Dr. Laws received degrees from the University of Missouri and Southern Illinois University. He is the former director of the Sex Behavior Laboratory at the Atascadero State Hospital in California . He was professor of crime and delinquency at the Florida Mental Health Institute at the University of Southern Florida and the director for the Center for the Prevention of Child Molestation in Tampa, Florida. He is currently affiliated with the Interpersonal and Family Skills Program in Edmonton, Alberta.

William D. Pithers, Ph.D.

Dr. Pithers received degrees from Edinboro State University and Kent State University. He founded and directs the sex offender treatment program for the Vermont Department of Corrections and is the director of the Vermont Center for the Prevention and Treatment of Sexual Assault. He is widely known for his work in adapting the Relapse Prevention model for use with sex offenders, and lectures, writes, trains, and consults internationally.

Stephen Price, B.A.

Mr. Price received his B.A. from Oglethorpe University in Atlanta, Ga. in liberal arts. He has worked with offenders and victims of sexual assault as a pastor /clinical chaplain and therapist. He interned as a pastoral counselor at Worchester Pastoral Counseling Center. He worked with sex offenders and mentally ill offenders in the South Carolina Department of Corrections. He has treated sex offenders at the Massachusetts Treatment Center and is currently a therapist with the Massachusetts Department of Corrections Sex Offender Treatment Program.

Barbara K. Schwartz, Ph.D.

Dr. Schwartz received her M.A. in psychology from the New School for Social Research in New York City. She received her Ph.D. in psychology/criminology from the University of New Mexico. She has been treating sex offenders since 1971, when she assisted in establishing one of the first community-based sex offender treatment programs in the United States (P.A.S.O. in Albuquerque, New Mexico). She founded and administered the New Mexico Department of Corrections' Sex Offender Treatment Program and the Washington Department of Corrections Sex Offender Treatment Program. Currently she is the clinical director for Sex Offender Treatment for Justice Resource Institute, Boston, Massachusetts, and in that capacity she directs treatment services for the Massachusetts Treatment Center for Sexually Dangerous Persons and the Massachusetts Department of Corrections Sex Offender Treatment Program. She is a consultant to the National Institute of Corrections and has consulted on program establishment and evaluation for Corrections Departments in Wisconsin, Arizona, Hawaii, Illinois, Indiana, Texas, New York, and Washington, D.C. She is an instructor for the National Academy of Corrections. Dr. Schwartz is the editor of *A Practitioner's Guide for Treating the Incarcerated Male Sex Offender* and has authored numerous articles, and conference presentations.

Roger Smith, D.Crim.

Dr. Smith received his undergraduate degree from Grinnell College, his master's degree from the University of Chicago and his doctorate in criminology from the University of California at Berkeley. He was active in the establishment of drug rehabilitation programs in the San Franciscan area before becoming the director of Correctional Programs at the Oregon State Hospital. Among the programs he directed in that position was the Sex Offender Treatment Program which was a model program in the field. For two years he was on loan to the National Academy of Corrections. He went on to become the director of sex offender treatment for the Hawaii Department of Corrections. Currently he is the Director of Forensic Mental Health Services for the State of Michigan. He consults internationally in the area of drug rehabilitation, sex offender treatment, and mental health services in corrections.

Nancy Steele, Ph. D.

Dr. Steele received her B.A., M.A., and Ph.D. from the University of Ohio. She founded and directed the sex offender treatment programs at several Colorado Department of Corrections facilities. She then became the director of the Transitional Sex Offender Program (TSOP) at Lino Lakes Correctional Center in Minnesota. This was one of the first prison-based sex offender programs focusing on the therapeutic community format and offering community aftercare. In 1993 she affiliated with the Medical/Legal Foundation in Indianapolis, Indiana and consulted with the Indiana Department of Corrections on sex offender treatment. She is currently with the Ohio Department of Corrections. She is a consultant with the National Institute of Corrections and an instructor for the National Academy of Corrections and has written, trained, and consulted throughout the country.

Introduction

During the past 30 years, the issue of sexual assault has been the focus of public attention. Movies, television specials, talk shows, and books have brought the problem out into the open. Citizens live with facts such as these: one in four girls will be assaulted before they are 18 years of age; one in six boys will be victimized; and patterned child molesters frequently have tragically high numbers of victims (perhaps several hundred).

Historically, society has responded by imposing restrictions on potential victims. The Israeli Parliament, for example, suggested addressing the increasing incidence of rape by enforcing a curfew on women. Golda Meier, then a member of Parliament, suggested that surely the curfew should be imposed on men rather than women. Other responses, advocated by groups such as Society's League Against Molesters or Washington's Tennis Shoe Brigade, include long prison sentences as retribution and as a deterrent.

Experts in this field suggest that most sexual offenders were molested during their childhood. Such offenders often exhibit a unique phenomenon known as the "Dracula Syndrome" in which the victim becomes the assailant. Thus, this syndrome causes the crime rate to grow exponentially. Given the large number of victims, the growth rate of this crime can be staggering if even a small percentage of the victims later become offenders. Indeed, the increase in the number of incarcerated sex offenders presents a major problem for corrections officials.

Response to Increase in Reported Crimes Includes Longer Incarceration and More Community Based Treatment Programs

On April 14, 1990, *The New York Times* reported that sex offenders represented 15% of the prison population. According to the July 1991 issue of Corrections Compendium, there was a 48% increase in sex offenders in U.S. prisons between 1988 to 1990. All other crimes increased by 20% increase over the same period. In Wyoming, sex offenders made up over one-third of the prison population. In 10 other states, they made up more than 20%. The increased rate is due to a variety of factors, including:

• More crimes are being reported because:

— Public attention has increased.

— Victims' rights groups have helped change the way members of the criminal justice system treat victims, and made it likelier that victims will report crimes.

— Teachers and youth workers are more aware of the possibility of sexual abuse. In many states, they are mandated by law to report suspicious circumstances.

- Many courts are handing out stiffer sentences.

- Parole boards are becoming more reluctant to release sex offenders if they have the discretion to hold them longer.

- In many states, offenders who refuse treatment serve longer sentences. Treatment while incarcerated may be mandatory prior to parole.

A number of strategies have developed in response to the problem of sexual assault. Along with longer sentences for the most serious offenders, there has been a virtual explosion of techniques for maintaining less serious offenders in the community. Today, programs ranging from mandatory counseling to electronic monitoring to involuntary commitment are in operation. There also has been a trend to close large institutional sex offender programs operated under mental health agencies. Responsibility for such programs is being shifted to corrections. At the same time, sex offender treatment programs in Departments of Corrections must fight long and hard, first to be established and then to continue intact.

Neither the public nor the media seem to want to scientifically ascertain whether therapy is effective. Instead, they prefer to debate a very different issue: whether sex offenders even deserve treatment. Apparently, they have decided that certain populations deserve treatment and others do not. The main criteria appears to be whether the individual had control over his or her condition. The more an individual is viewed as being responsible for his or her problems, the less deserving of help that person seems to be. Thus, those who have no control over their condition—for example, victims of natural disasters, children, etc.—merit treatment; individuals whose behavior was illegal or immoral are less worthy of help.

AIDS patients offer a classic example of how this philosophy works. The government's slow response to this serious health crisis coupled with the limited availability of funding probably reflects the initial perception of victims of this illness: they caused it themselves through their "morally unacceptable" behavior. Probably on the advice of public relations specialists, agencies seeking to promote AIDS education or raise funds for treatment use "innocent" victims—children, hemophiliacs, and women infected without their knowledge by a partner—to champion their cause.

Earlier in this century, victims of paralyzing illness faced the same kind of prejudice. They were considered responsible for their conditions and unworthy of sympathy. In FDR's *Splendid Deception*, Gallagher describes how revolutionary the atmosphere at his treatment center at Warm Springs, Georgia was. Previously, in a real although subconsciously motivated sense, the handicapped were viewed as flawed in moral character as well as in body. The physical handicap was as it were, "an outward sign of some inner weakness." R.C. Elmslie, a medical authority at the turn of the century, referred to crippled children as "individual(s) detestable in character, a menace and burden to the community, who is only too apt to graduate into the mendicant and criminal classes."

Treatment of Sex Offenders Should Focus on Alleviating the Problem Rather Than Whether Offenders "Deserve" Treatment

The focus should not be on whether sex offenders deserve treatment. Instead, it should be on reducing the cost, the recidivism rate, and the toll of human suffering caused by the problem.

The treatment of sex deviance is no more a perfect science than the treatment of any other complex physical or mental disorder. Furthermore, as a discipline, it is much younger than many other areas of therapeutic concern. Still, there is hope from a wide variety of sources that treatment can be effective. In fact, the availability of treatment programs may reduce recidivism as well as encourage reporting of these crimes. This is particularly true for intra-familial offenses. Families seem to be more willing to report an offense, victims to testify, and defendants to confess if treatment is a possibility. Conviction rates have risen in states that have comprehensive sex offender treatment programs in both the community and in prisons. In these states, judges do not have to weigh possible dangerousness against pleas for treatment. Furthermore, community treatment for low-risk offenders can save millions of tax-payers' dollars and yield more positive result than incarceration without treatment.

Background of the "Nothing Works" Philosophy

During the late 1970s and early 1980s, "rehabilitation" programs in corrections departments across the country were dramatically curtailed when R. Martinson published the two articles that became the foundation for the "nothing works" philosophy. Another article that is often quoted in this regard is a report entitled *Psychiatry and Sex Psychopath Legislation: The 1930s to the 1980s*, prepared by the Group for the Advancement of Psychiatry. This report addressed the problems inherent in assuming that sex offenders are mentally ill and attempting treatment in mental hospitals that usually did not offer specialized programs. Nevertheless, many people interpret this article as concluding that sex offenders cannot be treated.

These articles caused state legislators to begin shifting from indeterminate sentencing with parole based on program participation to a "just deserts" model requiring felons to serve set sentences regardless of whether they participate in rehabilitative efforts. Unfortunately, the movement to dismantle vocational, educational, and treatment programs for offenders continued despite the fact that Martinson later recanted his own research. All-or-nothing thinking, such as that reflected in the "nothing works" philosophy is self-indulgent. It gives the impression that there are simple answers to complex problems.

Few correctional professionals, politicians, or other policy-makers are aware of the impact of the nothing works theory. Even today, Martinson's articles are used to deny funding to criminal rehabilitation programs; research that corroborates the effectiveness of treatment is ignored.

In 1989, the *Psychological Bulletin* published an article by Furby, Weinrott, and Blackshaw, who did a mega-analysis on 42 studies evaluating treatment offered as far back as the mid-50s (only 26% of the articles dated from 1980 or more recently) and comparing outcomes to studies of untreated sex offenders (98% of the studies of untreated offenders were done in Europe). Although the authors acknowledged that there were numerous severe research errors, they nevertheless concluded that there was no evidence that treatment had been effective.

Critics have pointed out that this study may have reached a negative conclusion for two reasons: (1) the high recidivism rate for institutionally-based treatment programs may be due to the fact that these programs often attract the most at-risk offenders; and (2) the outcome rates may vary so dramatically because the study does not distinguish between different types of treatment. The identical problems were present in a study conducted in 1991 by the *Minneapolis Star-Tribune*.

Every treatment program—be it for substance abuse or appendicitis—has its failures. Still, citing the case of some nortorious re-offender who had undergone treatment at some time in the past is a popular way of discrediting sex offender treatment. Evoking the terrifying image of the serial rapist or the lust murderer is enough to radically sway public opinion. How many votes did Michael Dukakis lose because Willie Horton was furloughed during his term? Robert P. Casey, the former governor of Pennsylvania, found himself in a similar situation because his appointees paroled Reginald McFadden, a suspected serial killer. These stories always carry a subtle implication that the treatment program is partially to blame for the re-offense. It would be interesting to see what would happen to cancer treatment if oncologists were held to the same standards as sex offender treaters and blamed for every patient that succumbed to their disease.

Treatment Should Be Part of All Sex Abuse Prevention Programs

Numerous studies attest to the efficacy of sex offender treatment. However, as with all studies on psychotherapy, the research may show some methodological problems. Consider these examples: sex offender programs rarely occur in settings conducive to tightly controlled research; sponsoring agencies may be reluctant to deny treatment to amenable volunteers in order to maintain a control group; some offenders are systematically denied treatment because it is assumed that their offense record would be higher than the treated group; and the level of motivation or disclosure may vary radically between the two groups depending on such factors as a state's sentence structure or "good time" policy.

Administrative concerns may override therapeutic ones. Nevertheless, the success which individuals have experienced in treating sex offenders and which the criminal justice system has witnessed has led to the development of over 1,500 specialized programs for this population. Victims and potential victims deserve to have energy and resources committed to this problem. Treatment as a primary form of prevention should be part of any comprehensive plan to decrease sexual abuse. The reluctance to acknowledge this on the part of many, particularly certain representatives of the media, may have more to do with primitive human desires for revenge than a desire to do something constructive about the problem of sexual assault.

Few issues arouse more public disgust and outrage than this one, which combines society's anxiety over and fascination with sex and violence. Society can no more afford to ignore the problem of sexual assault than it can afford to dump raw sewage into its waterways. In both cases, the problem may no longer be in the community, but it will come back in one form or another.

Table of Contents

Chapter 2: Theories of Sex Offenses

Chapter 3: Characteristics and Typologies of Sex Offenders

Chapter 5: Female Sex Offenders

Chapter 6: Assessment and Treatment of the Adolescent Sexual Offender

PART 2: IMPLEMENTATION AND ADMINISTRATION OF PROGRAMS

Chapter 7: Sex Offender Program Planning and Implementation

PART 3: TREATMENT

Chapter 10: Comprehensive Treatment Planning for Sex Offenders

Chapter 11: Clinical Assessment of Sex Offenders

Chapter 12: Phallometric Assessment

Chapter 13: Psycho-Educational Modules

Chapter 14: Group Therapy

Chapter 15: Behavioral Techniques to Alter Sexual Arousal

Chapter 16: Enhancing Positive Spirituality, Sex Offenders, and Pastoral Care

Chapter 17: Life, the Life Event, and Theater—A Personal Narrative on the Use of Drama Therapy with Sex Offenders

Chapter 18: Psychopharmacological Options for Sex Offenders

PART 4: AFTERCARE

Chapter 19: Aftercare Treatment Programs

Chapter 20: Relapse Prevention: A Method for Enhancing Behavioral Self-Management and External Supervision of the Sexual Aggressor

Chapter 21: Community Management of Sex Offenders

PART 5: LEGAL ISSUES IN THE TREATMENT
OF SEX OFFENDERS

Chapter 22: Introduction to Legal Issues: How the Legal Framework Developed

Chapter 23: Washington's Sexually Violent Predator Act

Chapter 24: Right to Treatment

Chapter 25: Treatment Modalities and Consent

Chapter 26: Confidentiality, Privilege, and Self-Incrimination

Chapter 27: Liability and Negligent Release

Chapter 28: Duty to Protect

Chapter 29: Therapeutic Uses of Sexually Explicit Material and the Plethysmograph

Chapter 30: Registration and Scarlet Letter Conditions

Appendix

Part 1

Psychodynamics of Sex Offenders

The study of sex offenders and their treatment began after the mutilated bodies of a number of brutally murdered prostitutes were discovered in the Whitechapel District of London in 1888. The crimes, which have never been solved, obviously were committed by a sexual deviant. Interest was stirred in the psychological dynamics behind such acts. In the years that followed, a number of articles were written by physicians such as Kraft-Ebing. Thus began the study of sex offenders and their treatment.

Often, landmarks in sex offender treatment are preceded by brutal sex crimes. In the 1930s, for example, a senile man named Fish kidnapped a six-year-old girl on her birthday and subsequently killed, dismembered, cooked, and ate her. The public outrage over this act fueled support for Sexual Psychopath Laws. In the 1970s, Ted Frank, a newly released patient from California's Atascadero State Hospital's Sex Offender Treatment Program, kidnapped, tortured, raped, and murdered a two-year-old girl. California residents banded together to force the closing of the treatment program.

Historically, sex offenders were treated—or not treated—much the same way as mentally disabled persons were treated. The Mentally Disordered Sex Offender Laws were the direct outgrowth of Defective Delinquent Laws, and both reflected the belief that certain people committed crimes because they had some type of inherent deficit. While such persons should not be imprisoned, they should be institutionalized, perhaps for life. In most states, sex offenders were hospitalized along with the chronically mentally ill. Until mental health professionals began to develop therapeutic techniques in the 1950s and 1960s, both groups were confined with little effective treatment. Eventually, Florida, California, Wisconsin, New Jersey, and Washington, among others, began to institute specialized sex offender programs.

The late 1960s and early 1970s saw the beginning of the deinstitutionalization movement, which emphasized treating the mentally ill in community mental health centers, preferably on an outpatient basis. At about the same time, Philadelphia's Joseph Peters Institute began one of the first outpatient groups for sex offenders, and comprehensive programs such as Albuquerque's Positive Approaches to Sex Offenders (PASO) were developed. Many states began treatment programs for incestuous families.

The 1980s witnessed changes in several areas, including greater rates of reporting and more offenders being charged. In a number of states, judges began sentencing these individuals to prison rather than to hospital-based programs. The Washington State Legislature passed legislation transferring the sex offender treatment programs from Eastern and Western Washington State Hospitals to the Department of Corrections. A number of other states have followed suit.

Beginning in the mid-1980s, the National Institute of Corrections began providing major support for prison-based sex offender treatment through training and technical assistance grants to corrections departments throughout the country. The Association for the Behavioral Treatment of Sexual Abusers (later to become the Association for the Treatment of Sexual Abusers) emerged as a national organization for sex offender treatment providers around the world.

Now, in the 1990s, there are even more changes. States have continued to implement treatment programs and community programs have multiplied. Washington became the first state to (1) recognize sex offender treatment as a unique mental health profession and (2) certify sex offender treatment providers. In addition, that state's legislature, in a highly controversial move, revived the almost completely defunct concept of sexual psychopathy. As so often happens, this legislation was fueled by series of sensational sex crimes.

Recent studies, in the areas of sex offender and drug treatment, have contradicted the "nothing works" philosophy that deflated so many correctional treatment programs. Hopefully, the next stage in sex offender treatment will be the development of comprehensive treatment programs based on well-documented and carefully researched interventions and new developments will be logical outgrowths of further knowledge rather than emotional reactions to sensational crimes.

Chapter 1

Introduction to the Integrative Approach

by Barbara K. Schwartz, Ph.D.

Overview

The twentieth century discoveries that have revolutionized the way the universe is conceptualized impact on every field of human endeavor, including the treatment of sex offenders. This chapter discusses how the evolution of theories of sex offender treatment reflect the new paradigm emerging in the realm of the physical sciences, particularly physics.

Integrative Model Appreciates the Dynamic Nature of Human Behavior

During the past several years, four theories were published indicating a movement away from the single factor model (e.g., Relapse Prevention, conditioning, trauma) to a more integrated approach (Barbaree and Marshall, 1990; Prentky, 1993; Masters and Schwartz, 1993; Malamoth, Heavey, and Linz, 1993). These models stress slightly different components, but they all suggest that sexual deviancy is a multifaceted phenomenon that must be treated using a multimodal approach. Thus, the field seems to be moving away from simple cause-and-effect explanations to an appreciation of the dynamic nature of human behavior. Pithers (1993), a pioneer in the adaptation of the Relapse Prevention model from the substance abuse field for use with sex offenders, stated that:

> At this time, existing treatment approaches do not apply equally to all sex offenders, appearing less effective with rapists than pedophiles.... Because rape is a multiply determined act, a credible treatment design must be able to address issues such as personal victimization, cognitive distortions, behavioral treatment to alternate excessive arousal to sexually abusive fantasies, victim empathy, emotional recognitive and modulation, and attributional processes (p. 181).

Approaches to Modifying Therapeutic Models

The "Eclectic" Method. There are several approaches to modifying a therapeutic model. According to the "eclectic" method, if one treatment did not work, another is tried. Early critics of this approach argued that it represented a hodgepodge of methods tossed together without theoretical rationale. Strict adherents to various schools of psychology (e.g., Freudian, behavioral, etc.) were especially prone to ridiculing this approach. Still, therapists who did not follow single-factor models may have sensed the inherent inadequacy in traditional approaches to treatment. Not all human problems can be neatly explained or treated using a single approach. However, no available model responded to the wide diversity they saw in their everyday clinical practices.

The Additive Method. Another approach to expanding the treatment repertoire was an additive one. If a strict behavioral approach proved inadequate, add cognitive techniques: behavioral techniques + cognitive techniques = cognitive-behavioral techniques.

The initial edition of this work, *A Practitioners Guide to Treating the Incarcerated Male Sex Offender* (Schwartz, 1988), presented a multi-modal approach to the treatment of sexual deviance. Group therapy by itself had proven to be inadequate, but behavioral techniques were showing some efficacy so they were added to the therapeutic repertoire. Sex offenders also had problems with social interactions, anger management, and handling stress. Consequently, psycho-educational classes were added. Offenders also needed techniques to handle high risk situations, so Relapse Prevention also was included.

As long as cognitive-behavioral techniques were added, the modal remained consistent. However, what if one wished to add trauma work, techniques from the addiction model or dysfunctional family issues? Could these be added without violating the model's cognitive-behavioral orientation?

The Integrative Model. The integrative models that are advocated in this work are emerging from a radically different mind set. This new way of thinking is subtly influencing modern thought, from physics to religion to art. It involves a shifting of the world view from static to dynamic and from additive to integrative. To understand the emerging treatment model for sex offenders, it is necessary to understand the basic paradigm shift it reflects.

The New Paradigm in Natural Science: Relationship Between Classical Physics and Psychology

Psychology has always prided itself on being the most "scientific" of the social sciences, partially because it is modeled after physics, which arguably is the most scientific of all the sciences. Physics has been based on objective, quantifiable, predictable, and controllable occurrences. Psychologists have attempted to study human behavior in a way that is objective, quantifiable, predictable, and controllable.

Classical physics is based on certain assumptions, such as: (1) the universe exists in three-dimensional space; (2) time moves from the past to the present to the future; (3) the elements the world is composed of are made up of small, solid, indestructible particles; (4) forces and objects interact in understandable and predictable mechanical ways; (5) fundamental principles can be reduced to quantitative relationships; and (6) objective scientific observation is possible because there is a rigid distinction between mind and matter. Essentially, this view reduces the world to a series of independent building blocks that function together as a single unit. If any of the building blocks breaks, the unit cannot function properly until it is fixed. Psychologists have attempted to follow this model by studying and measuring human behavior in an objective, quantifiable, predictable, and controllable way. But what type of psychology arises from this model?

The search for clear-cut cause-and-effect relationships that can be objectively observed, measured, and understood is basic to all psychology. The early Structuralists believed they could objectively study their own minds and could analyze consciousness into its basic elements (Capra, 1982). Early behaviorists believed all human conduct could be understood, predicted, and controlled by manipulating the interaction between stimulus and response. Psychoanalysts adopted a mechanistic view. They held that maladaptive behavior results from cumulative early traumas that can be repaired by systematically evaluating the traumas and releasing the energy trapped in the experiences. These therapists functioned almost like engineers, analyzing and relieving the pressure on the system.

Over the past century, however, scientific breakthroughs created a new paradigm that began to change the way the world is perceived. Faraday, Clark, and Maxwell discovered electromagnetic fields that were not made up of little particles and could be studied without reference to any material bodies. Einstein discovered that observers who move at different velocities order events differently, depending on their own rate of motion. This meant that temporal sequence and spatial specifics (time and space) were determined by the observer and were constructs of the human mind (Capra, 1976). The discovery that light can be either a particle or a wave pointed out the incredible power of the observer to shape "reality." According to Briggs and Peat (1984):

> Two separate developments—that of relativity theory and atomic physics—shattered all the principle concepts of the Newtonian world view: the notion of absolute space and time, the elementary solid particles, the strictly casual nature of physical phenomenon and the idea of an objective description of reality. (Capra, 1976, p. 50)

According to physicist Geoffrey Chew's "bootstrap" approach to physics, the universe is a dynamic web of interrelated events. No properties of the web are more fundamental than any other. The structure of the web is determined by the overall consistency and meaning of each of the threads. Furthermore, "all natural phenomenon are ultimately interconnected and in order to explain any one of them, we need to understand all of them" (Capra, 1976, p. 277). A "bootstrapper" is someone who rejects the notion that events (including human behavior) can only be explained by one "true" theory. Since Chew's theory holds that all laws of the Universe are properties of the human mind, approximate and partial theories must be used to create a working picture of the world.

The great physicist, Neils Bohr, developed the concept of "complementarity" which meant that:

> The universe can never be described in a single, clear picture but must be apprehended through overlapping, complimentary and sometimes paradoxical views. (Briggs and Peat, 1984, p. 53)

This again reinforces the concept that the universe is comprised of complex, dynamic interrelationships that are constantly changing and shifting. It is not like a machine but much more like the Hindu concept of the universe—the dance of Shiva.

New Paradigm Calls for Researchers to Accept the Concept of Mutual Interactions and Adopt an Integrative Approach

According to many scientists, philosophers, theologians, and social scientists, society's view of the world is moving from one that stresses dualistic thinking (e.g., right and wrong, black and white, true and false), clear cause-and-effect reasoning, a mind-body split, and a mechanistic model to a dynamic, holistic, interrelated model that incorporates the physical sciences, religion, healing approaches, and so on. In effect, the old notion of a world constructed out of an infinite number of tiny building blocks is being replaced with a vision of the Universe as a void held together with dynamic interrelationships. After all, atoms are so small that if they were blown up to the size of St. Peter's Basilica, their electrons and neutrons would be the size of dust specks. If an orange was inflated to the size of the Earth, its atoms would be the size of cherries. Capra states:

> Because of the relativistic nature of subatomic particles, we cannot under-stand their propensities without understanding their mutual interactions and because of the basic interconnectedness of the subatomic world, we shall not understand any one particle without understanding the others (1976, p. 190).

The observer plays a critical role in that understanding because the values that person uses shape "reality" and illustrates the futility searching for the "right" answer. Heidenberg's Uncertainty Principle states that one can never know both the speed at which an object is traveling and the energy it is expending because these factors can-not be measured simultaneously. Studying one aspect only gives part of the answer. Similarly, it is rarely possible to study all aspects of a "real life" problem at the same time, and researchers of all types must acknowledge that their view—their answers—are only part of a vast, complex whole.

Feedback Ensures the Balance that Is Essential to Growth. Systems thinking is needed to understand the universe and all of its parts—from the atom to the molecule to the tissue to the organ to the individual to the family to the community to the soci-ety to the world to the universe. Taking a systems view means recognizing that all systems are dynamic and their activity involves interaction between multiple compo-nents. Functioning systems are flexible and elastic, responding adaptively to internal and external demands. Changes in systems are based on feedback that allows the sys-tem to be self-renewing and self-transcending. Living systems respond to a variety of demands from all of its levels by creating new structures and patterns of behavior. Feedback insures the balance that is the essence of life and growth.

The issue of balance has always been a core concept of Eastern religions. For example, Buddhists believe the world is a dynamic balance between Yin and Yang as described in Figure 1.1:

Figure 1.1
Dynamic Balance Between Yin and Yang (Capra, 1982, p, 38)

Yin	Yang
Feminine	Masculine
Contractive	Expansive
Conservative	Demanding
Responsive	Aggressive
Cooperative	Competitive
Intuitive	Rational
Synthesizing	Analytic

These characteristics, opposite but complementary, operate in all levels of systems from the individual to the society.

Integrative Thinking Impacts on Everyday Life. The new paradigm is having a subtle and profound impact on a wide variety of systems that affect everyday life. Here are some examples: Matthew Fox's Creation Spirituality seeks to transform Western religious tradition in terms of the new paradigm. Business and governmental agencies are turning to the teachings of Deming's Total Quality Management, which focuses on the dynamic interconnections between organizations with an emphases on creative responses to feedback. A struggling political movement based on the German Green Party is attempting to bring new paradigm thinking to economic and political structures. The ecology movement is focusing public awareness on the connection between humans and all aspects of their environment. Every time a family separates an aluminum can from the rest of the trash, they are wittingly or unwittingly operating on new paradigm thinking.

New paradigm thinking is apparent in the current interest in holistic approaches in the health field, where multi-disciplinary teams focus on all the various forces at work in an individual who has a serious disease. Traditional medicine concentrates exclusively on the diseased organ. One may temporarily "fix" a broken part, but the balance will not be reconnected unless the entire network of systems is considered.

Psychotherapy and the New Paradigm

Psychotherapists are also involved in a shift to the new paradigm. There is increasing interest in shamonic healing practices as well as Eastern traditions. Relating new physics to Eastern thought and its relation to psychotherapy, Atwood and Martin (1991), state that:

> The universe is seen as a dynamic web of interrelated events, all following from the properties of other parts. The overall consistency their mutual interrelations determines the structure of the entire web. It is evident that this idea is very much in the spirit of Eastern thought. The requirement of self-consistency that forms the basis of the new physics and the unity and interrelation of all phenomena, so strongly emphasized in Eastern mysticism, are just different aspects of the same idea, also exemplified by systems theory in psychology. The properties of any part are determined, not by some fundamental law, but by the properties of all the other parts. (p. 381)

These authors emphasize the need to assist patients in letting go of the past by accepting responsibility for their feelings and focusing on the present. Eastern philosophies stress going beyond the boundaries of one's self and accepting the pain and vulnerability of the human condition. According to Atwood and Martin (1991):

> This type of therapy creates psychological health, which is defined as the ability to live in harmony with one's self and nature, to understand one's relationship to the universe, to show tolerance and compassion to one's fellow human beings, to endure hardship and suffering without mental disintegration, to prize nonviolence, to care for the welfare of all sentient beings and to

Figure 1.2
Whole Systems Theory of Balance in Maintaining Health

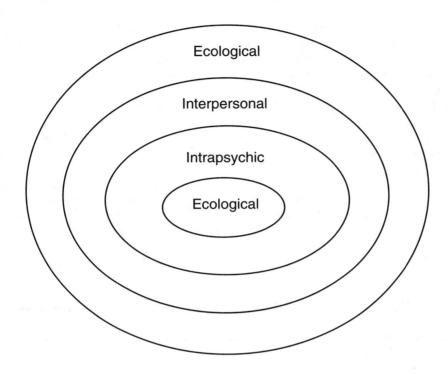

see a meaning and purpose in one's life that allows one to enter old age or to face death with serenity and without fear. (p. 374)

New trends in psychoanalysis replace the mechanistic drive-reduction theory formulated by Freud with a much more dynamic, interactional model of relations, such as Jung's concept of a collective unconscious that ties all humanity together. Many psychoanalysts, including Harry Stack Sullivan, Karen Horney, Abraham Maslow, and Carl Rogers stress the importance of human relations in the development of dynamic individual human beings. The relational model that has emerged from psychoanalysis stresses that "the most useful way to view psychological reality is as operating within a relational matrix which encompasses both intrapsychic and interpersonal relations." (Mitchell, 1988, p. 9)

Family therapy, particularly Systems Theory, is a perfect example of how the new paradigm operates in the mental health field. It has long recognized the crucial importance of the dynamic web of relationships that form the human family and each individual therein. The old mind/body dichotomy is breaking down. Mental health professionals attend to diet, exercise, relaxation techniques and other health-enhancing factors to improve one's emotional state. Physicians look at their patient's attitudes, outlooks, family relations, and role in society as critical to their physical health.

Healers of all types are seeking inspiration from shamonic traditions that "emphasize the restoration of harmony and balance within nature, in human relations, and in relationship with the spirit world" (Capra, 1982, p. 307).

Other new paradigm ideas for building an integrated model for health flow from this dynamic, holistic pattern. The bootstrap concept leads to the conclusion that a network of responses to the human condition can be used in a simultaneous and compatible manner to improve health.

At one time, it was considered rather shameful to label oneself as "eclectic" in outlook. It was preferable to state "I am a Freudian," or "I am a behaviorist," or "I am an existentialist." One was supposed to find one "true" model and subscribe to its dogma. Few professionals actually succumbed to this approach. Today, widely diverse approaches are used sequentially or simultaneously to assist individuals with their physical and/or emotional ailments.

Thus, maintaining a dynamic balance in one's life is the route to all health (see Figure 1.-2). Sickness comes from imbalance on a biochemical level, an interpersonal level, and an ecological level. In analyzing a dysfunction in any system, all aspects of that system must be analyzed and brought into balance. Then, the role of that system within other systems must be analyzed and balanced. Feedback about that balance must be constantly monitored and responded to. Only then will the system remain viable.

New Paradigm Makes the Observer's Role More Subjective

By changing the way the universe is perceived, the new paradigm also changes the observer's role. Under the new thinking, the observer's perception determines whether light manifests itself as a particle or a wave or in what sequence temporal events occur. Likewise, the way one human being perceives another establishes who that person is. It is well documented that one's beliefs about another person can dramatically impact that person's behavior. Mental health professionals deal constantly with maladaptive patterns that emerged when children respond to their parents' negative perceptions of them.

Therapists and physicians must constantly monitor how their internal perceptions are forming the person they are treating. They must always be aware of how subjective their "objective" view of their patient truly is. The therapeutic relationship is not just an objective observer "fixing" a malfunctioning unit but an elaborate dance in which each aspect of one partner impacts aspects of the other partner. Jung stated that:

> The therapist must at all times keep watch over himself, over the way he is reacting to his patient. For we do not react only from our consciousness. Also we must always be asking ourselves; how is our unconscious experiencing this situation? We must therefore observe our dreams, pay the closest attention and study ourselves just as carefully as we do the patient. (1965, p. 133)

Sexual Deviancy Treatment May Be Thought of as "Recycling"

It is quite a leap from quantum physics to the treatment of sexual deviancy. However, new paradigm thinking impacts directly on this field. Sexual abuse, which profoundly affects society as well as individual victims, will not vanish if offenders are given life sentences, pornography is banned, or prayer initiated in public schools. However, it may be diminished if society is willing to respond to the problem in a dynamic, interdisciplinary manner based upon an ecological model. The concept of "recycling" presents interesting parallels with the treatment of sex offenders. Communities are looking at inanimate objects and analyzing how each can be salvaged and revitalized for the benefit of society. Shouldn't this type of commitment to salvage and treat that which has been discarded apply to human beings as well? Incarcerated felons are off the streets and out of the public eye when they are in prison. However, without a serious effort to salvage and "recycle" those individuals, they will return to the community just as "toxic" as before, if not worse.

There should be an analysis of how and to what degree each offender needs to change to fit back into society, and a variety of techniques should be utilized in the change process. Certainly, some individuals should not be returned to the community. This raises the interesting issue of how to best utilize—or recycle—the assets of individuals who are too dangerous for release but still may have talents to contribute to society (e.g., female lifers at the Washington Correctional Center for Women train dogs to assist the handicapped).

A staggering amount of resources are being diverted from education, health, housing, and so on to prison beds for sex offenders. If we simply warehouse the increasing numbers of these individuals, we will be pouring money into a black hole—and have just as productive an outcome. Society cannot afford to lock up all sex offenders forever. Instead, it should determine how offenders can be rehabilitated using a "whole systems" or "integrative" approach to treatment. As illustrated in Figure 1.3, the offender, the victim, the family, and society all must be included in the process.

Figure 1.3
Systems Affected by the Problem of Sexual Assault

Offender	*Victim*	*Family*	*Society*
Police	Medical	Custodial	Legal
Legal	Therapeutic	Legal	Judicial
Judicial	Educational	Judicial	Correctional
Jail/Prison	Legal	Therapeutic	Therapeutic
Probation/Parole	Judicial	Financial	Financial
Therapeutic	Legislative	Informational	

In responding to this problem, it is imperative that programs avoid a piecemeal approach. Involvement from as many stakeholder groups as possible will construct a dynamic framework from which a viable system may evolve. Each of these groups has a particular perspective. Feedback and adaptation will determine whether the system will evolve or become stagnant. The bootstrap approach described earlier in this chapter suggests that each of these groups holds a piece of the "truth," and the kind of cooperation that comes from this approach will create a living changing system and provide the balance needed for survival.

Focusing resources and attention on some parts of the system to the exclusion of others can be disastrous. Nothing can kill sex offender treatment faster than the charge that it is being funded at the cost of victim's treatment. Thus, the system should be built so that different components depend on one another. For example, parole agents and therapists should serve complementary roles in supervision, and offenders could be ordered to pay for victims' treatment. This type of cooperation naturally leads to an understanding of the widely differing perceptions of the problem. Hopefully, in time, this will lead to abandonment of the many stereotypes and simplistic perceptions about the problems of sexual assault which are rampant in society today.

Integrative Approach to the Treatment of Sex Offenders

The Integrative Model presented in this book evolved from a series of workshops presented at the National Academy of Corrections entitled "A Systems Approach to Developing Sex Offender Programs." The basic tenets of these workshops is that sex offender programs exist within a complex web of agencies, communities, and interest groups. To succeed, they must recognize and respond to these diverse groups. If sex offender programs exist within and are themselves complex, dynamic, interactional systems, perhaps sex offenders also exist within and are themselves complex, dynamic, interactional systems.

The Integrative Model stresses balance as a prototype of health and views the individual as a dynamic, holistic system that interacts with other dynamic systems to form and interact with other, larger systems. These multi-faceted systems use many modalities to address a variety of issues. The union is the yin and yang, so that the masculine aspect is balanced by the feminine aspect, the passive with the aggressive, the conservative with the demanding, and the cooperative with the competitive. Additionally, the model stresses balance in the pedagogical, experiential, behavioral, and psychodynamic techniques that are utilized. By presenting therapeutic experiences in different formats, it is hoped that each of the senses and all of the different learning styles can be engaged in absorbing critical material.

Physiological Aspects of Treatment. Each individual life is composed of overlapping, interconnecting systems ranging from the molecular to the universal. Sex offenders are biochemical beings whose physiology may impact their offense patterns. Thus, an imbalance of testosterone, a history of head trauma, or an overly rapid uptake of serotonin may contribute to a pattern of acting out. Sexual arousal is a combination of physiological, psychological, and cultural factors. Deviant sexual arousal is itself a physiological response.

Many conditions thought to represent intrapsychic or intrafamilial conflicts (autism, many of the affective conditions, and so on) are now recognized as physiological in origin. Science is on the frontier of exploring the relationship between the brain and sexuality and violence. Aside from discovering a direct neurological or biochemical basis for sexual deviancy, it is readily apparent that numerous physical conditions (poor diet, various illnesses, lack of sleep, the influence of drugs or alcohol) can seriously compromise an individual's coping abilities.

Psychological and Emotional Aspects of Treatment. Sex offenders also are complex psychological beings whose thoughts, feelings, and behaviors interact to create patterns of sexual deviance. Typically, sex offenders have developed distorted beliefs and thoughts (cognitive distortions) that justify, minimalize, and rationalize their deviant behavior. For example, a rapist may believe that women in shorts are "looking for it," while a pedophile may believe that "it is better for her to learn about sex from me." These cognitive patterns must be challenged so that they will cease to support the assaultive behavior.

Often, sex offenders are emotionally frozen individuals from highly dysfunctional and abusive backgrounds. They respond by anesthetizing themselves from all feelings except anger. Male sex offenders may have grown up in dysfunctional families with assaultive male role models who repeatedly demonstrated that anger is the only acceptable feeling for a male. Sex offenders also tend to be filled with shame. Not shame over their behavior, but shame over who they are. This shame dates back to their earliest childhood. They may flee into addictive behaviors as a way of dealing with shame.

A major therapeutic task is assisting these individuals in releasing their emotions. A primary goal is helping them to feel legitimate shame and guilt over their behavior as well as the full range of emotional responses.

Behavioral Aspects of Treatment. Obviously, the behavior of sex offenders is most disturbing. Offenders not only have excessive dysfunctional behaviors, but they lack a positive behavioral repertoire as well. They may show deviant sexual arousal and lack appropriate sexual arousal. Behavioral techniques can help redirect their arousal patterns. Additionally, their dysfunctional behavior tends to organize itself in predictable patterns or cycles. If offenders and those around them become familiar with these destructive cycles, they can develop alternative behaviors that can be used to intervene in the deviant cycle.

Interpersonal Aspects of Treatment. Essentially, sex offenses are not intrapersonal problems like anxiety or even psychosis. Instead, they are interpersonal violations. Because sex offenders have no other model, they often enter into relationships with a scarcity mentality, particularly concerning power and control. They look at relationships as power games; if one person is feeling powerless, he can wrest power from the other person and thus have more for himself. There is little concept of inner power. Such disordered interpersonal relations are present in a variety of situations—not just sexual ones. The use of groups and therapeutic communities are particularly useful in this regard since they encourage offenders to learn how to deal with real, unsanitized relationships that are unlike those encountered in individual therapy. How the offender conducts himself in these situations is a much better indicator of his progress toward recovery than any psychological assessment.

Familial Aspects of Treatment. The families of sex offenders tend to be highly dysfunctional. Not only are the families of origin disturbed, but the marital relations and parenting patterns of sex offenders tend to repeat these disturbed patterns in both partners. The rage, trauma, and abuse (which is often sexual) must be recognized and dealt with. Couples and family therapy need to be utilized to help the offender's wife and children understand his pattern and develop safe, non-abusive relationships.

Societal Aspects of Treatment. In this country, sex offenders live in a society that fosters violence and distorts human sexuality. A review of any evening's television schedule reveals numerous shows that focus on sexualized violence. Advertisements use female bodies to sell products. Cultural stereotypes offer excuses for sexual violence of all types. The harsh fact is that this culture, along with many others, degrades its women and children. Unfortunately, one result of this is sexual violence toward the disempowered groups. Offenders need to be acutely aware of the messages that society is sending them.

Spiritual Aspects of Treatment. Sex offenders are notorious for distorting spirituality. For many, rigid, guilt-inducing religious attitudes towards sex contribute to the development of deviancy. The type of inflexible, black-or-white attitude fostered by some belief systems encourages the offender to split humanity into saints and sinners, the latter deserving of anything they get. Many offenders are so filled with shame and so convinced of their sinfulness that they cannot utilize spirituality to cope with their pain. Treatment of sex offenders should follow the Twelve-Step Programs for alcohol and substance abusers that rely upon connecting individuals with their spirituality as part of their recovery.

Helping Offenders Recognize Their Role in the Dynamic Web of Interrelations That Compose Humanity

One of the most fundamental goals of the Integrative Model is helping individuals recognize their role in the dynamic web of interrelations that compose humanity. Individuals must recognize that they can only survive as an intact system if their actions enhance, not destroy, that overall system. As Capra stated:

> An organism that thinks only in terms of its own survival will invariably destroy its environment and . . . will thus destroy itself. From the systems point of view the unit of survival is not an entity itself, but rather a pattern of organization adopted by an organism in its interactions with its environment. (1982, p. 289)

The following chapters focus on both the organization of sex offender treatment programs and the various components of treatment. It is assumed that these approaches will quickly evolve into more sophisticated ways of addressing the problem. The purpose of this book is less to present a series of policies or techniques than to encourage the creative and responsible exploration of ways of addressing the problem of sexual assault in the context of a dynamic universe.

References

Atwood, J.D. and Martin, I. (1991). Putting eastern philosophies into western psychotherapies. *American Journal of Psychotherapy*. XLV, (3), 368-382.

Barbaree, H.E. and Marshall, W.L. (1990). An integrated theory of the etiology of sexual offending. In W.L. Marshall, D.R. Laws, and H.E. Barbaree (Eds.), *Handbook of sexual assault: Issues, theories and the treatment of the offender*. New York: Plenum Press.

Briggs, J.P. and Peat, F.D. (1984). *Looking glass universe: The emerging science of wholeness*. New York: Simon & Schuster.

Capra, F. (1976). *The tao of physics*. Boulder, Co.: Shambhala Publication.

Capra, F. (1982). *The turning point: Science, society and the rising culture*. New York: Simon & Schuster.

Ellis, L. (1993). Rape as a biosocial phenomenon. In G. Nagayama-Hall, R. Hirschman, J.R. Graham, and M.S. Zaragozee (Eds.), *Sexual aggression: Issues in etiology, assessment and treatment*. Bristol, PA: Taylor & Francis.

Jung, C.G. (1965). *Memories, dreams, reflections*. New York: Random House/Vintage.

Malamoth, N.M., Heavey, C.L., and Linz, D., (1993). Predicting men's antisocial behavior against women: The interactional model of sexual aggression. In G. Nagayama-Hall, R. Hirschman, J.R. Graham, and M.S. Zaragozee (Eds.), *Sexual aggression: Issues in etiology, assessment and treatment*. (pp. 63–99). Bristol, Pa: Taylor & Francis.

Mitchell, S.A. (1988). *Relational concepts in psychoanalysis: An integration*. Cambridge, MA.: Havard University Press.

Pithers, W.D. (1993). Treatment of rapists: Reinterpretation of early outcome data and exploratory constructs to enhance therapeutic efficacy. In G. Nagayama-Hall, R. Hirschman, J.R. Graham, and M.S. Zaragozee (Eds.), *Sexual aggression: Issues in etiology, assessment and treatment*. (pp. 167–196) Bristol, PA.: Taylor & Francis.

Prentky, R. (In press). Treatment of sexual aggressors: Cost-benefit analysis and the design of treatment programs. In J. McGuire (Ed.), *What works: Effective methods to reduce re-offending*. Sussex, England; John Wiley & Sons, Ltd.

Schwartz, B.K. (Ed.) (1988). *A practitioner's guide to treating the incarcerated male sex offender*. Wash. D.C.: U.S. Department of Justice.

Chapter 2

Theories of Sex Offenses

by Barbara K. Schwartz, Ph.D.

Page

Overview

Not only are there numerous definitions of the term "sex offender," there are numerous theories regarding etiologies. All of the social sciences, as well as some physical sciences, have explored deviant sexual conduct. This chapter reviews a variety of explanations ranging from biological to holistic.

Definitions of "Sex Offender"

There are as many definitions of the term "sex offender" as there are individuals doing the defining. The definition of sex offender is shaped largely by the sexual mores of the times. Every state uses the label differently according to its legislative statutes. An act may be defined as a sex crime depending upon the degree of consent of the partner, his/her age, kinship, sex, the nature of the act, the offender's intention, or the setting. A behavior that in itself may be considered perfectly normal can become a serious criminal offense if it violates any of the above qualifiers. Numerous "blue laws" ban what is today considered perfectly acceptable sexual conduct. For example, in some states it is technically illegal to have sex without the intent to procreate. Other laws deal with activities our culture considers sexually bizarre—so-called "crimes against nature." However, a cross-cultural view of sexual taboos reveals that very few acts have been considered universally offensive (Wortis, 1939). This combination of factors causes the population of offenders to change constantly and makes studying the problem more difficult.

Perhaps the most useful definition of the term is offered by Gebhard, Gagnon, Pomeroy, and Christenson (1964) who define sex offenders as individuals who are ultimately convicted for committing overt acts for their immediate sexual gratification that are contrary to the prevailing sexual mores of their society and thus are legally punishable. Such individuals are distinguished from sexually deviant individuals who commit the same acts but have never been adjudicated in connection with their behavior.

The question of whether these individuals are suffering from a mental illness has generated considerable controversy. Karpman (1954) stated that sex offenders "are not conscious agents deliberately and viciously perpetuating these acts, they are victims of a disease from which many of them suffer more than their victims" (p. 482). However, DeRiver (1949) maintained that they are "endowed with free will, have equal opportunities to decide that they either will or will not commit certain unlawful and perverted acts" (p. x).

Most sexually deviant acts are classified as paraphilias. Nevertheless, each time the American Psychiatric Association meets to revise its classification of mental disorders, rival factions debate whether rape should be included. While many experts in the treatment of sex offenders maintain that rapists are mentally ill individuals who show similarities to pedophiles in their deviant behavior (e.g., compulsivity, possible deviant sexual arousal), others claim that rape is simply a criminal act.

The policy decision to treat sex offenses as crimes rather than illnesses shifted much of the responsibility for responding to this behavior to departments of corrections rather than departments of mental health. Just as this was becoming a clear trend, however, the Washington State Legislature passed a Sexual Predator Law providing for civil commitment in a treatment center for selected sex offenders identified as having a personality disorder or other mental disorder that would make it likely they would commit a sexually violent act. Suddenly the focus was again on sexual assault as the product of a mental illness. This allowed the state to institutionalize a person indefinitely for "treatment" rather than "punishment."

History of Societal Attitudes Toward Aggressive Sex Offenders

Attitudes Toward Rape. Reports of societal attitudes toward aggressive sexual assaults on both adults and children date back to early Egypt. Susan Brownmiller (1975) has suggested that sexual assault may have been the real basis of monogamous human relations from the earliest time. Women, fearful of gang rape, were forced to subjugate themselves to one man in return for his protection. This fear of rape has maintained women in a state of fear and passivity since that time (Griffin, 1971).

Both Brownmiller (1975) and Griffin (1971) theorize that rape laws exist to protect the rights of the male as the possessor of the female body. The first laws only addressed the rape of a virgin and existed solely to compensate fathers who, by theft of their daughters' virginity, were embezzled out of her fair market price. "The violation was first and foremost a violation of the male rights of possession, based on male requirements of virginity, chastity, and consent to private access as the female bargain of the marriage contract" (Brownmiller, 1975, p. 378). Perhaps the ultimate use of the female body as a show of political force was the medieval custom of jus primae noctis or droit du seigneur: the right of the manorial lord to devirginate any bride in his political sphere as a reminder of his powers over the lives of his people.

Others support the notion that rape does not exist. Amir (1971) noted the theory that it is impossible to rape a woman against her will has been reflected. throughout the history of Western civilization in such works as Chaucer's *A Miller's Tale*, Shakespeare's *Rape of Lucrece*, Balzac's *Droll Stories*, and Cervante's *Don Quixote*. Stories such as Updike's *Couples* and William Murray's *The Americano* illustrate the parallel concept that while rape may have its disadvantages, it can be sexually satisfying. As a jurist in the widely publicized Inez Garcia trial stated, "After all, they weren't trying to kill her; they were just trying to show her a good time" (Graduate Student Association, 1975).

Psychoanalytic literature on rape focuses on the unconscious motivation of the victim. Alexander (1974) stated, "Reflected in women is the tendency for passivity and masochism, and a universal desire to be violently possessed and aggressively handled by a man" (p. 10). A basic Freudian stance, according to Devereux (1939), holds that part of the woman's self is on the side of the rapist. Factor (1954) stated that a woman's guilt following an attempted rape is related to her desire to aid the man so that he can attack her successfully next time.

Psychiatrists also have postulated the phenomenon of "riddance rape" in which the victim seeks to rid herself of anxiety by doing that which is feared most—getting raped. This theory holds that to gain control over this fear, a woman may deliberately expose herself to dangerous situations so that she can feel a sense of power over the assault when it occurs.

Amir (1971) stated: "The psychiatric approach, using psychoanalytic concepts and reasoning, emphasized the pathological and deviant behavior of victims of sex offenses and rape; especially in young or adolescent girls of lower-class origins" (p. 297). Prior to 1970, most literature on rape assumed that "the ultimate proof of manhood is in sexual violence.... Men are aggressive as they take or make women, showing their potency (power) in the conquest. Women on the other hand submit and surrender, allowing themselves to be violated and possessed" (Astor, 1974, p. 201). Rape then may be seen as the logical conclusion of the culturally sanctioned male-female relationship.

Attitudes Toward Child Molestation. Attitudes toward sexual relations with children have varied through time and across cultures according to the particular definition of the age of consent. In Western literature, Dante fell in love with Beatrice when she was nine, and Petrarch's love, Laureen, was twelve. The Trobrianders of British New Guinea expect females to become sexually active between the ages of six and eight (Masters, 1962). In ancient Egypt, intercourse with prepubescent children was practiced as a religious ritual (Masters, 1962). Brothels in ancient Persia, China, and Japan retained small boys to satisfy the sexual desires of their clients. In ancient Rome, sadists could utilize infants kept at brothels (Masters, 1962). Masters also reported that brothels in 18th century England kept prepubescent females for males obsessed with deflowering virgins. Hartwell (1950) pointed out that some cultures believed that having sex with a child would restore potency or cure venereal disease. The most infamous pedophile was Gilles de Rey, a 15th century nobleman, who simultaneously sodomized and beheaded over 500 children (Revitch and Weiss, 1962).

Pedophiles were diagnosed as emotionally disturbed long before rapists, and they were described in the earliest clinical works (Krafft-Ebing, 1892). Child molesters were depicted as demented strangers lurking in the shadows, waiting to grab unsuspecting children. Today, we recognize that children are most frequently assaulted by individuals who are related to them. The media is overflowing with reports of outstanding citizens, religious leaders, judges, doctors, and so on who are molesting children.

History of Clinical Attitudes Toward Sex Offenders

It seems that there is increased interest in sex offenders after a sensationalized sex crime. In 1888, for example, a series of bizarre murders was committed in London's Whitechapel District. The killer was never found, but his memory remains a source of intrigue. "Jack the Ripper" was the first modern-day sex offender (Rumbelow, 1975). Over the next 10 years, three noted psychiatrists (Freud, 1893; Krafft-Ebing, 1892; Schrenck-Notzing, 1895) published pioneer works on sexual abnormalities.

Krafft-Ebing (1892) was the first to offer a classification of sexual problems. He postulated that individuals with these difficulties were genetically tainted; some suffering from acquired mental or cerebral diseases and others from retardation. Despite Krafft-Ebing's overemphasis on the evils of masturbation and didacticism, he offered some valuable insights into sexual abnormalities. He was the first person to establish the link between syphilis and insanity (Johnson, 1973). In addition, he (1) established the first pathology of sexual disorders, (2) found some types of sexual malfunctions to be correlated with problems in the limbic system, (3) urged that a person suffering from retardation, mental illness, "clouded consciousness," or an irresistible impulse

not be held legally responsible for a sex offense, (4) suggested that sexual abnormalities are partially formed by learning, and (5) advocated the decriminalization of
homosexuality. However, he pessimistically stated that, "There is no thought of treatment of an anomaly like these which have developed with the development of the personality" (1892, p. 576).

Schrenck-Notzing (1895) offered a lengthy description of the treatment of sexual
abnormalities by hypnosis. While he made some rather bizarre therapeutic suggestions (such as "severe mountain walks extending over months [p. 205]"), he also
pointed out some uses of hypnosis still are valuable. His earnest concern for individuals with these disorders may well be heeded today:

> Thanks to therapeutic nihilism, which unfortunately still finds numerous
> adherents among physicians, until now such patients have remained the life-
> long victims of their imperative feelings, and not infrequently have seen
> themselves placed before the alternatives of the prison or the asylum."
> (Schrenck-Notzing, 1895, p.x)

During the early part of the 20th century, Freud and his followers laid the foundation for the first highly developed theory of human sexuality. Their contributions
will be discussed later. The first American contribution to the literature on sex offenders was made by Karpman (1923), who published a case study of an obscene letter
writer.

Research conducted after 1930 can be roughly divided into that which occurred
prior to the passage of the Sexual Psychopath Laws in the early 1950s and that which
was published after that landmark. The earlier research was largely anecdotal, with
writers drawing largely from private practice or court experience. The later work was
able to draw from large numbers of individuals incarcerated under current statutes.

Early treatment of sexual deviants was primarily in the form of individual psychotherapy for the privileged few. The first center for the treatment of sexual devia-
tiants was the Institute of Sexual Science, which was established in 1918 in Germany
by Magnus Hirschfield. This pioneer therapist even urged treatment for lust murderers (Hirschfield, 1948).

In the United States, early treatment focused on the physical basis of sex and
offered such remedies as castration (Kopp, 1938) and large doses of testosterone
propinate. Incarceration as a method of treatment was advocated by East and Hubert
(1939), who wrote that "Prison acts as a deterrent to crime: It is frequently curative
(p. 110)," and by Cook (1949), who stated that "Imprisonment is a valuable therapeutic implement in treating certain types of criminal sexual psychopaths" (p. 140).
However, other early theorists disagreed with this position (Karpman, 1954; Kinsey
et al., 1948; Mullins, 1941; Richmond, 1933).

In 1947, following several widely publicized sex crimes, J. Edgar Hoover
announced that:

> The most rapidly increasing type of crime is that by the degenerate sex
> offender. A criminal assualt takes place every 43 minutes, night and day, in
> the U.S. In the last 10 years, arrests for rape increased 62%, commercial vice
> and prostitution—110%, other sex offenses—142% (p.15).

Public reaction to this statement demanded the enactment of tough laws against all types of sexual misconduct. Apparently, the rationale behind this was that harsh sentences would dissuade sex offenders because the enactment of stringent laws against kidnapping was followed by a decrease in that crime. Making reference to a particular case, Guttmacher and Weihofen (1952) responded:

> The fact that the particular crime (sex murder of a child) was carried out by an insane general paretic, who is about as responsive to law as a cat, is of no moment at such times. The supporters of such punitive measures often point to the decrease in kidnapping since more stringent penalties have been enacted. They totally neglect the fact that most crimes of kidnapping have, in part at least, an economic motivation and are largely under rational, conscious control, while brutal sex crimes against children are nearly always carried out in response to twisted, unconscious, and irrational impulses which the individual is incapable of understanding or controlling. (p. 56)

States began passing Sexual Psychopathy Laws based on numerous misconceptions. Hoover's statistics had included sexual acts between consenting adults and were in no way representative of serious sex crime (Karpman, 1954). Many believed that serious sex crimes were rampant. East (1946) pointed out that sexual felonies represented only 4% of reported crimes. Sutherland (1950) quoted statistics which indicated that in 1930, of the 324 women between 35 and 40 who were murdered, only 17 involved rape. More women were killed by policemen than by sex offenders. This does not dismiss the impact of these offenses, however, and sexual crimes certainly were more prevalent than these figures on reported felonies indicate (Wortis, 1939).

Several states' Sexual Psychopath Laws mandated that research be conducted on the efficiency of in-prison treatment programs. Studies were conducted at Sing Sing (Abrahamsen, 1950; Glueck, 1952), the New Jersey State Diagnostic Center at Menlo Park (Ellis and Brancale, 1956), the state prison in Waupun, Wisconsin (Glover, 1960), and Atascadero State Hospital in California (Frisbie, 1959). The studies reported a number of characteristics of sex offenders, but their populations differed according to the state laws defining criminal sexual behavior. Ellis and Brancale (1956) concluded that incarcerated sex offenders differ significantly from those convicted but not imprisoned, which seems to indicate that prison studies must not be assumed to represent all adjudicated offenders.

Several of these studies followed the participants after discharge and were able to report recidivism rates. An 8-20% rate was reported for treated offenders (Gigeroff, Mohr, and Turner, 1964; Guttmacher, 1952; Pacht, Halleck, and Ehrmann, 1962; Schultz, 1965; Selling, 1942; Turner, 1964). Studies of untreated offenders in England yielded a 20% rate versus a surprising 33% for those who received treatment (Radzinowicz, 1957). Several authors note that sex offenders have lower recidivism rates than other types of criminals (Guttmacher and Weinofen, 1952; Ploscowe, 1951; Sutherland, 1950).

Perhaps the greatest single advance in attitudes toward sex offenders is the revised view of homosexuality. The traditional attitude that homosexuality is a form of mental illness or a symptom thereof was first formally questioned in 1969, when Evelyn Hooker published the results of her classic study demonstrating that homosexuals do not differ from heterosexuals in psychopathology. She concluded that "Homosexuality as a clinical entity does not exist. Its forms are as varied as are those of heterosexuality. Homosexuality may be a deviant sexual pattern that is in the normal range, psychologically" (p. 45). Paul Gebhard, Director of the Institute of Sex Research, concurred: "The collective opinion of the members of the Institute of Sex Research....based on extensive interviewing and other data, is as follows....homosexuality is not a pathology in itself nor necessarily a symptom of some other pathology" (Hoffman, 1969, p. 44). Much of the earlier research on sex offenders was distorted by the inclusion of large numbers of individuals incarcerated for privately committing homosexual acts with a consenting adult. While homosexuality is no longer considered a mental illness by the American Psychiatric Association, there is still discrimination against gays and lesbians. Legislation forbidding the granting or overturning of established laws protecting the equal rights of gays and lesbians has been passed in Colorado and almost passed in Oregon, and the military continues to discriminate against these individuals.

Theoretical Explanations

Over the years, attitudes toward sex offenders have ranged from the belief that these individuals are congenitally malformed or morally depraved to the view that they are merely expressing a type of behavior that is subtly approved or even encouraged by their culture. The controversy as to whether sex offenders are suffering from some type of mental illness is as heated today as it was 90 years ago, and the efficacy of treating sex offenders continues to be hotly debated. Nevertheless, the number of treatment programs has grown dramatically to almost 1,600 specialized programs (Safer Society, 1993). The wide variety of theories supporting these disparate views are outlined below.

Biological Determinism. Several theories consider the possibility that some type of genetic, hormonal, chromosomal, or neurological biological process is responsible for sexually aberrant behavior.

Caesare Lombroso was the first proponent of this school of thought. He theorized that criminals were "atavists"—biological throwbacks to a more primitive species of homosapien. However, his analysis did not control for factors such as race, and he did not contrast his group of criminals with a group of normals. Nevertheless, Lombroso's views were echoed as late as 1949 by DeRiver, whose book included photographs accompanied by statements such as, "The facial structure clearly shows his contrasexual nature.... Note the dreamy neuropathic eyes often found among sexual criminals" (p. 97).

Some researchers have indicated that organic dysfunction related to epilepsy or head injuries may have a bearing on sexual misconduct (Radzinowicz, 1957; Selling, 1942). Rosen (1964) reported that sexually deviant behavior is linked with a variety of neurological disorders.

Tauber (1975) hypothesized that sexual perversions are a form of psychosomatic disturbance resulting from a lack of early touching and embracing. He felt this deficiency produced benumbed skin and muscles that do not respond to common types of erotic stimulation. Lindner (1973) presented the theory that psychogenic seizures are a defense against overwhelming anxieties related to unconscious incestuous desires.

Klinefelter's Syndrome and the XXY chromosome pattern are felt by some to be related to criminal behavior. However, Baker, Telfer, Richardson, and Clark (1970), compared subjects of all heights and chromosome patterns and did not find significant differences between the incidence of sex chromosome errors in penal and nonpenal populations.

Several researchers found that testosterone levels are associated with hostility and violence. In a study of rapists, Rada (1978) found that offenders judged to be the most violent had significantly higher testosterone levels, although this did not correlate with individual hostility scores. The highest testosterone level he found was in an individual who killed his victim.

Gaffney, Lurie, and Berlin (1984) conducted a double-blind family history study of 33 pedophiles and 33 depressed males. Pedophiles showed a significantly greater history of pedophilia. Nine pedophilic paraphiliacs showed a significantly greater family history of sexual deviancy not involving pedophilia. According to these authors, "That the syndrome is familial suggests, but does not prove, that genetic factors are responsible" (p. 547). Indeed, this is a classic example of the "nature-nurture" controversy and does not discount the possibility that behavior could have been learned—rather than inherited—from family members.

Researchers at Johns Hopkins Biosexual Psychohormonal Clinic are actively involved in studying biochemical approaches to the treatment of sexual deviation (see Chapter 18 on Psychopharmocological Interventions). The basic theory is to decrease the sexual libido by reducing testosterone levels. The most commonly used medication is MPA—medroxyprogesterone acetate—more commonly known by its trade name, Depo-Provera™. Berlin (1984) reports a recurrence of sexual behavior in three out of 20 patients (15%). When patients discontinued their medication, however, they tended to relapse.

Humans are basically biological creatures. Consequently, if the physiological dynamics underlying behavior were revealed, we could gain a truly comprehensive understanding of the problem. Prominent researchers Robert Prentky and Anne Burgess have formulated a theory of the "biological substrates of a fantasy-based drive mechanism for repetitive sexual aggression" (Prentky and Burgess, 1991). The authors hypothesize that the intrusive fantasies found in some sex offenders are based on traumatic childhood experiences which are encoded in the brain in a way that makes them extremely powerful and preoccupying. These traumas become deviant fantasies that may be stored in the visual cortex in a way that is unusually vivid and thus highly sexually arousing. The temporal lobes, limbic system, and hippocampus may also play a role in the maintenance of these deviant fantasies. Changes in brain chemistry, particularly in the adrenocortical hormones and catecholamines, may also influence the existence of intrusive, recurrent sexual fantasies. These researchers also relate the prenatal influence of testosterone to the later development of sexual deviance. This theory provides a theoretical basis for findings on the use of the serotonin reuptake inhibitors (Prosac™, Zoloff™) with sex offenders. However, more research is needed to clarify the biological foundations of sexual deviance.

Evolutionary Theories

The primary proponent of the "instinct theory," which is based on a large amount of animal research, was Clifford Allen (1940). Allen hypothesized that instincts can be altered by the environment even though they originate in reflex behavior. He also stated that instinctual responses should be allowed to emerge when they appear spontaneously. Allen pointed out that human beings are born with all the physical reactions necessary for sexual behavior and, as sexual desires awaken, individuals begins a trial-and-error search for satisfaction. Any set of conditions that satisfies these needs will be reinforced. As expounded by Allen (1940) and Pinkava (1971), the theory focuses on the frustration or mischanneling of sexual instincts, and stresses early marriage and the satisfaction of oral needs during infancy as prime preventive measures.

More recently, a sociobiological theory was proposed by Thornhill and Thornhill (1983), who stated that rape is an adaptive strategy used by certain males to fulfill an evolutionary urge to pass on their genes. Shields and Shields (1983) agreed with this theory, stating that: "During human evolutionary history, males that possessed a mating strategy that included rape as a facultative response were favored by natural selection over those that did not" (p. 123).

These sociobiological theorists further state that:

Copulation by a man with women who depend upon him or are under his control (e.g., a male employer copulating with his female secretary or a male slaveowner with his female slave) is not necessarily rape (or any other form of sexual conflict) by our definition because the female need not be denied the option of gaining benefits that exceed costs to reproduction—job security or salary (secretary); resources for self or offspring (slave). (1983, p. 141)

Evolutionary theories of rape assume that males seek to use any viable tactics to gain copulatory access to females, and they will rape if there is little risk of retaliation (Ellis, 1993). Humans are members of the animal kingdom and may retain biologically programmed patterns of behavior that should be identified and addressed.

Psychoanalytic Theory. In *Three Contributions of the Theory of Sex*, Sigmund Freud (1938) wrote:

Popular conception makes definite assumptions concerning the nature of qualities of the sexual instinct. It is supposed to be absent during childhood and to commence about the time of puberty; it is assumed that it manifests itself as an irresistable attraction exerted by one sex upon the other, and that its aim is sexual union or at least as would lead to such union. But we have every reason to see in these assumptions a very untrustworthy picture of reality. Closer examination indicates that they are based on errors, inaccuracies, and hasty conclusions. (p. 553)

Freud's response to these errors produced the first fully formulated theory of psychosexual development. His explanation of perversion is based on fixations at various psychosexual stages that result in the distortion of a sexual object or a sexual aim.

Psychoanalysts have focused on several major topics (see Table 2.1). The most popular causative factor is "castration anxiety." Freud theorized that when boys, usually during the Oedipal stage, discover the difference between themselves and females, they conclude that the jealous fathers of some boys have cut off their penises, thus producing girls. Supposedly, castration anxiety produces the resolution of the Oedipal conflict as boys decide not to compete with their fathers for their mothers. Should this fear remain unresolved, however, a male may develop a permanent aversion to females whose appearance arouses the fear. The individual may act-out sexually in order to symbolically obtain his father's penis by molesting boys or reassure himself of the power of his own organ through rape (Ostrow, 1974).

The image of the seductive mother is also considered an important factor in the development of the sexual deviation. Individuals may seek to preserve their childhood impotence in order to refute their incestuous cravings for their mothers. Fear of this seductive mother may produce phobias of pubic hair or of the "vagina dentata" (the belief that there is a set of teeth in the vaginal canal). The latter image arouses severe castration anxiety.

Another reason for the expression of sexually deviant thoughts may be a poorly developed superego. An individual may have been so impaired in his development that he can only relate to others as part-objects rather than as whole; as sets of genitals rather than as individuals. Socarides (1959) also saw inadequate ego development as a contributing factor. He felt that pedophiles experience early, excessive aggressive and libidinal internal drives. As a defense maneuver against these drives, the child projects the aggression he feels for his mother onto her so that she, the mother, is seen as the aggressor. In order to avoid internalizing this "bad" mother, he splits her into "good" and "bad" components. This produces an ego split that allows the individual to identify with a child and then play out the role of an erotic mother.

Gillespie (1956) indicated that the perverse act remains ego-syntonic because the ego is able to accept some part of infantile sexuality and repress the rest. This may be expressed in either rape or child molestation. By accepting some sort of behavior, the ego may be warding off destructive impulses toward the object. Thus, the ego may compromise with hostile impulses by allowing some sort of expression, such as "braid cutting," in order to control the rest of the impulse.

A number of analysts have observed that sexual assault may represent a fusion of aggressive and libidinous drives. Gardner (1950) stated that the rapist "enters puberty deriving equal pleasure from aggression and sexual impulses" (p. 50).

Psychoanalytic theory was the first formulation of a comprehensive, psychological explanation of human sexuality and its many variants. It recognized the importance of childhood sexuality and of early trauma. While it has limited usefulness as a treatment of choice for sex offenders, it has important historical significance in the development of the field.

Table 2.1
Summary of Psychoanalytic Theories of Sexual Deviancy

Theory	*Proponent*
Castration anxiety	Fenichel (1945) A. Freud (1965) Bak (1968) Ostrow (1974)
Reaction to seductive mother	Ostrow (1974)
Inadequate ego/superego	Gillespie (1956) Socarides (1959) Ostrow (1974)
Reenactment of sexual trauma	Ostrow (1974) Stoller (1975)
Confusion of aggressive and libidinal drives	Gardner (1950) Socarides (1959)
Narcissistic representation of self as child	Fenichel (1945) Bell and Hall (1971)

Ego Psychology. Ego psychologists maintain that the ego is not a secondary growth of the id. Instead, it is an autonomous structure with inborn processes oriented around perception, thinking, recall, language, object comprehension, motor development, and learning. Sexual deviations are produced by an impairment of one of the ego functions. Fenichel (1945) and Ostrow (1974) theorized that deviants form unusually vivid, eidetic visual experiences of some sexually traumatic event and become fixated at that point in psychosexual development. Any breakdown in the perceptual function may result in autistic behavior, a persistent state of primary narcissism, and difficulty in forming object relations (Fenichel, 1945).

Disordered cognitive functions may play a role in perversions by producing primitive thinking characterized by disorganization, tolerance of ambiguity, and emotionality (Fenichel, 1945; Hammer, 1968; Ostrow, 1974). Additionally, thought processes may take on a magical quality so that one believes that one can manipulate another's behavior by performing a "magical" gesture. The fetishist may be utilizing primitive symbolism, which is another characteristic of archaic thought processes. Ostrow (1974) and Hammer (1968) both pointed out that perverse behavior may be related to an inability to utilize organized abstract thought processes or substitute fantasy for action.

A. Freud (1965) and Glover (1960) suggested that perversions represent or serve to patch up flaws in reality testing. Fenichel (1945) suggested that a distortion of language development could be related to acting-out in that the individual would be unable to substitute thought for action. This proclivity may be related to a disturbance of motility so that the individual feels unable to effectively manipulate his environment.

Ego psychologists also stress that object development has a role in sexual perversion. If the mother is unable to act as a need-fulfilling and comforting agent, difficulties arise in individuation and the resultant separation anxiety causes the breakdown in object relations that is characteristic of these perversions. Blanck and Blanck (1974) stated that a breakdown in the mother-infant dyad may result in an inability to neutralize the sexual and aggressive drives. These drives then fail to become attached to a specific object, and an aggressive, sexual perversion develops. Gillespie (1956) hypothesized that the perversion may be a way of dealing with the danger of destructive impulses by allowing for their modified expression. Stoller (1975) felt that all perversions represent eroticization of aggressive impulses.

Ostrow (1974) pointed out that the perversion is expressed because the superego fails to exercise control. This, he stated, is due to its being weakened by the ego's tolerance of inconsistency. Hammer (1968) stated that witnessing the primal scene weakens the superego as the child no longer respects authority figures.

Ego psychologists have contributed the important concepts of the basic cognitive functions of the ego and the basic theory of object relations. The basic cognitive processing abilities of some sex offenders may indeed be impaired. Programs offering cognitive retraining techniques to criminal and delinquent populations are expanding. In the future, the neurological understanding of these cognitive processes may offer major breakthroughs for addressing a wide range of criminal behaviors. Sex offending is an interpersonal disorder, and the object relations theory reminds us that treatment of this disorder must always acknowledge that.

Neurosis Theory. Traditional psychoanalytic theory stresses the difference between the perversion, which is an act, and the neurosis, which represents a repressed conflict. However, other authors view sexually deviant acts as part of a neurotic process that usually is related to disturbances in personality development that leave the individual with intrapsychic conflicts and feelings of inferiority and insecurity. Although the term "neurosis" is outdated, it is the term many authors relied on. These authors often focused on the role of the seductive mother (Johnson and Robinson, 1957; Karpman, 1954; Littin, Griffin, and Johnson, 1956; Wylie and Delgrado, 1958). The parental role in unconsciously granting permission or exercising subtle coercion in the direction of sexual deviancy was stressed by Littin and associates (1956). Mathias (1972) blamed parents who failed to provide appropriate role models.

Feelings of inferiority were stressed by Bromberg (1948) and Mathias (1972), who stated that rapists "[conceive of] sexual intercourse as something no individual voluntarily engages in—especially with him" (p. 48). Rada (1978) stated:

> The major motive of the rapist is the desire for control; the means for obtaining this control is the commission of the rape event; the mode by which this control is effected may on one end of the continuum be primarily sexual; on the other end of continuum, primarily aggressive; or when these two meld in the middle, primarily humiliating. (Chap. 2, p. 6)

Glueck (1952) related the role of early developmental trauma to pedophilia, and stated that pedophiles experienced a continuously traumatic, prohibiting, and inhibiting sexual environment during their childhoods. Consequently, they grow up with pervasive difficulties relating to others and have impaired ability to use fantasy as an escape outlet for sexual conflicts due to impaired abstract thought processes. Torbert's (1959) general developmental theory states that a pedophile is:

> a person who, because of a sense of weakness, inadequacy and low self-regard, not unrelated to severe disruption of his family unit during childhood, finds a solution for his tensions in identification with the physically weaker and emotionally less sophisticated child. (p. 278)

Jungian Theory. Robert Stein (1973), in *Incest and Human Love*, presented a modified Jungian approach to sexual disorders. Initially, he differentiated Freud's basically Cartesian world view, which stresses logic and distrust of the instincts, from the Jungian approach, which theorized that creativity flows from the instincts. Stein stated that "Man's unique course of development, including ethical values and social organization, is based on an instinctively based disposition" (p. 14). He went on to say that "Nature, including human nature, contains a directing intelligence which is the source of all knowledge concerning the nature of man's being and becoming" (p. 19).

Stein also expanded the concept of the seductive parent's relationship to sexual deviation. He contended that the incest taboo functions to make the union between the mother and father sacred, therefore stimulating the formation of such archetypal images as the "sacred union of the divine couple," "the hierosgamos," "the royal marriage," "the sun and the moon," "the mandala," and a number of archetypes representing the union of opposites.

Meaningful sexual love is composed of phallos, "a sudden, powerful surge from within, flowing rapidly with the desire to make contact with another object" (Stein, 1973, p. 240), and eros, "the desire to merge and unite" (p. 241):

> In its pure form (phallos) tends to rape and ultimately destroy the object of its fascination.... The penetrating, dissecting quality of curiosity becomes destructive and antihuman without eros to preserve the integrity and mystery of the unknown object. (p. 83)

While the incest taboo allows archetypes representing this union to emerge, violation of the taboo splits the union. The individual may then identify with phallos and manifest only aggression and force, or he may identify with eros and remain passive, yielding, and impotent. The individual remains unaware of his incompleteness and has little desire to seek a love relationship with a nonincestuous female.

The Jungian analysts' focus on the universal masculine (phallus) and feminine (eros) principles meshes nicely with the gender issues that should be addressed with sex offenders. Additionally, this theoretical orientation may help offenders understand their power issues in a broader context.

Relational Theories. In his book, *Relational Concepts in Psychoanalysis: An Integration*, Mitchell (1988) stressed that a person is not a firmly fixed entity who emerges from childhood as a given set of personality characteristics. Instead, each human being is continually being changed by his encounters with other human beings. He states:

> Theorists emphasizing "relatedness by design" have contributed tools for understanding the specific interactions which transpire between self and other, focusing not so much on either pole, but rather on the space between them. (1988, p. 33)

Sullivan disagreed with Freud that the basic unit for the study of the emotional life was not the human mind but the interactional field. According to Mitchell (1988), Sullivan believed that:

> A personality is not something one has, but something one does. Consistent patterns develop, but the patterning is not reflective of something "inside." Rather the patterns reflect modes of dealing with situations and are therefore always in some sense responsive to and shaped by the situations themselves. (Sullivan, cited in Mitchell, 1988, p. 25)

Klein also focused on the continually interactive field of relationships. She rejected Freud's contention that early sexual development is inflexible and resistant to change. She viewed sexuality as a vehicle for playing out the full range of interpersonal relations in shifting and changing patterns. Other theorists emphasized the sense of self as the foundation of one's sexuality. Obviously one's sense of self changes continually as does one's relationship to one's sexuality.

Relational theorists including Fromm, Kernberg, Khan, and Lichtenstein all emphasize the critical role of relationships (Mitchell, 1988). Their theories have pointed the way to studying sexual deviance in an interactional manner.

Behavioral Theories. Many studies have used behavior therapy with cases of sexual deviation. Few have dealt with theoretical issues, however, because sexual deviations are considered another form of learned behavior. Allen (1940) theorized that sexual conditioning physically influences the hypothalamus, which in turn affects the endocrine mechanisms. The mother conditions the child to hold certain attitudes toward women. As the individual matures, he experiments with various types of sexual behavior, but retains the ones that were most reinforced.

McGuire, Carlisle, and Young (1965) theorized that sexual deviations are learned as a part of masturbation fantasies. The learning takes place as part of an initial seduction, which supplies a basic fantasy. If this seduction is deviant in nature, it is reinforced during each masturbation and may gradually become distorted and develop into more bizarre activities.

Sexual deviation can result from classical conditioning in which a repetitious or traumatic pairing of sexuality and some negative experience, produces some type of intensive emotional response that distorts subsequent sexual gratification. The cause might be either sexual assault or molestation in childhood or covert seduction at that time.

Operant conditioning may contribute to the learning of sexually deviant behavior. A child who is repeatedly molested in such a way that he is brought to climax will have that type of sexual conduct powerfully reinforced. As an adult, he may find that only the repetition of the pedophilic scene can produce sexual arousal.

Modeling also may produce sexually deviant behaviors. For instance, a boy who is aware of his father's incestuous behavior or adolescent participation in a "gang rape" may follow the example of these powerful role models.

Behavioral theories adapt readily to the development of behavioral techniques including covert sensitization, satiation, and aversive techniques.

Cognitive-Behavioral Theories. Cognitive-behavioral theorists explore how thoughts mitigate actions. Beck's (1979) work on depression points out how self-talk produces an emotional response that becomes self-perpetuating: an individual uses self-negating thoughts that cause him to feel depressed, which then produces more negative thoughts, and so forth.

Sex offenders may initially set-up negative emotional states by interpreting experiences in a negative way. They may relieve the depression or anxiety produced by these interpretations by preoccupying themselves with deviant fantasies. If the fantasies or the possible, subsequent behavior becomes uncomfortable, they minimize, justify, or rationalize their behavior by using "cognitive distortions." They may attribute blame to the victim (e.g., "she asked for it"), or they may blame alcohol or drugs. These distorted thought processes perpetuate the deviant behavior.

Samenow (1984) and his colleague, Yochelson, studied the thought processes of criminals. They identified certain thought patterns and beliefs (including entitlement, rationalization, victim stancing, among others) that comprise "the criminal mind." These patterns are often found in sex offenders, particularly those with histories of delinquency and property offenses and those who have been in prison for prolonged periods of time. The latter often subscribe to the values of the "con code," which is grounded in the thought patterns identified by Samenow.

Relapse Prevention is a cognitive-behavioral technique that was originally developed for use in the substance abuse field (Marlatt and Gordon, 1985). The language used in describing sobriety generally reflects the belief that one is either "on the wagon"—this is, abstaining and sober—or "fallen off the wagon" (i.e., drinking and drunk). This black-and-white thinking led to despair and hopelessness if one made the slightest slip. The Relapse Prevention model does not dwell on the deep, causative roots of dysfunctional behavior. Instead, it seek's to identify each individual's unique offense pattern and develop interventions to abort the cycle. Later in this volume Dr. William Pithers, who adapted this model for use with sex offenders, discusses the technique in detail.

Addictions Theory. With the growing use of the concept of addictions to address a variety of problems from overeating to organizational dysfunction, it is not surprising that addictions theory would be applied to deviant sexuality. Carnes (1991) has defined sexual addiction as the presence of the following:

1. A pattern of out-of-control behavior;

2. Severe consequences due to sexual behavior;

3. Inability to stop despite adverse consequences;

4. Persistent pursuit of self-destructive or high-risk behavior;

5. Ongoing desire or effort to limit behavior;

6. Sexual obsession and fantasy as a primary coping strategy;

7. Increasing amounts of sexual experience because the current level of activity is no longer sufficient;

8. Severe mood changes around sexual activity;

9. Inordinate amounts of time spent in obtaining sex, being sexual, or recovering from sexual experiences; and

10. Neglect of important, social, occupational, or recreational activities because of sexual behavior.

The origins of sexual addictions are found in the dysfunctional family patterns discussed in a later section. Individuals may progress through up to three levels of addiction. Both men and women can become sexual addicts, although many more men than women progress to the third level:

• *Level One* includes masturbation, heterosexual relationships, pornography, prostitution, and homosexuality. This category includes a wide range of behaviors with various cultural reactions. Many of these behaviors are appropriate in moderation but may take on a compulsive quality. Carnes (1983) states that for some behaviors there is a competing negative hero image of glamorous decadence. While these crimes lack a direct victim, psychological exploitation of a partner may be part of addiction. A vivid dramatization of the first level is presented in the movie, *Looking for Mr. Goodbar*.

• *Level Two* includes misdemeanor crimes such as voyeurism, exhibitionism, and obscene phone calls. While individuals who engage in these activities will be prosecuted if they are apprehended, they also may be the butt of jokes (e.g., the "flasher dolls" that can be bought in novelty shops). These activities may be a dire forewarning of more serious crime, especially if there is a pattern of escalating involvement with the victim.

• *Level Three* is marked by the felony sex offenses—rape, child molestation, and incest. There is a subgroup of sex offenders who clearly progress from Level One through Two to Level Three. It should be cautioned, however, that there is little indication of the number of sex offenders who show the compulsive pattern compatible with this construct.

Defining sexual addiction as "the substitution of a sick relationship to an event or process for a healthy relationship," Carnes points out that sex addicts subscribe to a set of core beliefs that distort reality (1983, p. 5). For example, they believe that they are not worthwhile enough for other people to care for them or satisfy their needs. They also believe that sex is the most important need in their life—their only source of nurturance, the origin of their excitement, the remedy for pain, and their reason for being.

The addictive cycle begins with distorted beliefs, progresses to impaired thinking, and progresses to an acting-out pattern similar to substance abuse, gambling, and/or eating disorders. While the acting-out is followed by despair, the guilt and remorse do not lead to reformation. Instead, it leads to an escape back into the addictive cycle.

The suggested treatment for the sexual addict is the utilization of self-help groups and the Twelve-Step Program originated by Alcoholics Anonymous and now widely used with a number of disorders. The program requires the individual to admit his behavior and that he is powerless to overcome it alone. The very admission of the problem removes the secrecy which can significantly contribute to the excitement. The addict then works on relating to a source of higher power. He shares his experiences, asks for forgiveness, and begins to make restitution for his sexual misconduct as well as for his past abuses of others. Sexaholics Anonymous and Sex Addicts Anonymous groups are springing up all over the country and may be used as a valuable resource for sex offenders in the community. These groups use an acronym— SAFE—to remind them when their sexuality is taking on a deviant or compulsive behavior:

1. It is a Secret.
2. It is Abusive to self or others.
3. It is used to avoid or is a source of painful Feelings.
4. It is Empty of caring.

Theorists disagree about using the concept of "addiction" outside of the substance abuse field where there is clearly demonstrable physiological dependence upon a chemical. However, Carnes (1991) makes the argument that there could be a biochemical connection based on the relationship between the endorphins, a peptid known as phenylethylamine (PEA), and monoamine oxidase (MAO), that produces a physiological dependence. This is, however, conjecture.

The addictions theory of sexual deviance has served to bring treatment of this condition more into the mainstream of therapy by aligning it with the treatment of substance abuse and related conditions. It would appear that the general public can identify with and tolerate the idea of a person being a "sex addict" rather than that person being sexually deviant.

Anthropological Theories. As mentioned previously, one of the major difficulties in defining sexual deviation is the variety of cultural attitudes toward acceptable sexual behavior. Even the various states in this country differ widely in their laws. One state may define incest as sexual relations with members of the nuclear family, while another might extend the definition to include third cousins. In some jurisdictions, homosexual unions are recognized as families for purposes of insurance or sick leave, but in other jurisdictions such unions can result in an indeterminate prison sentence.

Still, there is virtually no sexual behavior that some culture in some instance has not condoned (Masters, 1962). The Aranda of Australia and the Nambas of the New Hebrides approve of homosexual relations between adults and male children. The Keraki of New Guinea conduct initiation ceremonies involving homosexual conduct and allow marriage with prepubescent brides. The Ponapeons of the Caroline Islands use senile men to enlarge the genitals of prepubescent females (McCaghy, 1966). While Kluckholm pointed out that no society permits unlimited sexual contacts between adults and children (McCaghy, 1966), Brown (1952) indicated that only 23 of 110 cultures punish the act. Some groups, such as the Plateau Tonga of New Rhodesia, leave the punishment to divine forces (McCaghy, 1966), while the Ba-ila of New Rhodesia put the blame on the child. In studying 200 cultures, Ford (1960) found that there was no relationship between the types of sexual behaviors condoned and the level of development of the culture.

Societal changes may produce changes in the patterns of sex offenses within a culture. In Kenya, for instance, societal forces brought the tribes closer together so that males could have exposure to more potential sexual partners. The females were under severe formal restrictions against nonmarital relations, and economic factors act as barriers to early marriage. This produced sexual frustration among males in a society that equates sexual behavior with assault and aggression. Consequently, among the Gusii in southwest Kenya, the rape rate in 1959 was 47.2 per 100,000, as opposed to 13.85 per 100,000 in the United States (LeVine, 1959). The Gusii typically choose their wives from hostile tribes and their legitimate heterosexual encounters are "aggressive contests, involving force and pain-inflicting behavior related to hostility between clans" (p. 10). When the tribes were physically separated, rape was rare; however, as LeVine indicated, changing societal patterns broke down the cultural barriers controlling this behavior, resulting in the high 1959 rate.

Family Theories. A variety of family theories have contributed to the understanding of sexual deviance. Certainly, incest is a major indicator of family pathology. Freud's theory of infant sexuality was an attempt to explain incestuous themes in his patients. Today, there is a raging controversy about whether these themes emerged from fantasies or from real assaults.

The various family theories explain sexual deviancy differently. Some theories focus on the current family (e.g., relationship between husband and wife in the incest family) while others focus on the family-of-origin. Theories also differ in whether they emphasize the pathology of the individual within a family or the pathology of the family system.

Authors such as Bradshaw (1988), Miller (1990), Middleton-Moz and Dwinell (1986), and others associated with work with Adult Children of Alcoholics stress the development of maladaptive coping behavior in response to dysfunctional family systems. Individuals raised in these environments become enmeshed in codependent relationships forming new dysfunctional patterns characterized by addictive behaviors including sexual abuse.

The Family Systems Theory takes a "whole system" approach to family pathology. Its adherents (Minuchen, 1974; Haley, 1980; Satir, 1983) view problems as existing in the dynamics of the family network rather than in the pathology of the individual family members. In fact, an individual's apparent pathology may serve to maintain the coherence of the family. Whether sexual abuse in a family or sexual deviance in a family member is the product of a personal psychopathology or a pathological marital relationship or a pathological family network is a hotly debated topic.

Societal Theories. As McCaghy (1966) stated, "To violate the mores of society as to partner, time, place and form of sex act is to invite sanctions ranging from ridicule to death" (p. 4). In every society, the power structure is responsible for the formulation and enforcement of the legal code. Often, these enforcements are not representative of the dominant values. Lawmakers may be eager to adhere to the most puritanical sexual codes in order to present themselves as beyond reproach in this highly sensitive area and may be unwilling to vote for liberalization of these codes. Our sexual statutes are written so that 99% of adult males could be defined as sex offenders somewhere in this country (Kinsey, et al., 1948). As anthropological studies point out, no sexual behavior is universally recognized as deviant. "Deviance" is a label applied by a social group; it is not an inherent characteristic. As seen previously, the characteristics of a society may help to mold the type of sexual offenses prevalent to that culture.

In his study of rapists, Amir (1971) stressed the role of the "culture of violence" in explaining the predominance of ghetto black offenders. He hypothesized that this culture emphasizes and condones aggressive behavior. Amir also stated that these individuals may be subjected to early sexual stimulation due to crowded living conditions, and that sexual prowess may be used to gain status in the absence of other means. It should be pointed out, however, that Amir's statistics were drawn from court records, so his rapists may be more representative of individuals who are convicted of felonies in urban areas than rapists in general.

Social learning theorists have stressed society's role in fostering the learning of rape behavior. Ellis (1993) summarizes their work, stating:

> Rape is basically a form of male aggression that is learned through the following processes: (a) becoming desensitized to the harm caused by sexual violence, (b) coming to associate violence with sexual pleasure, and (c) becoming persuaded that sexual gratification can be gained via aggression towards women. (p. 19)

Thus, society may foster certain beliefs (e.g., women want to be raped) or present material through the media (e.g., pornography, "slasher" films) that desensitizes or sexually arouses the audience to rape.

Political Theory. The feminist movement produced a good deal of writing on sex offenses. Dealing with rape as the ultimate sexist act, Susan Brownmiller (1975) stated, "Rather than society's aberrants or 'spoilers of purity,' men who commit rape have served in effect as front line terror guerrillas in the largest sustained battle the world has never known" (p. 210). Rape is encouraged in this society because, "molestation isn't regarded seriously. It is winked at, rationalized and allowed to continue through a complex of customs and mores that applauds the male's sexual aggression and denies the female's pain, humiliation and outrage" (Rush, cited in Connell and Wilson, 1974). Rush went on to say that:

> Sexual abuse of children is permitted because it is an unspoken but prominent factor in socializing and preparing a woman to accept a subordinate role...to submit in later life to the adult forms of sexual abuse heaped on her by her boyfriend, her lover and her husband. (p. 163)

In *Understanding Sexual Violence: A Study of Convicted Rapists*, Scully (1990) states that "sexual violence and all its manifestations are the inevitable consequence of patriarchal social structure" (p. 166). This changes the question from "why are there sex offenders" to "why aren't there more sex offenders."

Certainly society has sexually typed women and men into specific roles. Melani and Fodaski (Connell and Wilson, 1974) stated "Men are again and again encouraged to show force and dominance, to disregard the weak refusals of the female, and when persuasion fails, simply overpower the passive partner with aggression and control" (p. 84). Women, on the other hand, are taught to be dependent, passive, weak, and fearful (Griffin, 1971). Men are portrayed as emotionally remote, superpotent playboys. They are subjected to the virility mystique which encourages them to separate their sexual responsiveness from their needs for love, respect, and affection (Russell, 1975). They are the victims of their own unrealistic sex role:

> Built on the lie of unattainable strength, will, cool, desire and self-realization, many men's egos are understandably fragile.... No longer forced to perform, no longer aspiring to emulate this hero or that playboy, perhaps men would learn to integrate sex and emotion, discover sensitivity, communicate deep feelings honestly and experience joy. (Russell, 1975, p. 256)

The above quote, written by a woman in the 1970s anticipated the Men's Movement and its recognition of the destructive roles gender stereotypes have produced. Increasingly, men are rejecting roles that emphasize dominance, aggression, and rationality at the expense of nurturance, acceptance, and intuition. The lyrics of two songs from the Men's Movement clearly illustrate this shifting concept of masculinity:

> My foggy, frozen self began to warm and clear
> When I discard dominance and threw away the fear
> Of softness and of gentleness and letting feelings flow
> And now I am a-changing as I go. (Kokopeli, 1988)

> For a change: when we're afraid let's not hide it.
> For a change: when we're hurt reach out our hand.
> Each one of us can be a solution
> If we love and work together for a change. (Morgan, 1984)

Integrative Theories. Theories of sexual aberrations reflect the bias represented by the particular discipline of the writer. Psychologists view the act as the product of psychopathology or the learning processes, both of which are intrapsychic processes. The anthropologist sees the behavior as part of cultural processes, while the sociologist and criminologist may seek explanations in subculture mores, differential associations, or a breakdown in societal controls. The political theorist sees the act as a means of subjugating a weaker group in order to control and exploit them. Susan Brownmiller (1975) states, "I believe that rape has played a critical function. It is nothing more or less than a conscious process of intimidation by which all men keep all women in a state of fear" (p.5).

Each discipline sees the problem through its own set of colored glasses. However, the current trend acknowledges that each discipline may hold part of the answer to the puzzle.

Integrated Theory of Rape. One of the first integrated theories of the development of sexually assaultive behavior, presented by Murphy and associates (1979), combined these theories and added the dimensions of perception and arousal to predict behavior. This dynamic model, which has implications for assessment and treatment, presents four general groups of individuals with numerous gradations between the groups. The first group includes highly psychopathological individuals who harbor intense hostility toward women, an inability to express anger appropriately, fear of rejection, or numerous other emotional conflicts. Rape is quite likely when these individuals accept myths regarding rape and violence, experience misperception of female behavior, and demonstrate arousal to aggressive sexual cues. The second group is similar to the first in all dimensions, but the degree of psychopathology is less. This group is apt to engage in criminal behavior, and rape may represent just one incident of taking by force. The third group (referred to as situational offenders in other systems) shows little psychopathology and limited antisocial inclinations. These individuals may occasionally rape, but they more frequently engage in coercive sexual behavior. The fourth group consists of males who are neither sexually assaultive or coercive.

This theory is refreshing in that it includes an explanation as to why there are men who are not rapists. While the authors do not explicitly differentiate rapists from other types of sex offenders, the theory can be easily adapted to explain a variety of deviant behaviors.

Integrated Theory of Child Sexual Abuse. Finkelhor (1984) developed a four-factor theory of child sexual abuse that incorporates characteristics of the offender, disinhibitors, the environment, and the victim. The first factor deals with basic motivations. Offenders frequently show deviant sexual arousal to children. It should be pointed out that, while all paraphiliac pedophiles as defined by the DSM-IIIR show deviant arousal, not all convicted child molesters do. Offenders may find relating to children emotionally congruent because it gives them a sense of power and control, while relating to adults produces feelings of inferiority and inadequacy.

Deviant arousal is often the product of sexual victimization of the offender himself. Offenders who have been sexually molested as children may engage in a reenactment of the trauma, identifying with the aggressor in an attempt to master the shock. According to Finkelhor (1984), any feature of a sexual event that makes it particularly prominent, including intense pleasure, pain, guilt, or anger, can make it a point of fixation. This fixation is then reinforced by becoming the focal point of a deviant sexual fantasy which is repeatedly reinforced for the victim, who then also becomes an offender. Particularly in cases of incest, sexual love and parental love may become fused so that any type of emotional arousal is interpreted as being sexual in nature.

Narcissistic identification with the child may cause the offender, in effect, to fall in love with himself. Feminist theorists point out that our society socializes men into being attracted to individuals smaller and younger than themselves.

Child molesters may be blocked in their attempt to gain peer-appropriate sexual satisfaction. These individuals are often timid, passive, unassertive, and socially awkward. They may come from familial or religious backgrounds that picture sex in sinful terms. The blockage may be developmental as with Groth's fixated offender, or situational as with his regressed offender.

The second factor (the disinhibitors) come into play before the motivational features can be translated into behavior. All but severely mentally retarded or organically impaired offenders know what types of behavior are not only culturally taboo but illegal. However, self-control may be impaired by psychoses, intoxication, or a simple lack of impulse control. Finkelhor (1984) suggests that the theory would have more flexibility if Groth's categories could be replaced by two continuums—strength and exclusivity.

Factors three and four (the environmental and victim characteristics) allow for the possibility of a variety of preventative approaches that can be utilized by parents, schools, social service agencies, and children themselves. According to this theory, victimized children may lack supervision. This lack may be the result of the physical absence of a protective adult or an emotional alienation that impairs trust and prevents the child from confiding in someone who could prevent the abuse. An emotionally alienated child may be easy prey to a molester who offers acceptance and affection. Children must be taught that adult behavior is not sacrosanct. It can be questioned and stopped by assertive responses.

Integrated Theory of Sexual Deviancy. Marshall and Barbaree's (1990) integrated theory of sexual deviancy is best summarized in their own words:

> Biological inheritance confers upon males a ready capacity to sexually aggress which must be overcome by appropriate training to instill social inhibitions toward such behavior. Variations in hormonal functioning may make this task more or less difficult. Poor parenting, particularly the use of inconsistent and harsh discipline in the absence of love, typically fails to instill these constraints and may even serve to facilitate the fusion of sex and aggression rather than separate these two tendencies. Sociocultural attitudes may negatively interact with poor parenting to enhance the likelihood of sexual offending, if these cultural beliefs express traditional patriarchal views. The young male whose childhood experiences have ill-prepared him for a prosocial life may readily accept these views to bolster his sense of masculinity. If such a male gets intoxicated or angry or feels stressed, and he finds himself in circumstances where he is not known or thinks he can get away with offending, then such a male is likely to sexually offend depending upon whether he is aroused at the time or not. All of these factors must be taken into account when planning treatment of these men. (pp. 270-271)

Causative Factors and Methods of Treatment

Prentky and Knight's (1993) research at the Massachusetts Treatment Center resulted in a model that identifies significant causative factors including:
- Caretaker instability during development
- Developmental history of abuse
- Hypothetical biological factors

They hypothesize that these factors interact in such a way as to produce an individual who may have a combination of the following problems:

- Impaired relationships with adults
- Global or misogynistic anger
- Cognitive distortions
- Deviant sexual arousal
- Lifestyle impulsivity

These factors interact to influence the individual's ability to experience empathy, the degree of expressive anger he harbors, the presence or absence of deviant sexual arousal, and the repetitiveness or compulsivity of the assaultive behavior. The treatment program would then diagnose which dynamics were operational in each sex offender and develop a treatment plan accordingly. For example, an individual who shows a high degree of cognitive distortions, a history of abuse, and a lack of peer or parent role models would receive the following treatments: cognitive restructuring; anger management; victim empathy training; assertiveness training; treatments aimed at enhancing self-esteem; and group/individual therapy addressing minimization and denial. An individual who experiences deviant sexual arousal due to a developmental history of abuse and impaired relationships with adults might have a treatment program that includes aversive conditioning, covert sensitization, systematic desensatization/ organismic reconditioning, and pharmacological/psychohormonal treatment.

This model is compatible with treatment programs that offer a variety of group, psycho-educational, and behavioral treatments and combine cognitive-behavioral techniques with psychodynamic approaches.

Theories Integrating Sexual Compulsivity and Cognitive-Behavioral Models. Schwartz and Masters (1993) combined psychodynamic, trauma-based theories of sexual addiction with cognitive-behavioral and addiction models to formulate an integrated theory of sexual deviance and a multi-modal therapeutic response to sexual compulsivity. This theory examines the impact of dysfunctional experiences upon John Money's concept of the "love map" (an erotic image encoded into the brain) (Money, 1986). Early childhood traumas affect one's ability to experience intimacy, form boundaries, develop self-esteem, trust, and gender identity, and may even produce neurological changes (Van der Kolk, 1989). Depersonalization may develop as a coping mechanism and a self-denigrating set of core beliefs further alienates these individuals from others.

This theory sees sexual compulsivity—including rape and child molestation—as rooted in early childhood traumas and maintained through cognitive distortions and behavioral reinforcements. The use of Relapse Prevention techniques flow naturally into this model as it was originally developed in the addictions field.

In summarizing their theory, Schwartz and Masters state that:

Deviant sexual arousal and compulsivity symptoms are the result of the influence of stigma and trauma to unfolding sexuality. The deviant arousal and behavior are always logical adaptations to the overwhelming stressors and become part of the dissociative survival-oriented symptoms to help the individual find some solution to the need to depend on other people whom they fear can injure or destroy them. Once deviant arousal is manifested, typically during adolescence, the symptoms become functional in dealing with anxiety, depression, loneliness and a myriad of other emotions, and thereby become "both necessary and distressing." The association with intense pleasure and other functional aspects of the symptoms results in addictive cycles which maintain and perpetuate the behavior. Therefore, both cognitive-behavioral, systemic, and 12-step approaches to treatment are required to control the symptomatology. Trauma-based approaches to treatment, including abreaction, catharsis, and cognitive restructuring are then useful in resolving the original issues for which the compulsivity symptoms had served as functional distorted survival strategies and anxiety, and keep the individual from having overwhelming intrusion of memory and cognition. By blending therapeutic approaches, treatment efficacy improves dramatically. (1989, pp. 23-24)

Ellis (1993) presented the Biosocial (Synthesized) Theory of Rape, which integrates feminist, social learning, and evolutionary theories. The theory is based on these three propositions:

1. There are two basic, unrelated drives related to rape (the sex drive) and the drive to possess and control.
2. Due to natural selection males have stronger sex drives than women.
3. The behavior of rapists is reinforced because it has proven to be successful in the past.

Interactive Model of Sexual Assault. Malamuth, Heavey, and Linz (1993) constructed the "interactive or confluence model of sexual aggression." They hypothesize that the following primary dynamics may be associated with sexual aggression: (1) hostile masculinity and (2) sexual promiscuity. They suggest that the probability for rape is high when the motivators and disinhibitors combine to form these two paths and the paths converge where an opportunity exists. Hostile masculinity acts to influence sexual promiscuity so that it is expressed coercively. Sexual promiscuity determines that one's anger toward women is expressed sexually. Both of these paths are traced back to early histories of parental violence and child abuse. These authors have empirically validated parts of their theory using the general male population rather than convicted individuals.

Dynamics of a Sexual Assault

In treating thousands of offenders of all types, this author has come to the conclusion that there are two components of any criminal act: a motive and a releasor that allows the motive to transcend personal and societal sanctions and be expressed. This theory uses the visual image of a dam and applies to all types of sex offenders (see Figure 2.1). It can also be modified to be used with any behavioral disorder. The reservoir of motivation can include a vast, complex network of beliefs, values, thoughts, feelings, and behaviors that set the stage for a variety of deviant sexual behaviors. What is perceived as comprising the reservoir will largely depend on the theoretical orientation of the therapist. The widest possible orientation allows for the widest possible exploration of the motivational reservoir. The anger, power, core beliefs, and deviant arousal of the sex offender may be explored by looking at issues around the dysfunctional family, the offender's own sexual victimization, family and peer attitudes and models, societal stereotypes, and origin and quality of sexual victimization. The offender may feel that he has been victimized by women. Significant role models in the offender's life may have been abusive toward others. Sexually deviant behavior may have been reinforced in a variety of ways. Each sex offender's motivational reservoir is unique to him.

Figure 2.1
Dynamics of Sexual Assault

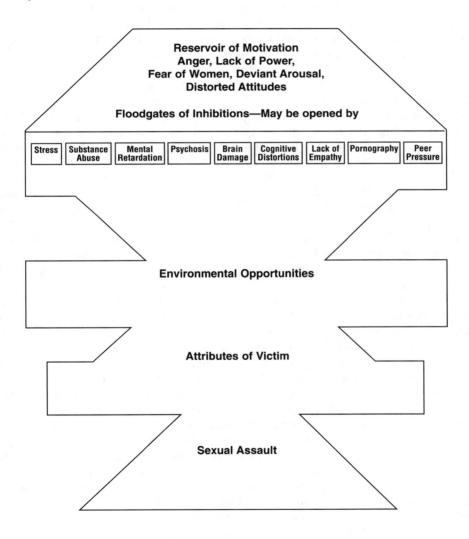

This motivational reservoir is held in check by floodgates (i.e., control factors) that may be opened by various influences. Stress impairs one's ability to maintain control by depriving him of the physical and psychological energy needed to exercise good judgment and maintain emotional equilibrium and a realistic perspective on the situation. Intoxication through either drugs or alcohol, on an acute or chronic basis, impairs judgment and enhances impulsivity. Mental retardation or organic brain damage can cause an individual to misread social cues or misjudge who is an appropriate peer. These conditions can also lead to feelings of inferiority, inadequacy, and isolation, that increase stress and contribute to the reservoir as well as to the opening of the floodgates. Some organic conditions impair impulse control.

Reality testing may be impaired by psychoses an individual might experience. Hallucinations or delusions may also contribute to a sexual assault (e.g., "that woman is possessed by a demon that I could exorcise by having sex with her").

Criminal thought patterns, first introduced in *The Criminal Personality* (Yochelson and Samenow, 1976), present a variety of rationalizations for antisocial behavior. Individuals with these thinking errors may take a victim stance ("she's rejecting me," "she asked for it"), or an "I can't" approach ("I can't control myself when I'm aroused"). They lack the concept of injury to others and empathy, and may also lack the willingness to put forth the effort to pursue their goals in a socially sanctioned manner. Entitlement, irresponsibility, mistrust, and unrealistic expectations play into the belief that one can simply take what one wants. These individuals have difficulty making decisions, establishing long-range goals, and evaluating progress toward those goals. They show an inordinate fear of being "put down" and, when they perceive this as happening, they release concomitant amounts of anger. They cannot acknowledge fear or deal with anger, and they are excited by power struggles. Any of these distorted beliefs can contribute to the acting out of deviant sexual motivation.

The lack of empathy can be generalized or quite specific. Empathy may vanish when one is angry or frustrated by another, or the basic ability may have generally failed to develop. Pornography might provide justification by leading the offender to believe that there is a community of individuals who share in deviant fantasies to the extent that businessmen fund the production of books, magazines, and films for that audience. Of course, the pornography itself is filled with justifications and rationalizations for the deviant behavior. In this model it is assumed that the deviant arousal is present prior to exposure to pornography so that it reinforces a pre-existing taste already established in the individual. There are, of course, certain situations where children are exposed to pornography, perhaps in the course of a molestation. The pairing of the pornography with sexual arousal could lay the ground work for the deviant pattern. Thus, it would be operating in the motivation stage of the model. For the sake of the model, pornography is specifically defined as material that fits an individual's deviant arousal pattern (e.g., child pornography for a pedophile and violent pornography for a rapist). Peer pressure can impair empathy, but it can also cause individuals to act in inappropriate ways through social or physical fear, the need for power, or the inability to exercise independent judgment.

When the floodgates open, varying amounts of motivational energy are released. When there is minimal energy, almost any type of environmental resistance will serve to halt the flow. For example, if the potential offender is not with a female whom he might readily assault, he may lack the motivational energy to seek one out and may content himself with a fantasy. When the amount of motivational energy is great, however, almost no environmental obstacle will deter him. Such an individual will fail the time-honored test of lack of control used in competency trials—the so-called "policeman at the elbow" test.

If there is sufficient energy to overcome environmental barriers, the would-be offender may still be stopped by certain attributes of the victim. Many potential rapists stalk the streets looking for such a particular victim with such specific attributes that they fail to find anyone before their motivational push recedes. However, when there is a vast amount of motivational energy, there may be no attribute of the victim that can stop the individual. He will assault literally anyone, which may explain why male rape may be committed by offenders with little, if any, homosexual orientation.

What other authors have referred to as "situational offenders" (Gebhard et al., 1964; Groth, 1979; Rada, 1978) may have a problem primarily with the floodgate portion of this system. There may be individuals who are under extreme chronic stress or chronic alcoholism. While any accumulation of anger, resentment, misreading of cues, or encouragement from society may be expressed through a sexually deviant act, such acts usually happen only where there is little environmental hindrance and when a victim is handy. With situational offenders, the lack of control may be enhanced in an additive manner by failures at many separate points (e.g., stress + intoxication + a momentary lack of empathy), or by the continual influence of one's disinhibitors (e.g. chronic alcoholism).

Patterned offenders have so much built-up motivational energy that the slightest weakness or the most momentary failure of their control systems may unleash the compulsive drive. In a few cases, the control system is almost totally destroyed so that the offender is always either committing a sexually deviant act or in the process of preparing to commit one.

This theory implies that there are many more potential sex offenders than actual ones. Many men and women who have intact control systems harbor tremendous amounts of deviant motivational energy. This conceptualization can explain the differences between an "expectant father" assailant suffering from a specific stress, a mentally ill or retarded offender, a criminal who takes a woman as he takes an object, an unexpectedly rejected college student whose empathy is impaired by societal myths and stereotypes, and a gang rapist.

Treatment implications revolve around draining the reservoir and strengthening the offender's floodgates, analyzing the environment to erect as many blockades to assault as possible, and assisting the offender to recognize whom he classifies as a victim and with behavioral and empathy and building techniques to eradicate that classification. The source of the motivational energy must be evaluated and dealt with therapeutically. It is here, in attacking the root of the problem, that behavioral techniques and group therapy come into play. Controls must be strengthened by equipping the individual with techniques to deal with stress, particularly social stress. Techniques such as social skills training, assertiveness training, and anger management are useful. Where applicable, substance abuse treatment also should be part of the program. Programs for the developmentally disabled and organically damaged may also incorporate educational approaches that deal with sexual and social issues as well as vocational rehabilitation, teaching basic cognitive processes such as analyzing and sequencing, and so on. Psychotic offenders may need proper medication. Victim empathy training may also be used to enhance control. School-based rape prevention programs may weaken peer pressure to act-out sexually. Relapse Prevention training can assist offenders in recognizing the building up of motivational energy or the weakening of control, and enable them to utilize appropriate techniques to deal with these problems.

Conclusion

The field of sex offender treatment is fortunate to be moving toward integration of its differing philosophical roots. Major theoretical orientations, including psycho-analysis, behaviorism, addictions theory, and family therapy, have evolved and devel-oped treatment models that converge with the model adopted by most institution-based sex offender treatment programs. Even psychiatry has shifted from treating only the severely mentally ill offender to an interest in studying and treating biologically-based factors related to sexual deviation.

Currently, comprehensive sex offender programs in institutions are most fre-quently housed separately in therapeutic communities that deal with abuse and trauma from the victim and the perpetrator's perspective and emphasize group therapy offer-ing behavioral interventions, cognitive retraining, and Relapse Prevention training. Typically, these programs also offer adjunct therapies such as substance abuse treat-ment.

There is a need to begin to identify which techniques are the most useful for dif-ferent types of offenders so that resources may be maximized. Only well-designed and constructed research will be able to answer this question. These issues must be responded to with knowledge rather than hysteria. The theories, characteristics, and typologies of sexual deviants is expanding and becoming more complex as the social sciences mature. There are many theories, but, as yet, few hard facts.

References

Abrahamsen, D. (1950). Study of 102 sex offenders at Sing Sing. *Federal Probation*, 14, 26-32.

Alexander, A.J. (1974). Simple question of rape. *Newsweek*, 84, 110.

Allen, C. (1940). *The sexual perversions and abnormalities: A study of the psychology of paraphilias*. London: Oxford University Press.

Amir, M. (1971). *Patterns in forcible rape*. Chicago: University of Chicago Press.

Astor, G. (1974). *The charge is rape*. Chicago: Playboy Press.

Bak, R. (1968). The phallic woman: The ubiquitous fantasy in perversions. Psychoanalytic study of the child. New York: International Universities Press.

Baker, R., Telfer, M., Richardson, R., and Clark, M. (1970). Chromosome errors in men with antisocial behavior: Comparison of selected men with Klinefelter's syndrome and XXY chromosome pattern. *Journal of the American Medical Association*, 214, 869.

Beck, A.T. (1979). *Cognitive therapy*. New York: Guilford Press.

Bell, A. and Hall, C. (1971). *The personality of a child molester: An analysis of dreams*. Chicago: Aldine-Atherton.

Berlin, F.S. and Meinecke, C.F. (1981). Treatment of sex offenders with antiandrogenic medication: Conceptualization, review of treatment modalities and preliminary findings. *American Journal of Psychiatry*, 138, 601-607.

Blanck, G. and Blanck, R. (1974). *Ego psychology: Theory and practice*. New York: Columbia University Press.

Bradshaw, J.E. (1988). *Healing the shame that binds you*. Deerfield Beach, CA: Health Communications, Inc.

Bromberg, W. (1948). *Crime and the mind*. New York: J.B. Lippincott.

Brownmiller, S. (1975). *Against our will: Men, women and rape*. New York: Simon and Schuster.

Carnes, P. (1983). *Out of the shadows*. Minneapolis, MN: CompCare.

Carnes, P. (1991). *Don't call it love*. Deerfield Park, FL: Health Communications, Inc.

Connell, N. and Wilson, C. (1974). *Rape: The first sourcebook for women*. New York: New American Library.

Cook, G.A. (1949). Problem of the criminal sexual psychopath. *Diseases of the Nervous System,* 10, 137-142.

DeRiver, J.P. (1949). *The sexual criminal: A psychoanalytic study*. Springfield, IL: Charles C. Thomas.

Devereux, G.H. (1939). The social and cultural implications of incest among the Mohave indians. *Psychoanalytic Quarterly*, 8, 510-515.

East, W.N. (1946). Sexual offenders. *Journal of Nervous and Medical Disease*, 103, 626-666.

East, W.N. and Hubert, W.H. (1939). Report on the psychological treatment of crime. London: H.M. Stationery Office.

Ellis, A. and Brancale, R. (1956). Psychology of sex offenders (pp. 15-41). Springfield, IL: Thomas.

Ellis, L. (1993). Rape as a biosocial phenomenon. In G. Nagayaman Hall, R. Hirschman, J.R. Graham, and M.S. Zaragozee (Eds.) *Sexual aggression:Issues in etiology, assessment and treatment*. Bristol, PA: Taylor and Francis.

Factor, M.T. (1954). Women's psychological reaction to attempted rape. *Psychoanalytic Quarterly,* 23, 243-244.

Finklehor, D. (1984). *Child sexual abuse: New theory and research*. New York: The Free Press.

Finkelhor, D. (Ed.) (1986). *A sourcebook on child sexual abuse*. Newbury Park, CA: Sage Publications.

Finkelhor, D. (Nov. 1993). Effectiveness of sexual assault prevention education. Paper presented at the meeting of the Association for the Treatment of Sexual Abusers, Boston, MA.

Ford, C. (1960). Sex offenses: An anthropological perspective. *Law and Contemporary Problems,* 25(2), 225-248.

Freud, A. (1965). *Normality and pathology in childhood: Assessment of development.* New York: International Universities Press.

Frisbie, L. (1959). Treated sex offenders and what they did. *Mental Hygiene,* 43, 263-267.

Gaffney, G.R., Lurie, S.F., and Berlin, F.S. (1984). Is there familial transmission of pedophilia? *Journal of Nervous and Mental Disease,* 172(9), 546-548.

Gardner, G.E. (1950). The community and the aggressive child. *Mental Hygiene,* 34, 44-63.

Gebhard, P., Gagnon, J., Pomeroy, W., and Christenson, C. (1964). *Sex offenders: An analysis of types.* New York: Harper & Row.

Gigeroff, A.K., Mohr, J.W., and Turner, R.E. (1964). A study of male sexual offenders charged in court over a twelve-month period: Report on the development of the study with an inventory of the data collected and a basic analysis. Toronto: Toronto Psychiatric Hospital.

Gillespie, W.H. (1956). General theory of sexual perversion. *International Journal of Psycho-Analysis,* 37, 396-403.

Glover, B. (1960). Control of the sexual deviate. *Federal Probation,* 24, 38-45.

Glueck, B. (1952). Study and treatment of persons convicted of crimes involving sexual aberrations: Final report on research project. Albany: New York State Department of Mental Hygiene.

Graduate Student Association. (1975). Women's law or how to stop the most commonly committed crime: Rape. Albuquerque: University of New Mexico Press.

Griffin, S.T. (1971). The politics of rape: An inquiry. *Ramparts,* 10(3), 26-36.

Guttmacher, M.S. (1952). Sexual offenses: Problem, causes and prevention. New York: Norton.

Guttmacher, M.S. and Weihofen, H. (1952). Psychiatry and the law. New York: Norton.

Haley, J. (1980). Leaving home: The therapy of disturbed young people. New York: McGraw-Hill.

Hammer, E. (1968). Symptoms of sexual deviation: Dynamics and etiology. *Psychoanalytic Review,* 55(1), 5-27.

Hartwell, S.W. (1950). A citizen's handbook of sexual abnormalities. Report to the Committee on Education of the Governor's Study Commission on the Deviated Sex Offender. State of Michigan.

Hirschfield, M. (1948). *Sexual anomalies: The origins, nature and treatment of sexual disorders.* New York: Emerson Books.

Hoffman, M. (1969). Homosexuality. *Psychology Today,* 15, 43-45.

Hoover, J.E. (1947). How safe is your daughter? *American Magazine,* 144.

Johnson, A.M. and Robinson, D.B. (1957). The sexual deviant (sexual psychopathy)—Causes, treatment and prevention. *Journal of the American Medical Association,* 164, 1559.

Johnson, J. (1973). Psychopathia sexualis. *British Journal of Psychiatry,* 122(56), 211-218.

Karpman, B. (1923). The sex offender (a case of obscene letter writing). *Psychoanalytic Review,* 10, 1-46.

Karpman, B. (1954). *The sexual offender and his offenses: Etiology, pathology and treatment.* New York: Julian Press.

Kinsey, A.C., Pomeroy, W.B., and Martin, C.G. (1948). *Sexual behavior in the adult male.* Philadelphia: Saunders.

Knight, R.A and Prentky, R.A. (1990). Classifying sexual offenders: The development and corroboration of taxinomic models. In W.L. Marshall, R.D. Laws and H.E. Barbaree (Eds.) *The handbook of sexual assault.* New York: Plenum. pp. 23–52.

Kokopeli, B. (1988). Changing as we go. In P. Blood and A. Patterson (Eds.) *Rise up singing* (p. 137). Bethleham, PA: Sing Out Corp.

Kopp, M.E. (1938). Surgical treatment as sex crime prevention measure. *Journal of Criminal Law and Criminology,* 28, 692-706.

Kozol, H.L. (1971). Myths about the sex offender. *Medical Aspects of Human Sexuality,* 11, 503-511.

Krafft-Ebing, R. (1892). *Psychopathia sexualis.* New York: Pioneer Publications, Inc.

LeVine, R.A. (1959). Gusii sex offenses: A study in social control. *American Anthropology*, 61, 965-970.

Linder, H. (1973). Psychogenic seizure states: A psychodynamic study. *International Journal of Clinical and Experimental Hypnosis,* 21(4), 261-271.

Littin, E.M., Griffin, M.E., and Johnson, A.M. (1956). Parental influence in unusual sexual behavior in children. *Psychoanalytic Quarterly*, 25, 37-45.

Lombroso, C. (1911). *Crime: Its causes and remedies.* London: Hernemann.

Malamuth, N.M., Heavey, C.L., and Linz, D. (1993). Predicting men's antisocial behavior against women: The interactional model of sexual aggression. In G. Nagayama Hall, R. Hirschman, J.R. Graham, and M.S. Zaragozee (Eds.) *Sexual aggression: Issues in etiology, assessment and treatment* (pp. 63-99). Bristol, PA: Taylor & Francis.

Marlott, G.A. and Gordon, J. (1985). Relapse prevention: *Maintenance strategies in the treatment of addictive behaviors.* New York: Guilford Press.

Marshall, W.L. and Barbaree, H.E. (1990). An integrated theory of the etiology of sexual offending. In W.L. Marshall, D.R. Laws, and H.E. Barbaree (Eds.) *Handbook of sexual assault: Issues, theories, and the treatment of the offender.* New York: Plenum Press.

Masters, R.E.L. (1962). *Forbidden sexual behavior and morality: An objective re-examination of perverse sex practices in different cultures.* New York: Julian Press.

Mathias, J.L. (1972). *Clear thinking about sexual deviation.* Chicago: Nelson-Hall.

McCaghy, C. (1966). Child molesters: A study of their careers as deviants. Doctoral dissertation, University of Wisconsin.

McGuire, R.J., Carlisle, J.M., and Young, B.G. (1965). Sexual deviation as conditioned behavior. *Behavioral Research and Therapy*, 2, 185-190.

Middleton-Moz, J. and Dwinell, L. (1986). *After the tears.* Deerfield Beach, FL: Health Communications, Inc.

Miller, A. (1990). *Banished knowledge: Facing childhood injuries.* New York: Doubleday.

Minuchen, S. (1974). *Families and family therapy.* Cambridge, MA: Harvard University Press.

Mitchell, S.A. (1988). *Relational concepts in psychoanalysis: An integration.* Cambridge, MA: Harvard University Press.

Money, J. (1986). *Love maps: Clinical concepts of sexual/erotic health and pathology, paraphilias and gender transposition, childhood, adolescence and maturity.* New York: Irving Publishers.

Morgan, G. (1988). For a change. In P. Blood and A. Patterson (Eds.) *Rise up singing* (p. 137). Bethleham, PA: Sing Out Corp.

Mullins, F.A. (1941). Prediction and parole. Journal of Criminal Psychopathology, 2(4), 59-63.

Murphy, W.D., Coleman, E.M., Haynes, M.R., and Stalgartis, S. (1979). *Etiological theories of coercive sexual behavior and their relationship to prevention.* Unpublished manuscript.

Ostrow, M. (1974). *Sexual deviation: Psychoanalytic insights.* New York: New York Times Book Co.

Pacht, A.R., Halleck, S., and Ehrmann, J. (1962). Diagnosis and treatment of the sexual offender: A 9-year study. *American Journal of Psychiatry,* 118, 802-808.

Pinkava, V. (1971). Logical models of sexual deviations. *International Journal of Man-Machine Studies,* 3(4), 351-374.

Ploscowe, M. (1951). *Sex and the law.* New York: Prentice-Hall, Inc.

Prentky, R.A. and Burgess, A.W. (1991). Hypothetical biological substrates of a fantasy-based drive mechanism for repetitive sexual aggression. In A.W. Burgess (Ed.) *Rape and sexual assault III* (pp. 235-256). New York: Garland.

Rada, R. (1978). *Clinical aspects of the rapist.* New York: Grune & Stratton, Inc.

Radzinowicz, L. (1957). *Sexual offenses: A report of the Cambridge Department of Criminal Science.* London: McMillan & Co., Ltd.

Revitch, E. and Weiss, R. (1962). The pedophiliac offender. *Diseases of the Nervous System,* 23, 73-78.

Richmond, W. (1933). *The adolescent boy.* New York: Farrar & Rinehart.

Rosen, I. (1964). *The pathology and treatment of sexual deviation: A methodological approach.* London: Oxford Press.

Rumblelow, D. (1975). *The complete Jack the Ripper.* London: W.H. Allen.

Russell, D. (1975). *The politics of rape: The victim's perspective.* New York: Stein & Day.

Safer Society. (1992). *Nationwide survey of juvenile and adult sex offender treatment programs and models.* Brandon, VT: Safer Society Press.

Samenow, S.E. (1984). *Inside the criminal mind.* New York: Time Books.

Satir, V.M. (1983). *Conjoint family therapy.* Palo Alto, CA: Science & Behavior Books.

Schrenck-Notzing, A. (1895). *The use of hypnosis in psychopathia sexualis.* New York: Institute for Research in Hypnosis Publication Society and Julian Press.

Schultz, G. (1965). *How many more victims?* Philadelphia: Lippincott.

Schwartz, M.F. and Masters, W.H. (1993). Integration of trauma-based, cognitive behavioral, systematic and addiction approaches for treatment of hypersexual pair-bonding disorder. In P.J. Carnes (Ed.) *Sexual addiction and compulsivity, Vol. I.* New York: Brunner Mazel.

Scully, D. (1990). *Understanding sexual violence: A study of convicted rapists.* London: Uniwin Hyman.

Selling, L.S. (1942). Results of therapy in cases of sex deviates. *Journal of Criminal Psychopathy,* 3, 477-493.

Shields, W.M. and Shields, L.M. (1983). Forcible rape: An evolutionary perspective. *Ethology and Sociobiology,* 4, 115-136.

Socarides, C.W. (1959). Meaning and content of pedophiliac perversion. *Journal of American Psychoanalytic Association,* 7, 84-94.

Stein, R. (1973). *Incest and human love.* New York: Joseph Okpakv Co., Inc.

Stoller, R.J. (1975). *Perversion: The erotic form of hatred.* New York: Random House.

Sutherland, E.H. (1950). The sexual psychopath laws. *Journal of Criminal Law,* 40, 543-554.

Tauber, E.S. (1975). Reflections on sexual perversions. *Contemporary Psychoanalysis,* 11(1), 1-14.

Thornhill, R. and Thornhill, N.W. (1983). Human rape: An evolutionary analysis. *Ethology and Sociobiology,* 4, 137-173.

Torbet, B. and Jones, P. (1959). Some factors related to pedophilia. *International Journal of Social Psychiatry,* 4, 272-279.

Turner, R.E. (1964). The sexual offender. *Canadian Psychiatric Association Journal,* 9, 533-542.

Van der Kolk, B. (1989). The compulsion to repeat the trauma: Reenactment, revictimization and masochism. *Psychiatric Clinics of North America,* 2, 389-411.

Wortis, J. (1939). Sex taboos, sex offenders and the law. *American Journal of Orthopsychiatry,* 9, 554-564.

Yochelson, S. and Samenow, S.E. (1976). *The criminal personality, Vol. 1.* New York: Aronson.

Chapter 3

Characteristics and Typologies of Sex Offenders

by Barbara K. Schwartz, Ph.D.

Overview

In 1990, the National Victim Center conducted a study that attempted to differentiate between the number of crimes that actually occurred and the number of crimes that were reported. Over 683,000 rapes were reported that year. After calculating how many rape victims would refuse to discuss their rape even in an anonymous survey, the Center suggested that the real rate may have been as high as two million victims (*Time*, 1992). That same year, the FBI reported that rapes were increasing four times faster than any other crime (Salhotz, 1990).

The United States has a rape rate four times higher than Germany, 13 times higher than Britain, and 20 times higher than Japan (Salhotz, 1990). In 1990, half of the states reported a record number of rapes. Using only figures for reported crimes, 16 attempted rapes and 10 completed rapes occur every hour (Madigan and Gamble, 1989). The National Victim Center estimates that of the 12 million women who were raped some time in their life, 61% were under 18 at the time of their assault and 30% were under 11 (*Time*, 1992).

This chapter describes epidemiology and demographic statistics on sex offenders' characteristics and typologies. Rather than listing various characteristics, a number of theorists have found it helpful to divide offenders into types. Some of these typologies are theoretical, while others are statistically derived. It may be helpful to match types to specific treatments.

Statistics on Female Victims

In large surveys of nonclinical female populations, up to 38% of the respondents reported being sexually abused before their eighteenth birthday (Salter, 1988). Earlier studies conducted between 1938 and 1965 reported comparably high rates (Salter, 1988). However, it should be recognized that the definition of "sexual assault" can vary widely. Not surprisingly, 24% of physically abusive mothers reported being victims of incest (Goodwin, McCathy, and DeVasto, 1981) and 81% of psychiatric inpatients reported histories of physical and sexual abuse (Jacobsen and Richardson, 1987).

The FBI reported that Black women are twice as likely to be raped as Caucasian women, and that 75% of victims come from low income families (*Time*, 1992). However, because these statistics appear to represent only reported rapes, they contain a disproportionately high number of assaults by strangers (about 80%) (Estrich, 1987).

Statistics on Male Victims

It should be remembered that females are not the only victims of sexual assault. Salter (1988) summarizes studies reporting that nonclinical samples of males reported a 5-16% rate of sexual assault, with older studies reporting a rate of 27-30%. Risin and Koss (1988) conducted a survey of 2,972 males in 32 colleges and reported that 30.7% of their respondents were victims of sexual assault which included penetration.

Date Rapes

Madigan and Gamble (1989) reported that half of all rapes occur in dating situations. Studies of female college students indicate that one in eight reported being raped in a date situation, and 25% reported having been the victim of some type of sexual aggression while on a date (Ledray, 1986). Four percent of college males in this study admitted having committed a sexual assault. Kamin and Parcell (1977) reported that 26% of their college male sample admitted having made a forceful attempt at sexual intercourse that caused observable distress in the women. Another study of college males reported that 15% admitted obtaining intercourse against the will of their dates (Rapaport and Burkhart, 1984), while Ledray (1986) reported that 30% of her sample admitted to similar behavior. A study at the University of California revealed that 54% of the males interviewed believed that forced sex was acceptable if the woman had initially consented even though she changed her mind. Forty percent stated that forced sex was acceptable if the man had "spent a lot of money" on her. Over 50% condoned force if the woman had "led him on," and one-third stated that it was acceptable to force sex if the man was "turned on" (Parrot, 1988). This study points to the clear need for education on appropriate sexuality even at a college level.

Again, as with other sexual assaults, women are not the only individuals to report being the victims of date rape. Struckman and Johnson (1988) reported that of 268 college men, 16% reported being victims of forced sex.

Marital Rape

Marital rape is being recognized as a crime throughout the country. Russell (1990) surveyed 930 women and found that of the 644 individuals who were ever married, 14% were raped by their husbands. A study of gay and lesbian couples done by Waterman and associates (1989) found that 12% of the men and 31% of the women had been victims of forced sex by their current or most recent partner.

Other Sexually Abusive Situations

A variety of relationships that were once considered acceptable are now being defined as sexually abusive due to the inequitable distribution of power in the relationship. Generally, these situations involve employers and employees, teachers and students, ministers and members of their congregations, and health professionals and their patients.

Gabbard's (1989) survey of mental health professionals and their rate of sexual contact with patients showed that 84 (6.4%) of the 1,442 psychiatrists in the survey reported having sexual contact with 144 patients. In addition, 4-5% of psychologist-respondents did not think that sexual contact with their patients was unethical. Currently, sexual contact is the single greatest complaint filed with the American

Psychological Association (Gabbard, 1989). Gechtman (1989) reported that 2.6% of male MSW's reported sexual contact with their patients, but 10% believed that it was acceptable under certain conditions. In a survey of professors in mental health training programs, 13% of the respondents reported having sex with their students (Pope, 1989). Finally, in a study of female incest survivors, 23% reported being sexually exploited by their therapists (Ainsworth, 1989).

Pastoral sexual abuse is particularly tragic as it ruptures not only the relationship with other humans but possibly with one's Higher Power as well. Rediger (1990, p.279) estimates that 2-3% of the clergy he has treated have been pedophiles. In speaking of the general population of clergy, he states that "approximately 10% of clergy (mostly males) have been engaged in sexual malfeasance." Berry references a study conducted at Fuller Theological Seminary which found that 38.5% reported having had some sexual contact with a church member, and 76.5% reported knowing another minister who had had sexual intercourse with a member (1992). Chandler of the *Los Angeles Times* (1990) reported that 2,000 cases of pastoral sexual abuse were pending in the courts throughout the country as of that date. A staggering amount of this activity floods the media and has become a national disgrace.

Statistics on Perpetrators

Although most convicted sex offenders are male, there is growing evidence that females commit a significant proportion of sexual assaults. Risin and Koss (1988) reported that 42.7% of the college males who reported being sexually abused were victimized by women. Fallen (1989) reported that 5-15% of perpetrators were females. Fromuth and Burkhart (1989) surveyed 582 college males in two universities. These authors included a wide range of sexual activities in their definition of sexual abuse. For example, the survey included sexual invitations to intercourse which occurred when the victims were 12 years of age or younger with the perpetrator being at least five years older; if the victim was 13-16 years old, the perpetrator was 10 years older. Using this criteria, 13% and 15% of the respondents reported having had at least one sexually abusive experience. These students reported that females were the perpetrators in 72% (midwest university) and 78% (southeastern university) of the incidents.

Another population of perpetrators, which has only recently been identified, are children who sexually assault other children. These perpetrators, who have themselves been victims of sexual abuse, are now being referred to as "abuse reactive" children. Friedrich (1988) reported that in his study of boy victims, 13% had committed a sexual assault by the time they were eight years old. Chasnoff and associates (1986) studied three cases of maternal-neonatal incest in which abuse stopped between four and 18 months. Two of the three victims had sexually assaulted another child by the age of three years. Females comprise a significant proportion of abuse-reactive children. Johnson (1989) reported that 21.6% of the children treated at the Support Program for Abuse-Reactive Kids (SPARK) at the Children's Institute of Los Angeles, California were females.

Table 3.1
Relationship of Perpetrator to Victim (Madigan and Gamble, 1989)

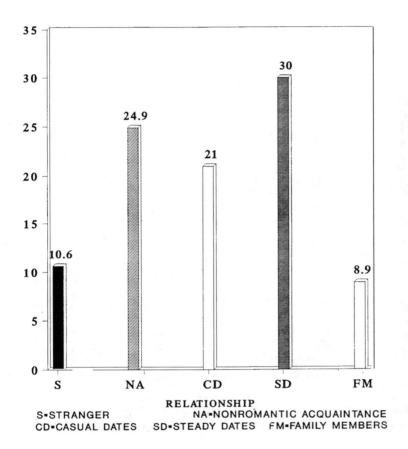

Table 3.2
Location of Rapes (Ledray, 1986)

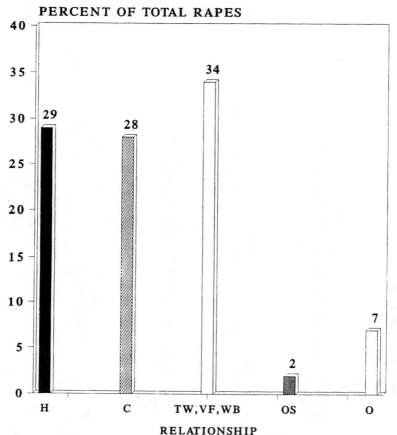

Characteristics of Sex Offenders

A number of researchers have studied both the demographic and psychological characteristics of sex offenders. However, there have been a number of problems with this research. Early studies used hospitalized or incarcerated samples whose descriptions may have been more reflective of individuals who end up in public institutions than of sex offenders as a group. In some states, homosexuals who had never committed what is now considered a sex offense were included in the research. Few studies used comparative samples. This early work is reviewed here for its historical value, but it is generally felt among treatment personnel that when sex offenders in community programs are studied, they resemble the general public in many ways.

They are much more likely to be educated, stably employed, and from working- or middle-class backgrounds than the typical felon (Van Kirk, 1984).

Factors Related to Age. Most studies reported the mean age of sex offenders is between 26 and 32. However, a number of factors could have contributed to this finding. A disproportionate number of youthful rapists might have been represented. Julian, Morr and Lapp (1980) found the average age of incest to be 42.3 years with 54% being between 36 and 45. Low reporting of incest or molestation by friends or relatives might have protected older offenders. While simply knowing how old the typical sex offender is means little or nothing, there are several related factors which are important. Waggoner and Boyd (1941) reported that in their sample, offenders had established a deviant sexual pattern between the ages of 10 and 16. These researchers were referring to a group of regressed or preferential pedophiles, although this concept had not been developed when their work was published. These individuals represent a significant percentage of sex offenders, and the clinician must always remember the likelihood that this pattern was established in childhood, often through molestation. One can frequently estimate the age the pattern was fixated by evaluating the pattern of ages of the victims.

Another feature relevant to the age of the offender is senility. This category was first recognized by Krafft-Ebing in 1892. The organic deterioration associated with hardening of the arteries often produces basic personality changes including the inability to control basic impulses such as anger and sexuality. The senile offender who is typically charged with child molestation may choose immature victims because they are vulnerable or because the offender has regressed developmentally to the point where he can no longer distinguish appropriate peers. Treatment is rarely recommended for this group. Placement in a suitable nursing home or other carefully supervised environment usually controls this behavior.

Mohr (1964) found that child molesters fall into three age groups. Adolescent offenders showed retarded maturation, immature social relations, and a lack of judgment. They tended to have unstable relations with other men and few, if any, relationships with females. The middle-aged group came from deteriorating families and often were experiencing vocational problems. The senescent group tended to be lonely and socially isolated. These findings are summarized in Table 3.3.

Table 3.3
Research Findings Based on Age

Researcher	*Findings*
Pollens (1938)	Mean age of 26-32.
Henninger (1939)	Senility a contributing factor.
Frosch and Bromberg (1939)	Senility a contributing factor.

Table 3.3 (continued)

Researcher	*Findings*
Waggoner and Boyd (1941)	Deviant pattern established between ages 10 and 16.
Hirning (1947)	Senility a contributing factor.
Frankel (1950)	Mean age of 26-32.
Guttmacher (1952)	Mean age of 26-32.
Glueck (1952)	Older than average.
Langley Porter (1953)	Younger than average.
Mohr (1964)	Trimodal age distribution for child molest 17, 37,57.
Julian et al. (1980)	Mean age of incest fathers: 42.3 years; 54% between 36-45.

Factors Related to Race and Ethnic Origin. The racial make-up of offenders varies with the geographical locale of the study. Frosch and Bromberg (1939), Frankel (1950), and Guttmacher (1952) found the majority of offenders to be native-born whites. A California study found the majority to be Spanish-surnamed (California Legislature Assembly, 1950). Julian, Morr, and Lapp (1980) found that the ethnic distribution of incestuous fathers replicated the racial composition of the United States. The racial distribution among convicted and uncarcerated sex offenders, as among all offenders, correlates highly with the poverty distribution in the locale for a number of reasons.

Table 3.4
Research Findings Based on Race and Ethnic Origin

Researcher	*Finding*
Frosch and Bromberg (1939)	Native-born white.
Frankel (1950)	Native-born white.
California Legislature Assembly (1950)	Spanish-surnamed.
Guttmacher (1952)	Native-born white.
Julian, et al. (1980)	Incest fathers replicate racial composition of U.S.

Factors Related to Cognitive Skills. While a number of studies have found below average intelligence quotients among sex offenders, this finding is suspect for a number of reasons. Here again, the sample was drawn from institutionalized individuals and cannot be assumed to be representative of all sex offenders. It should be noted that these findings refer to IQ scores, not the general concept of intelligence, and that these scores may be derived from different tests and from samples that may show a variation in the individual's test-taking ability due to language and other cultural factors. It has been this author's experience that sex offenders tend to be of above average intelligence, with many having college level or higher educations.

Cognitive skills encompass more than just intelligence quotient. A number of researchers have studied specific deficits and patterns in this area. Langevin and associates (1985) describe incest fathers as lacking in imagination, while Bennett (1985) stated that they tend to be illogical and simplistic although only 10% had an IQ of less than 69 (Lee, 1982). Child molesters show cognitive distortions which support their deviance (Abel, Becker, and Cunningham-Rathner, 1984; Conte, 1985; Gore, 1988; Howells, 1978; Stermac and Segal, 1990; Stermac, Segal, and Gillis, 1990).

Rapists demonstrate cognitive distortions reflecting negative views of women, condone violence and rape myths, and demonstrate "macho" attitudes (Abel, Blanchard and Becker, 1978; Segal and Stermac, 1990). In a study by Scully (1990) 45% of convicted rapists in her sample believed that some women like to be hit. A number of studies of sexually abusive men indicate that these individuals have difficulty accurately reading social cues from women (Abel, Blanchard. and Becker, 1978; Murphy; Coleman, and Haynes, 1986). In comparing the attitudes of rapists who denied their crimes with rapists who admitted offending, Scully and Marolla (1984) found that deniers described their victims as "seductresses" who were enthusiastic about having sex with them (31%), were willing (25%), or had sex with them for drugs or money. Over one-third believed that women say "no" when they mean "yes" and 100% stated that their victim meant "yes" even though 64% of the rapists used a weapon. The deniers used their victim's sexual background as a justification in 78% of the cases. However, only 16% of the deniers stated that they were blameless. Of the admitters, 77% of the men who had been drinking and 84% of the men who had used drugs blamed the substances. Admitters also blamed emotional problems (40%), childhood or marital situations (33%), and events involving wives or girlfriends (76%). Table 3.5 summarizes the studies in this area.

Table 3.5
Research Findings Based on Cognitive Skills

Researcher	*Findings*
Pollens (1938)	Below average.
Frankel (1950)	Normal.
Abrahamsen (1950)	Normal.

Table 3.5 (continued)

Research Findings Based on Cognitive Skills

Researcher	*Findings*
Durham (1954)	Above average.
Ellis and Brancale (1956)	Below average.
Abel, et al. (1978)	Rapists hold cognitive distortions which condone violence, support rape myths.
Larson (1984)	Rapists hold cognitive distortions which condone violence, support rape myths.
Mosher and Sirkin (1984)	Rapists hold cognitive distortions which condone violence, support rape myths.
Stermac and Segal (1990)	Rapists hold cognitive distortions which condone violence, support rape myths.
Stermac, et al. (1990)	Rapists hold cognitive distortions which condone violence, support rape myths.
Sullivan and Mosher (1990	Rapists hold cognitive distortions which condone violence, support rape myths.
Abel, et al. (1978)	Rapists have difficulty reading social cues.
Murphy, Coleman, and Haynes (1986)	Rapists have difficulty reading social cues.
Howells (1978)	Child molesters hold cognitive distortions which minimize, rationalize, and justify their behavior.
Becker and Cunningham-Rathner (1984)	Child molesters hold cognitive distortions which minimize, rationalize, and justify their behavior.
Conte (1985)	Child molesters hold cognitive distortions which minimize, rationalize, and justify their behavior.
Gore (1988)	Child molesters hold cognitive distortions which minimize, rationalize, and justify their behavior.

Table 3.5 (continued)

Research Findings Based on Cognitive Skills

Reseacher	*Findings*
Scully and Marolla (1984)	Denying rapists report that women seduced them and meant "yes." Admitting rapists blamed drugs, alcohol, wives, and girlfriends.
Marshall, Bates, and Rhule (1984)	Child molesters are deficient in judging social situations.
Barbaree, Marshall, and Connor (1988)	Child molesters are deficient in judging social situations.
Bennett (1985)	Incest fathers less logical, more simplistic.
Langevin, et al. (1985)	Incest fathers less imaginative.
Scully (1990)	Rapists believe that some women like to be hit.

Factors Related to Lifestyle. The concept of "lifestyle" incorporates a wide variety of activities that include educational and vocational achievements as well as criminal behaviors. Studies relating to personal achievement, such as educational and vocational achievement, are biased according to the population with those conducted exclusively in institutions showing lower overall functioning. However, even in these studies the findings were sometimes mixed. Glueck's (1952) sample had few job skills and tended to work alone, and also had more honorable discharges from the military, more consistent work histories, and fewer job-related problems than other types of offenders. As more individuals who have been referred to community alternatives are included in studies, it is predicted that overall level of achievement in this group will rise. As shown in Table 3.6, more recent studies reflect this trend. Finkelhor and Baron (1986) found no difference in economic standing between incestuous fathers and non-incestuous fathers. However, a number of other researchers have found that sex offenders tend to lead irresponsible, undirected, and often antisocial lives (Gebhard, Gagnon, Pomeroy, and Christianson, 1965; Marlatt, 1989; Pithers, Beal, Armstrong, and Petty, 1989; Thompson, 1989). The FBI's study of serial rapists found that during their childhood and adolescence, 71% were involved in stealing and shoplifting, 68% were isolated and withdrawn, 55% were assaultive to adults, 54% were chronic liars, 32% had enuresis, 24% set fires, and 19% were cruel to animals. A total of 63% showed either tantrums, hyperactivity, or alcohol abuse (Warren, Hazelwood, and Reboussin, 1991).

Table 3.6
Research Findings Based on Lifestyle

Researcher	*Findings*
Frankel (1950)	Less than 12% high school graduates.
Glueck (1952)	More honorable discharges, personal-service jobs, isolated jobs, consistent work histories. Fewer job skills, fewer job-related problems.
Langley Porter (1953)	Lower educational achievement.
Gebhard, et al. (1965)	Led irresponsible, undirected, antisocial lives.
Marlott (1989)	Led irresponsible, undirected, antisocial lives.
Pithers, et al. (1989)	Led irresponsible, undirected, antisocial lives.
Thompson (1989)	Led irresponsible, undirected, antisocial lives.
Van Kirk (1984)	33% have one or more years of college; 10% have graduate degrees.
Finkelhor and Brown (1986)	No difference in economic status between incest and non-incest fathers.
Warren, et al. (1991)	Serial rapists showed a variety of behavioral problems in childhood.

Factors Related to Marital Status and Sexuality. Research on marital status done with institutionalized offenders shows that fewer than average are married. However, it is not clear whether these offenders were single at the time of institutionalization or were divorced as a result of it.

The more recent research on marital status suggests that while sex offenders may have conflict-ridden relationships, they are able to acquire sexual and marital partners (Van Kirk, 1984). They are not, as stereotypes suggest, isolated degenerates, sexually frustrated and totally unable to find appropriate outlets. Some older studies have revealed some interesting marital dynamics. Schultz (1965) found that most married sex offenders claimed their wives were unfaithful regardless of the actual situation. Gebhard, Gagnon, Pomeroy and Christianson (1964) found higher divorce rates among offenders. Their general marital adjustment was characterized by fewer planned marriages, and the unions often showed an immature fantasy quality in which the offender related to his wife as if she were his mother (Glueck, 1952). It was also suggested that children were viewed as interfering with the adult relationship and were frequently made targets of the offender's hostility. Hartman and Nicolay (1966) found that in a sample of expectant fathers charged with crimes, 41% had been arrested for a sex offense compared to 16% of nonexpectant fathers arrested for sexual crimes. Most of those arrested were expecting their first-born. The authors felt that their crimes, rather than being attributable to sexual frustration per se, resulted from the arousal of maternal associations which impaired sexual performance. The rape then served to reduce anxiety about masculinity.

Incest offenders have serious marital difficulties (Saunders, McClure and Murphy, 1986). The marital relations of sex offenders in general may be impaired by their prudish attitude towards appropriate sexual behavior (Marshall, Christie, and Lanthier, 1979).

With the growth of interest in behavioral techniques and phallometric assessment, an interesting body of research has focused on the issue of deviant sexual arousal. Studies differ on whether incest fathers show deviant sexual arousal (Williams and Finkelhor, 1990). There was more consistency in reports of sexual dysfunction among incest fathers. Marshall, Barbaree, and Eccles (1991) report that 52.7% of child molesters admitted to deviant fantasies, with only 10% having such fantasies prior to 20 years of age. Forty-five percent admitted to molesting a child prior to that age. Only 21.7% admitted to having deviant sexual fantasies prior to committing their first crime. Of the 38.8% who showed strong deviant arousal on the plethysmograph, 96% admitted to deviant fantasies but only 44% reported deviant fantasies prior to their first crime. The presence of other paraphilias is less than previous studies have shown with 14% of nonfamilial offenders of girls reporting other paraphilias, but only 7.9% of incest offenders reporting more than one paraphilia (Marshall et al., 1991).

These findings contradict the research of Abel, Becker, Cunningham-Rathner, Mittleman, Murphy, and Rouleou (1987) who found high levels of deviant sexual fantasies (50% for nonfamilial molesters of boys) and higher incidences of other paraphilias (80% for nonfamilial child molesters and 70% for incest offenders) (Abel and Rouleau, 1990). Longo and colleagues (Longo and Groth, 1983; Longo and McFadin, 1981) reported that the onset of sexual deviance usually dated from early adolescence.

A number of studies use the penile plethysmograph to measure deviant arousal. If one controls for the number of sadists in a rapist population, there are few studies that show rapists demonstrating deviant sexual arousal. However, studies with a significant number of sadists do show arousal to sexualized aggression (Abel, Blanchard, Becker, and Djenderedjian, 1978; Barbaree, et al., 1979; Baxter, Marshall, Barbaree, Davidson, and Malcolm, 1984; Marshall, Barbaree, Laws, and Baxter, 1986; Murphy, Krisak, Stalgartis, and Anderson, 1984; Quinsey, Chaplin, and Upfold, 1984). However, penile plethysmography data is much more reliable in differentiating child molesters from normals (Abel, Becker, Murphy, and Flanagan, 1981; Murphy, Haynes, Stalgartis, and Flanagan, 1986; Quinsey, Chaplin, and Carrigan, 1979; Quinsey, Sternman, Bergerson, and Holmes, 1975). While there have been mixed results with incest offenders, studying individual profiles rather than group norms has revealed that some incest fathers have deviant arousal while others do not (Barbaree and Marshall, 1989; Marshall, Barbaree, and Christopher, 1986).

The FBI's study of serial rapists reported that 52% of the interviewees began fantasizing about rape between the ages of nine and 15 years, and 59% stated that there was no time lapse between the beginning of their fantasies and their first rape. The higher amount of deviant fantasies reported by this population may reflect the compulsive, and possibly sadistic, nature of this sample. This population also reported a variety of paraphilias with 68% admitting to voyeurism (Warren et al., 1991).

Table 3.7
Research Findings on Marital Status and Sexuality

Researcher	*Findings*
Shaskan (1939)	Fewer than average married.
Frankel (1950)	Fewer than average married.
Glueck (1952)	Fewer planned marriages; related to wife as a mother; children targets of anger at wife.
Durham (1954)	Fewer than average married.
Gebhard, et al. (1964)	Higher divorce rates.
Schultz (1965)	Most offenders claimed wives were unfaithful.
Hartman and Nicolay (1966)	Higher incidence among expectant fathers.
Marshall, et al. (1979)	Hold prudish attitudes toward sex.
Van Kirk (1984)	30-60% are married.
Saunders, et al. (1986)	Incest fathers have serious marital difficulties.
Glueck (1952)	Anxiety over masturbation; fewer but more bizarre fantasies; less sexual satisfaction.
Goldhirsch (1961)	More sexually explicit dreams among imprisoned sex offenders.
Gebhard, et al. (1965)	Higher rates of homosexual experience.
Johnson, et al. (1970)	Less exposure to pornography during adolescence.
Cook, et al. (1971)	Less exposure to pornography during adolescence.
Goldstein, et al. (1971)	Less exposure to pornography during adolescence.
Kercher and Walker (1973)	Rapists threatened by sexually explicit materials.

Table 3.7 (continued)

Researcher	*Findings*
Karacen (1974)	No significant difference in nocturnal penile tumescence between rapists and other prisoners.
Abel, et al. (1978)	High levels of deviant sexual arousal among sadists.
Barbaree, et al. (1979)	High levels of deviant sexual arousal among sadists.
Baxter, et al. (1984)	High levels of deviant sexual arousal among sadists.
Murphy, et al. (1984)	High levels of deviant sexual arousal among sadists.
Quinsey, et al. (1984)	High levels of deviant sexual arousal among sadists.
Langevin, et al. (1985)	High levels of deviant sexual arousal among sadists.
Marshall, et al. (1986)	High levels of deviant sexual arousal among sadists.
Warren and Hazelwood (1991)	High levels of deviant sexual arousal among sadists.
Longo and McFadin (1981)	Early onset of sexual deviance.
Longo and Groth (1983)	Early onset of sexual deviance.
Abel, et al. (1981)	Child molesters show significant amount of deviant arousal.
Quinsey, et al. (1975)	Child molesters show significant amount of deviant arousal.
Quincy, et al. (1979)	Child molesters show significant amount of deviant arousal.

Table 3.7 (continued)

Researcher	*Findings*
Murphy, et al. (1984)	Child molesters show significant amount of deviant arousal.
Attorney General's Commission on Pornography (1986)	Pornography related to the commission of sex crimes.
Carter, et al. (1987)	Subgroups of sex offenders differed markedly in use of pornography.
Linz, et al. (1987)	Sexually violent pornography related to sexual violence.
Abel, et al. (1987)	High levels of deviant fantasies among child molesters; high levels of other paraphilias.
Abel and Rouleau (1990)	High levels of deviant fantasies among child molesters; high levels of other paraphilias.
Barbaree and Marshall (1989)	Some incest fathers show deviant arousal.
Marshall, et al. (1986)	Some incest fathers show deviant arousal.
Williams and Finkelhor (1990)	Studies differ on deviant arousal in incest fathers but group shows much sexual dysfunction.
Marshall, et al. (1991)	Their sample of child molesters show less deviant fantasies than previous studies and fewer other paraphilias.

Factors Related to Mental Illness, Alcoholism, and Personality Disorders. The research on prevalence of mental illness again reflects the nature of the populations studied. As shown in Table 3.8, high levels of psychoses were reported by several early researchers. While most sex offenders show traits of personality disorders and while there are subgroups representing the seriously mentally ill and developmentally disabled, most sex offenders do not show major psychiatric disorders. Data is conflicting on the prevalence of alcoholism in this group. Various personality traits have been noted. A more extensive description of personality dynamics is included later in the chapter.

Williams and Finkelhor (1990) found that the research was mixed on the degree of psychiatric disorders among incest fathers but there was no pattern of serious mental illness. Langevin and associates (1985) did show elevated Pd (psychopathic deviate) scores on the MMPI for incest fathers but this sample did not have a history of criminal offenses other than incest. Various studies have reported that this population is anxious, depressed, passive, inadequate, and suspicious but other studies describe them as domineering and abusive (Williams and Finkelhor, 1990). These same authors report little evidence of substance abuse. However, excessive use of intoxicants among sex offenders was reported by Marques and Nelson (1989).

Some studies of child molesters have demonstrated problems in social skills (Overholster and Beck, 1986; Segal and Marshall, 1990). Not only do rapists show significant problems dealing with anger (Groth, 1979; Levine and Koenig, 1980; Pithers et al., 1988), but this applies to incest fathers (Paveza, 1987) and child molesters (Knight and Prentky, 1990) as well.

Table 3.8

Research Findings Based on Mental Illness, Personality Disorders, and Alcoholism

Researcher	*Findings*
Pollens (1938)	Infantile.
Shaskan (1939)	15% psychotic; 1% hysterical; 20% alcoholic.
Apfelberg, et al. (1944)	39% alcoholic.
Fenichel (1945)	Infantile.
Abrahamsen (1950)	11% psychopaths.
Gardner (1950)	Infantile.
Ploscowe (1951)	Immature.
Glueck (1952)	79% psychotic, with impaired judgment, reasoning, and reality contact.
Durham (1954)	Infantile.
Karpman (1954)	Infantile.
Rada (1978)	Alcoholism significant.
Groth (1979)	Rapists have problems with anger.

Table 3.8 (continued)

Researcher	*Findings*
Levine and Koenig (1980)	Rapists have problems with anger.
Pithers, et al. (1988)	Sex offenders have difficulty with developing empathy.
Seidman and Marshall (1990)	Sex offenders have difficulty with developing empathy.
Segal and Marshall (1985)	Problems in social skills with incest fathers.
Overholster and Beck (1986)	Problems in social skills with incest fathers.
Langevin, et al. (1985)	Elevated Pd scores on MMPI for incest fathers.
Paveza (1987)	Incest fathers have problems with anger.
Okami and Goldberg (1989)	No consistent findings of deficient social skills with sex offenders.
Marques and Nelson (1989)	Substance abuse high among incest fathers.
Knight and Prentky (1990)	Child molesters have problems with anger.
Williams and Finkelhor (1990)	Diagnoses mixed for incest fathers.

Factors Related to Sexual Abuse. Another area of hot debate among sex offender treatment providers is the true incidence of sexual abuse during their own childhoods. This was first identified by Bowman (1938) and elaborated on by Goldstein and associates (1971). Nicholas Groth (1979), studying incarcerated sex offenders, found that 45% described themselves as victims of sexual assault while an additional 18% remembered being pressured into sexual activity by an adult. Another 18% were involved in sex-stress situations where the family reacted with extreme anxiety to the discovery that the individual was involved in some type of sexual activity, usually childish sex play. Upsetting sexual activity was witnessed by another 39%. Finkelhor (1984) reported that 25% of his sample were victimized by women. He suggests that this figure probably is low because abuse by a female is less likely to be perceived as such. Often, it is perceived by the boy as reflecting a precocious ability to seduce an older woman or as an initiation rite in which the woman has done him the favor of performing. Such films as *My Tutor* and *Tea and Sympathy* reinforce this stereotype. Women are also able to mask inappropriate sexual behavior by disguising it as some caretaking function.

Baker (1985), Langevin and associates (1985), Pelto (1981), and Strand (1986) found a higher proportion of incest fathers had been sexually abused. Warren and associates (1991) found that 76% of their sample of serial rapists had been exposed to inappropriate sexual contact or conduct and an overlapping 76% had been sexually abused in some way. Of the latter group, 26% were forced to witness disturbing sexual occurrences, 22% were fondled or forced to fondle their abuser, and 52% of the abuse involved penetration. However, in studying child molesters, Hanson and Slater (1988) reviewed a number of studies and found an average abuse rate of 28%. Knopp (1984) reported rates varying from 22 to 82%. Some of the wide variance found in studies of this characteristic may be related to the varying severity of the samples being studied.

Table 3.9
Research Findings Based on Sexual Abuse

Researcher	*Findings*
Bowman (1938)	High incidence.
Goldstein, et al. (1971)	High incidence.
Pelto (1981)	High incidence among incest fathers.
Baker (1985)	High incidence among incest fathers.
Langevin, et al. (1985)	High incidence among incest fathers.
Strand (1986)	High incidence among incest fathers.
Finkelhor (1984)	25% molested by women.
Knopp (1984)	Sexual abuse studies range from 22-82% of sex offenders who were sexually abused.
Hansen and Slater (1988)	28% of sex offenders were sexually abused.
Warren, et al. (1991)	76% of serial rapists were sexually abused.

Factors Related to Parental Relationships. A great deal of research has documented the impaired parental relations often found among sex offenders. Patterns of neglect, physical and sexual abuse, and rejection were found. Disturbed parental sexual attitudes were stressed by Hartwell (1950) and Karpman (1954), who stated that:

> Fault lies with the parents, who, themselves products of unhealthy repression and much involved in sexual problems, do not know and cannot set themselves to be frank and open with the child whose naive and artless curiosity should be handled in an equally simple way. (p. 198)

Mandel (1986), Parker and Parker (1986), and Strand (1986) found high incidences of histories of physical abuse for incest fathers with four of the six studies showing an incidence of over 50%. Barker (1985), Berkowitz (1983), Langevin and associates (1985), and Strand (1986) found disturbed parental relationships to be a significant dynamic. Okami and Goldberg (1989) reviewed a number of research articles on pedophiles and found very few consistent findings. However, according to these authors, one recurring issue for this population was disturbed relationships with their mother.

Recently, the types of dysfunction associated with growing up in an alcoholic or otherwise dysfunctional family has gotten a lot of attention. While statistics specifically relating this to sex offenders are not immediately available, it has been this author's experience that a large number of offenders grow up in alcoholic homes. Adult children are described as suffering from psychic numbing, survivor guilt, lack of trust, being either totally irresponsible or overly responsible, having a strong need for power and control, and difficulty with intimate relationships. Many of these symptoms are relevant to the dynamics of sexual deviancy.

Table 3.10
Research Findings Based on Parental Relationships

Researcher	*Findings*
Bowman (1938)	Disturbed.
Pollens (1938)	Rejection.
Henry and Gross (1938)	Disturbed; rejection.
Menaker (1939)	Masculine, depriving mother and weak father; neurotic mother and tyrannical father; broken home.
Waggoner and Boyd (1941)	Disturbed; rejection.
Dushay (1943)	Rejection.
Hartwell (1950)	Disturbed parental sexual attitudes.
Glueck (1952)	Rejection; maternal seduction.
Karpman (1954)	Disturbed parental sexual attitudes.
Ellis and Brancale (1956)	Disturbed; rejection.
Glover (1960)	Disturbed; rejection; maternal seduction.

Table 3.10 (continued)

Researcher	*Findings*
Gebhard, et al. (1964)	Disturbed; rejection.
Schultz (1965)	Hostile fathers and unrealistic expectations for mothers; rejection.
Goldstein, et al. (1971)	Disturbed.
Fisher and Rivlin (1971)	Maternal seduction.
Berkowitz (1983)	Disturbed parental relationships among incest fathers.
Barker (1985)	Disturbed parental relationships among incest fathers.
Langevin, et al. (1985)	Disturbed parental relationships among incest fathers.
Strand (1986)	Disturbed parental relationships among incest fathers.
Mandel (1986)	Incest fathers show high rates of being physically abused.
Parker and Parker (1986)	Incest fathers show high rates of being physically abused.
Strand (1986)	Incest fathers show high rates of being physically abused.
Okami and Goldberg (1989)	Findings on family relations inconsistent with pedophiles; high rates of disturbed relationship with mothers.

Typologies of Sex Offenders

As the characteristics of any large population are studied, patterns start to emerge, and researchers begin to develop categories based on personal experience or statistical analysis. Typologies are useful in that they condense information and may form the basis for concepts that can be clinically useful and tested experimentally. The problem with typologies is that few are subjected to validation studies, and they often degenerate into stereotypes. Groth's (1979) pioneering work carefully differentiated between types of pedophiles, but others began extrapolating from his theory and drawing unwarranted conclusions. For example, the regressed pedophile is often considered to be a less serious or dangerous individual. However, the FBI's classification system takes into account the fact that a regressed pedophile, offending a child for the first time, may in some cases be quite dangerous as he is more likely to panic than the more patterned offender (Lanning, 1986).

Typologies can be quite useful in understanding clusters of dynamics and possibly in allocating and prescribing therapeutic interventions, but they must not be used to make sweeping generalizations or to overlook individual differences.

Typologies of Pedophiles

Pedophiles are individuals who turn to prepubescent children for sexual gratification. This happens for a number of reasons. Many researchers have attempted to classify these individuals (see Table 3.11).

Table 3.11
Typologies of Child Molesters

FINDINGS	Kraft-Ebing (1982)	Henninger (1940)	East (1946)	Fitch (1962)	Revetich & Weiss (1962)	Gebhard et al. (1964)	Mohr (1964)	McCaghy (1966)	Fehlow (1973)	Groth (1979)	Lanning (1986)
General Pedophiolia	X										X
Senility	X										
Alcoholic	X										
Organic Dysfunction	X	X							X		X
Antisocial			X	X				X			X
Regressed				X	X	X				X	X
Fixated				X			X	X		X	
Sexual Pressure										X	X
Sexual Force										X	X
Sadistic										X	X
Sexually Indiscriminate											X

Early Studies. In general, pedophiles are divided into several broad categories. In 1892, Krafft-Ebing classified pedophiles into those with acquired mental illness, senile individuals, chronic alcoholics, and individuals suffering from paralysis, epilepsy, head injuries, apoplexy, or syphilis. Antisocial offenders were found to have committed sexual offenses with adults and children, and to have committed more non-sexual crimes (McCaghy, 1966). Fitch (1962) described these individuals as "men with records of instability in many fields of behavior who felt themselves to be deprived and rejected by society and whose sexual offenses, generally committed on complete strangers, were impulsive acting-out of temporary aggressive moods" (p. 30). East (1946) apparently was describing this type of individual when he wrote that "some sexual offenders appear to belong to the constitutionally psychic inferior group of psychopathic personalities and are not necessarily sexual perverts in the narrow sense" (p. 46).

Fifty percent of Fehlow's (1973) sample of individuals arrested for sexually assaulting children were suffering from brain damage. This may be related to a high percentage of senile offenders. Henninger (1940) studied this type of offender and theorized that their relations with children were related to a desire to regain their youth. Mohr (1964) found a trimodal distribution in which one peak occurred between the ages of 55 and 59. While these individuals are probably not senile, they may share with the senile offender such characteristics as loneliness, emotional and sexual isolation, and impotence.

Individuals who are unable to identify with an adult sexual role are another type of offender (Fitch, 1962). Gebhard and associates (1964) considered this group the most disturbed in their sex offender population. These individuals were characterized as immature, underdeveloped persons who showed marked anxiety over potency and infe-riority. In retreat from adult challenges, they frequently established peer relations with children, who they found less threatening and judgmental (Revitch and Weiss, 1962).

Another group consists of individuals whose offenses seem to be a reaction against sexual or emotional frustration at an adult level (Fitch, 1962). Often, these individuals are incest offenders. Gebhard and associates (1964) found that this type typically was labeled as "heterosexual aggressors against children." Typically, these offenders had a history of broken marriages marked by restrained sexual activity with their wives. Mohr (1964) found that the group of offenders who first engaged in sexu-al activity with children between the ages of 35 and 39 usually had poor marital rela-tions and had been drinking heavily at the time of the offense.

Groth's Typology. Groth's (1979) typology of pedophiles actually consists of two parts. One concentrates on the degree to which the behavior is entrenched; the other stresses the basis of psychological needs.

The first part of Groth's typology distinguishes between fixated pedophiles and regressed pedophiles. Fixated pedophiles have been attracted to children throughout their lives and have been unable to attain any degree of psychosexual maturity. This profile contrasts with that of regressed pedophiles, who have related sexually to appropriate peers at some time in their life. However, a variety of situational stres-sors may undermine their confidence in themselves as men. Frequently the stressor is unemployment, which not only increases financial problems but undermines the identity which, particularly among males, revolves around a job. Physical illness can also impair regressed pedophiles' view of themselves as sexually adequate beings. Such individuals may engage in noncoital sex play with children, who are less threatening. In this individual, the behavior is much less fixated.

The other part of Groth's theory focuses on the degree of force used in the assault. This is related to the psychological needs fulfilled by the act. A sex-pressure offense utilizes enticement or entrapment. This offender, who is pursuing love and affection as well as physical contact, would prefer that the victim cooperate and usually is dissuaded if the child resists. These individuals frequently state that they are "in love" with their victims.

In contrast, a sex-force offense utilizes intimidation or physical aggression. These acts can be subdivided into exploitative assaults, which utilizes threat or force, and sadistic assaults. The former type of attack represents the use of the child as solely a sexual outlet. These offenders use only the amount of force necessary to accomplish the act, although this may even mean murder. These individuals are drawn to children primarily because they are easily overpowered and may present less resistance than an adult.

The most frightening type of individual—as well as the most dangerous—is the sadistic offender. This individual has eroticized violence. The sadistic child molester must inflict pain, degradation, and even death on the child in order to achieve sexual gratification. His compulsive behavior may involve complex, carefully planned, patterned rituals. While the most feared of all sex offenders, this type probably is the rarest.

Groth (1979) places incest along this dimension. Incest may be engaged in by either regressed or fixated individuals. It may be situational or it may reflect an effort on the part of the regressed pedophile to gain access to victims by pursuing a woman who has children whom he finds attractive. Incest may take place with one's natural children or with stepchildren. It does not inherently imply pedophilia as the victim could be an adult, even a consenting adult. However, since the latter is rarely reported, the type of incest which comes to the attention of the authorities often shows much pedophilic overlap.

FBI Typology. The FBI has developed a typology based loosely on Groth's work but expanded to include seven subgroups (Lanning, 1986). The classification system is designed for use in criminal investigations. Elaborating on the concept of the regressed pedophile, Lanning describes the situational child molester as an individual who does not have a defined sexual preference for children. Such individuals are stereotyped as rather benign persons who are relatively easy to treat. However, as Lanning points out, this subgroup may include highly predatory individuals. Situational offenders include the following types:

  • *Regressed*—Immature, socially inept individuals who relate to children as peers. These individuals may be experiencing a brief period of low self-esteem and turn to their own children or other available juveniles. This is the offender Groth described in his typology.

- *Morally Indiscriminate*—These are antisocial individuals who use and abuse everything they touch. Their victims are chosen on the basis of vulnerability and opportunity and only coincidentally because they are children.

- *Sexually Indiscriminate*—These individuals are referred to in the psychoanalytic literature as "polymorphous perverse." They have vaguely defined sexual preferences and will experiment with almost any type of sexual behavior.

- *Inadequate*—These individuals are social misfits who may be developmentally disabled, psychotic, senile, or organically dysfunctional. They rarely have contact with others and may see children as vulnerable objects with which to satisfy their sexual curiosity. These individuals have been known to murder their victims. However, any type of molester is capable of murder in order to avoid detection.

Preferential child molesters correspond to fixated offenders in Groth's system. These individuals show a strong sexual preference for children which has characterized their sexual attraction pattern throughout their lives. The subtypes include:

- *Seduction*—These individuals have exclusive sexual interest in children, and court and groom them. They usually are able to identify those children who will not divulge the sexual behavior.

- *Introverted*—These individuals have a fixated interest in children, but do not have the social skills to seduce them. Typically, they molest strangers or very young children or they may marry women with children in the age range of their preference.

- *Sadistic*—These individuals' sexual preference for children is coupled with a need to inflict pain in order to obtain sexual gratification. These individuals are obviously dangerous and fortunately, rare.

Meiselman's Typology. Meiselman (1978) devised a typology of incest offenders which identified the following groups:

Endogamic
Psychopathic
Psychotic
Drunken
Pedophilic
Mental defective
Situational

The group unique to Meiselman's typology is the first category, which is comprised of individuals who are heavily dependent upon their families to satisfy all of their emotional and sexual needs and are unwilling to satisfy any of these needs outside of the family structure. This type is divided between the personality disorder type and the subcultural type. The rest of the categories are self-explanatory.

Figure 3.1
Typologies of Child Molesters (Knight and Prentky, 1989)*

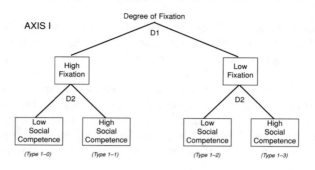

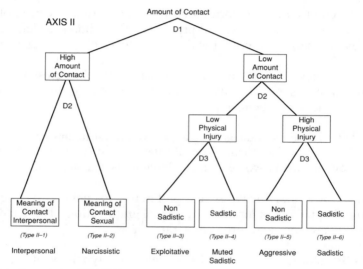

*Reprinted with permission of Ray Knight.

Knight and Prentky's Typologies. Using sophisticated statistical analyses, Knight and Prentky (Knight and Prentky, 1989) have developed typologies for both rapists and child molesters. These are being further refined and subjected to independent research. Their typologies are multidimensional. In analyzing child molesters one first evaluates the degree of fixation. The offender is then classified along the dimension of social competence. These two categories comprise Axis I. The amount of contact with children is then analyzed. Those with a high amount of contact are then analyzed according to the meaning of this contact. For some child molesters their contact with children fulfills a variety of social as well as sexual needs (Interpersonal Type). For others, the contact fulfills solely sexual needs and is usually genitally oriented (Narcissistic Type). Those with low contact are evaluated according to the amount of physical injury their victims sustain as well as the degree of sadism. This then creates a typology with 24 cells (see Figure 3.1).

Typologies of Rapists

Most researchers who have worked with rapists are impressed by the heterogeneity of the group. Consequently, they have tried to categorize not only the types of rapes but the types of rapists (see Table 3.12). One of the first to do this was Guttmacher (1952). Generally, researchers, who often depend upon their own orientation, classify rapists into the following three motivational systems:

1. *Situational:* Basically normal individuals who have certain cultural preconceptions about women and rape and who, under certain social situations or conditions of stress, may commit a rape.

Table 3.12
Typologies of Rapists

FINDINGS	Guttmacher (1955)	Gebhard, et al. (1964)	Howell (1972-73)	Cohen & Seghorn (1969)	Burgess & Holmstrom (1974)	Russell (1975)	Rada (1975)	Selkin (1975)	Groth (1979)	Hazlewood & Burgess (1987)	Nagayama-Hall (1992)	Kopp (19962)	Groth, Burgess & Holmstrom (1979)	Prentky & Knight (1992)
Sexual	X			X							X		X	X
Sadism	X			X			X		X	X			X	X
Antisocial Personality	X	X	X	X			X	X			X	X		X
Symbolic Reactions: Defense against homosexuality, incest, political condition	X			X		X	X			X				
Aggression		X		X	X				X	X	X			X
Stress		X						X						
Madonna/Whore		X						X	X					
Psychosis; Mental Retardation		X						X						
Fear of Women			X					X		X				
Power					X	X			X				X	
Ego splits												X		
Dependency														
Cognitive Distortions											X			
Opportunistic														
Vindictive													X	X

2. *Emotionally disturbed:* Rapists who may be compensating for feelings of inadequacy, expressing pent-up hostility, or duplicating a traumatic developmental experience.
3. *Criminal:* Criminal types who take sex the same way they would take money, cars, or television sets.

Note that not all researchers recognize all of these categories.

Groth's Typology. Groth (1979) and Burgess and Holmstrom (1974) were among the first theorists to discard the notion that rapists are motivated by sexual desire. Written during the height of the Women's Liberation Movement, their work obviously reflects a sensitivity to ways in which sex is misused to overpower and denigrate women.

Groth (1979) categorized rape as an act of anger, and then subdivided this emotion into (1) a simple discharge of intense anger, frustration, resentment, and rage, (2) a panic type of anger usually resulting from rejection, (3) aggression used as a way of dominating, controlling, mastering, and conquering a situation, and (4) eroticized anger. This typology is based primarily on the characteristics of the assault rather than the assailant.

Anger rape is intended to hurt, debase, and express contempt for the victim and is marked by gratuitous violence. The act is not sexually satisfying for the rapist, who often views any type of sexuality as offensive and thus an appropriate weapon. Rarely premeditated, this type of assault usually is committed in response to a precipitating stress. The rape serves as a discharge against some type of frustration either associated with the victim or utilizing the victim as a scapegoat.

Power rape serves as a means of exercising dominance, mastery, strength, authority, and control over the victim. There is little need for excessive physical force. These offenders, while less physically dangerous in their limited use of violence, may show more compulsivity, often engaging in fantasies or elaborate plans. Often, these offenders are influenced by the media-reinforced scenario of a victim who initially resists but then becomes aroused and is unable to resist the sexual prowess of the assailant. It is the endless seeking after this distorted fantasy that gives the behavior its compulsive quality. The act may be a way of reaffirming the offender's masculinity and these individuals are often highly homophobic.

Sadistic rape represents the most severe pathology as well as the most dangerous type of assault. The ritual of torturing the victim and the perception of suffering and degradation becomes eroticized, and as the assailant's arousal builds, so may the violence of his acts, progressing in some cases to lust murder. The pattern of the assault and the characteristics of the victim are repetitious and symbolic of something he wishes to humiliate and destroy.

Selkin's Typology. Selkin (1975) divides rapists into two categories. The first category, he said, are victims of what analysts call ego splits. They are married, young, employed, and living a life that one would not describe as typical of a person who is mentally ill. But their family life is disturbed, and they cannot relate successfully to their wives or parents. As youngsters they may have had problems with an older sister or an aunt who "messed on them." After the crime these men will deny their behavior. Typically they will say, "I don't remember," "It wasn't me," or "I felt like I was watching a movie" (p. 76).

The second category is predatory rapists. According to Selkin, "these men are out to exploit and manipulate others, and sometimes they do it through rape" (p. 76).

FBI's Typology. The FBI has developed a typology of rapists that utilizes four classifications. Type 1 is the Power-reassurance rapist who assaults to reassure himself of his sexual adequacy and his masculinity. This type of offender tends to show more "concern" for his victims, is less overtly angry, less violent, and more apologetic. Type 2 is the assertive rapist who has an aloof, "macho" attitude but usually does not resort to gratuitous physical force or violence. Type 3 is the angry-retaliatory rapist who may be comparable to Groth's sadistic type. This individual's sexual arousal is linked with the inducement of suffering in the victim (Hazelwood and Burgess, 1987). Type 4 is the anger-excitement type who shows characteristcs of a Type 3 rapist in that he derives pleasure and excitement from the victim's suffering.

Nagayama-Hall's Typology. Nagayama-Hall (1992) has presented a typology that divides rapists into four categories. Type 1 shows strong deviant arousal and impulsivity. Type 2 shows a significant amount of cognitive distortions which influence his interactions with women. This individual usually commits date rapes. Type 3 is the angry, impulsive individual who is subject to emotional outbursts. This type is the most violent. Type 4 tends to have a history of abuse and a variety of chronic problems and is usually a repeat offender with a variety of criminal behaviors.

Massachusetts Treatment Center's Typology. Knight and Prentky (1992) developed a statistically-based typology for rapists. (see Figure 3.2) Beginning with clinical observations by Seghorn and Cohen at the Massachusetts Treatment Center and adopted by Groth, these typologies were relied upon for many years. However, when they were subjected to statistical analysis, it became apparent that more refinement in the categories was needed. After three revisions, Prentky and Knight settled on a typology consisting of nine types derived from four basic categories (opportunistic, pervasively angry, sexual, and vindictive). Type 1 is an opportunistic individual with high social competency. Type 2 is also opportunistic but has low social competency. Type 3 is pervasively angry with a long history of antisocial behavior reflecting that anger. This individual is low in social competence and is impulsive. The overall category of the sexual-type offender is broken down along the dimension of sadism and then further divided according to social competence. Type 4 is overtly sadistic, high in antisocial behavior, and does engage in offense planning. Type 5 shows muted sadism which is not overtly expressed. This individual has little history of antisocial behavior but does engage in offense planning. Type 6 rapes for sexual gratification but shows little evidence of sadism and does have a fairly high level of social competence. This individual does not have a significant antisocial background but does engage in offense planning. Type 7 resembles Type 6 except that he shows low social competence. The last two categories are classified as vindictive. Both types focus their anger on women but Type 8 shows low social competence, while Type 9 shows high social competence (Knight and Prentky, 1992).

Figure 3.2
Typologies of Rapists (Knight and Prentky 1992)*

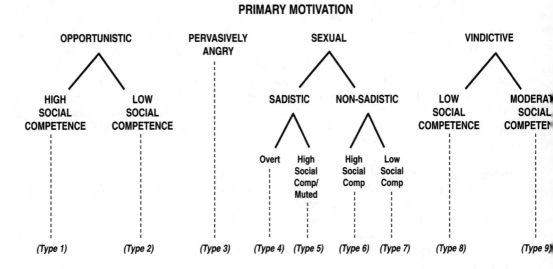

*Reprinted with permission of Ray Knight.

Escalators Versus Non-Escalators

Enhancing one's ability to predict behavior is a critical reason for developing typologies. Unfortunately, the field has not yet progressed to the stage where this is feasible. In order to identify the most dangerous offenders, research is being conducted by the FBI to distinguish between serial and solo rapists (Warren, Hazelwood, and Reboussin, 1991) and between "escalators" and "non-escalators." Serial rapists show a significant history of sexual assault in their childhoods. They show patterns of chronic acting-out on a variety of behavior dimensions. Their rape fantasies began in adolescence and they show multiple paraphilic behaviors. These individuals tend to assault strangers. The authors identified an interesting pattern in which the majority of serial rapists started out by committing "surprise" rapes but later switched to "confidence" rapes where they knew the victim and used deceit and manipulation rather than instrumental violence.

In studying those who escalate the degree of violence, Warren, Reboussin, Hazelwood, and Wright (1991) found that about one-quarter of their sample became more forceful and violent over time. They also found that the escalators had more victims (40 versus 22) over a shorter period of time (every 19 days versus every 55 days). The escalators tended to bind and transport their victims. They did not negotiate with or attempt to reassure their victims. They tended to act in what the authors describe as "macho" ways, showed greater planning, less impulsivity, and were colder and more detached. Finally, they maintained longer contact with their victims. Using this set of characteristics, the researchers were able to correctly classify 92% of the escalators. However, they are quick to caution that the results are preliminary.

Conclusion

Research into the characteristics of sex offenders can become a meaningless list of traits. Typologies may be reduced to labels that do more harm than good.

This information must be integrated into treatment in such a way that therapies become more refined and effective. The first treatment program simply placed sex offenders into generic psychiatric settings. This was probably more for confinement than for rehabilitation. Rudimentary therapies began to evolve when therapists and offenders recognized that sex offenders had little in common with severely psychotic or brain damaged patients. In some settings, the treatments kept a psychiatric orientation and stressed individual psychotherapy and groups which focused on early trauma or generic skill-building. However, over the past 20 years, the field of sex offender therapy has become as specialized as the field of substance abuse treatment. A basic set of techniques has come to be associated with the field, and participants have been offered as many of these treatments as setting, time, resources, and, in some cases, politics could afford to provide.

As a group, sex offenders have been identified as having unique needs. Now, therapists must strive to classify offenders into meaningful subgroups and devise appropriate interventions. This will open up a whole new field of research as the efficacy of different modalities are evaluated on different types of abusers. Indeed, this may be the focus of the next decade's development in the field of sex offender treatment.

References

Abrahamsen, D. (1950). Study of 102 sex offenders at Sing Sing. *Federal Probation,* 14, 26-32.

Abel, G.G., Becker, J.V., Cunningham-Rathner, J., Mittleman, M.S., Murphy, M.S., and Rouleou, J.L. (1987). Self-reported crimes of nonincarcerated paraphilias. *Journal of Interpersonal Violence,* 2, 3-25.

Ainsworth, M.W. (1989). Therapy of incest survivors: Abuse or support. *Child Abuse and Neglect,* 13, 549-562.

Abel, G.G., Becker, J.V., and Cunningham-Rathner, J. (1984). Complications, consent and cognitions in sex between children and adults. *International Journal of Law and Psychiatry,* 7, 89-103.

Abel, G.G., Blanchard, E.B., and Becker, J.V. (1978). An integrated treatment program for rapists. In R.T. Rada (Ed.), *Clinical aspects of the rapist* (pp. 161-214). New York: Grune & Stratton.

Abel, G.G., Blanchard, E.B., Becker, J.V., and Djenderedjian, A. (1978). Differentiating sexual aggressives with penile measures. *Criminal Justice and Behavior,* 5, 315-332.

Abel, G.G., Becker, J.V., Murphy, W.D., and Flanagan, B. (1981). Identifying dangerous child molesters. In R.B. Stuart (Ed.), *Violent behavior: Social learning approaches to prediction, management and treatment* (pp. 116-137). New York: Brunner/Mazel.

Amir, M. (1971). *Patterns in forcible rape.* Chicago: University of Chicago Press.

Apfelberg, C., Sugar, C., and Pfeff, A.Z. (1944). A psychiatric study of 250 sex offenders. *American Journal of Psychiatry,* 100, 762-769.

Astor, G. (1974). The charge is rape. Chicago: Playboy Press.

Baker, D. (1985). Father-daughter incest: A study of the father. Doctoral dissertation, California School of Professional Psychology, San Diego. Dissertation Abstracts International, 46(03), 951B.

Barbaree, H.E. and Marshall, W.L. (1989). Erectile responses among heterosexual child molesters, father-daughter incest offenders, and matched nonoffenders: Five distinct age preference profiles. *Canadian Journal of Behavioral Sciences,* 21, 70-82.

Barbaree, H.E., Marshall, W.I., and Connor, J. (1988). The social problem-solving of child molesters. Unpublished manuscript, Queen's University, Kingston, Ontario, Canada.

Baxter, D.J., Marshall, W.I., Barbaree, H.E., Davidson, P.R., and Malcolm, P.B. (1984). Deviant sexual behavior: Differentiating sex offenders by criminal and personal history, psychometric measures and sexual responses. *Criminal Justice and Behavior, 11,* 477-501.

Berkowitz, A.R. (1983). Incest as related to feelings of inadequacy, impaired empathy and early childhood memories. Unpublished doctoral dissertation, University of Southern California.

Berry, J. (1992). *Lead us not into temptation: Catholic priests and the sexual abuse of children.* New York: Doubleday.

Blanchard, W.H. (1959). The group process in gang rape. *Journal of Social Psychology, 47,* 259-266.

Bowman, K.M. (1938). Psychiatric aspects of the problem. Symposium: Challenge of Sex Offenders. *Mental Hygiene, 22,* 10-20.

Brownmiller, S. (1975). *Against our will: Men, women and rape.* New York: Simon and Shuster.

Burgess, A.W. and Holmstrom, L.L. (1974). *Rape: Victims of crisis.* Bowie, MD: Robert J. Brady Co.

California Legislature Assembly. (1950). Preliminary report of the subcommittee on sex crimes.

Carnes, P. (1983). Out of the shadows. Minneapolis, MN: CompCare.

Carter, D.L., Prentky, R.A., Knight, R.A., Vanderveer, P.L., and Boucher, R.J. (1987). Use of pornography in the criminal and developmental histories of sexual offenders. *Journal of Interpersonal Violence, 2,* 196-211.

Chandler, R. (1990). Sex abuse racks the clergy. Los Angeles Times, Aug. 3.

Chasnoff, M.D., Burns, W.J., Schnoll, S.H., Burns, K., Chisum, G., and Kyle-Spore, L. (1986). Maternal neo-natal incest. *American Journal of Orthopsychiatry, 56,* 577-580.

Cohen, M. and Seghorn, T. (1969). Sociometric study of the sex offender. *Journal of Abnormal Psychology, 74(2),* 249-255.

Conte, J.R. (1985). Clinical dimensions of adult sexual abuse of children. *Behavioral Sciences and the Law, 3,* 341-354.

Cook, R.F., Losen, R.H., and Pacht, A. (1971). Pornography and the sex offender: Patterns of previous exposure and arousal effects of pornographic stimuli. *Journal of Applied Psychology, 55,* 503-511.

Dushay, L.J. (1943). *The boy sex offender and his later career.* New York: Grune and Stratton, Inc.

East, W.N. (1946). Sexual offenders. *Journal of Nervous and Medical Disease, 103,* 626-666.

Ellis, A., and Brancale, R. (1956). *Psychology of sex offenders.* Springfield, IL: Thomas.

Estrich, S. (1987). *Real rape.* Cambridge, MA: Harvard University Press.

Fallen, K.C. (1989). Characteristics of a clinical sample of sexually abused children: How boy and girl victims differ. *Child Abuse and Neglect, 13,* 281-291.

Federal Bureau of Investigation. (1991). Uniform crime reports. Washington, DC: United States Department of Justice.

Fehlow, P. (1973). Causes and forensic assessment of sexual offenders. (Germ.) *Psychiatric, Neurologic and Medizinische Psychologic, 29(9),* 535-544.

Fenichel, I. (1945). *The psychoanalytic theory of neurosis.* New York: W.W. Norton & Co.

Finkelhor, D. (1984). *Child sexual abuse: New theory and research.* New York: The Free Press.

Finkelhor, D. and Baron, L. (1986). High-risk children. In D. Finkelhor (Ed.). *A sourcebook in child sexual abuse* (pp. 60-88). Newbury Park, CA: Sage Publications.

Fisher, G. and Rivlin, E. (1971). Psychological needs of rapists. *British Journal of Criminology, 11(21),* 182-185.

Fitch, J.H. (1962). Men convicted of sexual offenses against children: A descriptive follow-up study. *British Journal of Criminology, 3,* 18-37.

Frankel, E. (1950). Psychiatric characteristics of sex offenders: A statistical analysis of 250 sex offenders examined at the New Jersey State Diagnostic Center at Menlo Park. Trenton, NJ: Department of Institutions and Agencies.

Friedrich, W.N. (1988). Behavior problems in abused children: An adaptational perspective. In G.E. Wyatt and E.J. Powell (Eds.), *Lasting effects in child sexual abuse* (pp. 256-272). Beverly Hills, CA: Sage Publications.

Fromuth, M.E. and Burkhart, B.R. (1989). Longterm psychological problems in sexually abused children: An adaptational perspective. In G.E. Wyatt and E.J. Powell (Eds.), *Lasting effects in child sexual abuse* (pp. 256-272). Beverly Hills, CA: Sage Publications.

Frosch, J. and Bromberg, W. (1939). The sex offender: A psychiatric study. *American Journal of Orthopsychiatry,* 9, 761-777.

Gardner, G.E. (1950). The community and the aggressive child. *Mental Hygiene,* 34, 44-63.

Gebbard, G.O. (1989). *Sexual exploitation in professional relationships.* Washington, DC: American Psychiatric Association Press.

Gebhard, P., Gagnon, J., Pomeroy, W., and Christenson, C. (1964). *Sex offenders: An analysis of types.* New York: Harper & Row.

Gechtman, L.R. (1989). Sexual contact between social workers and their clients. In G.O. Gabbard (Ed.), *Sexual exploitation in professional relationships* (pp. 157-179). Washington, DC: American Psychiatric Association Press.

Geis, G. (1971). Group sexual assaults. Medical aspects of human sexuality, 5(5), 100-113.

Glover, B. (1960). *Psychoanalysis: A handbook for medical practitioners and students of comparative psychology.* London: Staples Press.

Glueck, B. (1952). Study and treatment of persons convicted of crimes involving sexual aberrations: Final report on research project. Albany: New York State Department of Mental Hygiene.

Goldhirsch, M. (1961). Manifest content of dreams of convicted sex offenders. *Journal of Abnormal and Social Psychology,* 63(3), 643-645.

Goldstein, M., Kant, H., Judd, L., Rice, C., and Green, R. (1971). Experience with pornography: Rapists, pedophiles, homosexuals, transsexuals and controls. *Archives of Sexual Behavior,* 1(1), 1-15.

Gore, D.K. (1988). Cognitive distortions of child molesters and the cognition scale: Reliability, validity, treatment effects, and prediction of recidivism. Unpublished doctoral dissertation, Georgia State University, Atlanta.

Griffin, S.T. (1971). The politics of rape: An inquiry. *Ramparts,* 10(3), 26-36.

Groth, A.N. (1979). *Men who rape: The psychology of the offender.* New York: Plenum Press.

Guttmacher, M.S. (1952). *Sexual offenses: Problems, causes and prevention.* New York: Norton.

Hartman, R. and Nicolay, C. (1966). Sexually deviant behavior in expectant fathers. *Journal of Abnormal Psychology,* 66, 232-237.

Hartwell, S.W. (1950). A citizen's handbook of sexual abnormalities. Report to the Committee on Education of the Governor's Study Commission on the Deviated Sex Offender. State of Michigan.

Hazelwood, R. and Burgess, A. (1987). *Practical aspects of rape investigation: A multidisciplinary approach.* New York: Elsevier.

Henninger, J.M. (1940). The senile sex offender: A consideration of therapeutic principles. National Probation Association Yearbook, 114-137.

Henry, G.W. and Gross, A.A. (1938). Social factors in the case histories of underprivileged homosexuals. *Mental Hygiene,* 22, 591-611.

Hirning, L.C. (1947). In R.M. Lindner and R.V. Seliger (Eds.), T*he sex offender in custody: A handbook of correctional psychology.* New York: Philosophical Library, 233-256.

Howell, L.M. (1972-1973). Clinical and research impressions regarding murder and sexually perverse crimes. *Psychotherapy and Psychosomatics,* 21(1-6), 156-159.

Howells, K. (1978). Some meanings of children for pedophiles. In M. Cook and G. Wilson (Eds.), *Love and attraction* (pp. 57-82). Elmsford, NY: Pergamon.

Johnson, T.C. (1989). Female child perpetrators: Children who molest other children. *Child Abuse and Neglect,* 13, 571-585.

Johnson, W.L., Kupperstein, L., and Peters, J. (1970). Sex offenders' experience with erotica. Commission on Obscenity and Pornography, Techn. Rep., Vol. 7. Washington, DC: Government Printing Office.

Julian, V., Morr, C., and Lapp, L. (1980). Father-daughter incest. In W. Holden (Ed.), *Sexual abuse of children: Implications for treatment* (pp. 17-35). Englewood, CO: American Humane Association.

Kamin, E.J. and Parcell, J.R. (1977). Sexual aggression: A second look at the female offender. *Archives of Sexual Behavior*, 6, 67-76.

Karpman, B. (1954). *The sexual offender and his offenses: Etiology, pathology and treatment*. New York: Julian Press.

Kercher, G.A. and Walker, C.E. (1973). Reactions of convicted rapists to sexually explicit stimuli. *Journal of Abnormal Psychology*, 81(1), 46-50.

Knight, R.A. and Prentky, R.A. (1990). Classifying sexual offenders: The development and corroboration of taxonomic models. In W.L. Marshall, D.R. Laws and H.E. Barbaree (Eds.), *Handbook of sexual assault: Issues, theories, and treatment of the offender* (pp. 23-54). New York: Plenum.

Krafft-Ebing, R. (1892). *Psychopathia sexualis*. New York: Pioneer Publications, Inc.

Langevin, R., Handy, L., Day, D., and Russon, A.E. (1985). *Erotic preference, gender identity and aggression* (pp. 161-180). Hillsdale, NJ: Erlbaum.

Langley Porter Clinic (1954). Final report on California sexual deviation research. Sacramento: Assembly of the State of California.

Lanning, K.V. (1986). *Child molesters: A behavioral analysis for law enforcement officers investigating cases of child sexual exploitation*. Washington, DC: National Center for Missing and Exploited Children.

Larson, R.M. (1984). Theory and measurement of affect intensity as an individual difference characteristic. Dissertation Abstracts International, 84, 22112.

Ledray, L.E. (1986). *Recovering from rape*. New York: Henry Holt and Co.

Lee, R. (1982). Analysis of the characteristics of incestuous fathers. Doctoral dissertation, University of Texas at Austin. Dissertation Abstracts International, 43, 2343B.

Levine, S. and Koenig, J. (1980). *Why men rape: Interviews with convicted rapists*. New York: Macmillan.

Luiz, D., Donnerstein, E., and Penrod, S. (1987). The effects of multiple exposures to filmed violence against women. *Journal of Communications*, 34, 130-147.

MacDonald, J.M. (1971). *Rape: Offenders and their victims*. Springfield, IL: Charles Thomas.

McCaghy, C. (1966). Child molesters: A study of their careers as deviants. Doctoral dissertation, University of Wisconsin.

Madigan, L. and Gamble, N.C. (1989). *The second rape: Society's continued betrayal of the victim*. New York: Lexington Books.

Mandel, M.D. (1986). An object relation study of sexually abusive fathers. Doctoral dissertation, California School of Professional Psychology, San Diego. Dissertation Abstracts International, 47(5), 2173B.

Marlatt, G.A. (1989). Feeding the PIG: the problem of immediate gratification. In D.R. Laws (Ed.), Relapse prevention with sex offenders (pp. 56-97). New York: Guilford.

Marshall, W.L., Barbaree, H.E., Laws, D.R., and Baxter, D. (September 1986). Rapists do not have deviant sexual preferences: Large scale studies from Canada and California. Paper presented at the Twelfth Annual Meeting of the International Academy of Sex Research, Amsterdam.

Marshall, W.L., Bates, L., and Rhule, M. (1984). Hostility in sex offenders. Unpublished manuscript, Queen's University, Kingston, Ontario, Canada.

Marshall, W.L., Christie, M.M., and Lanthier, R.D. (1979). *Social competence, sexual experience, and attitudes to sex in incarcerated rapists and pedophiles*. Ottawa: Solicitor General of Canada.

Meiselman, K. (1978). *Incest: A psychological study of causes and effects with treatment recommendations*. San Francisco: Jossey-Bass.

Menaker, E.A. (1939). Contribution to the study of the neurotic stealing symptom. *American Journal of Orthopsychiatry*, 9, 368-378.

Mohr, J.W. (1964). *Pedophilia and exhibitionism: A handbook*. Toronto: University of Toronto Press.

Mosher, D.L. and Sirkin, M. (1984). Measuring a macho personality constellation. *Journal of Research on Personality*, 20, 77-94.

Murphy, W.D., Coleman, E.M., and Haynes, M.R. (1986). Factors related to coercive sexual behavior in a nonclinical sample of males. *Violence and Victims*, 1(4), 255-278.

Murphy, W.D., Coleman, E.M., Haynes, M.R., and Stalgartis, S. (1979). Etiological theories of coercive sexual behavior and their relationship to prevention. Unpublished manuscript.

Nagayama-Hall, G. (Nov/Dec. 1992). Inside the mind of a rapist. *Psychology Today*, 25(6), 12.

Okami, P. and Goldberg, A. (1986). Personality correlated of pedophilia: Are they reliable indicators? *Journal of Sex Research*, 29(3), 297-328.

Overholster, C. and Beck, S. (1986). Multimethod assessment of rapists, child molesters and three control groups on behavioral and psychological measures. *Journal of Consulting and Clinical Psychology*, 54, 682-687.

Parker, H. and Parker, S. (1986). Father-daughter sexual abuse: An emerging perspective. *American Journal of Orthopsychiatry*, 56, 531-549.

Parrot, A. (1988). *Coping with date rape and acquaintance rape*. New York: Rosen Publishing Group.

Paveza, G. (1987). Risk factors in father-daughter child sexual abuse: Findings from a case-control study. Paper presented at the Third Annual Family Violence Research Conference. Durham, NC: Family Research Laboratory.

Pelto, V.L. (1981). Male incest offenders and nonoffenders: A comparison of early sexual history. Doctoral dissertation, U.S. International University, San Diego, 8118142. Ann Arbor, MI: University Microfilms.

Pithers, W.D., Beal, L.S., Armstrong, J., and Petty, J. (1989). Identification of risk factors through clinical interviews and analysis of records. In D.R. Laws (Ed.), *Relapse prevention with sex offenders* (pp. 77-87). New York: Guilford.

Pithers, W.D., Kashima, K., Cumming, G.F., Beal, L.S., and Buell, M. (1988). *Relapse prevention of sexual aggression*. Annals of the New York Academy of Sciences, 528, 244-260.

Pope, K.S. (1989). Teacher-student sexual intimacy. In G.O. Gabbard (Ed.), *Sexual exploitation in professional relationships* (pp. 67-89). Washington, DC: American Psychiatric Association Press.

Quinsey, V.L., Chaplin, T.C., and Carrigan, W.F. (1979). Sexual preferences among incestuous and nonincestuous child molesters. *Behavior Therapy*, 10, 562-565.

Quinsey, V.L., Chaplin, T.C., and Upfold, D. (1984). Sexual arousal to nonsexual violence and sado-masochistic themes among rapists and non–sex offenders. *Journal of Consulting and Clinical Psychology*, 52, 651-657.

Quinsey, V.L., Steinman, C.M., Bergerson, S.G., and Holmes, T.F. (1975). Penile circumference, skin conductance, and ranking responses of child molesters and "normals" to sexual and nonsexual visual stimuli. *Behavior Therapy*, 6, 213-219.

Ploscowe, M. (1951). *Sex and the law*. New York: Prentice-Hall, Inc.

Pollens, B. (1938). *The sex criminal*. New York: Macauley.

Rada, R. (1978). *Clinical aspects of the rapist*. New York: Grune & Stratton, Inc.

Rappaport, K. and Burkhart, B.R. (1984). Personality and attitudinal characteristics of sexually coercive college males. *Journal of Abnormal Psychology*, 93, 216-221.

Rediger, L. (1990). *Ministry and sexuality: Cases, counseling and care*. Minneapolis: Fortress Press.

Revitch, E. and Weiss, R. (1962). The pedophiliac offender. *Diseases of the Nervous System*, 23, 73-78.

Risin, L.I. and Koss, M.P. (1988). The sexual abuse of boys: Childhood victimizations reported by a national survey. In A.W. Burgess (Ed.) *Rape and sexual assault II* (pp. 91-104). New York: Garland.

Russell, D. (1975). *The politics of rape: The victim's perspective*. New York: Stein & Day.

Russell, D.E.H. (1990). *Rape in marriage*. Bloomington, IN: Indiana University Press.

Salhotz, E. (July 16, 1990). Women under assault: Sex crimes finally get the media's attention. *Newsweek,* p. 23.

Salter, A. (1988). *Treating child sex offenders and their victims.* Newbury Park, CA: Sage Publications.

Saunders, B., McClure, S., and Murphy, S. (1986). Final report: Profile of incest perpetrators indicating treatability. Part I. Charleston, SC: Crime Victims Research and Treatment Center.

Saunders, B., McClure, S., and Murphy, S. (1986). Structure, function and symptoms in father-daughter sexual abuse families: A multilevel-multirespondent empirical assessment. Paper presented at the Third Annual National Family Violence Research Conference, Family Research Laboratory, Durham, NC.

Schultz, G. (1965). *How many more victims?* Philadelphia: Lippincott.

Scully, D. (1990). *Understanding sexual violence: A study of convicted rapists.* London: Unwin Hyman.

Scully, D. and Marolla, J. (1984). Convicted rapists' vocabulary of motives: Excuses and justifications. *Social Problems,* 31, 530-544.

Segal, Z.V. and Marshall, W.L. (1985). Heterosexual social skills in a population of rapists and child molesters. *Journal of Consulting and Clinical Psychology,* 53, 55-63.

Selkin, J.R. (1975). Rape. *Psychology Today,* 8(8), 70-73.

Shaskan, D. (1939). 100 sex offenders. *American Journal of Orthopsychiatry,* 9, 565-569.

Stermac, L.E. and Segal, Z.V. (1990). Adult sexual contact with children: An examination of cognitive factors. Manuscript submitted for publication.

Stermac, L.E., Segal, Z.V., and Gillis, R. (1990). Social and cultural factors in sexual assault. In W.L. Marshall, D.R. Laws, and H.E. Barbaree (Eds.), *Handbook of sexual assault: Issues, theories, and treatment of the offender* (pp. 143-159). New York: Plenum.

Strand, V. (1986). Parents in incest families: A study of differences. Doctoral dissertation, Columbia University. Dissertation Abstracts International, 47(8), 3191A.

Struckman, C. and Johnson, K. (1988). Forced sex on dates: It happens to men too. *Journal of Sex Research,* 24, 234-241.

Sullivan, J.P. and Mosher, D.L. (1990). Acceptance of guided imagery of rape as a function of macho personality. *Violence and Victims,* 5(4), 275-286.

Time Magazine. (May 4, 1992). Unsettling report on an epidemic of rape, p. 15.

Thompson, J.K. (1989). Lifestyle interventions: Promoting positive addictions. In D.R. Laws (Ed.), *Relapse prevention in sex offenders* (pp. 219-226). New York: Guilford.

U.S. Department of Justice. (1986). The crime of rape. Bureau of Justice Statistics, Bulletin.

U.S. Department of Justice. (1986). Final Report of the Attorney General's Commission on Pornography.

Van Kirk, L. (writer/reporter). (January 1984). Men of ward 41A (TV documentary). Portland, OR: Station KGW.

Waggoner, R.M. and Boyd, D. (1941). Juvenile aberrant sexual behavior. *American Journal of Orthopsychiatry,* 11, 275-291.

Walters, D.R. (1975). *Physical and sexual abuse of children: Causes and treatment.* Bloomington: Indiana University Press.

Warren, J.I., Hazelwood, R.R., and Reboussin, R. (1991). Serial rape: The offender and his rape career. In A. Burgess (Ed.), *Rape and sexual assault III* (pp. 76-102). New York: Garland.

Warren, J.I., Reboussin, R., Hazelwood, R.R., and Wright, J.A. (1991). Prediction of rapist type and violence from verbal, physical and sexual scales. *Journal of Interpersonal Violence,* 6(1), 55-67.

Waterman, C.K., Dawson, M.A., and Bologna, M.J. (1989). Sexual coercion in gay and lesbian relationships: Predictors of gay rape. *Journal of Sex Research,* 26(1), 118-124.

Williams, L.M. and Finkelhor, D. (1990). The characteristics of incestuous fathers: A review of recent studies. In W.L. Marshall, D.R. Laws, and H.E. Barbaree (Eds.), *Handbook of sexual assault: Issues, theories, and treatment of the offender* (pp. 143-159). New York: Plenum.

Yochelson, S. and Samenow, S.E. (1976). *The criminal personality,* Vol. 1. New York: Aronson

Chapter 4

Cost Effectiveness of Treatment

by Nancy Steele, Ph.D.

Page

Overview

This chapter reviews recidivism rates for prison, community, and combined sex offender treatment programs as well as the cost effectiveness studies of several states that support treatment. The chapter is not meant to be a comprehensive review of all articles on program effectiveness. Instead, it looks at some programs in some settings that show promise of being effective. The chapter shows the differences in types of sex offenders being handled in different settings and the importance of separating these issues when trying to judge programs and make decisions. As different as many of these programs are, there is a similarity in their findings that is compelling and adds validity to each study. However, the differences make it obvious that there is a need for standardizing the terms used in this field so that the various findings can be compared more easily.

Research on Program Effectiveness Is Scarce

For many years, administrators and legislators have been concerned about budget constraints, public opinion, overcrowded prisons, and the expectations of greater public safety. One aspect of this concern centers on the effectiveness, cost, and possible benefits of sex offender treatment. Across the country, staff involved in sex offender programs have struggled to come up with answers.

Admittedly, there is a potential for bias when research is done by staff on their own programs. That is why the replication of findings is important. Gradually, data collected from various places over different time periods begins to show a picture of the benefits that sex offender programs can achieve. Funding for quality research into treatment effectiveness has been minimal, and many programs have had to struggle to conduct their own studies (Furby, Weinrott, and Blackshaw, 1989).

Problem Number 1: "True" Recidivism Rate Is Unknown. One of the main objections to recidivism studies is that they do not reveal the "true" recidivism of sex offenders. Both victim and offender studies show that many (if not most) sex crimes are unreported and undetected. Groth and Longo (1982) reported on a study done with 83 rapists and 54 child abusers incarcerated in two states. They asked these offenders to fill out an anonymous questionnaire indicating how many crimes they actually had committed. The results were compared to the number of convictions recorded in the offenders combined presentence investigation reports. The questionnaire reported an average of 14 undetected victims for each rapist and 11 unreported victims for each child molester. This is significant because it does not show undetected repeated events with the same victim.

Data reported by Abel, and associates (1987) indicates similarly high rates on undetected crimes when offenders are given a seal of confidentiality from the federal government. Most therapists working in the field also report that offenders who take treatment seriously confess to additional crimes.

Problem Number 2: Measuring Whether Treatment Works. Another problem with many recidivism studies is that they tend to simply ask whether treatment works with sex offenders. Looking at a specific group of treated offenders in a particular setting and then trying to apply the findings to all sex offenders in all settings and all types of programs only results in confusion. While it is the public's misconception that "nothing works," a review of meta-analyses on the efficacy of sex offender treatment found that nine out of ten studies reviewing up to eighty-seven (87) programs found affirmative evidence for sex offender treatment (McGrath, 1994). The one study that supported the pessimistic view was conducted by Furby and associates (1989). *Readers Digest,* unfortunately, then popularized this notion in an article of their own based on her survey of the research articles. Her original review looked at 42 studies from different settings using different kinds of sex offenders and dating back to the 1920s. As their control group they picked untreated sex offenders from Great Britain and Europe. Some newsstand magazines picked up on this review and have popularized the notion. There remains a need for major research for carefully controlled and statistically sound research in this area.

The rest of this chapter compares several studies of programs and recidivism from different settings. It also compares the cost of treatment with the dollar cost of a new sex offense.

Institutional Programs and Recidivism

The number of incarcerated sex offenders has risen dramatically in the last several years. In the United States, the number increased by 48% between 1988 and 1990. During the same time period, the total prison population increased by 20%. Overall, by 1990, 12.3% of the total U.S. prison population was incarcerated for sex offenses (*Corrections Compendium,* July 1991). These figures do not include the likely increase in the number of sex offenders who were convicted and sentenced to probation in the community. Presumably, many of these offenders remained in the community with treatment programming, county jail time, and community supervision as a part of their probation.

The results of this study probably do not reflect an increase in the number of sex offenses committed. Instead, it shows an increased awareness of, attention to, and concern about sex crimes. The public wants these crimes to be treated more seriously; they want offenders to be held more accountable. Prosecutors and elected officials are hearing this message loud and clear.

Recidivism Rates for Sex Offenders. The major problem in judging most treatment studies is the failure to compare matched groups of treated and untreated sex offenders. Without a base rate for comparison, one often is left guessing just how effective a reported treatment outcome is. Fortunately, in 1989, the National Institute of Justice (NIJ) published a study (Beck, 1989) on the recidivism rates of 108,580 inmates released from state prisons in 1983 in 11 states, including New York, Ohio, New Jersey, Texas, California, and Florida. Table 4.1 shows (1) 16 different types of crimes the offenders in the study served time for and (2) the rearrest and reconviction rates for these offenders three years after their release from prison. Rearrests and reconvictions were reported for all types of felonies, not only new sex offenses. The reported percentages give us a baseline with which to judge some treatment studies.

Table 4.1
Recidivism of Sex Offenders (Beck, 1989)

Type of Crime	% Rearrested	% Reconvicted
Rape	51.5	36.4
Other sex assault	47.9	32.6
All offenses, combined	62.5	46.8

Most of the prisoners in the study were not rearrested for the same type of crime they went to prison for. However, two groups had a much higher likelihood of repeating in kind. Beck (1989) reports that those released for rapes and other sexual assault are 10.5 and 7.5 times more likely to repeat the same crime than any other groups of offenders. This rationale might justify a specialized prison-based sex offender treatment.

Beck (1989) also confirmed the findings of other criminologists that men released from prison are most likely to be rearrested in the first year after release. Two-thirds of the men in this study were rearrested during that time. The rate of rearrest begins to drop off significantly after that. This is important because the length of time a sample of subjects is followed often is questioned. Although the rate of recidivism always goes up slightly the longer a group is followed, the rate undoubtedly is the highest in the first few years. It is not clear whether following releasees for 10 or 20 years would provide enough additional information to warrant the difficulty involved.

Another aspect of this issue is where the effects of institutional treatment end and the effects of what happens to the man in the community begin. Given the outside influences released prisoners are subject to, it hardly seems reasonable to assume the effects of a treatment program will last forever, even though we might wish it would. Even cancer studies only follow patients for five years before considering them "cured."

Comparison of Studies on Recidivism. Table 4.2 summarizes institution-based programs from five different states and Canada. Although some of these programs were carried out in state hospital settings, they drew their sex offenders largely from the prison population. The studies represent the longest follow-up periods (up to 15 years). However, they include individuals treated with outdated treatment modalities.

Critics who insist that efficacy studies report long-term follow-up periods assume that treatment will remain the same over time. Lumping offenders treated in 1962 with those treated in 1992 causes innumerable methodological problems in this rapidly changing field. Nevertheless, these treatments are likely to be similar in their approach to working with the most aggressive sex offenders.

Table 4.2
Recidivism Rates From Institutionally-Based Sex Offender Programs

	Years of Follow-Up	% New Sex Offenses	% Other Felonies	% Combined Offenses
Wisconsin N = 472 Year = 1962 (Furby, et al., 1989)	1-11	15.6	2.4	18
Avenel, NJ N = 324 Year = 1978 (Furby, et al., 1989)	0-10	9.3	11.7	21
Washington Western State Hospital N = 402 Year = 1979 (Furby, et al., 1989)	0-12	22.1		
Atascadero N = 382 Year = 1980 (Sturgeon and Taylor, 1980)	1-5			Treated 15.4 Untreated 25.0
Massachusetts Treatment Center N = 129 Year = 1985 (Prentky, 1992)	0-15			Treated 25 Untreated 40
Canadian Study N = 56 Year = 1988 (Lang, Pugh, and Langevan, 1988)	3			Incest 7 Pedophile 18

Table 4.2 (Continued)

	Years of Follow-Up	% New Sex Offenses	% Other Felonies	% Combined Offenses
Missouri N = 261 Year = 1989 (Mo. Doc.)	1-11	Completers 13.3 Noncompleters 25.5	9.57	12
Minnesota Transitional Sex Offender Program (TSOP) N = 428 Year = 1991 (Bittner, 1991)	1-11	Completers 16 Noncompleters 22	9.57	12

Note that three of the programs in Table 4.2 separate the percent of reconvictions for new sex offenses from those for other felonies, including parole violations. This writer has found this to be somewhat misleading in that the criminal justice system's practice of plea bargaining coupled with its eagerness to avoid trials often means that the sex offense portion of a charge is dropped. For example, an offender may plea bargain for assault, kidnapping, burglary, or robbery. Often, it is impossible to detect from the charge alone whether this behavior is a new type of crime or another sex offense. A great deal of valuable information will be lost if only new sex offenses are counted in recidivism studies.

Wisconsin Treatment Program. Wisconsin ran a prison-based treatment program for rapists and other aggressive sex offenders from 1950 through the 1970s. Their report on 475 men released from the program and followed up for between 1 to 10 years shows that 18% had violated parole or were convicted of a new felony. This number compares favorably with the approximately 34% of sex offenders who were reconvicted of a new felony within three years of release from prison as reported in the Beck's study (1989).

New Jersey Treatment Program. In New Jersey, which devotes an entire prison to the treatment of sex offenders, 324 men released after "emotional release" therapy showed a reconviction rate of 21% for new felonies. The follow-up period ranged from 0 to 10 years. This seems to be an improvement over the 34% reconviction rate reported by Beck (1989) for the prison group without treatment.

Western State Hospital, Washington. The State of Washington operated its program for "Sexual Psychopaths" at Western State Hospital until 1988. Their clients were convicted of criminal charges, and most would have been in state prison if they were not placed in the treatment program. This study reported recidivism only in the form of new sexual felonies. The rate is similar to the other programs in Table 4.2, but follow-up time of 12 years must be considered. It should also be remembered that many of these individuals were treated prior to the development of modern treatment techniques.

Atascadero, California. The first Atascadero State Hospital treatment program located in Atascadero, California ran for over 30 years. Over 2,000 sex offenders were released from this program. One of the better studies, published by Sturgeon and Taylor (1980), compared 260 offenders treated in the hospital program with 122 untreated sex offenders from prison. The releasees were followed for from 1–5 years. Results of this study are reported in Table 4.2.

Massachusetts Treatment Program. The Massachusetts Treatment Center treats civilly committed "Sexually Dangerous Persons." Theoretically, these individuals were selected for placement at the facility by the aggressive or repetitive nature of their crimes. They cannot be released until a judge rules that they are no longer sexually dangerous. Thus, while they may represent a more intractable population than sex offenders given a criminal sentence only, they may have been more closely screened prior to release. The statistics show a significant treatment effect.

Canada's Treatment Program. Lang and associates (1988) conducted a three-year follow-up of an inpatient Canadian treatment program that utilized a multi-modal approach combining behavioral, psycho-educational, and family therapy as well as psychodrama. Statistics are comparable to other programs reported in Table 4.2.

Missouri Department of Corrections. The Missouri Department of Corrections conducted a follow-up study of individuals completing Phase II of their sex offender treatment program. The program is housed in one prison and uses a cognitive/behavioral model without a therapeutic community milieu.

Minnesota's Treatment Program. In Minnesota, the Transitional Sex Offender Program (TSOP) began in 1978 in a medium-security prison and ran for almost 15 years.

This study (Bittner, 1991) reports data on 428 inmates who were followed-up for between 1-11 years after release. (see Table 4.2) The data compares 303 men who completed the program with 125 men who failed to stay with the program after their first few months of treatment in the prison. The program ran for 10-12 months during the offender's last year of incarceration. For some offenders, the program also included a four-month aftercare phase in the community. .

The 16% recidivism rate for offenders who completed the program is similar to that of other institutionally-based programs over a similar period of time. The 22% recidivism rate for the comparison group of noncompleters is significantly better than the base rate of 34%. This group was followed from 1-11 years. Since this program emphasized an intensive psycho-educational approach at the beginning of treatment, it is possible that the noncompleters benefitted from going through the beginning stages of treatment.

The TSOP data collected on return rates of program participants was reanalyzed by Steele (1993). Table 4.3 analyzes the data by subtype of offenders. This study's relatively short follow-up period may be a better measure of treatment impact. One would expect any treatment effect to decrease as the offender continues to live in the community with little or no follow-up treatment It also allows the recidivism data to be compared directly with that of the NIJ study. The rates were collected by the Minnesota Department of Corrections, Office of Research and Information, 1991.

Table 4.3
Percent of Sex Offenders Committing New Felonies Within Three Years of Release After Participating in the TSOP Program

Rapists	N = 204	48% of sex offenders
Completers	N = 138	14.49% new felonies
Noncompleters	N = 66	27.27% new felonies
Incest Offenders	N = 160	37% of sex offenders
Completers	N = 129	4.65% new felonies
Noncompleters	N = 31	6.45% new felonies
Child Abusers	N = 58	14% of sex offenders
Completers	N = 35	8.57% new felonies
Noncompleters	N = 23	20.83% new felonies
Other Sex Offenders	N = 6	1% of sex offenders
Completers	N = 1	0% new felonies
Noncompleters	N = 5	20% new felonies
Total	N = 428	
Completers	N = 303	9.57% new felonies
Noncompleters	N = 125	16% new felonies

Minnesota's program was one of the first to report an improved effect in treating rapists. Most community-based programs treat few, if any, convicted rapists. Although almost one-third of the participants failed the program, the recidivism rate of those that completed the program is nearly half of those that did not complete the program (14% versus 27%). The reasons offenders did not complete the program ranged from breaking institutional rules to waiving out to removal for not cooperating with treatment.

Rapists did not have nearly as high a failure rate as extra-family child abusers or other sex offenders, including exposers, voyeurs, and an obscene phone caller. Although most of these offenders were in prison for nonsexual felonies, they were placed in the program because their records indicated they also had problems in the area of sexual assault. Given their high rate of failure in the program (40% for the extra-family child abusers), it was surprising to see such a good effect for those who completed treatment. This group largely consisted of men who offended against male children, all of them outside the family.

In general, the incest offenders were the best behaved men in the program and were seldom, if ever, removed from treatment. Their lower recidivism rate is consistent with several studies of other programs that will be reported.

It is worth noting that Minnesota has the second lowest incarceration rate in the United States. This means that sex offenders who go to prison in Minnesota usually have committed fairly serious offenses. Four-fifths of convicted sex offenders are managed in the community.

The data includes a number of men convicted of murder and very serious mutilation of victims. Many of them responded well to treatment and have maintained success in the community years after release. The findings of this study contradicts an idea often mentioned in the literature that "sadistic" rapists cannot be treated. While it may be politically risky to attempt to treat the most violent offenders, particularly in the community, the data from this program seems to indicate that some rapists and other aggressive offenders can and do respond well to a treatment approach in a prison setting.

Comparison of Six Community-Based Programs

Outpatient programs in communities in the United States and Canada often treat less violent sex offenders (exhibitionists, voyeurs, non-violent pedophiles, incest offenders) as a condition of probation. However, most outpatient programs are reluctant to treat aggressive rapists because they fear repercussions on their program, if a re-offense brings a lot of publicity. Similarly, most courts choose to send the more violent rapists to prison rather than risk public criticism.

Table 4.4
Recidivism Rates from Community-Based Programs for Sex Offenders

Location	*Follow-Up Period*	*% New Sex Offenses*
Oregon (Maletzky, 1987) N = 2781	1–5 years	14.9 (See Table 4.5)
Kingston Sexual Clinic (Marshall and Barbaree, 1988) N = 184	4 years	Treated = 5.3 Untreated = 14.7 (See Table 4.6)
Abel and associates (1988) N = ?	1 year	12.2

Table 4.4 (Continued)

Location	Follow-Up Period	% New Sex Offenses
Dwyer and Myers (1990) N = 153	10 years	3.7
Johns Hopkins University (Berlin and Malin, 1991) N = 600	5 years	3
SSOSA Berliner and associates (1991) N = 613	5-6 years	Treated = 11.2 Untreated = 25.7 (See Table 4.7)

Some study results show that offenders who are treated in the community who commit less violent acts have higher recidivism rates than those who are sent to prison. An early study (Frisbie and Dondis, 1965) on the first Atascadero Hospital program reports that treated voyeurs were recidivating at 46% and exhibitionists at 41% with a 1 to 5 year follow-up. As shown in Table 4.5, Maletzky's (1987) study on 2,781 offenders in Oregon with a 14-year follow-up looks especially impressive.

Table 4.5
Community-Based Outpatient Treatment Program

Total No. of Offenders	Type of Offense	% New Sexual Crimes
N = 1719	Female child molesters	12.7
N = 513	Male child molesters	13.6
N = 462	Exhibitionists	6.9
N = 87	Less violent rapists	26.5

Clearly, the treatment approach being used by this clinic was successful with types of sex offenders who generally have a high rate of recidivism. The 6.9% recidivism rate for exhibitionists is quite a bit better than the 41% recidivism for exhibitionists reported in the Atascadero study. One reason for this may be that this community-based program, like most outpatient programs in the United States, treats sex offenders who are able to pay for their treatment. Generally, these men have more resources and support than those who are sent to institutions.

Similarly effective results were reported from The Kingston Sexual Clinic in Canada. The clinic, which treats offenders on an outpatient basis, presented their data in a study (Marshall and Barbaree, 1988) with a matched control group of untreated offenders. Participants in both the treated and untreated groups admitted their crimes and asked to be involved in treatment. The average follow-up period was four years. Their results are summarized in Table 4.6.

Table 4.6
Kingston Clinic Outpatient Program for Sex Offenders

Type of Offense	*Treated* *N = 126* *% New sex crimes*	*Untreated* *N = 58* *% New sex crimes*
Female child molesters	7.5	17.9
Male child molesters	5.5	19.2
Incest	2.9	7

The treated offenders have a lower recidivism rate. Male child molesters seem to have benefitted from treatment (5% compared to 19%), but the incest offenders have the lowest rate of recidivism. The lower rate for the incest offenders may in part be a reflection of the shorter average four-year follow-up period.

Abel, et al. (1988) reported a recidivism rate of 12.2% after a one-year, follow-up period of treated extra-familial child abusers who had abused boys, girls, or sometimes both. Abel may have found a higher recidivism rate because the self-reported offenders in this study were guaranteed immunity by the federal government and thus may have been more candid in admitting to crimes.

Berlin and Malin (1991) reported recidivism statistics from the Johns Hopkins Clinic in Baltimore. Their program followed 600 pedophiles, rapists, and exhibitionists for five years and reported an overall recidivism rate of less than 10% with the 170 pedophiles showing a rate of less than 3%. Their treatment combined group therapy with the antiandrogenic medication, medroxyprogesterone-acetate. There was no control group.

Dwyer and Myers (1990) reported an outcome study from their Minnesota community-based program which utilized behavioral, structural, and strategic family therapy, marital and sexual treatment, and psychopharmocology. They followed their 153 subjects for up to 10 years and found a 3.7% recidivism rate.

The State of Washington commissioned a study of its alternative sentencing laws for sex offenders (SSOSA) under which almost half of the state's sex offenders undergo community-based treatment from a variety of private providers rather than receiving prison sentences. The Harbourview Sexual Assault Center and the Urban Policy Center did a 5-6 year follow-up study on 613 SSOSA-eligible offenders (Berliner, Miller, Schram, and Milloy, 1991). The results are shown in Table 4.7.

Table 4.7
Special Sex Offender Sentencing Alternative Report (1991)

Type of Recidivism	Recidivism Rate (%) Treated Sex Offenders (N = 313)	Recidivism Rate (%) Untreated, Imprisoned Sex Offenders (N = 300)
Any rearrest	17.3	36.0
Sex offense rearrest	6.1	8.7
Any reconviction	11.2	25.7
Sex offense reconviction	5.1	5.3
Violent offense reconviction	3.8	9.3

The Washington study utilized the least dangerous offenders, most of whom were incest fathers. Few in the sample had serious substance abuse problems, extensive criminal histories, or employed weapons or gratuitous violence. Given this relatively low-risk population, it is not surprising that there was a low sex offense reconviction rate. The overall reconviction rate (11.2% versus 25.7%) is noteworthy. The program does not cost the state anything because the offenders pay for their own treatment.

Assuming that the imprisoned group would have re-offended at the same rate as the control had they received treatment, 32 men would have not re-offended. Estimating incarceration costs at $35,000 per year, the state would have saved $1,120,000 per year had these sex offenders originally been treated in the community.

In general, a number of studies suggest that outpatient treatment in the community of some sex offenders is effective. The cost of treating men on an outpatient basis in the community where they often pay for their own treatment is far less. If offenders are able to maintain their employment, keep their families off welfare, and the state does not have to pay for their incarceration, the savings for the tax payer will be considerable. The problem is balancing the economics involved with the risk level for the public. In several states where outpatient programs are available, incest offenders are considered the safest offenders to manage in the community. They often do not have a history of abusing children outside their own family and so the public at large is not at risk and children of the offender can be protected by restricting contact with them. If incest offenders demonstrate a willingness to avoid contact with their own children, they present the least risk for treatment in the community compared to other types of sex offenders.

Survey of Comprehensive Programs
(Institution with Aftercare)

California's Atascadero Research Project. Programs begun in the last few years have combined inpatient and outpatient services to their clients. Particularly worth noting is the current treatment program at the Atascadero State Hospital in California. In 1981, the California legislature eliminated their commitment statute to the state hospital and ordered all sex offenders sent to the state prison system. With funding support from the National Institute of Mental Health they created an experimental program that allowed the state to rigorously test methods of treating sex offenders. The 50-bed experimental program was started in 1985 with sex offenders who volunteered to come there from the prison system two years before their release from prison.

Since this program was funded primarily as a research program, the design always has included two control groups matched for age, type of crime, and severity of criminal history. One control group (Control group 1) consists of men who volunteered for treatment but were randomly selected to not participate. The other control group (Control Group 2) consists of sex offenders who did not volunteer to participate in treatment.

The program includes two years of institutional treatment following a Relapse Prevention model and a year of aftercare treatment in the community. They are seen twice a week in the community for a year by therapists trained in the Relapse Prevention model.

Recidivism rates are actively being collected on all three groups and will be for 10 years after their release. The recidivism percents are a combination of arrests and parole violations for sex offenses and other violent offenses. The results (Marques, 1993) are shown in Table 4.8.

Table 4.8
California's Atascadero Research Program (1993)

	Treatment N = 116	Voluntary Control Group 1 N = 126	Nonvoluntary Control Group 2 N = 121
Time at risk	38 months	38 months	38 months
Rapists (N = 78)	23.0%	48.0%	28.5%
Child molesters (N = 285)	7.8%	11.0%	13.8%
Total (N = 363)	11.2%	19.0%	14.9%

This program further reports that 21% of their clients failed to complete the program: 15% dropped out and 6% were removed for disciplinary reasons.

One statistic not included in Table 4.8 is the follow-up data on treatment failures, 100% of whom committed new sex offenses. Careful study of the characteristics of these individuals could have valuable predictive implications. The most immediate point obvious from this data is that if rapists volunteer for treatment, it would be a good idea to provide it. According to program staff, prisoners' willingness to volunteer often depends upon whether their families lived near to the hospital or prison they were in, by the type of prison job or schooling they had, their rate of pay, and other considerations that motivate people to move to another part of a very large state. It seems possible from this date that researchers have historically overestimated the importance of the "volunteering factor" as an outcome variable in effect of treatment. Type of offender, age, and severity of criminal history are probably the biggest factors which determine level of risk rather than initial motivation for treatment.

Overall, these arrest rates approximately three years after release would seem to compare favorably with the arrest rates in the Beck (1989) study. In that case rearrest rates were at 51% for the rapists and 48% for other sex offenders. Because Atascadero excludes men with three felony convictions or more, the group that probably accounts for the higher level of arrests within three years of release from prison, it is probably dealing with lower risk groups than Beck studied. This program should continue to yield valuable recidivism data of all sorts for the rest of this decade.

Vermont's Sex Offender Program. Another state with a continuous institution-based program and a long follow-up time in the community is Vermont. This program, like California, operates on a cognitive-behavioral model stressing Relapse Prevention. This is not a research program and it operates on a more modest scale. The institution program is a least a year long and the community phase is a year long. Pithers (1992) reports recidivism on new sex offenses with a 1-8 year follow-up. The report uses a very conservative estimate in that offenders were counted as recidivating if they were rearrested or believed by their parole officer or therapist to have committed a new sex offense. This criteria makes it difficult to compare results from this program with some of the others cited in this article. These results are presented in Table 4.9.

Table 4.9
Vermont's Sex Offender Program, Prison and Community
Involvement (1992)

Type of Offender	Number of Offenders	% New Sex Offenses
Pedophiles	195	7
Incest Offenders	190	3
Rapists	53	19
Untreated	—	38

For example, it is not possible to determine what percent of the sex offenders fail the institutional program or in community phase and what their recidivism might be. The results of this program are consistent with other studies in that the incest offenders have such a low recidivism and the program seems to be achieving success with the pedophiles based on reports from other programs.

Trends in Treatment Programs

It seems that the treatment of sex offenders is moving toward a model of treatment in an institution (typically a therapeutic community) followed by at least a year of follow-up in the community. Rapists particularly need continuity in treatment since the first few weeks after release are a particularly stressful time for them. The effectiveness of continuity in treatment even for a few months after release is supported by data from TSOP in Minnesota.

Both the California program at Atascadero and the program in Vermont offer a year or more of follow-up in the community after the offender leaves confinement. Additionally, the Atascadero program is considered a model in the country for research design. The legislature mandated random assignment as part of the test of treatment effectiveness. The offenders are recruited from the prison system. Results from these two programs have a shorter follow up period than some of the older programs because they have not been around as long.

A comparison of the recidivism rates for these comprehensive programs is shown in Table 4.10.

Table 4.10
Recidivism Rates for Comprehensive Programs

Location	*Follow-Up Period*	*% New Sex Offenses*
Vermont (Pithers, 1992)	1-8 years	Treated-7% Untreated-38% (See Table 4.9)
Atascadero (Marques, 1993) N = 363	3 years	Treated=11% Untreated=17% (See Table 4.8)

Cost Benefits of Successful Sex Offender Treatment

Treatment does not eliminate all sex crimes. At best, there are indications that it cuts the recidivism rate somewhere between 10 and 30%. How does this benefit measure up against the cost of treatment?

Prentky and Burgess (1990) sought to answer that question by looking at the cost of treatment in the Massachusetts program that has operated for years in the state hospital in Bridgewater, Massachusetts. They compared 129 child molesters treated in that program and released with a control group of untreated child molesters from

Canada. In both cases they looked at charges on new sex offenses in a five-year follow-up. They found that 25% of the treated child molesters were charged with a new
sex offense which compared favorably with 40% of the untreated abusers being
charged with a new sex offense.

They also computed the cost for a scenario in which there was a new, detected
sexual crime against one victim. They estimated that the cost for investigation, arrest,
prosecution, and incarceration for an average of seven years and no treatment for the
offender would be $169,029. Expenses for the victim which included treatment and
care came to $14,304. This assumes one victim. We can be sure that for every crime
they are caught for, there are probably some others that are not detected. This assumes
the person goes to prison for seven years on what might be a second or third conviction. Obviously, in some states he might go to prison for a much longer time.

This expense was compared with the cost of treating the offender in the
Bridgewater program. In Massachusetts prior to 1991 those who were released from
treatment were in confinement for an average of five years instead of the seven years
in prison. It turned out that the cost of treating one offender for five years in the hospital based program was $118,146, considerably less than the cost of one new sexual
offense which came to a total of $183,333.

While this seems high, the cost of one new sex offense as estimated in this study
is not too different from the $152,000 found in a Vermont study (Pithers, 1987). Pithers
included the costs for arresting, investigating, prosecuting, and confining the offender and supervising him on parole as well as the cost of services to the victim.

The cost factors associated with the Transitional Sex Offender Program in
Minnesota were figured in a different manner. Because this program is about 10
months long and all of the offenders were in prison anyway, the cost of incarceration
with treatment were compared to the cost of incarceration in the same prison without
treatment. The costs were averaged over a two year period (July 1989 through July
1991). The 41-bed program was largely run by using existing correctional staff that
were assigned to the living unit including correctional officers, plus three additional
treatment staff. The cost is shown in Table 4.11.

Table 4.11
Cost of Minnesota's Transitional Sex Offender Program

Salary—Three additional positions	$ 111,945.00
Travel Expenses	1,211.00
Supplies	1,093.00
Deaf interpreter	2,683.00
Total	$ 115,591.00
Prison cost per inmate per day	$67.21
Treatment cost per inmate per day	7.73

Treatment of one offender—$7.73 x 320 days = $2,473.60

Cost of new sex offense—$183,333.00

McGrath (1994) calculated the cost benefits of Vermont's community-based sex offender treatment program. The results are shown in Table 4.12.

Table 4.12
Cost of Vermont's Community-Based Sex Offender Treatment Program

Offender-Related (Pretrial Trial Incarceration (5 years),Incarceration Treatment)
Total $130,428

Victim-Related (Department of Social Services Hospital/Medical Evaluation Treatment (1 year)
Total $8,400

Offense Total $138,828

In Vermont offender treatment is subsidized at a rate of $345 a year for three years for up to 100 sex offenders. Thus, the cost to the state to provide outpatient treatment is $103,800. If recidivism is reduced by only 1%, the state saves $35,000 over the cost of the program. If recidivism is reduced by 8%, there is a $1 million savings to the state.

The recent trend toward giving mandatory life sentences to individuals convicted of three consecutive violent offenses can be used to illustrate the dramatic cost savings of successful treatment during a first or second offense. Assuming a sex offender was sentenced to a mandatory life sentence at the age of 30 and died at the age of 70, it would cost $1 million (40 years times $25,000 per year), not including any medical treatment for serious illnesses or inflation.

Almost every state spends a lot of money to prosecute and incarcerate offenders. As illustrated above, the additional cost of some treatment while incarcerated is small by comparison. For example, using the costs from the Prentky study as a guide for the Minnesota program, we can see that if the state program prevented one new sex offense offense among those men participating in the program, it could afford to treat 74 sex offenders. Treatment is only a little more expensive than simple incarceration and it has promise of improving public safety.

Most important, programs need to be researched as efficiently as possible to determine which elements pay off. For instance, while family may be critical for an incest offender in the community, it may be relatively unimportant in a prison setting with rapists. Perhaps rapists must begin their treatment within the confines and controls of a prison setting, but a longer follow-up time of treatment in the community after release would benefit both them and the community. Legislators and the public in general must pay careful attention to the costs and benefits of all types of interventions including prison, probation, treatment, education, and vocational programs before deciding how to allocate public funds. Otherwise, it will continue to be difficult to determine which programs in this difficult and emotionally charged area really increases public safety and which only give the appearance of "getting tough."

References

Abel, G.C., Becker, J.V., Mittelman M., Cunningham-Rathner, N., Rouleau, J.L., and Murphy, W.D. (1987). Self-reported sex crimes of non-incarcerated paraphiliacs (Final Report No. MH-33678). Washington DC: Public Health Service.

Abel, G.C., Mittleman, M.S., Becker, J.V., Rathner, J., and Rouleau, J.L. (1988). Predicting child molesters, response to treatment. *Annals of the New York Academy of Sciences,* 528, 223-234.

Beck, Allen J. (1989). Recidivism of prisoners released in 1983. U.S. Department of Justice. Bureau of Justice Statistics.

Becker, J. and Hunter, J. (1992). Evaluation of treatment outcomes for adult perpetrators of child sexual abuse. *Criminal Justice and Behavior,* 9, 74-92.

Berlin, F. and Malin, H. (1991). Media distortion of the public's perception of recidivism and psychiatric rehabilitation. *American Journal of Psychiatry,* 148, 1575-1576.

Berliner, L., Miller, L.L., Schram, D., and Milloy, C.D. (1991). *The special sex offender sentencing alternative: A study of decision-making and recidivism.* Seattle: Harborview Sexual Assault Center and Urban Policy Research.

Bittner, M. (1991). *Recidivisim data for TSOP.* Minnesota Department of Corrections (unpublished paper).

Corrections Compendium (July 1991). Survey: Number of sex offenders in prison. Volume XVI, No. 7.

Frisbie, L. and Dendis, E. (1965). *Recidivism among treated sex offenders.* Research Monograph No. 5. Sacramento, CA, California Department of Mental Hygiene.

Frisbie, L.V. (1969). *Another look at sex offenders in California.* Mental Health Research Monograph No. 12. Sacramento: State of California, Department of Mental Hygiene.

Furby, L., Weinrott. M.R., and Blackshaw, L. (1989). Sex offender recidivism: A review. *Psychological Bulletin,* 105, 3-30.

Groth, N., et al. (1982). Undetected recidivism among rapists and child molesters. *Crime and Delinquency,* 28, 450-458.

Lang, R., Pugh, G., and Langevin, R. (1988). Treatment of incest and pedophilic offenders: A pilot study. *Behavioral Science and the Law,* 6, 239-255.

Maletzky, B. (1987). Data generated by an outpatient sexual abuse clinic. Paper presented at the 3rd Annual Conference of the Association for the Behavioral Treatment of Sexual Abusers. Newport, OR.

Maletzky, B. (1991). *Treating the sex offender.* Newbury Park, CA: Sage Publications.

Marques, J. (1993). Atascadero, California Research Program.

Marshall, W., et al. (1991). Treatment outcome with sex offenders. *Clinical Psychology Review,* 11, 465-485.

Marshall, W.L., Jones, R., Ward, T., Johnston, P., and Barbaree, H. (1988). The long-term evaluation of a behavioral treatment program for child molesters. *Behavior Research and the Law,* 26, 499-511.

Marshall, W. and Pithers, W. (1994). A reconsideration of treatment outcome with sex offenders. *Criminal Justice and Behavior,* 21, 10-27.

McGrath, R. (1994). Cost effectiveness of sex offender treatment programs. Presented at the Annual Conference for Virginia Sex Offender Treatment Providers, Hampton Beach, Virginia.

Missouri Department of Corrections (1989). *Sex offender treatment program recidivism* (unpublished study).

Pacht, A.R., Halleck, S.L., and Ehramann. J.C. (1962). Diagnosis and treatment of the sexual offender: A nine year study. *American Journal of Psychiatry,* 118, 802-808.

Paper presented at the 12th Annual Conference of the Association for the Treatment of Sexual Aggressors. Boston, MA.

Pithers, W.D. (1987). Cost of a new sex offense and the relative cost of treatment. Paper prepared for the Safer Society Press.

Pithers, W.D., and Cumming, G.F. (1989). Can relapses be prevented? Initial outcome data from the Vermont Treatment Program for sexual aggressors. In Laws, D. (Ed.), *Relapse Prevention with Sex Offenders,* (pp. 313-325). New York: Guilford Press.

Prendergast, W.E. (1978). ROARE: Re-education of attitude and repressed emotions. Avenel, NJ: Adult Diagnostic and Treatment Centre Intensive Group Therapy Program.

Prentky, R. and Burgess, A.W. (1992). Rehabilitation of child molesters: A cost-benefit analysis. *American Journal of Orthopsychiatry,* 60, 108-117.

Saylor, M. (1979). A guided self-help approach to treatment of the habitual sexual offender. Paper presented at the 12th Cropwood Conference, Cambridge, UK.

Steele, Nancy M. (1991). Return rates collected by the Minnesota Department of Corrections, Department of Information and Analysis.

Sturgeon. V.H. and Taylor, J.(1980). Report of a five-year follow-up study of mentally disordered sex offenders released from Atascadero State Hospital in 1973. *Criminal Justice Journal,* 4, 31-63.

Chapter 5

Female Sex Offenders

by Barbara K. Schwartz, Ph.D. and Henry R. Cellini, Ph.D.

Page

Overview

This chapter discusses the most frequently ignored type of sex offender–female offenders. The incidence, demographics, and characteristics of female offenders are discussed as well as their similarities and differences from male offenders.

Years from now when you talk about this—and you will—be kind.

Deborah Kerr, *Tea and Sympathy*

These words were spoken by one of the world's most genteel actresses in her role as the middle-aged wife of the headmaster of a private boy's school as she initiated sex with an adolescent boy. The movie portrays the 45-year-old woman as a self-sacrificing heroine who gives herself unselfishly to enhance a 16-year-old boy's self-esteem. Now, let's switch genders so the scene is played by a 45-year-old man and 16-year-old female. The audience's reaction undergoes a dramatic shift—the movie is about the sexual abuse of children.

Studies of both clinical and non-clinical populations indicate a significant number of female offenders, even though most types of female offenders are ignored, denied, and minimized except in a few graphic instances. (See Tables 5.1 and 5.2.) Allen (l991) has calculated that roughly 1.5 million females and 1.6 million males have been sexually abused by females in this country.

Table 5.1
Non-Clinical Samples of Victims of Female Sex Offenders

Study	Percent of Female Victims Abused by Females	Percent of Male Victims Abused by Females
National Incidence Study (1981)	13%	24%
American Humane Assoc. (1978)	6%	14%
Finkelhor and Baron (1986)	0-10%	14-27%

Table 5.1 (continued)

Risin and Koss (1991)	42.7%	—
Fromuth and Burkhart (1989)	9-12%	—
Fritz, Stoll, and Wagner (1981)	60%	—

Table 5.2
Clinical Samples of Victims of Female Sex Offenders

Study	Population	Percent of Female Victims Abused by Females	Percent of Male Victims Abused by Females
Freeman-Longo (1987)	Rapists	—	4%
Groth and Burgess (1979)	Rapists (31% sexually abused)	—	41%
Burgess, et al. (1987)	Rapists (56% sexually abused)	—	56%
Johnson and Shier (1987)	Hospitalized adolescent males	—	44%
Groth and Burnham (1979)	Rapists	—	59%
Faller (1989)	Sexually abused children	5-15%	5-15%
Bera (1985)	Adolescent male sex offenders	—	20-25%

Table 5.2 (continued)

Study	Population	Percent of Female Victims Abused by Females	Percent of Male Victims Abused by Females
Dimock (1988)	Male victims	—	28%
Evans and Schaefer (1987)	Female substance abuse victims	25%	—

Societal Reasons for Denying Female Sexual Abuse

Despite these numbers, the problem of sexual abuse by females as been largely ignored. Mathis (1972) stated that "Women are viewed as harmless to children, what harm can be done without a penis?" (p. 54). With the exception of monographs published by the Safer Society Press (Matthews, Matthews, and Speltz, 1989; Knopp and Lackey, 1987; Allen, 1991), there are very few books on female offenders and fewer still on female sex offenders. Matthews and associates (1989) stated that:

> Although social awareness of sexual abuse increased greatly in the 1980s, the female sexual offender has been virtually invisible. Viewing females as perpetrators of sexual abuse, perhaps parallel to males as victims, challenges traditional cultural stereotypes. Females are thought of as mothers, those who provide care for others—not as people who harm or abuse others. (p. 275)

Craig Allen (1991) concurs: "Few behaviors deviate as far from cultural norms and deep-seated beliefs as those committed by women who sexually abuse children" (p. 11). He proposes the following reasons for the failure to acknowledge this problem:

1. Overestimating the strength of the incest taboo.
2. Overextending feminist explanations of child sexual abuse.
3. Overgeneralizing the empirical observation that the sexual abuse of children by women is rare.

If one subscribes to the theory that the masculine need to exercise power and promote the exploitation of more vulnerable members of society is at the root of sexual abuse, how can a female offender's behavior be explained? There does not appear to be an explanation as to why women would violate the incest taboo, since the taboo has always been presented as a way of controlling male sexual rivalry. Therefore, any woman who violates the taboo must be grossly disturbed.

Allen suggests that professionals have succumbed to societal stereotypes about female sexual abuse to the point where they have trouble seeing or acknowledging it. The result is a vicious cycle: the dirth of information causes more professionals to fail to ask relevant questions or diagnose dynamics related to female sexual abuse. There is also a tendency to believe that the relatively small number of female perpetrators (in comparison with male offenders) negates the importance of the problem. However, even low percentages translate into millions of individual victims.

Kasl (1990) pointed out that there may be confusion in defining sexual abuse by women:

> Descriptions cannot be extrapolated from definitions of abuse by males. Men cannot smother children against their breasts. Men do not usually walk around in sheer nightgowns flirting with their children. (p.260)

Women are naturally allowed a much wider range of physically intimate behaviors due to their care-taking role. It is almost impossible for a child to distinguish between legitimate concern with their health and hygiene and sexual abuse. By the time a child is old enough to recognize sexual intent, for example, the young male adolescent may already be subscribing to the gender stereotype that males are in control of all sexual encounters or that any sexual contact with a women is enjoyable. In working with male victims of female sexual abuse, these authors have noticed that it is often very traumatic when a man remembers that the sexual encounter was not an idealized encounter, like in the movie, *The Summer of '42*, but an unwanted, intrusive, shameful violation.

Female victims have had to endure both the trauma of the abuse itself and the realization that one cannot be safe with either sex. They may experience much the same gender confusion issues as males molested by men experience. Furthermore, they must cope with society's denial of the existence of the female perpetrator.

Kasl (1990) also pointed out that women may be loathed to discuss this problem:

> Women fear incurring the anger of other women who may believe that by exploring sexual abuse by females, we are apologists for men. There is also a fear that men will possibly coopt the subject or be recognized as the authorities and neglect to include a cultural analysis that takes power differences between men and women into account. (p. 261)

Another underlying cause of why the existence of female sexual perpetrators has been denied may be a deep-rooted fear of the sexual woman. A fertile—and thus sexual—woman was the prominent deity in many pre-Christian cultures. Christianity's focus on the "virgin mother" contributes to the splitting of the female image into the "Madonna" and the "Whore." Thus, the ideal mother becomes a biological impossibility and the sexual female becomes an object of fear and disgust.

In the Jewish and Southwest Hispanic cultures, living legends capture this split. Infants in Orthodox Jewish homes wear amulets with the words "Out Lilith" engraved on them. According to the Talmudic legend, Lilith was Adam's first wife. She is depicted as a headstrong individual who refused to be dominated by her mate and insisted that they were equals. Eventually, she was thrown out of paradise for pronouncing the name of God and began begetting offspring by demon lovers. Lilith, the sexual female, cannot be a nurturing mother and becomes a threat to every child. According to Schwartz (1988):

Since Lilith's flight from Eden she seeks her revenge by slipping beneath the sheets of men who sleep alone and trying to seduce them. So too does she attempt to strangle infants in their cradles. (p.6)

In New Mexico, children are still warned that if they frequent ditch banks after dark, they may be spirited away by La Llorona. There are over 42 versions of why this wailing woman haunts waterways looking for youngsters, but all of them involve her killing her own children so she could take a lover. Again, she cannot follow her sexual nature and nurture children simultaneously. Perhaps female sex offenders touch on some of our deepest psychic conflicts because they elicit the age-old image of the destroying sexual female.

Basic Gender Differences

Our culture makes some basic assumptions about how men and women differ:

• Men are more aggressive.
• Women are more empathetic and nurturing.
• Women are more emotional.
• Men are more achievement oriented.
• Women have better verbal skills.
• Women are more dependent.
• Men have better math skills.

Basic research into the differences between males and females may clarify the differences between male and female sexual offenders. Such studies must begin by noting the fundamental physical and psychological differences between the sexes as well as situational factors. Women may be perceived to be more nurturing because this is in some way an inherited trait or because of hormonal factors or biochemical influences or because they have been socialized to nurture others. However, believing these stereotypes might lead to certain conclusions about how female sex offenders should be evaluated and treated.

Aggressiveness. Over 48 studies reviewed by Oetzel (1966) and Maccoby and Jacklin (1974) confirm that men are more aggressive than women. However, Frieze and associates (1978) looked at other studies that may challenge this basic supposition. When "aggression" is defined as "physical force intended to inflict harm," then men may display more of that behavior. However, in studying verbal aggression, rejection of others, or hidden aggressiveness, then women equal or surpass men (Frieze, Parsons, Johnson, Ruble, and Zellman, 1978; Tauris, 1992).

Empathy and Nurturance. An equally strong belief involves women's inherent capacity for being nurturing and empathetic. When given written personality tests, women describe themselves as more empathetic than men do. However, after reviewing studies on whether men and women differ in empathetic behavior, Eisenberg and Lennon (1983) concluded that there is little evidence of innate differences.

Emotionality. Studies of emotionality reveal a similar pattern. Women tend to describe themselves as more emotional, particularly on ratings of fear, depression, and anxiety (Frieze, et al., 1978). When one studies actual physiological differences, however, the results are inconsistent. Furthermore, numerous studies show that men are seen as less masculine and less well-adjusted when they reveal their emotions (Robertson and Fitzgerald, 1990; Shields, 1987).

Achievement and Dependence. The research into differences concerning achievement and dependence abounds with problems. Here are some of them: Who is defining "achievement"? Who in this society is responsible for doling out the rewards for achievement and what are those rewards? Are individuals being self-effacing or modest when they describe their achievements? Are men self-confident or arrogant? As long as there are political and economic imbalances between the sexes, it will be difficult to study this issue.

Cognitive Differences. Cognitive differences have long been used as examples of how men and women differ. Men are better at math, and women have better verbal skills. Recent interest in differences in the brain structure of men and women have led to a refocusing on how this might effect thought processes. Kimura (1992) summarized studies indicating that males are better on certain spatial tasks, math, routing, and target-directed motor skills, but females are better in tests of perceptual speed, verbal fluency, math calculations, finding landmarks, and precision motor tasks.

Some theorists believe that testosterone levels may influence these abilities. Studies on individuals with Turner Syndrome, with androgen-sensitive females, and with congenital adrenal hyperplasia producing abnormally higher levels of androgens in females suggest that there may be a hormonal basis for certain spatial abilities (Bock and Kolakowski, 1973; Kimura, 1992). However, after reviewing 165 studies, Hyde and Linn (1988), concluded there were no gender differences in verbal abilities. A similar study on math skills suggest that males in the general population do not outperform females in math abilities although there are more highly gifted male mathematicians (Hyde, 1990).

Sexuality. The belief that men are more sexually oriented and active is one that needs close examination in the context of this article. Kinsey's (1953) landmark study found that women had fewer orgasms, viewed less pornography, and masturbated less then men. He believed that women had less "sexual capacity" for biological reasons. However, Masters and Johnson (1970) claimed that womens' capacity for multiple orgasms was evidence that their sexual capacity is greater than mens'.

Oral contraception allowed women to enjoy spontaneous sex without fear of pregnancy. Since then, women have been approaching men on almost every measure of "sexual capacity," including the number of extramarital relations they are having (Dennis, 1992).

Sexuality certainly does mean different things to different people, and may mean different things to the same person at different times in their life. Travis (1992) stated:

> [L]ook at the influences that make male and female sexuality more similar
> over the life span. Consider one difference long thought to be the hallmark
> of our species: that men generally want sex for the physical pleasure of it and

women want sex for the emotional intimacy of it. Studies of adolescents and young adults usually show this pattern, at least on the average. But people change over the years: more women start enjoying sex for the physical pleasure and more men start enjoying the emotional closeness. By observing such changes in the meaning and variety of sexual experience, we can see that sexuality is not necessarily inherent in the individual. (pp. 244-245)

Research on Inherent Differences Between the Sexes Not Always Conclusive

The research is contradictory whether one is studying gender differences in aggression, empathy, dependency, emotionality, sexuality, or cognition. Travis (1992) concludes that:

> By seeing the behavior of women and men in context as flexible capabilities rather than solely as steadfast qualities of the person, we move away from the unfathomable question of whether men and women are "really" essentially alike. (p.205)

Differences in Communication Styles May Have Implications for Therapy. Even though the research is not clear on the inherent distinctions between males and females, the same is not true of differences based on socialization. Recent publications have pointed out that the sexes' different communication styles may have implications for therapy. Tanner (1990) states that:

> Intimacy is key in a world of connection where individuals negotiate complex networks of friendship, minimize differences, try to reach consensus, and avoid the appearance of superiority, which would highlight differences. In a world of status, independence is key, because a primary means of establishing status is to tell others what to do, and taking orders to do, and taking orders is a marker of low status. Though all humans need both intimacy and independence, women tend to focus on the first and men on the second. (p. 26)

At least in their communication styles, they do. This is mirrored in the way males and females interact with each other. Tanner (1990) notes a study by Goodwin that compares play activities between boys and girls. She concluded that boys' play reflects a constant preoccupation with hierarchy and status while girls' play reflects concern with seeking out friends who are popular with others.

The differences thus far discussed may have some interesting implications for understanding the dynamics of female sex offenders and for their treatment. For example, the research on aggression suggests that male sex offenders would be more physically assaultive and females would be verbally abusive and, if they feel safe from disclosure, may be violent as well. Moreover, females may be more unwilling to discuss their deviance, particularly its physically abusive aspects.

The research on empathy and nurturing suggests that when female sex offenders talk together or describe themselves, they may sound more empathetic. However, their behavior itself should be closely monitored as they may be quick to reject each other in a group (Frieze, et al., 1978) or to develop intragroup jealousies (Tanner, 1990).

Studies on emotionality suggest that female sex offenders may be more open in discussing their feelings than male offenders. They may describe themselves as more depressed and anxious. This could be interpreted to mean that women are more distressed because they find their deviant behavior to be more ego-alien or it could merely reflect differences in communication styles.

Dependent Relationship May Impact on Commission of Offense. It is impossible to separate achievement and dependence in males and females from their political context in order to study their inherent characteristics. However, it can be readily observed that more women than men are in dependent relationships. Thus, few adult male sex offenders would be pressured into committing a sex offense as the result of being in a dependent relationship but women might find themselves in just such a situation. Indeed, this appears to be the case. (Men, however, might be dependent upon a group of other males such as a gang who might pressure them into acting-out.)

Group Therapy with Female Sex Offenders. The cognitive differences cited previously probably have little relevance to sexual deviance. Mens' apparent difficulty with the verbal milieu of therapy probably is related to their reluctance to discuss their emotions rather than their verbal abilities. However, while men may be adverse to talking about their feelings, they may not be embarrassed about discussing their sexual escapades. If a sex offender can justify his deviance to a point where it seems acceptable to him, he may consider talking about it "locker room talk." A bunch of males trading stories about sexual encounters is not considered unusual. Females may find this type of discussion of fantasies and behaviors much more uncomfortable because our culture does not openly sanction them. Consequently, while women may be more able to discuss their feelings and their patterns of socialization might readily lend themselves to a group therapy setting, the prospect of discussing their aggressive, abusive, and deviant behaviors in such a setting might initially be overwhelmingly threatening.

Balance Between Independence and Intimacy. The independence-intimacy balance also has interesting implications for understanding sexual abuse. The need to maintain independence and personal power in interpersonal relationships is a major theme among male sex offenders. In these authors' experience with male offenders, individuals who sexually assault both males and females constantly talk in terms of power. Men who rape adult females frequently speaks of being "put down" by women, being robbed of their power by women, or feeling vulnerable around women. Individuals who abuse children often say that children are not a threat to their feelings of power or that they are easily controlled.

Conversely, female sex offenders may be motivated by a desire to establish intimacy. While such a definition of intimacy is distorted and confused, it may have been molded by the offender's history of sexual abuse. Attention may have become interwoven with sexual assault. Other female offenders may have found themselves in abusive relationships with adult men, and may only be able to relate to younger males who are perceived as less threatening.

Whether it is due to inherent characteristics or situational factors, men and women in this culture do differ. However, they may not differ as much as society has assumed. The female sex offender is a stunning example of that. Discarding denial around this issue will lead the way to beginning to understand which differences are relevant in dealing with this problem.

Theories of Why Females Offend

Smart (1981) notes that researchers studying female offenders focus on two specific theories: (1) themes attributing antisocial behavior to physiological causes (specifically chromosomal and genetic abnormalities) and (2) theories suggesting that antisocial females have a strongly masculine psychological makeup. She also states that females are much more likely to be considered mentally ill than male offenders.

Physiological Theories. Caesare Lombroso is considered the first modern criminologist. A physician, he attempted to study the physical characteristics of criminals including moles, hair color, skull measurements, and brain capacity. In 1895, he published the first book on female offenders. Lombroso concluded that both male and female offenders are "atavists"—biological throwbacks to a less evolved subspecies. He noted that this group had certain obvious physical features:

> On looking at her photograph....one perceives that, although only nine years old, she [looks like a] born criminal. Her physiognomy is Mongolian, her jaws and cheek bones are immense; the frontal sinuses strong, the nose flat with a prognothous under-jaw, asymmetry of face and above all, precocity and virility of expression. She looks like a grown woman—nay, man.

> Precocity and virility of aspect is the double characteristic of the criminal-woman and serves more than any other feature to destroy and make her type. (1895, p. 99)

Lombroso also described seven types of female offenders:

1. The born criminal
2. The occasional criminal
3. The hysterical offender
4. The individual who commits crimes of passion
5. Suicides
6. Criminal female lunatics
7. Epileptic delinquents

Most of these types are self-explanatory. Hysterical offenders were described as easily hypnotized individuals who show mobility of mood, variable handwriting, a mania for lying (what is termed today as "la belle indifference"), and hypersexuality. Since Lombroso believed most offenders are biologically determined, he had little interest in rehabilitation.

Lombroso was not the only theorist to espouse a physiological explanation of female criminality. Healy and Brenner (1926) found that women offenders were physiologically overdeveloped. Smith (1962) explained female delinquency in terms of the mesomorph body type and early sexual development of runaway girls. Both Dalton (1961) and Lombroso (1895) felt that women were likely to commit crimes when they were menstruating. Dalton's research showed that half of his subjects committed most of their crimes either during or two days prior to their periods. D'Orban (1971) stated that there was a relationship between menopause and criminal behavior in women. Carver (1974) described chromosome disorders, including the XXY and XXX patterns, in this population. Cowrie, Cowrie, and Skater (1968) felt that genetics could predispose women to certain specific types of crimes. Recently, there has been an interest in the connection between crime and PMS (premenstrual syndrome). There has also been research into the effect of androgens on female behavior. Females with abnormally high levels of androgens who suffer from congenital adrenal hyperplasia demonstrate more aggressive behavior (Kimura, 1992).

Biological and Psychological Differences. Freud believed that personality differences between males and females were biologically determined by their gender differences and that male and female offenders following their preordained paths of sexual development would show unique characteristics. According to Freud (1933), females are less likely to engage in violent crimes:

> Differences emerge too in the instinctual disposition which gives a glimpse of the later nature of women. A little girl is as a rule less aggressive, defiant and self-sufficient; she seems to have a greater need for being shown affection and on that account to be more dependent and pliant. (p.150)

Females, Freud felt, were less able to develop a conscience because this mental structure is produced by the resolution of the Oedipal Complex which, of course, females do not experience. Thus, womens' asocial impulses are controlled by their natural passivity and their dependence upon men (Campbell, 1981).

Comparative Research Studies. Studies contrasting male and female perpetrators always compare the women with men who abused children rather than all male sex offenders. Women who molest children may represent a much more psychologically heterogeneous group than males who molest children. Also, there are so few women who have assaulted only adults that large scale research on this population has not been feasible. However, one may get some information by contrasting female adolescent sex offenders, a population that has a relatively violent and predatory group, with male adolescent offenders.

Wolf (1985) presented the first study contrasting male and female offenders. Wolf, who is affiliated with Northwest Treatment Associates, a large outpatient treatment program for male and female sex offenders in Seattle, Washington, compared women and men residing in the community and participating in treatment. She noted that: (1) the women in this sample had a co-defender half of the time; (2) females used dependency as a explanation of their dynamics much more frequently than males; (3) females used many of the same cognitive distortions as males; (4) both males and females in the treatment program used coercion rather than physical force; and (5) both groups were more likely to offend intrafamilialy than extrafamiliarly.

In Allen's (1991) study, females reported: (1) less parental stability and more parental criticism devaluation, disappointments, and physical abuse than males; (2) less marital satisfaction with their partner, and more satisfaction with their children; (3) more sexual satisfaction, more sexual partners; (4) more physical abuse suffered and more physical abuse perpetrated against their partners; (5) fewer offenses; (6) more of their own victimization; (7) more crimes against strangers; (8) more same-gender victims; (9) more abuse by males; (10) less acknowledgment of guilt and less ability to identify behavior as sexually abusive; (11) more maintenance of innocence, more anger toward informant, and less sorrow, guilt, relief at being caught.

Needless to say, womens' physiological characteristics make it more difficult for a woman to molest an adult man. In studies of situations where this occurred, the women often were able to physically restrain and then sexually manipulate their male victims by operating in gangs (Sorrel and Masters, 1982). Nevertheless, in some women, the degree of rage or the expression of the need for power and control may be closer to male rapists than male child molesters. Findings that women perpetrators are more sexually active, more assaultive, and angrier than male perpetrators may actually be measuring a rather homogeneous group of rather passive, sexually anxious, nonassertive male child molesters against a more diverse group of women.

Types of Female Offenders

Campbell (1981) discusses a variety of theories on female criminality, including the hypothesis that women learn to be deceitful because society demanded that they hide their interest in sex and their menstrual periods. Campbell notes the consistent suggestion that because women have fewer internal controls and must rely on society to control their behavior, they will become more criminal if they gain more equality. He also notes that females are socialized differently. For example, fewer of them know how to use guns, so they would be less likely to use one in a crime. Also, they either have less access to gangs or a strictly defined role in one, so they may not be involved directly in criminal behavior.

Several researchers have developed typologies of female offenders. Widom (1978), who studied women in the Massachusetts Department of Corrections, identified four subtypes:

Type I, psychopathic—hostile, poorly socialized, impulsive, aggressive, low in anxiety.

Type II, secondary or neurotic—resembles Type I but more anxious, depressed, guilt-ridden.

Type III, overcontrolled—denies problems, high degree of control.

Type IV, "normal" criminal—hostile, tense, not impulsive, little psychopathology. Butler and Adams (1966) developed a typology of delinquent girls that made the following classifications:
   • Disturbed—neurotic, guilt-ridden, anxious.

- Immature—impulsive, aggressive, manipulative.
- Covert manipulators—present as healthy.

Generally, female offenders are seen as having emotional problems or as being mentally ill. While males are labeled as "psychopathic," females are more often diagnosed as having hysterical or borderline personality disorders (Widom, 1978). Causes are sought in physical disorders that might masculinize the female. Judges and juries may be more receptive to psychological explanations such as the "burning bed" syndrome in which a woman kills an abusive partner or to post-traumatic stress disorder in which a female victim might murder someone who sexually assaulted her. As Chesler (1987) states:

> Men are permitted a greater range of acceptable behaviors before they are (psychiatrically) hospitalized, whereas women have traditionally been allowed a greater range of acceptable behavior before they are imprisoned. (p. 295)

In the long run, it is debatable whether it is better to be labeled as "bad" or as "mad."

Types of Offenses Committed by Female Offenders

Are the types of female sex offenders similar types to those found among male offenders? Certainly, child molesters are by far the largest subgroup of women offenders. Researchers looking closely at this category identified true pedophiles who show deviant sexual arousal to children (Cooper, Swaminath, Baxter, and Poulin, 1990), child molesters who do not have deviant sexual arousal (Matthews, Matthews, and Spletz, 1989), women who rape adult women (Sorrel and Masters, 1982), and women who coerce males into unwanted sex. In fact, in a national survey of 6,159 college students, 19% of the males identified themselves as victims of sexual coercion (Koss, 1988). There also are lesbians who sexually assault their partners. Waterman, Dawson and Bologna (1989) reported that 31% of the lesbians in the study reported being victims of forced sex by their current or most recent partners. Very little information is available on misdemeant female sex offenders who engage in frottage, exhibitionism, or the more obscure paraphilias (e.g., bestiality, etc.).

Researchers have devised typologies of female perpetrators, but none of these systems have been subjected to statistical analysis similar to the research with male offenders. Sorrel and Masters (1982) described four types of sexual assault perpetrated by women: (1) forced assault, where the sexual assault is marked by the use of physical restraints or believable threats of physical violence; (2) "babysitter," where there the abuse is perpetrated on a younger boy by a non-related female who uses direct or implied threats; (3) incestuous assaults, where relatives assault children; and (4) dominant women abuse, where a female makes an aggressive sexual approach to an adult male without direct physical force, which intimidates or terrifies the victim.

In 1986, McCarty published a description of three different types of female incest offenders:

1. *The Independent Abuser:* A single parent who usually uses a daughter who is perceived as an extension of herself. This type usually has been sexually abused as a child and frequently has serious emotional problems. This type generally is self-supporting.

2. *Co-Offender Abuser:* A highly dependent individual with marginal social functioning. This type of offender offenders with a male perpetrator who dominates her.

3. *Accomplice-Colluded Abuser:* This type of individual does not actually assault the victim but either colludes with the abuse or ignores it. This individual usually is more functional than the co-offender, but is as highly dependent.

Matthews, Matthews, and Spelt (1989 and 1993) described the following types of female child molesters:

- *Teacher/Lover:* The type of offender played by Deborah Kerr in *Tea and Sympathy*. This type of individual views herself as being involved in a romantic relationship with an adolescent male and tends to deny the abusive nature of her behavior.

- *Predisposed:* Individuals who tends to have a long history of being sexually abused, usually incestuously. This type of offender fears male peers in the same way many male pedophiles fear adult females. They have histories of addictive behaviors and tend to become involved in destructive relationships. They tend to be angry and abusive, particularly toward their children.

- *Male-Coerced:* This type of offender usually is a dependent individual who is passive, nonassertive, and locked into an abusive relationship with a male perpetrator. These women may later go on to molest on their own. These individuals usually offend against their own children, but they also occasionally offend against adult females.
- *Experimenter/Exploiter:* This type of offender generally is an adolescent or younger girl babysitting for a young boy. Such offenders tend to turn to those much younger than themselves because they are socially awkward and uncomfortable with their sexuality.

- *Psychologically Disturbed:* This type of offender, described by Faller (1987), often is psychotic. In Faller's sample, these females all abused younger female children or relatives.

McCarty (1986) reported that 52% of female perpetrators molested females (average age = 6.4), 35% molested males (average age = 9.6), and 10% molested both. Matthews and associates (1990) confirmed that female offenders more frequently molest females. Brown, Hull, and Panesis (1984), studying female rapists, and Grier and Clark (1987), studying incarcerated subjects, confirmed the preponderance of female victims.

Offenders' Attitudes Toward Their Crime

The studies show different perspectives on the attitudes of female offenders toward their crimes. (See Table 5.3.) The differences may be due to the sample rather than the distinctive characteristics of female offenders. Researchers have also come to different conclusions based on the same data. For example, Wolf (1985) reported that women used dependency on males as an excuse and justification for their behavior while Matthews and associates (1990) see this as "a reality in the lives of female offenders" (p. 288).

Matthews and associates (1989) saw their group, all women in the authors' treatment program, as empathetic and willing to take responsibility and acknowledge their guilt. Allen (1991) reported that the women in his more representative sample scored lower than male offenders on the issues of responsibility, empathy, guilt, and remorse and higher on anger. About 50% of Allen's sample had received treatment. Many of the women suffered harsher consequences than males, with more of them losing their children (51% versus 21% for males) and more receiving jail sentences (30% versus 25%). Reasonable inferences regarding this dynamic will only emerge from studying controlled samples.

Table 5.3
Attitudes of Female Offenders Toward Their Crime

Matthews, Matthews, and Speltz *(1989)*	*Allen* *(1991)*
• Most female sex offenders take responsibility for their actions.	• Few female sex offenders take responsibility for their behavior.
• Female sex offenders are generally empathetic.	• Female sex offenders recognize few behaviors as sexually abusive.
• Female sex offenders feel guilty about their behavior.	• Female sex offenders feel wrongly accused.
• Female sex offenders who acted alone admitted to deviant arousal.	• Female sex offenders feel angry at their accusers.
	• Female sex offenders feel little sorrow or guilt for their behavior.

Characteristics of Female Sex Offenders

Most descriptions of female sex offenders are based on studies of patients in treatment programs. This may produce skewed results. For example, outpatient programs may have less violent offenders, offenders with fewer victims, or individuals who are not in denial. Still, one recent study is particularly impressive in its sampling method (Allen, 1991). Allen utilized the state child abuse registries in Iowa and Missouri to locate a sample of men and women who had molested children while in caretaking relationships. Seventy-five male offenders and sixty-five female offenders were then paid to participate in an interview. Of course, the voluntary nature of participation in the study may have unavoidably biased the sample. The following paragraphs evaluate the conclusions of various researchers.

Childhood Experiences. In general, female sex offenders were raised in conflict-ridden families and were the victims of physical and sexual abuse. Researchers are in agreement about the dysfunctional backgrounds of these offenders. McCarty's (1986) study of 21 female sex offenders noted that 95% reported sexual or physical abuse, 29% had multiple caretakers, and 29% came from alcoholic families. Sixty-seven percent of independent offenders were molested by their brothers, while 86% of the co-offenders were abused by adult caretakers. Matthews and associates (1989) reported that all of their sample had been sexually abused. Allen (1991) reported that while slightly over half of the mothers of the female offenders had only one partner, which might suggest a modicum of stability, the offenders reported negative relations with both parents with worse relations with their mothers. Over half of the women reported being physically abused. Most of the offenders came from closed family systems. Nearly three-quarters (72%) of the women reported that they were sexually abused by more individuals than male victims were and that the abuse was more frequently committed by acquaintances. Females were 15 times more likely to be abused by a male than a female, whereas men were molested by women in 45% of the cases.

Marriage. McCarty (1986) indicated that 85% of her sample married while they were still in their teens with 31% being 15 or younger. Between 42% and 56% had a history of sexual promiscuity. In Allen's (1991) group, 37% of women reported being married once and less than 10% never married at all. Interestingly, the women reported above average satisfaction with their partners and even more satisfaction with their children. Furthermore, over 80% of the women reported moderate or above average sexual satisfaction and felt that their partners shared this opinion. They were more sexually active than the male offenders. Most of the women in Allen's group were apparently involved in physically abusive relations in which the partners assaulted each other. These abusive relations may have predated the relationships that the majority reported being satisfying. Some of these individuals did not see the abuse as negatively impacting the overall nature of the relationship.

Lifestyle. McCarty (1986) reported marginal functioning ability among her sample. Although 80% of the women had normal intelligence, 56% of those classified as co-offender type individuals functioned within the borderline region. Most physically and emotionally neglected their children. However, 75-80% were regularly employed. Matthew's group had much less stable work histories. They tended to be social isolates who engaged in promiscuous sex as a way of getting attention and approval. Allen's (1991) group tended to have low annual incomes and tended to work in service and clerical areas.

Mental Illness. There is considerable disagreement as to the percentage of female offenders who are mentally ill. Krug (1989), Marvasti (1986), and Matthews and associates (1989) all reported that no one in their samples suffered from serious mental illness. However, O'Connor (1987) and McCarty (1986) found that between 46-77% of their group had serious psychiatric disorders. Matthews and associates (1989) reported a variety of emotional problems, including depression, suicidal ideation, antisocial behavior, and anger among their patients. Some of these variations may be due to the different referral patterns or program acceptance criteria used by the service providers.

Substance Abuse. All categories of female offenders in Matthews and associates' (1989) study showed elevated scores on the MMPI MacAndrews scale, which is a measure of substance abuse. Allen's (1991) group reported lower rates of substance abuse with only 17% admitting to being alcoholics and 26% admitting to drug abuse. However, the MacAndrews scale is a broader and more subtle measure of addictive behaviors and thus may more accurately reflect the extent of this problem.

Nature of Assault. In Matthews' (1989) sample, 16 women had a total of 48 victims (20 boys, 27 girls, and one adult female). Six of the offenders molested both boys and girls. Eleven of the women had engaged in penetration. In Allen's (1991) group, the offenders were asked to self-report the number of victims. Thirty-six victims were reported by the women, with 66% claiming total innocence. The majority of acknowledged victims were the offenders' children or members of their extended families. Eight percent of the women identified their 13- to 16-year-old victims as their "boyfriends." Women admitted to more intrusive abuse than men, with 40% admitting to intercourse.

Characteristics of Adolescent Female Offenders

McCarty (1986) and Wolf (1985) reported that none of their sample had a history of sexual assaultiveness during adolescence. Relatively few female adolescents are reported for their crimes. However, the ones that do come to the attention of the authorities differ in significant ways from adult female offenders.

Fehrenback and Monastersky (1988) studied 28 adolescent female sex offenders referred for treatment at the University of Washington between 1978 and 1985. The mean age of these girls was 13.6. Most of these girls (53.6%) were charged with rape, versus 22.9% of male adolescents. Thirty-seven percent assaulted males, 57.1% assaulted females, and 7.1% assaulted both. All of these offenders acted alone. Hunter (1993) presented a contrasting picture, reporting that 40% of his sample of adolescent females assaulted strangers and 60% had victims of both sexes.

The National Adolescent Perpetrator Network (NAPN) (1993) identified four areas of controversy among experts studying this population:

1. Are female adolescent sex offenders more empathetic than male adolescent offenders?

2. Do female perpetrators show a greater degree of psychological disturbance?

3. What is the role of deviant sexual arousal in this population?

4. Do female adolescent offenders differ from male offenders in their "conscious awareness of connections between their own victimization and their abusive behaviors"? (p.62)

Characteristics of Abuse-Reactive Girls

Because children who sexually assault other children have almost universally been molested themselves, the term "abuse-reactive children" has been developed. The use of this term is somewhat controversial. The NAPN (1993) stated that "these behaviors were initially described as 'reactive' and the abusive nature was tradition-ally denied or rationalized" (p.63). However, the use of this term does not in and of itself dictate how seriously the abusive nature of the behavior is taken.

Along with problem terminology, there are problems with defining sexual abuse in children and distinguishing it from behavior that is purely exploratory. However, sexual abuse among children is not that different in its definition from adult sexual abuse. Essentially, it involves behavior that is coercive, nonconsensual, and exploits inequality in relationships (NAPN, 1993, p.64).

Johnson (1989) reported a study of 13 female child offenders, ages 4-13 years of age. All of these girls had been sexually abused, and they all molested family mem-bers wherever there were any available. The average age of the first offense was 6.9 years. These girls had an average of 3.5 mostly male victims.

Treatment Issues

There are important differences in treating male and female perpetrators. The fol-lowing specific recommendations made by the NAPN (1993) for adolescent female offenders are probably equally applicable to adults:

Treatment goals for sexually abusive female youth should be identical to those suggested in this report (i.e., accountability, empathy, and behavioral management) and many specific treatment tools such as the sexual abuse cycle, victim empathy development, and relapse prevention plans are the same. Consideration should be given to gender issues and treatment adaptations may be indicated by individual assessment, as is the case in appreciating the unique needs of every client (male and female). (p. 63)

While many treatment techniques are readily adapted to treating female offenders, behavioral techniques present a challenge. For example, do female sex offenders experience deviant arousal? Most of the female perpetrators in Matthews' treatment program who offended alone reported deviant arousal (Matthews, et al., 1989).

The use of some behavioral techniques may be useful, particularly covert and assisted covert sensitization. Orgasmic reconditioning focusing on the positive rein-forcement of appropriate fantasies could be utilized. In the absence of further research, the masturbatory satiation techniques that rely on the male refractory period in order to pair deviant fantasies with a state of nonarousal are not recommended for women.

Behavioral Treatment Techniques. Some behavioral techniques, such as minimal arousal conditioning, require the use of the penile plethysmograph. A comparable device, known as the photo-plethysmograph, is available for women. The device measures the engorgement of the vaginal walls by recording the reflection of light through a photosensor inserted into the vaginal cavity. The NAPN (1993) made the following recommendation regarding the use of this device:

> Objective measurement of female arousal patterns with photo-plethysmography is felt to be even more intrusive than plethysmography with males; and there is much less physiological research available on adult females than on adult males. Therefore, plethysmography is more controversial with female youth than with male youth and must be considered experimental and therefore approached only with extreme caution and oversight. (p. 6)

Use of Offender's Victimization. Currently, a lot of controversy in the sex offender treatment field concerns whether the offender's own victimization should be discussed. Most treatment programs for women described in the literature appear to have a psychodynamic orientation that stresses resolution of the offender's own sexual abuse. In Matthews' treatment program, for example, the major goals include developing: insight into sexual abuse; empathy for victims; understanding male dependency; and insight into the relationship between one's own abuse and the abuse one perpetrated.

Gender-Based Attitudinal Differences and Treatment Styles

The therapeutic philosophy in some of these treatment programs for female offenders differs from most programs for male offenders. Many statements made by Matthews and associates (1989) would be regarded by many as apocryphal if they were applied to male clients. Such statements include the following:

- The women repeatedly stated that the nonjudgmental atmosphere of the groups was most valuable to them. (p. 95)
- One key factor of the growth of the women was the acknowledgment and resolution of their own victimization. (p. 97)
- Confrontive "grouping on"....does not engender trust, openness, or a feeling of safety. (p. 99)
- Their progress in treatment was augmented by the therapists' genuine and direct love, care, concern, feedback, acceptance, and respect. (p. 99)
- Female offenders....understand that their behavior is wrong, exhibit empathy for their victims and rarely project blame onto their victims. (p. 100)
- There is no evidence to support that these women are intentionally malicious people. (p. 100)

These statements seem to show that therapists who treat female offenders view their patients or their role differently than those who treat male offenders. There is a definite move in the field to assist men with coping with their own victimization, but there is little evidence that sex offender treatment specialists view their role as "reparenting" as recommended by Matthews (1989).

We do not know how much of these attitudinal differences are based on gender stereotypes. One may stress cognitive-behavioral therapy with males because it is assumed they are more cognitively oriented. Females may be nurtured or parented because it is assumed they are more emotional or dependent. Conversely, one may skirt the use of nurturance in treating males because one does not believe that males respond to caretaking. Confrontation may be used with males because it is assumed that they are tough enough to handle it. Perhaps the central question concerns how much of the treatment of males is determined by the belief that they are "bad," and how much of the treatment of females is determined by the belief that they are "mad." These issues can only be clarified by systematic research into the various treatment techniques and therapeutic assumptions.

Conclusion

Acknowledging the existence of female sex offenders continues to be an issue fraught with controversy and deep emotional aversion. After all, accepting that women can be sexual deviants means recognizing that women—including one's mother—are sexual beings who can be cruel, aggressive, and violent. Ever since Lombroso's first works dealing with female criminality were published, researchers have attempted to explain this phenomenon by suggesting that female offenders are either extremely disturbed psychologically, are suffering from a physical illness that masculinizes them, or have been coerced by men. This theory but is still being explored today (Cooper, Swaminath, Baxter, and Poulin, 1990). Indeed, in some instances it may well be true. However, this behavior should be studied in the context of female psychology.

Failing to acknowledge the problem of female sex offenders ignores the extent of the trauma of sexual abuse. All studies suggest that the vast majority of female perpetrators were victims themselves. They did not survived unscathed. The trauma has caused deep-rooted and pervasive distortion of their own sexuality which is then passed on to others.

The biggest obstacle to working with female offenders may be the extent of their denial. This is easily understandable in the context of society's denial and the incredibly deep shame revelation of this behavior produces. Women are not socialized to talk about their sexual exploits the way men are. Add to this the deviant nature of this behavior, and it is not difficult to see why admission can be so aversive. Robert McGrath (personal communication) once pointed out that sex offender therapists who value the patient's ability to openly and candidly reveal all details of his or her deviance attract individuals for whom this behavior is totally ego-syntonic. Individuals who find their behavior ego-alien, highly shame-producing, and repugnant may flee into denial and silence. The latter group may be potentially the best patients, if they can only be reached.

The study of female sex offenders is still in its infancy, and studies of widely diverse subgroups have produced contradictory conclusions. A nationwide effort probably will be needed to gather a large and diverse enough sample of this population so that meaningful research can be conducted. As with male sex offenders, carefully gathered and applied data should drive the development of treatment for this problem.

References

Allen, C.M. (1991). *Women and men who sexually abuse children*. Orwell, VT: Safer Society Press.

Bock, R.D. and Kolakowski, D. (1973). Further evidence of sex-linked major gene influence on human spatial visualizing ability. *American Journal of Human Genetics*, 25, 1-14.

Brown, M.E., Hull, L.A., and Panesis, S.K. *Women who rape*. Boston: Massachusetts Trial Court.

Butler, E.W. and Adams, S.N. (1966). Typologies in delinquent girls: Some alternative approaches. *Social Forces*, 44, 401-407.

Campbell, A. (1981). *Girl delinquents*. New York: St. Martin's Press.

Chasnoff, M.D., Burns, W.J., Schnoll, S.H., Burns, K., Chisum, G., and Kyle-Spore, L. (1986). Maternal-neonatal incest. *American Journal of Orthopsychiatry*, 56, 577-580.

Chesler, M.S., quoted in Widom, C.S. (1978). Towards an understanding of female criminality. *Progress in Experimental Psychology Research*, 8, 245-308.

Cooper, J., Cowie, B., and Slater, E. (1986). *Delinquency in girls*. London: Heineman.

Crowe, R.R. (1974). An adoption study of antisocial personality. *Archives of General Psychiatry*, 31, 785-791.

Dalton, K. (1961). Menstruation and crime. *British Medical Journal*, 11, 1752-1753.

Dennis, W. (1992). *Hot and bothered: Sex and love in the nineties*. New York: Penguin.

d'Orban, P.T. (1971). Social and psychiatric aspects of female crime. *Medicine, Science and the Law*, 11, 104-116.

Eisenburg, N. and Lennon, R. (1983). Sex differences in empathy and related capacities. *Psychological Bulletin*, 94, 100-131.

Faller, K. (1987). Women who sexually abuse children. *Violence & Victims*, 2(4), 263-276.

Faller, K. (1989). Characteristics of a clinical sample of sexually abused children: How boys and girls differ. *Child Abuse and Neglect*, 13, 281-291.

Fehrenbach, P.A. and Monastersky, C. (1988). Characteristics of female adolescent sex offenders. *American Journal of Orthopsychiatry*, 58 (1), 148-151.

Fishbein, D.H. (1992). The psychobiology of female aggression. *Criminal Justice and Behavior*, 19 (2), 99-126.

Freud, S. (1933). *New introductory lectures in psychoanalysis*. New York: Norton.

Frieze, I.H., Parsons, J.E., Johnson, P.B., Ruble, D.N., and Zellman, G.L. (1978). *Women and sex roles: A social psychological perspective*. New York: Norton and Co.

Grier, P. and Clark, M. (1987). Female sex offenders in a prison setting. Unpublished manuscript. St. Louis: Behavioral Science Institute.

Healy, W. and Brenner, A.F. (1926). *Delinquents and criminals: Their making and unmaking*. New York: MacMillan.

Hyde, J.S., Fennema, E., and Lamon, S.J. Gender differences in mathematics performance: A meta-analysis. *Psychological Bulletin*, 107, 139-155.

Hyde, J.S. and Linn, M.C. (Eds.) (1988). *The psychology of gender: Advances through meta-analysis*. Baltimore: John Hopkins University Press.

Johnson, T.C. (1989). Female child perpetrators: Children who molest other children. *Child Abuse and Neglect*, 13 (4), 571-585.

Kasl, C.D. (1990). In M. Hunter (Eds.) *The sexually abused male: Prevalence, impact and treatment*. Vol. I. New York: Lexington Press.

Kimura, D. (1992). Sex differences in the brain. *Scientific America*, 267, 118.

Kinsey, A., Pomeroy, W., Martin, C.G., and Gebhard, P.H. (1953). *Sexual behavior in the human female*. Philadelphia: W.B. Saunders Co.

Knopp, F.H. and Lackey, L.B. (1987). *Female sexual abusers: A summary of data from 44 treatment providers*. Orwell, VT: Safer Society Press.

Koss, M. (1989). Sexual aggression and victimization in a national sample of students in higher education. In A. Burgess (Ed.) *Rape and sexual assault II*. New York: Garland.

Krug, R.S. (1989). Adult male report of childhood sexual abuse by mothers: Case descriptions, motivations and long-term consequences. *Child Abuse and Neglect,* 13 (1), 111-119.

Lombroso, C. and Ferrero, W. (1895). *The female offender*. London: T. Fisher Uniwin.

Maccoby, E.E. and Jacklin, C.N. (1974). *Stress, activity, and proximity seeking: Sex differences in the year old child*. Child Development, 44, 34-42.

Masters, W.H. and Johnson, V.E. (1970). *Human sexual inadequacy.* Denver: Little.

Mathis, R. (1982). Quoted in McCarty, L.M. (1986). Mother-child incest: Characteristics of the offender. *Child Welfare,* 65, 447-458.

Matthews, R., Matthews, J.K., and Speltz, K. (1989). *Female sex offenders*. Orwell, VT: Safer Society Press.

Matthews, R., Matthews, J., and Speltz, K. (1993). Female sex offenders. In M. Hunter (Ed.) *The sexually abused male: Prevalence, impact and treatment.* (pp. 275-293). New York: Lexington Books.

McCarty, L.M. (1986). Mother-child incest: Characteristics of the offender. *Child Welfare*, 65, 447-458.

National Adolescent Perpetrator Network. (NAPN). (1993). The revised report from the national task force on juvenile sexual offending. *Juvenile and Family Court Journal,* 44 (4), 1-120.

O'Connor, A. (1987). Female sex offenders. *British Journal of Psychiatry,* 150, 615-620.

Oetzel, R.M. (1966). Annotated bibliography in E.E. Maccoby. (Ed.) *The development of sex differences*. Stanford, CA: Stanford University Press.

Robinson, J. and Fitzgerald, L.F. (1990). The (mis)treatment of men: Effects of client gender role and lifestyle in diagnosis and attribution of pathology. *Journal of Counseling Psychology,* 37, 3-9.

Schwartz, H. (1988). *Lilith's cave: Jewish tales of the supernatural*. New York: Harper & Row.

Shields, S.A. (1987). Women, men and the dilemma of emotion. In P. Shaver and C. Hendrick (Eds.) *Sex and gender: 7*. Newbury Park, CA: Sage Press.

Smart, C. (1981). Criminological theory: Its ideology and implications concerning women. In L.H. Bowker (Ed.) *Women and crime in America.* (pp. 6-18). New York: MacMillan.

Smith, A.D. (1962). *Women in prison*. London: Stevens and Sons.

Sorrell, P.M. and Masters, W.H. (1982). Sexual assault of men by women. *Archives of Sexual Behavior,* 11, 117-131.

Tanner, D. (1990). *You just don't understand*. New York: Ballantine Books.

Tavris, C. (1992). *The mismeasure of women*. New York: Simon & Schuster.

Waterman, C.K., Dawson, M.A., and Bologna, M.J. Sexual coercion in gay and lesbian relationships: Predictors of gay rape. *Journal of Sex Research,* 8, 245-308.

Widom, C.S. (1978). Towards an understanding of female criminality. *Progress in Experimental Psychology Research,* 8, 245-308.

Wolfe, F.A. (1985). Twelve female sexual offenders. Presentation to the conference on Next Step in Research on the Assessment and Treatment of Sexually Aggressive Persons (Paraphilias), St. Louis, Missouri, March.

Chapter 6

Assessment and Treatment of the Adolescent Sexual Offender

by Henry R. Cellini, Ph.D.

Overview

Over the past few years, society has placed increased emphasis on the victims of sexual abuse and has encouraged victims to come forward and report the offenses. As a result, a substantial number of perpetrators under age 18 were identified and have received more attention from social service, mental health, and correctional agencies.

Several studies estimate that 20-30% of rapes and 30-50% of child molestations are committed by adolescents (Davis, Leitenberg, 1987; Matthews, 1987; Fehrenback, Smith, Monastersky, 1986). Studies also report that 47-58% of adult sex offenders committed their first offense during adolescence (Cellini, Schwartz, and Readio, 1993), and that the number of sexual offenses increases 50 fold as these offenders move into adulthood (Abel, Mittelman, and Becker, 1985; Apparthurai, Lowery, 1985; Davis, Leitenberg, 1987; Fehrenbach, Smith, Monastersky, 1986). Society can no longer ignore the problems associated with identifying and treating adolescent sex offenders.

This chapter discusses the special concerns associated with the management and treatment of juvenile sex offenders and makes suggestions for assessing risk level and placement. Special considerations in planning for treatment also are considered.

Characteristics of Adolescent Offenders

When adolescent offenders are divided according to racial, ethnic, and religious lines, the breakdown approximates the proportion of the particular groups in the general population. Although approximately 70% of all juvenile sex offenders are living in two-parent homes. When their abuse is discovered, over one-half report some parental loss such as divorce, illness, residential treatment, incarceration, or death. There is some speculation that adopted children may be over-represented in this population and that this might relate to either parental loss or difficulties relating to the childhood experiences prior to or after adoption (Ryan and Lane, 1991).

Most juvenile sex offenders attend school and achieve at least average grades. However, a significant number have special problems related to their schooling such as truancy, behavioral problems, and learning disabilities. The social characteristics of adolescent sex offenders range from social outcasts to popular athletes and/or academically gifted students to tough, delinquent youth. Studies indicate that fewer than 5% of these individuals were previously identified as suffering a major mental illness or psychosis, although there may be an over-representation of emotional and behavioral disorders among this group. About 30% of juvenile perpetrators were involved in other delinquent acts not related to deviant sexual behavior; 65% appeared to manifest their paraphilia without exhibiting any other observable personality or behavioral problems that set them apart from their peer group.

One study, conducted by the Safer Society in 1991 (National Council of Juvenile and Family Court Judges, 1993), indicated that youthful sexual perpetrators are between 5 and 19 years of age and that the median age is between 14 and 15. Fewer than 10% of the offenders in this study were female. More than 60% of their offenses included penetrating acts, and more than one-third involved physical force. Over 90% of the offenses were perpetrated against a youth the individual knew (e.g., a relative, acquaintance, or baby sitter). The median age of the victims was seven years. Females were three times more likely than males to be the victim.

Careful consideration must be given to every case where sexually abusive behavior has been observed. The age of the perpetrator and the age difference between the victim and perpetrator may limit legal intervention in some states. In some jurisdictions, juveniles under the age of 10 may not be charged criminally; in other areas the minimum age is 12. Where legal restraints preclude the criminal justice system from responding, law enforcement and child protective services must provide a systemic response and arrange treatment for the youth.

Coordinated Interventions Are Imperative

Intervening with sexually abusive youth must be considered a public safety issue, and public education is needed to clarify the implications of not holding juveniles accountable for their harmful sexual behavior. The need for early intervention and treatment is clear. Over the past decade, many social service systems around the country have refused to acknowledge the number of perpetrators and the severity of their impact on the victims. Some professionals and the lay public find it difficult to believe that a 14-, 15-, or 16-year-old youth would assault young children. Many professionals know that the number of juveniles committing this type of offense seems to be increasing (Cellini, 1993).

The investigation, apprehension, prosecution, control of future behavior, and treatment often fall under the authority of a number of agencies with different goals, policies, procedures, and statutory guidelines. None of these agencies can effectively control or intervene by themselves. Instead, the community must develop an interagency approach to sexual abuse intervention that includes direct cooperation and coordination between the judiciary, child protective agencies, defense counsel, law enforcement agencies, prosecutors, treatment providers, correctional agencies, victim treatment facilities, educators, youth leaders, probation and parole officers, and local media.

It is imperative to include qualified minority professionals on these intervention teams. These professionals should ensure that culturally sensitive treatment opportunities and alternatives are provided for minority youth perpetrators and victims of sexual abuse.

Phases of the Intervention Process

The importance of interagency coordination cannot be overstated. The coordinated effort must govern all phases of intervention, from the initial reporting of the abuse to the long-term monitoring of sexually aggressive, juvenile perpetrators. The intervention process can be broken down into the following phases (NCJFCJ, 1993):

1. Legal response
2. Assessment, evaluation, and placement
3. Treatment
4. Aftercare
5. Research and program evaluation

Legal Response: The Investigation Phase

The legal response phase ensures that all cases of potential sexual abuse perpetrated by children and adolescents are reported. It also ensures that a proper investigation is conducted using appropriate prosecutorial methods and procedures. This phase covers initial disclosure and reporting, the protective service and law enforcement investigation, and prosecution, defense, and sentencing issues.

Communities should formalize interagency agreements with written investigative protocols developed by the agencies and administrative bodies responsible for conducting these investigations. It is important that confidentiality issues are discussed and that a clear understanding is developed between various agencies.

Ideally, interagency coordination would enable the child protective services staff to conduct an investigation that culminates in placement in either community treatment or a secure facility. The different parts of the coordinated team would be able to consider various other issues. The police investigation would be directed at the collection of evidence, and the prosecutor would focus on legal accountability, community safety, and the imposition of placement that addresses juvenile risk levels. Treatment providers would consider clinical issues, risk assessment, and programmatic needs.

Assessment, Evaluation, and Placement Phase

This phase includes the assessment of risk and the clinical profile presented by each perpetrator. It also determines the appropriate placement for each youth and provides recommendations for treatment. The assessment process must be considered as on-going as the offender's moves through the criminal justice and social service systems. The various guideposts where assessments should occur are presented later in this paragraph.

None of the guidelines that have been offered as a basis for assessment have been systematically evaluated. Instead, a combination of clinical and actuarial (statistical) indicators are considered on a case by case basis during the assessment process. Only the development of accurate and well-developed assessment reports can offer adolescent offenders a chance to be matched with a treatment approach responsive to their needs. Unfortunately, the absence of validated research instruments and assessment protocols means that attempts to differentiate among types of offenders and their offenses should only be used in the treatment planning and placement phase. There simply is no way to make clinical assumptions about the risk of re-offense or progression of adolescents' deviant sexual patterns.

The lack of tools for assessing adolescent sexual perpetrators makes it difficult to accurately extrapolate cultural indicators. Culture should be viewed as a major component of the personality and identity development of the individual; however, the adolescent sex offender's identity is not just sexual. Identity development also occurs within the contexts of many economic, biological, cultural, interpersonal, personality, and environmental experiences. Unfortunately, little research is available to enhance the assessor's understanding of the cultural context in which sexually abusive behavior manifests across different racial or ethnic groups. Some youths who have experienced oppression due to their race or socio-economic status may exhibit defensive and protective reactions when they are being assessed. Assessors who are inexperienced at understanding cultural differences and diversity consider such behavior as rebellious and indicative of some behavioral or emotional problem or disorder.

Pretrial Assessment. Assessment during the pretrial investigative phase is essentially a forensic evaluation that is carried out by law enforcement and child protective services staff. Basically, these professionals are attempting to begin the data collection effort by evaluating the veracity and accuracy of the claims made against the adolescent. At this stage, investigators must be careful to ensure proper protection to the community. This is particularly important if a suspected adolescent sexual perpetrator is in a community-based program rather than a juvenile detention center or institution. All law enforcement and child protection workers who interview suspected adolescent perpetrators and their victims should be properly trained to interview youths at various stages of psychological development. The psychological assessment or treatment procedures used with an accused perpetrator during the pretrial phase must be voluntary. Clients and their families must be fully informed about issues of confidentiality, the need for legal counsel, statutory reporting requirements, and the individual's Fifth Amendment rights.

Presentence Assessment. If the adolescent is convicted, a comprehensive assessment should be completed before he or she is finally sentenced or placed. It is helpful to have a group of qualified therapists available for this purpose. Often, the assessor is required to provide the court with a concise, detailed report outlining the offense, the client's history (including an educational history explaining the client's involvment—or lack of involvment—in school-based programs), and specific treatment and placement recommendations. This is especially likely if treatment within the community is recommended.

If sophisticated sexual perpetrator programs are not offered in the geographic region, the assessment report should make it clear that the recommendation is simply the best available option for that client. An inappropriate or inadequate treatment plan or placement should not be recommended just because existing resources are limited.

During this phase, the assessor may be asked whether a particular offender is likely to re-offend during treatment or upon release. Risk assessment-be it short-, intermediate-, or long-term—is extremely difficult. Such assessments focus on the appropriate levels of supervision, security, and monitoring needed to safely allow the adolescent into either a community-based program or a home or foster-care setting. The criteria and typologies used in the assessment must be viewed cautiously because of the lack of scientific research on their utility. In most situations, clinical experience is the best basis for an assessment decision.

Assessment of Amenability for Treatment. The assessment must determine each individual's treatment needs, match them with the person's supervision needs, and recommend appropriate program placement. Thus, assessors must consider the issues and concerns related to a specific offender and the characteristics of their offense. The following guidelines (Ryan and Lane, 1991) give the assessor a brief overview of which issues to consider:

1. Does the perpetrator consistently deny the occurrence of his or her offenses?
2. Does the perpetrator have a major mental disorder?
3. Does the perpetrator show significant (as opposed to borderline) developmental disabilities?
4. Does the perpetrator show a pattern of ritualistic behavior?
5. Are the perpetrator's offenses sadistic? Has the perpetrator demonstrated that sexual arousal is related to inflicting pain on his or her victims?
6. Was physical aggression or violence used during the commission of the offenses?

When considering placement options for an adjudicated adolescent sexual perpe-trator, it is important for the community to provide a continuum of care that may include the following (NCJFCJ, 1993):

1. Short-term specialized psycho-educational programs for sexually abusive youths.
2. Home-based supervision while attending specialized outpatient treatment.
3. Foster-care homes where the foster parents are trained to manage sexually abusive youths while they attend specialized outpatient treatment in commu-nity-based programs.
4. Residential group homes with staff trained to manage sexually abusive youths while they attend specialized outpatient treatment in com-munity-based programs.
5. Residential group treatment facilities with sex offender specific treatment.
6. Residential group homes with specialized day treatment for sexually abusive youths.
7. Medium security training schools with specialized treatment for sexually abusive youths.
8. Secure residential treatment center (or secure group home) specially trained to manage and treat sexually abusive youths.
9. Inpatient psychiatric hospital units with specialized treatment for sexually abu-sive youths.
10. Maximum security with specialized treatment for sexually abusive youths.
11. Post-treatment support systems.
12. Supervised apartments.

Treatment Phase

This phase includes a wide range of treatment modalities, including offense-spe-cific treatment groups, family and individual therapy, and psycho-educational classes. Any and all therapeutic interventions should be fully discussed and consented to by the juvenile offender's parents and/or guardians. Parents should also be included in family therapy. The therapy should focus on (1) whether ongoing family dynamics are contributing to the sexually inappropriate behavior and (2) the juvenile's deviant cycle and Relapse Prevention plan.

Peer groups are the preferred method of treatment for 98% of the juvenile and adult programs currently being offered for sex offenders. Only 2% of juvenile service providers choose to use individual treatment alone, although many provide individual treatment for juvenile sexual perpetrators simply because of inadequate numbers of clients by gender and age (Knopp, Freeman-Longo, and Stevenson, 1992). When determining appropriate program placement for these individuals, the issues of safety of the community, security of the adolescent, appropriate supervision, and monitoring must be planned for and considered.

It is important to differentiate between treating adolescent sex offenders and treat-ing adult offenders. However, many of the techniques covered in this volume can be readily adapted for use with juveniles.

Treatment of juvenile sex offenders has a two-pronged goal: (1) teaching them to gain control over their deviant sexual behavior and (2) increasing their prosocial interaction with peers and adults. In other words, treatment is geared toward reducing the risk of recidivism through:

1. Increasing control of deviant sexual impulses, fantasies, arousal patterns, and behaviors;
2. Cultivating appropriate sexual impulses, fantasies, arousal patterns, and behaviors;
3. Managing high-risk situations, emotional states, and the deviant cycle; and
4. Assisting the juvenile in developing alternative coping mechanisms so that sex is no longer seen as a solution to nonsexual problems.

Accomodating Adolescents' Developmental Needs

One obvious difference between juveniles and adults is that juveniles have developmental needs that must be considered. Thus, treatment providers and assessors must be concerned with the changing developmental needs of their adolescent clients while simultaneously treating their sexually abusive behavior.

Some behavioral treatments can be controversial when used with adolescents. For example, masturbatory conditioning techniques (orgasmic reconditioning, masturbatory satiation) have not been researched with females and thus would not be appropriate for female adolescents. Young perpetrators who deny masturbating are not appropriate candidates for the above referenced interventions.

The use of phallometry with juveniles also is controversial (the ethical issues associated with this will be discussed later in this chapter). Juveniles, particularly older adolescents, can manifest deviant sexual arousal that may require behavioral treatment. It is difficult to administer these techniques without an adequate baseline and the ability to assess progress in modifying arousal which only the plethysmograph can adequately measure. However, the use of this instrument may be challenged.

Techniques that elicit strong emotional responses such as Drama Therapy should only be used in residential treatment environments that can provide the emotional support necessary after these sessions.

Treatment Models

In 1982, only 22 treatment programs for juvenile sexual offenders were identified (Knopp, 1982). By 1991, over 600 programs were in operation, and 480 of those were community-based. The treatment provided in these programs ranged from individual and group therapy to wilderness programs (Roberts and Camasso, 1991), however, most used similar treatment methods, including:

- Social skills training
- Assertive skills training
- Enhancing victim empathy
- Promotion of non-deviant sexual interests
- General sexual education

- Cognitive restructuring
- Understanding deviant cycles
- Self-monitoring strategies

Even though many programs utilize similar treatment methods, the current literature supports cognitive-behavioral and multisystemic models (Becker, Harris, and Sales, 1993). Sapp and Vaughn (1990) conducted a study of the various types of available treatment. The research revealed that most state correctional institutions prefer behavioral treatment approaches. In 1988, Knopp surveyed providers of juvenile sex offender treatment. Of the 574 respondents to that survey, 63% utilized a cognitive-behavioral model and 62% a psychosocioeducational model.

Cognitive-Behavioral Therapy Model. Becker, Kaplan, and Kavoussi (1988) tailored a cognitive behavioral approach specifically for juvenile sex offenders. The program has the following seven components, which are repeated each week:

1. Eight 30-minute sessions of treatment geared at verbal satiation;
2. Four group therapy sessions lasting one hour and 15 minutes;
3. One hour and 15 minute covert sensitization session, designed to disrupt the deviant cycle;
4. Four one hour and 15 minute social skills sessions;
5. Four one hour and 15 minute anger management sessions;
6. Two one hour and 15 minute Relapse Prevention sessions; and
7. Sex education and value clarification training session of unspecified length.

The authors did not research the recidivism rates among their treated population, but they did look at the overall change in their clients' deviant arousal patterns. The changes were measured using the erection response to non-deviant and deviant sexual stimuli before and after treatment. After treatment, the juvenile offenders showed a significant decrease in their sexual arousal to inappropriate stimuli.

Multisystemic Treatment Model. The multisystemic treatment model (Bourduin, Henggeler, and Stein, in press) was designed to consider that a factor or group of factors can facilitate a juvenile acting-out in a sexual manner. The interaction of these factors is considered very important. The treatment providers focus on different issues identified during the clinical assessment process. Generally, these areas are: peer relation, school performance, cognitive processes, and family relations.

A comparison of the recidivism rates of the multisystemic model and that of individual therapy showed a 12.5% recidivism rate for the model and a 75% rate for individual therapy. The individual therapy program consisted of 45 hours of treatment. The follow-up period ranged from 21 to 49 months, with the average period being about 37 months.

Assessing Progress in Treatment

In many individuals, sexual aggression can develop into a repetitive behavioral pattern. Treatment of adolescent sexual perpetrators is a crime control effort that focuses on the control and management of the behavior rather than attempting to cure the problem. Adolescent sexual perpetrators may participate in treatment, but they may also place themselves in high risk situations where they may re-offend. Consequently, it is important to track the progress of an individual in treatment. Treatment progress (or the lack of it) is determined by the individual's ability to meet certain, specific, measurable goals and objectives. The following list provides some basic guideposts for measuring success during the therapeutic process:

1. Acknowledgment of responsibility for offenses without denial, minimization, or projection of blame.
2. Ability to discern contributing factors to offending cycle.
3. Positive changes in or resolution of contributing factors of sexually abusive behavior.
4. Demonstration of empathy for their victims.
5. Ability to manage stress and modulate negative feelings.
6. Improvement in self-esteem.
7. Increases in positive sexuality.
8. Prosocial interactions and involvement with prosocial peers.
9. Positive family interactions.
10. Openness in examining thought processes, fantasies, and behavior.
11. Ability to reduce and maintain control of deviant sexual arousal.
12. Reduction of deviant fantasies and concurrent increases in healthy, non-abusive, prosocial sexual fantasies.
13. Ability to counter irrational thinking and thinking errors.
14. Ability to interrupt cycle and seek help when destructive or high risk behavior patterns begin.
15. Resolution of personal victimization or loss issues.
16. Ability to experience pleasure in normal activities.
17. Ability to communicate and understand behavior patterns in the treatment milieu and correlate them to behavior in the home and community.
18. Family's ability to recognize the risk factors (in the youth's cycle) and to help the adolescent seek help before they re-offend.

Ethical Issues of Treatment

Treatment providers must consider community protection as their highest priority. When the safety of the community conflicts with the rights or interests of an abusive client, the treatment provider must choose protection of the community as their highest ethical concern.

This raises several ethical issues that arise in the context of treatment. The use of graphic or sexually explicit materials during a phallometric assessment in the hope of changing deviant arousal patterns may be illegal with adolescent perpetrators in some states or county jurisdictions. Providers also must determine whether the use of such stimulus materials violates local or state child pornography laws. Some professional groups advise against the use of visual stimuli material in these situations, and recommend the use of audio-taped sets of stimuli instead (NCJFCJ, 1993).

Many professionals feel that deviant sexual arousal is one of the major contributing factors in sexually abusive behavior. Arousal patterns may be revealed by self-report or by plethysmography. Self-report information may be unreliable or provide insufficient information for the treatment provider. But is it ethical to use the penile plethysmograph, which is considered one of the most intrusive methods used in psychological or behavioral assessments, in the treatment of an adolescent sexual offender? Its use is controversial with even adult sex offenders. Nevertheless, according to Knopp, Freeman-Longo, and Stephenson, (1992), 168 juvenile sex offender treatment programs currently use this methodology. Research (Becker, Hunter, Goodwin, Caplan, and Martinez, 1992) suggests that penile arousal assessment in juvenile sexual offenders produces reliable patterns of responses.

Aftercare and Follow-Up Phase

This treatment phase includes providing on-going support, developing positive relationships, and monitoring the juvenile in relation to his or her risk factors, sexual offense patterns, and behaviors in order to prevent the individual from re-offending. This issue must be considered in light of the intervention strategies currently being offered to the youth.

Special attention must be given to teaching adolescent offenders the skills they will need to prevent and control their deviant fantasies. Thus, the treatment provider must work with the client to make use of both internal and external methods of monitoring their behavior. Internal self-monitoring is focused on understanding what triggers their deviant behavior and controlling it. External monitoring involves teaching family members, probation or parole officers, and others who can observe the adolescent to spot the early indicators of his or her starting their offense/deviant cycle.

Ultimately, treatment success is determined by the adolescent's ability to control his or her deviant sexual arousal and sexually abusive behavior when they return to the community. The goal is the same whether the youth was treated in a correctional institution, a residential treatment program, or an outpatient program.

Often, the public's perception is that an individual is cured once they complete treatment. Unfortunately, the harsh reality is that sex offenders are never completely cured even when their behavior is controlled. Consequently, follow-up services that maintain contact with and provide support for the adolescent sexual perpetrator must be in place. In addition, it is crucial to reinforce the self-monitoring techniques the offender learned during the more intensive phases of treatment. Offenders must know they must ask for help when they begin their deviant cycle.

Research and Program Evaluation Phase

This phase includes the development and collection of appropriate research data across the various phases described earlier and their relationship with judicial, legislative, and administrative bodies. This process is intended to recommend changes in the handling of cases by various agencies and administrative groups. It can ensure that the assessment, treatment, and aftercare components are effective for specific groups of offenders.

Conclusion

Professionals treating juvenile sex offenders need support form the various social service agencies and court systems involved with their client to provide the necessary coordination in treating these individuals and researching the effectiveness of that treatment. Considering the number of sex offenders who began their deviant behavior as adolescents, it is imperative that our society thake this issue seriously and begin to investigate the most efficient an cost-effective methods of intervening with this population.

References

Abel, G., Mittelman, M., and Becker, J. (1985). Sex offenders: Results of assessment and recommendations for treatment. In Ben-Aaron, S., Hucker, S., and Webster, C. (Eds.) Clinical criminology: *Current concepts*. Toronto: M & M Graphics.

Apparthurai, C. and Lowrey, G. (1985). Young sex offenders need early intervention. *OAPSW Newsmagazine* (November).

Becker, J., Harris, C., and Sales, B. (1993). Juveniles who commit sexual offenses: A critical review of research. In Hall, G. and Hirschman, R. (Eds.) *Sexual aggression: Issues, ideology and assessment, treatment and policy*. Bristol, PA: Taylor and Francis Press.

Becker, J., Kaplan, M., and Kavoussi, R. (1988). Measuring the effectiveness of treatment for the aggressive adolescent sexual offender. In Prentky, R. and Quinsey, V. (Eds.) *Human sexual aggression: Current perspectives*. New York: New York Academy of Science.

Becker, J.V., Hunter, J.A., Goodwin, D.W., Kaplan, M.S., and Martinez, D. (1992). Test-retest reliability of audio-taped phallometric stimuli with adolescent sex offenders. *Annals of Sex Research*, 5, 45-51.

Bourduin, C., Henggeler, S., and Stein, R. (in press). Multisystemic treatment of adolescent sexual offenders. *International Journal of Offender Therapy and Comparative Criminology*.

Cellini, H. (1993). Kids making history: Violence in the 90s. *Juvenile and Family Justice Today*, 2:1.

Cellini, H. (1994). Management and treatment of institutionalized violent juveniles. *American Corrections Association*, 56:4.

Cellini, H., Schwartz, B., and Readio, S. (1993). Child sexual abuse: An administrator's nightmare. School Safety Update (December). National School Safety Center.

Davis, G. and Leitenberg, H. (1987). Adolescent sex offenders. *Psychological Bulletin*, 101:417-427.

Fehrenback, P., Smith, W., Monastersky, C., and Deisher, R. (1986). Adolescent sexual offenders: Offender and offense characteristics. *American Journal of Orthopsychiatry*, 56:225-233.

Gilby, R., Wolf, L., and Goldberg, B. (1989). Mentally retarded adolescent sex offenders: A survey and pilot study. *Canadian Journal of Psychiatry*.

Gray, A. and Wallace, R. (1992). *Adolescent sexual offender assessment packet*. Orwell, VT: Safer Society.

Kahn, T. and Chambers, H. (1991). Assessing reoffense risk with juvenile sexual offenders. Child Welfare League of America.

Knopp, F. (1982). *Remedial intervention in adolescent sex offenses: Nine program descriptions*. Orwell, VT: Safer Society.

Knopp, F.H., Freeman-Longo, R., and Stevenson, W.F. (1992). *Nationwide survey of juvenile and adult sex offender treatment programs and models*. Brandon, VT: Safer Society Press.

Matthews, R. (1987). Female sexual offenders: Treatment and legal issues. In report by phase program of Genesis II. Minneapolis, MN.

National Council of Juvenile and Family Court Judges (1993). The revised report from the National Task Force on Juvenile Sexual Offending, l993 of the National Adolescent Perpetrator Network. Juvenile & Family Court Journal, l993.

Roberts, A. and Camasso, M. (1991). Juvenile offenders treatment programs and cost benefit analysis. *Juvenile and Family Court Journal.*

Ryan G. and Lane, S. (1991). Juvenile sexual offending: Causes, consequences and correction. Lexington, MA.

Sapp, A. and Vaughn, M. (1990). Juvenile sex offender treatment at state-operated correctional institutions. *International Journal of Offender Therapy and Comparative Criminology,* 34: 131-146.1.

Part 2

Implementation and Administration of Programs

In the following section, the authors offer suggestions for establishing policies, procedures, and programs that seek to reduce the incidence of sexual assault. In recent years a number of public policies have been initiated, some with careful study and some motivated by political advantage. Although sensational crimes may tempt legislatures to enact extreme laws that may in the long run threaten the basic civil rights of the entire population and do absolutely nothing to enhance public safety, the reasonable approach is to first take the time and effort to carefully assess the situation and consult the research.

The chapters in this part outline the history of the development of sex offender programs. It is pointed out that many programs may currently be at risk due to a conservative shift in the approach to corrections. The initiation of involuntary commitment programs which essentially add a preventive detention component to the old "sexual psychopath" laws is a recent development that will have far-reaching ramifications. The practical aspects of establishing sex offender treatment programs in institutional settings and the resources that are available for such programs in the criminal justice system also are discussed.

Community treatment providers may be available to provide treatment and aftercare services for offenders on probation. Mental health workers with various prisons may have already started treating sex offenders. Their efforts should be coordinated under a single treatment model. Chaplains can be help a or a hindrance, and thus need to fully understand the rationale behind therapeutic techniques. Probation and parole personnel need to be thoroughly trained in the supervisory models that are compatible with the treatment approach. Judges need to have a comprehensive knowledge of the nature of the treatment model so they can assess which offenders are appropriate to which part of the treatment process. It is an awe-inspiring task to coordinate all parts of such a system, yet there can be many benefits. Some states have found that report and conviction rates increased once treatment was established in both the community and the institutions.

Some of the information regarding the classification of sex offenders as well as some of the new public policies and technologies are discussed in the following chapters. Police departments, child protective service workers, lawyers, probation officers, judges, correctional classification officers, parole board members, and parole officers all must be made aware of the characteristics are that associated with dangerousness and risk of re-offending. Such knowledge will allow them to make rational decisions in the best interest of public safety.

The specific use of new technologies being used to monitor sex offenders, including the polygraph and electronic supervision, are discussed. The current trend toward registering sex offenders and notifying the public when a sex offender moves into the community also are reviewed. Some types of notification may be helpful. However, others may create a vigilante atmosphere, enhance fears, further victimize victims, and increase the chance of recidivism.

Careful program evaluation is essential in establishing sex offender treatment programs. However, the evaluation must be based on a sophisticated understanding of research design and statistical analysis. It is best if the research is conducted by a reputable third party who is experienced in summative research. Careful thought must be given to what type of outcome criteria will be measured. Traditionally, recidivism data has been used to measure treatment effectiveness. However, there are a variety of problems with this: Will rearrest or reconviction be the measure? Will recidivism be defined in terms of sex offenses or any crime? How long should offenders be followed before treatment outcome studies are reported. It must also be remembered that in some states there must be choice between sound research and departmental policy. For example, if treatment completion is required prior to release, then the possibility of having a matched sample of untreated offenders will be eliminated. Any research done within such a situation will be subject to criticism on a variety of methodological issues.

Chapter 7

Sex Offender Program Planning and Implementation

by Roger C. Smith, D. Crim.

Overview

This chapter addresses some of the issues facing criminal justice administrators, planners, clinicians, and others who are responsible for implementing, or modifying programs for incarcerated adult sexual offenders. The discussion focuses on programs that assess, treat, and provide transitional services to incarcerated felons. Such programs do not operate in isolation. Rather, they are one segment in a continuum of options that ideally are available at each stage of the criminal justice process.

History of Sex Offender Programs

Over the last two decades, much has been learned about assessing, treating, and supervising convicted sex offenders. Brecher (1978) found that many pioneering sex offender treatment programs of the 1970s were not coordinated with other public or private agencies. In addition, little agreement existed among criminal justice or mental health professionals regarding what constituted appropriate and effective treatment methods with sexual offenders, or whether effective treatment could even be conducted in a prison environment. Few studies showed that treatment for sex offenders, whether in corrections or in the community, was effective.

As recently as 1989, a major study of outcomes of sex offender programs concluded that there was no evidence that treatment reduced recidivism (Furby, Weinrott, and Blackshaw, 1989). Subsequently, numerous reviewers refuted these findings, pointing out serious methodological flaws in this study. Some reviewers noted that most of the programs surveyed by Furby, et al., did not employ currently accepted treatment methods. Most of the programs in the study have not survived.

More recent outcome studies in a variety of settings have yielded more optimistic results (Marshall and Pithers, 1994; Freeman-Longo and Knopp, 1992). Given the difficulty of conducting tightly researched outcome studies of sex offender treatment programs, particularly in prisons, therapy advocates always must be prepared to respond to the skeptics and to remain open to suggestions about improving efficacy.

Correctional Programs Face an Uncertain Future

The 1970s and 1980s were a time of innovation and refinement in methods for assessment, treatment, and supervision of sexual offenders. Correctional sex offender programs, often coordinated with community-based pre- or post-sentence programs, were initiated in many state systems. This author, as well as a number of other authors in this volume, participated in seminars at the National Academy of Corrections which promoted a "system approach" to the management of sexual offenders. During the eight years that these seminars were offered, most states sent teams of administrators, planners, clinicians, and others who were involved with state or local sex offender programs. Many participated in additional sex offender training. A survey of states participating in these seminars which was completed in 1993 showed the seminars were used largely to improve or expand sex offender programs that had already begun, particularly in prisons. Twenty-eight percent of the participants said they began totally new programs after attending the seminars. This parallels the growth in treatment programs reported by the Safer Society Press, a Vermont-based non-profit organization that keeps track of treatment programs and providers around the country. Safer Society reported that the number of specialized programs increased from 12 in 1976 to 1800 in 1992. Reportedly, the only two states that totally abolished their programs in the 1980s did so because of the loss of space resulting from prison overcrowding.

The 1990s may be characterized as a time of growing public and political impatience with criminals in general, and with violent sexual offenders in particular. Currently, state legislatures around the country are drafting legislation that responds to the public outrage against particularly heinous, high profile sexual crimes. Often, these crimes are committed by an offender paroled or released from the corrections system after serving a maximum sentence. Staff within corrections and parole agencies in most states have good reason to pause when making decisions regarding incarcerated sex offenders being considered for release into the community.

Impact of Post-Sentence Civil Commitment Statutes

Over the last few years, several states passed or considered laws permitting post-sentence civil commitment of sex offenders. With passage of the Community Protection Act of 1990, Washington became the first state to enact such legislation. This comprehensive Act included a controversial provision allowing for post-sentence civil commitment of individuals who met the criteria of "sexually violent predators." The civil commitment provision withstood a court challenge by two individuals who were civilly committed (*In re Young and Cunningham*, 1993). The courts also upheld Minnesota's Psychopathic Personality Commitment Act when it was challenged by a young sexual offender who was civilly committed to a secure state hospital for an indeterminate period of time following an examination by a psychologist prior to his release (*In re Phillip Jay Blodgett*, 1994).

Ethics and Confidentiality. Minnesota also committed several inmates who had spent decades in prison for sexual crimes and who successfully completed a voluntary prison program to a possible life sentence in the state hospital. The commitments, which occurred prior to the inmates' release from prison and while they were still living in the prison treatment program, were based on the original crimes they committed and the treatment records and notes from the prison programs. Therapists were subpoenaed and an effort was made to locate other inmates who had been in groups with these offenders for the purpose of bringing them to court to testify for the commitments. Fortunately, the other inmates refused. The proceedings were heavily publicized in the media. Reporters and TV cameras covered the trials and reported on the local news all of the day's happenings. One result was that men who were at the point of deciding whether to participate in the prison-based treatment program were dissuaded, and those who were already participating in the program were afraid to be open and talk about all of their issues.

Another result was that the treating professionals, who had acquired their information under one set of rules, were thrust into a huge dilemma about how the information was being used. In one of the most flagrant violations of ethical principles, "raw psychological test data" was subpoenaed directly to lawyers and judges who then read specific items from the MMPI and the Multiphasic Sex Inventory in open court. Reporters who were present proceeded to interpret the meaning of the offender's response. Not only did this potentially violate the copyright laws and validity of the tests, it put the psychologist's license in jeopardy. In both Washington and Minnesota, state professional boards and national professional organizations refused to act on behalf of treating psychologists who contended that ethical principles surrounding confidentiality were being violated by state legislation and departmental policies.

Passage of these statutes has affected voluntary treatment programs. For example, when Washington passed its civil commitment law, all confidentiality around prison treatment records was abolished. Those who had signed "Confidentiality Agreement Statements" suddenly were told that these agreements were null and void and that all of their records would be given upon request to the committee screening civil commitment referrals. Undoubtedly, this will have a negative impact on program participation because the treatment program collects a vast amount of information on participants, including phallometric assessment data, that would not otherwise exist. Such data can be used to make the case that an individual is a "sexual predator." Currently, only one participant among several hundred dropped out of treatment for this reason and one individual who successfully completed the treatment program was targeted for commitment.

Predictions of Future Dangerousness as Factor in Civil Commitment. Washington's sexual predator statute has sparked a highly charged national debate on the efficacy of using psychiatric predictions of future sexual dangerousness to indefinitely commit individuals who have completed a criminal sentence but are adjudged to remain sexually dangerous (Brooks, 1992). One might also speculate on the future of sex offender programs if civil commitment programs become widespread. Such programs, by definition, are civil rather than criminal, and thus are presumed to be the responsibility of mental health agencies instead of corrections agencies. Notably, this is not the case in Illinois, where civilly committed sex offenders are housed in a Department of Corrections psychiatric facility, or in Massachusetts, where the Department of Corrections has assumed control of the Civil Commitment Center for Sex Offenders.

Treatment as a Requirement of Parole

In some states, concern about releasing potentially dangerous sexual offenders from prison has led to policies that require prisoners who were convicted and sentenced for sexual crimes to participate in either educational or treatment programs before they can be considered for parole. While correctional treatment programs have historically employed a blend of coercion and incentive to "motivate" otherwise recalcitrant individuals, caution must be exercised to ensure that such blanket requirements do not dilute scarce clinical resources on offenders who lack motivation or capacity to profit from educational or treatment programs. Such policies may destroy the credibility and legitimacy of programs for both prisoners and clinicians. Sex offender programs could simply become an annoyance, a hoop through which prisoners must jump to obtain a parole, and a necessity for correctional systems forced to move prisoners toward parole release as quickly as possible to minimize overcrowding. Correctional systems have historically found themselves in the position of offering mandatory "treatment" programs that have had no impact on post-release behavior, but which have destroyed the credibility of prison-based treatment and rehabilitation programs.

Programs Must Be Pursued Wholeheartedly. Sex offenses are crimes that reflect distorted interpersonal relationships, and correcting dysfunctional social patterns may require a variety of techniques including planning and participating in positive social experiences (e.g., parties, celebrations, rituals, etc.) that demonstrate to the resident that fun, joy, spontaneity can be experienced in a positive interpersonal atmosphere—

not just through alcohol or drugs or deviant sexuality. Consequently, correctional facilities that decide to implement treatment programs must make them an integral part of the operations of the department. Care must be taken to place the program in a facility that promotes all aspects of treatment.

The efficacy of the program may be compromised if treatment and security staff begin warring over permission to conduct therapeutic activities. The staff's energy will be diverted and hostility and skepticism will ensue if legitimate treatment activities are interfered with because a power struggle is going on.

Training and Experience Required for Those Who Treat Sex Offenders. Sex offender assessment and treatment is a unique and specialized professional field. To enhance retention of qualified clinical staff, it is essential that opportunities for continuing education and training are available, and that networking is encouraged and supported. Attendance at conferences, workshops, and seminars reduces the professional isolation experienced by many clinicians working in corrections.

The Association for the Treatment of Sexual Abusers (ATSA), an international professional organization, has taken the lead in developing standards of care for the treatment of sex offenders, including standards of professional competence. They acknowledge that possession of an advanced degree and appropriate licensure in one of the behavioral sciences does not imply competence in working with sex offenders. Thus far, Washington and Texas were the only states to establish certification standards for those who work with sex offenders, although other states are moving in that direction. In addition, few clinicians are exposed to specialized training in sexual deviance in graduate programs. Instead, expertise must be obtained through workshops, reading, clinical experience, and networking with others in the field.

Finally, state civil service systems rarely acknowledge specialized training and certification. Thus, clinicians who otherwise meet requirements for state employment may not be prepared to provide adequate assessment or treatment services. For this reason, many systems rely heavily on contractual services with specialists who have the requisite training and experience.

Planning Sex Offender Treatment Programs

Effective public policy planning and program development require the involvement of knowledgeable legislators, as well as representatives of the judiciary, law enforcement, victim service advocates, and public and private programs that provide services to sex offenders. In many respects, sex offender treatment programs are similar to the educational or therapeutic programs most correctional systems have managed for decades. Whether planning and implementing a continuum of services for substance abusers or mentally ill inmates or providing educational and vocational training services, correctional systems adhere to similar processes for planning and implementation. Administrators establish goals and objectives, determine human resource needs, assign staff, and establish mechanisms that allow for management oversight and program evaluation.

Major Goals of the Program Planning Process

The National Task Force on Correctional Substance Abuse Strategies (1991) set out strategies that correctional agencies could use in planning and implementing effective programs for substance abusers. Because there are many similarities between this population and sex offenders, the major goals and the program planning process described in that report are adapted below.

Goal 1. Assess all sex offenders entering the corrections system to determine their need for specialized intervention.

The assessment of sex offenders for the purpose of determining their need for program services should begin during the intake or reception process. In most instances, the presentence investigation provides details of the offense, a summary of past criminal offenses, and social history data (including information related to mental health, substance abuse, or other special needs). In jurisdictions that have probation officers who are trained to conduct specialized presentence investigations on sex offenders should also acquire information on sexual history, prior victimization, previous treatment, and an assessment of dangerousness and amenability to treatment.

Goal 2. Conduct intensive clinical assessment on all offenders who require and can profit from specialized programming.

Assessment should be an ongoing process. It is nearly impossible to conduct comprehensive clinical assessments of prisoners during the intake and classification process. A standardized clinical assessment may occur when a prisoner is within a specified number of years or months before consideration for parole release, or it may be triggered by other factors (e.g., ordered by a parole board).

Clinical assessment with specialized instruments should be initiated when a prisoner is being considered for admission to an educational or treatment program where a specific plan of treatment will be developed. This assessment might include a variety of paper and pencil tests, clinical interviews, and, when available, phallometric assessment utilizing the penile plethysmograph. Normally, corrections systems do not conduct intensive clinical assessments on sex offenders who are not potential candidates for specialized interventions, nor would such assessments be practical with recalcitrant individuals.

Goal 3. Provide a range of high quality programs for incarcerated sexual offenders responsive to level of service need and individual differences.

Within the limits of available resources, corrections systems should develop a range of educational and treatment programs to meet the diverse needs and capabilities of sexual offenders. A comprehensive treatment plan, such as the one described below, should be developed for each sex offender considered eligible for educational or treatment services. The plan should consider sexual deviancy, substance abuse, educational and vocational needs, physical and mental health problems, and other areas which might impact on the offender's ability to successfully participate in treatment. Sex offenders should also have access to other correctional programs consistent with their individual needs. For example, they should be encouraged to participate in work activities, religious, educational, vocational, and recreational programs, and other activities offered to prisoners.

A continuum of specialized programs should be available. The continuum may be designed to provide services in a variety of settings, with different levels of intensity. Each program within the continuum may be taken in sequence, or prisoners may participate in one phase only, based on need, amenability, and motivation to participate. A typical sequence might include the following service delivery models.

Educational Classes. Educational programs may be required to meet minimum parole requirements, or they may be a first step for prisoners entering more intensive phases of treatment. Such classes generally are intended to provide information about sexual deviancy, the impact of sexual assault on victims, and an understanding of sex offender treatment. Normally, prisoners are not required to disclose specific aspects of their crimes. If educational programs require that participants complete homework assignments, these assignments can be used to screen for motivation, or capacity to read and understand written materials. A popular monograph series developed by Safer Society Press (Freeman-Longo and Bays, 1988, 1989, 1990) is used by many states during this phase of sex offender programming.

Outpatient Psycho-Educational Programs. Psycho-educational programs are designed to develop specific life skills. For example, cognitive skills training (Ross, Fabiano, Ross, 1986) is intended to enhance the basic cognitive skills that enable sex offenders to better utilize psychotherapies requiring at least average cognitive or reasoning abilities. Other psycho-educational programs might include:

- Sex education
- Victim empathy
- Drug and alcohol education
- Social and interpersonal skills training
- Anger management
- Relapse Prevention
- Assertiveness training
- Stress management
- Dating skills
- Self-esteem
- Criminal thinking errors/cognitive distortions

Educational and self-help materials in these areas have become widely available in bookstores. Carefully scripted lesson plans, videos, and participant workbooks are also commercially available. Many commercially designed psycho-educational packages also have pre- and post-tests that are helpful in quantifying participant learning.

Nonresidential Group Psychotherapy. Group therapy is the recommended mode of treatment for sex offenders. It is during this phase that offenders are required to disclose their offenses and address issues related to their deviancy. The groups may be designed to teach and practice Relapse Prevention methods, they may be behavioral, or they may be confrontational. Yet all of these groups have some things in common:

they require that group membership to be stable, confidentiality rules to be strictly enforced, and a physical environment that is conducive to open and frank discussion.

In correctional systems where the physical environment or resource deficiencies preclude separate residential treatment programs, nonresidential group psychotherapy represents the most intensive phase of treatment for the incarcerated offender. Nonresidential programs are defined as treatment which is offered to offenders living in the general prison population. This is not the most effective way to offer treatment unless it is actually a pre-treatment model meant to be followed by placement in a therapeutic community. The nonresidential models do not have the positive therapeutic interaction which occurs when offenders are housed together.

Residential Programs Housed in State Mental Hospitals. Traditionally, state mental hospitals have been the site of residential sex offender treatment programs. Indeed, despite an abysmal early history of failure in effectively treating sexual offenders, many of the creative pioneers in the field of sex offender treatment began their work in such programs. For example, at Western State Hospital in Washington State, Dr. George McDonald revolutionized sex offender treatment by emphasizing client responsibility, developing peer self-help groups, defining steps of progress through treatment, and implementing graduated release programs (Brecher, 1978).

Currently, several states operate sex offender treatment programs in mental health facilities for offenders who are near release. Because they are separated from the values and pressures of traditional prisons, such programs are able to create therapeutic environments, break down barriers between staff and prisoners, and institute procedures, such as phallometric assessment and behavioral treatment and gradual release strategies that might not be supported in a typical correctional facility.

Sex offender treatment programs housed in mental health facilities are often viewed as pariahs. Administrators may see sex offenders as criminals masquerading as mental patients and draining much needed resources from needy patients rather than as legitimate clients of their agency. The public may think sex offenders who are housed in hospitals as being "coddled."

Viewing sex offenders as psychiatric patients also can lead to assumptions that are at odds with mainstream sex offender treatment philosophy. Sex offenders in hospitals may spend inordinately long periods of time in treatment (10, 15, 20 years) with little access to educational and vocational progams. When disciplinary matters arise, these patients are treated rather than disciplined. Consequently, the clear-cut procedures that characterize prison policies are replaced by subjective sanctions devised by therapists. Such subjectivity often plays into the very pathology being treated. Endless discussions of one's deepseated motivations for having a dirty room may be less rehabilitative and more punitive than mopping the floor for an hour. Therapists in some hospital sex offender programs find themselves forced to refer to their clients as "consumers" and submit their treatment programs to "consumer satisfaction surveys."

Residential Programs Operated in Correctional Institutions. Residential treatment programs also are operated in minimum through maximum security correctional institutions. These programs have been successfully implemented in separate facilities or in converted cellblocks. Corrections-based residential programs use an integrated staffing approach in which both clinical and custodial staff interact with program participants. Some corrections departments have been quite receptive to implementing highly sophisticated treatment techniques.

Preparing prisoners for transition back into the community is a major task of residential programs. Prior to release, participants should have completed a continuing plan of care, made contacts with treatment programs in the community, and developed skills necessary to sustain themselves in the community. Some states have integrated elaborate networks of pre-release and work release programs and halfway houses as well as community-based treatment into their overall therapy programs.

Special Needs Offenders. Most incarcerated sex offenders have the intellectual capacity and skill necessary to participate in sex offender programming. However, some groups require special services for their unique needs. Mentally ill, mentally retarded or intellectually low functioning individuals, persons with physical limitations, and those with language problems are examples of such groups. Relatively few existing programs are designed specifically for mentally ill sex offenders. Generally, persons with severe mental illness are treated to control their psychiatric symptoms before they are referred to available programs. Some programs for mentally retarded or low functioning individuals have demonstrated significant impact on sexual misconduct (Haaven, Little, Petre-Miller, 1990). Corrections departments must be careful to cite programs that are accessible to the handicapped and make provisions for those with vision and hearing problems.

Goal 4. Provide parole boards with relevant information on community treatment and supervision needs, progress attained, potential risk, and specific stipulations enhancing successful community adjustment.

Sex offender programs must be able to objectively document progress around specific, measurable goals instead of vague, subjective therapeutic impressions. Many sex offender programs have met with serious problems because they made specific recommendations for parole rather than commenting on documentable progress.

Institutional treatment staff may provide specific recommendations to parole boards regarding desirable conditions to be imposed on sex offenders during parole supervision. Such stipulations might include regular urinalysis testing and prohibitions against dating single women with children, living in areas near children, working in jobs involving children, volunteering to coach youth sports, teaching religious classes, driving school buses, or engaging in other activities that put them in close proximity to potential victims.

Goal 5. Prepare sex offenders to return to the community; establish links to appropriate community-based resources for treatment and supervision.

Establishing effective links to public and private agencies that provide treatment and supervision services for released sex offenders is an essential component of an integrated, comprehensive continuum of sex offender treatment and supervision services. Often, the staff's ability to communicate with one another is the difference between success and failure. Effective working relationships between institutional and community services providers is enhanced by regular staff meetings, joint planning efforts, and training. In many jurisdictions, the lack of coordination between government agencies presents a barrier to effective offender treatment and supervision. It may be reassuring to draft formal policy agreements relating to the specific responsibility of each agency or facility.

Many community mental health agencies refuse to treat sex offenders for a variety of reasons ranging from the clinical staff's lack of specialized training or expertise, to statements that their primary responsibility is providing services for seriously mentally ill clients, to their concern about potential liability issues or negative public response. Many corrections systems find aftercare programs that use contract clinicians in conjunction with parole officers trained in specialized treatment and management techniques are effective.

Correctional facilities must share all relevant clinical and risk assessment data, treatment progress, and information on supervision needs with the clinicians or agencies that will be assuming responsibility for aftercare of the sex offender. Relapse Prevention plans, if available, are important for supervisory and clinical purposes. Offenders must (1) be aware of their responsibilities during aftercare and (2) be clear on the expectations treatment agencies and parole officers will have. Pre-release contacts between institutional and community staff and the offender are an effective way of communicating needs and expectations.

Goal 6. Create a workplace environment that attracts and retains qualified clinical staff.

Correctional facilities properly regard custody as their primary responsibility. However, professionals employed in secure correctional settings often assert that their expertise is neither appreciated nor supported. The challenge for corrections is to create an environment that both attracts and retains qualified professional staff. In many states, the geographical isolation of correctional facilities makes it difficult to attract qualified clinical staff. However, this can be mitigated by offering sex offender programs only at facilities located in areas where qualified staff can be recruited.

Another key to attracting and retaining qualified clinical staff is their recognition by key facility administrators (wardens, assistant wardens, security directors, and shift commanders) who both understand and communicate their support of program goals and methods to subordinate staff. Line correctional officers reflect the attitudes of their supervisors. Training custody and other staff not directly involved in sex offender assessment and treatment also can be important in creating a supportive work environment for clinical staff.

Goal 7. Create environments within correctional facilities which promote effective delivery of educational and treatment services.

Few feel that prisons are the optimal therapeutic environment for addressing psychological or behavioral problems. The values espoused by most prisoners are antithetical to those which are generally associated with positive therapeutic environments—that is, open, trusting, supportive, and respectful. Certainly, the despised status of the child molester in prisons does not encourage such offenders to seek help in programs that might expose their status to peers. Nevertheless, most sex offenders are housed in secure correctional facilities. The negatives implicit in this environment should not deter placement of educational or therapeutic programs, however. Some of the barriers to effective therapeutic programming can be minimized by creating treatment program space separate from other general population activities.

Other environmental issues can be addressed by ensuring that all staff have a clear understanding of the program, its goals and methods, and the expectations of all staff who have contact with sex offenders involved in educational or treatment activities.

Goal 8. Establish and maintain data systems facilitating tracking of offenders, program process and outcome evaluation, and program planning.

Program accountability is most often conceived of in terms of recidivism data comparing treated and non-treated sex offenders. This measure of program effectiveness is of interest to the public, the correctional or mental health agency supporting the program, and the legislatures who fund them. However, recidivism is not the only measure of accountability.

Ideally, accountability measures should be designed into every sex offender program plan. Data should be compiled at entry into the criminal justice system and track the offender's progress until his or her discharge from legal supervision. At a minimum, data collection systems should include the following areas:

1. *Assessment of Need:* Information should be collected on the numbers of sex offenders entering the corrections system, the nature of their conviction, previous convictions for sexual and other criminal behavior, the presence of other risk factors (substance abuse, mental illness or retardation, history of violence, etc.), length of sentence, and assessed level of service need. This data assists the corrections system determine the size and types of programs required to meet the needs of the corrections population. Such data is also used to justify budgetary requests with administrators and legislative committees.

2. *Process Evaluation:* Process evaluations are designed to measure the extent to which the program achieves stated goals. They are an important managerial tool that measures whether the program staff performance is adequate, the program philosophy and methods are sound, and the extent to which program participants are progressing in measurable ways to achieve therapeutic goals. Process evaluations include formal mechanisms such as quality assurance programs, systematic review of pre-post test scores before and after each psycho-educational modules, participant success in reducing deviant sexual arousal, or successful completion of various stages of the program. It makes little sense to conduct outcome evaluations or make attributions to programs that fail to implement program goals because they are chaotic, poorly staffed, fail to provide educational or therapeutic interventions of sufficient length or intensity, etc.

3. *Outcome Evaluation:* Typically, correctional programs evaluate the relative recidivism rates of sex offenders who have completed therapeutic programs, those who entered but did not successfully complete, and those who were similar in background, but did not participate in treatment. Outcome measures may distinguish between sexual and nonsexual recidivism, or in the severity of the subsequent criminal behavior, number of victims, and other indicators of change in patterns of criminal behavior which might be attributed to program participation.

The monograph *Intervening with Substance-Abusing Offenders: A Framework for Action* (U.S. Department of Justice, 1991) suggested that our understanding of why or how programs for offenders work is hampered by the fact that most evaluation focuses on a single dimension or intervention, while programming is multidimensional. Drug abuse interventions, for example, might include group therapy, drug education, self-help support groups, and urinalysis. This study concluded that our understanding of the effectiveness of various treatment approaches with offenders remains rudimentary, and proposed the following approaches to program or outcome evaluation:

- Outcome monitoring measures success or failure of a program on the basis of indicators such as recidivism rates, sexual crimes, etc. The use of such indicators make it difficult to determine the causal relationship between program interventions and subsequent behavior of participants.

- Quasi-experimental approaches most often utilize matched control groups, in an attempt to statistically control for the differences in outcome.

- Pure research experiments involve the random assignment of sex offenders to either a treatment or non-treatment group. Since the experimental and control groups are presumed to be comparable, differences in outcome are attributed to treatment. While this approach has the potential for meaningful evaluation of program efficacy, it raises a number of ethical issues related to denying treatment for sex offenders who would be released, untreated, back into the community. Marques, et al. (1993) are currently conducting a study which compares three matched groups (matched volunteers assigned to treatment or non-treatment and non-volunteers matched to volunteer groups).

Conclusion

Over the past 20 years or so correctional systems nationwide have experienced a dramatic rise in the numbers of incercerated sex offenders. The number of programs designed to provide educational and treatment services to these offenders have also increased.

It is clear that the technology for sex offenders is improving and that treatment has been demonstrated to be effective with some incarcerated offenders under some circumstances. However, it remains to be seen whether prison environments are viable settings for effective therapeutic programs for sexual offenders. Pressures on overcrowded institutions to process large numbers of sex offenders through perfunctory educational or treatment programs, which qualify essentially untreated sex offenders for parole release or label them as "treated," do a disservice to the field of sex offender treatment and to public safety. Given the current trend toward longer sentences for repeat offenders, comprehensive, adequately staffed and funded programs can pay for themselves over the long run and diminish the terrible suffering experienced by victims.

References

Bays, L. and Freeman-Longo, R.E. (1989). *Why did I do it again? Understanding my cycle of problem behaviors*. Orwell, VT: Safer Society Press.

Bays, L., Freeman-Longo, R.E., and Hildebran, D. (1990). *How can I stop? Breaking my deviant cycle*. Orwell, VT: Safer Society Press.

Brecher, E.M. (1978). *Treatment programs for sex offenders*. Washington, DC: National Institute of Law Enforcement and Criminal Justice.

Brooks, Alexander D. (1992). The constitutionality and morality of civilly committing violent sexual predators. *University of Puget Sound Law Review,* 15:709.

Furby, L., Weinrott, M.R., and Blackshaw, L. (1989). Sex offender recidivism: A review. *Psychological Bulletin,* (1)105.

Freeman-Longo, R.E. and Bays, L. (1988). *Who am I and why am I in treatment? A guided workbook for clients in evaluation and beginning treatment*. Orwell, VT: Safer Society Press.

Freeman-Longo, R.E. and Knopp, F.H. (1992). State-of-the-art sex offender treatment: Outcome and issues. *Annals of Sex Research,* 5.

Governor's Task Force on Rape and Sexual Assault (New York 1990). Rape, sexual assault, and child sexual abuse: Working toward a more responsive society.

Haaven, J., Little, R., and Petre-Miller, D. (1990). *Treating intellectually disabled sex offenders: A model residential program*. Orwell, VT: Safer Society Press.

Marques, J., Day, D., Nelson, C., and West, M. (1993). Findings and recommendations from California's experimental treatment program. In G.C.N. Hall, R. Hirschman, J. Graham, and M.S. Zaragoza (Eds.), *Sexual aggression: Issues in etiology, assessment and treatment,* Taylor and Francis, Washington, DC (pp. 197-214).

Marshall, W. and Pithers, W. (1994). A reconsideration of treatment outcome with sex offenders. *Criminal Justice and Behavior,* Vol. 21, No. 1, 6-27.

Minnesota State Supreme Court (1992), In re Phillip Jay Blodgett, C-9-92-844.

National Task Force on Correctional Substance Abuse Strategies, (1991). Intervening with substance abusing offenders: A framework for action. Washington, DC: U.S. Department of Justice: National Institute of Corrections.

Ross, R., Fabiano, E., and Ross, R. (1989). *Reasoning and rehabilitation: A handbook for teaching cognitive skills*. Ottawa, Ontario: University of Ottawa.

Washington State Supreme Court (1993). In re Young and Cunningham, No. 57837-1.

Chapter 8

Decision Making with Incarcerated Sex Offenders

by Barbara K. Schwartz, Ph.D.

Overview

Sex offenders, once hospitalized under various sex offender statutes, are being incarcerated. This, coupled with deinstitutionalization of the mentally ill and mentally retarded, has resulted in new demands on correctional departments. This chapter discusses the many policy decisions—from presentence evaluations to parole board recommendations—made by correctional administrators and therapists. These decisions directly impact on the public safety. In addition, special legislation, court actions, community pressure, and/or a desire to be responsive to the needs of a growing subgroup of the prison population has resulted in the initiation of various treatment programs for sex offenders. A number of treatment options currently are available, each with its own pros and cons.

Although the treatment of sex offenders is still in its early developmental stage as a technique and continues to be controversial, a number of states have devoted substantial time and resources to the development of innovative programs. As mentioned in other chapters, the kinds of programs that are offered may depend on (1) whether the program will be housed in a maximum, medium, or minimum security prison, or in all three simultaneously, (2) the type of physical facilities available, (3) the characteristics of the prison population, (4) the department's classification system, and (5) state law. Also, state laws that limit sex offenders' participation in community release programs present a major obstacle because this population is particularly in need of transitional programs.

Ideally, programs want individuals who are highly motivated, accept responsibility, do not have antisocial personalities, and are not substance abusers, psychotic, mentally retarded, or sadistic. The community and the rest of the criminal justice system want the most dangerous offenders treated. The taxpayers have provided funds with the hope that sex offender treatment programs will alleviate some of their fears by rehabilitating individuals who are the greatest risks. However, the programs are painfully aware of the disastrous results that follow a re-offense committed by a "treated" sex offender. Consequently, fear for their own survival may force programs to treat only the least dangerous offenders. Society must recognize that some sex offenders will always re-offend, no matter how good the therapy. Treatment rarely, if ever, causes recidivism; it can lessen the extent and harm done in the next offense.

Education of the public and responsible media coverage will do much to alleviate the tendency to blame the program for the failure to "cure" what in some cases is an intractable condition. Then, programs will begin to accept and learn to treat those now considered untreatable. This chapter stresses that programmatic decisions must be based on a thorough knowledge of each state's particular characteristics, needs, and resources.

Controversy Over Treatment

There is considerable disagreement about whether sex offenders can be treated. Several early authors theorized that certain types of offenders are more responsive to treatment than others; however, none of these theories has been explored through research (Schrenck-Notzing, 1895; Pollens, 1938; Shaskan, 1939; Brande, 1950, Ploscowe, 1951; Rosen, 1964). Allen (1940) stated that sexual deviations are as easily treated as neurosis if the individual is not obtaining some type of secondary gain. He felt that a younger age, shorter duration of symptoms, higher IQ, desire for a cure, and absence of alcoholism were factors which predicted success. Kozol, Cohen, and Garofalo (1966) felt that successfully paroled sex offenders could be characterized as showing compassion for others, having few hostilities, and possessing a fairly positive self-image. Mathias (1972) stated that the unresponsive offender tends to be unreliable, manipulative, unmotivated, and inclined to handle anxiety with acts of sexual deviation which tranquilize him and thus reinforce the behavior.

Rosen (1964) listed the following criteria for successful treatment: younger; first offense; no previous treatment failure; high IQ; ability to express self and good abstract thinking; socially well adjusted; depression, shame, disgust, and guilt related to deviant fantasy or action; healthy social environment; married, bisexual, or past heterosexuality; desire for cure; sincere effort to control behavior; acceptance of responsibility; socially discreet; absence of coexisting perversion; not neurotic, psychopathic, or psychotic; not homosexual or pedophilic; and shy with women. The reader is cautioned that "homosexual" in Rosen's content probably refers to males who assault boys. These individuals may not be interested in adult homosexual relations and are often married.

Marcus (1971) suggested that the following criteria be used to identify potentially dangerous offenders who would be inappropriate for outpatient therapy: bedwetting; firesetting and cruelty to animals; delinquent acts between the ages of 8 and 13; escalation of sex offenses; interrelated criminality with sexual offenses; sustained excitement prior to and at time of offense; lack of concern for victim; bizarre fantasies with minor offenses; explosive outbursts; absence of psychosis; absence of alcoholism; high IQ; lack of human warmth or humanitarian depth; and lack of social know-how.

It is apparent that therapists disagree about whether high intelligence is an asset or a liability in the treatment of sex offenders. Basically, it is a factor that can be used or abused. Limited intelligence may prevent an individual from remembering, assimilating, or utilizing what he has learned in treatment. It may be difficult to rely on heavily verbal modalities or aim for the acquisition of insight. Some states, including Oregon, are developing specialized programs for low-functioning sex offenders. However, individuals of high intelligence who lack true motivation, abdicate responsibility, or lack remorse may use their innate abilities to manipulate others. They may be able to learn all the appropriate jargon and theories and say exactly what therapists wish to hear. Individuals at both extremes of the intellectual spectrum present a special challenge for treatment programs.

Sentencing Policies

Sentencing structure is an issue that is of critical importance to correctional departments seeking to establish treatment programs. Basically, states have either indeterminate sentencing in which an individual's sentence represents a range of time (e.g., 2-10 years, 10-50 years, 25-100 years) that may be shortened by parole, or fixed sentences that may be shortened by the accrual of "good time." Some states have a hybrid of the two systems. For example, Oregon can transfer incarcerated sex offenders to a hospital-based program during their last two years and then request extension of their parole.

In states with indeterminate sentencing, sex offenders may view therapy as a pre-requisite to parole. Consequently, their participation will be based on gaining their freedom rather than on treating their problem. Such program participants may become quite adept at manipulating the staff and presenting the image of the "ideal inmate" so they will be paroled.

Fixed sentencing automatically screens out individuals who see treatment as the path to release. Still, treatment programs should be quite cautious about awarding time off an individual's sentence for participation, as this usually leads to the same manipulation associated with indeterminate sentencing. When an individual's sentence is completed, the individual is released regardless of his potential dangerousness. Since treatment is time-based rather than criteria-based, the failure rate is probably higher in states with determinate sentencing. Presently, no research is available to confirm this, but it is realistic to assume that a program whose participants must successfully complete a course of treatment will do better than one where some patients complete 100%, some 50%, and some 25% of the same program. While indeterminate sentences have their own set of problems, they also provide the opportunity to keep incarcerated those individuals who are obviously dangerous. They also serve initially to motivate individuals who can respond well to treatment. They may provide more control and more leverage for encouraging appropriate behavior.

Treatment professionals must remember that they will never succeed with all patients. Inevitably, some individuals will re-offend after they leave a treatment program. If the media picks up on this, the treatment program may be blamed for recommending release. Thus, it is imperative that treatment personnel refrain from advocating the parole of participants. Completion of treatment must be rigidly and objectively defined and parole boards must continuously be cautioned that completion of treatment does not guarantee success in the community. Outside consultants may be used to evaluate an inmate's progress in treatment and readiness for parole.

Sentencing Procedures Vary

Several different procedures are used for determining the sentence of a sex offender. Some states have court clinics where publicly employed mental health evaluators make impartial recommendations to the court or the probation department regarding sentencing issues such as dangerousness or amenability for community treatment.

Other states accept recommendations made by private providers retained by the defendant. For example, Washington State has a legal provision known as the Special Sex Offender Sentencing Alternative (SSOSA). This alternative to incarceration allows roughly 45% of the state's sex offenders to enter community-based treatment. Since offenders pay for their own evaluation and treatment, this farsighted program saves taxpayers millions of dollars in costs of incarceration, and its participants show no higher recidivism rate than those who have been incarcerated without treatment (Berliner, 1992).

SSOSA's decision-making process has a serious flaw, however. The judge's decision is based on evaluations done by private practitioners who perform the assessment and provide the treatment. If one evaluation concludes that an individual is not amenable to treatment, the defense attorney can squelch that evaluation and seek out another—as long as the defendant can pay for it. Consequently, the more money the offender has, the likelier it is that a positive assessment will be acquired.

Some states offer an option that allows judges to bring convicted felons into the prison to be evaluated as to whether they are suitable candidates for probation. The evaluation, which may last from several weeks to several months, is often used as "shock incarceration" to deter felons from further crime. In the case of sex offenders, mental health professionals and others involved in the classification and evaluation process may be called upon to make a determination of amenability for community treatment. The evaluators must realize that sex offenders are a specialized population and must not be overly influenced by the fact that many of these individuals have been law-abiding citizens in the past.

Segregation of Sex Offenders

There may be both positive and negative repercussions if an individual correctional department decides to segregate sex ofenders or offer a segregated treatment program. Segregation probably is the most economical approach since establishing physiological assessment laboratories at a number of institutions could be quite costly.

In segregated programs, the entire staff can be specially trained and can devote their full energies to this problem. Also, correctional officials involved with this population can serve as part of the therapeutic team. Another positive aspect of segregated programs is that they can provide a therapeutic atmosphere. Residents do not have to be concerned about hiding their crimes or about ridicule or physical assault once their crimes are revealed.

Segregated programs also have some negative aspects. For example, they may be limited in the range of rehabilitative programs they can offer. In addition, participants may not be eligible to participate in educational or vocational programs due to security, classification, or location. Finally, the stigma of participation in sex offender treatment programs may be so great that these individuals cannot be returned to the general population and must remain in the program regardless of their adjustment. Creative efforts will be needed to overcome these problems and establish suitable alternatives.

Problems with Prison Environments

Numerous problems exist with any attempt to provide psychological treatment in prison. Knopp (1984), points to the attitudes of secrecy, defensiveness, and denial that the prison value system encourages. Idle time is spent reinforcing deviant attitudes and fantasies. Expressing emotions or admitting problems is perceived as weakness. Individuals may acquire certain problems while they are in prison that they did not have before they entered the institution. These problems include drug abuse, alcoholism, criminal thought patterns, bitterness, and anger toward the system.

Here are some of the inherent differences between prisons and treatment:

1. Prisons encourage dependency while treatment focuses on responsibility.
2. Prisons often isolate men from women, while treatment tries to facilitate more appropriate interaction with women.
3. Prisons encourage distrust, while treatment encourages trust.

In making decisions regarding treatment and release, mental hospitals may not be able to accommodate sex offenders for either the length of time or at the level of security that the crime warrants. Judges may resent being placed in the position of having to choose between treatment and incarceration. The community may perceive commitment to a hospital program as exoneration of the offender. Correctional departments, however, are obligated to respond to all of these situations. These problems might tempt one to abandon the idea of treating sex offenders. However, studies cited throughout this volume support the efficacy of sex offender treatment.

Making Treatment Decisions

There are severe problems inherent in evaluating sex offenders. Dreiblatt (1982) points out that there is no way to identify sex offenders within the general population. One may or may not have an admission of guilt and the situation may be more or less incriminating. Before attempting to predict amenability for community treatment, one must be fully cognizant of the limitations in this area. Accuracy may be improved if the factors associated with the crime are carefully defined.

It is helpful to know something about the base rates of different types of offenses. There is a strong feeling among clinicians that sadistic offenders and patterned same-sex offenders are the most intractable. The sadistic offender may be diagnosed by the police report; the crime will be particularly brutal and degrading and marked with a certain ritualism. The scene of the crime may have been prepared in advance with confining devices and instruments of torture. Any pattern that suggests that sexual arousal was linked with inflicting pain on the victim should be carefully analyzed.

Note that the term "same-sex offense" is used rather than the term "homosexual." That is because the latter term usually refers to a developed, adult sexual preference. The fixated same-sex pedophile may be stuck at the immature stage of development prior to developing an interest in the opposite sex or may have repressed a homosexual preference out of shame or humiliation.

Dreiblatt (1982) points out that practitioners doing presentence evaluation with sex offenders should bear in mind that:

- After the sex offender is apprehended, there is a suppression effect which should not be confused with a substantive change in behavior.
- Sex offenders are quite heterogeneous and do not show one or even several consistent profiles.
- Many sex offenders have a highly habituated sexual preference, and their disorder may best be viewed as an addiction.
- Sexually deviant behavior is extremely complex, with multiple causes.
- Treatment selection must be matched specifically to the offender, and a multifaceted approach should be used. (p. 4)

Assessing Dangerousness and Amenability

Like corrections officials, mental health professionals involved with this population must make certain critical decisions. For instance, specialized knowledge is needed to identify which sex offenders are too dangerous to be referred to community programs. Within the prison, a decision must be made as to whether individuals who wish to participate in the treatment program but whose degree of dangerousness makes them extreme treatment risks will be allowed to participate.

Individual state policies, court orders, legislative mandates, and/or consent decrees may demand that treatment be offered to everyone who does not specifically refuse it. Nevertheless, the recidivism of one notorious sex offender can destroy a treatment program regardless of how conscientious program staff were or whether they had input into the offender's release.

Nicholas Groth (1979) offers several suggestions for evaluating the dangerousness of pedophilic offenders for purposes of placing them in community programs. His suggestions can easily be modified to aid in assessing rapists for the same purpose. Groth suggests that the evaluation must disclose (1) how much of the offender's criminal behavior is the result of external situational factors and how much is due to psychological determinants and (2) the circumstances under which the assault occurred and the chances and conditions of recurrence. In order to evaluate these questions, one must determine:

- Frequency of offending (from police records, family reports, hospital records, and perhaps the offender himself);
- Appropriate sexual outlets;
- Questionable sexual outlets (e.g., pornography or prostitution);
- History of misdemeanor sex crimes;
- Access to victims; and
- Specificity of victims.

Any drug or alcohol problems should be evaluated and taken into account. If present, these problems provide an added challenge to treatment because substance abusers are less predictable.

Family, friendships, and employment also may be major factors in determining risk. An offender who is a transient, alcoholic derelict with no means of support probably is less inclined to pursue treatment than an offender who has a stable job, family, and friends. The latter is a better risk and more likely to pursue treatment that is offered as an alternative to incarceration. Treatment resources may substantially lower the risk of re-offending.

Myths regarding different types of offenders need to be unveiled. Pedophiles are often seen as passive individuals who entice and cajole their victims into cooperating. However, Abel and associates (1981) found that 58% of child molesters use excessive force. Even if the offender did not use excessive force because the victim acquiesced, it is still advisable to evaluate whether he is aroused by violence. This information may be obtained through a physiological assessment.

Incest offenders should be evaluated to determine whether they actually are pedophiles with strong deviant arousal. This may also require physiological assessment.

It is important to remember that these measures are not foolproof, because deviant arousal may be suppressed. Thus, in the case of incest offenders, one might look for a pattern of multiple marriages to, and divorces from, women with children of similar ages. Sudden, unexplained moves also may indicate a patterned offender who is constantly on the verge of being apprehended and is quickly leaving an area.

There is considerable controversy regarding how much overlap exists among types of sex offenders. Abel and associates (1987) found significant crossover. Large numbers of rapists had committed child molestation. Pedophiles raped adult women. Some incest offenders had done both.

Marshall, Barbaree, and Eccles (1991) reported much less overlap. Their study reported that only 7.9% of incest offenders reported other paraphilias. It is not known, however, how much of the variance in these two studies can be attributed to the extraordinary care which Abel and his associates took to maintain confidentiality.

Evaluating Amenability

Amenability to treatment is another issue that calls for astute professional judgment. One individual may be amenable but judged too dangerous to participate, while another may be considered to be less dangerous but not amenable. Both of these clinical decisions will influence program participation.

Outpatient Programs. Many outpatient treatment programs have established set criteria for admission. Pacific Professional Associates in Sherman Oaks, California insist that therapy candidates recognize that they (1) are sexual deviants, (2) are capable of being aroused by stimuli judged to be inappropriate by contemporary community standards, (3) have trouble controlling their deviant urges, and (4) are highly motivated to change their behavior. These professionals prefer that their patients be between 18 and 40 years of age, have an IQ above 80, speak, read, and write English, and not be taking medicine that may interfere with their thought processes or autonomic nervous system. These criteria actually screen in many patterned offenders because deviant arousal is a criterion. Many situational offenders do not show deviant arousal (Marshall, et al., 1991).

The Multnomah County Community Corrections Sex Offender Treatment Program in Portland, Oregon accepts pedophiles and incest offenders who have no prior history of offending. There should not be a history of antisocial behavior or an escalation of this behavior. Those who are accepted may not presently have a substance abuse problem, psychosis, or severe mental illness. Candidates must accept responsibility for their actions and should not have a history of placing themselves in a position where they can contact victims. Offenders should have stable family relations, friendships, and work histories. Finally, it is preferable that the offender had only one victim and that victim was not inordinately young or physically or emotionally handicapped.

The Positive Approaches to Sex Offenders (PASO) Program in Albuquerque, New Mexico was one of the few programs to treat violent rapists successfully on an outpatient basis. A four-year follow-up study of 58 patients was conducted to differentiate between those who successfully completed the program and those who terminated or recidivated before its completion (Schwartz, 1977). Four offenders (7%) recidivated; another 13 (21%) left the program for a variety of reasons but did not recidivate. The offenders were evaluated on 27 different factors. Five factors frequently associated with response to treatment did not differentiate responders from nonresponders. These were measures of emotional distress, motivation, denial, empathy, and frequency of crime. For child molesters, 74% of the group could be correctly categorized by using the variables of environmental stress, previous criminal convictions, alcoholism, and intact marriages. Using the Rorschach Genetic-Level Score, intact marriage, stable employment, and honorable discharge from the military, 93% of the rapists could be correctly categorized. Notably, 77% of the nonresponding pedophiles were alcoholics. Clinicians should be cautious in assuming that the same factors will predict amenability to treatment among all types of sex offenders. In general, responding pedophiles were individuals with normal heterosexual histories who committed the crime during a period of extreme stress (e.g., the loss of a job). Responding rapists were individuals who had a history of responsible behavior.

Prison-Based Programs. While the major emphasis for evaluating amenability is on placement in a community-based program, prison-based sex offender programs may also have criteria for admission. For example, the Vermont Treatment Program for Sexual Aggressors at Chittenden Correctional Facility in South Burlington, Vermont has established an admission policy that selects offenders with demonstrated histories of prosocial behaviors, and those who do not have problems that threaten their sense of self-control (e.g., alcoholism). Candidates must accept responsibility and acknowledge the harm done. Sadistic offenders are excluded.

Assessment Device Being Developed. Prentky and Knight are currently developing an assessment device that incorporates some of the better predictive indices including the Hare Psychopathy Scale. The Multidimensional Assessment of Sexuality and Aggression (MASA) was developed at the Massachusetts Treatment Center under a grant from the National Institute of Mental Health in connection with the authors' work identifying sex offender typologies (see Chapters 2 and 3). It should prove to be a major asset in the decision-making process. Much more research is needed in this area to establish amenability criteria for different groups in relation to treatment.

Evaluating for Classification

Decisions relating to classification also have significant program impact. If the treatment program exists in only one facility, prospective participants must meet certain security-rating criteria or the criteria must be written to allow for this. Once a program participant is at the appropriate facility, decisions must be made about specific housing assignments. In many institutions, sex offenders are at risk for abuse by other inmates, and housing assignments may make the difference between participation in the program or protective custody.

How well classification is handled may determine whether treatment can even be conducted. Many departments utilize classification systems that are based solely on past history and focus on issues such as prior escapes, detainers, and criminal record. However, it may be more helpful to have a system that focuses on current functioning. Sex offenders, from the highly predatory career criminal to the passive, deferent college professor, probably are more heterogeneous than any other group.

Quay (1984) devised a classification system based on both behavioral ratings and some social history data done by correctional officers and case managers. It divides offenders into five categories along a continuum—heavies, con-artists, moderates, dependent, and neurotic/anxious. Table 8.1 identifies the major characteristics of these groups, and Table 8.2 offers some suggestions for programming. In some situations, this classification system may be best used to segregate individuals. In other cases, it may be best used to integrate weaker individuals with stronger, nonpredatory ones.

As mentioned earlier, whether sex offenders are treated in maximum, medium, or minimum security institutions will have major implications for treatment. There may be more opportunities for therapeutic communities in maximum security prisons where mixing the general population can be restricted. Therapeutic communities may make it somewhat easier for sex offenders to participate in group therapy. Individuals are not stigmatized and there is less fear that the revelation of their crime or its details will place them in physical jeopardy. In such an environment, offenders can begin to learn trust, as well as have more opportunity to practice the social skills many of them lack.

In a medium security prison, the safety of the sex offender program's site depends primarily on the characteristics of the particular prison. In such a facility, there will be more contact with the general population even if the program is placed in special units, and there will also be less supervision.

Many states have laws or policies forbidding the placement of sex offenders at minimum security facilities. Where possible, however, a minimum security placement has many advantages. For instance, the rest of the population may feel that they have too much at stake to harass other inmates. Also, there may be a much needed opportunity for transitional programs such as work or school release and/or furloughs. These are quite valuable in the therapeutic process.

Table 8.1
Characteristic Behaviors by Group*

I ----------Heavy ------------II		III —Moderate	IV ----------Light ----------V	
• Agressive	• Sly	• Not excessively aggressive or dependent	•Dependent	• Constantly afraid
• Confrontational	• Not directly confrontational	• Reliable, cooperative	• Unreliable	• Anxious
• Easily bored	• Untrustworthy	• Undustrious	• Passive	• Easily upset
• Hostile to authority	• Hostile to authority	• Do not see themselves as criminals	• "Clinging"	• Seek protection
• High rate of disciplinary infractions	• Moderate to high rate of disciplinary infractions	• Low rate of disciplinary infractions	• Low-to-moderate rate of disciplinary infractions	• Moderate rate of disciplinary infractions
• Little concern for others	• "Con artists," manipulative	• Concern for others	• Self-absorbed	• Explosive under stress
• Victimizers	• Victimizers	• Avoid fights	• Easily victimized	• Easily victimized

*This table is reprinted with permission of Herbert Quay and the American Correctional Association.

Table 8.2
Differential Programming by Group Assignment*

	Education	Work	Counseling	Staff Approach
Heavy (*Groups I & II*)	• Individualized • Programmed learning	• Non-repetitive • Short-term goals • Individual goals	• Individualized (behavioral contracts)	• By the book • No-nonsense
Moderate (*Group III*)	• Classroom lecture plus research assignments	• High level of supervised responsibility	• Group and individual (problem orientation)	• "Hands off" • Direct only as needed
Light (*Groups IV & V*)	• Classroom lecture plus individual tutoring	• Repetitive • Team-oriented goals	• Group and individual (personal orientation)	• Highly verbal • Supportive

*This table is reprinted with permission of Herbert Quay and the American Correctional Association.

Determining Whether an Offender Should Be Released

Perhaps the riskiest decision the treatment professional makes is when, or if, treatment should be terminated. Unsuccessful termination can be a fairly objective process that occurs when the individual fails to attend or actively participate, is disruptive, or violates confidentiality. Therefore, when the therapist is called upon to state whether the person has successfully completed treatment and is therefore ready for release, then it is vital to be able to rely on a set of objective criteria. (See Appendix A.)

Regardless of whether the state has indeterminate sentencing, determinate sentencing, or some combination of the two, therapists need to have some measure of progress in therapy so they can determine whether the offender should be released. The treatment program in the Chittenden facility in Vermont requires offenders to do the following before they are eligible for release:

• Explicitly describe the situations that pose an increased risk of his acting-out in a sexually aggressive manner.
• Verbalize without hesitation the coping responses that he will enact in order to refrain from sexual aggression.
• Anticipate future risk situations and use problem-solving techniques to devise effective coping responses.

- Discern and modulate an adequate range of emotions.
- Express anger verbally and appropriately.
- Understand that every person in society has a right to define his or her own sex role as long as that role is not illegal.
- Show decreased arousal to deviant stimuli and increased arousal to appropriate stimuli.

Pacific Professional Associates, a community-based program, can more easily measure response to treatment in real life situations. They are able to evaluate where improved social coping skills are being put to use in establishing appropriate relationships. They also use measures of deviant arousal, which must be below 20% on 10 consecutive evaluations, and for nondeviant arousal, which must be above 80% for 10 consecutive evaluations.

Systems that offer transitional programs have the advantage of being able to evaluate the offender's response to real life challenges (e.g., socializing with females, responding to unexpected frustrations, being exposed to old temptations). However, they also give offenders the opportunity to re-offend while still actively participating in the program. More research is needed to help correctional professionals decide who is ready for a community release program. When treatment programs are tied to release, it may be best to have evaluations conducted by independent professionals.

This author has developed a set of treatment goals that include the individual steps that must be taken to reach each one. The goals include:

- Overcoming denial
- Understanding motivators
- Understanding disinhibitors
- Developing a Relapse prevention plan
- Correcting cognitive distortions
- Modifying deviant arousal
- Developing a transition plan and
- Participating appropriately in the therapeutic community

These goals are geared to the author's programs and reflect that orientation. However, every treatment program should be able to identify and objectify its goals.

Selecting Treatment Providers

Systems that emphasize community-based treatment can be risky. Many therapists are not specifically trained to deal with sex offenders. In fact, their training may actually be counterproductive. Therefore, when a community decides to turn an offender over for treatment rather than incarceration, that community had better be certain that the treatment and those providing it are as effective as possible.

In treating sex offenders, particularly in the early stages of recovery, one may be dealing with involuntary patients or individuals whose motivation for treatment is highly questionable. These individuals may attempt to manipulate, intimidate, and/or flatter their therapist into inadvertently colluding with them. For example, such offenders are notorious for distorting religious beliefs to make themselves look better.

Washington State's SSOSA program, which was discussed earlier in this chapter, allows certain less dangerous sex offenders to receive community treatment at their own expense. Forty-five percent of the state's sex offenders are placed on SSOSA. This saves the state approximately $6 million annually in the cost of incarceration; only about one-sixth of that amount is needed to finance an intensive prison treatment program.

The states handle this issue in different ways. Some states ignore it and hope for the best. Others, such as Hawaii, provide the treatment to all offenders through contracts with certain providers. Still other states have established lists of approved providers. Some of these states have been threatened with "restriction of trade" lawsuits. It is possible, however, to establish agreements between the state and private providers if the therapists agree to charge certain rates in exchange for referrals from probation, prison, or parole.

Licensing of Sex Offender Treatment Providers. Washington State was the first state to license sex offender treatment providers as a separate mental health discipline (Washington Administrative Code, 246-930-2330, 1991). Texas has passed similar provisions, and other states, including Iowa, are in the process of licensing such providers. Individuals wishing to obtain such a license must be licensed or certified health/mental health care providers with 2,000 hours of experience in the treatment of sex offenders, 500 of which must have been in evaluation. This experience must have been acquired within the past five years. All candidates must pass a written examination. There is no grandfather provision. The law only applies to those treating sex offenders in the SSOSA program. The process attempts to ensure that all treatment providers have a common base of knowledge, regardless of their theoretical approach to treatment.

Standards for Treatment Established in Washington State. The same legislation mandated the establishment of standards for treatment. This was a challenging task as the orientation of therapists from Freudian analysts to radical behaviorists needed to be accommodated. Washington State's Recommended Treatment Goals (Washington Administrative Code 246-930-220 (1991) are as follows:

- Address client's deviant sexual urges and recurrent deviant sexual fantasies as necessary to prevent sexual re-offense;
- Attempt to educate clients and the individuals who are part of their support systems about the objective risk of re-offense;
- Attempt to teach clients to utilize self-control methods to avoid sexual re-offending where applicable;
- Consider the effects of trauma and past victimization as factors in reoffense potential where applicable;
- Address client's thought processes that facilitate sexual offense and other victimizing or assaultive behaviors;
- Attempt to modify client's thinking errors and cognitive distortions where possible;
- Attempt to ensure that clients have accurate knowledge about the effect of sexual offense upon victims, their families, and the community;

- Assist clients to develop a sensitivity to the effects of sexual abuse upon victims;
- Address client's personality traits and personality deficits that are related to re-offense potential;
- Address client's deficit coping skills in present life situations where applicable;
- Include and integrate the client's family into the therapy process where appropriate;
- Attempt to maintain communication with client's spouse and family where appropriate to assist in meeting treatment goals.

It is particularly important to note that the standards for certification and treatment were established by Washington's Department of Health. Neither corrections nor probation/parole departments should attempt to certify treatment providers. That is beyond their area of expertise and should be handled as a health licensing issue. However, it is possible for corrections departments to enter into contractual agreements with providers. For instance, Vermont has established a network of community providers who have agreed to undergo special training in return for referrals.

Utilizing Technologies

In attempting to establish standards, three issues regarding modern technology will undoubtedly arise. These technologies are penile plethysmography, polygraphy, and electronic monitoring.

Plethysmography. Basically, penile plethysmography is a biofeedback measure that is used to analyze sexual arousal patterns by measuring penile engorgement (see Chapter 11). It is commonly used as an evaluation technique, a measurement of the effectiveness of therapeutic techniques, and to administer certain behavioral modalities. The use of plethysmography as part of a comprehensive assessment is mandated as part of Washington State's standards for sex offender evaluations (Washington Administrative Code, 246-930 (1991)).

This issue is easily sensationalized, and many individuals faced with the option of approving plethysmography, particularly in public institutions, may shy away from it. However, there tends to be public acceptance when this and some of the more intrusive behavioral treatment components have been endorsed in a "master plan."

Interested groups should have access to ongoing education around these issues. Professional groups involved in sex offender treatment should be alert to the unethical use of the instrument (e.g., as evidence of guilt or innocence, as evidence in custody battles, or in making exaggerated claims about its validity or predictive ability).

It should also be emphasized that the plethysmograph should not be utilized as a polygraph. Both Marshall (1975) and Quinsey (1983) report that indices of deviant sexual interest did not predict outcome (Marshall, Laws, and Barbaree, 1990, p. 381). Therefore, plethysmograph results alone should never be used as a basis for continuing or terminating individual or community supervision or to make parole or other release decisions.

Polygraphy. Polygraphy is another technology that is relevant to the treatment of sex offenders. Polygraphs are widely used with the sex offender population in the Pacific Northwest, but are vehemently opposed in some other parts of the country.

There are two basic approaches to polygraphy. The first attempts to discover whether the person being evaluated has information only a guilty party would have. The second compares direct accusations to control questions. In three strictly controlled evaluations of the accuracy of this approach, the results range from 30 to 92% (Harts and Perry, 1992). Iacono and Patrick (1987) state that:

> After decades of continuous debate surrounding the validity and appropriate uses of polygraph tests no consensus has emerged on their accuracy or how they should and should not be used. It is our feeling that it will be impossible to reach a consensus with the existing (almost nonexisting) data base. (p. 486)

However, a federal court has ruled that "the science of polygraphy has progressed to a level of acceptance sufficient to allow the use of polygraph evidence in limited circumstances where the danger of unfair prejudice is minimized" (*State v. Wilson*, 17 Ore. App. 375, 521 P.2d 1317 (1974), cert. denied 420 U.S. 910 (1975)).

Sex offender treatment specialists are dealing with a population that is prone to distortion and minimization, so it is understandable that the polygraph would be seen as a valuable instrument for improving disclosure. A study conducted with adolescent sex offenders at the MacLauren School in Oregon found that 71% of their residents failed the polygraph and subsequently disclosed another 92 offenses (Ogard, Abrams, and James, 1987). Another study indicated that admission of deviant acts among eight offenders rose from 2,085 acts to over 10,000.

It is this author's experience that the use of the polygraph as an aid to treatment is most successful when (1) the therapist and the polygrapher cooperate in developing the specific questions, (2) the patient is read the questions and given a chance to respond prior to administering the polygraph, and (3) there is some arrangement with the area district attorney regarding which new disclosures will or will not be prosecuted, and this is clearly communicated to the patient.

Regardless of its value, polygraphy will remain controversial until matters regarding invasion of privacy and self-incrimination issues are settled. As Jones (1993) states:

> Currently, programs are experiencing litigation on both sides of the issues. Sex Offenders have appealed against the use of the polygraph, while victims have filed lawsuits against providers who do not use the polygraph. It is a controversy of which providers must be aware. (p. 6)

Electronic Monitoring. Electronic monitoring is another technological advance with implications for supervising and monitoring sex offenders. The activities of such offenders are of great concern to the therapist, the police, and probation or parole officers. It is very useful in keeping close track of newly paroled offenders who are at their greatest risk in the first few weeks after their release.

The use of an electronic bracelet linked to a computer that monitors an individual's movement may make it possible to place on supervision offenders who would otherwise be imprisoned and, in doing so, save the taxpayer thousands of dollars. Usually, offenders are somewhat grateful to be spared a prison sentence and may even pay the cost of the surveillance.

Civil Commitment

Obviously, the involuntary civil commitment of sex offenders is the most extreme form of monitoring. In 1990, Washington State responded to a series of horrific sex crimes by instituting a process by which a sex offender who could demonstrate that his past sexually predatory behavior was a product of a mental disorder could be placed in a treatment center. The commitment process is typically evoked at the end of a prison sentence. This form of preventive detention is fraught with problems and has yet to demonstrate that it enhances public safety more than traditional sentencing options such as undeterminate sentencing or sentence enhancements.

Public Notification

Public notification is another issue encountered by any comprehensive approach to the problem of sexual assault. Many communities have been shocked to find out after a crime has been committed that a recently released sex offender has been residing in their midst. The subsequent outcry has led to a variety of responses.

In many states, the victim is notified of an offender's upcoming Parole Board hearing. This may give the victim the opportunity to provide the story of his or her trauma as part of the overall decision making process, but it may also make it impossible for the offender to present evidence of change to an objective board. Other states notify victims only upon the imminent release of the offender. Some jurisdictions simply maintain a file that is open to the public containing information supplied by the Corrections Department on sex offenders in the area.

There is little objective data to indicate how helpful public notification is to the victim. The way the victim is notified may impact on whether notification is helpful. For example, a form letter may produce a different response than a supportive phone call. Some programs have the offender write a letter to the victim but mail it to the district attorney who is charged with notifying the victim. When the district attorney contacts the victim, he or she can tell the victim about the letter and, if requested, can read it to the victim.

Depending on the philosophy of the notifying authority or the notoriety of the offender, the media may be notified, bulletins may be posted in the offender's neighborhood, school children may be warned, the offender's picture may be displayed on buses, and so forth. While this may make the public feel more secure, it may make it nearly impossible for the offender to find employment or housing. The offender also may be physically threatened or harmed. In one recent case, an offender's house was burned down. In another, someone's house was burned down because the wrong address was publicized and the perpetrator thought the offender was going to live there.

There is no way public notification can be conducted without subjecting the offender's family, friends, and, in the case of incest, the victim to shame, hostility, and possibly vengeful acts. Public notification may contribute to a "vigilante" atmosphere and escalate violence and lawlessness.

Registration with Law Enforcement Authorities

At least 28 states currently require sex offenders to register with the local sheriff's department. The offender is required to update that registration each time he moves. The registration process provides the authorities with a ready list of suspects if a crime does occur. However, it is most helpful if sufficient information about the individual's offense cycle is known. Violation of a sex offender registration act can also be used to arrest offenders who suddenly and unexpectedly move without updating their registration and without discussing the move with their therapist or parole/probation officer. This type of behavior is definitely a warning sign.

In this author's opinion, registration is most useful as a way of monitoring whether the sex offender is taking responsibility for his or her behavior. Is the offender complying with the law, or is the offender in rebellion from the moment of release? Individuals may be capable of handling details such as registration and still recidivate. However, failing to register, particularly upon release, can alert authorities immediately.

Conclusion

Corrections and treatment professionals must make a number of decisions, each of which may require a knowledge of different dynamics. Mental health professionals, classification officers, and security personnel should all become familiar with the research in this area. Treatment planning and programming must be based on a thorough evaluation of the offender population and the specific environment in which these policies and/or technologies would be instituted. In addition, educating all concerned segments of the community may make it easier to make decisions in an informed and professional manner, rather than in an atmosphere that is based on fear and societal pressure.

References

Abel, G.G., Becker, J.V., Mittelman, M.S., Cunningham-Rathner, J., Rouleau, J.L., and Murphy, W.D. (1987). Self-reported crimes of nonincarcerated paraphilias. *Journal of Interpersonal Violence,* 2(6), 3-25.

Abel, G.G., Becker, J.V., Murphy, W.D., and Flanagan, B. (1981). Identifying dangerous child molesters. In R. Stuart (Ed.), *Violent behaviors: Social learning approaches to prediction, management and treatment.* New York: Brunner/Mazel.

Allen, C. (1940). *The sexual perversions and abnormalities: A study of the psychology of paraphilia.* London: Oxford Press.

Berliner, L. (1991). *Evaluation of the special sex offender sentencing alternative.* Seattle, WA: Harborview Medical Center.

Brande, J.M. (1950). The sex offender and the court. *Federal Probation,* 14(3), 17-22.

Dreiblatt, I.S. (May 1982). Issues in the evaluation of the sex offender. Paper presented at annual meeting of the Washington State Psychological Association, Seattle.

Groth, A.N. (1979). *Men who rape: The psychology of the offender.* New York: Plenum Press.

Honts, C.R. and Perry, M.V. (1992). Polygraph admissibility. *Law and Human Behavior,* 16, 357-379.

Iaceno, W.G. and Patrick, C.J. (1987). What psychologists should know about lie detection. In I.B. Weiner and A.B. Hess (Eds.), *Handbook of forensic psychology* (pp. 460-489). New York: John Wiley & Sons.

James, B. (1993). Polygraphy: A current perspective. *Cooperative Newsletter of the National Adolescent Perpetrator Network*. Denver, CO: Henry Kempe Center.

Karpman, B. (1954). *The sexual offender and his offenses: Etiology, pathology and treatment*. New York: Julian Press.

Knopp, F.H. (1984). *Retraining adult sex offenders*. Syracuse: Safer Society Press.

Kozol, H.A., Cohen, M.L., and Garofalo, R.M. (1966). The criminally dangerous sex offender. *New England Journal of Medicine*, 79, 275-281.

Marcus, A.M. (1971). *Nothing is my number: An exploratory study of dangerous sex offenders in Canada*. Toronto: General Publishing.

Marshall, M.L. (1975). Relapses after treatment of sexual deviants. Unpublished manuscript, Queen's University, Kingston Ontario, Canada.

Marshall, W.L., Laws, D.R., and Barbaree, H.E. (1990). *Handbook of sexual assault*. New York: Plenum Press.

Mathias, J.L. (1972). *Clear thinking about sexual deviation*. Chicago: Nelson-Hall.

Ogard, E., Abrams, S. and James, B. (1987-1989). Juvenile study. Unpublished manuscript, MacLauren School, Oregon.

Oregon Court of Appeals. State v. Wilson, 17 Oregon App. 375, 521 P.2d 1317 (1974), cert. denied 420 U.S. 910, 95 S.Ct. 829, 42 L.Ed.2d 83 (1975).

Ploscowe, M. (1951). *Sex and the law*. New York: Prentice-Hall, Inc.

Pollens, B. (1938). *The sex criminal*. New York: McCauley.

Quay, H.C. (1984). *Managing adult inmates: Classification for housing and program assignments*. College Park, MD: American Correctional Association.

Quinsey, V.L. (1983). Prediction of recidivism and the evaluation of treatment programs for sex offenders. In S.N. Verdum-Jones and A.A. Keltner (Eds.), *Sexual aggression and the law* (pp. 27-40). Burnaby, BC: Criminology Research Centre Press.

Rosen, I. (1964). *The pathology and treatment of sexual deviation: A methodological approach*. London: Oxford Press.

Schrenck-Notzing, A. (1895). *The use of hypnosis in psychopathia sexualis*. New York: Institute for Research in Hypnosis Publication Society and Julian Press.

Schwartz, B.K. (1978). Factors associated with response to treatment among aggressive sex offenders. Doctoral dissertation, University of New Mexico, 1977. Dissertation Abstracts International.

Washington Administrative Code 246-930-2330, 1991.

Part 3

Treatment

Many misconceptions surround the treatment of sex offenders. The public may view this activity as ranging from the coddling of offenders, where therapists work to erase guilt and offer unqualified acceptance, to scenes from *A Clockwork Orange*, where rapists receive near-lethal electrical shock. Many of the techniques utilized may sound somewhat bizarre to the general population. Thus, therapists and administrators must do everything possible to enlighten the community and dispel any misconceptions. Four areas of misunderstanding are repeatedly encountered—homosexuality, passive or misdemeanor sex crimes, "violent" crimes, and rape as a paraphilia.

In the early 1900s, treatment of sex offenders began with individual psychoanalysis for those few, privileged paraphiliacs whose conduct caused them or their families sufficient discomfort to expend considerable money and time on individual treatment. Rarely had these individuals been arrested. Prior to the publication of the DSM-III, homosexuals were commonly included among those labeled and treated as sexual deviants. Many of the earlier writings on the topic of deviancy included large numbers of homosexuals, along with pedophiles, exhibitionists, voyeurs, and rapists. Homosexuals who engage in sex between two consenting adults are not considered to be sexually deviant. Their behavior rarely results in imprisonment, although it may still be illegal in many states. This conduct is no longer considered to be a mental illness by the American Psychiatric Association except where it causes significant personal distress. It is a popular misconception that men who molest young boys are homosexuals. This is rarely the case. These individuals are frequently heterosexual in their sexual relations with adults.

Individuals who become aware of homosexual yearning in adolescence may respond with panic, shame, and fear of familial rejection. These individuals may turn to children rather than acknowledge their homosexual orientation, in the same way that individuals for whom adult heterosexual behavior is anxiety-provoking. Adults who are able to acknowledge their sexuality and engage in mature, responsible sexual relations are society's best protection against child molestation.

Another area that may cause confusion is the outdated distinction between passive and aggressive sex offenses. Almost all of the incarcerated sex offenders in treatment today are rapists or child molesters, either incest offenders or pedophiles. Exhibitionists, voyeurs, frotteurs, or those who make obscene phone calls may be jailed on misdemeanor charges and referred for counseling but are rarely imprisoned unless their behavior involves other criminal conduct. A decade ago, these individuals were considered to be essentially nuisances, passive individuals who presented little real threat. However, these offenses are now recognized as frequently comprising an escalating pattern of deviant behavior. The sexual addictions model emphasizes the increasing severity of crimes in the development of many sex offenders. Additionally, the actual intent of the individual arrested for a misdemeanor sex offense is frequently difficult to ascertain. The voyeur caught at someone's window may be on the verge of climbing in and committing a rape. Treatment personnel must examine the histories of all sex offenders for patterns of a variety of sex offenses. In those cases where the individual is incarcerated purely for exhibitionism, voyeurism, etc., these behaviors may be treated in the same way as the more serious types of sexual crimes.

Yet another issue that causes considerable misunderstanding among the public is the use of terms such as "violent rape" or "sadistic sexual assault." Any aggressive act falls along a continuum from those involving threats of violence to threats with weapons to various degrees of physical harm to death. Every sexual assault is a violent act. However, references in this work to "violent rape" or child molestation refer to situations where a considerable amount of unwarranted physical damage is done to the victim. Sadistic sex crimes are very specifically defined as sexual assaults which are usually elaborately planned with a distinctively ritualistic quality. Pain and degradation are systematically inflicted on the victim. Fortunately, sexual sadists represent a very small proportion of sex offenders.

The question of whether rape is a paraphilia is more of a political controversy than a therapeutic one. The most official definition of mental illness is the American Psychiatric Association's Diagnostic and Statistical Manual which officially lists all conditions considered to be mental illnesses ranging from psychosis to nicotine addiction. While pedophilia, exhibitionism, voyeurism, and numerous other types of deviant sexual behaviors are listed as "paraphilias," rape is not. Yet it resembles these conditions in many ways. Rapists may have deviant patterns of sexual arousal. They may have intrusive deviant sexual fantasies. Their acting-out may have a readily identifiable build-up phase followed by remorse and regret. Their behavior may be obsessive-compulsive in nature. Rapists are at times treated with a variety of drugs. They are most commonly treated with the same techniques and usually in the same programs and groups as all the other sex offenders who carry the label of "paraphiliac." Yet for some reason they are excluded unless they fit the definition for "sexual sadism" which most do not. Factions who oppose the inclusion of rape in DSM may perceive that labeling a behavior as an illness leads to the coddling of criminals who are "bad," not "mad." The matter makes little difference for most sex offender providers but does have legal, financial, and administrative implications. A rapist may not have a "right to treatment" comparable to that of a pedophile who can claim that he has a significant mental illness. A rapist may not be able to utilize insurance benefits to reimburse his therapist unless he is diagnosed under the "Paraphilia, Other" category. Administrators considering Involuntary Commitment proceedings which require the existence of a mental illness as well as dangerousness may have to identify other behaviors (substance abuse) or other personality dynamics to confine a highly dangerous individual. This quandary is largely a result of the utilization of a medical model. Dealing with behaviors rather than abstract theoretical models may someday clarify this issue.

Sex offender treatment is challenging enough without the massive misunderstandings which surround the field. Consequently, professionals in this area must be constantly updating their own knowledge and making this knowledge available to the public. Keeping abreast of the changes in this field is particularly crucial because in many areas the methods are still in their infancy. Because sex offenses have multiple causes even within a single individual, the problem must be addressed on a number of different levels.

Because sex offenders are such a diverse group, treatment must begin with an evaluation of individual assets and deficits. After this is completed, treatment planning can address specific areas of need. A lack of knowledge, particularly in the area of human sexuality, as well as a lack of coping skills can be addressed through psycho-educational modules. Where deviant arousal plays a part, behavioral techniques can be used to recondition sexual preferences. Group therapy can integrate a variety of approaches and address a number of issues simultaneously. Individuals confront their destructive values and thought patterns, work through their own victimization, examine their deviant cycle, and learn empathy while improving their social skills.

In prisons different types of treatment can be offered during different phases of treatment. While many offenders are in denial when first convicted, a significant proportion have admitted their guilt and are highly motivated. Some type of treatment should be offered to these men before they retreat back into denial. At this initial stage, the principal question is "Why?" "Why would I do such a thing?" Didactic presentations on the origins of sexual deviation, as well as classes in stress management, anger management, and communication skills, can provide only the basic information for the individual to begin his personal exploration. For those individuals in denial, sometimes all that is needed to break this down is the permission given the individual by the group to admit the deed. Even discussing sexual assault in the abstract can open one up to personal admission.

The middle stage of treatment can continue with the psycho-educational modules while beginning the group process. The final stage, which should probably be started no sooner than two years prior to release, should focus on intensive treatment. Behavioral techniques can be initiated. Offenders may be moved into therapeutic communities and group work intensified. The transitional phase leading to aftercare is crucial in assisting the individual through this difficult period of readjustment.

In the community the therapist is faced with a very limited amount of time (often a group lasting a few hours a week) to address numerous problems in an individual who may be at constant risk to re-offend. It is imperative that only those sex offenders who can structure their lives so as to avoid access to High Risk Situations prior to having learned control through treatment be kept in the community. Although few programs exist in jails as opposed to prisons, this could be an ideal place to begin treatment as many offenders in jails are eventually released on probation.

Eventually residential programs similar to the thousands available for substance abusers may fill this gap. These programs will offer intensive treatment and skill building in a structured setting while reserving costly prison cells for the most dangerous.

Administrators are frequently concerned about who should provide sex offender treatment. A psychiatrist in a consulting role should be involved in medication, either specific to sex offenders or utilized to treat accompanying mental illness, will be needed. Since there is very little specific training in sex offender treatment available through any mental health degree program, no discipline is recognized as particularly proficient in this area. The leaders in this field include psychologists, social workers, rehabilitation counselors, criminologists, and educators. Both professionals and paraprofessionals make a valuable contribution. Correctional officers can be trained to facilitate groups and teach modules. Correctional counselors or caseworkers can do this as well. The inmates themselves can also be trained to assist in providing certain treatment techniques under supervision.

The personality of the staff member is probably more important than his/her degree. Even their gender is important. Where possible, male-female teams should be used for a variety of reasons:

- The offender needs an appropriate male role model to demonstrate correct social skills and attitudes toward females.

- The offender needs an appropriate female figure with whom he can practice social skills, as well as work through anger, power, or other issues.

- The offender needs a male-female dyad to model appropriate interactions, conflict resolution, and nonsexual relationships.

Therapists should be able to be confrontive but caring. If the treatment staff do not communicate to the offender their commitment to him as an individual, then when heavy confrontation begins, the offender will usually drop out of therapy outright or withdraw into himself. Substance abuse counselors often do quite well in this work, as many of the dynamics of the two conditions are similar. Staff should be screened for individuals who have unresolved conflicts relating to sexual assault.

A final issue in dealing with this type of treatment is not to oversell it. This is a new, challenging, and controversial area. Many people do not accept its efficacy and are just waiting to discredit any program which overstates its effectiveness. Every program will have its failures, and the failures are the ones that will make the front page of the newspaper. The program should be sold, but cautiously.

Chapter 9

Sex Offender Treatment Program Evaluation

by Randy Green, Ph.D.

Overview

Over the past 15-20 years, our society has witnessed a massive increase in the incidence of reported sexual crimes. The criminal justice system and the mental health community have attempted to respond to this epidemic in a variety of ways, ranging from punishment and incarceration to the extensive use of probation. Treatment responses include small, intensive, secure residential programs as well as large community-based programs. Correctional and mental health program managers are under significant pressure to protect the community and "cure" sex offenders before they return to society. At the same time, several of the nation's leading sex offender programs have been closed down over the past few years.

Another problem is that this is an era of declining state economies that is fostering a pronounced shift in who is responsible for treating each distinct population. As children's protective services and mental health divisions are restricting their services to their primary client groups, correctional divisions are taking over more treatment responsibility. Consequently, treatment programs with a multitude of assessment procedures and innovative interventions are becoming more widespread in correctional settings. These multimodel treatment interventions include group and family therapies, psycho-educational modules, behavioral treatment, cognitive-behavioral paradigms, Relapse Prevention strategies, and drug therapies.

The convergence of these therapeutic advances with increased populations and limited resources creates a necessity for the incorporation of program evaluation components at each level of service delivery. From any vantage point, either pragmatic, ethical, or professional, it is incumbent upon managers of correctional mental health programs for sex offenders to establish and maintain program evaluation components within their treatment initiatives.

The necessity for such evaluation efforts is enhanced by additional considerations. Typically, people-changing programs within corrections divisions have been guided by trial and error and intuitive approaches, rather than by program efficacy data. In addition, Glaser (1973) emphasized the need (1) for differential offender typologies that can be used as a basis for more appropriate classification and (2) treatment efforts that take into account the limited available resources. Such typologies can guide policymakers in decisions that pertain to those individuals entering limited-space treatment facilities or those returning to the community.

Another important reason for making program evaluation an integral part of sex offender treatment programs centers around the fact that there still is a need for scientifically collected information regarding the efficacy of sex offender treatment, in terms of recidivism and behavior change. At this time, it has not been established which treatment works best with what type of offender—fundamental data which is potentially vital to program managers, agency policy makers, and legislators. Therefore, data collection and program evaluation integrated into treatment programs becomes advisable in anticipation of future scrutiny. This scrutiny, though sometimes threatening, helps foster an attitude of accountability and objectivity.

This chapter develops and emphasizes the concept of program evaluation. Methodological obstacles in program evaluation and analysis are discussed. Finally, different types of program evaluations are examined in regard to the evaluation objectives. Program managers are provided with a number of evaluation options that can be pursued as thoroughly as their priorities and resources allow.

The Concept of Program Evaluation

Program evaluation is designed to be a systematic process for eliciting clear and objective feedback regarding the following primary issues:

- Which type of treatment is most effective with what type of offender and at what cost; and
- To what degree is the program achieving success in accomplishing its established goals and objectives.

Evaluation components should be integrated into treatment programs at their beginning or as soon as possible for already-established operations. During the establishment phase, administrative and clinical staff should be concerned with the following foundational concerns:

1. What is the task or mission of this treatment program?
2. What is the profile of the offender to be treated?
3. What specific interventions will be employed?

4. What are the expected outcomes of these interventions?
   a. To what degree will recidivism rates be a measure of program success?
   b. Is the sex offender expected to be crime-free, or demonstrate reduced seriousness of new crimes?
   c. What social/psychological changes are expected in the sex offender?
5. How can activities be defined and measured? As clients begin to participate in the program, additional questions should be asked periodically:
   a. To what degree are clients meeting the program's expectations?
   b. What types of clients are actually being treated? (For example, several pioneering sex offender programs have been receiving more chronic, refractory clients, as community-based alternatives have become increasingly available for incest offenders and other more amenable clientele.)
   c. What programmatic changes would enhance the treatment process?
   d. Is the program keeping abreast of the latest research?

The experiences of two states that pioneered sex offender treatment program development illustrate the need for these questions to be anticipated, rather than asked retrospectively. What happened in these states is instructive because the issues can be so readily generalized.

Western Washington State Hospital's Sex Offender Program, recognized nationwide as an innovative pioneer in this field, boasted an escape rate substantially less than comparable medium security institutions within the state. In 1985, however, a very dangerous rapist escaped from the unit. Following an enraged community and legislative reaction, an automatic program lockdown was effected for the nearly 225 residents. The lockdown lasted several months, during which time the Legislative Budget Analyst Office conducted an independent program evaluation. The program evaluation mandate was broad but did include an examination of the degree to which the sex offender programs were operating in a manner consistent with legislative intent, combined with an assessment of program effectiveness in accomplishing statutory objectives. Among other findings, authors of the report noted that earlier in-house program evaluation recommendations had been ignored. In addition, they concluded that the following action should be taken:

> Development of a comprehensive plan pertaining to the operations of the Sex Offender Programs ... [that] should address, but not necessarily be limited to such issues as: the development of appropriate goals and objectives; treatment methods; organizational and supervisory issues; and staff training needs. In order to provide for future program evaluation, the plan should also emphasize data and statistical requirements as well as procedures for collecting and reporting same (Washington State Legislative Budget Committee Report, 1986, p. 74).

They incorporated several other recommendations that could be generally instructive to other programs. Specifically, they recommended that more realistic staffing and funding levels be established consistent with program responsibilities. They recommended that the programs should be authorized to consider amenability as a criterion for program involvement and that programs be able to control their own admissions.

The sex offender programs at both Eastern and Western Washington State Hospitals were phased out, and the Washington State Department of Corrections was mandated to develop a treatment program to fill the gap. An elaborate plan included a therapeutic community to be housed at the Monroe compound, treatment in work release programs, and six follow-up programs.

In the mid 1970s, Ted Frank, who had been a model resident of the Atascadero State Hospital's Sex Offender Treatment Program, was released and shortly thereafter kidnapped, tortured, raped, and murdered a two-year-old girl. The child's grandmother formed a citizens' lobbying group, Society's League Against Molesters (SLAM), which called for lengthy prison sentences for sex offenders.

The California State Legislature passed a bill in 1978, requiring the Department of Mental Health to evaluate the "adequacy and value of such counseling" of convicted sex offenders within the state prisons (California Senate Bill No. 1716, 1978). Following the results of this evaluation, a subsequent bill was passed which repealed the law requiring commitment of sex offenders to state hospitals (California Senate Bill No. 278, 1981). The new law required that sex offenders be delivered to the Department of Corrections after sentencing.

In conclusion, two state legislatures, prompted by public concern and demands for accountability, retrospectively assumed responsibility for sex offender program evaluation. They determined that the responsibility to collect and analyze data is an inherent function of such treatment programs. A small pilot research project on sex offender treatment is now being conducted at Atascadero. Such lessons should not be lightly dismissed by program managers in other states. Unless programs have kept careful records and established sound quality assurance programs, they will be in constant jeopardy.

Program Evaluation Implementation

As previously mentioned, program evaluation must be directed by the program objectives and specific purposes of the research. Differential targets of evaluation can include reviews of program inputs, efforts (activities), and results or project efficiency (Hudson and Galaway, 1979). Each of these aspects will be addressed at length in relationship to sex offender program evaluations.

Input Evaluations. These evaluations focus on an examination of all resources utilized within the treatment program itself. The concept of "inputs" pertains to every resource available for the program, including funding, staffing, and client population demographics. Therefore, an input evaluation might legitimately review the following areas:

1. What funds are allocated for the individual program components of facility, security, staff?
2. What is the cost per client in capital outlay, treatment material, etc.?
3. What is the staff/client ratio?
4. What are the academic, experiential and attitudinal characteristics of the staff?
5. How is the staff organized to accomplish programmatic, statutory, and clinical objectives?

6. What are the sources of referral of clients to the program?
7. How well do the referral sources understand the intent and capabilities of this program?
8. Is there a need to educate referral sources about those amenable to the type of treatment that this program provides?
9. Do the statutes and policies pertaining to the program need to be changed?
10. What are the demographics of the client population? Client demographics are very important for interpreting outcome and output studies, when comparing the results to those of nonprogram participants and for comparing data between treatment programs. At the minimum, it is recommended that the client demographic variables listed in Table 9.1 be collected on admission to the program.
11. What are the demographics of those sex offenders who, either by choice or refusal, do not participate in the program?

It is advisable to expend effort to obtain basic demographic data regarding these individuals in order to allow for possible comparisons in subsequent outcome studies intended by the agency or program.

Table 9.1

Client Demographic Variables

Social Security Number
Age
Race
Educational Level
Marital Status
Prior Criminal Convictions, non-sex-related
Prior Criminal Convictions, sex-related
Prior Incarcerations
Prior Commitments, mental hospital
Current Offense
Weapons or Use of Physical Abuse
Number of Years, sexual acting-out
History of Sexual or Physical Abuse (as victim)
Age Range of Victims (include options for more than one category)
Sex of Victim
Relationship of Victim to Offender
Chemical Abuse Patterns
Expressed Attitude Toward Sexual Problems
Expressed Motivation Toward Treatment
Sex Offender Typology (include options for more than one category)
Relevant Psychometric Findings

Effort Evaluations. Effort evaluations examine the process by which inputs are channeled into program output. The following questions can clarify process-oriented issues for a sex offender treatment program:

1. How is staff time allocated among administrative, security, public relations, documentation, training, assessment, and treatment tasks? How do these statistics reflect priorities and expectations?
2. How are decisions made regarding acceptance of an offender into treatment?
3. How are potential clients identified and offered treatment within an institution? How effective are these efforts?
4. How are decisions made regarding advancing, graduating, and terminating offenders?
5. How many groups, modules, behavior therapy sessions, activity groups, family or marital therapy sessions are being conducted on a monthly basis?
6. How is treatment planning conducted?
   a. How is input from staff solicited regarding an offender's treatment status?
   b. How is information communicated to other staff members regarding treatment plans?
   c. How is peer group incorporated into the feedback process?
7. What measures are taken within an institution to insure privacy for sex offenders participating in treatment?
8. How are security issues considered in the program? If applicable, how does this apply to community access? How do risk assessments measure the changing levels of risk as a client responds to treatment in either direction?

Questionnaires can be tailored to specific programs in order to assess the manner, quality, and efficiency of a program's efforts or activities. In addition to questionnaires, quality assurance checklists can be designed that reflect key operational areas and gauge whether certain minimal standards are being met. Alternately, the Correctional Institutions Environmental Scale (Moos, 1974) could be used to determine the subjective perception of the environment from the viewpoint of the client/inmate. Any of these indices can be useful in providing program management with feedback regarding the process through which program input is transformed into program output.

Output Evaluations. Output evaluations provide managers with data regarding the immediate accomplishments of the program. Examples of output data to which program managers need to have regular access include the following:

1. Number of clients residing in the treatment unit (average daily population).
2. Number of clients being assessed or treated per month.
3. Number of clients being terminated, identified by type of termination:
   a. Successful completion of the program.
   b. Maximum benefit (a term used to designate clients who have been cooperative and motivated but about whom treatment staff continue to have serious reservations regarding prognosis). Persons being terminated from treatment as "maximum benefit" should have these concerns identified with risks and any recommendations for disposition clarified.

      c. Administrative termination (e.g., transferred because of overcrowding, because a more appropriate unit has been identified, or because an individual has "flat-timed" out of the program).

      d. Unsuccessful termination (i.e., failure to cooperate with treatment, major rule infraction, escape, etc.).

4. Number of clients entering aftercare programs (if applicable):

      a. Specify type and intensity of correctional supervision and treatment follow-up;

      b. Employment status;

      c. Living arrangements;

      d. Estimated degree of community support system;

      e. Status with family.

5. Number of criminal justice system, legislative, or community members who may have been trained, toured, consulted, etc., during the relevant time period. This output can become particularly significant as a program becomes better known and recognized as a regional resource. The opportunity to influence public policy and opinion cannot be ignored by program managers of sex offender units. It is important to monitor continually how much time is being channeled into this endeavor. The value of output data, in part, comes from comparing output to specified program priorities and mandated tasks.

Evaluation of the Results

This level of program evaluation focuses on the longer term program goals for which the program has been established. For most correctional treatment programs, especially for sex offender treatment programs, recidivism rates are the central issue. For this reason, methodological issues pertaining to recidivism data will be incorporated into this discussion.

California Senate Bill 278 (1981) recognized that there was a great need for controlled experimental research studies to establish the efficacy of sex offender treatment. Therefore, it is also required that a formal controlled program for 50 sex offenders be conducted by the Department of Mental Health in order that "the most effective, newest and promising methods of treatment of sex offenders be rigorously tested" (Marques, Murrey, and O'Connor, 1985). Consequently, a controlled design study was established at Atascadero State Hospital involving a volunteer treatment group, an untreated volunteer group, and an untreated control group. The program primarily utilized a Relapse Prevention model and assisted covert sensitization as the treatment intervention. A 10-year follow-up on offenders who spent two years in residential treatment is continuing (see Chapter 19, Aftercare Treatment Programs).

Direct, meaningful comparisons between groups of treated and untreated sex offenders are, however, very misleading. Outcome studies reported by sex offender programs have not employed classical experimental designs. The nonequivalence of samples makes it impossible to determine whether the various groups differ significantly in terms of other unspecified independent variables. For example, volunteers for treatment programs may differ significantly from those who do not volunteer. Conversely, staff might admit into treatment those who are most promising or amenable to treatment.

The classical controlled study is hindered in applied clinical settings by a variety of obstacles. Glaser (1978) noted that controlled experimental designs are complicated by several factors, including the following:

1. Legal and ethical problems with postponing treatment for motivated sex offenders who are randomly assigned to a control group;
2. Drop-out tendencies from volunteers who may be randomly assigned to a high-intensity, demanding treatment intervention;
3. A "Hawthorne effect" which threatens external validity by influencing those being evaluated to respond in a different manner from those in a nonevaluated treatment program which offers the same interventions;
4. Administrative pressures to keep bed spaces full, or to transfer unhappy, complaining clients, irrespective of research design considerations;
5. Insufficient numbers to provide a large enough sample for control and experimental groups;
6. Consent decrees which would forbid denial or postponement of treatment to a control group or limit some research design.

No Standard Definition for "Recidivism"

At this point, we should address another methodological issue encountered in reporting outcome recidivism data. Because the definition of "recidivism" varies greatly, the term must be redefined each time it is reported. For example, the public might subjectively define "recidivism." One escape or re-offense can result in generalizations about the worth of the entire program. A recidivism rate of one can be entirely unacceptable to the public. This underscores the importance of collecting accurate follow-up outcome data to minimize the destructive impact of such subjective interpretations.

Many sex offender treatment outcome reports alternately define recidivism as rearrests, reconvictions, reincarcerations, or as any criminal justice system contact. Some definitions further refine these categories by specifying "all crimes" or "sex-related crimes only." Reports must also acknowledge that treated offenders may be continuing to commit sex crimes which are undetected.

While attempting to compare outcome studies, Weinrott (1982) encountered comparability problems resulting both from different states' definitions of crimes and from vague or unstated definitions of recidivism within the report data. New York's Department of Corrections found that changes in state statutes, over time, can also confound results. Statisticians noted the rate of convicted rapists skyrocketed when compared to data available five years earlier. On closer inspection, it was discovered that a less stringent standard for prosecution of rapists accounted for most of the increase in convictions (D. MacDonald, personal communication, September 1986). Learning from the limitations and weaknesses of the current status of available outcome data, those involved in sex offender program management can redress some of the concerns identified here.

General Recommendations for Collecting Recidivism Data

General recommendations for recidivism data collection by sex offender program managers include the following:

1. Program managers should commit to allocating staff time and funding for data collection.

2. When possible, program managers should match treated volunteers with an equal number of untreated sex offenders in state institutions. Demographics from the treated sample will provide some guidelines regarding sample size, age range, or type of crime. Random samples, or stratified random samples, would enhance comparability considerations. In some states, random samplings may even be taken from a group of volunteers on a waiting list, who are subsequently released without treatment because their period of incarceration lapses prior to being accepted into treatment.

3. Follow-up should cover at least a five-year time period. Longer or more frequent intervals of time are more desirable, but a five-year period is considered a minimum adequate standard for such follow-up.

4. At a minimum, FBI and state "rap sheets" should be used as a source for recidivism data collections. However, Weinrott (1982) notes that the use of such sources alone tends to underestimate re-offense rates and recommends use of independent evaluators who engage in field investigation, review police report data, and self-report forms from the sample group. Interested readers are referred to Weinrott's NIMH research proposal for further details. It is apparent that one can increase the confidence in re-offense data by going beyond the use of rap sheets. Specific states may have additional follow-up possibilities already accessible to researchers.

5. The definitions of actual crime behaviors and "re-offense" or "recidivism" should be clearly stated. No single definition is problem-free. Conservatively, re-offense could be defined as reconviction for sex-related crimes. More liberally, tabulation of rearrests could compensate for the underidentification problem, recognizing that an arrest is, of course, not a conviction.

6. Because it is based upon the time in which the offender had an opportunity to recidivate, the time-at-risk (or life-table) method of figuring recidivism rates will provide a more realistic picture (Soothill and Gibbens, 1978; Weinrott, 1982). There are two such methods of calculation. The cumulative method divides the sample's total number of re-offenses by the total number of at-risk months in the study. In contrast, the successive method identifies the number who were actually at risk during specific time periods and enables the tabulator to calculate an unbiased re-offense rate for each period (e.g., month or year).

A more extensive statistical analysis, developed by Maltz and McCleary (1977), is the failure rate analysis which examines the trend or pattern of re-offenses over the time period. It is possible that a major difference between treated and untreated sex offenders might be the length of time prior to re-offending. Follow-up data incorporating these recommendations would begin to provide a greater degree of standardization of sex offender outcome research.

Goal Attainment Scaling is a clinical outcome measure offering an individualized means of evaluating, as well as perhaps enhancing, the process of change in the sex offender. This process, originally developed by Kiresuk and Sherman (1968), has been applied in more than 800 mental health centers in the United States and Canada. One application of this process has been made to sex offender treatment programs (Lang, Lloyd, and Fiqua, 1985). In their study of 46 sex offenders in a forensic hospital treatment setting, Lang, et al. (1985) utilized this method of individualized outcome assessment to measure the achievement of specific treatment goals. From a total of 180 individual goal statements, 88% of the goals were either met or exceeded by 38 of the clients. The other eight individuals failed to achieve expected levels of success, defined as achieving two or more individual goals.

Rosenberg's Self-Esteem Scale (1965) can serve as a measure of change in self-concept. The Social Skills Checklist (Barlow, Abel, Blanchard, Bristow, and Young, 1977; Becker, Abel, Blanchard, Murphy, and Coleman, 1978) and the Interpersonal Behavior Checklist are measures which can reflect change in social skills, empathy, or assertiveness.

Conclusion

One of the more neglected aspects in the field of sex offender treatment is program evaluation. Tremendous innovations and creative developments have taken place within the past two decades. Methods of determining effectiveness of treatment methodologies have lagged behind. It is clear that technology must be developed prior to its being rigorously tested. Also, field constraints, limited resources, and multiple jurisdictions have exacerbated problems in the adequate evaluation of sex offender treatment.

This chapter reviewed general issues and components of program evaluation and suggested means by which program managers can assess their progress. The proposition has been advanced that sex offender program evaluation is not an option. Rather, the choice becomes when will the evaluation be conducted and what source will initiate it. The case has been advanced, furthermore, that program evaluation be coordinated with sex offender programs at the earliest juncture. Data gleaned from the evaluation efforts have the potential to enhance the efficacy of both the individual program and the field in general. The more emphasis that programs can provide for quality evaluation, the greater the potential for meaningful comparisons across programs and jurisdictions. Such a trend could contribute much to the longer term outcome to which every program subscribes, the reduction of future victims in our society.

References

Barlow, D., Abel, G. Blanchard, E., Bristow, A., and Young, L. (1977). A heterosexual skill checklist for males. *Behavior Therapy,* 8, 229-239.

Becker, J., Abel, G., Blanchard, E., Murphy, W., and Coleman, E. (1978). Evaluating social skills of sexual aggressives. *Criminal Justice and Behavior,* 5(4), 357-367.

Brecher, E.M. (1978). T*reatment programs for sex offenders*. Washington, DC: National Institute of Law Enforcement and Criminal Justice.

California Senate Bill No. 1716 (Robbins). (1978). Legislative Counsel's Digest.

California Senate Bill No. 278 (Rains). (1981). Legislative Counsel's Digest.

Cohen, B. (1979). Reliability and validity issues in evaluation research: The community corrections experience. In Proceedings of the 1979 Research and Evaluation Conference on Criminal Justice in Minnesota. St. Paul, MN: The Crime Control Commission.

Glaser, D. (1973). *Routinizing evaluation: Getting feedback on effectiveness of crime and delinquency programs*. Rockville, MD: National Institute of Mental Health.

Glaser, D. (1978). Evaluation of sex offender treatment programs. In E. Brecher (Ed.), *Treatment programs for sex offenders*. Washington, DC: National Institute of Law Enforcement and Criminal Justice.

Hudson, J. and Galaway, B. (1979). Evaluability assessments: Toward useful program evaluations. In Proceedings of the 1979 Research and Evaluation Conference on Criminal Justice in Minnesota. St. Paul, MN: The Crime Control Planning Board.

Kiresuk, T. and Sherman, R. (1968). Goal attainment scaling: A general method of evaluating comprehensive community mental health programs. *Community Mental Health Journal,* 4, 443-453.

Lang, R., Lloyd, C., and Fiqua, N. (1985). Goal attainment scaling with hospitalized sex offenders. *The Journal of Nervous and Mental Disease,* 173(9), 527-537.

Maltz, M. and McCleary, R. (1977). The mathematics of behavior change. *Evaluation Quarterly,* 1, 421-438.

McHugh, G. (1979). Sex knowledge inventory (Form X, revised). Saluda, NC: Family Life Publications, Inc.

Marques, J., Murrey, C., and O'Connor, D. (1985). The sex offender treatment and evaluation project: First report of the legislature in response to PC 1365. Sacramento, CA: Department of Mental Health.

Moos, R. (1974). *Correctional institutions environment scale manual*. Palo Alto, CA: Consulting Psychologists Press.

Perkins, D. (1987). A psychological treatment programme for sex offenders. In McBurk, B.J., Thornton, D.M., and Williams, M. (Eds.), *Applying psychology to imprisonment: Theory and practice*. London: Her Majesty's Stationery Office.

Rosenberg, M. (1965). *Society and the adolescent self-image*. Princeton, NJ: Princeton University Press.

Soothill, K. and Gibbens, T. (1978). Recidivism of sexual offenders: A reappraisal. *British Journal of Criminology,* 18, 267-276.

Washington State Legislative Budget Committee. (1986). Report on Washington State Sex Offender Treatment Programs.

Weinrott, M. (1982). Evaluating sex offender treatment programs. (NIMH Grant No. R01MH32669). Rockville, MD: National Institute of Mental Health.

Chapter 10

Comprehensive Treatment Planning for Sex Offenders

by Randy Green, Ph.D.

Overview

The delivery of treatment services to sex offenders is a complex and specialized field. Therefore, those involved in therapeutic interventions with sex offenders should have a general therapeutic background, specialized training, and an understanding of the unique dynamics of the sex offender. Inadequate treatment planning or a lack of understanding about sex offenders can result in the mistaken judgment by therapists that an offender has successfully completed treatment and is safe to live in the community. Reinforcement of offenders' denial or minimization problems is often the result of such misunderstanding. While issues of planning, documentation, and evaluation may be perceived as either luxuries or scourges by therapists, they are necessary to the establishment and continuation of quality treatment.

This chapter discusses the importance of good treatment planning in plotting the course of treatment and as a method of quality control documentation. The use of Goal Attainment Scaling as a quantitative tool for objectively measuring progress is presented.

Advantages of Comprehensive Treatment Planning

Contemporary treatment programs for sex offenders use a multimodal intervention model that relies on the premise that the causes of sexually deviant behavior are complex and multidetermined (Groth, 1983). A responsible treatment plan might best be defined as a remediation plan that, based on the sex offender's identified resources, problems, needs, and/or deficiencies, uses the most effective, appropriate, and available treatment methods to achieve the offender's treatment goals.

In addition to simplifying the flow of complex interactions and issues, such a plan offers several other advantages:

- Individuals who are involved with the sex offender are informed as to what treatment has been offered the client and can see documentation regarding response to that treatment. A comprehensive treatment plan identifies issues that are yet to be addressed or resolved. Such a plan provides a logical and standardized basic of providing feedback on the offender's treatment status to the offender himself, treatment personnel, and concerned agencies.

- Accountability and professional quality assurance standards can be enhanced by an established treatment planning and documentation process. Such a system invites the clinician to think continuously of needs and objective goals.

- An established treatment plan guides the clinical staff and the client toward a series of treatment objectives. Given the varied clinical issues and staff with diverse training, an effective clinical treatment plan reduces the likelihood of legal liability for clerical errors. Without a treatment plan that continually refocuses everyone on the central concerns, staff and client efforts may get sidetracked from core issues onto more peripheral ones. Resources are inevitably limited, so it is important that staff be able to distinguish between necessary issues and issues that are desirable but not critical. Goal setting and periodic review help to keep staff focused on realistic goals for clients.

- A good treatment plan provides an opportunity to trace the progress of the offender on each goal throughout the treatment record. Periodically, summaries of treatment interventions, coupled with the offender's responses to treatment, should be written in the file. This facilitates a ready reference for anyone desiring a general overview of the offender's treatment.

Comprehensive Treatment Planning Process

A treatment planning process for a sex offender treatment program includes four steps: assessment of treatment needs, synthesis of data, determination of clinical interventions, and review and evaluation of the treatment process. Each of these steps is described below.

Assessment of Treatment Needs. All types of sex offender treatment flows from a thorough assessment of a sex offender's resources, needs, and deficiencies. It is imperative that treatment providers either have performed or have access to a thorough assessment (see Chapter 11, Clinical Assessment).

Synthesis of Data. The synthesis of data obtained during the evaluation helps the staff develop a comprehensive plan for treatment intervention. The staff should develop preliminary conclusions regarding the dynamics of the offender, problems and needs that should be addressed in treatment, and the strengths and assets the offender brings into treatment. Risk management issues, motivation for treatment, intellectual or psychiatric impairment that might influence response to treatment (such as borderline or mild mental retardation, mood, personality or thought disorders) also should be considered in developing a comprehensive perspective on the offender.

From this synthesis, target goals should be established for treatment. The goals should be prioritized and sequenced. For example, the emotional involvement of the offender in treatment is sometimes enhanced by a victim-empathy focus early in the treatment process. In addition, information regarding sex offender dynamics and cognitive distortions frequently is handled early in the treatment process to provide the offender with a general awareness of concepts and vocabulary used in the program. Goals should be stated in clear, specific, observable terms that can be understood by the staff and the client. They should be realistic, time-limited, and developed in active coordination with the client.

Determination of Clinical Interventions. Once the specific goals are identified, methods must be selected which are likely to accomplish them. The range of approaches used in a comprehensive treatment program include, but are not limited to, the following components:

- *Psycho-Educational Modules:* A series of didactic-experiential educational modules focused on clinically related topics, such as sex offender dynamics, anger management, Relapse Prevention, etc. (see Chapter 13, Psycho-Educational Modules).
- *Interpersonal Techniques:* Either group, family, marital, or individual (see Chapter 14, Group Therapy).
- *Psychological and Behavioral Diaries:* Written logs and journals, autobiographies.
- *Assignments:* Any number of books and articles on the topics of incest, rape, anger management, assertiveness training, irrational beliefs, etc. can be given as assigned reading. These can be constructive treatment adjuncts for offenders who are able to read. Many of these materials can be put on audiotapes for offenders who cannot read.
- *Reconditioning:* Overt or covert methods of counterconditioning, behavioral rehearsal, and/or masturbatory reconditioning (see Chapter 15, Behavioral Techniques).
- *Cognitive-Behavioral Techniques:* Relapse Prevention methods, identification of deviant cycle, and evaluation of basic incorrect assumptions and perceptions (see Chapter 20, Relapse Prevention).
- *Pharmacological Treatments:* The employment of neuroleptic or antiandrogenous medication. Typically, these methods are deemed highly intrusive and

are prescribed only when other methods appear to be ineffective in remediating the relevant symptom behavior. Clinical use of this method is now being questioned by many professionals in the field (see Chapter 15, Behavioral Techniques and Chapter 18, Psychopharmacological Options for Sex Offenders).

• *Aftercare Needs:* Job search, preparation of a Relapse Prevention plan, and establishment of an ongoing support system to reduce the likelihood of re-offending (see Chapter 19, Aftercare Treatment Programs).

Review and Evaluation of Treatment Progress. Every two or three months, or as the need dictates, the offender's progress should be reviewed in light of the established goals and assigned treatment. In preparation for the review, it may be helpful to request a relevant assessment. In addition, the offender should be prepared to discuss his or her progress toward each goal. Treatment staff, the offender, and peers involved in the treatment group(s) can all be helpful and desirable participants in such a review.

If an offender is not responding to treatment, the treatment goals should be revised. If limited space is available in the program, those clients who are most cooperative and motivated must be given priority. The clinical treatment planning process is most effective when used regularly and when modified as the need arises. In the process, it keeps treatment relevant and targeted toward the needs of each offender.

Major Treatment Goals for Sex Offenders

The major goal of sex offender treatment is to reduce victimization, with the hope of reducing victimization for any given offender to zero. Usually, there are a number of steps between getting offenders into treatment and discharging them into the community with some confidence. Most treatment programs only take offenders who admit their guilt. However, some states mandate that all sex offenders go through treatment. One way to handle this requirement is to place all clients into psycho-educational classes where information on sexual assault, effects on victims, and the dynamics of sexual deviation are discussed. As clients see that these topics can be discussed in a rational, open manner and hear other clients begin to admit their guilt, others may begin to open up. However, even offenders who refuse to admit their guilt may be exposed to information which they can process on their own.

The goals of treatment progress from owning up to one's deviant behavior to exploring its origins to identifying its precursors and substituting alternative coping mechanisms. These goals can be specified on a treatment plan using the Goal Attainment Scaling format (Kiresuk and Sherman, 1968), which weighs the goals for importance and scores them according to objective criteria. Each plan must be individualized and may include extended work on substance abuse, family relations, or other special problems (see Table 10.1, Sample Goal Attainment Scaling). Five broad goals are outlined below.

Goal I: Admitting Guilt. The offender should be able to openly acknowledge guilt. This admission is a basic requirement for meaningful participation. Offenders who proclaim their innocence make other participants uncomfortable and suspicious.

Table10.1
Sample Goal Attainment Scaling

GOAL WEIGHTS

OUTCOME VARIABLES	I. Admitting Guilt	II. Accepting Responsibility	III. Understanding dynamics	IV. Identifying deviant cycle	V. Making restitution
Most unfavorable treatment outcome thought likely. (-2)	Insists on innocence.	Admits crime, but blames it on seduction behavior or claims victim was not deviant.	Minimizes dynamics, denies importance.	Denies that crime precursors.	Refuses to make restitution.
Less than expected success with treatment. (-1)	Admits some part of crime but attributes to victim or rationalizes nature of deed.	Admits guilt but attributes it to alcohol, drugs or claims it was one-time occurrence.	Superficially denies dynamics but shows little understanding.	Unable to identify.	Minimizes ability to make restitution.
Expected success. (0)	Admits guilt.	Accepts responsibility.	Understands dynamics.	Identifies cycle.	Makes some type of restitution.
More than expected success with treatment. (+1)	Admits guilt and exonerates victim.	Accepts responsibility, recognizes need for help and shows victim empathy.	Recognizes and understands dynamics.	Identifies cycle and begins to develop coping skills.	Makes restitution; empathizes.
Best anticipated treatment. (+2)	Admits guilt for offense & other offenses. Exonerates victim, recognizes deviant motivation.	Accepts responsibility, recognizes need for help, understands dynamics without placing blame, demonstrates empathy.	Idependently identifies dynamics and works to resolve them.	Identifies cycle and uses coping strategies.	Makes restitution in a variety of ways.

Their participation has a voyeuristic quality to it. They may be viewed as a threat to the confidentiality of the group as they may remain closed and aloof. However, sophisticated therapy groups may welcome the challenge of breaking down denial. This goal can be outlined for Goal Attainment Scaling as follows:

-2 Insists upon innocence. States that it is a case of mistaken identity or revenge on the part of the victim.

-1 Admits that some sort of act may have occurred but insists that either the motivation was not sexual (e.g., hygiene rituals, etc.) or that an adult victim was fully consenting.

 0 Admits guilt.

+1 Admits guilt and exonerates victim from any type of complicity.

+2 Admits guilt for current offense as well as other offenses, exonerates victims and recognizes deviant motivations.

Goal II: Accepting Responsibility. Not only must an offender admit his guilt but he must accept full responsibility for it. Offenders frequently acknowledge the deed but blame alcohol, drugs, provocative victim behavior, or other outside factors. The offender must be able to distinguish between understanding the dynamics of his behavior and blaming the behavior on some contributing factor, e.g., his own victimization. Levels of attaining these goals include:

-2 Admits that he performed deed but blames seduction or claims that it is not deviant behavior (e.g., a teacher who molests postpubescent students).

-1 Admits that he performed deed but attributes it to alcohol or drugs or claims that it was a one-time occurrence that will never happen again.

 0 Accepts responsibility.

+1 Accepts responsibility and recognizes need for help. Shows some victim empathy.

+2 Accepts responsibility, recognizes need for help, understands dynamics without placing blame. Demonstrates high degree of victim empathy.

Goal III: Understanding Dynamics. Once offenders acknowledge their guilt and assume responsibility for their behavior, they may feel extremely guilty. They may spend a good deal of time ruminating over their crimes and castigating themselves. This energy can be put to much better use investigating the dynamics behind the behavior. Often a major part of dealing with dynamics is dealing with an offender's own victimization. The levels of this goal include:

-2 Minimizes dynamics, claims that since crime was only a situational quirk and will never happen again, there are no underlying dynamics.

-1 Identifies a few superficial dynamics but shows little clear understanding of relationship between dynamics of acts or blames his crime on dynamics.

0 Understands dynamics.

+1 Independently recognizes how dynamics are involved in crime.

+2 Independently identifies dynamics and works actively to resolve these dynamics.

Goal IV: Identifying Deviant Cycle. It is often tempting for mental health clients to focus on dynamics, going over and over traumas of the past and assuming a victim stance. Clients must be encouraged to deal with and lay aside past traumas, victimizations, and injustices, and identify the chain of immediate precursors to their acting-out. Deviant sexual arousal may be a crucial part of the cycle and will need to be addressed with behavioral techniques (see Chapter 15, Behavioral Techniques to Alter Sexual Arousal). Other deficits related to precursors must be remedied. The levels of this goal include:

-2 Denies that crime was anything but a purely impulsive deed with no recognizable precursors.

-1 Unable to identify cycle through cognitive deficits or claims that alcohol has fogged his memory of the event.

0 Identifies deviant cycle.

+1 Immediately identifies deviant cycle and is in process of identifying techniques for averting it.

+2 Readily identifies deviant cycle and can readily substitute alternative coping strategies.

Goal V: Making Restitution. The final goal of any victimizing behavior should be to make amends to the victim, either concretely or symbolically. It is not always possible to make actual restitution to the victim. However, clients should be encouraged to do so whenever the victim is available and amenable. Restitution can be in the form of money or a letter of apology that is delivered by the victim's therapist or another third party. If the victim is a family member and the family plans to reunite, much work needs to be devoted to mending the relationship while maintaining the safety of the victim. If the victim is unavailable, offenders may make restitution by supporting victims' assistance groups financially or through in-kind support (e.g., building dollhouses to be used in play therapy), by participating in media presentations on sexual assault, or by helping other offenders. The levels of this goal include:

-2 Refuses to make restitution, even through helping peers in group therapy.

-1 Minimizes ability to make restitution by offering various excuses.

 0 Makes some type of restitution.

+1 Makes restitution based on understanding of victim's pain.

+2 Makes restitution based on empathy for victim in a variety of different ways.

Other Goals. Many other goals may be included over the course of treatment. The individual may need substance abuse treatment, social skills training, vocational training, or family therapy. The Goal Attainment Scaling (GAS) technique has the advantage of being readily translated into numerical scores which can then be compared (see Table 10.1). A score based on a ceiling of 100 can be calculated using the following formula:

$$GAS = 50 + \frac{10\Sigma_{i\,=\,1}^{n} w_i x_i}{\sqrt{(1-p)\Sigma_{i\,=\,1}^{n} + p(\Sigma_{i\,-\,1}^{n} w_i)^2}}$$

x_i = raw score or outcome level on the ith scale

w_i = relative weight attached to ith scale

p = weighted average intercorrelation of scales (usually set at .30)

n = number of scales

This system can provide evidence of progress or lack of it to the patient and a method of quality assurance to the program. It is invaluable in research and in improving sex offender treatment.

Conclusion

Comprehensive treatment planning for sex offenders is a complex process requiring trained staff who understand the key components of such treatment and who have an organized process to systematically deliver the core treatment methodologies. While these components are often viewed as fixed integral parts of a sex offender treatment program, they essentially represent state-of-the-art concepts of a skill developing speciality field. The field could look very different in the near future and will only be improved by continuous self-examination and program evaluation. Extensive program evaluation must yet take place to determine which methodologies work best with which individuals. Chapter 9 on program evaluation reviews this issue in greater detail.

References

Burt, M.R. (1980). Cultural myths and supports for rape. *Journal of Personality and Social Psychology,* 2, 217-230.

Field, H.S. (1978). Attitudes toward rape: A comparative analysis of police, rapists, crisis counselors, and citizens. *Journal of Personality and Social Psychology,* 36, 156-179.

Greer, J. and Stuart, I. (Eds.), *The sexual aggressor: Current perspectives on treatment.* New York: Van Nostrand Reinhold Co.

Groth, N. (1983). Treatment of the sexual offender in a correctional institution. In J. Greer and I. Stuart (Eds.), *The sexual aggressor: Current perspectives on treatment.* New York: Van Nostrand Reinhold Co.

Kiresuk, T. and Sherman, R. (1968). Goal attainment scaling: A general method of evaluating comprehensive community mental health programs. *Community Mental Health Journal,* 4, 443-453.

Knopp, F. (1984). *Retraining adult sex offenders: Models and methods.* Syracuse, NY: Safer Society Press.

Krulewitz, J. and Payne, E.J. (1978). Attributions about rape: Effects of rapist force, observer sex, and sex role attitudes. *Journal of Applied Social Psychology,* 8, 291-305.

Lang, R., Lloyd, C., and Fiqua, N. (1985). Goal attainment scaling with hospitalized sex offenders. *The Journal of Nervous and Mental Disease,* 173(9), 527-537.

McHugh, G. (1979). Sex knowledge inventory (Form X, revised). Saluda, NC: Family Life Publications, Inc.

Mosher, D.L. (1966). The development and multitrait-multimethod matrix analysis of three measures of three aspects of guilt. *Journal of Consulting Psychology,* 30, 25-29.

Paitich, D., Langevin, R., Freeman, R., Mann, K., and Handy, L. (1977). The Clarke sex history questionnaire: A clinical sex history questionnaire for males. *Archives of Sexual Behavior,* 6, 421-436.

Thorne, F.C. (1966). The sex inventory. *Journal of Clinical Psychology,* 22, 367-374.

Yochelson, S. and Samenow, S. (1976). *The criminal personality.* New York: Aronson.

Chapter 11

Clinical Assessment of Sex Offenders

by Michael J. Dougher, Ph.D.

Overview

This chapter outlines the process of assessing sex offenders, including the use of offenders' social history, a variety of different psychological tests, and the use of the penile plethysmograph in conducting a physiological assessment.

Comprehensive, In-Depth Assessment Is Prelude to Effective Treatment Planning and Implementation

The following three assumptions are the basis for much of what is discussed in this chapter. The first is that sex offenders comprise an extremely heterogeneous population that cannot be characterized by single motivational or etiological factors. Recent attempts to develop classification schemes and explanatory theories of sex offenders have cogently argued that sexually offensive behavior is varied, complex, and multiply determined (Finklehor, 1984; Prentky, Cohen, and Seghorn, 1985; Carter and Baird, 1986). Accordingly, any attempt to explain or treat sexually offensive behavior must consider the specific factors pertinent to an individual's offense and the psychological characteristics of the individual offender.

Second, with current techniques, some, but not all, sex offenders can be effectively treated. Reviews by Kelly (1982) and Lanyon (1986) show that treatment enjoys an encouraging success rate with many types of child molesters. Previous work by Abel, Blanchard, and Becker (1978) reports success with some types of rapists. However, other research suggests that excessively violent or sadistic offenders, sociopathic offenders, and offenders not motivated for treatment are almost impossible to treat (Hobson, Boland, and Jamieson, 1985). Thus, the task then for those faced with treating sex offenders is determining who is and who is not amenable to treatment.

The third assumption is that adequate treatment involves a comprehensive and individually tailored treatment program that takes into consideration the acts committed by the offender as well as his or her motivations and psychological characteristics. Thus, treatment should be tailored to the needs of individual clients. A variety of other issues or areas of concern also need to be addressed in treatment. Deviant sexual arousal, social skills deficits, irrational beliefs and attitudes, anger and stress management, and self-esteem problems are all areas that may demand therapeutic intervention (Barlow, 1974; Abel, Blanchard, and Becker, 1978; Dreiblatt, 1982).

If valid, these assumptions emphasize the importance of a comprehensive, in-depth assessment of the offender prior to effective treatment planning and implementation. Decisions about treatment amenability, target areas for intervention, and selection of treatment procedures require an adequate information base that can only be acquired through assessment procedures. Given that many, if not most, sex offenders tend to lie about their offenses and are unreliable and deceptive in their verbal reports, the value of a thorough assessment cannot be overemphasized.

Assessment Issues

With already limited resources, many correctional mental health workers might be tempted to cut corners in the assessment process or feel that comprehensive assessment is beyond available means. However, there are ways to gain a great deal of information at relatively low cost. The point is to get as much information as possible from as many sources as possible.

Generally, assessments in the area of sexual diversity are concerned with five issues:

1. Assessment of sexual diversity in society (Kinsey, Pomeroy, and Martin, 1948; Kinsey, Pomeroy, Martin, and Gebhard, 1953; Hite, 1981);

2. Identification or diagnosis of sex offenders, usually subsequent to arrest for an alleged offense (Laws, 1984);

3. Identification of sex offender characteristics or a sex offender profile (Marsh, Hilliard, and Liechiti, 1955; Toobert, Bartelme, and Jones, 1959);

4. Determination of treatment amenability and identification of target areas for therapeutic intervention (Laws and Osborn, 1983);

5. Evaluation of treatment outcome (Travy, Donnelly, Morgenbesser, and MacDonald, 1983).

Information regarding the specific offense(s) committed by a sex offender is extremely important to the determination of treatment amenability and the formulation of a treatment program. Factors to be evaluated and their clinical significance determined, as well as suggested interventions, follow.

Nature of Specific Offense. Did the crime involve fondling, masturbation, exhibitionism, rape, beating, sadism, or murder? Generally, any crimes involving extreme violence and sadism should serve as a warning sign and the offender should be more thoroughly assessed.

Victim Characteristics. What are the demographic factors such as age, sex, and physical characteristics of the victim(s)? Pedophiles who exclusively assault boys tend to be more resistant to treatment, as are offenders who choose very young victims. Victim characteristics should be used when constructing offense cycle analyses or when using behavior therapy techniques to alter sexual arousal patterns (see Chapter 15, Behavioral Techniques and Chapter 20, Relapse Prevention).

Antecedents of the Offender's Crimes. Were alcohol or drugs involved? Was the crime committed under conditions of stress or in a particular psychological state such as depression? Was the crime premeditated or spontaneous/impulsive? The antecedents of an offense are useful in helping the client identify the offense cycle, to target related behavioral or psychological problems, and to gain some information about the type of offender. For example, if stress is a reliable antecedent such as with regressed or situational pedophiles, then stress management procedures may be indicated. Likewise, if drugs or alcohol are typically used before a crime, then drug or alcohol treatment may be warranted. Premeditated offenses tend to be associated more with fixated-preference pedophiles than regressed-situational pedophiles. Offenses with impulsive features may suggest that the offender needs training in impulse control.

Previous Offenses. In general, the best predictor of future offenses is the number of previous offenses (Dreiblatt, 1982; Tracy, et al., 1983). Thus, the number of previous offenses, especially those resulting in arrest, is a good predictor of treatment outcome. If there are previous offenses, it is useful to determine whether the modus operandi and antecedent conditions are similar. Compulsive and ritualistic offenders may require different intervention strategies than first-time offenders or those with no particular offense pattern.

Level of Psychopathology. The presence of psychopathology, apart from the offender's actual crime, has important relevance for treatment. If a psychosis is present, medication may be required and treatment techniques will be limited. Some behavioral methods cannot be utilized if the client's physiological functioning is affected by medication. Career criminals and others with entrenched antisocial personalities rarely respond positively to treatment.

Developmental History. It is important to assess such factors as the nature of the offender's relationship to his parents and siblings. In particular, information should be gathered about any abuse, neglect, or trauma suffered, parental death or abandonment, methods of discipline, use of ridicule, family sexual behavior, and the adequacy of parental role models. These areas have obvious implications in the development of the offender's characteristics. Insight-oriented therapy, flooding or desensitization techniques may be warranted to deal with the emotional remnants of the offender's abuse.

Educational History. This characteristic varies tremendously among offenders. Specifically targeted areas should include school performance and level of education, classroom behavior, intelligence level, and the presence of any learning disabilities. School performance gives some information about the offender's ability to persist at long-term goals and his self-discipline and self-esteem. These characteristics correlate with positive treatment outcome. Continued education may become a treatment goal. A lack of intellectual ability might preclude certain verbal therapies or imagery-based behavior therapy.

Social History. There is likely to be considerable variation among offenders concerning their social histories. Of particular importance are the nature of the offender's relations with peers, the nature and duration of the offender's friendships, the relative age of the offender's friends, the nature and extent of social isolation, stability in relationships, and whether the offender was active or passive in social relations.

Interpersonal relations are of central concern when dealing with the sex offender. If the offender is lacking in social skills, then social skills training may be in order. If debilitating social anxiety is present, especially in social settings with women, desensitization may be warranted. Passivity or, alternatively, dominance may characterize the offender's social relations and may thus serve as targets of intervention through group therapy. Extreme social isolation may also indicate a more severe psychopathology or personality disorder.

Sexual History, Experience, and Knowledge. Despite the nature of their crimes, it is not unusual for sex offenders to have limited sexual experience and knowledge.

Also common is an excessively rigid and puritanical attitude about sexuality. Assessment should focus on the nature, quality, and quantity of previous sexual experiences. Age and type of first sexual encounter should be determined as well as the nature of masturbatory fantasies and the use of pornography. Additionally, assessment should be made of any sexual trauma or victimization. Any history of sexual dysfunction should be ascertained. Information on the history, severity, and frequency of sexually deviant and offensive acts should be gathered. Sex education or sex therapy may be appropriate therapeutic interventions. Information about sexual fantasies and deviations should be included in the development of specific behavioral interventions aimed at sexual arousal patterns.

Religious Beliefs. Religious beliefs should be thoroughly evaluated with this population. Offenders frequently come from religious backgrounds which instill repressive sexual attitudes, fear of adult sexuality, and a lack of accurate sexual knowledge. Other individuals escape from the guilt and responsibility of their crimes by suddenly becoming extremely religious. They often state that they no longer need treatment because they have been forgiven for their sins. Individuals of certain denominations may express religious objections to certain types of assessment or treatment procedures including the viewing of sexually explicit materials or techniques using masturbation.

Occupational History. It is useful to obtain a record of the offender's work history, including types of jobs, job performance, level of responsibility, and employment stability. As with educational history, an occupational history can reflect a person's ability to persist at a task or pursue long-term goals. Job stability may also indicate good frustration tolerance, as well as the ability to cooperate with others, especially authority figures. Occupational training may be warranted as part of treatment.

Level of Anger. Many sex offenders harbor substantial anger, which often is directed toward women. While this is most prevalent in rapists and exhibitionists, it is also present in many pedophiles. Since anger may serve as a primary source of motivation for many sex crimes, it is an important target area for assessment and treatment. Insight-oriented therapy or anger management training may be used (Novaco, 1975).

Level of Responsibility and Ability to Empathize. All too often, sex offenders are unwilling to take responsibility for their offenses or fail to understand the traumatic impact on their victims. Pedophiles tend to blame children for being too seductive or interested in sex while claiming that their own sexual activities with children are educational and in the best interest of the child. Rapists may blame their attacks on the sexually provocative style of their victims or on the worn-out and offensive assertion that women secretly wished to be raped. Moreover, it is not unusual to find that rapists are surprised by the traumatic effects of their crimes.

An offender's failure to take responsibility for his or her actions or to empathize with their victim's plight is a primary target for assessment and treatment. Group therapy and cognitive-behavioral techniques are useful methods of confronting the irrational beliefs held by sex offenders regarding their own psychopathology. Empathy training or victim confrontation techniques can be useful in enhancing offenders' awareness of the often devastating effects of his crime.

Awareness of Emotions. A common problem with sex offenders, especially regressed-situational pedophiles, is the lack of awareness of and inability to cope with their emotions. Feelings of anger, tension, sexual arousal, inferiority, and so on, are often denied by offenders until it is too late. Consequently, effective means of coping with these emotions are not employed. Verbal insight therapy, group therapy, and stress inoculation (Meichenbaum and Novaco, 1978) or stress management procedures can all be useful in helping offenders identify the source and presence of emotional reactions and effectively respond to them.

Cognitive Distortions About Men, Women, and Children. Sex offenders often have irrational beliefs about who is responsible for their sexual offenses and the impact the crimes have on their victims. These irrational beliefs are frequently concerned with what it means to be a man, the psychology of women, and the inherent vulnerability of children. A desire to project a "macho" image or, conversely, low self-confidence regarding one's masculinity is common among offenders. Ridiculous beliefs, such as all women are rejecting, domineering, and calculating are also typical. Finally, the idea that children benefit from and enjoy sexual encounters with adults is a very common belief, particularly among fixated-preference pedophiles. Sex education, group therapy, and cognitive-behavioral techniques may be useful procedures in dealing with these problematic beliefs.

Sexual Arousal. It is widely accepted that deviant arousal plays an important role in the commission of sex crimes. Barlow (1974), Abel and his colleagues (1976, 1978) and Laws (1984) have all argued cogently that sexual arousal must be a primary target of intervention in the comprehensive treatment of sex offenders. Moreover, as early as 1965, McGuire, Carlisle, and Young argued that deviant sexual fantasies, coupled with masturbation, play an important etiological role in sexually deviant behavior. Finally, Quinsey (1981) argues that the best available predictor of long-term therapy success is the reduction of deviant sexual arousal coupled with an adequately high level of appropriate sexual arousal. Deviant sexual arousal is a primary target area for assessment and treatment. Behavior therapy techniques are particularly useful in modifying deviant arousal patterns (Quinsey and Marshall, 1983). (See also Chapter 14, Behavioral Techniques.)

Assessment Procedures

A variety of techniques are used to assess and evaluate sex offenders. These techniques include clinical interviews, self-reporting, psychological tests, questionnaires, rating scales, and physiological measures. It should be mentioned, however, that whenever possible a medical and/or neuropsychological exam also should be conducted since some medical and neurological disorders manifest as sexually deviant behaviors (Berlin, 1983).

Clinical Interviews. Clinical interviews are by far the most commonly used assessment procedure. It may also be the most important. However, it is important to remember that sex offenders are notoriously unreliable and deceptive in their verbal reports, and all information so obtained must be viewed with skepticism. In this regard it is useful to obtain as much collateral information as possible when conducting an interview. Such information includes police reports, arrest records, any previous psychological and medical reports, previous statements made by the offender, and any information that can be obtained from others who know the offender. The information obtained can then be used to corroborate the offender's statements in an attempt to assess their veracity and reliability or to confront the offender when discrepant information is uncovered.

The goal of the clinical interview is to obtain as much information as possible with as much detail as possible. As this can be a time consuming process, alternatives and supplements to the interview process can be helpful. Having the offender create a detailed autobiography or completing specific questionnaires are some ways of accomplishing this. Nevertheless, these should never substitute completely for the interview because so much additional and useful information can be obtained through the personal interaction with an interviewer. For example, behavioral observations, follow-up detail questions, and exploration of discrepancies between what the offender has reported and what is included in official records can best be obtained in this setting.

Clinical interviews should be comprehensive. The interview should begin with the offender's earliest recollection of his or her childhood and family situation and progress through the offender's educational, social, sexual, and occupational history. (See appended evaluation, Appendix C.) The interview should also include detailed probing into the nature of the offender's sex crimes with an emphasis on their antecedents. An excellent model for the clinical interview is the autobiographical outline used in the Transitional Sex Offender Program at Lino Lakes, Minnesota. (A copy of the outline may be found in Appendix B.)

Psychological Tests. The use of psychological tests with sex offenders has a long history, although their use has primarily been to identify personality characteristics of offenders or to create a psychological profile of the sex offender. Unfortunately, these attempts have not been very successful. One reason for the lack of success in accomplishing their intended goals is that the tests were not constructed for use with sex offenders. Another reason is that they require a high degree of inference which reduces their reliability. Nevertheless, psychological tests can be useful in combination with other assessment procedures to create a clinical picture of an offender and to identify target areas for clinical interventions.

The tests that are most frequently used with offenders will be discussed below. However, mental health workers who deal with sex offenders are encouraged to use whatever assessment procedures are considered helpful, as long as those procedures are used appropriately. No test should be the sole source for identifying, diagnosing, or classifying sex offenders; rather, it should be used as part of a more comprehensive assessment procedure and as an aid in identifying target areas for clinical intervention.

Projective Tests. Early work with sex offenders focused heavily on the use of the Rorschach to identify the underlying dynamics of the population and to determine whether there were signs or responses that differentiated sex offenders from other populations (Pascal and Herzberg, 1952; Hammer, 1954; Hammer and Jacks, 1955). The reliability and validity of these procedures never held up, however (Laws, 1984). Generally, projective techniques should only be used as part of a more comprehensive assessment procedure to aid in obtaining general clinical information.

Objective Tests. The Minnesota Multiphasic Personality Inventory (MMPI) is the psychological test most frequently used with sex offenders. Early efforts with this test attempted to identify a profile characteristic of sex offenders (McCreary, 1975) and to develop scales comprised of selected items which seemed to discriminate sex offenders from other populations (Marsh, et al., 1955; Toobert, et al., 1959). Although these profiles and scales often are generated through sophisticated statistical procedures, they have not been shown to differentiate sex offenders from other populations reliably (Rada, 1978). Consequently, as is the case with projective tests, the MMPI should not be used as a means for identifying, diagnosing, or classifying sex offenders. This does not mean that the MMPI cannot be valuable as an assessment tool, provided it is used to identify personality characteristics and relevant clinical issues for individual offenders.

Obvious uses of the MMPI with sex offenders include identifying those who have psychotic processes or personality disorders. However, the usefulness of the MMPI is not restricted to offenders with severe pathology. Even when all scale scores are within normal limits, interpretation can be useful. Graham (1977) and Greene (1980) provide useful interpretations of profiles and high-point pairs even when all scores are within the normal range. For example, if an offender produces a profile with high-point pairs on Scales Four (psychopathic deviance) and Three (hysteria), or on Scales Four and Ten (social isolation), this information has clinical implications. With the former pairing, one might be more concerned with the offender's level of repressed hostility or unrecognized stress; with the latter, issues around social withdrawal and social anxiety might be more prevalent.

The validity scales can also be of value. The extent to which an offender is dishonest, defensive, or malingering has obvious implications for treatment amenability and prognosis.

Some objective tests have been specifically constructed to gather information about sexual knowledge, experiences, attitudes, interests, and behaviors. One example is the Sex Knowledge and Attitude Test (Lief and Chapter 20, Reed, 1972). While not particularly useful in identifying or classifying offenders, this test can help determine an offender's knowledge and attitudes about sexuality.

The Sex Inventory (Thorne, 1966) and the Clarke Sexual History Questionnaire (SHQ) (Paitich, Langevin, Freeman, Mann, and Handy, 1977; Langevin, 1983) are inventories that tap specific sexual interests and activities. The Thorne Inventory also measures sexual conflicts, fixations, repressions, control, confidence, and promiscuity, while the Clarke SHQ measures the frequency of various sexual behaviors as well as disgust for any sexual behaviors. The clinical utility of the tests is obvious when trying to assess offenders' sexual histories, proclivities and attitudes or designing a specific treatment plan. Moreover, both tests have been shown to be able to differentiate offenders from nonoffenders, although only the Clarke SHQ has been able to differentiate among offenders.

A particularly promising test for measuring sexual interests and behaviors is the Multiphasic Sex Inventory (MSI) developed by Nichols and Molinder (1984). The MSI is a 300-item, true-false test with 14 clinical and validity scales. Three of the clinical scales measure sexually offensive behavior (rape, child molestation, exhibitionism), five measure sexual deviations, four measure sexual dysfunction, one measures sexual knowledge and attitudes, and one scale is a measure of the offender's treatment attitudes. One positive aspect of the MSI is that it has been normed on populations of sex offenders. In addition, the test enjoys good psychometric properties and comes with an elaborate interpretive guide. Although more research with the MSI is needed, especially regarding cross-validation, it holds particular promise for clinicians working with incarcerated sex offenders.

In addition to the use of psychological tests, sexual interests and behaviors can be assessed in a less formal way. For example, Laws (1984) describes a card-sort procedure in which offenders are requested to sort a set of cards, each of which describes some sexual activity, into piles corresponding to the level of sexual arousal. The activities described include homosexuality, heterosexuality, rape, masochism, sadism, male pedophilia, female pedophilia, voyeurism, and exhibitionism. In addition, several treatment facilities have developed extensive questionnaires which ask for specific details of various sexual experiences.

Assessment of Social Skills

Most clinical descriptions of sex offenders refer to a deficiency in the area of social skills (Cohen, Seghorn, and Calmas, 1969). Specific aspects of social skills, such as assertiveness, can be tapped by relevant inventories such as the Rathus Assertiveness Scale (1973). However, more global social skills assessment generally involves role playing (Bellack, 1983), where clients are typically instructed to act out some contrived scenario in the presence of others. These scenarios are then either videotaped or observed by raters who judge the level of specific skills. Often clients view the videotapes themselves and generate corrective solutions to their observed deficiencies. There is a considerable body of literature concerned with social skills assessment and training which may prove useful to clinicians working with sex offenders (Turner and Hersen, 1981).

Psychophysiological Procedures

The discussion thus far has been restricted to psychological assessment techniques. While these techniques are certainly useful and should be used, they are not sufficient in themselves. It has become increasingly clear that deviant sexual arousal is an essential aspect of a comprehensive assessment procedure and may even be the single most important measure (Wincze, 1982; Earls and Marshall, 1983; Laws and Osborn, 1983; Laws, 1984). Direct measures of penile erection appear to be the only reliable and valid measure (Zuckerman, 1971). Measures of penile circumference are most commonly used (Geer, 1980; Earls and Marshall, 1983; Laws and Osborn, 1983).

The most common approach to the measurement of sexual arousal involves having offenders attach a gauge around their penises. Deviant and nondeviant sexual stimuli are then presented to the offender, and changes in the circumference of the penis are recorded on a strip chart recorder. The strip chart produces a record of changes in the offender's erection to each of the stimuli presented. In this way, differential sexual arousal can easily be observed.

There are a few private companies that manufacture and sell complete systems for assessing sexual arousal (sometimes called a penile plethysmograph). With some knowledge of electronics, however, virtually any strip chart recorder can be adapted to measure and record penile responses.

Sexual stimuli can be presented to offenders through three modalities: slides, audiotapes, and videotapes. Some researchers argue that slides usually are more arousing than audiotapes (Laws and Osborn, 1983), but there tends to be considerable variation among researchers as to which modality elicits the strongest responses. It is a good idea to try different methods with an offender in order to determine which one is maximally arousing for that particular person. Regardless of the method, offenders should be presented with a variety of deviant and nondeviant stimuli in order to be sure of the presence and extent of their arousal pattern. Often, offenders are unwilling or even unable to reveal their arousal to deviant stimuli or activities. For this reason, it is useful to expose the offender to as wide a range of stimuli as is practical.

Deviant and appropriate slides can be obtained from commercial sources or from various treatment programs around the country. Explicit child pornography can be difficult to obtain, but local law enforcement agencies — or even the offenders in treatment — may be good sources for this type of material. It is advisable to inform local legal authorities that one has such materials and why. Most state statutes against the possession of obscene materials permit the possession of such materials for research and treatment.

Audiotapes are the easiest source of stimuli to produce. Both appropriate and deviant sexual activities can simply be described and recorded. Offenders' deviant and appropriate experiences and fantasies can serve as an excellent source for these tapes. These tapes can be continuously refined to produce maximum levels of arousal and to minimize boredom with repeated presentations.

Except for child pornography, videotapes of virtually any kind of sexual activity can be easily obtained. Rape, sadism, bestiality, bondage and discipline, and a variety of other deviant as well as mutually consenting and nondeviant sexual activity are readily available. Abel (Abel and Blanchard, 1976) produced a series of videotapes depicting mutually consenting sex, rape, and assault that may be particularly useful for assessment purposes. These tapes attempt to minimize extraneous sexual stimuli by eliminating sound and scenes of exposed genitalia that might in themselves elicit sexual arousal.

Regardless of the modality, deviant stimuli are typically presented for two and three minutes. Several stimuli can be presented within a given assessment session although care must be taken not to satiate offenders with sexual stimuli that may diminish their responsiveness. Unfortunately, there is little research on the physiological assessment of sexual arousal. Therefore, it is not possible to give specific guidelines for the number of stimulus presentations per session or even the length of an assessment session. One study (Julien and Over, 1984) suggests that habituation was not a problem when normal males were presented with eight 12-minute depictions of sexual activity, even over a five-day period. Nevertheless, caution is urged when presenting large numbers of stimuli. It is best to schedule repeated assessment sessions over several days.

Usually, sexual arousal is reported in terms of the percentage of maximal erection. Clients are generally instructed to masturbate to 100% erection and measurement of maximum penile circumference is then taken. Subsequent arousal levels are then calculated as a percentage of the maximum erection. Laws and Osborn (1983) offer a guide to interpreting arousal levels. They have subdivided arousal levels as follows: 0-20%, no arousal; 20-40%, low arousal; 40-60%, moderate arousal; 60-80%, high arousal; and 80-100%, very high arousal. They argue that at least a moderate level of arousal is necessary for clear judgment and evaluation of treatment possibilities.

It is important to note that the presence of deviant arousal alone is not an indication of sexual preferences or deviant tendencies. Deviant arousal must be considered in relation to the magnitude of nondeviant arousal. If appropriate arousal is low, then moderate levels of deviant arousal may warrant treatment. Conversely, if appropriate arousal is high, then moderate deviant arousal may not be of any clinical concern. Abel (1976) has developed a rape index that is used to differentiate rapists from other offenders and normals. The index is a ratio of the percentage of an offender's arousal to rape stimuli compared to the percentage of arousal to mutually consenting sex.

Although direct physiological monitoring of sexual arousal is probably the best available measure, it is certainly not infallible. To some extent, offenders can exert control over their arousal and thus create an appropriate-looking record. While all faking cannot be eliminated, some steps can be taken to minimize the offender's tendency to fake. It is advisable to observe offenders periodically while they are undergoing assessment in order to be sure they are not manipulating themselves or the gauges. It is necessary to determine whether the offenders are attending to the stimulus materials being presented and not to some fantasy of their own. One technique to evaluate this is to have them describe the slides or videotapes or to answer factual questions about the stimuli after presentation. Offenders should also be asked to give subjective ratings of their arousal, which can then be compared to the objective rating and assist in detecting any obvious discrepancies. Offenders who show strong arousal to deviant stimuli but give low subjective ratings may be trying to deceive the examiner, and their records should be viewed as suspect.

Finally, stimuli should be presented under two different instructional conditions. For certain stimuli, offenders should be told to try to enhance their arousal; for others, they should be instructed to suppress their arousal. Difference in arousal levels between the two instructional conditions can then be used as an indicator of the degree to which cognitive suppression of arousal is possible for that particular client.

While the data obtained from physiological procedures is objective and useful, caution is urged in interpreting it. It should be remembered that the setting in which this data is obtained is quite different from the real world. There will be some inherent variation within subjects over time and this data is susceptible to cognitive influence. As discussed earlier, this data should never be used exclusively to identify, diagnose or classify offenders but must be interpreted cautiously and within the context of the offender's history, available records, and psychological characteristics.

Conclusion

The assessment procedures for sex offenders described above should provide a comprehensive base of information that can be useful in generating effective treatment programs for individuals. While no assessment procedures are capable of identifying offenders apart from their criminal history, these procedures can be used to create a clinical picture of the offender and to identify specific target areas for clinical intervention and treatment.

References

Abel, G.G. (1976). Assessment of sexual deviation in the male. In M. Hersen and A.S. Bellack (Eds.), *Behavioral assessment: A practical handbook*. Elmsford, NY: Pergamon Press.

Abel, G.G. and Blanchard, E.B. (1976). The measurement and generation of sexual arousal in male sexual deviates. In M. Hersen, R.M. Eisler, and P.M. Miller (Eds.), *Progress in behavior modification: Vol. 2*. New York: Academic Press.

Abel, G.G., Blanchard, E.B., and Becker, J.V. (1978). An integrated treatment program for rapists. In R. Rada (Ed.), *Clinical aspects of the rapist*. New York: Grune & Stratton.

Barlow, D.H. (1974). The treatment of sexual deviation: Towards a comprehensive behavioral approach. In K.S. Calhoun, H.E. Adams, and K.M. Mitchell (Eds.), *Innovative treatment methods in psychopathology*. New York: Wiley.

Bellack, A.S. (1983). Recurrent problems in the assessment of social skills. *Behavior Research and Therapy,* 27(1), 29-42.

Berlin, F.S. (1983). Sex offenders: A biomedical perspective and a status report on biomedical treatment. In J.G. Greer and I.R. Stuart (Eds.), *The sexual aggressor: Current perspectives in treatment*. New York: Van Nostrand Reinhold.

Carter, D.L. and Baird, L.A. (1986, August). A new method for classification of child molesters. Paper presented at annual meeting of the American Psychological Association, Washington, DC.

Cohen, M., Seghorn, T., and Calmas, W. (1969). Sociometric study of the sex offender. *Journal of Abnormal Psychology,* 74(2), 249-255.

Dreiblatt, I.S. (May 1982). Issues in the evaluation of the sex offender. Paper presented at annual meeting of the Western Psychological Association. Seattle, Washington.

Earls, C.M. and Marshall, W.L. (1983). A current state of technology in laboratory assessment of sexual arousal patterns. In J.G. Greer and I.R. Stuart (Eds.), *The sexual aggressor: Current perspectives in treatment*. New York: Van Nostrand Reinhold.

Finkelhor, D. (1984). *Child sexual abuse: New theory and treatment*. New York: Free Press.

Geer, J.H. (1980). Measurement of genital arousal in human males and females. In I. Martin and P.H. Venables (Eds.), *Techniques in psychophysiology*. New York: Wiley.

Graham, J. (1977). *The MMPI: A practical guide*. New York: Oxford University Press.

Greene, R.L. (1980). *The MMPI: An interpretive manual*. New York: Grune and Stratton.

Hammer, E.F. (1954). A comparison of H-T-P's of rapists and pedophiles. *Journal of Projective Techniques,* 18, 346-354.

Hammer, E.F. and Jacks, I. (1955). A study of Rorschach flexor and extensor human movement responses. *Journal of Clinical Psychology,* 11, 63-69.

Hite, S. (1981). *The Hite report*. New York: Dell.

Hobson, W.S., Boland, C., and Jamieson, B. (1985). Dangerous sexual offenders. *Medical Aspects of Sexuality,* Vol. 19, 104-123.

Julien, E. and Over, R. (1984). Male sexual arousal with repeated exposure to erotic stimuli. *Archives of Sexual Behavior,* 13(3), 211-222.

Kelly, R.J. (1982). Behavioral reorientation of pedopiliacs: Can it be done? *Clinical Psychology Review,* 2(3), 387-408.

Kinsey, A.C., Pomeroy, W.B., and Martin, C.E. (1948). *Sexual behavior in the human male*. Philadelphia: Saunders.

Kinsey, A.C., Pomeroy, W.B., Martin, C.E., and Gebhard, C.E. (1953). *Sexual behavior in the human female*. Philadelphia: Saunders.

Langevin, R. (1983). *Sexual strands*. Hillsdale, NJ: Erlbaum.

Lanyon, R.I. (1986). Theory and treatment in child molestation. *Journal of Consulting and Clinical Psychology,* 54(2), 176-182.

Laws, D.R. (1984). The assessment of diverse sexual behaviors. In K. Howells (Ed.), *The psychology of sexual diversity*. Oxford: Basil & Blackwell.

Laws, D.R. and Osborn, C.A. (1983). Setting up shop: How to build and operate a laboratory to evaluate and treat sexual deviance. In J.G. Greer and I.R. Stuart (Eds.), *The sexual aggressor: Current perspectives on treatment*. New York: Van Nostrand Reinhold.

Lief, H.I. and Reed, D.M. (1972). Sex knowledge and attitude test. Philadelphia: University of Pennsylvania, Department of Psychiatry, Center for the Study of Sex Education in Medicine.

Marsh, J.J., Hilliard, J., and Liechiti, R. (1955). A sexual deviation scale for the MMPI. *Journal of Consulting Psychology*, 19, 55-59.

McCreary, C.P. (1975). Personality differences among child molesters. *Journal of Personality Assessment*, 39, 591-593.

McGuire, R.J., Carlisle, J.M., and Young, B.G. (1965). Sexual deviation as conditioned behavior: A hypothesis. *Behavior Research and Therapy*, 2, 185-190.

Meichenbaum, D. and Novaco, R.W. (1978). Stress innoculation: A preventative approach. In Spielberger and I. Sarason (Eds.), *Stress and Anxiety: Vol. 5*. New York: Halstead Press.

Nichols, H.R. and Molinder, I. (1984). The multiphasic sex inventory. Unpublished manuscript. Tacoma, WA.

Novaco, R.W. (1975). *Anger control: The development and evaluation of an experimental treatment*. Lexington, MA: Lexington Books.

Paitich, D., Langevin, R., Freeman, R., Mann, I., and Handy, L. (1977). The Clarke SHQ: A clinical sex history for males. *Archives of Sexual Behavior*, 6, 421-436.

Pascal, G.R. and Herzberg, R.I. (1952). The detection of deviant sexual practice from performance on the Rorschach Test. *Journal of Projective Techniques*, 10, 366-373.

Prentky, R., Cohen, M., and Seghorn, T. (1985). Development of a rational taxonomy for the classification of rapists. *Bulletin of the American Academy of Psychiatry and the Law*, 31(1), 39-70.

Quinsey, V.L. (October 1981). Prediction of recidivism and the evaluation of treatment programs for sex offenders. Paper presented at Sexual Aggression and the Law: A Symposium. Vancouver, Canada.

Quinsey, V.L. and Marshall, W.L. (1983). Procedures for reducing inappropriate sexual arousal. In J.G. Greer and I.R. Stuart (Eds.), *The sexual aggressor: Current perspectives on treatment*. New York: Van Nostrand Reinhold.

Rada, R.T. (1978). *Clinical aspects of the rapist*. New York: Grune and Stratton.

Rathus, S.A. (1973). A thirty-item schedule for assessing assertive behavior. *Behavior Therapy*, 4, 398-406.

Thorne, F.C. (1966). The sex inventory. *Journal of Clinical Psychology*, 22, 367-374.

Toobert, S., Bartelme, K.F., and Jones, E.S. (1959). Some factors related to pedophilia. *International Journal of Social Psychiatry*, 4, 272-279.

Tracy, F., Donnelly, H., Morgenbesser, L., and MacDonald, D. (1983). Program evaluation: Recidivism research involving sex offenders. In J.G. Greer and I.R. Stuart (Eds.), *The sexual aggressor: Current perspectives on treatment*. New York: Van Nostrand Reinhold.

Turner, S.M. and Hersen, M. (1983). Disorders of social behavior: A behavioral approach to personality disorders. In S.M. Turner, K.S. Calhoun, and H.E. Adams (Eds.), *Handbook of clinical behavior therapy*. New York: Wiley.

Wincze, J.P. (1982). Assessment of sexual disorders. *Behavioral Assessment*, 4, 257-271.

Zuckerman, M. (1971). Physiological measures of sexual arousal in the human. *Psychological Bulletin*, 75, 297-329.

Chapter 12

Phallometric Assessment

by William D. Pithers, Ph.D. and D.R. Laws, Ph.D.

Overview

Traditionally, a client's self-report of symptoms was the primary method through which a therapist evaluated treatment needs and outcome. Although many clients accurately perceive and report their current functioning, others may be unable or unwilling to do so. The thought processes of some individuals experiencing major psychiatric disorders may be affected to such an extent that self-reported information cannot be considered reliable. In other cases, an evaluation occurs under circumstances in which the client has a vested interested in the outcome (e.g., competence to stand trial) that might affect their symptom presentation.

Regardless of functional level and evaluative circumstances, some response bias in self-reported information is always to be expected. In an effort to minimize inaccuracies of self-report, many psychometric devices include specialized validity scales intended to detect overly self-protective or self-disclosing response tendencies.

Assessment of sexual aggressors poses difficulties beyond those encountered with traditional mental health clients. In most instances, sexual aggressors do not enter therapy on their own accord. More typically, sex offenders reluctantly seek therapy after their abuse of others has been discovered by authority figures. Offenders may view their behavior as problematic solely because it resulted in arrest, conviction, and imprisonment. For such individuals, leaving treatment as soon as possible, rather than achieving attitudinal and behavioral change, may represent the goal of therapy. These characteristics make a sexual aggressor's self-report a particularly suspect measure of change.

Since many sexual aggressors prefer to describe their deviant sexual interests inaccurately, therapists must have access to an evaluative procedure that objectively and reliably measures an individual's sexual arousal pattern. Phallometry is regarded by experts in the treatment of the sexual aggressor as the only ethical, reliable, and valid means of assessing a male's pattern of sexual arousal.

Phallometry is an essential technology in the assessment and treatment of the sexual aggressor. Dr. James Breiling, of the Violence and Traumatic Stress Branch of the National Institute of Mental Health (personal communication, July 11, 1983), stated that any restrictions imposed on a specially trained clinician's ability to employ phallometry in assessing and treating sex offenders "would be analogous to depriving a physician the right to obtain x-rays in cases of bone injuries." This assessment procedure offers information about one specific aspect of an individual's treatment needs and provides a clear criterion of his response to treatment.

The information in this chapter is intended to be an introduction to the basic concepts of phallometry. It summarizes the rationale for employing phallometry as well as the types of information that may be derived from this technology. Factors that may affect validity of evaluations are also presented. The text also emphasizes the importance of integrating this assessment technique with data from other evaluative procedures. The chapter also discusses current uses and potential abuses of phallometric assessment.

This chapter is not intended to prepare clinicians to conduct phallometric evaluations. The need for mental health professionals to obtain specialized training prior to employing phallometric assessment is strongly encouraged. Only supervised experience will provide professionals with the requisite skill to conduct this component of a comprehensive psychosexual assessment.

Phallometric Assessment of Sexual Interest

Behavioral assessment and treatment techniques appear to represent significant components in work with sex offenders. A recent national survey identified 735 treatment programs for adolescents who had engaged in sexually abusive acts and 726 programs for adult sex offenders (Knopp, Freeman-Longo, and Stevenson, 1992). Despite the fact that many of the providers included in this survey devote only a small percentage of their practice to work with sexual abusers, behavioral methods were used to assess and treat disordered arousal in many of the programs. Phallometry was used to measure sexual arousal in 24% of the adolescent and 32% of the adult programs. Covert sensitization, the most commonly used behavioral treatment procedure, was employed in 41% of the adolescent and 45% of the programs for adults. Olfactory aversive conditioning occurred in 16% of the adolescent and 23% of the adult programs. Thus, measurement of sexual arousal, and treatment of disordered arousal, are widely recognized as important components of sex offender programs.

Phallometry assesses genital arousal in response to stimuli depicting a variety of sexual acts or "objects" of each gender at various ages. The client places around his penis a small electronic ring called a penile transducer. It detects changes in the size of the organ from a state of no sexual arousal (flaccidity) to a state of complete arousal (full erection). Audiotapes depicting both abusive and affectionate sexual scenarios are then played to the client while his sexual arousal is monitored by the penile transducer. The changes in arousal measured by the penile transducer are continuously registered by a chart recorder in another room. By comparing the differential amplitudes of response associated with audiotapes depicting various types of sexual activity, the clinician is provided an indication of the client's sexual interests, preferences, and inhibitions.

This technology may be used in two ways. First, it may be used as an assessment technique to evaluate the client's relative interest in or preference for various abusive versus nonabusive sexual activities. Second, phallometry is used as one of a variety of measures to index the success or failure of treatment for sexual deviance. In effective treatment, one expects to see a progressive decline in deviant sexual arousal and/or an incremental increase in sexual arousal to consenting sexual acts.

The work of Masters and Johnson (1966) showed that a variety of physiological responses occurred concurrently during sexual behavior. However, responses such as increased heart rate, increased respiration, flushing, sweating, and changes in galvanic skin response all occur in the same form in other states of heightened physiological arousal. For purposes of assessment and treatment of sex offenders, penile erection response serves as the best single dependent variable. For maximum effectiveness, phallometric measures should be supplemented by other data, such as subjective estimates of levels of sexual arousal, self-reports of the percentage of abusive and nonabusive sexual fantasies, frequency of masturbation and content of the accompanying fantasies, card sorts, and other indicators of sexual interest and performance.

Including phallometry in comprehensive treatment programs for sex offenders offers numerous advantages. These advantages include: (1) identification of individuals who manifest excessive arousal in response to stimuli depicting sexual abuse, (2) discernment of lack of arousal to stimuli of consenting sex, (3) identification of offenders whose arousal disorder necessitates specialized behavioral therapies, (4) minimization of distortions evident in self-reported levels of arousal, (5) evaluation of therapeutic efficacy, and (6) enhancement of certain forms of behavioral therapy.

Identification of Excessive Arousal to Stimuli of Sexual Abuse

Many have tried to explain the etiology of deviant sexual behavior (Laws, 1993). Certainly, sex offenses typically are predisposed by the interplay of numerous factors (e.g., emotional mismanagement, self-hatred, cognitive distortions, inadequate social skills). In most cases, no single factor represents the causal agent. Therefore, the assessment of sexual aggressors must be wide ranging, including measures of the offender's emotions, knowledge, behaviors, and beliefs. In this fashion, the specific factors predisposing each offender's abusive sexual acts may be determined and ameliorated by prescriptive therapies.

A major factor predisposing sexually abusive acts of some offenders is a disordered sexual arousal pattern. While one may reasonably speculate that most adult males prefer adults females as consenting sexual partners, research demonstrates that a significant subset of offenders harbor preference for sexual acts with children or acts that express sexualized violence.

In a review of assessment data from a random selection of 200 sex offenders (Pithers, Kashima, Cumming, Beal, and Buell (1987, 1988)) found that 69% of the rapists and 57% of the pedophiles exhibited deviant sexual preferences during phallometric evaluation. It is important to note that only 17% of the rapists and 51% of the pedophiles self-reported the perception that they experienced greater sexual interest in abusive sexuality than affectionate sexuality with adults.

Thus, some rapists experience greater sexual excitement in response to situations containing a fusion of violence and sexual activity than to depictions of sexualized affection. Attempts to victimize children may be driven by a sexual preference for those who have not yet developed secondary sexual characteristics. Although such individuals may periodically engage in consenting sex with peers or reveal a history of occasional attempts to do so, their predilection is toward sexual abuse of children. Once excessive arousal to abusive fantasies has been discerned through phallometric evaluation, highly specialized treatments may be implemented to decrease arousal to abusive acts.

Identification of Lack of Arousal to Stimuli of Consenting Sex

Stimuli depicting consenting sexual acts with peers may evoke little arousal from some offenders. Rather than expressing the pleasures of intimacy and an ultimate acceptance of another person, sex may represent the risk of a frightening exposure of personal inadequacy to individuals afflicted by diminished self-esteem. For men whose lives are imbued with hatred, the notion of sexually expressing affection and respect for another may seem acutely alien. Regardless of its etiology, lack of arousal to consenting sex with peers may be problematic. Minimally, such a dysfunction may be frustrating. Maximally, offenders may rationalize their abusive behaviors as being attributable to their inability to participate in consenting sex with peers.

In a study examining precursors to sexual offenses, sexual dysfunctions were noted in 11% of both the rapist and pedophile samples (Pithers, et al., 1987; 1988). Since most sexually dysfunctional males do not victimize others, dysfunction obviously cannot be considered a causal factor of sexual abuse. However, in conjunction with other factors, inability to engage in affectionate sexual relationships with peers appears related to some offenders' crimes.

Increasing sexual arousal to consenting relationships with peers may provide offenders with an opportunity to communicate effectively sexually, rather than attempting to meet their emotional needs through behaviors damaging to others. A combination of specialized behavioral treatment (e.g., orgasmic reconditioning) and psycho-educational group therapy (e.g., sexuality training, social skills) may enable sex offenders to develop increased levels of arousal to depictions of consensual sex.

Determination of Need for Specialized Behavioral Therapies

Identifying offenders who have disordered sexual preferences is essential to enabling effective treatment. Existence of a disordered arousal pattern does not signify an offender is untreatable but is an indication that specific forms of behavioral therapy may need to be undertaken to assist the offender to alter his arousal pattern. These behavioral interventions are described in other chapters of this volume.

Neglecting to evaluate an offender's arousal pattern may result in failure to treat a central etiological factor of that offender's abusive behaviors. In such a situation, the offender may accomplish changes in many aspects of his therapy but continue to possess preference for sexual abuse. For example, if pedophiles harboring sexual preference for children participate only in group therapy to enhance communication skills, treatment will likely yield a pedophile with social skills. In the absence of specialized intervention, disordered arousal patterns are unlikely to change and the offender may be at high risk of relapse. Clearly, failure to evaluate sexual arousal patterns, and neglecting to provide appropriate therapy for individuals manifesting preferences for sexual victimization, may be viewed as major shortcomings in any treatment program for this population. Such neglect may lead to avoidable relapses and unnecessary risk to potential victims.

Objective Evaluation Minimizes Subjective Misrepresentation

Sex offenders are notorious for misrepresenting their favorite fantasies and behaviors. Minimization of one's sex offense is not an unusual event, particularly during the early stages of therapy. Since phallometry does not rely entirely on honesty of self-report for accuracy, the assessment procedure may yield information that the offender has been reluctant to disclose. Phallometry represents the only objective, valid method of assessing an offender's sexual arousal pattern.

Once an accurate representation of the offender's sexual preferences has been gained through phallometric evaluation, confronting the offender with this information encourages increased honesty and fosters additional self-disclosure. In one study,

55.5% of a sample of 90 offenders acknowledged additional paraphilias when confronted by a variety of assessment data, with phallometry being the source of 62.2% of the added admissions (Abel, Cunningham-Rathner, Becker, and McHugh, 1983). In clinical application, the results of a phallometric evaluation often enable denying offenders to accept responsibility for their crimes.

Although phallometry is critical to assessment and treatment of sexual aggressors, it seldom should be the only procedure employed in evaluation of such clients. While phallometry may be used alone to examine changes in arousal pattern as a result of behavioral therapy, integration of data derived from personality assessment, behavioral observation, self-report, evaluation of functional skills, and assessment of the client's attitudes and values remains the only method of obtaining a comprehensive representation of an individual's functioning. However, assessment of a sexual aggressor cannot be considered complete until information about his sexual arousal pattern has been acquired.

Objective Evaluation of Behavioral Change

In some instances, offenders acknowledge deviant sexual preferences during an initial interview, without need of phallometric evaluation. Although such an admission may be viewed as a favorable prognosticator for change, clinicians are advised to avoid the pitfall of assuming that, since the offender forthrightly attested to his deviant interests at the onset of therapy, he will be equally honest later on.

If attaining a "normal" arousal pattern is a criterion for completing treatment and if completing treatment is necessary for parole, even well-intended offenders will be tempted to deny the existence of any interest in abusive acts. Dependent clients may deny experiencing deviant fantasies, in a misguided effort to please an admired therapist. Individuals paying for outpatient therapy may report an absence of abusive fantasies in order to end this expensive endeavor. Thus, even offenders who honestly disclose abusive fantasies at the onset of treatment have powerful incentives to report dishonestly later on.

Even when offenders openly acknowledge an obsession with abusive fantasies at the beginning of treatment, completing a phallometric evaluation is necessary to gain a baseline against which the results of later assessments may be contrasted. In this fashion, the effects of treatment may be documented objectively.

Phallometric Monitoring Enhances Some Behavioral Therapies

While phallometry is used primarily as an assessment technique, some forms of behavioral therapy may be performed most effectively when phallometry is employed to monitor treatment sessions. Olfactory aversive conditioning represents one behavioral intervention that may be facilitated by use of phallometry.

In olfactory aversive conditioning, arousal to stimuli depicting sexual abuse is paired with a noxious odor. Typically, presenting the unpleasant odor leads to rapid detumescence. After repeated pairings of the aversive odor and deviant stimulus, abusive stimuli no longer elicit arousal.

Research on aversive conditioning has demonstrated that the effects of treatment vary depending on when the noxious stimulus is presented. When the stimulus is repeatedly presented after the client has developed a relatively high level of sexual arousal, the offender simply becomes less responsive to the abusive stimulus. However, if the aversive stimulus occurs when response to abusive sexual scenario is at a low level, sexual response to stimuli depicting consenting sexual acts is paradoxically heightened. Thus, the plethysmograph must be employed to determine the timing of administering the aversive stimulus. Consequently, the impact of some forms of behavioral therapy may be increased through utilization of phallometry .

Setting Up a Laboratory

The need to create a contrived, or laboratory analogue, situation in order to study the sex offender may seem strange. The unreality of it, its isolation from the real world, is actually its strength. In such a situation, the behavioral problems of the sexual abuser, which are believed to be mirrored in his sexual arousal patterns, may be systematically disassembled and studied in their component parts. With this information at hand, treatment strategies that are directly targeted on highly specific problems can be devised and implemented.

Some therapists disagree with the laboratory analogue method, regarding measurement of deviant arousal as having little relevance to sexually abusive behavior. Laws and Osborn (1983, p. 295) observed:

> A frequent complaint against this laboratory analogue approach is that it is the commission of deviant sexual acts, not sexual arousal, that is the "real" problem. Further, it is argued, because a direct causal relationship cannot be established between the two, it makes no sense to treat deviant sexual arousal. This objection ignores the rather obvious fact that deviant sexual arousal is deviant sexual behavior and is worthy of attention in its own right as a key link in the chain of behaviors leading to sexual offenses. The erection response is measured because it is the one behavior in the chain that can be objectively measured.

Most traditionally trained mental health professionals have never seen a behavioral laboratory and have little idea of its essential components. The basic requirements are quite simple. A relatively secluded area, containing at least two rooms, is needed. A variety of electronic equipment is necessary so that one can talk and listen to the client, present slide, audiotape, and videotape stimuli to him, and record his erection response data. The following paragraphs detail each of these requirements.

Space Considerations. Small areas can be effectively used as laboratory space. A clinic area with small examination rooms along a hallway represents an ideal area since no building modification would be required. One room could be used for equipment and a second as the testing room. Since the client and technician are in separate rooms, electronic equipment may need to be connected through wall-mounted interfaces.

Client Rooms. The client space should be sufficient to house a reclining chair with disposable examination paper on the seat, a headset with a boom microphone, and a wall-mounted interface panel containing an operator call button and two electrical jacks into which the headset and transducer leads are plugged. The area needs to be temperature controlled. Adequate ventilation is critical, particularly if the room will be used as a site for olfactory aversive conditioning.

These basic components are desirable but not absolutely necessary. Wiring could be shunted under the door or sent above suspended ceiling tiles rather than connected through a wall panel. Audiotapes could be played through a speaker rather than a headset. Creativity may be exercised as long as the client's privacy and clinical integrity are assured.

Control Room. The control room contains the chart recorder or computer that records the measurements from the penile transducer, an audiocassette tape deck, an intercom, and stimulus tapes. All of these materials may be arranged on a desk. A second headphone can be connected to the tape deck via a Y-adapter so that the technician can ensure that the client is hearing the correct stimulus tape. A storage cabinet can also be useful for supplies.

Ideally, the control room will contain a sink so that the process of sterilizing the penile transducer after every use may be facilitated. As a further precaution against sexually transmitted diseases, the technician is advised to wear surgical gloves when handling the transducer.

Recording Devices

Laws and Osborn specified the basic requirements for measurement devices:

The basic measurement system requires a sensing device called a penile transducer, to detect the behavior and send an electronic signal to some type of recorder that can read out the minimum, maximum, and all intermediate values of the response. Preferably, to reduce operator error, the recording device should produce a hard copy of record whether that be a pen tracing of the response or a digital readout in percentages. . . . Transducers are relatively cheap while recording devices are expensive (1983, pp. 300-301).

There are basically two types of recorders used in these laboratories: strip chart physiological recorders and computer-driven systems.

Strip Chart Recorders. Strip chart recorders have the longest history of use in this type of work. These are basically multichannel recorders which trace an analogue of a physiological response on a moving strip of paper. The resistance change from the penile transducer is sent through a special coupler to the amplification system of the recorder which converts the signal and produces a tracing of the response on a graduated chart.

Strip chart recorders permit the technician to identify changes in sexual arousal moment-by-moment. This enhances the technician's ability to discern arousal that has been evoked by specific elements of the stimulus tapes. In turn, the specific elements of the stimulus tapes can then be addressed in behavioral therapy. The analogue tracing of the chart recorder also increases the technician's ability to identify artifacts that may affect the validity of the evaluation.

Computer-Controlled Devices. Computerized assessment procedures have been introduced. In these systems, all programming, stimulus presentation, recording, and data analysis are controlled by software. The system runs itself but must be monitored by an operator who can intervene at any point. Some of these units permit simultaneous monitoring of the erection response and three additional physiological responses such as heart rate, galvanic skin response, and respiration rate. The utility of these additional measures in the assessment of sexual abusers has not yet been defined. However, some researchers are hopeful that the additional measures may function in a manner akin to the validity scales of psychometric devices, permitting reliable identification of clients who attempt to distort their appearance on the assessment.

Since computerized phallometric assessment remains a relatively recent innovation, licensed health care professionals are advised to check that the manufacturer's technology has received approval for use with sex offenders from the United States Food and Drug Administration (FDA). The FDA approval process is intended to insure the safety of the client and technician. Therefore, only equipment that has been reviewed and approved by the FDA should be considered for purchase.

Sensing Devices

Two types of penile transducers are most frequently employed: the metal band strain gauge and the mercury-in-rubber strain gauge. Both operate on the same electrical principle of variable resistance.

Metal Band Transducer. Looked at from the side, the metal band resembles a man's ring that is flat on the top and open at the bottom (Barlow, Becker, Leitenberg, and Agras, 1970). An electronic strain gauge is glued to the flat portion and its electrical leads run directly to the recorder. The client fits the ring to his penis with the flat section on top. An electrical current is passed through the gauge. As he becomes sexually aroused, the two side pieces gradually spread apart, straining the gauge on the flat section and producing a change in electrical resistance. This resistance change is amplified, and then converted by the recorder into some sort of printed copy. The metal band transducer is reliable and extremely durable, but expensive. If carefully handled, the life of the gauge is indefinite. For that reason, the metal band gauge may be the choice of laboratories that assess clients infrequently.

Mercury-In-Rubber Transducer. The mercury-in-rubber strain gauge is the most widely used device, probably because it is the least expensive (Bancroft, Jones, and Pullan, 1966). The mercury gauge is a loop of flexible silicone tubing, filled with mercury and plugged at both ends by electrodes. The electrical leads run directly to the recorder. Its operation is identical to the metal band gauge. Electrical current is passed through the mercury. When the client becomes sexually aroused, the mercury column is thinned out, creating heightened resistance. These gauges have a realistic life of only one to two months.

A variation of the mercury-in-rubber transducer, the indium-gallium gauge, is apparently not yet in wide use. Its construction is the same as the mercury unit but the tubing is filled with indium-gallium.

Reliability of Gauges. Reliability tests have shown that the mercury and indium-gallium gauges possess identical levels of linearity (Murrin and Laws, 1986). However, the metal band transducer is somewhat less linear in its measurement characteristics than the mercury and indium-gallium transducers (Murrin and Laws, 1986), although Laws (1977) initially reported those characteristics to be nearly the same.

Stimulus Materials

An effective stimulus is required to elicit sexual arousal. Although the role that pornography might have in the etiology of sexual abuse remains the topic of substantial debate, sexual abusers often have had protracted exposure to explicit sexual material. Our experience has been that the more graphic and detailed the erotic stimulus and the closer it comes to capturing the interests of a specific group of sex offenders such as pedophiles or rapists, the more likely it is to elicit sexual arousal that is indicative of a particular client's interests. Historically, three stimulus modalities have been used: photographic slides, audiotapes, and videotapes. Although two of these modalities are no longer used widely, all three are discussed in this chapter.

Slides. Photographic slides were the first stimuli employed to elicit sexual arousal during phallometric assessments. Research demonstrated that slides were the weakest stimulus modality in terms of eliciting high levels of sexual arousal (Abel, Blanchard, Barlow, and Mavissakalian, 1975). They were used mostly to determine age and gender preferences (Freund, 1963, 1967a, 1967b; Quinsey, Steinman, Bergerson, and Holmes, 1975). Laws and Osborn (1983) reported that they found them useful with about two-thirds of their clients, particularly pedophiles.

Although slides were once the most commonly employed stimulus in phallometric evaluations, significant ethical problems have been identified in the use of slides depicting actual children. In recent years, federal and state statutes have been enacted that broadly define and severely restrict possession and use of sexually explicit depictions of children. In some states, exemption from child pornography statutes for medical or scientific purposes may be gained from the Attorney General.

Although obtaining an exemption from a state Attorney General may make the materials legitimate for use legally, the ethics of using stimuli of children in phallometric assessments of sex offenders are highly questionable. In essence, we believe that children and their parents cannot truly provide informed consent for the taking of photographs that could be considered sexually explicit. Although one vendor marketing such stimuli purportedly had obtained informed consent from the children and the children's parents, after failing to demonstrate that informed consent actually existed, the vendor reached an agreement with the state Attorney General that resulted in police-supervised burning of the child pornography slides.

Some practitioners report using photographic stimuli obtained by police during the seizure of evidence from individuals arrested for sexual abuse allegations. We strongly oppose the use of photographs of child sexual abuse victims as stimuli for a plethysmographic evaluation. We regard this as unethical practice.

Given the legal and ethical concerns, practitioners are cautioned against using sexually explicit photographs of children in the phallometric assessment of sexual abusers. Alternatives to slides of children clearly must be pursued.

Two options to photographic stimuli are apparent: artists' renditions and computer generated images. These procedures would obviate the concern about exploiting children since no images of actual children would be employed. Legal considerations about possession of these materials may remain, but potentially could be addressed through the "scientific and medical uses" exemption to child pornography statutes.

Videotapes. Videotaped stimuli were used for assessment of rapists (Abel, Blanchard, Barlow, and Guild, 1977) with great effectiveness for a number of years. These were the only videotaped stimuli that were ever found useful with sex offenders. This was a tailor-made assessment which showed simulated sequences of consenting sexual intercourse, rape, and physical assault without sexual activity. A controversy remains as to whether this is an effective technique, and its original authors have abandoned its use (Abel, Blanchard, Becker, and Djenderedjian, 1978). A revision was made by Crawford and Bonham (1981) but it received limited use in the United States.

Some workers abstract particularly graphic and sexually strong sequences from X-rated and R-rated films and use these as assessment tools. Although they are no doubt powerful, this approach is not advisable as the sequences are filled with extraneous stimuli, such as inane dialogue and poorly recorded music. In addition, many of these films contain an unrealistic representation of acts which begin as a sexual assault but which evolve into supposedly consenting acts. Under such circumstances, one cannot discern precisely to what the client is responding.

Audiotapes. Audiotaped descriptions are the modality of choice for most applications. Pioneered by Abel and his colleagues (Abel, Levis, and Clancy, 1970; Abel, et al., 1975; Abel, et al., 1977), the method is very flexible in that stimuli may be prepared that are applicable to a particular offender group (Abel, et al., 1977; Avery-Clark and Laws, 1984; Laws, 1986) or may be tailored to the unique interests of a single offender. The flexibility lies in the fact that one may vary any parameter of the stimulus (e.g., age of victim, modus operandi of the offender, use or nonuse of violence, etc.) in order to relate different levels of arousal to different components of the stimulus (Abel, et al., 1975; Laws, 1984).

An attempt has been made to standardize these stimuli. Laws and colleagues have developed sets of tapes to evaluate female and male pedophilia, female and male incest, rape, and exhibitionism. Each script consists of three paragraphs of 15 lines each. Each script is exactly three minutes long, as Avery-Clark and Laws (1984) demonstrated this to be the probable optimal stimulus duration. Recently, the Association for the Treatment of Sexual Abuse (ATSA) improved the recording quality of these audiotapes and began marketing them to its membership. Individuals interested in joining the ATSA can write to its headquarters for an application: Connie Isaac, Executive Director, Association for the Treatment of Sexual Abusers, Box 866, Lake Oswego, OR 97034-0140.

The use of audiotaped descriptions also minimizes the legal issues mentioned previously. There is no question about the source of the materials. They are prepared by adult clinicians for an exact purpose with adult clients. No one is exploited in their production, no one earns illicit profit from the effort.

Protecting the Client: Issues of Informed Consent

Many sex offenders repeatedly perform behaviors most persons find reprehensible. However, this does not mean they are undeserving of concern or should expect less than the best standard of professional treatment.

While phallometry is a highly specialized behavioral assessment procedure, its use occurs in a more general therapeutic context. Therefore, one must specify to the client the purpose of phallometric evaluation and how the assessment data may be used. Among the issues that must be addressed are: clients' fears, confidentiality, and informed consent.

Clients' Fears. Sex offenders do not ordinarily see themselves as psychologically troubled people. While a small percentage may self-refer to mental health clinics, most enter treatment under coercive circumstances and many vehemently deny any involvement in abusive sexual activity upon the initial interview.

When such offenders discover that they will be required to engage in a phallometric evaluation, they may become anxious or frightened. Often the offender may view phallometry as a sexual lie detector which will reveal things that he would prefer that no one know. The best way to handle concerns about the nature of phallometry, and treatment in general, is to be quite frank about it.

Offenders have a right to know the nature of the assessment and what they may expect to gain from it. They should be made aware of exactly what engaging in the procedure will entail. They should be informed that they will be asked for detailed information about their past and present experiences. They should also be instructed that they cannot be forced to respond sexually and that they are participating in this procedure consciously and freely.

Confidentiality. Issues of confidentiality are controversial in sex offender treatment programs. Some treatment providers insist on total confidentiality to increase the chances of an offender detailing all his criminal sexual acts. Other providers advocate no confidentiality, requiring offenders to sign full and irrevocable waivers prior to entering treatment, in the belief that reporting sexual offenses to authorities might enable intervention for victims.

Regardless of a program's philosophy about confidentiality of information provided by a client during therapy, phallometric evaluation data should be treated with confidence. Such information would have little meaning to other agencies. However, providing the offender feedback about his sexual arousal pattern may motivate him to accept responsibility for the current offense, and hopefully to disclose additional victimizations. In such cases, confidentiality may be protected only if sufficient details to identify the victim is not provided. However, where such details are disclosed, treatment providers are required by law to report this information to legal authorities.

Informed Consent. As with confidentiality, various beliefs exist regarding the necessity of obtaining informed consent prior to phallometric evaluations. Some providers consider phallometry to be only one of many psychometric techniques employed during a psychosexual evaluation, none of which requires a special informed consent document. Other professionals regard signature of a special informed consent document to be essential.

In order to decide the optimal procedure in a particular setting, therapists may request information about the basic elements of an informed consent document from the National Institute of Mental Health (Parklawn Building, 5600 Fishers Lane, Rockville, MD 20857). With this information, administrators, attorneys, and the ethics committee of one's state professional group to review your situation may be asked to consult on this issue. If informed consent appears essential, the drafted document should be submitted to an institutional review board or correctional administrator for approval.

Avoidable and Unavoidable Limitations on Phallometry

Validity of information derived from phallometric assessment may be compromised by both avoidable and unavoidable influences. Detrimental but avoidable factors include examiner incompetence, over-interpretation of data, and failure to adhere to administrative standards. Efforts by offenders to suppress arousal to preferred but deviant sexual stimuli and restrictions imposed by laboratory measurement of real-world behaviors represent the principal unavoidable pitfalls.

Avoidable Pitfalls

Examiner Incompetence. The FDA has classified phallometric assessment instrumentation as a "prescriptive" medical device. According to the FDA, prescriptive medical devices can only be employed by licensed providers living in states where the licensing statute governing their profession authorizes them to use such technology. Phallometry should be employed only by licensed mental health professionals who have received thorough training in the procedure. Professionals concerned about their ability to use phallometry should contact their state licensing board.

Since phallometry is a relatively esoteric assessment not covered in graduate training programs for mental health practitioners, opportunities to gain experience are limited to internships in treatment programs utilizing the procedure. As a result, some practitioners may be tempted to purchase the necessary equipment and pursue on-the-job training. Attempting to conduct phallometric evaluations without the needed training is not only unwise, but also violates professional ethics. Incompetent evaluations may lead to erroneous conclusions about an offender's arousal pattern, possibly prolonging an individual's treatment needlessly or enabling an offender to gain access to situations in which he may create yet another victim.

Over-Interpretation of Data. Because of the high face validity of the data, it is easy to over-interpret the significance of the information and make unwarranted conclusions. Laws and Osborn summarized the problem this way:

Does the presence of high levels of arousal to rape, pedophilic, or other deviant stimuli in a laboratory mean that surely the person will rape, molest children, or otherwise disport himself in a deviant fashion? Of course, it does not. Undeniably, sexual arousal is considerably more than just penile erection. The erection response is not even present during the commission of some deviant sexual acts and, when present, the offender may or may not use his genitals in the act itself. Nonetheless, if in an assessment . . . a male shows a very large erection response to a deviant sexual stimulus, and very little or no response to a nondeviant stimulus, this is more than presumptive evidence that he is more sexually attracted to the former than the latter. This would be a particularly reasonable conclusion if the man had a known history of sexual deviance. Such data, however, do not mean that he will necessarily act upon his arousal; they do mean that he may be at risk to do so, and in the case of a known sex offender, that is reason enough to justify therapeutic intervention. ... Deviant sexual arousal is deviant sexual behavior. That is what the data show (1983, p.373).

Thus, the way to use and not abuse phallometric data is simply to report what was done and what was found. If this can be unequivocally related to known behaviors of the client, and particularly if the client admits to the accuracy of the measured pattern of sexual response, it is permissible to report that. It is not legitimate, given the current state of the science, to make any prediction whatever concerning future behavior of a specific client or to comment about questions of guilt or innocence. It is recommended that all reports summarizing phallometric evaluations contain such disclaimers.

Failure to Adhere to Administrative Standards. Several studies comparing arousal patterns of incarcerated sex offenders and non-sex offenders have neglected to evaluate the extent of overlap between the two groups (i.e., sex offenders who have a history of frequent nonsexual crimes and non-sex offenders who have engaged in sexual aggression in the past). Recently, it was discovered that some studies failing to differentiate rapists from normal subjects had employed stimuli that showed the victim initially resisting the assault but later deriving pleasure from it. When more realistic depictions of the victim's constant abhorrence of the assault are used, rapists appear more aroused than normals.

When appropriate procedures are employed, information derived from phallometry is usually reliable and valid. The test-retest reliability coefficient for baseline measurement of penile circumference has been reported to be 0.94 (Farkas, Evans, Sine, Eifert, Wittlieb, and Vogelmann-Sine, 1979). On the basis of this reliability estimate, phallometry appears to match or surpass the reliability of the most highly regarded psychometric techniques: the Wechsler Adult Intelligence Scale-Revised and the Minnesota Multiphasic Personality Inventory. Rates of diagnostic accuracy have been estimated to be as high as 90% (see Knopp, 1984).

As with any assessment procedure, failure to comply with administrative and interpretive standards lessens the adequacy of the resulting information. Before all evaluations, examiners must provide clients with detailed information about the procedure in order to allay anxiety that could inhibit arousal. Instructions to the offender should be standardized. Equipment must be calibrated for each client before and after the session. Clients must be given adequate time to become flaccid before presentation of another stimulus. The client should be instructed to self-report his estimated level of arousal after each stimulus so that his subjective estimate can be compared to the objective measurement. Opportunity should be provided for debriefing upon conclusion of the session. If one follows accepted procedures, information from phallometric assessment is usually accurate.

Use with Inappropriate Clients. With adult and older adolescent clients, as long as guidelines for appropriate administration and interpretation of data are followed and the client is compliant, information derived from phallometric assessments generally may be considered reliable and valid. However, phallometry cannot be used meaningfully with pre-pubescent clients. The Association for the Treatment of Sexual Abuse adopted the following position statement in 1992 in an effort to restrain practitioners:

> The Association for the Treatment of Sexual Abusers does not endorse the use of plethysmography or olfactory aversive conditioning with pre-pubescent children who have engaged in sexually abusive behaviors. No scientific basis exists for the use of these procedures with pre-pubescent children. Any use of these procedures with pre-pubescent children must be considered experimental and, therefore, subjected to scrutiny by Institutional Review Boards or other professional review groups which serve to ensure that the safety and rights of experimental subjects or clients are protected fully.

Practitioners need to exercise good judgment, using assessment and treatment procedures in a manner that is professionally and ethically responsible. Any effort to extend assessment and treatment procedures to populations with whom they have not yet been shown to be effective requires the oversight of an Institutional Review Board or a professional review panel.

Unavoidable Pitfalls

Suppression of Deviant Arousal. The major unavoidable pitfall of phallometry is that tumescence may be subjectively controlled. To some extent, males can control their sexual arousal. A male's ability to suppress arousal to a preferred stimulus is usually greater than his ability to generate arousal to a nonpreferred one (Laws and Rubin, 1969; Henson and Rubin, 1971; Laws and Holmen, 1978; Alford, Wedding, and Jones, 1983). An individual who is predisposed to sexually abuse children may be able to inhibit his arousal to children and, perhaps, appear normal. Thus, failing to identify pathology when it exists is essentially the only error in classification resulting from phallometric assessment.

Concern about response suppression is particularly great when phallometry is employed with incarcerated offenders. Imprisoned offenders have extensive opportunities to exchange information about specific stimuli and suppression strategies.

The instructional set may be varied to estimate the extent to which a client has tried to suppress arousal. Clients may be requested to allow themselves to become aroused to a second stimulus set. If little difference in arousal exists under the two instructional sets, one may hypothesize that the client attempted to suppress arousal throughout the evaluation, regardless of instructional set. Preparing several sets of stimuli may also alleviate this problem.

Precautions may be taken to minimize response suppression during phallometric evaluations. If in spite of these measures suppression should occur, the examiner is often able to discern suppression through the presence of certain artifacts in the recording of the arousal response. For example, attempts to influence the outcome by covert masturbation, or by mechanically attempting to manipulate the transducer, are readily apparent on the record (Laws and Holmen, 1978). Although no foolproof method for detecting faking yet exists, the phenomenon continues to be investigated (Quinsey and Chaplin, 1987).

False positive errors (i.e., identification of a disordered arousal pattern in a normal individual) are extremely rare and have been found only under experimental conditions when subjects, in a laboratory setting, have been instructed to attempt to respond physiologically. Even though experimental subjects can generate sexual arousal to a non-preferred gender or age group, irregularities in the response recording are typically apparent. Since strong incentives against faking a disordered arousal pattern exist for sex offenders (i.e., incarceration or prolongation of probation), not a single instance of an offender feigning abusive preferences has been reported in the clinical literature.

Limitations of Laboratory Analogue Approaches. People responding in a laboratory situation, and particularly those who are already in confinement, are not exposed to the real temptations of society. It is important to remember that, however extensive the data collected, no more than an approximate picture of the offender's deviant and nondeviant sexual interests will be obtained.

Concern is growing that phallometry may be less applicable to rapists than pedophiles. Essentially, phallometry does not differentiate rapists and nonrapists sufficiently. In contrast, phallometric assessments appear quite useful in differentiating pedophiles and nonpedophiles, and may even assist differentiation among child abuser subtypes (Barbaree and Marshall, 1989).

Essentially, arousal patterns of pedophiles resemble "traits" while rapists' arousal patterns may be "state dependent." By definition, pedophiles experience strong and enduring sexual attraction toward children. The pedophile's sexual desire for children may be altered to some degree by various emotional states, but across emotional states the pedophile's strongest sexual interest remains focused on children.

However, with rapists, arousal patterns may be altered dramatically by different emotional and cognitive states (Barbaree, 1990). The abusive interests of some rapists may emerge only after a potentiating event occurs. Only in the presence of these variables does a latent abusive belief system become evident in arousal to sexually violent stimuli. These potentiating events differ across rapists. Among the influences that have been shown to disinhibit sexual arousal to stimuli depicting rape are victim blame due to clothing and location (Sundberg, Barbaree, and Marshall; cited in Barbaree, 1990), anger (Yates, Barbaree, and Marshall, 1984), alcohol intake (Barbaree, Marshall, Yates, and Lightfoot, 1983), and exposure to aggressive pornography shortly before assessment (Seidman, Marshall, and Barbaree, 1989). Since professional ethics constrain clinicians' freedom to create the circumstances that may activate sexually abusive interests and enable their identification, the ability to precisely measure rapists' sexual interests is compromised.

What the physiological recording indicates is a precise measurement of what is happening within a specific individual, in a given laboratory, on a certain day, under a set of controlled circumstances. But what may be present one day may be absent the next, then reappear a week or a month later, then disappear again. However, it is reasonable to expect that, over time, evidence of fixed behavioral patterns will appear. What one must look for is consistency over time. In this manner, phallometry can assist the clinician's ability to accurately assess treatment needs and progress.

References

Abel, G.G., Blanchard, E.B., Barlow, D.H., and Guild, D. (1977). The components of rapists' sexual arousal. *Archives of General Psychiatry,* 34, 895-903.

Abel, G.G., Blanchard, E.B., Barlow, D.H., and Mavissakalian, M. (1975). Identifying the specific erotic cues in sexual deviation by audiotaped descriptions. *Journal of Applied Behavior Analysis,* 8, 247-260.

Abel, G.G., Blanchard, E.B., Becker, J.V., and Djenderedjian, A. (1978). Differentiating sexual aggressives with penile measures. *Criminal Justice & Behavior,* 5, 315-332.

Abel, G.G., Cunningham-Rathner, J., Becker, J.V., and Mchugh, J. (1983). Motivating sex offenders for treatment with feedback of their psychophysical assessment. Paper presented at the World Congress of Behavior Therapy, Washington, DC.

Abel, G.G., Levis, D., and Clancy, J. (1970). Aversion therapy applied to taped sequences of deviant behavior in exhibitionism and other sexual deviation: A preliminary report. *Journal of Behavior Therapy and Experimental Psychiatry,* 1, 58-66.

Alford, D.S., Wedding, D., and Jones, S. (1983). Faking "turn ons" and "turn offs": The effect of competitory covert imagery on penile tumescence responses to diverse extrinsic sexual materials. *Behavior Modification,* 7, 112-125.

Avery-Clark, C.A. and Laws, D.R. (1984). Differential erection response patterns of sexual child abusers to stimuli describing activities with children. *Behavior Therapy,* 15, 71-83.

Bancroft, J., Jones, H.G., and Pullan, B.R. (1966). A simple transducer for measuring penile erection, with comments on its use in the treatment of sexual disorders. *Behaviour Research and Therapy,* 4, 239-241.

Barlow, D.H., Becker, J., Leitenberg, H., and Agras, S. (1970). A mechanical strain gauge for recording penile circumference change. *Journal of Applied Behavior Analysis,* 3, 73-76.

Crawford, D.A. and Bonham, E. (1981). A videotaped procedure for the assessment of sexual arousal in rapists. Crowthorne, Berkshire, England: Psychology Department, Broadmoor Hospital.

Farkas, G.M., Evans, I.M., Sine, L.F., Eifert, G., Wittlieb, E., and Vogelmann-Sine, S. (1979). Reliability and validity of the mercury-in-rubber strain gauge measure of penile circumference. *Behavior Therapy,* 10, 555-561.

Freund, K. (1963). A laboratory method for diagnosing predominance of homo- or heteroerotic interest in the male. *Behaviour Research and Therapy,* 1, 85-93.

Freund, K. (1967a). Diagnosing homo- and heterosexuality and erotic age preference by means of a psychophysiological test. *Behaviour Research and Therapy,* 5, 209-228.

Freund, K. (1967b). Erotic preference in pedophilia. *Behaviour Research and Therapy,* 5, 339-348.

Henson, D.E. and Rubin, H.B. (1971). Voluntary control of eroticism. *Journal of Applied Behavior Analysis,* 4, 37-44.

Knopp, F.H. (1984). *Retraining adult sex offenders: Methods and model.* Syracuse, NY: Safer Society Press.

Knopp, F.H., Rosenberg, J., and Stevenson, W. (1986). *Directory of juvenile and adult sex offender treatment programs in the United States.* Syracuse, NY: Safer Society Press.

Laws, D.R. (in press). A theoretical formulation of the etiology of sexual deviance. In W.L. Marshall, D.R. Laws, and H.E. Barbaree (Eds.), *Handbook of sexual assault.* New York: Plenum.

Laws, D.R. (1977). A comparison of the measurement characteristics of two circumferential penile transducers. *Archives of Sexual Behavior,* 6, 45-51.

Laws, D.R. (1984). The assessment of dangerous sexual behavior males. *Medicine and Law,* 3, 127-140.

Laws, D.R. (1986). Prevention of relapse in sex offenders. Unpublished monograph. Tampa, FL: Florida Mental Health Institute.

Laws, D.R. and Holmen, M.L. (1978). Sexual response faking by pedophiles. *Criminal Justice & Behavior,* 5, 343-356.

Laws, D.R. and Osborn, C.A. (1983). How to build and operate a behavioral laboratory to evaluate and treat sexual deviance. In J.G. Greer and I.R. Stuart (Eds.), *The sexual aggressor.* New York: Van Nostrand Reinhold.

Laws, D.R. and Rubin, H.D. (1969). Instructional control of an autonomic response. *Journal of Applied Behavior Analysis, 2,* 93-99.

Masters, W.H. and Johnson, V.E. (1966). *Human sexual response.* Boston: Little, Brown.

Murrin, M.R. and Laws, D.R. (1986). Linearity characteristics of three penile transducers. Unpublished raw data. Tampa, FL: Florida Mental Health Institute.

Pithers, W.D., Kashima, K.M., Cumming, G.C., Beal, L.S., and Buell, M.M. (January 1987). Sexual aggression: An addictive behavior? Paper presented at a meeting of the New York Academy of Sciences, New York, NY.

Pithers, W.D., Kashima, K., Cumming, G.F., Beal, L.S., and Buell, M.M. (1988). Relapse prevention of sexual aggression. In R. Prentky and V. Quinsey (Eds.), *Human sexual aggression: Current perspectives* (pp. 244-260). New York: New York Academy of Sciences.

Quinsey, V.L. and Chaplin, T.C. (1987). Preventing faking in phallometric assessment of sexual preference. Unpublished manuscript.

Quinsey, V.L., Steinman, C.M., Bergerson, S.G., and Holmes, T.F. (1975). Penile circumference, skin conductance, and ranking responses of child molesters and "normals" to sexual and nonsexual stimuli. *Behavior Therapy, 6,* 213-219.

Chapter 13

Psycho-Educational Modules

by Randy Green, Ph.D.

Overview

Many sex offender treatment programs use cognitive-behavioral theory as a foundation for a major component of their treatment methodology. This treatment component is an educational intervention strategy designed to provide information to the offender on pro-social beliefs and attitudes as well as knowledge, skills, and abilities which the offender lacks. Typically, this intervention takes place through the use of psycho-educational modules.

Uses of Psycho-Educational Techniques with Sex Offenders

The theory behind psycho-educational programs is that individuals may be prevented from achieving optimal adjustment due to certain deficits or maladaptive behavioral patterns. In most communities, one can find programs which teach parenting skills, communication techniques, assertiveness, etc. These courses feature a didactic presentation by a trainer who is not necessarily a therapist and often uses workbooks and homework assignments. The format is nonthreatening as it takes place in a class setting rather than a group therapy session. This technique is readily adaptable to sex offender treatment programs and can be tailored to address a number of different areas, ranging from cognitive distortions to the enhancement of social skills.

Each offender has acquired a set of beliefs, attitudes, and expectancies which have contributed to the victimization of others. For example, a child molester may operate under the assumption that female children enjoy having their genitals stimulated by adult males. Similarly, a rapist may maintain a belief that women enjoy having rough sex. An exhibitionist may assume that he is impressing women with his physical display of masculinity and virility. These examples serve to illustrate that there are certain cognitive distortions which can directly contribute to the victimization of others.

Offenders may also maintain other stylized, well rehearsed "thinking errors" or irrational beliefs which reinforce their victim-creating and/or irresponsible behavior patterns. These beliefs can be very powerful in undermining constructive changes in the offender's repertoire of responses. Yochelson and Samenow (1976) have identified these thinking disturbances in their work, *The Criminal Personality*. An example of a criminal error in thinking is the concept of "instancy," in which the individual "wants what he wants when he wants it," without regard to the impact on anyone else. An example of an irrational belief or misconception might be an offender's belief: "I must be loved and approved by everyone in my sphere of acquaintances. If I am not, I'm worth nothing. I'll be rejected, and that would be catastrophic." This thinking process creates a context within which the individual continuously perpetuates a sense of frustration and rejection. The offender may then turn to more accepting, less threatening, and more vulnerable children for acceptance. Albert Ellis (1956), among others, has identified other misconceptions or irrational beliefs which can exist in the cognitive belief systems of offenders.

Additionally, each individual who sexually victimizes another frequently has certain deficiencies or distortions which impair his ability to manage his life responsibly or constructively. For example, child molesters may have poor social skills and shyness, leading to avoidance of female or male peers. Feeling alone and perceiving himself to be isolated from socially appropriate partners, the pedophile may seek primary social gratification and acceptance from children. He resorts to children for intimacy and to gain a sense of competency and/or adequacy.

As noted in the chapter addressing treatment planning issues, current sex offender treatment approaches attempt to target these problem areas in a variety of ways. Psycho-educational modules can teach a variety of skills which the sex offender lacks. Besides the clinical benefit derived from the use of psycho-educational modules, this mode of intervention has additional advantages. The format for such modules can be useful in establishing the authority and credibility of those who teach them. The psycho-educational module can also be useful in providing the instructor with data regarding the offender who lacks motivation. Thus, the modules may serve as a preliminary screening tool to convey initial information about sex offender dynamics and need for treatment and to determine whether an offender is interested in and amenable to more intensive and costly intervention.

The psycho-educational module can be an unobtrusive recruiting tool for encouraging offenders to participate in further, more intensive treatment. For those states required to provide treatment, such a module becomes a means of following legislatively mandated treatment requirements. It also provides an initial test of motivation. Consequently, an orientation module on "Dynamics of Sexual Offenders" provides staff with a way to document those who profess a desire for treatment but whose behavior/performance shows the opposite. It also allows the participants to learn how to communicate in a group and to begin discussing the sensitive topic of sex. Another benefit derived from this method is that such modules can provide common language and therapeutic concepts which can be useful in all other aspects of the treatment program.

Finally, psycho-educational modules are a cost-effective means of first-line therapeutic intervention. Such modules allow for ratios of one staff member per 12 to 15 offenders. Communicating substantial amounts of information, the offenders are prepared for more intimate and intense group experiences which focus on personal application, self-disclosure, and confrontation. These latter treatment components require higher levels of commitment from the offender. The modules may be taught by anyone trained in that particular area, including the offenders themselves.

The content for a psycho-educational module can be varied. Modules lend themselves to a broad range of topics which can be developed and utilized to address the diverse needs of sex offenders. The types of psycho-educational modules frequently used in treatment follow.

Types of Modules

Sex Offender Characteristics. This module focuses on the general typologies of sex offenders, elaborating on their psychodynamics and behavioral patterns. Various classifications such as those discussed by Groth (1979) and Finkelhor (1984) are introduced. The causes of sexually deviant behavior are addressed. Issues including compulsivity, escalation of offense behavior, and principles of addictive behavior patterns are presented. Issues relating to victim empathy are discussed. An explanation of various treatment concepts and interventions is reviewed. Goals for such a course include the following:

- Provide an opportunity for the offenders to see themselves as individuals who are in serious need of help in order for behavioral change to occur.

- Give hope to those troubled by sexually deviant behavior and/or its consequences.

- Confront cognitive distortions and misperceptions.

- Make a convincing statement to sex offenders regarding their need for treatment which is necessary to the prevention of future victims.

- Learn about the variety of cognitive and behavioral treatment methods available (including masturbatory reconditioning, satiation, covert sensitization, other aversive conditioning methods, and fantasy logs), and the rationale for their use.

Victim Awareness/Empathy. This course is designed to provide the offender with an awareness of the impact of his criminal behavior on others—emotionally, physically, relationally, and sexually. This focus on the victim is an attempt to confront the offender with myths such as, "if the child doesn't resist, she/he doesn't mind it," etc. Information will be provided to the offenders regarding victim dynamics, such as why children, for example, tend to respond the way they do to certain engagement strategies and eventual victimization. Goals should include:

- Identification of the long- and short-term impact of sexual assault on the victim.
- Recognition of the myths which society reinforces which perpetuate sexual assault.
- Identification, where possible, of the specific impact on the offender's victim.
- Involvement in some type of restorative activity, e.g., the payment of restitution, donating to a rape crisis center, participation in a media presentation or public information campaign, etc.

An initial attempt is frequently made in this module to assist those offenders who were themselves victims of physical and/or sexual abuse. A substantial percentage of offenders have, in fact, been victimized and sexualized at early developmental ages. The primary point in identifying this phenomenon as an issue is to assist the offenders in the development of empathy for their own victims, to shift their focus from self-centeredness to other-centeredness. The context in which this powerful and sensitive area is handled should never excuse the offender's behavior. At a later time, the offender's own victimization should be dealt with more thoroughly to assist him in gaining some insight into this area. However, the primary rationale for its inclusion here is to assist the perpetrator in using his own pain as a bridge to empathy and concern for others. At this point, the staff should always be aware of the possibility of depression or suicidal ideation.

Another topic dealt with in a victim awareness class is the victim clarification process. Whether or not victims ever actually receive a clarification letter routed through their own therapists, the process of multiple rewrites of the clarification letter can have the effect of generating a sense of ownership, remorse, and guilt in the offender. This is a constructive goal which serves to provide a potential inhibitory effect.

Cognitive Restructuring. This course focuses on the beliefs, values, and thought patterns which allow the offender to initiate and then rationalize a sexual assault. The goals are to:

- Assist the sex offender in identifying irresponsible beliefs or thinking errors.
- Recognize those errors which each offender utilizes most frequently.
- Learn alternative thought patterns to dispute or replace the distorted ones.
- Provide all offenders with a language of accountability and change within the treatment program.

In addition to the above, keeping a journal to record daily thinking errors can augment the scope of the course and provide the offenders with practice in identifying those errors and then intervening. This technique also provides an opportunity for staff to assess an offender's motivation and degree of self-awareness.

Since many sex offenders are rather concrete in their thought structures, they often find models such as these very helpful in effecting change and for holding themselves and others accountable.

Deviant Sexual Acting-Out (Pre-Assault Cycle). Presuming that each offender has one or more identifiable pre-assault cycles, this psycho-educational module emphasizes the recognition of those patterns. The instructor will assist an offender in gaining insight regarding his motives, emotions, fantasies, thoughts, and actions by recording the antecedents for each separate type of crime or victim category. Sharing this information with the class and receiving feedback from staff and peers can facilitate honest disclosure. By observing class members manifesting their deviant cycle, appropriate confrontation methods and interventions can be learned. It is hoped that offenders can later identify, intervene, and halt their cycle prior to the commission of another offense.

Relapse Prevention must be addressed prior to an offender's release. Relapse Prevention is defined as a "therapeutic approach specifically designed for the maintenance phase of behavior change programs ... toward helping the client maintain control of the behavior over time and across situations" (Pithers, Marques, Gibat, and Marlatt, 1983, pp. 215-216). (see also Chapter 20, Relapse Prevention.) These authors cite a study which found that 75% of the relapses were preceded by situations which evoked a negative emotional state, and 20% of the sample relapsed following interpersonal conflicts. A Relapse Prevention module attempts to accomplish the following goals for the offender:

- Dispel any misconception that treatment will eliminate all problems with future sexually deviant behavior.
- Identify situations which create a high risk for relapse and the subsequent chain of responses culminating in re-offense.
- Identify cognitive and behavioral skills which will enable the offender to control his behavior and reduce the likelihood of relapse.
- Demonstrate the use of these Relapse Prevention strategies.

Anger Management. Many offenders have serious difficulties with the appropriate expression of anger. Their failure to manage anger in a responsible manner increases the likelihood of displacement through aggression toward others. The goals of such a module include:

- Assisting the offender in becoming aware of both the dimensions and determinants of the anger problem (Novaco, 1976).
- Assisting the offender in learning the role that anger plays in the acting-out pattern.
- Assisting the offender in learning and implementing a stress inoculation approach to anger management.

Assertiveness Training. Subassertive or passive communication patterns are frequently found among sex offenders who perceive themselves to be inadequate or inferior both to their peers and to those in authority. Fearful of expressing their thoughts or feelings and risking rejection, they often suppress their emotions, which then manifest themselves through passive-aggressive, aggressive, or direct victim-creating behavior. Goals of a module of this type are similar to those of anger management and include:

- Assisting the offender in identifying passive, aggressive, and/or passive-aggressive patterns of behavior.
- Assisting the offender in relating these maladapted communication patterns to the acting-out cycle.
- Assisting the offender in learning and demonstrating assertiveness skills, with an end to being able to practice these skills with those who appear to be most threatening or intimidating.

Substantial material is available for assertiveness training module presentation. In 1960, Stevenson and Wolpe taught clients that assertive expression of one's feelings is incompatible with social anxiety; they taught these individuals how to be more disclosing and transparent through the technique of behavioral shaping.

Social Skills Training. Another psycho-educational module which focuses on communication styles is related to social skill development. While some sex offenders are quite socially adept, others cannot sustain appropriate social interactions with peers and cannot respond to the disclosures of others. Inaccurate perceptions of women and misinterpretation of their responses are additional social skill problems manifested by offenders. Although this relationship is not yet proven, such deficiencies may alienate them from others and may tend to reinforce victim-creating patterns of behavior (Becker, Abel, Blanchard, Murphy, and Coleman, 1978). Goals for social skills training modules frequently include:

- Identification of verbal and nonverbal social skill deficiencies through the use of interview techniques, observation, collateral contacts, and the Social Skill Assessment Scale (Barlow, Abel, Blanchard, Bristow, and Young, 1977; Becker, et al., 1978) and the Empathy Assessment Scale (Truax and Carkhuff, 1967; Becker, et al., 1978).
- Identification of the relationship of social skill deficiencies to the pre-assault cycle of the offender.
- Development of appropriate cue discrimination.
- Development of pro-social skills, characterized by appropriate voice, conversation, affect, and motor behavior responses, for those situations in which the offender has the most difficulties (Becker, et al., 1978).

Surveys of heterosocial skill training (Abel, Blanchard, and Becker, 1976, 1978) found that many programs utilize female staff or volunteers during semistructured sessions. "Minimal dating" or "heterosexual shyness" research has used such specific techniques as a dating manual, group discussions of dating practice behaviors, heterosocial behavior practice, contact with female volunteers, semistructured social problems involving real life contact with community women, arranged simulated dates with both positive and negative feedback, role modeling, videotaping, and social reinforcement shaping (Becker, et al., 1978).

Social skill training with developmentally retarded sex offenders is even more critical since their level of social functioning is often very low (Murphy, Coleman, and Haynes, 1983). Similar techniques to those described above can be used with this population. However, the staff must begin at more basic skill levels and use more learning trials (Matson, 1980; Matson, Kazdin, and Esveldt-Dawson, 1978).

Psychological Models for Behavior Change. A psycho-educational module in this category would include presentation of certain personality or psychological models which offenders can use in describing their own personalities, their relationships, their learned maladaptive responses, and their goals for more adaptive behavior. Examples of such helpful models include but are not limited to Transactional Analysis, Rational Emotive Therapy, and Cognitive Behavioral Theories. The goals of this component would assist the offender in the following ways:

- Understanding specific models of intrapersonal and interpersonal dynamics/behavior which would be of assistance in understanding oneself and others more realistically.
- Demonstrating insight into oneself and others by relating current life experiences in terms of these models.

Autobiographical Awareness. Assigned autobiographies provide a method through which a participant can present a summary of key issues, patterns, or themes in his life which may have influenced his current lifestyle, assumptions, and coping patterns. The facilitator must avoid reinforcing "poor me" or "victim stance" responses from the offender, assisting the offender in distinguishing insight from excuse-making. Some goals of a module of this type include:

- Understanding oneself and others more clearly in terms of maladaptive, victim-creating behavior symptoms.
- Understanding which nonsexual needs may have been met through inappropriate sexual behavior.
- Reexamining and updating past history by replacing erroneous assumptions with current reality-based, pro-social beliefs.

Sex Education. Many sex offenders are poorly informed regarding human sexuality. They hold attitudes and myths which frequently reflect their lack of information. This, in turn, reinforces their avoidance of intimate mutually consenting sexual relationships and their treatment of victims as objects rather than as persons. Groth (1979) cites an example of one offender who claimed that raping a woman was better than consenting sex between two males because it was normal. Goals of a human sexuality psycho-educational module attempt to assist the offender in the following ways:

- Identifying myths, inaccurate unhealthy values, and/or role stereotypes which have obstructed healthy psychosexual and sex role development.

- Identifying how these beliefs/attitudes have related to deviant sexual acting-out.
- Replacing unhealthy beliefs or attitudes with constructive, nonvictim-creating beliefs or attitudes.

The content of human sexuality modules includes information on myths and misunderstandings regarding human sexuality, anatomy and physiology of sex, values and attitudes, reproduction, methods of contraception, sex roles and gender identity issues, masturbation, variations of sexual behavior involving mutuality and consent, and the relationship of fantasy to sexual behavior.

The Sex Knowledge Inventory (McHugh, 1979) can be used as a pre- and post-intervention measure for this module. For developmentally disabled sex offenders, the Sexual Knowledge Inventory (Edmondson, McCombs, and Wish, 1979) is available. In addition, the Essential Adult Sex Education Curriculum (Zelman and Tyster, 1979), was designed for the developmentally disabled (Murphy, et al., 1983).

Stress Reduction/Relaxation Management. Many sex offenders lack healthy, adaptive coping responses when they experience stress, anxiety, or frustration. For some offenders, the entry into their pre-assault pattern is their primary method of stress reduction. Others use some form of chemical abuse which, in turn, may be part of the pre-assault pattern. Consequently, goals of this module include the following objectives for the offender:

- Identifying the dimensions in which stress manifests itself in all aspects.
- Identifying the primary determinants of stress.
- Identifying the maladaptive methods used to cope with stress.
- Identifying how stress is involved in the pre-assault pattern.
- Identifying constructive alternatives to reduce external stress.
- Identifying and developing constructive methods of stress reduction and relaxation.
- Demonstrating competency in using those particular methods in terms of actual stress.

Chemical Abuse. Alcohol abuse has been found to be prevalent among sex offenders; however, its influence is best understood as a contributing factor which varies in importance according to the different types of sex offenders (Tracy, Donnelly, Morgenbesser, and MacDonald, 1983). In addition, the use of other chemicals can be involved as part of a sex offender's pre-assault pattern. Researchers agree, however, that while drugs may act as general disinhibitors of behavior, they do not account for the fact that an offender acts-out in a sexually deviant manner. Given the contributory relationship of chemical abuse with many sexual offenses, many treatment programs provide a module on chemical abuse for those who have an identified problem in this area. Goals for the offender to accomplish in such a module include:

- Accepting the reality of one's chemical abuse pattern.
- Identifying one's own dynamics/patterns of chemical abuse, especially as they relate to sexually deviant behavior.
- Developing a commitment to abstain from chemical use of any type.

- Developing interventions for Relapse Prevention.
- Establishing a support system in the community to augment strategies for Relapse Prevention.

Sexuality and Religious Belief Systems. Therapists who work with sex offenders are likely to encounter religious beliefs which may initially appear to complicate or even obstruct treatment efforts. In the development of their attitudes toward sexual expression, many offenders have struggled with the integration of their religious beliefs with their sexuality. They may have grown up with highly rigid and suppressive proscriptions against experiencing any sexual thoughts, emotions, or arousal. Others have distorted healthy religious precepts, using them improperly to instill exaggerated and unrelenting guilt, self-deprecation, depression, diminished self-esteem, and diffuse anger into their daily experience. Others, upon a conviction for sexually deviant behavior, profess instant healing and new life and a total lack of need for treatment since they have been cured spiritually. Finally, many offenders express in religious terminology a strong resistance toward homosexuality or masturbation as viable alternatives to their established patterns of sexual deviancy. They state that their beliefs allow for only the adult heterosexual expression of sexuality in the context of marriage.

These are some of the major issues which therapists for sex offenders are likely to encounter. It can be useful, in a module or group, to enlist one or more clergy or pastoral counselors sympathetic with program goals to join with the primary therapist in treatment. In that content, certain goals can be established which will assist the offender in the following ways:

- Identifying conflicts which may have developed over sexual identity and practice with spiritual beliefs.
- Resolving in a constructive manner religious concerns regarding behavioral treatment modalities.
- Reconciling and integrating a healthy concept of sexuality within one's spiritual belief system.
- Using spiritual beliefs and resources to establish a healthy foundation for victim-free behavior.

Conclusion

The use of psycho-educational modules as a topically focused, time-limited, and cost-effective intervention has been reviewed. This structured group method is widely used in many current sex offender treatment programs. These modules can be readily adapted to the needs of each specific population. Psycho-educational modules can be utilized as an appropriate and efficient introduction to a comprehensive treatment program.

References

Abel, G., Blanchard, E., and Becker, J. (1978). An integrated treatment program for rapists. In R. Rada (Ed.), *Clinical aspects of the rapist*. New York: Grune and Stratton.

Abel, G., Blanchard, E., and Becker, J. (1976). Psychological treatment of rapists. In S. Brodsky and M. Walker (Eds.), *Sexual assault*. Lexington, MA: Lexington Books.

Barlow, D., Abel, G., Blanchard, E., Bristow, A., and Young, L. (1977). A heterosocial skill checklist for males. *Behavior Therapy*, 8, 229-239.

Becker, J., Abel, G., Blanchard, E., Murphy, W., and Coleman, E. (1978). Evaluating social skills of sexual aggressives. *Criminal Justice and Behavior*, 5(4), 357-367.

Edmondson, B., McCombs, K., and Wish, J. (1979). What retarded adults believe about sex. *American Journal of Mental Deficiency*, 84, 11-18.

Ellis, A. and Brancale, R. (1956). *Psychology of sex offenders*. Springfield, IL: Thomas.

Finkelhor, D. (1984). *Child sexual abuse: New theory and research*. New York: The Free Press.

Groth, N. (1979). *Men who rape: The psychology of the offender*. New York: Plenum Press.

Marlatt, T. and Gordon, J. (Eds.) (1985). *Relapse prevention*. New York: The Guilford Press.

Matson, J. (1980). Acquisition of social skills by mentally retarded adults training programs. *Journal of Mental Deficiency and Research*, 24, 129-135.

Matson, J., Kazdin, A., and Esveldt-Dawson, K. (1980). Training interpersonal skills among mentally retarded and socially dysfunctional children. *Behavior Research and Therapy*, 18, 419-427.

McHugh, G. (1979). *Sex knowledge inventory (Form X)*. (rev. ed.) Saluda, NC: Family Life Publications, Inc.

Murphy, W., Coleman, E., and Haynes, M. (1983). Treatment and evaluation issues with the mentally retarded sex offender. In J. Greer and I. Stuart (Eds.), *The sexual aggressor: Current perspectives in treatment*. New York: Van Nostrand Reinhold Co.

Novaco, R. (1976). Therapist's manual for stress inoculation training: Therapeutic interventions for anger problems. Unpublished manuscript. University of California, Irvine.

Pithers, W., Marques, J., Gibat, C., and Marlatt, G. (1983). Relapse prevention with sexual aggressives: A self-control model of treatment and maintenance of change. In J. Greer and I. Stuart (Eds.), *The sexual aggressor: Current perspectives in treatment*. New York: Van Nostrand Reinhold Co.

Stevenson, I. and Wolpe, J. (1960). Recovery from sexual deviation through overcoming nonsexual neurotic responses. *American Journal of Psychiatry*, 116, 737-742.

Tracy, F., Donnelly, H., Morgenbesser, L., and MacDonald, D. (1983). Program evaluation: Recidivism research involving sex offenders. In J. Greer and I. Stuart (Eds.), *The sexual aggressor: Current perspectives in treatment*. New York: Van Nostrand Reinhold Co.

Truax, C. and Carkhuff, R. (1967). *Toward effective counseling and psychotherapy: Training and practice*. Chicago: Aldine.

Yochelson, S. and Samenow, S. (1976). *The criminal personality*. New York: Aronson.

Zelman, D. and Tyster, K. (1979). *Essential adult sex education for the mentally retarded*. Madison, WI: The Madison Opportunity Center.

Chapter 14

Group Therapy

by Barbara K. Schwartz, Ph.D.

Overview

Interpersonal techniques of treatment, which included individual and group psychotherapy, were the first approaches used in treating sexual deviants. For many years, psychoanalysis was the only approach available—and that was available only to the wealthiest. Around the turn of the century, Schrenk-Notzing, a German physician, established an institute to treat paraphiliacs with techniques such as hypnosis and various programs similar to the Outward Bound wilderness experiences currently used with offenders. Group experiences, both formal and informal, played an important part in that program. Many advances have been made using behavioral techniques to enhance the treatment of sex offenders, but interpersonal techniques, particularly group therapy, remain the core of almost all programs.

This chapter discusses techniques for dealing with the sex offender in group therapy. Major steps in treatment are outlined, as are specialized group techniques such as victim empathy training.

Individual Versus Group Therapy

Sexual deviation, even when not conceptualized as an addiction, certainly has much in common with the traditional addictions, particularly as regards denial, guilt, and secrecy. It is these characteristics that make sex offenders especially difficult to treat in individual therapy. Because these offenders often lie, minimize, and rationalize their behavior, it is quite a task for a lone therapist to muster the strength or the evidence to confront their defenses. Just as the use of groups in treating addictive disorders is viewed as particularly useful in breaking down barriers, so it is with the sex offender. The group members are able to recognize their own patterns and may provide confrontation and support far more effectively than could the individual therapist.

Individual therapy may replicate the dynamics of the sexual assault. The offender and the therapist are in a "secret" (confidential) relationship. The theme of the relationship deals with the sexually deviant conduct. The sex offender is fairly certain that no matter how graphically he retells his crime that the therapist will not flee the room or even show discomfort regardless of how he or she may actually feel. In fact, the more "truthful" the offender is about the details of his acts, his fantasies, even his fantasies about the therapist, the better patient he may be perceived to be. Many sex offenders have covertly sexually assaulted their individual therapist and exercised power and control in the relationship without the therapist being aware of the dynamics.

A recurrent problem for sex offenders is that they have great difficulty maintaining normal social relationships. The more aggressive ones demand that others meet their needs and if this does not happen, they act-out. The more passive individuals may be terrified to assert themselves enough to establish any type of relationship and so they turn to weaker, less threatening partners. Individual therapy does little to improve this because an individual therapeutic relationship does not replicate a social relationship. In fact, it may even reinforce an unrealistic standard. A good therapist by the usual criteria is understanding, fair, trustworthy, reliable, etc. A potential partner is much less consistent. A therapy group, however, is a much more realistic social unit because each member brings his interpersonal problems to the situation. In learning to cope with the interactional problems of various group members, the sex offender learns how to manage real life relationships.

Unfortunately, group therapy cannot always be conducted in a prison system. Offenders may doubt whether confidentiality is possible in such a setting. They may realize that in certain institutions, being stigmatized as a sex offender is tantamount to being given the death sentence. Other offenders are so socially isolated and inept that group participation is simply beyond their ability. Individuals who may have committed extremely bizarre crimes may need much individual work before they are ready for a group. There are also situations in institutions which may limit group therapy. Physical barriers such as lack of privacy or the lack of enough appropriate participants may preclude this form of treatment. In such cases, individual therapy may be the only choice, but this should only be utilized as a method of involving offenders until systematic changes can be made to facilitate group participation or to overcome the initial reticence and anxiety of the offender. It should also be noted that individual therapy perpetuates the "sexual secret" and may provide an opportunity for the offender to play at a seduction game, either in fantasy or reality. Individual therapy can be useful as an adjunct; however, it should be recognized that individual therapy may undermine group participation. The offender may be able to resist group pressure to open up if he can instead form an alliance with an individual therapist. The therapist, therefore, should constantly emphasize the importance and even pre-eminence of the group as the primary interpersonal treatment tool. Table 14.1 sets out the pros and cons of individual therapy.

History of the Use of Group Therapy

One of the earliest uses of group therapy was at Atascadero State Hospital in California, where a program known as the "Emotional Security Program" was instituted during the mid-1950s. Patients in the program participated in group therapy. Self-governing committees made important therapeutic decisions regarding the program participants (Schultz, 1965). Several prisons with inmates committed under Sexual Psychopathy Laws have offered group therapy, although this often has been simply a method to provide token treatment to large groups of inmates.

At Western State Hospital in Washington, offenders, desperate for treatment directed specifically toward their problems, approached Dr. George McDonald with a request to establish their own group therapy. This technique became known as Structured Self-Help. Often, no therapist was present. Instead, the therapist reviewed the session either on videotape or from notes made by a group member serving as a scribe. However, problems can easily arise as participants wrestle and abuse power in the group setting.

The first reported use of outpatient group therapy with sex offenders was conducted at Philadelphia General Hospital. Mostly, that program treated primarily exhibitionists who were on probation or parole. It was assumed initially that the sex offender has both a low tolerance for anxiety and a fear of authority. Therefore, in one-to-one treatment, the therapist would be viewed as an anxiety-arousing authority figure. Consequently, the patients would fail to show up or would withdraw into passive resistance (Peters and Roether, 1972). The program assumed that many trained therapists would have communication difficulties with individuals who have poor educations and limited verbal skills (Peters and Sadoff, 1971). Individuals convicted of sex offenses often show both of these characteristics. More intellectually and economically stable offenders may be able to avoid criminal convictions. The use of the group was viewed by the Philadelphia project as a means of helping to bridge the verbal, educational, and cultural gap between patient and therapist (Peters and Roether, 1972).

The groups acted to counteract the social isolation of the members. Communicating with others of his status tended to build up the member's self-esteem and subsequently his respect for others. The groups also acted to exert pressure in the direction of social conformity and to reinforce control of impulses (Peters and Sadoff, 1971).

Follow-up of the Philadelphia General Hospital project, comparing 92 offenders in group therapy with 75 under general supervision, found a recidivism rate of 1% for the patients treated in groups versus a 5% rate for the others. Of the general supervision group, 27% committed crimes other than sex offenses, as opposed to 3% of the group therapy patients (Peters, Pedigo, Steg, and McKenna, 1968).

Table 14.1
Pros and Cons of Individual Therapy

Pros	*Cons*
1. Provides more individual attention.	1. Therapist more easily manipulated.
2. May provide more confidentiality.	2. Denial may be more easily maintained.
3. May be used to develop trust and basic	3. Therapeutic dyad perpetuates the social skills for extremely with drawn or "sexual secret."
4. May be provided in variety of physical settings.	4. More opportunity for attempts at seduction on the part of the client.
5. May be used on short term basis overcome initial reticence and anxiety.	5. Less opportunity to practice to and develop social skills.
6. May be used where crime is extreme,unusual or stigmatized, e.g., sadism, coprophilia, necrophilia.	6. Less opportunity to learn empathy or help others.
7. May be used where offender is mentally retarded or mentally ill and has trouble cognitively functioning in a group or is disruptive.	7. Less therapeutic confrontation by peers.
	8. Creates unrealistic social expectations.
	9. May be dangerous for therapist.
	10. Is more costly.
	11. Undermines the power of the group or Therapeutic Community.
	12. Is not supported by research findings.

Unfortunately, further long-term follow-up showed a reversal in the trend. In two different studies conducted by the J.J. Peters Institute, the sex offenders who received probation and group therapy did worse than those who received probation alone (Peters and Roether, 1971; Peters, 1980). The reasons behind the dramatic reversal in the trend from 1968 to 1971 are unknown.

An interesting approach to dealing with the traumas found so frequently in the childhoods of sex offenders was developed at the Adult Diagnostic and Treatment Center at Avenel, New Jersey. Developed by Dr. William Pendergast, the technique is known as Reeducation of Attitudes and Repressed Emotions (ROARE). Of the rapists treated at this program, 90% were sexually abused during childhood (Pendergast, 1978). The method uses a marathon format and was conducted in the facility's fully equipped television studio where a tape was made of the session. With this technique, the group begins to confront the selected member, badgering him until he flies into a rage, at which point other members make physical contact with him. According to Pendergast, the individual then regresses to a reenactment of the memory of his own sexual trauma and undergoes a cathartic experience. Later, the tape of the session is reviewed with the therapist and the patient.

Stages of Group Therapy

Sex offender groups function much like any other groups in process, if not in content. Groups go through various stages and manifest various problems. These stages and problems may depend on whether the group is closed or open-ended. Most sex offender groups are open-ended as new members come into treatment and old members move on. Although this makes for constant change, it is unavoidable in most cases. It may even help members learn flexibility and how to cope with loss.

Groups have various stages of growth including: forming, norming, storming, and performing. Silence may be the initial norm and the facilitator may wish to introduce some simple trust-building exercises. In the "norming" stage, the group or group member may begin exploring the boundaries of the unit. What are the rules? Are they enforced? What can one get away with? In the "storming" stage there is a good deal of conflict as individuals challenge the leader, jockey for status, and begin initial confrontation. Some groups remain stuck in this stage or retreat into dependency or passivity. In the "performing" stage the group coalesces and begins real therapeutic interactions.

Program planners are faced with deciding whether the groups should be structured or unstructured. It has been this author's experience that, because the entire concept of group therapy is so threatening to incarcerated individuals, the intentional structuring of groups tends to be a good introductory technique. Utilizing lectures, audiovisual aids, guest speakers, and workbook materials can allow the participants to begin processing highly threatening and emotionally arousing materials without being preoccupied with issues of trust and confidentiality. As the materials are discussed, emotionally charged issues tend to emerge until the group needs less structure or individuals are transferred to more advanced groups.

Building a Functioning Group

When sex offender groups are conducted outside of a therapeutic community, care must be exercised to protect the members. If the other inmates identify a certain building, office, or therapist as associated with the sex offender program, then there will be a stigma attached to that place or program. Therefore, other less controversial activities should be scheduled for that place and/or assigned to that staff member. Expanding the program to include other types of offenders is another way of minimizing this problem. Many psycho-educational classes/groups can be offered to the general population without sacrificing their value for the sex offender. This is especially valuable with issues such as family dynamics where common histories of abuse can be processed by sex offenders and non-sex offenders together. An empathy may develop that leads to more acceptance of sex offenders by the general population.

Therapeutic communities can even include a mix of sex offenders and non-sex offenders who have other issues such as substance abuse in common. However, the participants must agree to accept each other regardless of offense. Additionally, specialized treatment must still be provided to the sex offenders.

Process of Group Therapy

Dealing With Denial. The course of sex offender treatment seems to be fairly predictable. Most of these individuals respond to accusations with denial. If they were not caught actually committing the act, they plead innocence for a variety of offenses because either they were not the offender, or the act involved mutual consent and the victim is playing a vindictive game, they were too drunk to know what happened but they are sure that they never could have done such a thing, or they were "set-up" by another adult who had some motive for hurting them. If the offender was caught in the act, it was all a terrible misunderstanding. The therapist or the treatment program staff must carefully evaluate how much of their resources can be expended on breaking down denial. Individuals who claim that the situation was one of mistaken identity are rarely successfully confronted. Programs or therapists sometimes choose to treat only those making a full confession. However, paper-thin defenses will crumble once the individual understands that the therapist will not reject him and brand him as a sex-crazed pervert.

Ignoring Deniers. One way of coping with denial is to simply ignore it. One may place an individual in a group and deliberately keep the focus away from the denier. He may bond with the group and even begin to contribute around other members' issues. As he begins to trust the group, his denial may begin to crumble. Locking horns with an offender in denial may back him into an intractable stance.

Some programs offer orientation sessions that utilize paradoxical intent. The offender is specifically instructed not to discuss his offense. He is then inundated with information regarding sexual assault, its dynamics, its effect on victims, and so forth. By the end of the session, which may last for several hours a week and up to four weeks, the participants may often be barely able to contain the urge to relate the material to their own behavior.

Hypnosis. Hypnosis may be useful in breaking down denial. Occasionally, an individual may have truly repressed the details of the offense and may be able to retrieve them under hypnosis. Alternatively, even if the participant does not actually enter a trance state and recover unconscious material, the procedure may provide him with a face-saving way to admit to material which he consciously denied. Later in his treatment he should be held accountable for lying about the incident.

Confrontation. The best time to confront the offender in denial is when he is at his most vulnerable. An individual who has maintained his innocence is at his most vulnerable on his first night following a guilty verdict. If a system can be devised in which a representative of the treatment program meets with him then, he can be offered the treatment program as a supportive activity to pursue while serving his sentence or, in the case of residential programs, a safe place to do his time. Often people who enter treatment with the most banal of reasons emerge as the most committed.

Inducing Guilt. Once denial is broken down, there may or may not be empathy for the victim. Here, it is helpful to utilize the many victim accounts, written or available as audiotapes or movies, to educate the offender as to the effects of sexual assault. At this point, it is the therapist's job to induce guilt. This is the most dangerous point in the therapy. The offender may re-erect his defenses. He may become seriously depressed, even suicidal. He may unleash vast quantities of anger and frustration onto the therapist.

While the feelings of shame and self-recrimination experienced at this point may be a healthy sign of empathy, offenders cannot be permitted to wallow in interminable guilt. At times offenders turn this process into a type of self-pity which stultifies progress. This person may claim that he cannot deal with the issue because he feels so sorry, so remorseful that he wants to kill himself. The therapist must attempt to discriminate between true emotional responsiveness and sentimentality, which is one of Samenow's criminal thought patterns (Yochelson and Samenow, 1976).

Using Guilt as a Motivational Force. Guilt can serve as the motivating force behind the inquiry into the dynamics of the crime. Referring to an earlier theory outlining this author's theory of sexual deviation, the process now becomes one of exploring the motivational reservoir (see Chapter 3). This may include family dynamics, childhood victimization, developmental difficulties, traumas in later sexual experiences, as well as attitudes, values, and beliefs. Having the offender write an extensive autobiography is often helpful. At this point, exploration of deviant fantasies can begin. It is usually best to wait until the offender has a realization of how devastating and deep-rooted his behavior is before starting on the behavioral techniques. Even without the use of physiological assessment techniques, one can do some behavioral reconditioning. Covert sensitization, masturbatory satiation, and thought stoppage can be utilized if the individual is highly motivated. Whenever possible, physiological measurements should be used to assess progress in modifying deviant arousal.

The last stage of therapy should focus on strengthening the floodgates, as described in Chapter 3. By this time, the individual should have begun to have an awareness of his deviant cycle, and Relapse Prevention techniques can be taught. He may have to learn assertiveness training, anger management, or social skills. He may have to confront the criminal thought patterns which have enabled him to rationalize his abuse of others or begin to deal with other addictive behaviors. Most important, he must understand that as a person he will always be at risk regarding this type of behavior and must be forever vigilant.

Different Types of Groups

Sex offender groups have many common goals. Costell and Yalom in discussing group therapy for sex offenders state that group psychotherapy provides an arena in which their symptoms or offenses may be translated into the interpersonal context and in which disturbed interpersonal relationships may be appreciated, understood, and altered. The group is able to provide the participants with motivation, hope, and the realization that their individual problems are not unique, as well as an opportunity to help others. The members can develop socializing techniques, utilize positive role models, and experience emotional release (Resnik and Wolfgang, 1972, p. 119).

However, groups may utilize many different theoretical foundations and formats. Some groups, such as those at Minnesota's Transitional Sex Offender Program, have a psychodynamic structure. Others, such as those at Northwest Treatment Associates in Seattle, Washington, have a Relapse Prevention orientation with a very structured format. Some groups use a cognitive restructuring model based on Yochelson and Samenow's (1976) work. Most programs do incorporate several different types of treatment techniques and thus it would be extremely difficult to contrast the efficacy of various techniques. The one approach which does appear to have been all but totally abandoned is exclusive reliance on long-term individual psychoanalysis.

At the Oregon State Hospital program, the group is highly involved in helping its member recognize and record their own individual deviant cycles. Each individual's cycle is divided into two parts: recognition of his deviant arousal pattern coupled with his observable behaviors and thought processes during that cycle. This information is recorded on large charts posted around the group room, and all members are expected to recognize and confront an individual who slips into that cycle. Because these individuals can earn community passes, it is important that each group member closely monitor his peers. These individuals are well aware that one individual's deviant behavior can destroy a program, as it did at Atascadero.

Sexaholics/Sex Addicts Anonymous. Carnes' (1983) work on sexual addiction led to the founding of Sexaholics/Sex Addicts Anonymous groups throughout the country. These groups adapt the 12-step approach used by Alcholics Anonymous. A variety of curriculum packets geared to this approach are available, and volunteers who are active in the community may be recruited to establish self-help groups within programs. These groups can also provide a natural transitional program for offenders being released to larger communities.

Victim Empathy Groups. Empathy for others is one of the basic mechanisms that helps control negative impulses. Offenders as a group lack empathy for a variety of reasons. For one thing, there is little opportunity to develop empathy for the victim once the offender is arrested. For another, the offender may or may not ever see the victim again. Also, an offender who goes on trial may be entirely focused on renouncing everything the victim says and attempting to impugn the victim's character. Programs take different approaches to helping offenders experience the impact of their behavior on the lives of others.

Empathy-focused groups should begin in a slow, nonthreatening way in order to avoid the retreat into defense mechanisms caused when offenders are flooded with guilt. Both professional and personal victim account books currently are available. Offenders often start out with materials available through local rape crisis centers that deal with the rape trauma syndrome and child sexual assault and then move on to personal accounts, such as Brady's *Father's Days* (1981) or Morris's *If I Should Die Before I Wake* (1982). Movies further personalize the trauma of the victim. Films such as *Something About Amelia* and the Canadian Film Board's *A Scream from Silence* and *A Matter of Consent* are excellent dramatic presentations. If the group is working up to direct victim confrontation, *Rape! Face-to-Face* is another excellent documentary. The therapist may prepare an audiotape based on police reports or on victim impact statements which retell the event from the victim's perspective. This can be expanded into role playing with the offender playing the role of the victim.

The cooperation of local victim groups should be actively sought. If counselors of victims can present the offending behavior from the victim's viewpoint, it can have an impressive emotional and intellectual impact.

The final stage is an actual confrontation between victims and offenders. This is usually done with victims of different offenders. It is important that the victims are fully oriented to the entire experience—everything from procedures for entering the prison to the goals and techniques of the sex offender program. If at all possible, they should come in as a group, accompanied by their counselor so that they may later have the maximum opportunity to process the experience. The offenders should be fully prepared for the amount of rage which will probably be directed at them. This technique should only be used with advanced groups where the members have abandoned their denial and are able to cope with their anger and the anger of others.

In this author's former program at Twin Rivers Corrections Center in Monroe, Washington, a therapist contacted the program requesting that she be allowed to bring the members of an Incest Survivor's group to the prison for a confrontation session. This was arranged and the group faced a carefully chosen group of incest perpetrators. Because the offenders were able to tolerate the rage of the survivors, the survivors group returned and they returned again, and again once a month, and then twice a month for three years. Not only did the offenders benefit by being faced with the repercussions of their behavior, but the victims benefited as well. The program itself was able to provide free treatment for the survivors. The group dynamics were fascinating as over time the two factions discovered that their common experiences outweighed their differences and they bonded on a very deep level.

Whenever possible, group energies should be directed toward assisting community efforts in combating sexual assault. The group may make video presentations aimed at the general public or at potential offenders. They might raise money to contribute to an agency working with victims or, as individuals, voluntarily agree to pay or increase restitution to their victims. They might connect with programs for juvenile offenders, either by contributing money, sharing resources, or exchanging video tapes. Caution should be exercised not to allow personal relationships to develop between adult and juvenile perpetrators.

Speciality Groups. A comprehensive treatment program may identify issues that only apply to a sub-group of the population or that need special attention but cannot be adequately accommodated in a primary group. Victims' confrontation group such as the one described above are examples of such groups. Individuals who have other major issues such as substance abuse, mental illness, or Vietnam War Post-Traumatic Stress Disorder can be assigned to specialty groups within an institution or referred for adjunct community treatment as long as there is adequate cooperation between the various therapists.

Individuals struggling with their sexual orientation or individuals who are "coming out of the closet" also can benefit from support groups focused on these issues. Volunteers from the gay men's community can be particularly helpful in serving as appropriate role models.

Specialty groups do not only focus on specific issues. They may focus on specific techniques that reinforce basic sex offender issues. Behavioral techniques can be processed in a group format. For instance, art, music, and drama therapy can focus on victim empathy, Relapse Prevention, and/or cognitive distortions.

Devoting Time to the Offender's Own Victimization

There is a major conflict in the field of sex offender treatment as to what percentage of offenders have been the victim of childhood sexual abuse or other early trauma and how much time should be devoted to dealing with the offender's own victimization and early traumas. Programs range from focusing almost exclusively on this to forbidding any discussion whatsoever.

The Integrative Approach (see Chapter 1) demands that all aspects of an individual be considered in planning treatment including any childhood sexual abuse or other early trauma. If these issues play a significant role in the dynamics of the offense, they must be dealt with—to do otherwise is to promote denial. A favorite rationalization for child molesters who themselves sustained abuse is "It didn't hurt me. I didn't think it would hurt them [the victims]." For the therapist to minimize the offender's own victimization is to reinforce the denial that leads to the offending behavior.

Logistics of Providing Treatment. The logistics of providing treatment for the offender's victimization may be tricky. The issue is whether treatment should be part of the regular group or a specialty group. It is recommended that if the regular group is doing autobiographies as part of its format that initial processing of early trauma be in that context. However, an individual who needs more intensive work in this area may be referred to a specialty group. It is not recommended that sex offenders in early stages of treatment in the community be referred to regular Survivor's Groups or Adult Children of Alcoholics (ACOA) groups. These community groups may not be prepared to accept an offender, particularly if that person still is wrestling with offender issues and is in denial or is minimizing and justifying his or her own assaultive behavior. After finishing treatment, the offender may be able to fit in with such a group provided he is able to accept the possible negative reception he might initially receive.

Another important issue is when offenders should be treated for their own victimization. Some programs insist that participants deal with their offender issues first and in a sense "earn the right" to deal with their own issues. Individuals who start off dealing with their own issues may get stuck there and continue to wallow in self-pity, blaming their abusers rather than taking responsibility for their own behavior. Others, however, are so emotionally repressed over their own abuse that they cannot begin to develop empathy for their victims for fear that they will be overwhelmed by their own trauma. In these cases identifying the trauma that resulted from their own victimization may facilitate the recognition of the trauma they have caused others.

Offender's Victimization Must Be Linked to Victim's Trauma. A primary principle in treating offenders' own victimization is to continually link it to their own victims. The therapist must continually intertwine the offender's feelings of fear, powerlessness, and anger to how his victims must have felt. However, the therapist should be careful not to be so confrontational that the offender becomes defensive and blocks out the effect.

This type of treatment is not intended to facilitate a victim stance on the part of the offender. Believing that one is a "victim" can lead to the rationalization of even the most outrageous behavior. One must recognize and acknowledge the trauma, move past the initial rage and resentment, grieve the loss and the injustice, and then learn to become a survivor.

Treatment of Offender and Family Members

Family therapy can be utilized with sex offenders in several ways. In the more general context, it is a modality that should be made available to every sex offender involved in a comprehensive program. The anger and resentment toward women characteristic of the rapist and the fear and immaturity associated with many pedophiles are often associated with dysfunctional family interactions that may still be occurring or are replicated in other relationships. The work being done with adult children of alcoholics has expanded to include individuals raised in a variety of disturbed familial environments and may be directly applicable to many sex offenders. Working on issues of grief, anger, and forgiveness may assist in freeing the offender from his pattern of displacing his rage onto innocent victims. Learning new communication techniques is vital, not only in improving existing relationships but in building a support system which can be utilized to interrupt the deviant cycle. Improving marital relationships, both sexual and nonsexual, will assist in reinforcing appropriate outlets. Conjugal visits, where allowed, can be utilized as part of the therapeutic process. In situations where this is not an option, traditional marital, conjoint, or family therapy can be employed as well as couples or family groups, which can be either educational, therapeutic, or a combination of both. Dr. N. Steele's former program at Lino Lakes, Minnesota features at least one family session where all members of the extended family participate in an attempt to help them understand the offender's situation and to provide additional information about his background.

Another type of family therapy reinforces Relapse Prevention. When family members as well as all members of an offender's support system are fully aware of his re-offense cycle, they can act to reinforce it. In conducting this type of group, certain family and support system members who acknowledge the offender's guilt and are willing and able to assist him are educated in the offender's Relapse Prevention Plan including his high risk situations and his interventions. This type of monitoring is more fully explained in Chapter 20.

Another way to provide treatment to family members is to focus more specifically on their needs. Who could possibly be more shunned and emotionally isolated than the wife of an incarcerated rapist or child molester? Not only does she find herself lonely, bereft of emotional and possibly financial support, and angry not only at a violation of the law and the marital contract, but she is subtly blamed by society and possibly herself. After all, it is a common misconception that sex crimes are perpetuated by sex-starved individuals who are deprived of suitable gratification. Therefore, who else is to blame but the partner who failed in some way to provide suitable sexual satisfaction? This unfounded guilt may be compounded by real sexual trauma related to her own victimization. There are no studies at present on the incidence of marital rape in families of rapists, but it may be quite high. In this author's experience, wives of sex offenders had a phenomenally high rate of childhood sexual abuse, with up to 80% being victims of incest. These individuals may also be entangled in co-dependent relations with their spouse's acting-out. Carnes's (1983) work on the addiction model of sexual deviancy provides valuable insights into working with co-dependency in these situations.

Another, more specific way of dealing with families is in the area of incest. Perhaps the best known work in the field has been done by Henry Giarretto, Ph.D., of the Institute for the Community as Extended Family, Child Sexual Abuse Treatment Program (CSATP) in San Jose, California (Mayer, 1985). This program is community-based, providing group treatment to the offender, wife, and victim(s). Self-help is provided through Parents United, Daughters and Sons United, and Adults Molested as Children United. Giarretto (personal communication, 1984) reports:

- About 90% of the children avoid foster or institutional placement and are reunited with their families.
- The recidivism rate among father-offenders has remained at less than 1%.
- Child victims treated by CSATP do not persist in the self-abusive behavior reported by adults who were molested as children who did not receive individual and family therapy.

While one advantage of this program is that it is largely community-based, the fathers often serve an initial period in jail, and are released on furloughs to attend treatment. Sex offender programs in jails or in minimum security facilities may be able to take advantage of similar programs throughout the country. Where community participation of this sort is not possible, programs may still be provided for families. Marital and family therapy can be arranged in most settings, and marital and family groups meeting at least once a month are incorporated into many programs. It should be remembered that in states without sex offender treatment programs even incest offenders with supportive family systems amenable to treatment may end up in prison. In states with programs which interact with the courts and social service departments to provide alternatives to incarceration, offenders serving prison sentences for incest may primarily be antisocial individuals with prior criminal records or fixated pedophiles who have long histories within and outside the family patterns of child molestations. Neither of these types is particularly suited to family-centered therapy aimed at family reconciliation.

Therapeutic Correctional Communities

Therapeutic communities are residential programs whose aim focuses on rehabilitation rather than mere incarceration. All staff involved with these residents become part of the treatment team, and every aspect of daily interaction becomes the focus of therapeutic intervention. The Therapeutic Communities Association has issued a definition for such programs (see Figure 14.1).

Fenton, Reimer, and Wilmer (1967) describe such correctional communities as "a method of social therapy in which staff and inmates make a conscious effort to utilize all experiences in all areas of their lives in a therapeutic manner" (p. 1). These authors point out that the staff in a typical institution influences the residents in only one specialized area, such as security, mental health, education. This creates an environment that is ripe for manipulation and for playing staff members against each other. In a correctional community, all staff play a therapeutic role with individual disciplines uniting in common goals. The residents form a community that holds its members accountable.

Incarcerated individuals usually deal with their imprisonment with suppression, rationalization, anger at society, withdrawal, and/or manipulation (Fenton, Reimer and Wilmer, 1967). Institutions filled with these individuals may adapt many of these same characteristics. The staff may be isolated from each other, deviant behaviors may become the norm, and antisocial values may become predominant. Therapeutic communities can combat many of these trends. For perhaps the first time in their lives, program participants are exposed to a group of people who cooperate and communicate. An expression and acceptance of emotions are valued, and an atmosphere is created where the appropriate expression of emotion is reinforced, resulting in an atmosphere of mutual help. This is particularly important for the sex offender who may be unable to find other residents to confide in due to the nature of their crime.

Staff must learn to function in ways that are alien to the traditional correctional model; their role is that of adviser rather than enforcer. Even when in an authority role, the staff member needs to be able to explain the meaning behind the rules and enlist the cooperation rather than the coercion of the community.

The community must begin to assume responsibility for the conduct of its members. Initially, this may fly in the face of the most basic prison code—the dictate against "snitching." The members must come to appreciate how the conduct of one reflects upon all the others. The very existence of the community relies on the degree to which its members are willing to confront one another. This becomes increasingly the case if community release is part of the program. For this reason, therapeutic communities such as the one at Oregon State Hospital force members to learn everyone's deviant cycle and to confront each other when that cycle surfaces.

To date, therapeutic communities for sex offenders only exist in a few states, including Oregon, Minnesota, Washington, Wisconsin, Massachusetts, and Vermont. Other states house sex offenders together but not in therapeutic communities.

A number of factors determine whether a therapeutic community could or should be established in a prison setting. A primary duty of any institution is to make sure that its residents are physically safe. Because the existence of a therapeutic community for sex offenders would stigmatize the residents, each state's corrections department must determine whether this is a wise undertaking. One factor that must be considered is whether the personality of the prison will allow residents to be segregated from the rest of the prison population without depriving them of other services, such as educational opportunities and recreational facilities. The personality of an institution may change drastically due to factors such as overcrowding or media attention that results from a sensational sex crime. Any situation that increases tension among the residents will be reflected in the treatment of sex offenders by the rest of the population.

Where therapeutic communities are possible, they are cost-effective and provide a facilitative environment in which psychological and social growth may occur. It should also be noted that if these programs are not constantly monitored and revitalized they may become just another cell-block with a fancy name.

Figure 14.1
Definition: Therapeutic Community

The primary goal of a Therapeutic Community is to foster personal growth. This is accomplished by changing an individual's lifestyle through a community of concerned people working together to help themselves and each other.

The Therapeutic Community represents a highly structured environment with defined boundaries, both moral and ethical. It employs community imposed sanctions and penalties as well as earned advancement of status and privileges as part of the recovery and growth process. Being part of something greater than oneself is an especially important factor in facilitating positive growth.

People in a Therapeutic Community (T.C.) are members, as in any family setting, not patients, as in an institution. These members play a significant role in managing the T.C. and acting as positive role models for others to emulate.

Members and staff act as facilitators, emphasizing personal responsibility for one's own life and for self-improvement. The members are supported by staff as well as being serviced by staff, and there is a sharing of meaningful labor so that there is a true investment in the community, sometimes for the purpose of survival.

Peer pressure is often the catalyst that converts criticism and personal insight into positive change. High expectations and high commitment from both members and staff support this positive change. Insight into one's problems is gained through group and individual interaction, but learning through experience, failing and succeeding and experiencing the consequences, is considered to be the most potent influence toward achieving lasting change.

The T.C. emphasizes the integration of an individual within this community, and the progress is measured within the context of that community against that community's expectations. It is this community, along with the individual, that accomplishes the process of positive change in the member. The tension created between the individual and this community eventually resolves in favor of the individual, and this transition is taken as an important measure of readiness to move toward integration into the larger society.

Authority is both horizontal and vertical, encouraging the concept of sharing responsibility, and supporting the process of participating in decision making when this is feasible and consistent with the philosophy and objectives of the Therapeutic Community.

—*from the Therapeutic Communities Association credentialing packet*

Conclusion

In conclusion, sexual offenses are violations of interpersonal relations. They represent a violation of trust, betrayal of intimacy, and dissolution of boundaries. Treatment must involve establishing an awareness of what appropriate relations represent. Often sex offenders have little, if any, awareness of normalcy in this area. Violated as children, abused or neglected, many have little opportunity to observe and learn anything other than exploitive interactions. Relearning involves confrontation, acknowledging one's own pain, and generalizing this recognition to the pain of others. It then involves relearning how to change one's thought patterns, appropriately channel one's emotions, and control one's behavior.

References

Anderson, R.E. (1969). The exchange of tape recordings as a catalyst in group psychotherapy with sex offenders. *International Journal of Group Therapy, 19*, 214-217.

Brady, K. (1981). *Father's days*. New York: Dell.

Carnes, P. (1983). *Out of the shadows*. Minneapolis: CompCare.

Costell, R.B. and Yalom, I.D. (1972). Institutional group therapy. In H.L. Resnik and M.E. Wolfgang (Eds.), *Sexual behaviors: Social, clinical and legal aspects*. Boston: Little, Brown and Co.

Fenton, N., Reimer, E.G., and Wilmer, H.A. (1967). *The correctional community: An introduction and guide*. Berkeley: University of California Press.

Marcus, A.M. (1971). *Nothing is my number: An exploratory study of dangerous sex offenders in Canada*. Toronto: General Publishing.

Mayer, A. (1985). *Sexual abuse: Causes, consequences and treatment of incestuous and pedophilic acts*. Holmes Beach, FL: Learning Publications, Inc.

Morris, M. (1982). *If I should die before I wake*. Los Angeles: Tarcher.

Pendergast, W. (1978, January). Paper presented at ROARE Conference, University of Tennessee.

Peters, J.J. Institute (1980). *A ten-year follow-up of sex offender recidivism*. Philadelphia: Author.

Peters, J.J., Pedigo, J., Steg, J., and McKenna, J. (1968). Group psychotherapy of the sex offender. *Federal Probation, 32*, 41-46.

Peters, J.J. and Roether, H.A. (1971). *Success and failure of sex offenders*. Philadelphia: AATS.

Peters, J.J. and Roether, H.A. (1972). Group psychotherapy for probationed sex offenders. In H.L. Resnick and M.E. Wolfgang (Eds.), *Sexual behaviors: Clinical and legal aspects*. Boston: Little, Brown and Co.

Peters, J.J. and Sadoff, R. (1971). Psychiatric services for sex offenders on probation. *Federal Probation, 35*, 33-37.

Resnick, H.L. and Wolfgang, M.E. (Eds.) (1972). *Sexual behaviors: Social, clinical and legal aspects*. Boston: Little, Brown and Co.

Schultz, G. (1965). *How many more victims?* Philadelphia: Lippincott.

Yochelson, S. and Samenow, S.E. (1976). *The criminal personality, Vol. 1*. New York: Aronson.

Chapter 15

Behavioral Techniques to Alter Sexual Arousal

by Michael J. Dougher, Ph.D.

Overview

The behavioral techniques discussed in this chapter are those that have been used to alter patterns of sexual arousal with sex offenders. Specifically, these techniques are used to increase arousal to appropriate sexual stimuli and to decrease arousal to deviant or inappropriate sexual stimuli. While appropriate and inappropriate sexual stimuli and activities are culturally defined, in the context of this paper "inappropriate sexual stimuli" are those which involve children, or exploitive, or violent sexual activities. "Appropriate sexual stimuli" are those involving consenting adults in non-exploitive or nonviolent activities.

Sexual arousal is the focus of intervention in many sex offender programs simply because it is believed to be a factor in sexually abusive behavior (Laws and Osborn, 1983; Quinsey and Marshall, 1983; Finkehor, 1984; Laws, 1984). No claim is made that it is the case that sex offenders of various types can be differentiated from each other and from nonoffenders on the basis of their patterns of sexual arousal (Quinsey, Steinman, Bergerson, and Holmes, 1975; Abel, Blanchard, Becker, and Djenderedjian, 1978; Quinsey, Chaplin, and Varney, 1981; Laws and Osborn, 1983; Laws, 1984). Moreover, a reduction of deviant sexual arousal does enjoy some measure of predictive validity in terms of recidivism rates among offenders and allows for more predictability of post-therapy success than any other measure yet developed (Quinsey and Marshall, 1983).

The purpose of this chapter is to briefly describe the behavioral methods and the mechanisms underlying their effectiveness. The clinician will be provided with suggestions for the implementation of these therapeutic methods. The behavioral techniques discussed are covert sensitization, assisted covert sensitization, olfactory conditioning, the satiation therapies, aversive behavioral rehearsal, and arousal reconditioning. The first five methods are designed to decrease inappropriate arousal; arousal reconditioning is utilized to increase appropriate arousal patterns.

Theoretical Bases for Behavioral Techniques

These techniques have a reasonably good track record. Three reviews of the research on sex offender treatment suggest that behavioral interventions appear to have the best success rate (Kelly, 1982; Kilmann, Sabalis, Gearing, Bukstel, and Scovern, 1982; Lanyon, 1986). While there are more and better studies examining the effectiveness of behavioral techniques, there is still a relative lack of adequately controlled treatment outcome studies. Obviously, more research is needed in this important area.

There has been some controversy, or at least disagreement, about how these procedures actually work. For example, Cautela (1967), the developer of covert sensitization, views this procedure as an imagery-based operant or instrumental punishment procedure. Rachman and Teasdale (1969) argue that these stimuli function as conditioned suppressors which inhibit sexual arousal. Neither of these explanations has fared well. In a series of experiments, Dougher, Crossen, Ferraro, and Garland (1986a, 1987, 1988) have shown the Cautela assumption to be untenable. Also, Quinsey (1973) has shown that the formulation of Rachman and Teasdale is not supported by the results of clinical studies using these procedures. As an alternative, Dougher, et al. (1987, 1988) suggest that covert sensitization is a classical counterconditioning procedure by which means deviant sexual stimuli simply lose their capacity to reinforce sexual behavior. The experimental findings support this explanation.

While this discussion may seem to be primarily academic and theoretical, there is real significance for the practical use of these procedures. It is suggested that these procedures must be implemented according to the parameters of classical conditioning. Failure to adhere to these theoretical parameters may result in ineffective treatment interventions.

A final word before turning to the techniques. Except for arousal reconditioning, all of the techniques discussed here are examples of counterconditioning procedures in that they attempt to reduce deviant sexual arousal by pairing sexually deviant stimuli with unpleasant stimuli. Because of this, it is essential that they be used with strict adherence to ethical and legal guidelines, such as prevailing consent decrees or court orders. Informed consent must include detailed descriptions of the procedures and possible side effects. Clear criteria for termination of the procedures should be developed, and a clear rationale for their use should be given.

Types of Techniques

Covert Sensitization. Covert sensitization was first developed by Cautela in 1966 and has been used to treat a wide variety of disorders, including alcoholism, obesity, smoking, and sexual deviance (Cautela and Kearney, 1986). A number of studies have reported the successful use of covert sensitization procedures with sex offenders and the reader is referred to them for procedural details (Barlow, Agras, Leitenberg, Callahan, and Moore, 1972; Callahan and Leitenberg, 1973; Harbert, Barlow, Hersen, and Austin, 1974; Brownell, Hayes, and Barlow, 1977; Barlow and Abel, 1981; Kelly, 1982; Laws and Osborn, 1983).

Essentially, covert sensitization is an imagery-based counterconditioning procedure in which clients are instructed to imagine some deviant sexual act or stimulus followed by the imagining of some negative reaction, usually either severe anxiety, terror, or nausea. In the fantasy, the imaginary pairing is often accompanied by relief from the imagined aversion, contingent upon the offender's turning away from the deviant act or stimulus. Avoidance scenes are also employed in which offenders curb negative images by imagining themselves avoiding deviant acts and stimuli.

Scenes should be constructed individually for each offender according to his sexual fantasies and specific nausea response. (The reader is referred to Abel, Blanchard, and Becker (1978) for a detailed covert sensitization scene with a rapist.) However, scenes should use words and descriptions that are arousing to the offender, and the characteristics of the victim and nature of the sexual activity should fit his fantasies and previous offenses. Descriptions of sexual arousal and nausea (or anxiety) should be graphic, and emphasis should be given to detailed descriptions of bodily reactions rather than the stimuli that elicit them.

In line with the theoretical processes underlying covert sensitization, the procedure must use nausea scenes that function as unconditioned stimuli. By themselves, these scenes must elicit strong nausea reactions. Offenders should be observed to grimace, swallow, squirm, and show general signs of nausea. If possible, it is useful to measure physiological correlates of nausea, such as heart rate, skin conductance levels, or respiration. With repeated presentations, the nausea scene should be introduced progressively earlier in the deviant sexual scene until it is introduced upon the first mention of deviant sexual arousal. If an offender is unable to clearly imagine the deviant scene or generate nausea to the nausea scene, conditioning will not occur and the treatment will not be effective.

While the duration of the scenes varies somewhat, typical presentations are about two to three minutes. The number of scene presentations per session also varies, but it is not uncommon to find as many as 10-15 scenes per session. Care must be taken, however, to avoid habituation. There are also no clear guidelines in the literature regarding the number of scenes that should be presented to ensure maximum efficacy. Forty scenes is common, but psychophysiological measures of arousal should be used to be sure that the procedures have, in fact, produced significant decreases in deviant sexual arousal. In addition, booster sessions should be scheduled about six months after treatment (Maletzky, 1977).

Assisted Covert Sensitization. Assisted covert sensitization was first used as treatment for a sexual offense by Maletzky (1974). It is used to enhance the effects of covert sensitization, especially when the offender is not capable of generating sufficiently strong nausea reactions to make basic covert sensitization effective. Assisted covert sensitization employs a noxious odor to aid in the development of a nausea response. Different sources of noxious odors have been used, but most procedures use valeric acid or cultured (rotting) placenta. These odors can engender particularly strong nausea reactions.

The underlying mechanisms of assisted covert sensitization can be safely assumed to be similar to basic covert sensitization. Accordingly, the same parameters should be followed. That is, pairing should continue until deviant arousal is significantly reduced. Maletzky (1974) reports satisfactory results with an outpatient population using 10-12 bimonthly office sessions, coupled with 15-25 triweekly "homework" sessions during which clients are instructed to practice the techniques in extra therapy sessions. Booster sessions may be warranted about six months after treatment.

Olfactory Conditioning. Olfactory conditioning is very similar to assisted covert sensitization except that clients are not required to imagine either sexually deviant or nausea scenes. Instead, inappropriate sexual stimuli are presented to clients via slides, audiotapes, or videotapes, followed by the presentation of a noxious odor. The first report of the use of olfactory conditioning was by Laws, Meyer, and Holmen (1978). Since then it has been used by Marshall, Keltner, and Griffiths (1974) as a treatment with two cases of fetishism. Although a promising technique, more research is needed to be sure of its long-term effectiveness and limitations.

The Satiation Therapies. Two particularly promising techniques for reducing inappropriate sexual arousal are masturbatory satiation (Marshall and Lippens, 1977; Marshall and Barbaree, 1978; Marshall, 1979; Abel and Annon, 1982) and verbal satiation (Laws and Osborn, 1982).

Masturbatory satiation involves first having the offender masturbate to ejaculation to an appropriate sexual fantasy. The offender should be required to verbalize the fantasy aloud to be sure that the fantasy is, in fact, appropriate. The offender should be encouraged to embellish the appropriate fantasy with feelings of affection, tenderness, and warmth. Following this, the offender is required to continue masturbating for a period ranging from fifty minutes to two hours while verbalizing deviant fantasies. At times, the continued masturbation will result in arousal, at which time the offender is instructed to switch to an appropriate fantasy. This process can be minimized if the offender is required to masturbate to ejaculation twice to appropriate fantasies before beginning the satiation procedure. Abel and Annon (1982) report significant reductions in deviant arousal within 12 sessions.

Verbal satiation procedures are similar to masturbatory satiations, except that the offender is simply required to continuously verbalize deviant fantasies after masturbation, and ejaculate to appropriate fantasies. Continuous verbalization is required for at least thirty minutes not less than three times per week. According to Laws and Osborn (1982), significant reduction in deviant arousal occurs within 40-60 sessions. The two satiation techniques have not yet been compared directly for their effectiveness or efficiency.

Aversive Behavioral Rehearsal. Aversive behavioral rehearsal (ABR) was first used as a treatment for exhibitionism but has been extended to the treatment of pedophilia and rape (Wickramasera, 1976). It is an extremely powerful technique but intrusive and potentially humiliating for offenders. Its goal is to decrease sexually deviant behaviors and arousal by making the behavior publicly observable. Because of the nature of ABR, therapists are urged to inform the offenders of the exact procedures to be used, the possible side effects, and available treatment options. Wickramasera (1976), however, reports this technique to be effective with clients where other techniques, including those discussed in this chapter, have failed.

There is no single ABR procedure. Variants on the technique have been employed by different therapists to suit the needs of the offenders with whom they work. What is described here is a general procedure using the techniques common to the various specific procedures.

The procedure starts by having offenders describe in detail the types of sexual offenses committed and the situations in which they have occurred. From this description, the therapist can determine what props (e.g., mannequins, clothing, apparatus, etc.) should be used in subsequent reenactments of the offense.

Next, the offender spends approximately 30 minutes reliving the offense in the presence of the therapist, other offenders, significant others, and/or other treatment staff. Often these sessions are videotaped. The offender is encouraged by the therapist to relive the offense with as much detail as possible. The offender is required to verbalize his plans for the offense, the method of stalking and controlling his victim, how he was dressed, how he felt at various times during the offense, his thoughts, etc. This process can create an exceptionally emotional session, and some time is usually needed to debrief the offender and help him cope with his reactions to the session. These sessions may be repeated to deal with other offensive acts or fantasies.

During the next phase of treatment, the videotape is viewed by the client, therapist, and a group which includes other offenders, treatment staff, or the offender's significant others. The offender is required to narrate the tape, explaining his thoughts, feelings, and actions. In subsequent sessions, the tape may be viewed again by the client, therapist, and others. Wickramasera (1976) recommends follow-up sessions at two, six, nine, and twelve months, then once each year as needed to maintain treatment gains.

This technique is extremely intrusive and often results in serious side effects. Common iatrogenic reactions include depression, anxiety, nightmares, secondary impotence, and a general disinterest in sex. Fortunately, these reactions usually dissipate within a few weeks. Some offenders attempt to avoid the powerful impact by cognitively withdrawing from the procedure, or thinking of something else. The therapist can minimize this response by forcing the offender to verbalize in detail his thoughts, feelings, and the circumstances of the offense.

Arousal Reconditioning. To this point, the procedures described were designed to reduce inappropriate sexual arousal and behavior. However, it is the case that simply eliminating inappropriate arousal without enhancing appropriate arousal will produce only short-term effects. In fact, Barlow and Abel (1976) recommend that the best clinical strategy is to increase appropriate arousal before decreasing inappropriate sexual arousal. One straightforward method of increasing appropriate arousal is simply to pair masturbation with appropriate sexual stimulation or fantasies. This procedure has reportedly been successful in the treatment of sadomasochism (Davison, 1968; Marquis, 1970) and pedophilia (Annon, 1971).

One problem with this technique is that many offenders, particularly pedophiles, do not exhibit sufficient sexual stimulation to appropriate sexual fantasies to allow for arousal and orgasm. To address this issue, Davison (1968) and Marquis (1970) have employed a thematic shift method in which offenders begin masturbating to deviant fantasies or stimuli but shift to appropriate fantasies at the point of orgasmic inevitability.

Because of the popularity of this procedure, Conrad and Wincze (1976) reviewed the literature and found a disturbing lack of methodological rigor. In a carefully controlled evaluation of this procedure, they were not able to attribute behavioral change to it and concluded that the procedure by itself was suspect.

In response, Abel, Blanchard, Barlow, and Flannagan (1975) and VanDeventer and Laws (1978) have used a procedure of fantasy alteration between masturbatory sessions rather than within sessions. Thus, clients are instructed to masturbate to ejaculation alternately to appropriate and inappropriate fantasies. This procedure produces a simultaneous reduction in deviant arousal and increase in appropriate arousal, although the mechanisms responsible for these effects are unclear (Laws and O'Neil, 1981; Foote and Laws, 1981).

The fantasy alteration approach seems preferable to simple orgasmic reconditioning as it is more reliably effective and more efficient, having the advantage of simultaneously increasing appropriate arousal while decreasing inappropriate arousal. The same, however, is true of masturbatory satiation, as discussed earlier. It seems, then, that therapists are offered a choice between fantasy alteration and masturbatory satiation to increase appropriate arousal. There may be a slight preference for the masturbatory satiation procedure since it is theoretically more straightforward and avoids the problem of having offenders masturbate to inappropriate fantasies.

Conclusion

The behavioral techniques for altering sexual arousal patterns have good track records in the psychological literature and should be included in any comprehensive treatment program. However, by themselves, they are not enough as a treatment program. They must be coupled with other treatment modalities discussed elsewhere in this volume.

References

Abel, G.G. and Annon, J.S. (1982, April). Reducing deviant sexual arousal through satiation. Workshop presented at the 4th National Conference on Sexual Aggression, Denver.

Abel, G.G., Blanchard, E.B., Barlow, D.H., and Flannagan, B. (1975, December). A case report of the behavioral treatment of a sadistic rapist. Paper presented at the meeting of the Association for the Advancement of Behavior Therapy, San Francisco.

Abel, G.G., Blanchard, E.B., and Becker, J.V. (1978). An integrated treatment program for rapists. In R. Rada (Ed.), *Clinical aspects of the rapist*. New York: Grune & Stratton.

Abel, G.G., Blanchard, E.B., Becker, J.V., and Djenderedjian, A. (1978). Differentiating sexual aggressives with penile measures. *Criminal Justice and Behavior, 5*, 315-332.

Annon, J.S. (1971). The extension of learning principles to the analysis and treatment of sexual problems. *Dissertation Abstracts International, 32*(6-B), 3627.

Barlow, D.H. and Abel, G.G. (1981). Recent developments in assessment and treatment of paraphilias and gender-identity disorder. In W.E. Craighead, A.E. Kazdin, and M.J. Mahoney (Eds.), *Behavior modification: Principles, issues and applications* (2d ed.). Boston: Houghton Mifflin.

Barlow, D.H. and Abel, G.G. (1976). Sexual deviation. In E. Craighead, H.E. Adams, and K.S.

Calhoun (Eds.), *Handbook of behavioral assessment*. New York: Wiley.

Barlow, D.H., Agras, W.S., Leitenberg, H., Callahan, E.I., and Moore, R.C. (1972). The contribution of therapeutic instructions to covert sensitization. *Behavior Research and Therapy,* 13, 45-50.

Brownell, K.D., Hayes, S.C., and Barlow, D.H. (1977). Patterns of appropriate and deviant sexual arousal: The behavioral treatment of multiple sexual deviations. *Journal of Consulting and Clinical Psychology,* 45, 1144-1155.

Callahan, E.I. and Leitenberg, H. (1973). Aversion therapy for sexual deviation: Contingent shock and covert sensitization. *Journal of Abnormal Psychology,* 81, 60-73.

Cautela, J.R. (1967). Covert sensitization. *Psychological Record,* 20, 459-468.

Cautela, J.R. and Kearney, A.J. (1986). *The covert conditioning handbook.* New York: Springer.

Conrad, S.R. and Wincze, J.P. (1976). Orgasmic reconditioning: A controlled study of its effect upon the sexual arousal of adult male homosexuals. *Behavior Therapy,* 7, 155-166.

Davison, G.C. (1968). Elimination of a sadistic fantasy by a client-controlled counter conditioning technique. *Journal of Abnormal Psychology,* 73, 84-90.

Dougher, M.J., Crossen, J.R., Ferraro, D.P., and Garland, R.J. (1987). Covert sensitization and sexual preference: A preliminary analogue experiment. *Journal of Behavior Therapy and Experimental Psychiatry,* 18, 231-242.

Dougher, M.J., Crossen, J.R., and Garland, R.J. (1986a). An experimental test of Cautela's operant account of covert conditioning. *Behavioral Psychotherapy,* 14, 226-248.

Dougher, M.J., Ferraro, D.P., Diddams, A., and Hill, R. (1988, November). The effect of covert sensitization on behavioral preference for sexual stimuli. Manuscript submitted for publication.

Finkelhor, D. (1984). *Child sexual abuse: New theory and treatment.* New York: Free Press.

Foote, W.E. and Laws, D.R. (1981). A daily alteration procedure for orgasmic reconditioning with a pedophile. *Journal of Behavioral Therapy and Experimental Psychiatry,* 12, 267-273.

Harbert, T.L., Barlow, D.H., Hersen, D.M., and Austin, J.B. (1974). Measurement and modification of incestuous behavior: A case study. *Psychological Reports,* 34, 79-86.

Kelly, R.J. (1982). Behavioral reorientation of pedophiliacs: Can it be done? *Clinical Psychology Review,* 2(3), 387-408.

Kilman, P.R., Sabalis, R.F., Gearing, M.L., Bukstel, L.H., and Scovern, A.W. (1982). The treatment of paraphilias: A review of the outcome research. *Journal of Sex Research,* 18(3), 193-252.

Lanyon, R.I. (1986). Theory and treatment in child molestation. *Journal of Consulting and Clinical Psychology,* 54(2), 176-182.

Laws, D.R. (1984). *The assessment of diverse sexual behavior.* In K. Howells (Ed.), *The psychology of sexual diversity.* Oxford: Basil & Blackwell.

Laws, D.R. and O'Neil, J.A. (1981). Variations on masturbatory conditioning. *Behavioral Psychotherapy,* 9, 111-136.

Laws, D.R. and Osborn, C.A. (1982). A procedure to assess incest offenders. Proposal submitted to research committee, Atascadero State Hospital, Atascadero, California.

Laws, D.R. and Osborn, C.A. (1983). Setting up shop: How to build and operate a laboratory to evaluate and treat sexual deviance. In J.G. Greer and I.R. Stuart (Eds.), *The sexual aggressor: Current perspectives on treatment.* New York: Van Nostrand Reinhold.

Laws, D.R., Meyer, J., and Holmen, M.L. (1978). Reduction of sadistic sexual arousal by olfactory aversion: A case study. *Behavior Research and Therapy,* 16, 281-285.

Maletzky, B.M. (1977). "Booster" sessions in aversion therapy: The permanency of treatment. *Behavior Therapy,* 8, 460-463.

Marquis, J. (1970). Orgasmic reconditioning: Changing sexual object choice through controlling masturbation fantasies. *Journal of Behavior Therapy and Experimental Psychiatry,* 1, 263-270.

Marshall, W.L. (1979). Satiation therapy: A procedure for reducing deviant sexual arousal. *Journal of Applied Behavior Analysis,* 12, 10-22.

Marshall, W.L. and Barbaree, H.E. (1978). The reduction of deviant arousal: Satiation treatment for sexual aggressors. *Criminal Justice and Behavior,* 5, 294-303.

Marshall, W.L., Keltner, A.A., and Griffiths, E. (1974). An apparatus for the delivery of offensive odors: A description and its clinical application. Unpublished manuscript. Queen's University, Kingston, Ontario, Canada.

Marshall, W.L. and Lippens, K. (1977). The clinical value of boredom: A procedure for reducing inappropriate sexual interests. *Journal of Nervous and Mental Disease,* 165, 283-287.

Quinsey, V.L. (1973). Methodological issues in evaluating the effectiveness of aversion therapies for institutionalized child molesters. *Canadian Psychologist,* 14, 350-361.

Quinsey, V.L., Chaplin, T.C., and Varney, G. (1981). A comparison of rapists' and non-sex offenders' sexual preferences for mutually consenting sex, rape, and physical abuse of women. *Behavioral Assessment,* 3, 127-135.

Quinsey, V.L. and Marshall, W.L. (1983). Procedures for reducing inappropriate sexual arousal. In J.G. Greer and I.R. Stuart (Eds.), *The sexual aggressor: Current perspectives on treatment.* New York: Van Nostrand Reinhold.

Quinsey, V.L., Steinman, C.M., Bergerson, S.G., and Holmes, T.P. (1975). Penile circumference, skin conductance, and ranking responses of child molesters and "normals" to sexual and nonsexual stimuli. *Behavior Therapy,* 6, 213-219.

Rachman, S. and Teasdale, J. (1969). *Aversion therapy and behavior disorders: An analysis.* Coral Gables, FL: University of Miami Press.

VanDeventer, A.D. and Laws, D.R. (1978). Orgasmic reconditioning to redirect sexual arousal in pedophiles. *Behavior Therapy,* 9, 748-765.

Walker, P.A. and Meyer, W.J. (1981). Medroxyprogesterone acetate treatment for paraphiliac sex offenders. In J.P. Hays, T.K. Roberts, and K.S. Salwaz (Eds.), *Violence and the violent offender,* pp. 353-373. New York: S.P. Medical and Scientific Books.

Wickramasera, I. (1976). Aversive behavioral rehearsal for sexual exhibitionism. *Behavior Therapy,* 7, 167-176.

Chapter 16

Enhancing Positive Spirituality, Sex Offenders, and Pastoral Care

Stephen Price, B.A.

Overview

This chapter focuses on the healthy and unhealthy roles that spirituality plays in the lives of sex offenders. Special emphasis is given to group work, which can facilitate a healthy analysis of the role spirituality has played in the lives of sex offenders, and the use of the "Religious Assessment" is discussed.

Healthy Versus Unhealthy Spirituality

The scene was one familiar to any professional with experience working with sex offenders. The offender, a convicted pedophile, was in the midst of an evaluation interview when he held up his hand to stop the interviewer's questions:

This is all well and good for some of these other fellows, but you, being a man of faith yourself, will understand when I tell you that I don't really need therapy. It's all been taken care of. You see, I've been born again, and Jesus has taken the urge to be with young boys away. It's just not a problem for me any more.

The offender appeared shocked when the interviewer challenged his faith stance by suggesting that being a religious individual might actually call him into the process of therapy. To distance himself from this challenge, the offender avoided speaking to the interviewer whenever possible.

Encounters such as the one described above make many professionals wary of any talk of faith or spirituality on the part of sex offenders. Consequently, what could become a doorway into treatment and an integral part of recovery is often overlooked, or worse, actively avoided and disdained.

The simplistic solution of believing the offender's religious issues and needs have been addressed because a program allows religious volunteers to come in or employs a part-time chaplain is just as ill-advised. Such an approach does little to address the real issues at hand. It may, in fact, impede the treatment process:

> [T]he untrained volunteer may do more damage to the offender's recovery than good, because he/she will often oversimplify the offender's issues and in the few minutes he/she has to work with the offender gives the offender easy solutions to his problems. (Stack, 1993, p. 29)

For spirituality to be taken seriously as a vital part of the treatment of sex offenders, one may need to have some clear picture of the differences between healthy and unhealthy spirituality; a model for entering into a diagnostic process around these issues; and some basic ideas about how to proceed once diagnostic impressions are formed.

Unhealthy spirituality, or "religiosity," has as a primary characteristic the support of a fragmented world. The offender splits experiences into worldly/spiritual, saints/sinners, real people/objects of deviance, and good/evil. Compartmentalizing in this way keeps these experiences from ever touching one another and protects the offender from the painful crisis that such a confrontation would engender. Unlike healthy spirituality, which encourages people to make responsible choices and "do unto others as you would have them do unto you," religiosity tends to support distortions that minimize responsibility and inhibit empathy.

Some offenders are so stuck in a sense of their sinfulness and their belief that they cannot be forgiven that they are unable to utilize the supportive resources of spirituality and faith to aid their journey into treatment. Others seem to find support for their deviancy in the rigid, guilt-inducing attitudes they learned as children in faith communities or family systems that were devoid of a sense of Grace. Such a support for deviancy is noted in offenders who divide the world into "saints" and "sinners" and see themselves as deliverers of a deserved retribution. Comments such as "any woman who goes out after midnight dressed like that deserves to be raped" exemplify this mindset.

An interesting juxtaposition occurs when deviancy and religious expression are viewed from the perspective of traumatic events and environments in early childhood. The theory that early trauma and victimization contribute to later criminality and sexual deviancy is widely held:

> [A]lthough not all victims become perpetrators, behind each perpetrator is some sort of victimization. (Carlson, 1990, p. 249)

> It would seem senseless to debate the frequency in which the transition from victim to offender occurs among boys and men. It seems more reasonable to acknowledge that according to research, it occurs with some frequency and causation is attributable to a variety of variables.... (Gerber, 1990, p. 154)

Some object relations theorists have explored the idea that the concept of God springs from childhood experience (Rizzuto, 1979), while others have taken this work forward to research the effects of victimization on the individual's concept of God (Doehring, 1993). Understanding the interrelationship of these dynamics provides fertile ground for creative efforts in pastoral care with the offending population. Because the internal anguish of early traumatic experience may cause the child to engage in the fragmentation discussed earlier as a defensive, survival mechanism, the adult is left in the tenuous position in which distorted and false perceptions of ultimate authority are directly linked with erroneous definitions and beliefs about one's self, one's identity, and one's worth (Jordon, 1986, p. 30).

When these distorted perceptions and erroneous beliefs are challenged, it often feels to the offender like a death. The very things that enabled these offenders to survive their early trauma are the things they are being asked to give up. A recovering offender eloquently voiced this view when he said, "All through the abuse of my childhood, the two things that kept me going were sex and the church. Now it feels like I have to give them both up." Because this offender could not imagine any other way of expressing himself sexually or religiously than the unhealthy ways he had learned in childhood, he felt as though he was losing his only options.

Treatment providers see offenders' avoidance of struggling with this dilemma as a lack of receptivity to information that would contribute positively toward Relapse Prevention. Two prime examples of this are an unwillingness to define "lapse" behaviors and overconfidence about the possibilities of re-offending. If life has no "gray" areas, if the world is divided sharply into saints and sinners, and if closeness to God is based on one's behavior, then discussing or allowing for the possibility of slipping—or worse—failure, is threatening indeed. Responsibility becomes projected outward. The offender may say things like "When I am guilty of a sinful act, or when someone else does me wrong for no reason at all, this is the work of Satan...." When this offender's response is coupled with an understanding of a childhood history of abandonment, abuse, and institutionalization, his or her difficulty in preparing a Relapse Prevention plan that provides for lapse behavior becomes more understandable. Hopefully, it also becomes more workable. It is offenders who, in their religiosity, stay locked in this stance toward treatment and recovery who suffer the most.

Identifying and Promoting Healthy Spirituality

> If the religious sex offender is looking for easy solutions or ways of behaving that help cover up his pain and weakness, while embracing a doctrine that proposes health, wealth, and prosperity, but without the accompanying dedication to a life of commitment, then he has truly sold himself short by his distorted thinking. (Stack, 1993, p. 32)

If religiosity is thus defined, how do we identify and promote healthy spirituality in the context of treatment?

Healthy spirituality is a spirituality that brings the possibility of reconciliation to the fragmented portions of life. It trusts that the Creator—by whatever name one calls out to the Divine Mystery—desires the healing of humankind and consequently can be trusted with the failures, sins, and shortcomings of one's life. Healthy spirituality builds bridges: between one's inner and outer world, between one's self and others, and between one's self and God.

> If one is willing to accept that a mature relationship with one's parents is pos-
> sible, then a mature relationship with the God representation should also be
> possible ... It has to do with the individual's total psychic transformation and
> reworking in each stage of the life cycle. Those who are capable of mature
> religious belief renew their God representation to make it compatible with
> their emotional conscious, and unconscious situation, as well as with their
> cognitive and object-related development. (Rizzuto, 1979, p. 46)

Persons with a healthy spirituality have a spirituality that grows along with the rest of their life. Healthy spirituality is able to create this space for the growth of the emerging, maturing self because it is rooted in a faith that claims "The nature of God's love is to affirm each person's unique identity and to provide a holding, caring environment for each, that each might blossom in his or her own special way" (Jordan, 1986, p. 70). Thus, healthy spirituality affirms that God meets us where we are and calls us toward wholeness, inviting us constantly toward healthier, more mature relationship and faith as we go.

C.B. Stack points out some of the ways in which this kind of healthy spirituality gets lived out in the day-to-day life of the recovering offender in treatment.

> An offender who is truly in recovery will seek out religious teaching that is
> not only not in conflict with his recovery, but will tend to bolster it. His reli-
> gious associations and choice of chapel services will be those which hold up
> God, as well as man, as being helpful in his recovery process. The idea is that
> God can and delights to use others to help us down the path in this journey
> called recovery. (Stack, 1993, p. 31)

"Paul Evans," a recovering offender, wrote about what the journey through recovery looked like to him from a spiritual standpoint. Although the language may seem alien to some treatment providers, the goals of breaking down denial, victim empathy, and relapse prevention are consistent with the treatment goals in all sex offender treatment programs:

> The next step is determining how to create opportunities within our programs
> for recovering offenders to move from unhealthy religiosity to the concept of
> healthy spirituality expressed above. This goal is especially important as we
> realize that an integrative view of treatment affirms that damage in one area
> of the individual's life will impact other areas as well, and that healing in one
> area (i.e., spirituality) will have positive repercussions in other areas such as
> relationality, self-image, and capacity for empathic response.

One way of accomplishing this goal is giving offenders the opportunity to share and discuss their faith journey in a group context. Under the guidance of a clinician who is conversant with both the language of faith and the modes and goals of sex offender treatment, this spiritual self-examination allows group members to confront denial and distortions and supports the wholeness that is the goal of spiritual growth. Such groups also can provide the basis for other pastoral care.

Spirituality and 12-Step Programs

Twelve-step recovery programs are modeled after the 12-step recovery process first initiated by Alcoholics Anonymous. These steps were outlined by recovering alcoholics at a time when the difficulties incurred by their drinking behaviors did not have the benefit of either medical research or extensive treatment programs. These steps, which were built on the premise that "what works, works," were outlined as what works. Similar groups have sprung up around other compulsive behaviors, such as gambling, narcotics, and eating disorders. Individuals have found that the community of the 12-step group and the spiritual discipline of "working the steps" are essential to their maintaining abstinence or sobriety.

There has been some disagreement in the field as to whether 12-step programs are compatible with a Relapse Prevention approach. Certainly the first step, which refers to being "powerless" over one's condition, is not compatible with the Relapse Prevention approach which teaches that one is in control of one's behavior. However, the 12-step program's statement —"Admitted that we were powerless over our addiction and that our lives had become unmanageable"— is essentially about humility. It stands in stark contrast to the offenders' narcissistic stance that they have everything under control, that they could handle it if everyone would just get out of their way. In comparison:

> Our lack of success in managing our addiction, our loss of control, had become an established fact. We had experienced over and over the mind-altering effect which had sapped the strength of our resolve to free ourselves from sex and love addiction. Thus we approached the prospect of surrendering our sex and love addiction with real humility, for we had no way of knowing if such a surrender was even possible.

> Each of us, regardless of individual circumstances, was now willing to go to any lengths, a day at a time, to stay unhooked. This decision was unilateral. (SLAA 1086, pp. 70, 73)

The powerlessness addressed in the 12-steps is the humbling realization that there is no way for the individual to engage in this behavior in a "controlled" fashion, that it has made their life unmanageable and untenable.

The faith in a Higher Power is also a controversial issue. Many people find the spirituality of step programs to be incompatible with their beliefs and for them, approaches like Rational Recovery may be more palatable. However, many sex offenders do find a spiritual approach to be meaningful. Unfortunately many of these individuals may quickly turn to the idea of instant cures by suddenly turning their life over to God. They may maintain that they have been "born again" and thus have no need for treatment. They may feel that they only need to ask for forgiveness from God and all will be well. However, this represents religiosity rather than spirituality and is addressed by 12-step programs.

Nevertheless, the fact that we needed faith in some Power, since we could not trust ourselves to be consistent in either behavior or motive, left some us us feeling even more shaken. Where would we find even the rudiments of a faith that could carry us through this dissolving and reconstruction of our whole personality? If there was no Power greater than ourselves, it would be impossible! (SLAA, p. 75)

For may recovering offenders that Higher Power is not "God" in the sense of a deity. For many, their Higher Power, at least in the beginning, is the example and support of a community of persons with similar issues and struggles who have been able to achieve and maintain some degree of abstinence and recovery. In trusting that "if they can do it, perhaps I can too" many offenders find the strength and courage to engage in the difficult work of coming to terms with one's behavior and the changes necessary for maintaining a non-offending lifestyle. In fact, it has been my experience that for some offenders, the time in their 12-step program when they begin working on their fourth step (made a searching and fearless moral inventory of ourselves) is also the time when they rewrite their Deviant Cycle in a more open and honest fashion.

Finally, we need to realize that the differences between 12-step approaches to recovery and the behavioral maintenance strategies of Relapse Prevention are not an either/or proposition, but a both/and partnership. Programatically, perhaps we need to find creative ways to integrate 12-step modalities into the treatment process for those men who desire to be involved in them.

We need also to remember that the 12-step communities offer another valuable gift to the offenders with whom we work. As we think of recovery or behavioral maintenance as a continuum that extends beyond incarceration, we realize that the support systems from which the offender can draw are few. Particularly in those cases, and they are many, where there is no family support, 12-step groups such as SLAA and SA will be one of the few places where the recovering offender can find acceptance and support as they continue in their recovery. The other possibility, is the offender's faith community. But first we need to address the issue of assisting the offender in treatment to develop a healthy spirituality from the perspective of traditional religious practice.

Group Processing of Religious Values

When suggestions for working with the spiritual issues of the offender are put forward, some raise valid questions about involving therapists who do not share the offender's faith tradition or who do not know how to quote scripture by chapter and verse (as many offenders trapped in their religiosity are prone to do). The answer is that an interested therapist can usually find pastors in the community who are more than willing to discuss their tradition and to provide resources and sometimes more personal involvement to the effort of supporting healthy faith. As for the questions around scripture, it is sometimes helpful not to know too much. Asking offenders to point out the passage they are quoting often is a non-threatening way of helping them see that they have actually misquoted a passage or taken it out of context in such a way that promotes their distortions. If this is done in the group context, the group leader can say something like this: "That's an interesting way of approaching that verse, is that how the rest of you guys see it?" A question such as this facilitates the growth of the therapeutic culture in the group and breaks down the "privatization of faith" that is so often seen in persons with religious distortions.

The Religious Assessment

In 1985, this author and Timothy H. Little published a Religious Assessment (see Appendix F) which we had found valuable in the diagnosis and treatment of persons in a psychiatric facility (Little and Price, 1985). Over time, this assessment tool has been refined and modified for use with sex offenders and prison populations. Allowing each member of the group to fill out the questionnaire and then, over a period of weeks, share portions of it with the group can be the catalyst for the type of self-examination and faith development described previously. This happens in part because the structure of the assessment invites the telling of stories. The process of sharing the responses in group become a journey made together through the history and feelings which surround an individual's experience of their faith. It is, in many ways, an intimate experience. It gives the individuals involved in working through it a common set of shared memories. The members of the group become a part of one another's story to the extent that the sharing of story and the hearing of story are allowed to impact their lives. To this extent, the group becomes a small faith community in which the hard questions can be asked without fear of condemnation or abandonment, and where the work of transformation can take place in a safe holding environment.

As this group process unfolds, the following framework helps to identify the points along that process:

1. As the group carefully attends to both the individual story and the narratives of the faith community out of which the individual comes (be they Jewish, Christian, Muslim, or Native American) a critique is made of the current situation and the individual beliefs which support it. Out of that critique, there is lifted up and disclosed the reality of the disturbances in relationship—between self, God, and others.

2. Within the context of this group/faith community there is found a loyal relationship which will not abandon the sufferer, but will be present even to the point of suffering themselves as the pain of this disruption is embraced and articulated. (Students of Hebrew Scripture will be quick to see that the group in this instance embodies the "oracle of presence" used to respond to public psalms of lament.)

3. In the speaking and sharing of these feelings of pain and rage and the claiming of one's own role in the creation of the disruption, they are transformed into energies for creative imagination which envisions and searches for new forms of relationship and community shaped more like the Divine Intention expressed in the individual's original faith community.

It must be pointed out that the creation of such a "faith community" in an offender's group in a correctional/treatment setting is neither quick nor easy. Some members drop out. Others launch "anti-group" campaigns in response to the perceived (or real) threat to their faith—for they are being asked to engage in change at the most profound of levels. However, such communities can be created and such change can take place. And, in the dynamic web of interrelations that comprises treatment, the gains made here will permeate their way through the various other treatment components, enhancing and enliving the growth and recovery of the individuals who move through the program and back out into the community.

A basic understanding of how to interpret the assessment will aid the group facilitator in helping group members to peel back the layers of meaning of their responses. This understanding should not, however, stop group leaders from pushing further as they aid group members to explore their faith journey and its implications for their recovery.

The first five questions in the assessment invite an exploration of one's religious roots:

- Religious background of client and family. What did you like most about it? What did you like least?

- Have there been changes in your religious activity and/or affiliation? What precipitated these changes?

- What has most influenced the way you feel about religion? What people? What experiences?

- What do your parents think about God and about religion?

- What is your earliest memory of a religious experience or belief?

Sometimes the responses to these questions are fairly basic. But other times they open up discussion or stories of one's earliest feelings of God's care and compassion—feelings that have carried the individual through a lifetime of difficulties and need to be honored, or early feelings of shame and unworthiness which will grow increasingly evident throughout the questionnaire.

The next three questions approach one's cognitive understanding of God and the role of faith:

- What does religion mean to you?

- What is the most important thing that God does?

- What is the most important thing that religion teaches?

It is important to note how congruent this cognitive understanding is with later answers of a more personal nature. Between these and the more personal questions one can also begin to discover the kind of cognitive distortions which can interfere with an individual's ability to move toward a more healthy, whole relationship with God, self, and others in the community of faith.

Questions 9 through 12 explore both the individual's connection with the Biblical material (or the scripture of their faith community, if not Judeo-Christian) and where he feels some identity with that material:

• What is your favorite Bible verse? Why?

• What is your favorite Bible story? Why?

• Who is your favorite Bible character? Why?

• What Bible character are you most like? How are you like this character?

These questions can also be a projective tool for identifying basic themes in the person's life and faith journey. Another area where the projective identification explored in these questions can be valuable in the offering of hope and guidance to the individual from outside their faith tradition. Suppose the offender answers the question about what biblical character he is most like by saying that he is most like the Old Testament character David. He then goes on to recount how his life has been spent "taking on giants" of one form or another. The therapist can point out the real strength and courage of David (and by connection the offender) in facing the giants of life, and then speculate as to whether that same courage made it possible for David to take on some of the more personal giants which interfered with him being a good king. One "giant" sure to strike close to home is the biblical story of Nathan, the prophet, confronting David with his sexual misconduct when he had Bathsheba's husband killed so that he could take her as his wife. Such an approach to the biblical connection made by the offender provides the opportunity to affirm strength, confront denial, and offer hope all within a framework which provides less grounds for resistance than a more direct method of approaching the same goals.

The next 13 questions are a potpourri designed to look at the here-and-now feelings about the individual's relationship to God and faith as well as assumptions about God's attitude toward them personally.

• How does God function in your personal life?

• When in your life did God feel closest?

• When did God feel furthest away?

• How do you think God feels about you right now?

• What does prayer mean to you?

• If you pray, what kinds of things do you pray about or for?

• What is the worst sin that a person could commit?

• What is the most religious thing that a person could do?

• What do you think about bad things that happen in the world?

• What are your ideas of an afterlife, what do you think happens after you die?
• If God would grant you any three wishes, what would you want?

• What do you see as your number one goal in life?

• Do you feel like God approves of this goal?

Asking when God felt furthest away may bring out feelings connected to the offender's arrest and trial or may provide the first real opportunity to talk about childhood victimization. One offender responded to this question by saying, "[It was] when I quit believing. I kept praying for it [the abuse] to stop, and when it didn't, I figured God had deserted me." Questions of guilt and acceptance may also rise to the surface in this part of the questionnaire.

Having set the stage with an understanding of the individual's personal sense of faith and God's involvement in his or her life, the next several questions attempt to engage a specific biblical story in a concrete way. Taking the New Testament account of Jesus's healing of a paralyzed man, the questions ask:

• What do you think about this story?

• Who would you be in the story?

• How do you think this man felt about being forgiven?

• Who would carry you the way that the four friends carried their
  paralyzed buddy?

• Who would you be willing to carry this way?

This series of questions helps to focus on the offender's sense of community or lack of it. The therapist should beware of sweeping generalizations such as "I'd be willing to carry anyone who needed it" or "I've got lots of folks who'd be willing to carry me." Such answers may point more to the offender's grandiosity than any reality. Pushing for specific people in these roles may cause the offender to look at who they really can count on as well as pointing up the relational breaks caused as their offending behavior alienated the people they cared most about.

These questions may have another valuable insight for the therapist. Observing the strengths and shortcomings in the offender's ability to integrate learning from one setting (the story) to another (questions about what he would do) may reveal whether the offender's response is marked by fragmentation or all-or-nothing thinking or whether the offender is able to carry the lesson of the story into new territory and apply it specifically to his or her own life and current situation.

The final questions seek to address the unspoken covenants that individuals often have with God:

- If you were to sum up what you want from God in a short prayer, what would that Life Prayer be?

- What would it sound like if you finished the sentence, "God, I am your person (if, when because). . . ."?

- Were there any questions that made you anxious?

- Is there anything else you think it important to say about your faith or your religious experience?

Covenants are rooted in life stories. They are often promises made to one's self to cope with trauma or anxiety in childhood or to give meaning to otherwise fearful circumstances. Often, they are the unconscious remnants of magical thinking and are designed to ward off the final abandonment—the abandonment of God. Such covenants need to be brought to light, examined, and intentionally claimed or discarded. Some covenants are healthy while others are clearly immature or pathological. But when they are held unconsciously, they exert a power far beyond what is needed or necessary and often function as a source of spiritual and emotional imprisonment rather than a conduit for God's grace to make itself known.

One way to judge the health of a covenant statement is to look at its structure. Unhealthy covenants tend to sound like a magical incantation: "I do this or that thing, therefore God must do this thing." Power and control lie with the individual who dominates the actions of God by his behavior. Healthy covenants sound more like those from scripture. In scripture, covenant stories often begin with phrases like, "I am the Lord your God who . . . [did this thing] . . . therefore . . . [you shall do this]." The story is retold as grounds for the demands of the covenant. In this instance, however, power and control flow from God to the community of faith and/or the individual. The individual lives in response to God's graceful action, not in an attempt to appease God's anger or control God's behavior.

The final questions allow the opportunity for clearing the air of leftover issues. Sometimes an individual will be aware that a certain question or set of questions made them particularly anxious and open the door to further work in that area. It also allows offenders to have a last word concerning what they want you to understand about their faith. Allowing this level of control is important, especially since most offender treatment is done in settings where very little control or autonomy is left to the offender in treatment.

It may seem strange, at first, to think of a sex offender treatment program as "Sacred Space." But if one looks at the literature in religion and anthropology, one finds this concept alive as the internal and external place where an encounter with the Holy occurs and transformation takes place. It is what James Fowler, drawing from the work of William Bridges, speaks of as the "neutral zone":

The neutral zone bears some resemblance to what St. John of the Cross referred to as the "dark night of the soul." . . . One is dislocated in time and space, and the structures of meaning have been shaken or emptied. . . . Biblically speaking, it is the 40 years in the wilderness with the liberated Hebrews, living day to day on manna and following the pillars of cloud and fire wherever they may lead. Or it is the 40 days in the wilderness with Jesus, struggling with the demons of temptation and trying to fathom the meaning of a calling. (Fowler, 1987, p. 109)

Fowler points out that from the standpoint of faith development this is the place where change takes place and new beginnings are initiated. It is in these new beginnings that the goals of pastoral care of the offender and the larger goals of treatment find common ground. By joining in the exploration of the offender's faith journey, with all its wounds and triumphs, strengths and weaknesses, we participate in creating a safe place that has the raw materials for change. Doing this in a group setting helps the members of the group to see that their journey is not unique, but has much in common with the journey of others. Offenders involved in this process also discover, perhaps for the first time, that they are capable of helping to create a genuine community of faith.

Conclusion

The goals of recovery and sex offender treatment are consistent with the development of a healthy faith and spirituality. A serious consideration of spirituality and/or pastoral care as a vital part of treatment has a great deal to offer the larger treatment process. By engaging in a structured model for assisting offenders in treatment to explore their religious journey, we give them the opportunity to develop that faith as a growing part of their recovery.

References

Carlson, S. (1990). The victim/perpetrator: Turning points in therapy. In M. Hunter (Ed.), *The sexually abused male,* Vol. 2. New York: Lexington Press.

Doehring, K. (1993). *Internal desecration.* Boston: University Press.

Evans, P. (January-February 1993). Old lies and new beginnings. The other side (pp. 57-63).

Fowler, J.W. (1987). *Faith development and pastoral care.* Philadelphia: Fortress Press.

Gerber, P.N. (1990). Victims becoming offenders: A study of ambiguities. In M. Hunter (Ed.), *The sexually abused male, Vol. 1.* New York: Lexington Press.

Jordan, M.R. (1986). *Taking on the gods: The task of the pastoral counselor.* Nashville: Abingdon Press.

Little, T.H. and Price, S.G. (1985). The use of religious assessment in an adolescent psychiatric unit. *Cura Anamarum I* (1).

Rizzuto, A. (1979). *The birth of the living God.* Chicago and London: University of Chicago Press.

Stack, C.B. (1993). From religiosity to spirituality: A guide for the recovering sex offender. Unpublished manuscript.

Chapter 17

Life, the Life Event, and Theater: A Personal Narrative on the Use of Drama Therapy with Sex Offenders

John Bergman, M.A., R.D.T.

Overview

"We act our lives. We make up our dialogue and create ourselves as we go along." (Geese Company, 1986)

This chapter explores the use of drama therapy with sex offenders. The Geese Theater has developed techniques utilizing role playing and props (including masks) specifically designed for this population. Special attention is paid to Relapse Prevention.

Role Playing as a Treatment Strategy

When I talk to therapists and counselors about their treatment strategies with sex offenders, somewhere along the line they always mention role play. Few staff members seem to know role play is one of the more crucial elements in the canon of drama therapy, however. It is a mainstay of psychodrama and sociodrama as well as a proven strategy with a wide variety of clients. But, if I suggest to those same counselors that they should seriously consider using drama therapy in their work, I can be sure of a look of something approaching acute anxiety. Drama therapy frightens people. These are a fair sample of some of the fears I have heard over the years:

- How do I start?
- What am I looking for?
- Isn't it dangerous?
- What happens if a client goes out of control?
- Am I doing psychodrama?
- What do I do?
- Where do I get more training?
- Do I tell them that I don't know what I am doing?
- How do I know that they aren't just using this therapy to secretly enhance their fantasies?
- What if this just confuses their sense of what is and is not real?

Many practitioners in the field of sexual offender treatment recognize the strength of drama therapy as a treatment tool. Privately, many treatment providers have talked to me about the high drama when the sex offender first breaks his denial and makes a cathartic admission. Many therapists wish that they could access this affect more readily. They can. But those frequently asked anxious questions about drama therapy, psychodrama, or role play seem to shrink their will. If this chapter does anything, I hope that it puts confidence into would-be users of drama therapy and persuades many of the fainthearted that this skill is a tool that is basic to doing therapy with sex offenders.

Drama therapy is a therapeutic variation of theater. Theater is condensed life in a box. Theater concerns itself with everything in life. Tennessee Williams looked at themes of decay, alcoholism, and fear—certainly the life themes of some prisoners. Shakespeare dramatized jealousy, patricide, and suicide. "All in the Family," with its focus on the minutiae of daily life in Queens, New York explored racism, sexism, abortion, and family relations. Walt Disney's films have dealt with everything from loss and bereavement to how to hold one's temper. All of it is theater, and all of it is about the real world.

Drama therapy's topics are all of the above and everything that can have relevance to a client's life and mental health. Drama therapy is the therapeutic highlighting of psychological experiences, traumatic events, and life experiences in a "theatrical space and time." Despite the complexity of sex offenders' life experiences, theater is capable of representing those events and drama therapy of investigating them. All you really need to make either theater or drama therapy is a room, two "actors," and someone's life.

In my work with sex offenders I have concentrated on creating specific drama techniques that interact with the thinking, feeling, and life experiences of these men. We are using new strategies to deal with what can be put into the empty space of the therapy room, as well as extending the search for the inner themes that are the dramatic story of sexual offending. Part of this chapter is a mini-narrative about using these techniques that focuses on:

1. The special metaphors of the sex offender and how to use them in drama-based cathartic techniques.
2. Creating dramatic rituals using props like the belt and the mask to produce the hidden effect of sexual offending.
3. Using role play as a rehearsal for a relapse-free life.

I have arrived at these techniques by applying the basic rules of theater to the special life behaviors of the sex offender. I have used their imagery, their acts, as the subject of the theater event and the therapeutic investigation. I have put the sex offender's life into the theater box.

While it is clear to me that theater really is life in a box and drama therapy the investigation of the meaning of that life in the box, it does not always seem so clear to others. One of the keys to doing drama therapy comfortably is to realize the elegant simplicity of theater as life and therapy combined. How does one visualize the actions of theater and life simultaneously? It helps to think of basic terms like script, dialogue, actors, and roles. I begin by just thinking of a space.

Imagine a big open box with one side cut away so that you can see into the box. This is a little like the picture of your old school theater.

Imagine Figure A walking into the box. He or she stops. Another figure, B, enters the box. B, too, stops. The figures look at each other. A says, "Hello." B turns, looks carefully, smiles, and leaves. A watches, turns, and then also leaves.

One must ask some questions to understand what was happening:

• Why didn't B say anything?
• What was their relationship?
• Why did this meeting happen in this particular space?
• What is this place?
• Where did they come from?
• Is this just a dream, a scene inside a man's head?
• If this were a fantasy, what would A and B be doing?

- Does that door lead to darkness?
- Is the darkness a fear of being swallowed?
- What was that shadow?
- Is it just a child?

In a simple way, this is all that theater is. People moving in space and time. People meeting somewhere, responding to each other, talking, whispering, answering, interacting, and then leaving. Theater is a slice of life, done right now.

Theater draws entirely on life. My guess is that we could take a slice out of your home life and that it would hold up well as a piece of theater. We might collapse the time frames a bit, but we would still see the daily dramas of paying bills, having mis-understandings, loud televisions, and just plain irritating married life.

Theater happens everywhere. If we look carefully at the events in our lives we see a manipulating boss punishing an employee, a car crash, a harried transaction between a cashier and a customer. Each of these events is a mini-drama with roles, scripts, and actors. I define it as "life-in-a-box." It is crucial that the neophyte drama therapists really pay attention to that life because it has an intricate pattern and many layers of meaning.

When people get together, work, ignore, run, and talk, it is complex living even though we think about these actions as being ordinary life acts. I wake up, put on my slippers because the floor is cold, go to the bathroom, get my cigarettes, go down-stairs, and put on the coffee. My wife starts to get up. I can hear her. The dogs go to the door. Told neutrally, these actions are merely part of the event of waking. But, suppose I wake up angry because I have to go to a meeting. The floor is cold because the heating went off in the middle of the night. I get my cigarettes even though I said I would quit and I feel guilty because I have not stopped. I put the coffee on but drop the lid of the coffee pot on my toes. I think that my wife should take the dogs out. And so on. The script has changed, even though the actions are still the same.

If I was talking to the actors about their actions, I would ask more than, "What happened then?" I would ask "What did you feel about her?"

When I re-run an event using a record of the actions as a guide, I am making the-ater with a script. I must be very careful to ask all the right questions about the script, roles, and actions in order to see the real significance of the events.

Yesterday I went to an auction. I bought my wife a piano for $90. It was an action in life. If today I decide in a room in a prison to repeat the events of the auction, I would need the auctioneer, the other bidders, my wife's presence, and my actions. If we merely repeat this event, it is a simple piece of life-in-a-box. But, if the purchase of the piano was part of a neurotic but repetitive psychological process of buying when I feel discontented, then re-playing the event with an acute focus on all of my actions and all the nuances of script and role will give me a chance to examine my actions and feelings more closely. That is both life-in-a-box and therapy. And that is part of the science of drama therapy.

Let's look at my example of buying when I feel depressed. Could we change my play? What happens if one of the "actors" changes the script? What if the actor play-ing the auctioneer refuses to acknowledge my bid? What happens if one of the peo-ple in this script is not there. Can we make other changes? Is it possible for me to act someone else's role in the play? Is it possible to act like any of the other people/char-acters in this life action/scripted drama? How could I teach others to "act" my role in that script? These questions will unlock my automatic portrayal of myself in life and give me some measure of objectivity. Could we do the same with your script, or with the script and roles of someone else?

As you become more comfortable in asking the theater questions, you will begin to see that the sex offender has only one script and one role. Both the script and the role are very well hidden. It is the trick of theater and drama therapy that makes these hidden private acts and roles public. Theater and drama therapy can re-create any script, even if the actors are fantastic, tortured, or from another country. All of this can come to life in the therapy space. Once the offender describes his inner theater to you, the questions of theater and the probing tools of drama therapy will open up the script.

With special clients like sex offenders, theater begins when we see how they do their own life interactions when they are the directors. We need to see who the people/actors are in their life events. We need to know their secret inner stage directions. We need them to show us the actions and the interactions. Because of the danger-ousness and often the repetitive quality of their acts, we need to see single life events but in great detail. Theater is such an elastic structure that if we want to see how an offender is doing at any given minute, we can create a place and people/actors and make him enact immediately and in front of us. This is both life and live theater. As a piece of life, the event can have profound meaning for the client. As theater, it can be seen as merely an event captured and created in this time and this place and there-fore safe because it is an act with roles and a script. It is not life, and yet for the offender it may be the first healthy moment in his life.

How can a sex offender change his tragedy and experience that healthy moment? Let us begin with a simple anxiety and fear: a son talking to his father about his report card.

> *You are nervous. You hear your father come in the door. He goes upstairs. He calls for you. What does his voice sound like? How should you walk in? How will you cope with his feelings? What role can you put on? He shouts at you and you experience shame, and then you shout back with all your strength.*

The offender learns that an old event can be played out with a different ending. It can be learned and repeated. It can be changed to make the moments violent, tranquil, humane, and decent. The actors can put their own interpretations into the slice of life/theater. Or they can be given new interpretations for this slice of life. Our clients can enact their own victimization and change their roles. The victimized boy can repeat this life event and become the father victimizer. He can discover what was hid-den in his house. He can explore the sounds of repression, or the empty wind that lived in his mind when he was being assaulted. He can learn what being hurt by him feels like. He can learn and rehearse new actions so that those other dangerous life acts can be changed. He can practice a decent life.

Drama therapy is merely a set of techniques to help clients discover, enact, and reinforce new actions. Drama therapy helps put the focus/spotlight on the client's actions and interior actions with clarity. Creating the interior monologue in one place at a specific time can be exhilarating, painful, shameful, cathartic, and even boring. Drama therapy asks the client to give us a different script from talk therapy. The focus is on action, interaction, and experience. The focus is on feeling, terror, re-enacting in public the endlessly enacted private shame. Language is the tool of analysis, but theater and drama therapy is the medium for behavior and the experiment with changed actions.

The Secret and Its Metaphors

By activating the offender's secret universe, drama therapy can be a crucial part of the treatment of the sexual offender. Drama therapy forces the offender to marshall his daily defenses against a dramatic "real" event in real time, but without the consequences of re-offending against a victim in the public.

It is the reality of any event that is so threatening: the reality of appropriate responses, of dealing with healthy affect, real criticism, and of having to create healthy role responses. In the real world, the offender only has the power of his secret dreaming. In the face of the real world event, he feels ineffective, overwhelmed, shamed.

Theater can make the hidden meaning of events come to life. It can work in metaphors that ordinary language cannot do. And it is sometimes the elastic quality of metaphor that allows offenders to trust and investigate.

I have intentionally couched this next section in some of the language that works with drama therapy. It may seem strange to the therapist, but it is often the stuff of a good cathartic session.

The Pedophile and the Secret

The sex offender fights all attempts at acknowledging the consequential real world. His denial is total. He cries, begs silently, and then falls back into a truculence that has the strength of years of living in his secret universe. This secret world is central to his survival. Without it, the sex offender has little to fill his life except an almost animal resistance. His hidden universe is the power that protects the self, protects his needs, and supports and excuses the sexual assaults. The tension between the secret and the real world is huge and painful.

A child victim is a triumph, a release, a pleasure that is sexual and a source of empowerment. It is a release from failure. The victim is a nexus for the reconciling of his shamed weakness and will for domination. Here in the act with the child is the true release of an ancient but ongoing rage. This rage electrifies the secrecy: "You hurt me and I will make myself feel better;" "You hurt me and I will find a way to get even."

The drama therapist must use his tools to force the offender's secret world into the open. Secrecy is the enemy.

The priest who must always hide his sexual needs soon learns to sublimate the urgency within a powerful set of guilt ridden sexual dreams. Unable to let even his peers know what he is experiencing, and ashamed that he is not strong enough to be able to combat them, the priest may ultimately give in to them. He must hide his obsessions in order to believe that he faces the world with respectability. He attempts to bury his secret in a chamber surrounded by oblivion and masked with outward care and concern. He is decent. He may even become a type of super-priest actively engaged in all of the parish's business. He will work long hours, proving to himself with his exhausting 20th century mortification that he is good and decent.

But distortions run parallel to this workaholic ethic. The priest's mind becomes a carefully calibrated balance for justifying his deviance:

- I have done this amount and I deserve to have this thrill.
- I am always doing good deeds.
- This child is the product of my good deeds.
- This is an act of love.
- It goes along with my work.

If the pressure of repression is too great, the priest can attack his victims with lightning speed—and later talk helplessly about feeling overwhelmed by his monster within. It is as if he is a Dr. Jekyll and Mr. Hyde. And, in a way, he is. He lives with such a high degree of emotional self-denial that the release of self-control feels almost explosive.

Most therapeutic programs for sex offenders can gradually pry open the secret places, but there is always the danger that the secret is only half opened. The offender may insist on holding onto the controls found in the final bits of the secret. The drama therapist must try to set in motion a language of action and metaphor that bypasses the secret controls.

The Rapist and the Secret

The result can be catastrophic for the victims of offenders with explosive tempers who mix rage generated by anti-social beliefs with unresolved family dynamic experiences and sexual fantasies. This combination of drives is often seen in adult rapists. Intriguingly, adult rapists receive much less focus than the more malleable pedophiles. Providers are sometimes intimidated by the rage or manipulated by the criminality of these rapists. Adult rapists generally can find support for their acts from the criminal fraternity, and they use their sociopathy as a basis for their defiant rejection of change. Playing to a criminal crowd, the adult rapist can distort and demean women and believe that "she really wanted it, most women do."

In my experience, rapists always are an unknown force. Their rage is palpable, and they have a carefully calculated gauge for violence. Rapists sometimes seems sexually sensitized by every stimulus and act with an underlying edge of hysteria. Where pedophiles hide from life, rapists pretend to be in it. They stick to their pretence with charm and the threat of intimidation. But, in their fantasies they may be drawn to the blood on the skin, the rope burn, and the scream. Rapists live as deeply in their fantasies and interpersonal emptiness as pedophiles. Often, it is the female staff at a facility who can best sense a rapist's violence. They feel it when they have to apply institution rules to them. In prison, rapists feed on the rage of the facility to gain an endless supply of violent fantasy.

I am highlighting the language of metaphor and analogy to describe some offenders' mental landscapes. Really effective drama therapists must constantly search for the linguistic mind key that will open the sex offenders' shamed doors. For instance, we found one offender who responded strongly to the phrase, "screaming into the abyss." During lengthy sessions with this man, we focused his affective attention on the meaning of the abyss and especially its effect on his victims.

We have found that such language greatly strengthens the therapist's creativity. The offenders learn all too quickly the games of therapy survival. They glibly speak of cycles, grooming, and deviance. They compliantly participate in treatment swearing like addicts that they are all better. But, the drama therapist has a tool that can put the offender anywhere; in the mind of the victim, in the grip of his brutalizer's hands, and in an empty lonely box. The therapist must only observe and lead.

The Trance

Drama therapy can use the language of description and objectivity, but it is the poetry of active language like "warfare," "the shadow," "earth and fire," "the watcher," and "the judge" that forces the offender to enter whatever world the therapist can intuit onto the landscape of the offender's deviance. Drama therapists must use everything they know. They must search for clues to the secrets and the violent fantasies in every gesture, nuance, and intonation. They must try to tunnel into the landscape of deviance. The therapist must be a chameleon, a bull, and a serpent. At one moment, the therapist may be part of a ritual of defrocking for an angry, offending priest; at another he or she may be a 30-year-old housewife with a penchant for gossip who is the secret alias of the gender-confused pedophile. At yet another moment the therapist may be a cold victim lost in a terror that finally reminds the offender of the horror in his own past and the hell he has caused others.

The key to the success of this modality is the profound ease with which sex offenders enter into these altered states or trances. Drama therapy, like theater, produces altered states for the actor and for the audience. When I watch a production about the Holocaust, such as *The Investigation* by Peter Weiss, I experience the terror of the victims being tortured. It is as if I am being tortured. Even though I know I am in the safety of the theater, I fear the door opening to the SS. I can always close my eyes and remember that I am in the theater. But, I am still potentially in a trance—a changed state where my identity is temporarily displaced. When this happens, it is possible that my most controlled defenses to my most repressed fears can become unprotected.

The same is true for a sex offender, who may experience this changed state with almost alarming speed. The sex offender seems especially susceptible to altered states. His passivity and blurred ego boundaries let him breach his own defenses and change his tenuous hold on the world. This effect is one that gives drama therapy the force to bypass the linguistic denial of deviance and the numb wall of shame. Fortunately, the drama therapist can always bring the offender back to the safety of the therapy space. The ability to engender the trance is one of the great powers of drama therapy. The potency of this modality is that it is convincing, dangerous, and safe. It can lead to very cathartic sessions—experience of remembering and flooding that opens and cleanses.

Tools of Drama Therapy: The Hiding Place

The biggest tools in your drama therapy arsenal should be humor, courage, sensitivity, creativity, good ears, and some luck. Drama therapy is a little like cooking and entertaining guests at your house. It takes preparation, an eye to the environment that will promote intimacy and depth, the smooth transition of food and conversation, and an ability to improvise around unfolding relationships.

In practice, the only tools a good drama therapist needs are an empty chair, a door, and two clients. The chair is the grandfather of old props and theater tools. Think of who might be in that chair: a mother never met, an abusive uncle, a manipulative boss. The chair can also hold things: a bottle that will not leave, the memory of the first beating, the buried child, or the assaulted self.

The therapist's tools become catalysts of the affect that he or she seeks from the client. The client sees the prop and, if it is potent, creates an immediate set of associations. The therapist must see the client "see." The therapist must be with the client in the act of associating and see with the offender's inner eye:

> *The client sees a teddy bear. He has not held one for 30 years, but his memory of the bear is tactile, kinesthetic, and active. He automatically remembers and feels the bear. He wants to fall to the ground, play, become three years old. And we want this also. If he can regress, he may lose 35 years of defenses and allow himself to experience the moment of his victimization.*

> *The therapist asks the client to hold the teddy bear just like he wants to be held by others. The teddy bear instantly becomes a metaphor of abandonment. He must learn to play with this forgotten self.*

The original hurt, rage, and shock leading to the consequent lonely dissociation surfaces in the conflict between the acting-out of the wounded self and the safe process of play. When the offender can begin to play, he begins to chance ridicule. He re-experiences his past but changes the message of shame and failure. It is the process of leaving the victimized adult/child and beginning the painful task of integration. And the process can begin with a "charged" prop like the teddy bear.

Potent props like the teddy bear, a baby's rattle, a picture of an empty bed, or a black glove are like a shaman's tools. They spit out the fantasy aloud, not in the shamed secret dungeons that fortify the violent sexual secrets, but in the healthy light of the therapeutic milieu. The potent prop invariably leads the offender and the therapist to the earliest child metaphor, the hiding place:

> *The hiding place is the earliest safe house. It is yours. It has a sense of safety. It has in it only the people and friends that you invite to it. It can fly away. It hears crying. It knows how to make you feel warm. It never rejects you. It is there always no matter what is happening somewhere else. No one else can claim it. You are invisible.*

If the therapist can establish a link with the client's hiding place, then it is possible to enter many of the client's cognitive escape processes. The hiding place metaphor is rich with associations. When we talk to offenders, we often discuss the hiding place in these terms:

> *Think about this: What can a hiding place be for you? Start at the beginning of your life. Count up the number of different ways that the hiding place resonates. Hiding at the breast, hiding from a peek-a-boo from the adult figure, hiding with your friends from the adult world, hiding from school peers, hiding from your abuser, hiding from your physically abusive parent, hiding and masturbating, hiding with your*

pornography, hiding your abused difference from everyone, hiding your revenge, day-dreaming/fantasizing in your safe shame-proof mental bunker. Hiding until you do not need a place anymore, merely the experience and memory of that place. You need to make it a safe shelter for others. You make a false cocoon for your victim. Wasn't your hiding place really unsafe? Didn't he find you there? Was anywhere ever really safe? Was anyone ever safe from you?

The following is a short precis of a session with a client that began with a check-in disclosure about losing a job and beginning the effect of a deviant cycle. We used the hiding place as one of the tools of learning and disclosure.

That chair is the hiding place. Sit in it. Take me there. Show me it's boundaries. What does that part do? Where is the door? When do you close and open the door? You said today that you felt hurt by what the supervisor said to you. Where did you go to feel better? Show me where that is in this hiding place.

Has the hurting just begun? Choose someone who can double for the hurter. Your supervisor said what? He told you that you were daydreaming on the job? Show me the scene. Who here looks and acts like him? Give him the script. What was going on? What was the environment like? Who else was there? Are they important to this event? Set the scene for me. Make sure that the door to your hiding place, the one in your head, is not blocked.

Where is the door that the supervisor came through? Use that chair for the desk. Do the scene. Get someone to double for the moment when you go into the door of your hiding place. Now let's do it again but with you playing the boss. Only let's have you as the boss talking about what his business concerns are.

Let's see what else you are afraid of. Let's do the scene again and let's have you being the thoughts that you are having while the boss is talking. Take me to where you hid in your mind as he was talking to you. Who were you hiding from? There was the boss and who else? Another co-worker? What about him? And anyone else? Hmm, what were you feeling—ashamed, anxious, afraid? What do afraid, anxious, and ashamed look like? Make someone here look like Mr. Afraid. Become Mr. Afraid and chase after you. So you are on the run. Who are they? Where are you? Closing the door?

Does your hiding place protect you from the worst of these feelings? But don't you start fantasizing then? So the actions of someone else produce these feelings which put you on the run. You out-distance them and go to your hiding place. But isn't this the special hiding place? Isn't this the offending hiding place? Isn't this where you begin to picture children? Isn't this the same place that you go to when you want relief and revenge? It's dangerous. Let's go there again. Let's look at this hiding place again. Remember it is very old. Do you remember its beginning? Do you remember why you went there?

In this session the client was able to connect the dissociative response to his work experience with his ancient self-protecting escape to his early hiding place. In doing so he reached back into the traumatic site of his own victimization and set up the next session for a journey into the originating trauma.

A Journey with the Baby's Shoes, the Mask, and the Belt

In drama therapy, a prop is an unconscious extension of memory and action. When I visit my mother, she shows me old photographs of myself as a child. I am here and there at the same time. The photo is a prop that guides my memory to a specific place. If I look at a picture of my old bicycle, I have an instant sensory recall of the weight of the bike, the feel of the saddle, the feeling of being free. The prop seems to bypass my forgetfulness or repression for a moment. It bypasses the concreteness of language and its function as a tool of communication and survival.

For the offender, language can act as a trap. The offender often learns to make the inchoate appear to be sensible and appropriate. His secret may be a maelstrom of deviance, but his daily language in therapy or at work and at home seems "normal." His language is often seductive, passive, or therapeutically correct. Sex offenders are skilled at becoming treatment slick. In conventional therapy, the sex offender may present himself as a paragon of propriety, claiming that his upbringing was perfect and his behavior as exemplary as that of any middle-class man. His presentation can be as seductive as the grooming process he uses with his victim. He has covered up his tracks with words, but the fear and anxiety are still there. Therapists who can by-pass the words of control, can find the past and the pictograms of terror. Often, this non-linguistic associating, sensing, and remembering is generated by a prop. The prop box can become a critical part of the breakdown of denial, the onset of catharsis, and the role-taking necessary for a healthy return to society. I know practitioners in the field who have baby's coffins, bloody sheets, and very realistic looking dolls. My theater company travels with an assortment of male and female dolls, toy figures, telephone parts, a tablecloth, an empty photo frame, and so on. We find that the more ordinary the prop, the easier it can be for the client to remember, dissociate, go into a trance. Three of our most devastating tools are the belt, the baby's shoes, and the mask.

Each of these props generates a devastating sense of being in the past and in the present. Baby shoes are rife with memories, guilt, sexual victimization, and the memory of hiding and abandonment. Although the baby's shoes might correspond in reality to a one-year-old's shoes, offenders associate them with any age between 0 and 5 years old. Sometimes the shoes are filled with the judge and jury. Other times I ask the offender to hold the shoes to his ears and listen for the screams of his victims. These props overwhelm the offender's language denial and focus him on the crux of his life.

The mask cannot adequately be dealt with in this chapter. It is a multi-faceted tool with an awesome power to focus sex offenders on the identities that they use to gain the confidence of their victims, or to lead offenders to painfully recognize the nature of the "beast" within. The masks we use range from totem masks to emotion masks to realistic face masks. Totem masks have a symbolism that offenders recognize as traits. For instance, we have one mask with a brick wall on its face. Offenders variously identify it as a portrait of their stubbornness, a picture of denial, the painful wall of terror around their own victimization, or the inside of the tunnel vision that the offender experiences when he is victim-focused. Because masks are so powerful, it is not easy to use them. Offenders need to be gradually acclimated to their meanings and their use, and work sessions must be carefully created to maintain the masks' meaning. Not all props need to be treated with such care.

One of the most devastating and simple props is the belt. For many offenders the belt is rich with association. Ask an offender to put the belt in the place where it used to be kept at home or tell him to put the belt in the place where he was punished. He will almost immediately pick up the belt and walk to the place where it hung when he was a child. The belt has as many associations as metaphors like "the dinner table."

This affect-rich prop automatically jars loose the memory of pain and repression. Offenders seem to immediately have picture memories that are almost as strong as their deviant fantasies. Therapists who use the belt as a prop see the offender quickly go into the "trance" effect and can begin to ask very powerful questions:

- How old are you?
- What had you done?
- Is he coming to the door?
- Where are you going?
- When is he going to come in?
- Is it him now?

Sometimes the offender is so overwhelmed with fear that one may have to use a double or become the unspoken voice:

Oh God, please. Daddy, I didn't do it, I didn't do it! I love you! I hate you! I'm not a sissy. I'm not! Mummy, Mummy please!

The belt shows the therapist more of the family structure, and particularly who was considered "safe." Unfortunately, most offenders seem to have few memories of a caring adult. Too often, the mother figure is distant, dissociated from the gestalt of the family through a meticulous attention to tasks. She has no words for sexuality. She has a permanent umbrella to ward of the emotional climate changes.

The belt opens up the world of angry feelings and the sense of injustice that some sex offenders have refined to a microscopically accurate analysis of fairness and the righteous response:

Was it fair of that man to hurt you with the belt? Do you remember what you were being punished for? Do you remember how you made the pain go away? How do you make the pain go away now? Talk to the belt. Tell the belt everything that you have stored away in your mind. I know that it seems dangerous, but we are all here. It is safe in this room here. Whisper to me what you want to say. Say it louder. Push against my body as if it were the belt itself. Remember everything that you are feeling now. Is it fair?

It is never fair. But without being able to master those original experiences, without a concerted attempt at internalization, the old unfair experiences continue to be part of the matrix of the client's personality and the client's passive behaviors merely continue the humiliations that are the dynamo of revenge and the victimization of others. Powerlessness is the hard rock of righteous judgment and sexual rage. That passivity is a fine machinery for supporting deviance. The offender's heightened responses to daily living create an endless dread of consequences that are ancient and automatic — but invisible. We only see the passivity, fear, and, sometimes, the victimizing.

The therapist must affirm the injustice, the old wounds, and the repressed rage. With this affirmation, the offender can move from the hellish memories of the belt and his own victimization to his victim's pain and, finally, to victim empathy. Drama therapists help the offender make this journey through props like the baby's shoes and the mask. Each stage of prop catharsis is the underpinning for the next stage. In the following session, the props allowed the offender to see the intimate relationship between his rage and his attacks on his victims.

Walk me through the event, the last time you sexually assaulted your victim. No, you must do this alone in the space but we will all be with you. Your victims are here. And, you will be able to hear their cries.

He is ashamed and resists. Talk to him. Tell him why he must do this. Reach for a mask of a child, ask another offender to put it on and sit on the floor like a child and continue with:

Look at the child. What is he saying to you? Is he crying? Tell him what you did. Tell him about how you planned this. Tell him how you said that you loved him and it wasn't true.

Sometimes, when the shame is too great, the offender can do the grooming in mime. But, eventually he must put words to his actions. At this point, the therapist's objectives must be very clear: the actual sexual assault is not the only psychological act committed against the child; the victim's entire safe world is destroyed; and this act of "love" is an act of extraordinary rage and violence.

The latter point bears some analysis. Pedophiles often content themselves with distortions that their acts were motivated by love. Further, some pedophiles take refuge in the idea that they are merely addicted. It is a comforting notion because their offending then has the ring of a compulsion and the sense that the responsibility for the act is outside themselves. It is an extraordinary denial. Incapable of finding meaning in an adult world that threatens them with a constant recreation of the original act of their own victimization; like a school bully, they look for someone to beat up then blame that person.

The victim becomes their possession, their other repressed self to be hurt with the self-same lies that hurt them. To carry off such a thinking/behavior process, the offender must be able to merge his persona with children in such a way that he can blot out the real world signals of appropriateness.

Many pedophiles show poor boundaries. Their modes of attack and defense are predicated on subtle acts of seduction that blur the boundaries of what is acceptable. It is so automatic for offenders to emotionally fuse themselves with others that I remind therapists to be wary of what they see in an offender's eyes. Pedophiles sometimes seem to have the passive eyes that one associates with startled deer in the forest. Offenders see themselves in the victim's mask and play for survival with their seduction. It is interesting to speculate that early victimization may so traumatize the offender that his actual physiological growth is changed and he fails to assertively mature.

The painful part of drama therapy is in opening the door for the offender to glimpse the rage he feels at his victims, at their helplessness, and at his own helplessness. Each successful sexual assault reinforces a picture of victims as mere sacks of flesh.

The pedophile's photo gallery is an instrument of dehumanization. These offenders firmly believe that each victim can say "No!" They expect their victims to fight back as they believe they never did. Each victim is a chance to die with shame, and yet the core shame is reinforced with a numbing indifference.

Pedophiles often shock therapists by their rank indifference and a sort of brutal sullen defiance: "I am not going to do this any more. I am not even going to talk." This can seem like a mere passive resistance, but, offenders who are pressed about this resistance can be guided into a real rage that they will not forget. It is the rage that is denied yet always there. It is easy enough to get the tears from a pedophile, but it is the rage and its electric linkage to fantasy and offense that is so critical.

Then comes the final part of the session. The offender must find the mask that is the mask of sexual violence. Behind that mask, I put the baby shoes. Here, the offender must confess the rage to the victim and recognize the mask of hate:

I am the victim. I am the child. I am the powerless one. Tell the mask what you feel. Tell the mask how much you hate it.

And eventually it comes: "Push against my shoulders very hard." As he does, the old fears come back, the memory of trying to push his own rapist away from him. He touches base with the rage. He shouts at the old memory and the fused child-self molester. At the height of this rage, the mask is pulled away and there are the baby shoes:

I hate him for what he did to me! I hate that child. I hate that it is me and it's too weak to push me away. I can't push him away. I can't push you away. I hate that child so much.

The rage focuses on the victim and on himself, the rapist, and on his victimization and weakness. He cries. He floods with memories. Now is the time for words. He can speak. He can return back to the therapy session and name the flooding memories and thoughts. He must now make whatever peace he can with these props. They have come alive and will remain active in his mind and therapy for months to come.

In a way, this type of drama therapy resembles shamanic rituals. The drama therapist is the safe vehicle for ancient presences to be exorcised. The ritual allows everyone safe access to the original creation of the past matrix and its continued presence in therapy.

The pedophile has often been sexually victimized himself. Without a confidante, he has had only his mind to survive the past. He has learned how to make pain go away. He shuts off some of the painful memories. He covers the past in numbness, but circulates unconsciously and constantly around the scene of his crime. He becomes ultrasensitive to any act that even vaguely weakens him and that unconsciously duplicates his own early victimization. He collects sea shells of the past and keeps one part of his ear attuned to the memory. Locked into this trance defense and offense, he is consciously very sensitive to returning to this place. His very being can feel under attack. After all, he has spent many years refining his defended self. But through suggestion and the lightest of trance states, he can bypass his normal defense mode and be quickly sucked into the moment of his own victimization. This can have powerful results.

He is now locked into the source moments of his pain. Here in very quick time is the dramatic key to opening insight. Turned back into those moments, he experiences not only the terror, the weakness, the oppression but also the soul of his victimizer. Here he can be brought to see the unexpressed but deeply felt and repressed rage. His victimizer was bigger, stronger. He manipulated with sexual touch. He hurt the victim and did not care. He threatened in words and acts that no five-, six-, or seven-year-old could understand except that those words were a terrifying message from the real world. The threat alone will become emblematic of all adults. He is now alone without any adult hearing him, no one. He is alone, defenseless, deeply afraid, and incapable of expressing the anger at this new differentness. Young children who begin to process their own sexual victimization often go through violent attacks on other children. One wonders what would happen if they could attack adults, smear feces on walls, violently masturbate, or self-mutilate. The sexual switches have been turned on, yet they do not live in an age appropriate world where they experience response and parity. A five-year-old child has no sexual peer because sexuality has no function for a child.

Locked into a child's body alone, there is only fear and then a slowly building rage at the complete madness of it all. Repressing begins immediately. The wound is thrown into a mental pit and then covered with trance stuff. It will be a major player in the world of the violated/violator.

Drama therapy can open the secret world of the past and bring it into the present. In Figure 17.1 you can see a diagram of a two-story house we have created with questions that bring back both kinetic memories of the past and figure in the offender's own sexual assaults. In a therapy session we transform the phrase in the diagram, "Is he back? Listen!" from a discussion with the client about that moment in that room in his childhood past, to a scene in which we enact the footsteps of the rapist and let the client/victim give a running commentary of what must come next. His hidden memories closely coalesce with the memories of his own offenses. The hidden becomes public. The memory becomes concrete.

But the offender must also learn how to harness his dread and fear. He must learn to fight the lure of the secret universe and look for new strategies of psychological survival.

Teaching Real World Skills

Sex offenders must be readied for the real world. Pedophiles are often highly under-socialized, repressed, and chronically incapable of assertive relations. Adult rapists often have a cluster of anti-social thinking distortions mixed with poor interpersonal skills and a negative attitude to authority that make for dangerous coping skills in the "free" world. Most systems pay lip-service to providing real, tangible goals and skills for offenders. Society is equally ill-served by correctional and public attitudes that are more interested in the front end of punishment than the back end of returning offenders to society. The majority of the public refuses to accept the responsibility for insisting on real reintegration skills for adapting to a complex society, even though it acknowledges that prison/punishment does not work.

Offenders leave the frightening but monotonous world of the penitentiary for the safer but completely unpredictable world of society. Out there, offenders must have a place to stay, pay rent, find work, arrange their days to accommodate treatment, and

Figure 17.1
The House of Memories

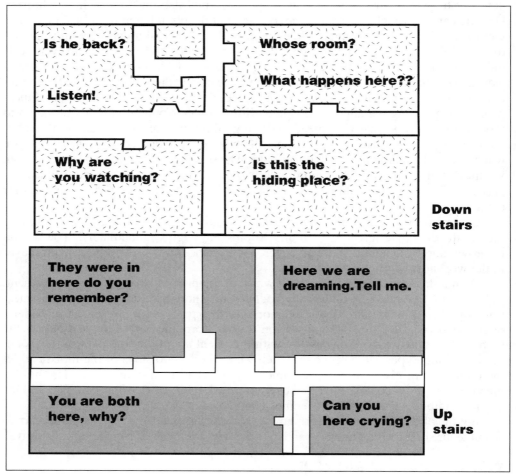

so on. They must learn to deal with social service organizations that keep them wait-ing and then never see them. They have to buy clothes, get on buses, and find some-thing to do on those long weekends when the mind can drift too easily to fantasy.

Sex offenders must learn how to deal with the world as it often is—stressful, un-directed, sometimes lonely, and always challenging to the core of the offender's life. An employer can unknowingly trigger the offender's abuse cycle merely by giving that offender a mild criticism. Sex offenders rarely have well-developed interpersonal skills. They cannot separate, for example, a criticism of their work habits from a sense that they are being criticized as a human being. They have learned how to get by with the minimal amount of attention and an ability to deflect interpersonal con-frontation or emotional pain.

A low profile is the necessary "cover" for the high roar of the hidden fantasy. Offenders are supersensitive, and they often convert perceived inequities into a cycle of hurt, depression, disassociation, fantasy, anger, planning, and acting-out. A directed role play/drama therapy session can surface the entire cycle both cognitively and affectively "in vivo" by focusing on every aspect of a high-risk, real-world situation.

Laying Out a Picture of Change

I often talk to sex offenders about role playing and role taking for their very life. It is crucial for them to understand that their thoughts and feelings in group sessions or in drama sessions are a measure of their present dangerousness. Offenders need to rehearse new behaviors no matter what part of the process of change they are in. However, offenders are masters of deception who are very resistant to doing something new.

For some offenders this will be the first time that they have ever been in treatment. That does not necessarily mean that they have escaped the social systems. Often from a young age, these men have gone to special education classes, alternative high schools, juvenile detention centers, and other specialized facilities. But this may be the first time they had to recognize their dangerous core beliefs and connect their private world with its consequences. It will be the first time that they have ever stripped down their lives to the tiny steps of thought, picture, action, feeling, and physical sensation.

Therapy is an implicit challenge to the offender's secret world that must be phrased in such a way that he feels confident enough to attempt new behaviors. Especially in drama therapy, it is critical to find a language of challenge and change that engages the client. The following is part of a session whose primary aim was experiencing the therapeutic objective:

Imagine a man who looks like you. Where is he? Is that a room, a bedroom, a kitchen, the dining room? Who is sitting in the room with you? Do you know him/her? Is he smiling, frowning? How do you feel about this person? Does it feel OK to be there? Is there anything that you want to say to him? Say it any way that you want. Did the person change? Would it help to bring this person here to this room?

Look around you. Is there anyone here who could double for this person? What information do you have to give them? For instance, what is the relationship between you two? Parent, relative, or friend. What are his qualities: open, friendly, judgmental, cynical? What is the nature of this unfinished business? Do you feel comfortable enough to take this on? Would you like someone to double for you? What does he have to know about this situation?

You have started to go into your secret fantasy place. What is happening? Is the other person safe from you? What are you doing now? Is the other person still safe?

What did you think and feel during this? Where was the transforming moment? How did that moment feel? Why wasn't that young person safe? What do you have to remember going into the situation? Can you remember what has been in your thoughts for so long? What thoughts, feelings? What type of pictures? So what will you do if those types of pictures, thoughts, feelings, and physical sensations occur again?

What is that type of intervention? Is this typical? Is this type of problem a major type of problem in your life? Where? We call this a pattern or wheel. These thoughts, pictures, and feelings all go together to end up giving us an experience that is painful to us or to others.

Because you have repeated this pattern throughout your life, it will be diffi- cult to break. You will find that other events/situations which seem to be dif- ferent may contain the seeds of this same pattern. If you can "rehearse" new behaviors in the safety of this classroom, and you can tolerate what may seem to be very emotionally dangerous, you have a chance of being able to do the same thing in the outside world.

Many offenders experience this moment of therapy as a powerful and dangerous challenge. Highly defended offenders will do everything they can to throw you and themselves off the scent. They will make phony contracts. They will swear that they are making changes and then cut the entire process down the moment they leave the treatment room. They will refuse to speak to you hoping to prevent you from ever focusing on them. They will swear they have already changed and may even enjoy the idea that they have. They may even behave as if they have changed. Meanwhile, deep inside the unconscious, an active and fragmented self is fighting to resist even the slightest change. Remember, change hurts. Everything the offender knows, every secret that has been protected, every wriggle of the fragmented self is alert and fighting.

Despite all these defenses, the offender must be encouraged to listen to why our social way of doing things is better and to hear how we deal with a difficult world. The offender must recognize that the world is safe—or at least safer—if it is handled in this new way. The offender must want to do more than just comply, which is gen- erally a ploy. The offender must go beyond simply feeling hurt and victimized. The offender must choose to make the new behaviors the focus of his life. It is very hard.

We are, after all, talking about change. People are afraid of change. For exam- ple, people who are depressed understand how to deal with their depressed state. Depression is what they know. Changing so they can live life happily may well be an overwhelming and frightening concept. The tenacity with which people fight change can also be seen in offenders who demonstrate pronounced sentimental feelings even though they are simultaneously most distrustful and very closed to change. This is the man who believes that he is "good" and yet is emotionally alienated and cold. They are the complex men in the prison yard who seem attached and sentimental about ani- mals. They sometimes are seen alone "publicly" in the yard, talking to and feeding stray cats and dogs. They genuinely believe they love these animals. They shower them with all the attention that they believe is love. But they also believe that these animals love them as humans cannot. There is an implied statement that people are not better than these animals. There is the further implication that other people are not to be trusted, that they will take and not love. There is no fight with animals. The inmate, who controls all the cards of social interaction, is telling you, "Go away, I am watching for you always." The inmate's early fractured self is en garde, ever judging, and hypervigilant. The created self that substituted for the absent reflection of the parent chaotically shuts the doors against perceived extinction. The result is a willful and hostile defiance.

This inmate finds it is very painful to come in out of the cold. Because he is in the emotional cold, he lays the blame for this aloneness on the world. He reinforces his perception of the facts of his life with minute bits of memory and observation that he distorts and squirrels away in a bag of resentment. If he ever comes to group it is only to reinforce what he already believes. And he will swear that black is white to support the emotional safety of being out in the cold. He will be hypersensitive to anything said or done to him. He will cut his own throat rather than see how twisted up his reasoning and feelings have become. We can only continue to keep the door open and the mirror clear and clean. That is our task. This inmate will become furious if his stray cat or dog goes up to someone else. The enormous need for attention or the enormous need for control overwhelms anything that might be like the sometimes painful experiences of sharing with someone else and all the frightening possibility that he will be abandoned, overlooked, or even shamed. He cannot bear psychic or intrapsychic pain. He runs from it to sex, opiates, easy money, or other men who see the world in this infantilized way. "I feel bad and I want something to make me feel better right now!" We must tell him that change will be painful. He will challenge us to be faithful to all of his needs all the time. And, he must learn that this is not possible. He is a three-year-old and who must learn to become twenty-three.

The weight machines are one of the few places where some of these men will work with anything resembling pain. At the weight pile they can preen and display themselves. The offender tells the always active inner monologist that he looks good, dangerous, powerful. Nothing can get through this permanent mirror that the offender maintains. Our criticism, our therapeutic ploys, are often all for nought. Remaining safe is the offender's task. The power of his early abandonment focuses his life very keenly. The knowledge of his distortion of every event in life is guarded, suppressed, dismissed, and buried. All he knows is that knowledge creates fear, anger, and pain that cannot be controlled.

Sex offenders must know that we understand and empathize with fear. They must be made to see that there is no other way. The role work is a test and a rehearsal that they must face and pass. Change is based on paying attention and fighting the biggest battle of their life against their worst enemy — themselves.

Role Work

Once the groundwork with rituals, catharsis, and metaphor have been done, the emphasis can shift to the real world. But role play, like all drama therapy, has one great danger: it is very easy to get sidetracked. It is helpful to keep a clear set of goals for doing drama therapy/role play with sex offenders. We find that the easiest way to remain focused is to make objectives that specifically relate to the cycle of deviancy and the precursors to relapse. The therapy must help the offender to:

1. Learn what situations, triggers, feelings and thoughts are the precursors to deviancy.
2. Learn the re-enforcers, stressors, that accompany the wheel of acting-out.

3. Identify high risk situations thoughts and feelings which are dangerous and then find and rehearse real coping strategies.
4. Learn to take new roles and reject the depressed cycle of fantasizing and offending.
5. Confront the strangle-hold of his past victimization.
6. Develop strategies to meet his emotional needs in a safe way.

These types of objectives are also comfortable for clients, who can chart their success and rehearse and experience their new skills with drama therapy. However, no therapy is that cut and dried. Sex offenders very often get stuck for months on end, especially as they work out the details of their own victimization. Similarly, offenders can remain quite overwhelmed by any effect, if they have spent years assiduously tamping down feelings into a daily numbness. Work with props can leave an offender with months of processing. Still, the basic strategy of using role play is simple.

The role play is just a simple key to open the door to memory, experience, and action. The action needs to be simple, because offenders must be able to clearly record their active perceptions. The more unstructured the role play the more the offender has to record and the greater the likelihood of confusion. The role play must be able to generate issues that are relevant to the offender's understanding. Finally, the role play must teach an experiential change. Conflict is a catalyst for this type of role learning.

The most basic role play has two characters and a conflict:

- I want the car for the night but my father wants me to stay in because I am grounded.
- I want to take a sick day but my employer is short-handed and wants me to come to work.
- I am picking up my car from the garage. I need it tonight, but when I get there the mechanic tells me he did not get around to it.
- I have just finished painting the kitchen blue. My partner walks in and says she does not like the color.
- I am a busy waiter. The customer claims that he has been charged for squid which he did not order.

The conflict is clear in each of these cases. Remember, though, that these conflicts may be difficult, or even shame-provoking, for the offender. It is important not to confuse the conflict by using analytical terms. If you begin your directions to the actors by saying, "Your character is into power and control," you miss the opportunity to see how the offender understands, perceives, solves, and responds to the simple conflict situation.

Character. Greater differences in station, authority, and class will create more potent conflicts. If the two characters are policeman and thief, cook and waiter, supervisor and employee, teacher and pupil, and father and daughter, then the differences in power will generate different needs in the conflict. By being simple and clear about the conflict and the characters, you give offenders a real opportunity to show you how they deal with fears, authority, humiliation, and the daily wear and tear of life.

Remember, in role play work, offenders will tend to play their own answers. That is, most people that are confronted with real life situations will solve problems as they themselves understand how to cope. Similarly, unless the client is very skilled at deception, the role answer in a simple role play will always be the offender's gut reaction. And that gut reaction contains the seeds of relapse and dissonance. Analyze what you see.

Situation. It is vital that offenders know where the action is set. They are used to "fudging" all the basic details of life. It is characteristic of their deception. Again, be basic: the situation takes place in the garage, at a supermarket, in the sitting room at your house, in the office, outside the movie house. Being very specific about "where" supports people in using their more typical thought and action responses.

The directed role play is successful only to the degree that it encourages the client to disclose or participate fully. Offenders tend to leave out significant personal experiences of an event for many reasons, including these:

- The memories are so automatic that offenders do not recognize that they are there.
- The memories are lost in the rewind process.
- The memories, thoughts, feelings, and actions are deliberately suppressed.
- The offender edits the experiences because he may be embarrassed, or feel that the real memory may affect his image.
- He does not think that these thoughts are important to the cycle.
- The offender has difficulty in finding words for the thoughts or feelings.
- The still active shame at the event interferes with the objective re-telling of the event.
- The offender misses vital physical action-based clues that are intimately tied to his outcome behavior. For instance, some offenders automatically escalate their rage by tightening their jaw muscles and fists. This automatic physical cue reinforces the cognitive statements of revenge.

But the crux is that the offender must learn the habit of reporting objectively every element of the entire experience. This is a skill that is difficult for many of us. Role play work:

- Recaptures forgotten elements of an experience.
- Re-reminds the offender after all the years of incarceration that his old and ineffective pattern of coping, understanding, and interpreting is extensive and still very much alive and well.
- Gives the offender a more sophisticated sense, memory and more skilled cognition.

If a Relapse Prevention contract is to be successful, the therapist and the offender must have the sensation that they have all the facts, pictures, thoughts, feelings, and physiological sensations. The offender's sensory memories will increase along with his or her participation in basic role plays. Sometimes, the new memories or the attempt to put sensations into words is just as important as evoking forgotten experiences. The therapist and the offender must both, in their own ways, be courageous. The therapist needs to go beyond the client's angry resistance, and the client must find the courage to investigate, report, and understand an ancient fear. The simple role play and a simple session outline are key to the success.

A Typical Session. A typical session begins with each member pairing up and doing a simple mirror exercise. That is, one offender begins a series of movements and the other offender imitates them. Nominally, this is a non-threatening exercise, but in some cases even this minimally affective exercise can trigger a sense of being overwhelmed.

The paired offenders are then asked to make the subject of their mirroring exercises the actions they took prior to one of their assaults. This is intended to both highlight the cycle and to see whether the offender can battle a sense of powerlessness and vulnerability to his own feelings. An offender who can clearly and painfully get through to the end of the offense cycle is considered ready to begin the work of intervention and learning new interpersonal skills.

The mime cycle could begin by asking an offender who feels slighted at work to show us this scene. Beginning with his actual work actions, progress to his looking startled by a comment from a co-worker, the shutting down of the healthy social interactions, getting depressed and perhaps being on a bus, obviously fantasizing, arriving at a playground, and beginning to scan for children. I stop the process here. Mime as a memory exercise is very intense and intriguingly mimetic of the processes of the pedophile. The molester imitates being in the world while being really in his mind. In fact, it is his frightened inability to be in the world that we must address.

We then go back to the moment when the co-worker seemed to make fun of him. Working from his phenomenological report of his subjective experiences during his "humiliation," we repeat the experience with the co-worker. This time, the offender must simultaneously shout out what he is thinking. He does it again. Then he gets ready to use the intervention that he has been developing in group and in assignments with other therapists. We try to use the simplest and most potent interventions such as "Stop, what is the other person feeling?" or "I can handle these feelings without getting mad." He announces where he is going to use the intervention. We reconstruct the scene again and he uses the intervention.

Then we raise the pressure up yet another notch by setting a scenario that is sufficiently like the original that the offender is likely to experience somewhat the same cycle of thoughts, feelings, and physiological change. However, the scene will have a twist or heightening effect so that the offender must be very vigilant and skilled in the use of his intervention. For instance, a disgruntled employee might be added to the employer/employee scenario. This employee might tell the boss that "This new guy doesn't work hard enough. All he does is daydream." This added event may be too much for the offender to manage. If it is, he must go through the process again of identifying precisely where he needs to intervene in this new scenario. This offender also may need to work on the skill of dealing with someone else's emotions while remaining within the role boundary of a co-worker. Each step is based on his disclosure of his comfort and how fast he runs to his "hiding place."

Each time the offender is successful, the level of information, role complexity, interpersonal skill levels, and assertiveness are raised. Once the offender can come up with a plan for the first six weeks of being in the real world, we gradually move toward issues like family relationships, children, drugs, and alcohol. At each step of the way, the offender has to match the role play with a real awareness of how he thinks, where to intervene, and what new measures to take.

It is important to note that the intervention is only a stop-gap measure. In order to do more than just white-knuckle his way through the universe, the offender must learn new interpersonal skills. We find that Arnold Goldstein's book, *The Prepare Curriculum*, to be one of the better primers on the active teaching of interpersonal skills. Goldstein's book is tailor-made for rehearsal. He splits up skills into small easily learned steps and often includes a real life situation for enactment.

The Therapist's Discomfort

It is crucial that skills like discussing complex feelings, problem solving in a non-victimizing way, or itemizing and prioritizing interpersonal responsibilities, all need to be rehearsed. It is unfortunate that too many brilliant therapists miss the chance of using the drama therapy skill because they are either afraid of looking foolish or fear a possible loss of control. I do not want to minimize their feelings in the slightest. Even after all these years of doing this work, I still feel occasionally threatened or uncomfortable. Still, this therapy is not that complex.

In part, role play is the ability to choose other temporary personae that facilitate mutual needs. Role play helps the wheel of life roll around more peacefully. It is the daily glue that we all use to help our friends, lovers, and employees to accept differences and take new directions. It is a temporary state. One does not need to remain that person in order to continue one's own life. It is very common in our lives.

Every married couple has probably experienced a scenario like this: "I know you don't get on with my father, but please, for my sake, can you just try to be charming? I know he's not easy. . . ." Long before the father-in-law's arrival, the spouse-in-law will have decided how he or she is going to act. I always go back to my private school days: stiff upper lip and lots of self control.

Here is another example. When you speak to your boss in private, your friendship may break the role relationship of boss/subordinate. But when you meet your boss in a public work place, you act the boss/worker role. Sometimes we have very little information to support our roles. A worker coming into a new situation looks all at sea, or, a little shaky and wobbly. We can see that this worker has settled down when he or she seems to more comfortably do what is expected.

Occasionally, we find ourselves in situations where we have to take on roles that are very uncomfortable for us. For example, someone who is unassertive by nature who is suddenly thrust into a situation where he or she must be very emotionally potent, can find it very hard to break years of old behaviors. In the same way, some offenders, no matter what the situation, use violence to solve the problem and find it difficult to take a backseat to anyone. Similarly, many sex offenders are so afraid of rejection that they respond to anger and disappointment with hurt and shame. They do not take on the role of being assertive. Their thoughts and feelings are so powerful that they easily become converted into the raw material of offending.

Therapists are artists of the emotions even though some therapists understandably fear their clients' emotions. When ancient repressed rage and outrage is finally released, it can be very frightening. But clients must know that they can discharge their feelings and be heard and held.

We have to follow the mind of the offender. Sometimes, we have to step in as the punishing father with the belt in a role play about dangerous child rearing: "If you don't get up those stairs, you'll get a whipping before and after dinner." Sometimes we must play the part of the child/victim in a scene about grooming: "Will you play with me today? My mum has left me on my own." And sometimes we have to be the voice of social service's alienation: "I'm sorry, sir, but your check hasn't come in. Come again next week. Have a nice day." We all know the roles. But this knowledge is sometimes threatening. We can only remember that these roles are the stuff of the real world that the offender must navigate with his bird of death on his shoulder. We learn that the enemy is sometimes within us and that we use a variety of roles to control the self. The drama therapist must teach how to take a role and how to play a role. It is exactly like life.

Conclusion

Drama therapy is a potent tool in the arsenal of any therapist or counselor working with sex offenders. Once you begin to use drama therapy, you will quickly develop your own props, ideas, exercises, and rituals. I caution you to begin by getting a basic grounding in some of the terms and concepts. Good training, especially in a group setting, can be invaluable.

Like all good therapy, doing drama therapy will extend your own affective skills. You will begin the fascinating process of examining your own interpersonal processes in action. It can be exhilarating. Look for the unspoken dialogue, the unsaid experience. Sometimes, you will have to find the hidden pictures amidst a host of denial. The drunk gives you his side of the story, but what about the bottle? What does the bottle have to say to the drunk? What does the fantasy have to say to the offender? What does the offender's eye have to say? What does the orgasm have to say?

Drama therapy is first and foremost experience. Good drama therapy creates experiences. What are the experiences that this offender has never had? Has he ever just played? Has he held a truck in his hands? Has he played baseball, soccer? Has he ever just stood up and done something silly, something unarmored? Has he lived without hurting?

Drama therapy is the home of those experiences. It is the place to practice life safely. It is the place to see life, to feel, to hurt, to celebrate. It is a concentrated, clear-eyed but forgiving place to begin to forgive, make the deepest of apologies, make amends, and heal. It is life-in-a-box in the real world.

Chapter 18

Psychopharmacological Options for Sex Offenders

William B. Land, M.D.

Overview

This chapter discusses a variety of psychopharmacological approaches that may be helpful in some cases of sexual deviancy. Both antiandrogens and antidepressants, particularly the serotonin reuptake inhibitors have shown some promise when utilized in a comprehensive treatment program.

Psychiatrists have traditionally prescribed various psychotropic medications to control deviant and aggressive sexual activity, including antipsychotic medication, antiandrogens, and mood stabilizers. However, most research on the effectiveness of these agents with this population has methodological limitations. Researchers have used small samples and often have not employed scientific protocols such as placebo or comparative controls. Recent research using larger samples and employing placebo controls does report beneficial results. This chapter reviews recent studies and issues involving the prescription of specific medications, including dosage and potential side-effects.

Antiandrogens

Medroxyprogesterone Acetate. The most famous drug used specifically with sex offenders is the antiandrogen medroxyprogesterone acetate (MPA or Depo-Provera™). This drug has been the subject of a good deal of controversy due to a popularly held belief that it is "chemical castration." MPA was first used with sex offenders in 1966 (Money, 1968). It can legally be prescribed for sex offenders even though the Food and Drug Administration (FDA) has not specifically approved its use for this purpose. Physicians had previously used MPA as a female contraceptive and to treat a variety of medical conditions including gynecologic cancer (Smith, 1992).

Mechanism of Action and Side Effects. MPA inhibits the release of luteinizing hormones (LH) from the pituitary. This hormone normally causes the testicles to produce androgens. When MPA is administered, there is a subsequent decrease in androgen levels, especially testosterone. Through this mechanism, MPA presumably suppresses or lessens the frequency of erection and ejaculation. It also lessens desire for sexual behavior including deviant sexual behavior. However, men receiving MPA are still capable of achieving erections, engaging in sexual intercourse, and ejaculating. When patients discontinue MPA, their androgen levels return to normal within seven to 10 days (Money, 1987).

During treatment, the sexual accessory organs (including the prostate and seminal vesicles) temporarily decrease in size. Other possible side-effects include weight gain, lethargy, headaches, hot/cold flashes, nightmares, hyperglycemia, insomnia, nausea, muscle cramping, irritability, and shortness of breath. The long term effects of MPA are unknown. This medication may also have carcinogenic properties, although this has not been firmly established (Smith, 1992). MPA must be used with caution, particularly in patients with pre-existing diabetes, obesity, or pulmonary disease.

Dosage. The starting dose for MPA is usually 500 mg. intramuscularly every seven days. After four weeks the dose can be lowered in 50 mg. increments. The maintenance dose is adjusted according to the patient's subjective report of decreased paraphiliac urges and ideation. Most men usually receive between 150 and 800 mg. per week and tolerance apparently does not develop (Money, 1987).

Finally, in a recent study by Gotestein (1993), psychiatrists prescribed low dose oral medroxyprogesterone acetate for seven patients. Five of the patients had noncontact paraphilias (i.e., voyeurism, exhibitionism, compulsive masturbation, masochism, telephone scatologia, transvestite fetishism) and three patients had contact paraphilias (i.e. pedophilia, sexual sadism, rapism, zoophilia). Six responded at 60 mg. per day over a period of approximately 15.33 months. All patients described fewer paraphiliac fantasies. No patient reported engaging in paraphilic behavior. In addition, none of the patients displayed significant side-effects. The authors conclude that low dose oral medroxyprogesterone acetate be considered in patients who meet any of the following conditions:

1. Patients who are not court mandated for pharmacological treatment. Because court-mandated sex offenders and/or paraphilics theoretically represent significant social danger, they are not candidates for low dose MPA. Given the

consequences of noncompliance with treatment, high dose depot (injectable) MPA is more appropriate initially in these cases.

2. Patients with preexisting hypertension, obesity, or family incidence of diabetes mellitus, who otherwise would be considered for high-dose treatment.

3. Patients with proven compliance records in therapy for a paraphiliac condition where failure to alter behavioral manifestations of the paraphilia has been the case.

4. Patients with known histories of low-frequency, noncontact paraphilias (i.e., exhibitionism, fetishism, voyeurism) and where the social danger of the paraphiliac behavior is minimal.

5. Patients with contact paraphilias (i.e., pedophilia, sexual sadism including rapism and/or masochism, frotteurism, toucherism, etc.) whose sexual deviancy is restricted to fantasy alone. These would all be classified as DSM-III-R "mild" forms of this disorder.

6. Patients who have a history of failure to respond to a variety of other treatment for paraphilias.

Efficacy Studies. Cooper (1986) reviewed studies on the use of progesterones including medroxyprogesterone acetate and cyproterone acetate and concluded that these drugs were reasonably effective in suppressing sexual desire and arousal in men. The best results were in self-referred, non-recidivist, hypersexual males with good social support systems. Several more recent studies report therapeutic benefit with MPA. Federoff (1992) reported a retrospective, self-report study of 46 male patients in the Johns Hopkins Sexual Disorders Unit who met criteria for at least one paraphilic sexual disorder using DSM-III-R criteria. Paraphilics were combined into three diagnostic groups: pedophilia, exhibitionism, and voyeurism, and other paraphilics. All patients were followed in the clinic for at least five years and received group psychotherapy. Experimental subjects also received MPA. The relapse rate for experimental subjects was 15% whereas that for control subjects was 68%. However, the authors emphasized that the study was an open retrospective investigation conducted in a clinic that has considerable experience prescribing MPA. For this reason, they encourage replication of the study's findings in a multi-center, double-blind treatment protocol.

Meyer (1992) compared 40 men aged 16 to 78 years old who took MPA for between six months and twelve years with a control group of 21 men who refused MPA and were treated with psychotherapy instead. The men receiving MPA included 23 pedophiles, 7 rapists, and 10 exhibitionists. The control group consisted of men with similar types of offending behavior. Of subjects prescribed MPA, 18% re-offended while on the medication and 35% re-offended after stopping it. In the control group 58% re-offended. The authors conclude that MPA is useful in decreasing offending sexual behavior in carefully selected, motivated, and well-informed men.

Emory (1992) sheds further light on conditions under which MPA is likely to be effective. He reviewed the use of the drug in Texas between 1980 and 1990 in pedophiles, rapists, exhibitionists, and voyeurs. Factors associated with re-offense were (1) high initial plasma testosterone, (2) regressed behavior type (Groth, et al. 1982), (3) exhibitionism, (4) continued substance abuse, and (5) past history of major head trauma. Emory also cautions that MPA should only be used in carefully selected patients. For example, he does not accept patients who admit the sexual offense, but blame drugs, alcohol, fatigue, or their own abused childhood for MPA therapy.

In a smaller study, Kiersh (1990) reported his work with eight court-committed sexual offenders (two rapists and six pedophiles) who served as their own controls. MPA injections for 16 weeks were alternated with saline injections for 16 weeks. Although MPA decreased sexual drive, it did not change the object of the sexual drive (i.e., pedophiles remained interested in children).

There are obvious limitations to many of these studies including reliance on self-reports, termination of patients who experience serious side-effects, and the lack of comparison groups receiving either a placebo or another drug. Federoff (1992) proposed other criteria for a fair trial of MPA, as for any medication including subjects (1) being sufficiently ill that therapy is considered necessary, (2) followed long enough follow-up for relapse to occur, (3) opportunity for relapse (i.e., subjects should not be incarcerated or otherwise unable to commit sex offenses) and, (4) being sufficiently motivated to accept treatment.

Mood Stabilizers

Antidepressants. Recent developments in the psychopharmacological management of sex offenders have focused on the use of antidepressant and antiobsessional medications such as fluoxetine (Prozac) and clomipramine (Anafranil). Jenike (1989) suggested that compulsive sexual behavior and obsessive-compulsive disorder may both involve the neurotransmitter serotonin. Obsessive-compulsive disorder and paraphilias both involve a build-up of tension that is relieved through a compulsive act. Therefore, could medications used for obsessive-compulsive disorders also be helpful for sex offenders?

Fluoxetine. Although published reports describe encouraging results using antidepressants and anti-obsessional agents with sex offenders, the studies have mostly included case reports and open studies with a small number of patients. For example, Kashkan (1990) prescribed fluoxetine for 10 sex offenders who were not responding to concomitant behavioral therapy. Sexual fantasies, urges, and contacts decreased in all subjects and re-emerged when subjects reduced or discontinued fluoxetine. Perilstein (1991) reported favorable results in three patients prescribed fluoxetine: a pedophile, an exhibitionist, and a patient diagnosed with voyeurism/frotteurism. He suggested that this beneficial effect occurred because fluoxetine may decrease the patient's paraphilic urges or directly decrease sexual activity, a side-effect noted in patients receiving fluoxetine. Other case reports describe successful use of fluoxetine with patients suffering from paraphilic coercive disorder (a rapist), (Kafka, 1991), exhibitionism (Bianchi, 1990), and voyeurism (Emmanuel, 1991).

Dosage. Kafka (1993) treated over 150 paraphiliac men with fluoxetine in doses commonly prescribed for depressive disorders (e.g., 10-100 mg/day.) In his experience, when effective, fluoxetine mitigates sexual impulsivity but preserves "normative" sexual desire. Kafka usually starts patients on 20 mg. per day of fluoxetine. A discernable effect on sexual as well as depressive symptoms is usually apparent within four weeks. The fluoxetine dose can be titrated every 4-5 weeks. Most patients tolerate fluoxetine but common side-effects include nausea, tremor, headache, sweating, drowsiness, and nervousness.

Clomipramine. Psychiatrists have also treated obsessive-compulsive disorder and sexual disorders with clomipramine, a tricyclic antidepressant with strong serotonergic properties. Four patients diagnosed with exhibitionism (Wawrose, 1992; Casals-Ariet, 1993; Torres, 1993) responded positively to clomipramine. Of note, one of these patients (Casals-Ariet, 1993) had been treated with fluoxetine, up to 80 mg/day, with some improvement of mood, but no change of behavior. Rubey (1993) reported the successful use of clomipramine in two patients: a 25-year-old male who complained of frequent visits to female prostitutes and preoccupation with pornography and in a 19-year-old male with borderline mental retardation who complained of a constant "need for sex," and said he was "going to get some or rape someone." The authors concluded that clomipramine was useful for obsessional sexual preoccupation and compulsive sexual behavior in patients who did not meet formal criteria for obsessive-compulsive disorder. This effect may be due to a decrease in sexual preoccupation or to a physiologic decrease in sexual function. Both results have been described in patients prescribed clomipramine.

Krusie (1992) sought to determine if similar effects could be obtained with desipramine, a traditional tricyclic antidepressant with only weak serotonergic properties. In his study, 15 paraphilics entered a double-blind crossover comparison of clomipramine versus desipramine proceeded by a two week placebo period. Four patients responded to the placebo. Three others failed to complete the study for other reasons. The eight remaining subjects all responded positively to both drugs, with no preferential response to clomipramine, the more serotonergic drug. The authors conclude from this negative result that paraphilias may not be part of the Obsessive-Compulsive Disorder spectrum. However, because the result for both medications were greater than for a placebo, the authors also conclude that both medications may have a role in the treatment of sexual disorders.

Dosage. Most psychiatrists prescribe clomipramine at a starting dose of 25 mg. daily with gradually increased, divided doses to approximately 100 mg. daily for the first two weeks. The dose can be gradually increased over the next several weeks up to 250 mg. daily. Common side-effects include dry mouth, somnolence, tremor, dizziness, and constipation. In addition, clomipramine may lower the seizure threshold.

Conclusion

Because of the small number of studies that have been done, the conflicting results that have been found, and methodological limitations, psychiatrists should be cautious in using these drugs with sex offenders. In addition, patients should only receive medication after appropriate informed consent is obtained and documented. Kafka (1993) offers the following caveats: (1) patients with sexual impulsivity may not readily acknowledge a sexual disorder because of guilt, shame, distrust, or fear of legal consequence, and (2) although drugs may ameliorate paraphilias, persons with sexual impulse disorders may also benefit from group therapy, behavior therapy, and comprehensive Relapse Prevention programs. Further research is clearly needed, using larger samples and employing double-blind, placebo-controlled studies.

References

Bianchi, M. (1990). Fluoxetine treatment of exhibitionism (letter). *American Journal of Psychiatry*, 147:8, 1089-1090.

Casals-Ariet, C. and Cullen K. (1993). Exhibitionism treated with clomipramine (letter). *American Journal or Psychiatry*, 150:8, 1273-1274.

Coleman, E., Cesnik, J., Moore, A.M., and Dwyer, S.M. (1992). An exploratory study of the role of psychotropic medications in the treatment of sex offenders. In Pallone, N.J. (Ed.) *Sex offender treatment: Psychological and medical approaches*. New York: The Haworth Press, Inc.

Cooper, A.J. (1986). Progestens in the treatment of male sex offenders: A review. *Canadian Journal of Psychiatry*, 31, 73-79.

Emmanuel, N.P., Lydiard, R.B., and Ballenger, J.C. (1991). Fluoxetine treatment of voyeurism (letter). *American Journal of Psychiatry*, 148:7, 950.

Emory, L.E., Cole, C.M., and Meyer, W.J. (1992). The Texas experience with Depo-Provera: 1980-1990. In Pallone, N.J. (Ed.) *Sex offender treatment: Psychological and medical approaches*. New York: The Haworth Press, Inc.

Federoff, J.P., Wisner-Carlson, R., Dean, S., Berlin, F.S. (1992). Medroxy-progesterone acetate in the treatment of paraphyliac sexual disorders. In Pallone, N.J. (Ed.) *Sex offender treatment: Psychological and medical approaches*. New York: The Haworth Press, Inc.

Gotestein, H.G. and Schubert, D.S.P. (1993). Low-dose oral medroxy progesterone acetate in the management of paraphilias. *Journal of Clinical Psychiatry*, 54, 182-188.

Groth, A.N., Jobsoh, W.F., and Gary, T.S. (1982). The child molester: Clinical observations. In Conte, J. and Shore, D.S. (Eds.), *Social work and child sexual abuse*, pp. 129-144. New York: The Haworth Press, Inc.

Jenike, M.A. (1989). Obsessive-compulsive and related disorders. *The New England Journal of Medicine*, 321:8, 539-541.

Kafka, M.P. (1993). Personal communication.

Kafka, M.P. (1991). Successful treatment of paraphiliac coercive disorder (a rapist) with fluoxetine hydrochloride. *British Journal of Psychiatry*, 158, 844-847.

Kashkin, K. (1990). Sex offenders treated with fluoxetine: preliminary results. Poster presentation at the American Psychiatric Association Annual Meeting, May 1990. APA: New York: New research program and abstracts. American Psychiatric Association, Washington, DC. 1990, 170.

Keirsch, T.A. (1990). Treatement of sex offenders with Depo-Provera. *Bulletin of the American Academy of Psychiatry and the Law*, 18:2, 179-187.

Kruesi, J.M.P., Fine, S., Valladares, L., Phillips, R.A., and Rapoport, J.L. (1992). Paraphilias: A double-blind crossover comparison of clomipramine versus dosipramine. *Archives of Sexual Behavior*, 21:6, 587-593.

Meyer, W.J., Cole, C., and Emory, E. (1992). Depo-Provera treatemnt for sex offending behavior: An evaluation of outcome. *Bulletin of the American Academy of Psychiatry and the Law*, 20:3, 249-259.

Money, J. (1987). Treatment guidelines: Anti-androgen and counseling of paraphiliac offenders. *Journal of Sex and Marital Therapy*, 13:3, 219-223.

Perilstein, R.D., Lipper, S., Friedman, L.J. (1991). Three cases of paraphilias responsive to fluoxetine treatment. *Journal of Clinical Psychiatry*, 52:4, 169-170.

Rubey, R.A., Brady K.T., and Norris, E.T. (1993). Clomipramine treatment of sexual preoccupation. *Journal of Clinical Psychopharmacology*, 13:2, 158-159.

Smith, R. (1992). The use of medroxy-progesterone acetate (Depo-Provera). In Schwartz, B.K. (Ed.) *A practitioners handbook for treating the incarcerated male sex offender*. Washington, DC.: National Institute of Corrections.

Torres, A.R. (1993). Exhibitionism treated with clomipramine. *American Journal of Psychiatry*, 150:8m 1273-1274.

Wawrose, F.E. and Sisto, T.M. (1992). Clomipramine and a case of exhibitionism (letter). *American Journal of Psychiatry*, 149:6, 843.

Part 4

Aftercare

Aftercare is perhaps the most crucial part of the treatment of sex offenders. Institutionalized offenders have little opportunity to re-offend. Children are not roaming unsupervised around prisons and while there are usually female or male staff members who could be assaulted, the other precursors to rape are rarely present. This is unlike the substance abuser who may be able to measure the effectiveness of his treatment by his resistance to the alcohol and drugs which are usually readily available in prisons.

By gradually transitioning sex offenders into the community, the offender, the therapist, his classification officer, parole officer, and support system members can slowly evaluate whether he or she is able to utilize the interventions which he/she has been taught in the treatment program. Sex offenders who are released into the community without appropriate supervision and treatment may be overwhelmed by the stress inherent in the process and consequently withdraw, isolate, and return to his or her high risk methods of handling stress. Even though no individual or group wants to be targeted as having recommended the release of an individual who then goes out and commits a highly publicized re-offense, those charged with the responsibility of making these decisions must not forget that public safety is best served by conditional release programs versus waiting for an offender to be released without conditions.

The chapter on Relapse Prevention has been placed in this section because it discusses not only the use of Relapse Prevention as a treatment technique but as a specialized supervisory approach. The use of this method can maximize the efficient use of supervisory resources by focusing on the specific precursors to relapse for each sex offender. These precursors are much more subtle and varied than those seen in a more generic group of offenders.

An entire chapter deals with the various issues related to community supervision of sex offenders. States may choose to train a cadre of specialized probation and parole officers to supervise sex offenders. Release conditions must also be individualized based on an individual's relapse cycle.

Chapter 19

Aftercare Treatment Programs

by Nancy Steele, Ph.D.

Overview

Treatment of sex offenders in a secure setting teaches new behaviors and increases control over the older assaultive behaviors. Hopefully, when offenders are released, they will not harm others again. If the lessons taught in treatment are to be transferred to the new and less controlled setting of the community, aftercare or follow-up within that community is essential. Treatment then becomes a vehicle for easing the transition between the artificial living arrangements of confinement to the more realistic living arrangements outside the institution.

This chapter outlines how sex offenders can be gradually transitioned from a prison program into the community with the use of halfway houses. The discussion emphasizes the importance of this final step in the treatment of sex offenders.

Re-Offense Rate Measures Treatment Program's Effectiveness

A measure of a treatment program's effectiveness is the re-offense rate of its graduates. The problems of detecting recidivism in sex offenders are frequently mentioned in the literature of the field and are well documented in a study by Groth, Longo, and McFadin (1982). The few available studies seem to show that the highest rate of known repeated offenses occurs within the first two years of release from a correctional facility (Christiansen, Elers-Nielson, Lamaire, and Sturup, 1965; Soothill and Gibbens, 1978).

In 1979, Minnesota began a study that carefully followed the behavior of 74 untreated sex offenders released from the state prison. In the first year, 35 of them (47%) either absconded or were arrested on a new offense. While not all of these arrests resulted in convictions, they indicated varying degrees and types of problem areas the offenders experienced during their initial release period. These problems ranged from fights with wives and girlfriends to stabbings to new felony-level sex offenses. The average time to rearrest was 5.1 months after release. Six offenders were arrested on new sex offenses within the first six months; two of these offenses occurred within two weeks of release.

Given these indications that sex offenders just released from prison are at a high risk to re-offend, it seems clear that strong aftercare is a necessary component of institutional treatment programs.

Community Reintegration Programs Reduce Recidivism

Some research, as well as accepted correctional practice, points to the need for a gradual return of all offenders to the community. LeClair (1981) has reported on a study completed in the Massachusetts Department of Corrections covering releases of 8,121 inmates in a seven-year time period. Recidivism rates for all types of offenders dropped from 25% to 16% with the establishment of a community reintegration model in the correctional system. (In this study, recidivism was defined as a return to prison, for any reason, within one year after release.) The model used decreasing levels of security, the introduction of a furlough system, and a pre-release program that allowed offenders to live in the community where they could find jobs and/or educational opportunities.

The continuation of treatment combined with the increased exposure to the community allows for the transference of learning to the setting where it needs to be implemented. The individual establishes trust with the new community therapist and the group, and his uneasiness, which increases upon release from the correctional facility, can be dealt with in a much more effective way. In addition, the treatment becomes more relevant when the individual is exposed to the community in a gradual, controlled way. The urge to act-out sexually rarely manifests itself within the institution but sometimes floods the individual when he is first exposed to life outside. If he is honest at this point and if the therapist is skillful, it is a great opportunity for him to get help in strengthening his controls. Conducting treatment exclusively in a secure, controlled institutional setting is like teaching someone to swim in a bathtub.

Much of the information about aftercare in this chapter was derived from work with the Transitional Sex Offender Program (TSOP), which has always had a strong community aftercare component. This Minnesota program was administered through a medium security prison about 20 miles north of the Twin Cities. The men, who were in their last 10 to 12 months of incarceration, were involved in an institutional residential treatment program. The TSOP participants agreed to complete four months of aftercare in a halfway house in Minneapolis. While living in the halfway house, they found jobs and began to spend more time with their families and friends. Their roommates were men with whom they had gone through treatment. Participants attended group sessions one night a week and had an individual or couples session with their TSOP therapist once a week.

After moving from the halfway house, the participants attended the group every other week for three months, Thus, over a period of seven months, they gradually decreased their contact with TSOP and its staff. By the time they completed the program, they were living in the community, reporting to their parole officers, and had established a social support network. This could include referral to community outpatient treatment, which was sometimes necessary, especially for incest families who wished to reunite.

TSOP's strong approach to structure and aftercare has yielded promising results. Recently a study was completed by the Research Office in the Minnesota Department of Corrections (Welfling, 1987). It compared return rates to prison of 111 sex offenders who completed TSOP with those of 64 offenders who either quit or were removed from the program and were not involved in the aftercare phase. Two years after release 5% of the TSOP graduates returned to prison with new criminal convictions, and 14% of the program failures returned. This still compares favorably with the general return rate to prison for all adult offenders in Minnesota, which shows a new conviction rate of 20% after two years. This may suggest that while some treatment inside of prison helps, completion of the aftercare component improves the success rate considerably.

Other institutional programs, frustrated with the need for an aftercare component, have begun to bring parole and mental health staff in from the communities in order to train them and develop the needed liaisons for aftercare. One of the biggest problems in developing only institutional programs is that people who could be treated in the community may be sent to prison for treatment. This is not only more expensive for the taxpayer but is also destructive to the individual and the families involved. The best way to protect against this is to develop resources in the community that integrate with institutional services, thus providing continuity of care and control.

Facilitating Release from the Institution

Many mechanisms were built into TSOP to ease the sex offenders' transition back into the community and to help them generalize what they had learned in treatment to situations in the community. About six weeks before their release date, which was established by their sentence, the men began to attend the outpatient group that met one night a week at the halfway house where they would be living. Time spent with their inpatient group decreased slightly at this point. The outpatient group gave the men a chance to see where they would be living and to hear the problems and concerns of those who were further along in the program. In general, the more one knows about an upcoming situation, the better one can prepare for it. The men were driven to the halfway house by the TSOP staff who ran the group. The staff also returned them to the institution after each session. In many programs, outpatients return to the inpatient setting where they underwent treatment as another way to accomplish the same linkage. However, in those instances the treatment emphasis was on the concerns of those in the institution and the focus may not have been so much on community adaptation. In group sessions, if the outpatients were being realistic about their concerns and feelings, the inpatients had a chance to preview their own exits from the institution.

Twice a month the participants in the transitional phase reported to men still living in the treatment cottage about how the outpatients were doing. More detailed, informal discussion went on outside the group and cottage meetings, which kept the inpatients aware of the progress of the men in the halfway house. Participants' failures were rarely hidden or downplayed. When the progression of a failure could be traced, especially in those few cases where a new sex offense had been committed, it was reported to the cottage residents in a way that helped them better understand what the man himself could have done differently and emphasized how each person can learn from the failure of another.

From the program's inception, there has been a call-in line that enables men in the community to contact inmates or staff 24 hours a day, seven days a week. Although this was first conceived of as a crisis line and is occasionally used that way, it primarily functions as another supportive link between the correctional facility and the community. It allows men to maintain friendships they have made in treatment, to exchange information about the outside world, and to make plans for the future.

Furloughs or day passes are another way for inmates to maintain some contact with the outside world. The use of passes is encouraged so the men can attend AA meetings, visit their families, or participate in social and recreational activities in the community. Sometimes the inmates are encouraged to go out on passes with one another as a way to strengthen their bonds. Some of these friendships and activities have continued for many years after release from the program and have been a healthy influence on the men's readjustment. Feelings, urges, and impulses that arise on these community excursions make excellent topics for group discussion. Thus, the whole group benefits.

Leaving a prison, hospital, or secure treatment setting is a major event in such an individual's life. The longer the sex offender has been confined, the more momentous and frightening the departure. This is especially true if confinement has been since adolescence. The less time the individual has spent successfully in the community, the more he fears another failure and doubts his ability to succeed—no matter how good his intentions. While few inmates will reveal that they want to stay, most of them are ambivalent about leaving. They are familiar with and comfortable in their setting. If they have had a good experience in treatment, they are attached to some of the other inmates and, to a lesser extent, some of the staff. These attachments are very important, and it is necessary for the men to voice their feelings about leaving those to whom they are close. For some, particularly those who have been lonely and alienated most of their lives, the attachments formed in treatment may be the closest and most genuine relationships they have ever realized.

A graduation ritual developed in which the exiting man makes a brief speech during his last inpatient meeting. He talks about what he has learned in treatment, what has helped, and what he will miss. He summarizes what the treatment has been like for him and specifically discusses each group member's contribution to his growth. He may also suggest directions for each member of the group and give final input on how he perceives the other individuals. Learning to say goodbye is an important part of the process of leaving. The cottage members will often shake the departing man's hand or hug him and wish him well. Sometimes the cottage shares a special meal in his honor.

The anticipation of change begins to affect inmates about three to four months before their release. In the treatment milieu, there are changes in how they interact and function in their daily living. These changes resemble regressions. Some of their worst behaviors begin to reappear—behaviors they may have exhibited when they began inpatient treatment. They may become more quiet or secretive. Sometimes tempers flare and arguments erupt. They may challenge authority or "the system" to remove the focus from themselves. They may not want to talk about their sexual feelings, thoughts, or crimes. For sex offenders who deal with their anxieties through sex, their sexual fantasies, urges, and use of pornography may begin to increase. They may become reluctant to talk about their cycle of sexual assault. These patterns are unique, fixed, and repetitive for each offender. Feeling apprehensive, they are particularly afraid to tell staff anything that might be detrimental to their release.

Not talking about feelings or impulses is one of the more common methods offenders use to control their stress. Unfortunately, it also might contribute to their acting-out. From the beginning of treatment, staff needs to stress that these feelings, impulses, and fantasies will recur from time to time and that the appropriate method of dealing with them is to talk about them and get some help in working through them. Sex offenders who deny or hide these feelings could be near the brink of a dangerous cycle that will lead to a new sex offense. However, talking about a frightening impulse or fantasy can make it less powerful. If there is some understanding and trust between clients and staff and if staff is willing to ask about the existence of these symptoms and impulses in a nonpunitive way, they can be talked about, worked through, and, to some degree, defused. It should also be noted that other offenders are often better than therapists at sensing these feelings in one another. If the group culture is healthy, group members will encourage each other to talk openly.

Frequently, sex offenders manifest their exiting jitters by fighting with their best friend over some trivial issue or with a staff member on whom they feel too dependent. Such fights trigger a cool-down of the relationship which in turn lessens the pain of saying goodbye. This rather primitive and childish way of dealing with the end of a relationship is typical of many sex offenders' past behaviors and the patterns that led them to the acts of violence for which they were incarcerated.

Once the therapist recognizes and understands the individual's behavior, it can be used in a therapeutic manner. The treatment for all these symptoms is similar: the underlying fear or uncertainty must be analyzed. Sex offenders who are given permission to be afraid and to doubt themselves can discuss their worst fears. The more accurately the therapist can pinpoint the particular fear, the more helpful the therapy will be. For example, is the individual worried about looking for a job, fighting with his wife, or performing sexually? Is he concerned about the health of a parent for whom he feels responsible? Does he trust the therapist and/or the group enough to tell them what is really going on? He must learn that disclosure is his best chance for help and that talking about the situation will allow him to master his behavior now and after his release.

It is also important for the therapist to continue to mention how many sessions remain. This gives the individual some time during the last few weeks to talk about how he feels about leaving. The goodbye process spans many sessions. As previously mentioned, each individual's last inpatient meeting is devoted to his saying goodbye.

Community-Based Residential Facility

From a treatment strategy standpoint, it is ideal to have a residential setting in the community at which to conduct treatment and in which the offenders leaving an institution can live for a few months while they adjust to life outside prison walls. However, establishing such a facility is not easy. It takes an administration with a fair amount of courage and persuasive ability.

In places where this has been done, it has happened gradually. If a halfway house already exists in the community, it is a matter of persuading its administrators to take a chance on admitting sex offenders.

It is essential to be honest and straightforward with other agencies and staff. The program participants' projected behavior should never be guaranteed or oversold. Staff should not take responsibility for what the offenders do—good or bad. It is often better to underpredict the probability of success.

If the first few participants do well, it will leave a good impression and will cushion the program against the more difficult cases which may follow. Credibility and trust are built over time through a willingness to share with other staff and honestly talk about one another's doubts and concerns. Weiser (1986) describes a model program of interagency cooperation in a community-based incest treatment program. However, ultimately the offenders are the only ones responsible for and able to control their behavior.

Whatever the arrangement with the supervising agent, it is important that each participant understands that he must not keep secrets from the group and that all pertinent information relating to his current behavior will be shared, if necessary, with those officers responsible to the court.

A necessary component of aftercare in the community is a mechanism that ensures attendance. Participants must have a clear understanding that if they miss one appointment without permission, their parole officer will be contacted immediately.

Therapy should concentrate on how the offenders are adjusting to the community. What are their feelings, concerns, and fears? What are their sexual fantasies, urges, and behaviors? Loneliness is often the most persistent problem. Offenders should learn to use the group to plan actions with which to combat these feelings. Aftercare is a safety net from which to build new social networks. Offenders who try to meet these social needs by relying on sex or counting too heavily on one woman or one individual are setting themselves up for failure.

Group members need to believe that the therapist will act to confine or curtail the movement of a participant if it appears necessary. They will lose confidence in a therapist who is not willing to intervene. When such action is necessary, it is best for the therapist to be as straightforward as possible with everyone concerned, individual and group, about what is being done and why, and what the consequences will be. Sex offenders depend on staff to help them when they cannot control themselves.

Periodically, the therapist must bring up the issues, especially sexual issues, and ask questions. One of the best ways to encourage offenders to talk about their more shameful impulses is to confirm their feelings, for example: "I know it is hard to talk about.... I can see how bad you feel about it. It takes a lot of courage to share things sometimes. I have a lot of respect for you for being able to say the worst things. I know you don't want to do anything to hurt anyone."

Re-Offense Warning Signs

A treated sex offender who is on the verge of committing another offense probably is displaying many signs. More than likely, the offender is failing in treatment, either by becoming more distant about his immediate concerns or by becoming very hostile, belligerent, and uncooperative with the staff. Obvious signs are missed appointments and tardiness.

In general, sex offenders rely too heavily on sex to fill needs that should be met socially or in other ways. Thus, if the group is aware of the individual's increasing problem, they can help him develop plans to change his social and recreational patterns.

If there has been a sudden increase in responsibilities, either on the job or within the family, the sex offender needs to talk about it. He probably has doubts and fears and may need to hear that even if he fails, he will still be a valuable, worthwhile person. Also, it is not uncommon for a sex offender to fail when he suddenly experiences great success on the job or in other areas of his life.

Pedophiles. The therapist and group members need to be aware if a member who is a child molester is spending more time with children than with adults. Does he seem to prefer the company of children and become animated when he talks about children or a particular child? By contrast, does he seem flat or disinterested when he talks about his adult friends? Is he befriending and wanting to live only with women who have children? Does he seek out jobs that will put him in contact with children? The therapist needs to ask how the person is functioning sexually, either with his partners or in his fantasies. Is he having trouble getting an erection or ejaculating? Can he accomplish this only by thinking of children? Is he feeling sexual demands or pressures from an adult and does this overwhelm or frighten him? Is he self-confident enough to turn someone down sexually and still feel good about himself? Is he involved with a partner who never wants to have sex with him? It is also important for the therapist to notice if the child molester is feeling sorry for himself and blaming others for his problems. This could definitely signal a re-offense.

If an incest family wishes to reunite, it is a bad sign if the offender, or any of the family members, begins to minimize or downplay the original conviction. An article by O'Connell (1986) describes in detail rules for incest families who wish to reunite. These rules could be required reading for an incest offender and his family. They could also be discussed specifically with the family before the beginning of home visitations.

The therapist and group members should always have knowledge of each participant's offense pattern and the events that preceded or triggered the last offense. For example, in one case the sex offender picked up a child in a park and raped her two weeks after his wife had a baby. When he was released six years later, he met a woman, moved in with her and, two weeks after the birth of their child, raped again. Although the parole officer knew it was a vulnerable time for this man and did his best to question him carefully about his feelings and impulses, the offender all along continued to deny adamantly that anything was wrong. This last occurrence took place nearly a year after the offender had finished treatment, but apparently he did not trust anyone enough to be honest about his feelings.

Rapists. The most common trigger for a rapist is rejection by a woman upon whom he is emotionally dependent. This can be perceived either as sexual rejection or a rejection of the entire relationship. An important sign is the rapist's escalating anger. He may become very hostile with a therapist or group member for little or no reason. He might refuse to talk about any sexual issues and become irrationally angry when asked to do so. Abuse of alcohol or other drugs is very common for a few days or weeks before a rapist's re-offense.

A rapist motivated by a desire for power will be overwhelmed with feelings of inadequacy and incompetence. He may experience a recurrence of deviant fantasies or fetishes. He may try to force his sexual partner to comply with increasingly bizarre sexual behavior. In general, the rapist is likely to feel helpless in his relationship with a woman. It is possible that he feels he has lost control or is being used. He may be reluctant even to bring up or work on these issues or to deal directly with the woman involved. Nevertheless, the therapist must pursue these points.

A rapist may succumb to a strong urge to visit prostitutes, massage parlors, or to use pornography. He may begin cruising certain neighborhoods where he had previously found victims. Again, it is very important for the therapist and other group members to be aware of prior assault patterns.

Staff should not be afraid to meet, discuss, and, in a sense, perform an "autopsy" on failures. Whatever is learned should be shared with program participants. The offenders are usually as upset, if not more so, than staff. Group discussion of their fellow member's recent sex offense will help control their own fears of a relapse.

The therapist should be willing to talk to the relapsed offender. Although the therapist might be angry or disgusted, too much valuable information is lost if the therapist is unwilling to do so. For example, a new session can reveal trouble signs that the offender may have been exhibiting and that the therapist missed, or a use of chemicals that went unnoticed, or a discomfort or frustration with the group that kept the offender from being honest and seeking help. It is possible to learn far more from a single failure than from a string of successes.

Treatment Termination

An implicit part of the treatment contract is that it will terminate when some goal is achieved and/or when a set period of time has elapsed. One of the objectives of treatment is to prepare the sex offender for the time when he will no longer need a therapist. When the individual enters the final stages of treatment, the therapist should periodically mention how many sessions he has left so the individual and the other group members will be well prepared. The same process was used to condition the offender for release from prison.

In some cases, the sex offender and his family may be referred to another therapist or agency in the community. It is helpful for the two therapists to do a combined session or two. It encourages the individual to relinquish his dependency on the first therapist, and it sanctions the transference of this dependency so the client does not feel confused about his loyalties. Because different therapists may use different methods, the combined session(s) can be used to help the individual feel comfortable with the new therapist's techniques. It is essential for the old therapist to share the offender's pertinent treatment history so the new therapist does not have to cover the same ground.

If treatment is going to end without further therapy, the final sessions should be gradually spaced out. Participation in Sexaholics Anonymous/Sex Addicts Anonymous (SA/SAA) groups could be encouraged. These are self-help groups led by people who have completed treatment and want to continue to be involved helping others. Functioning like Alcoholics Anonymous, SA/SAA groups are common in various parts of the country, and all indications are that they will continue to spread and develop. Along the West Coast, a similar group called Parents United includes a support network for the entire family. If a group makes use of the 12-step model developed by AA, it can be very effective. Sometimes sexual issues are even discussed in AA groups, but this is risky for the sex offender who could be ridiculed for talking about these matters. It is possible that in some communities, AA will be the only support group available to the sex offender; but, if the therapist believes it could be helpful, participation should be encouraged.

It is a good idea to maintain a telephone crisis line for formerly treated offenders in desperate need. Just a chat with a former therapist can be quite helpful. At other times the individual may need a referral for treatment on a new or related problem.

Sometimes the therapist has to make it very clear to the offender that his therapy has ended and that if the individual needs further treatment, he will have to go elsewhere. Although it is flattering to the therapist to feel needed, such a dependency can be destructive for the sex offender.

Some programs have developed annual reunions so clients can renew old acquaintances and let staff know how they are doing. This is a good morale booster for the staff, who are generally all too aware of failures but seldom of successes. It can also be helpful for the current program participants to see that former group members are succeeding after therapy. These reunions can be especially important for men who have spent a good portion of their lives in prisons or institutions and who have no family or other support system in the outside world. Their contact keeps staff abreast of events and successes in their lives. And for staff, this can be the greatest reward of all, a reminder of why they chose to be therapists in the first place.

References

Christiansen, K.O., Elers-Nielson, M., Lamaire, L., and Sturup, G.K. (1965). *Recidivism among sexual offenders: Scandinavian studies in criminology.* London: Tavistock.

Groth, N.A., Longo, R.E., and McFadin, J.B. (July 1982). Recidivism among rapists and child molesters. *Crime and Delinquency,* 450-458.

LeClair, D.P. (March 1981). Community reintegration of prison releases: Results of the Massachusetts experience. Research Unit, Massachusetts Department of Corrections.

O'Connell, M.A. (September 1986). Reuniting incest offenders with their families. *Journal of Interpersonal Violence,* Vol. I, No. 3, 374-386.

Soothill, K. and Gibbens, T. (1978). Recidivism of sexual offenders: A re-appraisal. *British Journal of Criminology,* 18, 267-276.

Weiser, M., General description of the family incest treatment program of Eau Claire and Chippewa County, Wisconsin. Eau Claire, WI: The Guidance Clinic.

Welfling, M. (1987). Follow-up study of untreated sex offenders. Unpublished report. St. Paul, MN: Minnesota Department of Corrections.

Chapter 20

Relapse Prevention: A Method for Enhancing Behavioral Self-Management and External Supervision of the Sexual Aggressor

by William D. Pithers, Ph.D. and Georgia F. Cumming, B.S.

Page

Overview

All therapeutic interventions for sexual aggressors share the same goal: deterring subsequent victimization. Some sex offenders will start their therapeutic journey in prison, others receive their initial treatment in the community. Regardless of the setting in which treatment initially takes place, the safety of society will be maximized if sex offenders participate in a tightly-integrated system of specialized treatment and supervision.

This chapter depicts procedures that may be employed to enhance community safety by supporting maintenance of change in treated sex offenders. To function most effectively, these procedures require the collaborative efforts of sex offenders, mental health professionals, probation and parole officers, and community members. The safety of society can be reasonably assured only if the sexual aggressor gets continued treatment and supervision upon his return to an informed community. The treatment and supervisory model presented in this chapter is called Relapse Prevention. Three overall goals of Relapse Prevention are: (1) to increase the clients' awareness and range of choices concerning their behavior; (2) to develop specific coping skills and self-control capacities; and (3) to create a general sense of mastery or control over their lives. To attain these goals, Relapse Prevention includes intervention procedures that are designed to help clients anticipate and cope with the occurrence of lapses and to modify the early antecedents of lapses. The interventions to be used with a particular client are determined by assessing his High Risk Situations and coping skills. Thus, the Relapse Prevention treatment program is not a standardized package, but an individualized program tailored to meet each client's unique needs.

Relapse Prevention begins by dispelling misconceptions that the client may have regarding the outcome of treatment and by describing more realistic goals. For example, many sex offenders expect treatment to eliminate their desire for unacceptable sex acts or objects, while the Relapse Prevention model expects clients to participate in forming the procedures designed to reduce his deviant interests and arousal patterns and prepares them for the possible return of these problems.

Thus, clients are informed that no cure exists for their disorder but that the return of a deviant fantasy does not necessarily mean that they are going to re-offend. Clients learn that a critical part of their treatment involves learning what to do when they feel attracted to deviant sexual activity again. We instruct clients that they will discover a variety of situations in which they make Seemingly Unimportant Decisions (SUDs) that actually lead them closer to offending again or which take them away from that danger. They are encouraged to develop an ability to recognize these situations and enact alternatives which will reduce the likelihood that they will act out their unacceptable.

Importance of Identifying Precursors to Sexual Aggression

A central premise of Relapse Prevention is that sexual offenses are rarely impulsive acts. Nevertheless, many offenders engage in careful planning to make it appear their acts were unplanned. Others engage in substance use prior to offending in an effort to appear exculpable or to break down the final inhibitions against performing a desired abusive act. Although abusers may choose victims opportunistically, the activity performed during the assault generally has been fantasized about for a long time. These fantasies constitute planning sessions in which future behaviors can be refined.

There is a corollary to the premise that precursors to sexual offenses exist. It is that identifying these factors may enable the development of enhanced treatment and supervision of offenders. Pithers, Buell, Kashima, Cumming, and Beal (1987) analyzed case records, psychological assessments, and physiological evaluations of 200 sexual offenders who had been convicted of felonious assaults. These offenders' files were randomly selected from the clinical files of the Vermont Treatment Program for Sexual Aggressors. Of the 200 offenders included in this study, 136 had sexually abused children and 64 had raped women during their index crime. In reviewing each subject's data, the authors identified a number of precursors that may have been related to commission of the crime. It should be noted that the risk factors identified in this study may be applied to other, less severe populations.

Generally, these data suggest that precursors to sexual offenses are identifiable. Some of the risk factors do not appear to be disproportionately represented between rapists and pedophiles, while others are distributed more uniquely among one of the two groups. The nature of these precursors suggests that truly impulsive, unplanned sexual offenses are exceptionally rare.

However, the greatest value of identifying risk factors is not apparent in group comparisons, but rather in the analysis of specific precursors for each unique offender. When discerned individually, precursive risk factors may provide information about the client's relapse process that enhances the efficacy of treatment and parole supervision. Risk factors that occurred within six months of the subjects' offenses appear in Table 20.1. Risk factors that took place earlier, and which may have generally predisposed deviant behavior, are shown in Table 20.2. These tables report data for "pedophiles" and "rapists." Because these categories are so broad, they include offender subtypes whose precursors might differ.

Risk Factors Occurring Within Six Months Prior to Offense. Several differences in the immediate precursors of rape and pedophilic acts are apparent in Table 20.1. A greater percentage of rapists than pedophiles exhibited generalized anger (88% of rapists versus 32% for pedophiles), anger toward women (77% versus 26%), acted in opportunistic situations rather than after protracted (i.e., grooming) interactions (58% versus 19%), and engaged in substance use prior to offending (56% versus 30%). In contrast, depression seemed more common among pedophiles (38%) than rapists (3%), and pedophiles were more likely than rapists to acknowledge having planned their offenses (73% versus 28%). During the clinical evaluation, a greater proportion of pedophiles (51%) than rapists (17%) acknowledged harboring deviant sexual fantasies.

(continued on page 20-6)

Table 20.1
Immediate Precursors to Sexual Aggression

Precursor	*Rapists**	*Pedophiles**
Anger		
At event	3	3
Interpersonal conflict	3	4
Generalized, global	88	32
Anger toward women	77	26
Anxiety	27	46
Assertive skills deficit	42	23
Boredom	45	28
Cognitive distortions	72	65
Compulsive overworking	0	8
Depression	3	38
Deviant sexual fantasies	17	51
Disordered sexual arousal pattern	69	57
Divorce	2	2
Driving car alone without destination	17	1
Emotionally inhibited/overcontrolled	58	51
Interpersonal dependence	30	48
Low self-esteem	56	61
Low victim empathy	61	71
Opportunity (e.g., finding a hitchhiker)	58	19
Peer pressure	2	3
Personal loss	6	14
Personality disorder	61	35
Photography as new hobby	0	4
Physical illness	14	6
Planning of sexual offense	28	73
Pornography use	2	7
Psychiatric hospitalization	0	7
Sexual knowledge deficit	45	52
Social anxiety	25	39
Social skills deficit	59	50
Substance use/abuse		
Alcohol	42	23
Other substances	14	7

*Percentage of sample

Table 20.2
Early Precursors to Sexual Aggression

Precursor	Rapists*	Pedophiles*
Cognitive impairment (IQ < 80)	9	10
Divorce (more than 5 years before act)	14	15
Exposure to violent death of human or animal	22	2
Familial chaos	86	49
Late sexual experience (older than 25 at initial activity)	0	4
Limited education (< grade 9 completed)	44	26
Maternal absence/neglect	41	29
More than one prior sex offense	14	17
More than one known victim	30	60
Parental/marital discord	59	45
Paternal absence/neglect	59	54
Physically abused as child	45	7
Pornography use (habitual)	14	33
Precocious sexuality (< 12 years at time of first act of penetration not considered abuse)	14	30
Prior arrest for nonsexual offense	44	15
Sexual anxiety	39	58
Sexual dysfunction	11	11
Sexual victimization		
Prior to age 12	5	56
Between ages 12 and 18	11	6
Use of female prostitutes	30	8

*Percentage of sample

Some of the factors identified in this analysis did not appear in differential proportions among rapists and pedophiles. Variables occurring in relatively high proportion among both samples included: cognitive distortions (72% of the rape sample and 65% of the pedophiles), low self-esteem (56% and 61%), and emotional inhibition or over-control (58% and 51%). Upon clinical evaluation, the majority of both groups exhibited a disordered sexual arousal pattern (69% of the rapists and 57% of the pedophiles). The discrepancy between the percentage of rapists who self-reported deviant fantasies (17%) and the percentage yielding deviant arousal during physiological assessment of sexual arousal patterns (69%) is greater than that evidenced in pedophiles (51% self-reporting deviant fantasies and 57% demonstrating disordered arousal patterns). However, it should be noted that, for both groups, the number of subjects self-reporting deviant fantasies was less than the number exhibiting deviant sexual arousal during an objective, behavioral evaluation.

Risk Factors Occurring More Than Six Months Prior to Offense. Examining early precursors to sexual offenses (see Table 20.2), a greater proportion of rapists than pedophiles experienced the violent death of a human (e.g., hunting accidents) or animal (e.g., pig slaughtering) during childhood (22% versus 2%), chaotic family lives involving parental altercations or extramarital affairs witnessed by the subject (86% versus 49%), and physical abuse as a child (45% versus 7%). Pedophiles revealed a greater proportion of sexual victimization prior to age 12 than rapists (56% versus 5%). In contrast, a slightly greater proportion of rapists than pedophiles were sexually victimized during adolescence (11% versus 6%).

Common Sequence of Precursors to a Relapse

The data also showed that sexual violence frequently was the result of a common sequence of risk factors. Initially, the offenders experienced an emotional change. While they usually could not define this change precisely, their comments revealed that pedophiles typically felt depressed and rapists generally experienced an exacerbation of chronic anger.

The next stage of the relapse process was marked by an increase in the frequency or strength of deviant sexual fantasies. Often, these fantasies occurred as offenders masturbated in a dysfunctional effort to cope with their negative emotional state. The acquisition of pornography was common, probably as a means of heightening arousal during repetitive masturbation to deviant fantasies.

Deviant sexual fantasies were transformed into cognitive distortions in the third stage of relapse. Offenders often rationalized their fantasies, saying things like "All women are whores at heart" and "Since my teenage daughter is about to start dating and experimenting sexually, she should learn about sex from someone who cares about her rather than some teenager who'll take advantage of her."

As the relapse process unfolds, offenders "passively" develop a plan to enable commission of their fantasized behavior. Usually, the planning was accomplished while fantasizing. Nuances in offense setting, timing, and behavior were developed that might enable victimization without detection by authorities.

The plan is enacted in the final stage of the relapse process. In instances where substance use was a factor, it generally served to anesthetize any anxiety that may have interfered with commission of the offense and to minimize the offender's perceived responsibility for an offense. Often, these offenders initially denied any memory of the act. (Later in treatment, however, such offenders frequently acknowledged having vivid recollections of the abuse.)

Thus, a distinct sequence of offense precursors was often discerned:

Affect -> Abusive Fantasy -> Passive Planning -> Cognitive Distortion -> Disinhibition -> Abusive Act

The risk of relapse grows as the offenders progress through the various stages of the relapse process.

Differential Utility

While specific precursors to offenses are observable in both child abusers and rapists (Pithers, Kashima, Cumming, Beal, and Buell, 1988) the importance and usefulness of these factors may vary with the different categories of offenders. Two factors that may affect the utility of risk factors with specific offenders are: (1) the number of precursors involved in the relapse process and (2) the rapidity with which the offender progresses through the relapse process.

Clinical experience suggests that while considerable variation exists across individual offenders, the number of risk factors does not differ dramatically between groups of rapists and child abusers. Also, while the number of offense precursors does not appear to differ for child abusers and rapists, rapists appear to progress through the relapse process more quickly than pedophiles.

Several studies have found that rapists have the highest risk of relapse during the first year after release and that the number of re-offenses declines after that (Frisbie, 1969; Pithers and Cumming, 1989; Sturgeon and Taylor, 1980). This finding may reflect the influence of anger and power as the predominant motivations for sexual violence. Eruptions of anger and feelings of disempowerment have precipitous, explosive onsets and loss of behavioral control can take place rapidly. Consequently, maintenance strategies that rely on the ability to detect and respond to risk factors may be less effective with rapists than child abusers (Gray and Pithers, 1992).

Most child abusers take a lot of time establishing a trusting relationship with their intended victim. Since pedophiles' behaviors may manifest risk factors for a longer period of time, they have more opportunity to inform others that they have engaged in behaviors related to offending and permit the members of their prevention teams increased opportunity to witness these precursive behaviors. Therefore, treatment programs employing Relapse Prevention strategies may find more favorable treatment outcomes with child abusers than rapists.

Potential Uses of Identified Offense Precursors

Identification of precursive risk factors by mental health clinicians may serve several important functions. The analysis of risk factors by clinicians may assist delineation of behavioral excesses and deficits that must be addressed therapeutically. By monitoring risk factors during treatment, therapists may be better able to (1) confront clients about elements of their relapse processes and (2) assess the efficacy of treatment on an ongoing basis.

The Relapse Prevention model asserts that offenders engage in prodromal behaviors to sexual assault and that these premonitory signs represent distinct changes from the offender's typical behaviors. Probation and parole officers may be able to tell when an offender is at high risk of relapse by monitoring for the presence of these high-risk factors. Since probation and parole officers monitor specific risk factors related to the client's sexual offenses (rather than attempting to oversee all his behaviors, many of which have no bearing on his offending), and can develop collateral contacts (e.g., employers, spouses) to assist monitoring of the offender's risk factors, their efficiency is increased.

The Relapse Process

Relapse Prevention proposes that the variety of factors presented in Table 20.1 influences whether a sexual offender will successfully avoid committing another abusive act. It is important to remember that a sexual aggressor who enters treatment is essentially taking a vow of abstinence. While abstinent, the offender believes he or she has the self-management skills that will allow life's difficulties to be handled without undue distress. Occasionally, this attitude may grow to an unrealistic level of superoptimism that encourages inattention to behavioral maintenance.

High Risk Situations. This self-assuredness is tested when the offender encounters a high risk situation—that is, a set of circumstances that threaten the individual's sense of self-control and increase the risk of relapse. For example, a rapist who, driving his vehicle to escape an angry interaction with his spouse, spots a female hitchhiker and a pedophile who is asked to baby-sit for a neighbor are in potentially high risk situations. Abstaining offenders who manage to cope with such situations will have a better sense of self-management and more realistic expectations about how to handle future situations.

The probability of relapse increases, however, if the offender fails to respond adaptively to a high risk situation (e.g., purchases pornography while in a book store). The offender's sense of self-management will decrease and there will be a tendency to passively yield to the temptation of the next high-risk situation ensues.

Generally, each time an offender fails to cope with a high-risk situation, he will engage in the one of the precursive behaviors involved in the relapse process. For most sexual offenders, the initial return of deviant sexual fantasy is the earliest identifiable lapse.

Seemingly Unimportant Decisions. Thus far, the relapse process has been depicted from the point at which a person encounters a high risk situation. It is important to note, though, that the Relapse Prevention model also examines events that precede such situations. Although some sex offenders lapse in situations that would have been difficult to anticipate, the majority appear to set the scene for lapses by placing themselves in high risk situations.

One can covertly set up a lapse, or relapse, by making a series of Seemingly Unimportant Decisions (SUDs), each of which represents another step toward a tempting, high-risk situation. Each SUD, taken by itself, may seem unrelated to re-offending. However, it is those choices that lead the aggressor to the point where a decision must be made: to re-offend or not to re-offend.

Offenders who are not prepared to cope with a SUD-precipitated lapse may attempt to hide their error from therapists and parole officers. The offender may believe that acknowledging even a momentary deviant fantasy will be viewed as an indication that he or she is totally out of control and lead to the revocation of parole. However, the offender's effort to bury a lapse usually leads to additional lapses that are closer still to re-offending. Thus, the probability of re-offending is increased. In the Relapse Prevention model recurrence of deviant sexual behavior defines a relapse.

Distinguishing Between a Lapse and a Relapse: The Abstinence Violation Effect

A concept referred to as the "Abstinence Violation Effect" determines whether a lapse really is a relapse. The conflict between the offender's definition of him- or herself as an "abstainer" and recent indulgence in a behavior that is part of the relapse process is a major component of this effect. Offenders may resolve this dissonance by deciding that treatment was a failure and that they still are sexual offenders. Another component of the Abstinence Violation Effect is whether the offender attributes the lapse to personal failures. Offenders who do this will develop an expectation of continued failure that will culminate in the ultimate failure, relapse.

A third factor influencing the extent of the Abstinence Violation Eeffect is the individual's selective recall of positive aspects of having engaged in deviant sexual behavior in the past. An angry rapist may focus on the gratification derived from the violent release of hostility during past assaults. A socially isolated pedophile may recollect moments of perceived intimacy from prior victimizations of children. The probability of relapse increases to the degree that aggressors selectively remember positive outcomes of prior sexual offenses, forgetting the delayed negative consequences (e.g., loss of self-respect, arrest, dissolution of family). This aspect of the Abstinence Violation Effect is so strong that it has its own title, the Problem of Immediate Gratification—or the PIG phenomenon.

The last factor affecting the Abstinence Violation Effect is the individual's expectations about the likelihood of encountering lapses. If the offender believes that all treatment is successful only if it eradicates any vestige of deviant desires, the effects of a momentary loss of control may be devastating. In contrast, an offender who accepts that there are no "cures" for sexual offenders and views lapses as opportunities to enhance self-management skills through inspection of acceptable mistakes, may successfully return to abstinence after a lapse with improved coping skills. A lapse may even give such an offender a more accurate perception of the need to be vigilant for the earliest signs of a relapse process.

Case Study of the Relapse Process

Al, 34, was recently released from prison. He had served two years in prison on his first conviction for committing lewd and lascivious behavior with a child while intoxicated. He participated in individual therapy while in prison and, even though his sexual attraction to children was rarely discussed, he believed himself "cured." As Al left prison, he stated that he was glad he had taken care of his problem so that he would not have to "worry about that stuff anymore."

During his incarceration, Al longed to return home to his spouse, despite the problems they had experienced. He recalled thinking that living with the wreck of Hesperus would be rewarding compared to prison. Once he was out and he and his spouse begin fighting again, prison no longer seemed so awful. He felt that everyone was bossing him around. Al went for a walk.

"Never could stand up for myself," he thought. He found himself thinking about just what Betty, his spouse, did during her long absences away from home. He recalled her comment about going shopping, and wondered what she was shopping for.

While he was in prison, he felt lonely, but at least he could imagine being close to Betty when he got out. Now, he felt a loneliness he never knew existed. Unable to express his emotions to Betty, he decided to do the next best thing and entered a corner store to buy a beer or two. When he came out of the store, he sulked into depression. His energy waning, he slumped onto a park bench to rest, hardly noticing the nearby school. He wished there was something in life to look forward to, something or somebody that would make him feel alive. Someone who would appreciate everything he did for them. A relationship in which he felt equal and loved, not some servant to be bossed around.

Lost in thought, he scarcely noticed the clanging bell dismissing school. Turning his vacant gaze toward an ever increasing clamor, he saw happy children surging away from the school building. "Damn, I shouldn't be here," faintly passed through his thoughts. However, before he could muster the determination to get moving, a softball rolled up to his feet, followed closely by an impish little boy with a coy smile and dirty clothes. As he reached out to hand back the ball, the boy looked directly into his eyes, met his gaze for several long moments, and smiled broadly. Al thought about how cute the kid looked, "Real friendly smile. Reminds me a lot of myself at that age. Wonder if he's as lonely as I was then. Parents probably don't take care of him right. Probably could use a friend." He recalled how being close to a child always made him feel better when he was depressed.

Noticing that the boy glanced in his direction, Al thought, "That little rascal. He must have known what I was thinking about." His depression beginning to dissipate as he wondered whether the boy was interested in him. Al got up from his bench and walked toward the boy. He was thinking about sharing a soda, and possibly more, with this cute, good-natured boy.

Al's story illustrates the relapse process:

• He minimized the difficulty of abstaining from child sexual abuse (Seemingly Unimportant Decision). He returned home with an unrealistic expectation of his relationship with his wife (Seemingly Unimportant Decision). When his expectation of the relationship went unmet, he felt dominated, resentful, and depressed (High Risk Situation).

• Al chose not to express his dissatisfaction to his spouse (Lack of Coping Response), taking walks to avoid her whenever he felt lonely or depressed (Seemingly Unimportant Decision).

• When walking did not dissipate his negative emotions, Al imbibed alcohol in an effort to deaden them (High Risk Situation).

- Already engaging in a high risk behavior by drinking, he exacerbated the situation with a Seemingly Unimportant Decision to sit on a park bench, "hardly noticing the nearby school." Seeing the schoolboy's smile, he interpreted a friendly expression as one implying seduction, attributing adult intent to a child (Cognitive Distortion).

- Rather than responding constructively to this lapse, he remembered the immediate comfort he had experienced from his past sexual abuse of a child (Fantasy and Abstinence Violation Effect). Remaining in the High Risk Situation, instead of leaving it immediately, he felt overwhelmed by an urge to approach the boy (Abstinence Violation Effect).

- Although he excused his approach as an innocent offer of a soda to a boy who obviously was not cared for adequately by his parents (Cognitive Distortion), he used the offer as a method of grooming his victim for sexual abuse (Plan and Act).

Clearly, each of these decisions brought Al closer to a situation where he was in imminent danger of relapse. Yet, during his initial interview with a therapist upon returning to prison for child sexual abuse, Al sadly shook his head and commented, "It just happened." Al seemed unaware of the chain of choices and behaviors that enabled him to establish an opportunity to re-offend.

Beginning Relapse Prevention with Sexual Aggressors

Whether one is a mental health clinician or probation and parole officer, Relapse Prevention begins in the same fashion. Clients must be disabused of common misconceptions about the likely outcome of treatment and be provided a more realistic description of reasonable therapeutic goals. Relapse Prevention continues by engaging the client in a thorough assessment of his high risk situations, which are the conditions under which relapse has occurred or is likely to occur in the future. SUDs that may have set up each High Risk Situation are explored. The initial assessment also includes an analysis of the client's coping resources, since any situation can be considered high risk only to the extent that the client is unprepared to cope with it. After the SUDs, High Risk Situations, and coping resources have been identified, a specific therapeutic intervention is designed to train the client how to minimize the frequency and strength of lapses, and how to prevent lapses from becoming a relapse.

Rather than beginning therapy with confrontational techniques designed to break through denial and force clients to admit responsibility for their crimes, Relapse Prevention therapists encourage responsibility on the part of the client by fostering an atmosphere of cooperation. This firm, but nonabusive, approach has several goals:

1. Encouraging clients to serve as their own co-therapists creates a greater sense of objectivity in the clients' consideration of their own behaviors. As a result, they are freer to discuss threatening emotions and behaviors.

2. By adopting an objective and detached approach, the client and therapist mutually may begin to explore problem behaviors without the extreme defensiveness that otherwise might be engendered. The absence of a condemnatory confrontation of the client's personality enables the client to see that sexually aggressive behavior is an unacceptable act rather than an indication of something he or she is (and always will be), a sex offender.

3. Using a nonconfrontational introduction in order to encourage the client, from the beginning of therapy, to play an active part in determining the program's pace and content.

Two Models of Relapse Prevention

Relapse Prevention was originally developed as a technique for enhancing the maintenance of change by clients who have been in treatment for compulsive behavioral disorders (e.g., substance abuse, compulsive gambling, etc.). As originally articulated by Marlatt and colleagues (Chaney, O'Leary, and Marlatt, 1978; Marlatt, 1982; Marlatt and Gordon, 1980, 1985; Marlatt,1982), Relapse Prevention was designed to strengthen self-control by providing clients with methods for identifying problematic situations, analyzing decisions that precipitated situations enabling return to the compulsive behavior, and developing strategies to avoid, or cope more effectively with, these dangerous circumstances. Thus, as originally proposed, Relapse Prevention represented a method of enhancing self-management skills.

Internal, Self-Management Dimension. As originally modified for application to sexual aggressors (Pithers, Marques, Gibat, and Marlatt, 1983), Relapse Prevention remained solely a means of enhancing offenders' self-control. The initial application of Relapse Prevention, in the Vermont Treatment Program for Sexual Aggressors (Pithers, 1982), demonstrated that the maintenance model appeared effective in aiding self-management. A state-wide network of outpatient group therapists, who participated in Relapse Prevention training and continual supervision regarding treatment of sex offenders, was established to assist client maintenance. Relapse Prevention successfully accomplished the goals of increasing the client's awareness and range of choices concerning his behavior, developing specific coping skills and self-control capacities, and creating a general sense of mastery over life. This aspect of the modified Relapse Prevention model is referred to as the Internal, Self-Management Dimension.

Unfortunately, sexual aggressors sometimes neglect to employ skills they acquire at certain critical moments. Although the importance of acknowledging lapses to therapists and probation and parole officers was repeatedly stressed during therapy, and the mythical goal of attaining behavioral perfection was dismissed frequently, clients leaving the inpatient treatment unit still thought they were expected to maintain self-managerial perfection. Offenders either believed that acknowledging lapses would lead to their being returned to prison for parole violations or that problems would go away if they just did not acknowledge them. Occasionally, lapses were reported to the treatment team by a released offender's spouse, friends, or co-workers, but not by the client himself. The trend toward secrecy at critical moments remained even when offenders recognized that other clients who self-reported lapses were reinforced by receiving therapeutic intervention, and while those whose lapses were reported by third parties received punitive consequences. Thus, although the Internal, Self-Management Dimension of Relapse Prevention was beneficial in enhancing self-control, it was not enough.

External, Supervisory Dimension. Since offenders are, at times, unreliable informants regarding lapses, creating other methods of gaining access to information about their functioning is essential to enhance community safety. To accomplish this, an External, Supervisory Dimension was developed and added to the Relapse Prevention model (Pithers, Kashima, Cumming, Beal, and Buell, 1987; 1988). This dimension has three functions:

1. Enhancing efficacy of supervision by monitoring specific offense precursors;
2. Increasing the efficiency of supervision by creating an informed network of collateral contacts which may assist the probation officer in monitoring the offender's behaviors; and
3. Creating a collaborative relationship with mental health professionals conducting therapy with the offender.

Probation or parole supervision of sexual offenders is very challenging. Traditionally, gaining the information essential to adequate supervision of a sexual offender was considered nearly impossible. Sex offenders were generally reported to be "hard workers" by employers. Parole violations noted frequently among other types of offenders (e.g., new offenses, intoxication, neglect of supervision appointments, failure to pay restitution) were rarely noted among sex offenders. Often, the lack of detailed information about the offender's behaviors produced a feeling of supervising in a vacuum—a disquieting position in this age of heightened professional liability.

In contrast, using the Relapse Prevention model to specify an offender's SUDs, High Risk Situations, and offense precursors provides probation and parole officers with identifiable indicators of impending danger of relapse. Probation or parole officers who detect the presence of an offense precursor can assume that offender is involved in the relapse process. Since offense precursors appear most commonly in the distinct sequence discussed earlier, the type of precursor exhibited provides an indication of the imminence of potential relapse. This information can be used to determine the type of intervention required by the lapse. The possibilities range from additional conditions of parole to consultation with offender's therapist to parole revocation.

A second element of the External, Supervisory Dimension involves the instruction of collateral contacts. All members of the collateral network (e.g., spouse, employer, co-workers, friends) are informed about SUDs, High Risk Situations, Lapses, the Abstinence Violation Effect, and offense precursors.

Relapse Prevention requires the offender to inform network members about his offense precursors. The probation and parole officer later request each network member to summarize what he or she was told. This accomplishes two things: (1) it allows the probation or parole officer to check the accuracy and completeness of the information presented by the offender (thus enabling the officer to estimate how well the offender understands these precursers); and (2) destroys the secrecy necessary for the commission of sexual aggression. Network members learn that their assistance in identifying the factors involved in the offender's relapse process increases the likelihood that the offender will avoid re-offending. Network members are encouraged to report lapses to the parole officer or therapist in the offender's presence. At some level, this process creates an extended supervisory network.

Care must be exercised in evaluating the ability of collateral contacts to serve this function. Consider these situations: a fearful spouse, who has been battered into total submissiveness, is unlikely to disclose information about her husband if she fears additional abuse; spouses who are overly dependent on their husbands may be reticent to risk any information that could potentially get him into trouble; employers who treasure the compulsive work habits of some sexual offenders may be reluctant to mention information that could lead to loss of cheap labor; certain religious individuals, who believe they can show their love for others by forgiving their misdeeds, may be reluctant to share information; community members who express hatred for the offender may fabricate reports of the offender's misbehaviors in an effort to damage him. Managing the collateral network demands good judgment.

Professional Liaison. The final element of the External, Supervisory Dimension is the liaison between the probation or parole officer and the mental health professional. Regularly scheduled meetings involving the probation officer and mental health professional are essential. By reviewing case specific information together, these professionals may discern previously unknown aspects of the offender's behaviors. It is not unusual to discover that offenders have discussed an important issue with only one of the professionals involved in their care or that offenders have depicted the same event differently to each professional person in the treatment and supervision network.

Regular meetings between these professionals allow the extent and consistency of the offender's disclosures to be compared. It also enables detection of the client's efforts to split his supervisory team. In addition to regularly scheduled meetings, telephone calls and messages can be used to deal with critical events that occur between meetings.

Specialized Teams of Professionals

In practice, creating specialized teams of probation and parole officers who supervise sex offenders has proven beneficial. A small group of specially trained officers allows the development of a frequent supportive collaboration with mental health professionals. In a small, specially trained network, the professionals can always contact someone who is known relatively well. This can help alleviate the "burn out" that sometimes occurs when working with difficult populations.

The combined functions of specially trained probation professionals, collateral contacts, and the collaborative relationship between probation and mental health professionals establishes additional resources that are vital to the adequate treatment and supervision of sex offenders. Taken together, the two dimensions of Relapse Prevention offer improvements over traditional treatment approaches.

Relapse Prevention Assessment Procedures

The clinical psychology literature often makes an artificial distinction between assessment and treatment when in reality the two endeavors are inextricably intertwined. Typically, assessment precedes treatment so that specific problems requiring therapeutic intervention can be identified. However, evaluative procedures should be repeated during treatment in order to determine the extent of change accomplished.

Because Relapse Prevention is a highly individualized approach to treatment and supervision of sex offenders, it begins with thorough assessment of the client's assets and deficits. In addition to the specialized psychometric devices described elsewhere in this volume, Relapse Prevention employs assessment procedures that can be conducted equally well by mental health or probation and parole professionals. These procedures include the analysis of case records, structured interviews, direct behavioral observation, self-monitoring, and self-report measures.

Analysis of Case Records. The professionals assigned to the case should begin to assess the offender's risk factors even before meeting the client. By carefully analyzing background information, such as prior offenses listed in a computerized criminal record, police reports, victims' statements, the offender's statement, psychological or psychiatric evaluations, and presentence investigations, the examiner may gain information pertinent to discrimination of offense precursors. For instance, the professional may discover that the client performed other sexually aggressive acts that were plea bargained to lesser, nonsexual offenses. Thus, a first time date rapist, who arguably might receive outpatient treatment under carefully sculpted conditions of probation, may have performed numerous other sexual assaults that were legally processed as simple assaults. A pedophile arrested for the first time in a given state may possess a vocational history containing numerous short-term periods of employment. This type of work history may reflect movement of a fixated pedophile who has sexually abused many children over the years and moved to a new location each time his secret world was threatened by a victim's report. A stepfather arrested for sexually abusing his stepdaughter may have had several prior marriages, each to a partner who had a daughter his preferred age. Thus, a thorough inspection of the offender's records may yield important information and reveal issues for further exploration in a structured interview.

Structured Interview. After reviewing all available information about the offender's history, the probation and parole officer or mental health professional is prepared to conduct a thorough interview. In order to create a relatively comfortable environment that may maximize initial disclosures, the interview should begin with nonthreatening topics. Deciding how to begin the interview can be difficult because "safe" topics are not the same for everyone. Some offenders may be totally at ease discussing their educational background, while other may view their academic performance as the worst embarrassment of their lives. Generally, safe topics can be discerned during the case record review.

Responses to questions such as the ones listed below may yield important insights concerning the treatment and supervision of the offender and help determine whether treatment should occur in the community or in a secured facility:

- Does the offender openly discuss most issues but become suddenly reticent when his sexual or criminal behaviors are questioned?
- When summarizing his sexual offense, does the offender become more animated, develop the glazed appearance of complete absorption in a revivified event, or evidence self-disgust?
- How socially adept does the individual appear?
- To what extent does the offender accept responsibility for his sexually aggressive acts (e.g., total denial, displacement of responsibility for offense onto victim, acceptance of factual responsibility for an offense but denial of harm to the victim, minimization of harm, acknowledgment of physical and emotional trauma)?
- To what degree does the offender's story correspond to the victim's report of the abuse?
- Does this person seem to have always been walking on the edge of criminality?
- How does the offender's affect compare to the topic being discussed?
- Has the offender glossed over any periods of time?
- How does the offender respond to confrontation, support, or expressions of incredulity about some aspects of his or her responses?

In a structured interview, clients are requested to detail circumstances associated with past offenses. Situational and personal (cognitive and affective) antecedents should be identified as should any SUDs (Seemingly Unimportant Decisions) made en route to the offense. Since the concept of SUDs may be new to the client, it should be introduced with an explanation. The following scenario is an example of such an explanation:

Each of us makes many decisions each day which seem so minor that they could have absolutely no significant impact on our lives. Yet regardless of their apparent irrelevance, some of these decisions profoundly alter the range of behaviors which are subsequently available to us. The cumulative effect of all of these "Seemingly Unimportant Decisions" can dramatically alter the major events of our lives. An example may help to clarify this point.

Let's take the case of George, an alcoholic who has recently sworn never to drink again. Imagine him walking down a dimly-lit city sidewalk close to midnight. As he walks, he reaches into his pocket for a cigarette and discovers that he doesn't have any. He anxiously looks around for a store and notices a flashing neon sign up ahead. As he draws closer, he realizes that the sign says "Beer." He pauses a moment to deliberate but decides that he really needs a cigarette. He enters the bar and goes directly to the vending machine. Then he realizes he has no change. He asks two men playing pool if they can change a dollar, but they both say "No." As he turns toward the cash register at the bar to get change, someone calls his name, "George!

Turning toward the sound, he stares through the drifting blue cigarette smoke and recognizes the foreman of a construction crew he works with. The foreman immediately turns to the bartender and says, "Fill up a brew for

George!" Debating only a second, George begins to sip the foaming beer. That was the first of many he took that night.

Now that you've heard this story, you may be able to see that George made a series of decisions that led up to his final decision to drink beer. At any one of these points, George could have made a different decision that would have taken him away from a dangerous situation. Did he really have to have a cigarette? Did he have no alternative but to enter the bar? Could he have refused the beer his foreman bought him? I think you can see that some of the decisions George made appeared to be irrelevant to his abstaining from alcohol, but each of which brought him closer to finally taking the drink of beer. Looking at your decision to have a sexual relationship with a female child in this way, can you tell me the earliest point at which you decided to seek that out? (Pithers, Marques, Gibat, and Marlatt, 1983)

At this point, the client may provide any of a wide range of responses, none of which should be severely criticized or ridiculed. If the client responds with a statement such as, "I didn't decide, it just happened," the therapist can offer another example (perhaps one closer to home), or proceed with other questions designed to clarify the client's High Risk Situations, such as "If you were to become sexually involved with a child again in the future, how might it occur?" or "What particular situations or events would make you feel like raping again?"

Direct Behavioral Observation. Some sexual offenses are motivated by disordered sexual arousal preferences. That is, some pedophiles are driven to victimize children at least partly because they experience much greater sexual attraction to children than to adults. For these individuals, the notion of sexual intimacy with a peer is far less interesting than abuse of children. Similarly, some rapists regard acts that fuse sexuality and violence to be more desirable, at least under certain precursive conditions (e.g., anger, alcohol consumption), than sexual expression of affection and intimacy. Certainly, such sexual arousal disorders must be regarded as factors predisposing sexual abuse.

Research has demonstrated that direct, behavioral observation often allows those who harbor disordered arousal patterns to be distinguished from those who do not. The technology enabling behavioral assessment of sexual arousal patterns is phallometry. This technology, which measures a client's sexual responses to audiotaped or visual depictions of various sexual scenarios, must be administered by trained personnel under laboratory conditions. The results may reveal high risk factors that the client has not recognized or has been unwilling to self-report. If excessive sexual arousal to stimuli of child abuse or rape is discovered, specialized behavioral interventions presented elsewhere in this volume may effectively diminish the disordered preference. However, one must avoid the pitfall of assuming that, once a sexual arousal pattern has changed, the arousal pattern remains altered. Follow-up evaluation, supervision, and "booster" sessions remain essential.

Self-Monitoring and Self-Reporting. In many settings, it is not possible to use direct behavioral measurement of sexual arousal, and therapists and parole officers must rely on self-report measures, such as questionnaires, structured interviews, or self-monitoring records. Skilled interviews may elicit self-report of precursors to sexual offenses. Predisposing factors, such as cognitive distortions that objectify women or attribute adult qualities to children, the excessive need for power over others, hatred of self or others, victim stancing, the lack of recognition of trauma induced by sexual victimization, rigid structures about gender appropriate behaviors, deficient social skills, or an inability to modulate emotional experiences, all may be explored during interviews with the offender or those who know him.

Questionnaires. Since individuals entering treatment still may experience urges to perform the problem behavior with high frequency, encouraging offenders to self-monitor their behaviors may enable offense precursors to be identified. Questionnaires have been designed to assess many qualities that may be related to sexual offenses. For example, the Clarke Sexual History Questionnaire (Langevin, 1983; Paitich, Langevin, Freeman, Mann, and Handy, 1977) may be employed with admitters to acquire a comprehensive depiction of the offender's sexual experiences and preferences. Salter (1988) offers an excellent source for professionals who wish to obtain an extensive array of inventories for use with sexual offenders. Corcoran and Fischer (1987) provide a compendium of questionnaires, several of which are useful with this population.

Documentation of the Occurrence of Precursors. Documentation is an essential aspect of self-monitoring. Analysis of self-monitoring records may reveal a pattern of precursors that is associated with urges to engage in the relapse process. Whenever offenders detect an urge to engage in any aspect of their relapse process (e.g., affect, fantasy, cognitive distortion, planning, behavior), they should chart (or tape record) the following information:

- time of day,
- description of internal events (feelings and thoughts that preceded and accompanied the urge),
- a detailed review of the external situation,
- the numerical rating of the strength of the urge,
- how difficult it was to tolerate the urge, and
- the resulting mood.

Although self-report and self-monitoring can yield useful information from individuals who want to alter their damaging behaviors, those who wish to obfuscate the assessment process can distort. Therefore, information from additional sources should be sought to confirm, or disconfirm, the offender's representations.

Situational Competency Test. The Situational Competency Test evaluates an individual's ability to cope with High Risk Situations. The client is required to respond to descriptions of a variety of High Risk Situations and to articulate the first coping response that comes to mind. The offender's response is scored along several dimensions, such as response latency, length, content, adequacy, and number of coping alternatives mentioned. Problematic situations are considered to be present when the offender cannot formulate a coping strategy, responds only after a prolonged delay, describes a response that would not realistically minimize risk, or elaborates the described High Risk Situation by detailing a related sexual fantasy or past crime.

The Situational Competency Test was developed after examining numerous pre-sentence investigation reports for common offense precursors. Scenarios may be tailored to the individual offender. For example, the following scene might be described to a same sex pedophile:

You have been taken to religious retreats, on furlough from the prison, for several weeks by the same volunteer. The volunteer really seems to have developed an interest in your welfare. You appear to be developing a friendship with him. Finally, he invites you to his home for Sunday dinner with his family. He has never mentioned his family to you before and you are surprised to hear him speaking proudly about his nine-year-old son. At that moment, you recognize that you have never informed him about the details of your offense. You begin to say that you need to talk with him about your offense, but he interrupts, saying, "I don't need to know all about your offense, I know you as a person already and that's all I need to know." What do you do?

Analysis of the offender's response to this scenario enables the probation officer, therapist, and offender to discern whether the offender is prepared to deal effectively with this High Risk Situation.

Relapse Fantasies. Relapse fantasies may be used to assess clients' coping skills and openness to acknowledging the limitations of their self-management skills. This procedure requires offenders to imagine a variety of precursors that would surmount their coping resources and evoke a relapse. Typically, offenders who have recently entered treatment are unable to accomplish this task. However, individuals who meaningfully participate in therapy generally are able to depict some set of circumstances that would overwhelm their ability to cope.

In introducing this assignment to the offender, the probation officer or therapist might say something like this:

You and I have been working hard together to help you develop skills that may enable you to keep from raping again. I'm sure we both hope this work will prove successful. However, you and I both know that your self-management skills will never be so good that you'll be able to handle all life's problems without difficulty. It would be helpful to our work together if, for the next few minutes, you allow yourself to imagine that you're no longer in treatment (under supervision) and that you're having trouble keeping the thoughts and moods of raping under control. Just close your eyes, ease back into your chair, breathe deeply, and allow yourself to develop this situation in your mind for these few moments. When you are able to describe fully the events that have led to your having the urge to rape again, just allow yourself to begin talking and describe them as vividly as you can.

Relapse Prevention Treatment Procedures

Relapse Prevention covers a wide variety of intervention procedures that can be divided into two major categories: (1) procedures for avoiding lapses and (2) techniques for preventing a lapse from precipitating a relapse. Although the concept of offense precursors, or risk factors, are introduced during the early phases of therapy, Relapse Prevention treatment strategies are not broached until the offender recognizes the trauma his acts have inflicted upon his victims. Since Relapse Prevention employs highly cognitive interventions, employing them too early in treatment may encourage denial of the actual extent to which his victims were harmed. The development of empathy for victims is an important aspect of any therapeutic program and an essential element motivating offenders to refrain from future sexually abusive acts.

Interventions to Avoid Lapses

Identification of Offense Precursors. Although some lapses in self-management are unavoidable, Relapse Prevention contends that assisting sexual offenders to avoid lapses entails teaching them to accurately recognize offense precursors involved in their relapse processes. Although this task is introduced as an assessment technique, the identification of High-Risk Situations, Seemingly Unimportant Decisions, and offense precursors continues throughout treatment. Therapy will teach the client to discern behavioral and attitudinal subtleties that previously were not regarded as related to his offenses. Continued self-monitoring and analysis of case examples in group therapy sessions foster the offender's ability to detect offense precursors.

These assignments should enable the client and therapist to identify the specific offense precursor that constitutes a "lapse," that is, the precursor that is the earliest indication that he has resumed his relapse process. For many offenders, an emotional state (e.g., intense isolation or anger) will constitute a lapse, but for others, the lapse may be a specific thought (e.g., "all women are whores at heart"), behavior (e.g., looking for hitchhikers when driving), or some combination of these precursors (e.g., masturbating to rape fantasies when angry).

The identification of lapses is necessary, but it is not enough to deter relapses. Offenders must be trained to identify the "warning signals" that tell them that they are getting into trouble. The difference between Relapse Prevention and many other treatment programs is that Relapse Prevention does not stop at teaching clients to recognize the warning signals. Instead, it goes on to provide offenders with strategies to minimize frequency of lapses and to prepare them to cope more effectively with momentary breeches in self-management. Offenders are instructed to think of lapses as opportunities to enhance self-management by learning from mistakes rather than as signs of failure.

This is how the program works toward that goal. Once a lapse is reported, the offender and the therapist analyze the circumstances that preceded it and determine which factors overwhelmed the offender's self-control. Coping behaviors then are developed to decrease the likelihood of lapses occurring again in similar situations. This process teaches the offender what to do to prevent a lapse from becoming a relapse.

Stimulus Control Procedures. If external stimuli elicit lapses, self-control must be enhanced by removing these stimuli from the offender's daily environment. For example, a rapist whose anger toward women is made more salient by alcohol use should be prohibited from possessing alcohol or residing in a location where it is present. Similarly, individuals whose deviant sexual fantasies are evoked by pornography (or a children's clothing catalog) may be advised to remove these items from his surroundings.

Avoidance Strategies. Avoidance strategies are similar to stimulus control procedures. Treatment and probation conditions are developed to mandate avoidance of the specific circumstances that may elicit lapses. For instance, pedophiles should be prohibited from developing relationships with women who have children of the gender and age that they have victimized. Rapists who have predatorially driven in search of a hitchhiking female should be restricted to using a vehicle only for traveling to and from work within a specified time frame or when accompanied by an adult the probation or parole officer deems responsible.

Escape Strategies. No matter how thorough the preparation, it is impossible to predict every situation that could precipitate a lapse. Thus, offenders must be prepared to employ an effective escape strategy as soon as they recognize they have encountered a High Risk Situation they are not prepared to handle. Offenders who wait, hoping that the risk will go away if they ignore it, are often referred to as recidivists.

The most important aspect of an escape strategy is the speed with which it is enacted. A quick response may not be elegant, but it may interrupt a chain of events leading to disaster. After reaching safety, survivors can take time to review the situation, identify the source of danger, and consider how to defuse the situation if it arises again.

Programmed Coping Responses. Programmed coping responses may be devised for high-risk situations that can be anticipated. In such cases, clients are asked to participate in the following problem-solving process: constructing a detailed description of the problematic situation; brainstorming to generate potential coping responses; evaluating the likely outcome of each potential coping response; and estimating their ability to perform the required coping behavior. The most adaptive response that the client can perform should be selected.

Once the ideal coping response has been identified, the offender should be given ample opportunities to practice it and get feedback. The repeated practice of coping behaviors is like the instructional drills used by piano teachers who seek to have pupils' hands dance naturally across a keyboard or athletic coaches who drill players to exhaustion so that they will respond instinctively in important game situations. These "natural" and "instinctive" skills are the result of intensive, repetitive work. Hopefully, the continuous practice of coping behaviors over time, in different situations, and in many moods, will result in the same type of automatic responses for treated offenders.

Coping with Urges. Within the offender's phenomenology, acts of sexual aggression generally result in some sort of immediate gratification. Power rapists may regard their ability to coerce their victims into uttering favorable comments about their sexual performance as a sign of personal superiority. Socially isolated pedophiles may feel pleased that they have finally found someone with whom they perceive intimacy.

Typically, the negative consequences of sexual abuse are delayed. Realistic fears of arrest, social disapproval, and incarceration occur only after the temporary gratification from the act has vanished. The rapist's self-disgust does not emerge until the satisfaction of feeling powerful during a rape has faded. The pedophile may not become depressed until he recognizes that his "intimate relationship" must be kept secret from everyone else in the world.

Selectively remembering the gratifying aspects of offenses, while neglecting the negative aftereffects, increases the probability of relapse. In compulsive behavioral disorders these positive outcome expectancies are experienced as urges to perform a prohibited behavior. Positive expectancies are especially problematic if they occur when an individual is in a High Risk Situation. For example, an abstaining smoker who is distressed may only think about how relaxing it is to smoke a cigarette, the struggle to quit smoking to avoid developing lung cancer may be forgotten.

To deal with positive outcome expectancies, or urges, the Relapse Prevention model reinforces the biphasic nature of responses to sexual aggression: initial gratification is followed by a delayed negative effect. Offenders are told that, contrary to their expectation, urges do not increase in intensity over time, do not become more difficult to resist, cannot be viewed as overwhelming one's better intentions. Offenders are taught that when they give into an urge, they are making an intentional choice for which they are responsible. They also are instructed that the urge will grow weaker and pass away with time if they can refrain from submitting to it. Making self-statements, such as "Rape doesn't leave anyone feeling good" or "Two minutes of power isn't worth 20 years of prison," may be used to counter urges. Aversive images and outcomes are other potent methods for dismantling urges. For example, offenders may be encouraged to visualize their favorite deceased relative looking over their shoulder as they contemplate an urge to fellate a boy. Such images may deter a tendency to passively submit to an urge and create sufficient delay to consider the negative consequences of the act.

Skill Building Interventions. When sex offenders do not have adequate abilities in interpersonal relationships, anger management, problem solving, stress tolerance, sexual knowledge, interpersonal empathy, and basic survival skills, comprehensive treatment programs should provide opportunities to remediate these deficits. Since these global interventions are described in the general psychological literature, readers are referred to those works for additional information.

Interventions to Prevent Lapses from Becoming Relapses

Lapses in self-management will occur regardless of the adequacy of the treatment. Offenders who adopt this belief are better able to mitigate the negative impact of the Abstinence Violation Effect if a lapse is encountered. Simply providing the offender with this expectation may lessen the likelihood of a lapse precipitating relapse. In addition, Relapse Prevention employs several specific treatment procedures to enable offenders to pull out of a downward spiral before they crash and burn.

Cognitive Restructuring. In order to counter the self-defeating cognitive and emotional aspects of the Abstinence Violation Effect, offenders are instructed to cognitively restructure their interpretation of lapses. Offenders are encouraged to recognize that a lapse may remain a single event, as long as they decide to cope with it, not necessarily a predictor of impending doom.

The Relapse Prevention model prepares offenders to view lapses as mistakes that present the opportunity to learn something new about their relapse process and deficiencies in coping skills. Lapses are not attributed to invariable, negative personal characteristics (e.g., "I am a monster"); instead they are viewed as a slip in self-management. Offenders may be asked to summarize their ability to restructure their interpretation of lapses on a reminder card that must be carried in their wallets at all times. When a lapse is encountered, the offender should immediately remove the card and review it. The card should contain items such as:

1. A lapse is a slip in self-management, not an irreversible loss of self-control.
2. A description of the Abstinence Violation Effect and the negative self-attributions that may accompany it.
3. Reassurance that the offender does not need to yield passively to deviant urges, but that they will weaken over time.
4. Instructions to examine the precursors to the lapse in an effort to discern what might be learned from the event to enhance personal control in the future.
5. A list of coping responses that may be enacted if the offender needs additional assistance to refrain from relapsing.
6. Some offenders list telephone numbers of therapists, treatment group members, and supportive friends on this card for use when they have difficulty coping with a lapse.

Contracting. A therapeutic contract, signed by offenders upon entry into treatment, specifies the limits to which they may permit themselves to lapse. The therapist and offender work together to identify the "lapse limit," but the therapist must make certain that this limit is not "beyond the point of no return." The following shows a portion of a treatment contract for a pedophile, for whom acquisition of child pornography is an offense precursor.

1. When feeling an urge to leave my current location and go out to purchase pornography, I agree to wait 30 minutes before leaving my location. During this time, I agree to pause and consider my desire and the risks it may pose to my re-offending. If, at the end of this 30 minute period, I decide to leave my location to purchase pornography, I will be making an intentional choice, rather than passively yielding to an uncontrollable urge.

2. If I decide to travel to a location where I may purchase pornography, I will buy only one magazine. I also agree to inform my probation officer and therapist about this lapse at my next meeting with each of them. I promise to give possession of the pornography to whomever I meet first (i.e., probation officer or therapist). At that time I will also donate to the local victim/witness program, an amount of money equal to the purchase price of the pornography.

The contract specifies the limits to which lapses will be tolerated by the treatment team (i.e., probation officer and therapist), requires offenders to view their behavior as a clear choice, mandates a delay during which the urge to perform the offense precursor may wane, limits the offender's exposure to a stimulus predisposing sexual abuse, and demands that some penalty is paid for the choice to lapse. In addition to these contingencies, offenders are required to address the lapse during their next treatment group. The contract may also specify that the offender's probation may be revoked if a lapse is reported to the treatment team by someone other than the offender.

Maintenance Manuals. Each offender can work on developing a maintenance manual that may be used to refresh their memory after the intensive phase of treatment has concluded. Depending on the client, the manual may contain the offender's reminder card, the rationale for avoidance and escape strategies, emergency telephone numbers, as well as a list of Seemingly Unimportant Decisions, High-Risk Situations, and offense precursors, self-statements, and self-monitoring forms.

Maintenance manuals are particularly useful when offenders undergo a transition from residential treatment to outpatient therapy. In such cases, the manuals may enhance maintenance of change and assure continuity of treatment. Offenders should update their maintenance manual periodically to remain vigilant for the development of new risk factors.

Relapse Prevention Compared to Traditional Treatment Models

Multiple Sources of Information Versus Reliance on Self-Report. Exclusive reliance on a sex offender's self-report to assess the extent and maintenance of behavioral change is a flawed concept. Sex offenders have many incentives to misrepresent their progress in treatment. If release from prison is dependent on "completion" of treatment, any sane individual would try to impress others by showing that progress was made. Clients who like their therapists and wish to please them may be tempted to say that they have made great progress when they have not. Individuals who are paying their own way through outpatient treatment may need to justify (or attempt to end) their expenditure by making a fictitious claims of attitudinal and behavioral change.

Traditional treatment relies almost exclusively on a combination of self-reports and therapists' intuition to evaluate improvement. Since sex offenders have strong incentives to favorably misrepresent their gains and therapists' intuition has never been empirically validated, additional sources of information are helpful. Relapse Prevention formalizes mechanisms for acquiring information from collateral contacts (e.g., family members) who frequently observe the offender's behaviors. This allows a more thorough examination of the offender's behavioral maintenance and therapeutic compliance. Ultimately, the result is that the treatment team is less likely to base important decisions about the offender on misinformation.

Relapse Prevention Versus Other 12-Step Models. Not all sex offender treatment models based on therapeutic approaches to addictive behaviors are similar. The following comparison of Relapse Prevention and other "12-step" programs that are based on the famous Alcoholics Anonymous (AA) 12-step program reveals major differences in orientation and implication.

12-Step Programs Are Rigid. Carnes (1983) provides superb insight into the phenomenology of "sex addicts." He proposes that sex addicts can be treated using a program that is adapted from AA's 12-step program. Under Carnes' treatment model, participants attend self-help groups, and "co-addicts" (i.e., spouses) receive ancillary treatment. Offenders are encouraged to subscribe to tenets advocating total abstinence from all behaviors remotely related to sexual victimization. As mentioned previously, enabling offenders to refrain from additional acts of victimization is the principal goal of all forms of treatment with sexual aggressors.

One of AA's central beliefs, "one drink makes a drunk," is particularly well-known. The premise behind this tenet is that imbibing even one sip of a forbidden beverage increases the likelihood of a full-blown relapse. Such statements motivate many individuals to maintain abstinence. However, they also imply that troubled individuals always must be in total control of their problematic behavior. There are no intermediate stages. Anything less than total control is considered total failure. In some individuals, this all-or-nothing approach can trigger a relapse. After all, no one can maintain absolute control over their behaviors at all times and in all situations. At a given moment, behavioral management may fall anywhere between complete control and total lack of control. The ability to exert behavioral control is contingent upon many internal and external variables. Encouraging an individual to believe that there are only two possible behaviors and that they are expected to have absolute behavioral control is an unrealistic and possibly dangerous goal.

There are other difficulties in the AA approach. For one thing, other than telling participants to call other members for support, the model does not offer any specific coping procedures that can be invoked if there are lapses. Participants learn to recognize signs of impending trouble, but they are not taught skills that will enable them to lessen the chances of encountering problems in the first place.

Another problem is that the AA model appears to advocate contradictory beliefs. At the same time that the goal of absolute behavioral control is advanced, the premise that "addicts are powerless over their behavior" is espoused (Carnes, 1983, p. 12). In effect, this model tells sex addicts they should seek perfection but that they are powerless to attain that goal. Doubtlessly, this dichotomous tenet appeals to sexually aggressive clients who would like to convince the court, the therapist, friends, and victims that they were "powerless" to refrain from the victimization. This argument does not deny the existence of a subgroup of compulsive sexual offenders who genuinely are unable to attenuate deviant fantasy. However, psychopharmacological intervention, with concomitant group therapy to enhance self-management, is advocated for such clients. This offender subgroup should not be treated with cognitive-behavioral therapies alone.

Yet another dilemma is posed when offenders are asked to rely totally on their Higher Power for their recovery (Carnes, 1983, p. 151). Although total reliance on a Higher Power is a noble goal that may benefit a select group of people, countless sex offenders have found that this tenet neglects the adage, "God helps those who help themselves." For some offenders, the pattern of being forgiven and sinning anew may be considered a phase of their relapse process. Thus, although Carnes provides an excellent picture of how sex offenders view the world, the 12-step treatment model cannot be considered appropriate as an initial intervention with sexual aggressors.

Relapse Prevention Is More Flexibile. Relapse Prevention offers a more realistic approach to enhancing maintenance of behavioral change. Contrary to the 12-step model, Relapse Prevention proposes that individuals always fall somewhere along a continuum of behavioral control. Rather than frightening participants into maintaining abstinence through the use of doomsaying slogans, individuals are provided with specific skills that can be employed to enhance self-control in problematic situations. In addition, instead of offering a single approach that is applied uniformly to all, Relapse Prevention offers a wide range of therapeutic activities that may be instituted prescriptively to meet the unique behavioral assets and deficits of each individual.

Finally, Relapse Prevention does not postulate dichotomous states of control and dyscontrol without any intermediary stages. Instead, it proposes that relapse is a process that occurs over time. A central tenet of this model holds that abstaining offenders make many decisions, with options influenced by internal and external factors, that lead them closer to, or farther away from, High Risk Situations that may cause a relapse.

Terminology

Relapse Prevention differentiates between two different usages of the term "relapse" (Marlatt and Gordon, 1985). Relapse, as a noun, refers to a terminal state about which little may be done. It represents "a slip back into a former state, especially illness, after a period of improvement" (Webster's New World Dictionary, 1971). This definition corresponds to the dichotomous view espoused by treatment models such as AA.

The same word has far different significance as a verb, where it connotes an active process that occurs over time. Instead of representing a black-and-white dichotomy of abstinence-relapse, the process definition of relapse encompasses a continuum of behaviors that range between those two extremes. Thus, there is room for small errors in self-management. Recognizing that clients frequently experience relatively minor setbacks in self-control that do not yield the severe consequences of total relapse, the Relapse Prevention model refers to minor setbacks as "lapses." Since the first lapse does not necessarily signify total failure (e.g., buying pornography represents a less severe violation of abstinence than raping), clients have the opportunity to exercise damage control. As Marlatt and Gordon (1985) conclude:

> [R]elapse is viewed as a transitional process, a series of events that may or may not be followed by a return to baseline levels of the target behavior. Rather than adopting a pessimistic view in which relapse is viewed as a dead end, treatment failure, or a return to the disease state, the RP model views the occurrence of a lapse as a fork in the road, with one path returning to the former problem level (relapse or total collapse) and the other continuing in the direction of positive change.... Not every lapse eventuates in a relapse, however. In some cases, we actually benefit from a lapse.... An individual who is attempting to change a habit pattern may sometimes find that a lapse provides useful information about both the cause of the event (e.g., a formerly

unknown stressful situation) and how to correct for its occurrence in the future (e.g., to plan remedial action).... Whether or not a lapse is followed by a relapse...depends to a large extent upon the individual's personal expectations and underlying model of the habit change process. (pp. 32-33)

Continuum of Treatment Versus Treatment Solely in Institutions

Assisting sexual offenders to initiate cognitive and behavioral changes may not appear exceptionally difficult, particularly if treatment takes place exclusively within a total institution in which therapists and security personnel have complete control over reinforcement contingencies (Goffman, 1961). Offenders who know they will get a second weekly visit with their spouse if they conform (i.e., demonstrate the ability to change) are likely to conform. Similarly, if an early parole hinges on the "completion" of treatment, the sexual offender's ability to accomplish substantial behavior modification may be stunning.

In many prisons, life is not easy for sex offenders, who are viewed with contempt and harassed by many prisoners. Some incarcerated sexual offenders would have us believe that survival in a correctional facility is one of life's most arduous tasks. In many cases, such claims amount to the offense-related cognitive distortion of victim stancing (Yochelson and Samenow, 1977). Maintaining a gratifying lifestyle in prison may be problematic, but surviving in society generally is more constantly challenging. In prison, residents are not required to exhibit many of the survival skills needed to exist in free society.

Some inmates actually find that their level of tension is lower in prison than in society. These inmates may attribute this to internal change rather than to a changed environment. Another group of offenders may think their new-found tranquility is due to religious rebirth. In either case, these individuals may decide that, given their increased comfort, they can make it on the outside without more work on the problems that predisposed their instant crimes.

It can be difficult to differentiate between offenders who are meaningfully engaged in treatment because they want to stop damaging others' lives and avoid returning to prison from those who attend treatment regularly to get some short-term benefit such as an extra visit with their spouse. Both clients and therapists can be fooled into believing that behavioral change has occurred, when the change really is attributable to compliance with expectations in a less demanding, artificial environment.

The major challenge in treating sexual aggressors comes after the offender has left prison and has returned to a society that is full of distressing life events, risk factors, and potential victims. Thus, the actual impact of treatment may not be discerned until after the individual is released from prison. Inpatient programs that do not include prolonged periods of specialized outpatient treatment and supervision are doomed to fail.

Therapeutic and Supervisory Control Versus Therapeutic Cure

Historically, many treatment programs for sexual aggressors operated exclusively within prisons or maximum security state hospitals. These programs adhered to the traditional belief that effective treatment enables cure. This model works well for many disorders: bacteria causing diseases can be annihilated, ruptured appendices can be removed, weak hearts and lungs can be replaced. However, cure is not always possible. Sometimes control is the best available choice. For example, epilepsy cannot be cured, but it can be controlled with medication. If the patient does not take his or her medication, it is likely that he or she will suffer a seizure.

Sex offenders cannot be cured, either. Permitting offenders (and anyone treating them) to have hope of complete, irreversible eradication of their disorder establishes an expectation that assures failure. Often, a program's failure to prepare clients for lapses (i.e., a return to the moods, fantasies, and thoughts encountered during the relapse process) is due to either (1) the belief that treatment can cure sex offenders or 2) the fear that predicting recurrence of lapses licenses the offender to have them freely. Both of these possibilities appeal to narcissistic mental health providers who enjoy the power inherent in their ability to cure. Parole officers are well advised to avoid permitting such therapists to remain involved in treatment of sexual aggressors. Offenders who have been treated by such therapists may say things like this:

Doc, you've helped me in a way that no one else ever has. If I had you for my first therapist, I never would have re-offended. I kind of look at you as a father, you mean so much to me. I'm thinking of naming my first child after you. The past six weeks of therapy have changed my life, helped me to know things about myself I never would have realized alone. I think I've got a handle on life now, Doc. My schedule is getting kind of tight, but, if you wouldn't mind, I'd like to be able to come in to see you every few weeks, or maybe give you a ring whenever I need you again.

The dire prognosis for affecting cure may lead one to conclude that any attempt to treat sexual aggressors is misguided. However, just as medication can control, but not cure, epilepsy, specialized treatment interventions for sexual offenders can empower them to gain enhanced control over their disorder. If prison systems neglect to provide sex offenders access to treatment programs that are broad enough to meet the specific needs of each individual, the probability of relapse is unacceptably high. Estimates of relapse rates for untreated sex offenders range as high as 80% (Freeman-Longo, and Wall, 1986). In contrast, the relapse rate for the Vermont Treatment Program for Sexual Aggressors, which employs Relapse Prevention in three inpatient treatment units and nearly 40 outpatient groups, currently has a 6% relapse rate.

Integration of Parole and Mental Health Versus Mutual Distrust

All too frequently, mental health practitioners and correctional professionals do not work well together. Clinicians view correctional agents as hardbitten, militaristic agents of authority who are intent upon destroying inmates will and spirit. Correctional workers think mental health professionals are fuzzy thinking, bubble-headed, ivory tower liberals who need to get real jobs.

These opposing views probably developed because the two professional groups seldom work together in an integrated fashion. Instead, they work independently with the same difficult clients, and they both feel frustrated at their own perceived lack of efficacy in helping clients change (clinicians' perspective) or monitoring their criminal behaviors (correctional professional's perspective). Each profession blames the other for undermining their efforts. In addition, each group makes different assumptions about the client. Mental health providers are thought to regard clients with genuineness, empathy, and warmth; while correctional workers are believed to consider clients manipulative, callous, and shallow. This incompatibility extends to the terminology used by each profession. A psychologist might describe a client as "experiencing an ego-dystonic, abreactive, catharsis of an anal-retentive fixation," while the correctional officer might consider him "one upset dude."

Relapse Prevention uses professionally neutral language and concepts to help mend this professional chasm. Since neither profession can lay claim to terms like Seemingly Unimportant Decisions, High Risk Situations, Lapses, and Offense Precursors, both groups can employ the concepts with equal levels of understanding and ownership. Relapse Prevention helps disaffiliated professional groups develop a mutually supportive collaboration with the common goal of preventing sexual victimization.

Effectiveness of Relapse Prevention: Outcome Data

The Vermont Treatment Program for Sexual Aggressors (VTPSA) was the first to use Relapse Prevention with sexual offenders. Currently, the treatment program consists of three inpatient units housed in community correctional facilities and 40 outpatient therapy groups. Between 1982 and 1993, 473 offenders participated in outpatient treatment. They are described in Table 20.3

Table 20.3
Offense Categories of Participants in the Vermont Treatment
Program for Sexual Aggressors (1983-1993)

	Number of Participants	*Percentage*	*Recidivism*
Incest	190	40%	3%
Pedophiles	195	41%	7%
Rapists	53	11%	19%
"Hands off" (exhibitionists, voyeurs)	34	8%	3%
Total	473	100%	6%

Thirty of the 473 offenders are believed to have engaged in another sex offense. The recidivism rate across offender subtypes is 6%. Offenders were included in the recidivist category if (1) they were reconvicted of another sex offense, (2) they were arrested or arraigned for another sex offense, (3) the primary therapist or probation/ parole officer believed the client engaged in another sex offense (even though no arrest occurred).

Specialized treatment and supervision for sex offenders, particularly child sex offenders and noncontact offenders, appears highly efficacious. Relative to the low recidivism rates of child sex offenders and noncontact offenders, treatment of rapists appears less effective. However, it must be noted that treated rapists had one-half the recidivism rate of untreated sex offenders (19% versus 38% respectively).

These data suggest that the VTPSA appears to effectively assist sex offenders in learning new skills that enable offenders to avoid further abuses. Additional attention should be devoted to modifying interventions so that the treatment and supervision needs of rapists may be addressed more adequately.

Conclusion

Relapse Prevention provides sexual offenders with specific procedures to facilitate behavioral self-management. In addition, this model of behavioral maintenance enhances the efficacy of offender treatment and supervision. Since probation and parole officers monitor the presence of specific precursors to offenses, rather than all the offender's behaviors, the efficiency of their supervision is increased. Relapse Prevention facilitates development of a network of professional and nonprofessional collateral contacts who may assist in checking the offender's offense precursors, enabling the probation or parole officer to perform more efficiently. In addition, the Relapse Prevention model enhances communication between professional groups that often appear disaffiliated. Since probation or parole officers and mental health professionals provide each other with information that makes their work more effective, mutual respect, and appreciation are engendered.

With a brief training period, probation and parole officers, clinical psychologists, and social workers who deal with delinquent adolescents all are able to employ the Relapse Prevention model. Research data showing a low overall recidivism rate for participants indicates that this approach holds promise for enhancing the safety of society. Despite the generally favorable findings, Relapse Prevention appears differentially effective across subgroups of sex offenders, with rapists being less effectively treated than all other sex offender subtypes. Even with rapists, however, treated offenders are significantly less likely to recidivate than untreated offenders.

References

Carnes, P. (1983). *Sexual addiction*. Minneapolis, MN: CompCare Publications.

Chaney, E.F., O'Leary, M.R., and Marlatt, G.A. (1978). Skill training with alcoholics. *Journal of Consulting and Clinical Psychology* 46:1092-1104.

Corcoran, K. and Fischer, J. (1987). *Measures for clinical practice: A sourcebook*. New York: Free Press.

Freeman-Longo, R. and Wall, R. (1986). Changing a lifetime of sexual crime. *Psychology Today*, 20, 58-62.

Frisbie,L.V. (1969) Another look at sex offenders in California. Research Monograph No. 12. Sacramento: California Department of Mental Hygiene.

Goffman, E. (1961). *Asylums: Essays on the social situation of mental patients and other inmates*. Garden City, NY: Anchor Books.

Gray, A.S. and Pithers, W.D. (1992). Relapse prevention with sexually abusive adolescents: Three applications to treatment and supervision. In Barbaree, H.E., Marshall, W.L., and Hudson, S. (Eds.), *The juvenile sex offender*. New York: Guilford Publications.

Guralnik, D.B. and Friend, J.H. (Eds.) (1971). Webster's new world dictionary. Cleveland, Ohio: Simon and Schuster

Langevin, R. (1983). *Sexual strands: Understanding and treating sexual anomalies in men*. Hillsdale, NJ: Lawrence Erlbaum Associates.

Marlatt, G.A. (1982). Relapse prevention: A self-control program for the treatment of addictive behaviors. In R.B. Stuart (Ed.), *Adherence, compliance, and generalization in behavioral medicine*. New York: Brunner/Mazel.

Marlatt, G.A. and Gordon, J.R. (1980). Determinants of relapse: Implications for the maintenance of change. In P.O. Davidson and S. Davidson, (Eds.), *Behavioral medicine: Changing health lifestyles*. New York: Brunner/Mazel.

Marlatt, G.A. and Gordon, J.R. (1985). *Relapse prevention*. New York: Guilford Press.

Paitich, D., Langevin, R., Freeman, R., Mann, K., and Handy, L. (1977). The Clarke SHQ: A clinical sex history questionnaire for males. *Archives of Sexual Behavior*, 6, 421-436.

Pithers, W.D. (1982). Vermont Treatment Program for Sexual Aggressors. Vermont Department of Corrections. Waterbury, VT.

Pithers, W.D., Buell, M.M., Kashima, K., Cumming, G.F., and Beal, L.S. (1987). Precursors to Sexual Aggression. Paper presented at the Association for the Behavioral Treatment of Sexual Abusers. Newport, OR.

Pithers, W.D. and Cummings, G.F. (l989) Can relapses be prevented? Initial outcome data from the Vermont Treatment Program for sexual aggressors. In Laws, D. (Ed.) *Relapse prevention with sex offenders*, 313-325 New York: Guilford Press.

Pithers, W.D., Kashima, K., Cumming, G.F., Beal, L.S., and Buell, M.M. (1987). Relapse prevention of sexual aggression. Paper presented at the New York Academy of Sciences. New York.

Pithers, W.D., Kashima, K., Cumming, G.F., Beal, L.S., and Buell, M.M. (1988). Relapse prevention of sexual aggression. *Annals of the New York Academy of Science*. New York: New York Academy of Sciences.

Pithers, W.D., Marques, J.K., Gibat, C.C., and Marlatt, G.A. (1983). Relapse prevention with sexual aggressives: A self-control model of treatment and maintenance of change. In J.G. Greer and I.R. Stuart (Eds.), *The sexual aggressor: Current perspectives*. New York: Van Nostrand Reinhold.

Salter, A. (1988). *Treatment of child sexual abuse*. Beverly Hills, CA: Sage Press.

Sturgeon, V.H. and Taylor, J. (1980). Report of a five-year follow-up study of mentally disordered sex offenders released from Atascadero State Hospital in 1973. *Criminal Justice Journal*, 4, 31-63.

Yochelson, S. and Samenow, S. (1976). *The criminal personality, Vol.1: A profile for change*. New York: Jason Aronson.

Chapter 21

Community Management of Sex Offenders

by Randy Green, Ph.D.

Overview

Even the best and most comprehensive treatment program for sex offenders will fail in its objective if the offender does not know how to apply what he has learned in the treatment program to his life after discharge. Adequate aftercare strategies are developed by translating generalized coping skills to each offender's particular dynamics and helping him implement those skills over a lifetime. Communication between the offender, therapist, correctional personnel, and the offender's support system is essential in the early stages of community reintegration and desirable thereafter.

Issues relating to sentencing conditions, community-based correctional settings, and transition back into the community by the offender will be discussed in this chapter. It is the purpose of this chapter to encourage maximum interagency awareness and cooperation in the aftercare management of sex offenders in order to minimize the likelihood of future instances of sexual assault.

Aftercare Defined

Following the most active phase of treatment intervention for the sex offender, whether in a correctional institution, residential facility, or community-based treatment program, there is an inevitable reduction in the intensity of treatment and supervision. In the initial and most optimum end of the continuum, treatment has been comprehensive and intensive, but treatment and supervision are gradually reduced with the demonstrated responsibility of the offender. At the most pessimistic end of the continuum, treatment becomes quite fragmented until both treatment and supervision are finally terminated. In either case, the after component of a treatment program should be viewed not as an afterthought but rather as an integral part of a comprehensive rehabilitative and case management program for the sex offender

Aftercare is essentially that portion of the offender's program in which positive changes which have been made are maintained on a day-to-day basis. A responsible aftercare approach should assume that the sex offender is never "cured." There is no point in time that a sex offender or case management personnel can relax and conclude that the offender will never perpetuate another sexual crime. In fact, the first sign of a possible relapse might occur when the offender adopts the optimistic posture that he will "never let it happen again." Such professions of overconfidence, frequently made with all sincerity and often believed by the offender's personal support group, can nonetheless signal the first significant erosion of the offender's defenses against re-offending. This attitude, unfortunately, is quite prevalent and highly resistant to being dislodged. Treatment personnel, therefore, attempt to let the offender know from the outset that his efforts toward rehabilitation will not be easy. The hope to "maintain without pain" has just as many adherents as those who hope to "gain without pain." Sex offender programs should endeavor to prepare the offenders with a reality-based view that responsible living, though difficult, is far easier than the alternative.

Statistical support for the contention that sex offenders should always consider themselves at risk to re-offend comes from several sources. Soothill and Gibbens (1978) reported that, after 22 years, the reconviction recidivism rate for 174 untreated British incest offenders, rapists, or sexual abusers was 48%. Significantly, they reported that the highest reconviction rate occurred during the first two years following an initial conviction. In that high-risk time, 16.8% of the total group, or one-third of the recidivist group, were reconvicted. However, their study also revealed some other significant findings. One such finding was that the recidivism rate continued to increase an average of 2-3% annually, with nearly 25% of the reconvictions occurring more than 10 years after the initial conviction. According to this information, there is no point at which it can be assumed that untreated offenders are no longer at risk. It is probable that this is more true of child molesters than of forcible rapists. Jurisdictions throughout the United States are grappling with the phenomenon of the grandparent child molesters being potentially very protracted. Furthermore, statistics kept on those offenders who have been treated for sexual deviancy reinforce the conclusion that there is never immunity from offending.

A treatment program should incorporate as great a degree of control, structure, treatment intensity, and correctional supervision as possible. As an offender demonstrates motivation, commitment, trustworthiness, follow-through, and integration of treatment principles into behavior patterns—including arousal patterns—it becomes possible to gradually reduce program control and increase the offender's own sense of responsibility for daily life management. This process is best-facilitated in residential programs in which the offender's access to the community is restricted until such time as appropriate insight, stability, maturity, and responsibility are demonstrated. Then the offender can enter a gradual community transition and a subsequent aftercare phase. Institutional programs in which there is no access to the community until after discharge, handicap the inmates who are progressing in treatment. Some assimilation into a community, like a halfway house, is vital.

Community programs, on the other hand, attempt to work with the lower risk, less impulsive, less antisocial clients from the outset. They have a lower capacity to monitor their offenders in treatment but do have an early opportunity to observe the degree of self-motivation and follow-through which the offender himself is willing to provide. Much earlier in treatment, there is a need to address how the offender can successfully manage in the community. Because the offender who is initially sentenced to outpatient care is usually without any prior treatment for sexual deviancy, it is advisable that sentencing orders be particularly clear about the limits of contact and movement for those individuals. The treatment and community corrections personnel, as well as the offender, need all the rules clearly defined.

Sentencing Issues

Nearly all sex offenders are referred to treatment through court mandate. That being the case, the manner in which the court order is written for such a mandated client is critical. The best of intentions by the court may translate into either glaring omissions or, alternately, extremely rigid and inflexible orders.

As defined by law and within the limitations of resources available for treatment, incarceration, and community supervision, it is desirable to create the optimum conditions to accomplish a two-fold purpose:

1. Encouraging those who are amenable for treatment to actively participate in available treatment, while
2. Identifying those currently unamenable to available treatment and separating them from society for the maximum time possible.

With regard to sentencing, whenever possible it is advisable to have a presentencing report available for the court. This report should include an assessment from an experienced clinician regarding the specific issues which are addressed earlier.

Additionally, it has proven helpful in Oregon for treatment providers and specialized probation/parole personnel to develop a list of possible sentencing conditions which can be included in the sentencing order (see Appendix D). This list provides a set of conditions which can be tailored to the specific dynamics of each individual sex offender.

The concepts and sentencing provision options can be shared with the state judiciary. The State Judiciary Association or the State Supreme Court, as well as the parole board, could provide a helpful agency through which these issues and concerns can be addressed and communicated. Many judges and parole board members are also struggling with how best to respond to this societal problem. Many may welcome assistance in the preparation of possible sentencing or release conditions which can be effectively incorporated into their sentencing orders.

Topical areas addressed in the list would include general probation/parole conditions addressing the recommended frequency of contact between probation/parole officer and the sex offender, community access, the offender's contact with children or significant others, limitations on high-risk or pre-assault behaviors, conditions related to drugs, and conditions specifically involving low-functioning sex offenders. This list is clearly nonexhaustive and can be made available to any other state agencies who control the offender's access into the general community. A state's parole authority would be a primary example.

Aftercare Issues for Agencies Involved with Recovering Offenders

The overriding issue for public or private officials involved with treating or monitoring the recovering offender is to insure that they have taken the proper steps to best perform this duty. In setting a proper tone in the relationship, the therapist or community correctional officer is advised to inform the recovering offender of the manner in which questionable or potentially problematic situations will be handled, including the procedures to warn or report. A signed statement to that effect may be helpful to prevent law suits for alleged violation of confidentiality. Should any questionable situation arise, the staff person should immediately consult with another professional and discuss the matter with the recovering offender, carefully documenting each action taken. In cases where there is potential harm to an identifiable victim, the therapist has the responsibility to notify that victim and/or the police/community corrections officer immediately (see Chapter 26, Confidentiality, Privileges, and Self-Incrimination).

In this era of malpractice suits, no one feels safe or immune from the potential risks which can arise in the area of aftercare and community management of the recovering offender. Awareness of statutes, sentencing orders, and typical case management issues, coupled with a practice of clear, direct, assertive communication, minimizes the likelihood of difficulties in this sensitive area. A willingness to obtain consultation and to provide accurate documentation is also vitally important.

Aftercare Components

When a recovering offender is transitioning into a community, even in a probation situation involving community-based therapeutic intervention, the therapist should develop a community contract as soon as possible. Primary responsibility for development of the contract rests with the recovering offender, who works within a general format and philosophy provided by the therapist. Approval prior to implementation should be obtained by the recovering offender's probation or parole officer and should be appropriately shared with significant others who will be involved in the recovering offender's life.

A sample "Discharge Contract" is provided by F. Knopp (1984). The primary components of the contract include the following:

- A thorough description of the recovering offender's sexually deviant outlet. Range of ages and sex of victims are identified. The pre-assault process, observable behavior cues, fantasy and thought patterns, and actual sexually deviant activities are enumerated in detail. In addition, the recovering offender should state those specific interventions at each stage which have the greatest likelihood of interrupting the pre-assault pattern. Support system personnel should be listed with their phone numbers and addresses.

- Methods to avoid relapse: Behaviors, activities, persons, situations, or locations which are likely to sabotage the aftercare plan should be listed and avoided as specified. Use of chemicals and pornography should be specifically addressed (see Chapter 20, Relapse Prevention).
- Plans to pursue therapeutic support as well as accountability and practice assigned behavioral "booster sessions" should be specified. Pre- and post-probation/parole plans regarding these responsibilities should be listed.
- Plans for employment and/or education should be specifically identified.
- Living arrangements should be described fully.
- Social/vocational goals should be developed in detail.
- Current relationship plans should be discussed.
- Budget and transportation arrangements should be clearly developed

This document should be one which is shared with any therapist, case manager, significant other (such as spouse, fiance, or live-in partner), roommate, or treatment group with whom the recovering offender interacts. In order to remain viable, the contract should be revised whenever there are significant changes, updating so that anyone reading it would have a current and accurate picture of the recovering offender's community living plan.

Aftercare/Community Case Management Components

Interagency cooperation is imperative. Traditional concepts of confidentiality should always be defined by a clear awareness of the potential danger to identifiable victims, including children of incest offenders wishing to reunite with the children. Under the best of circumstances, coordinating case management of recovering offenders is very challenging. Interagency hostility and poor communication can create a situation in which the offender or the family members can manipulate the system to serve their own purposes.

There appears to be a developing trend toward specialization among probation/parole officers which is worth mentioning. These specialists have a real interest in providing responsible intervention and case management duties for sex offenders. Those individuals with an interest in working with sex offenders, either in treatment or case management, may be motivated by a desire to directly impact on this major societal epidemic. These individuals may wish to update their skills through continuing education.

In addition to capitalizing on increased motivation and commitment, there are other arguments for more specialized training for both treatment providers and probation/parole personnel. Knowledge of offender dynamics, typologies, differential risks to the community, unique case management issues, and pre-assault cycle patterns is highly desirable for personnel working with these individuals. Knowledge of the strengths and limitations of available behavioral interventions and psychophysiological technology is also very desirable. Quality evaluations, both clinical and pre-sentence, as well as ongoing intervention and supervision, are enhanced when there are knowledgeable and experienced personnel trained to do this work. Specialists also become more aware of community resources and support systems and can be more effective in coordinating with the network.

If a community correctional agency works toward the development of specialized officers for sex offenders—and perhaps other types of offenders as well—it should also develop a policy statement regarding the scope of the officer's authority. When probation/parole officers become highly involved, committed, and specialized, there can be a tendency to blur role distinctions, for example, between case worker and therapist. Where such a line is drawn is a matter for each agency to decide and depends upon its mandate, resources, and workload issues, among others. Clarification of the issue at the outset can possibly avoid later frustrations.

In certain jurisdictions where specialization has occurred, probation/parole officers have co-led supervision/therapy groups with a clinician who specializes in this area. This maximizes their communication and provides the officer with an opportunity for participation in group supervision. It provides the officer with the added perceptions of the sex offender's peer group, who also provide direct feedback and monitor behavior. Of course, this presupposes probation/parole officers who are comfortable in such roles and able to be empathic and facilitative, as well as confrontive, in group situations. Pre- and post-sessions between the probation/parole officers and the therapist provide the necessary time to review and plan.

In Oregon, specialized community correctional officers have actually formed a nonprofit professional association in which topics of mutual concern are discussed. Meeting periodically, they may invite another colleague or a clinician to discuss particular topics. In addition, this motivated group, with the support of correctional administrators, has been actively involved in lobbying for a change in state laws pertaining to the sentencing process and probationary guidelines for sex offenders. One specialized probation/parole officer was faced with the unenviable addition to his caseload of five indigent sex offenders who were in denial and who had been determined unamenable for treatment in other settings. He established a group composed of "deniers" who were on probation and, within two months, had utilized the group forum to break through the denial problem, thus preparing the group members for subsequent treatment interventions. Needless to say, this will not always happen, but it does serve to illustrate the potential of such groups for a state system grappling with such desperate problems.

For those sex offenders in aftercare following institutional or residential treatment or those who began their probation within the community itself, it is useful for community correctional personnel to establish an approved list of recognized clinicians who are experienced in the assessment and treatment of sex offenders. Furthermore, it is helpful to clarify the specifics regarding communication between probation/ parole personnel and the therapist. Guidelines, such as phone or written contact once every three months to update corrections regarding the sex offender's status, are advisable. In addition, any change in behavior or situation suggestive of a lapse, or a change of situation which could possible place the offender in a High-Risk Situation should be communicated to the probation or parole officer.

In essence, community corrections is best served by identifying its philosophy of case management of sex offenders, by clearly articulating that philosophy and concurrent expectation, and choosing those assessment and treatment providers who are willing and able to work compatibly with those standards.

Aftercare Issues for Recovering Offenders

Recovering offenders must be able to balance the precariousness of their situations with their worth and significance as human beings. They also must accept that, despite the reality of the past and the potential for sexually deviant fantasies and behavior in the present and the future, they can still achieve a sense of belonging and acceptance from others in order to make their lives worthwhile. Many recovering offenders have an understandably difficult time keeping this tension in balance, but it is important for them to learn to do so.

Recovering offenders must retain some trust in order to be able to appropriately "disclose" to potentially significant others in their community. This group would typically include prospective employers, prospective dating partners, and close friends. Such issues are filled with emotionality, explosiveness, and danger. The following general guidelines are useful in most instances:

- Though it goes without saying, the recovering offender should abide by any statutory or sentencing requirements in terms of reporting or disclosing information to specific individuals.
- In job-search situations, the recovering offender should be encouraged to prepare functional resumes which emphasize skills and experience, in contrast to the chronological resume which would more likely highlight gaps in time. Generally, minimal information regarding criminal history is sufficient unless the nature or location of the job opportunity would make it appropriate to be more disclosing.

Disclosure to prospective friends or dating partners is no less sensitive. In general, it appears to be appropriate if the recovering offender does not disclose to casual friends. Those who are seen on a frequent basis, who are demonstrating a sensitivity and trustworthiness, and with whom the offender would like to spend more time, should probably be told. Disclosures at this stage may avert uncomfortable situations in a longer term friendship where the friend feels betrayed by having had such information withheld.

Disclosure becomes even more critical with sexually intimate companions. It is preferable to disclose general information in the early stages of a potentially serious or ongoing relationship. This is especially true whenever the recovering child molester desires to date someone with children. It is reasonable that the other party make the decision to date a recovering offender on the basis of "informed consent."

Conclusion

In conclusion, this chapter has reviewed issues pertaining to community management of the sex offender. Neither public nor private officials involved with treatment or supervision should be complacent regarding the need for daily maintenance of acquired behavioral changes. A comprehensive, informed interagency network at the community level is essential to maximize the achievement of the goal. The cooperation of the state's legislative, judicial, correctional, and mental health resources is needed to minimize future victimizations. Approaching the task from a clear problem-solving perspective at state and local levels can replace counterproductive "turf" issues with the mutual collaboration needed both to protect society and to rehabilitate those who may be reintegrated back into that society.

References

Knopp, F.H. (1984). *Retraining the adult sex offender: Methods and models*. Syracuse, NY: Safer Society.

Soothill, K. and Gibbens, T. (1978). *Recidivism of sex offenders: A reappraisal*. British Journal of Criminology, 18, 267-276.

Part 5

Legal Issues in the Treatment of Sex Offenders

Laws related to sex offenders and their management span the field of criminal law, mental health practice and liability statutes. Recently a number of constitutional issues have also been raised in the areas of preventive detention, self-incrimination and privacy issues. In this section Fred Cohen gives an overview of the current issues of most concern to those involved in the treatment and management of sex offenders.

Books on sex offenders published in the 1980s spoke of the abolition of Mentally Disordered Sex Offender Laws (also known as Sexual Psychopath or Sexually Dangerous Persons Laws) which had led to the civil commitment of certain groups of sex offenders, usually in state hospitals. In only one year, 1989, was there almost unanimous agreement that these types of statutes were based on flawed logic and no conducive to treatment. However, in 1990 the State of Washington reinstituted civil commitment for certain sex offenders. However, whereas previous MDSO legislation had provided for commitment in connection with a specific sex offense, the Washington legislation was directed at crimes which might be committed in the future as they were meant to be applied after an individual had finished a period of institutionalization. The constitutional challenge to this law is now working its way through the courts.

The issues concerned with the provision of treatment are also reviewed. Do sex offenders have a "right" to treatment? Would those child molesters who meet the criteria for "pedophilia" according to the American Psychiatric Association Diagnostic and Statistical Manual-IV have a right to treatment as individuals suffering from a mental illness? Can individuals be forced to admit to their guilt as a stipulation of court-ordered treatment?

There are also issues related to the responsibilities of those who treat and supervise this population. The "duty to protect" is discussed as are liability issues related to release and supervision.

Considerable controversy has been generated lately around the stimulus materials utilized in phallometric assessment. One such issue focuses on whether the materials currently in use are illegal and what materials would be least likely to be legally challenged.

Sex offenders maintain many rights associated with theirstatus as patients of mental health practitioners, including certain confidentiality rights, and the right to give consent to certain treatments. Since sex offender treatment is significantly different from traditional mental health treatment in a variety of approaches, it is important that practitioners understand how these different approaches legally intersect and how patient rights can be maintained without compromising public safety.

Finally, a number of states have instituted various public notification statutes, such as New Jersey's so-called "Megan's Law," that exempt sex offenders from the right to privacy enjoyed by other citizens. Undoubtedly, the constitutionality of these laws will be challenged.

Chapter 22

Introduction to Legal Issues: How the Legal Framework Developed

by Fred Cohen, D.J.P.

Overview

Persons who violate laws involving sexual misconduct no doubt plague society more than the laws themselves. Nevertheless, the laws surrounding this area of misconduct constitute a troublesome body of legal problems that encompass both criminal and civil law. These problems range from fundamental questions such as who is a sex offender to more concrete issues such as the value of using allegedly obscene material in behavioral modification-type programs.

While this chapter touches on all of these matters, some of the discussion must necessarily be abridged. In order to provide a full discussion of the legal issues associated with "sex offenses" and "sex offenders," one would have to engage in an elaborate analysis of Sexual Psychopath (or Mentally Disordered Sex Offender) Laws that still exist, the entire range of correctional law problems as they touch on sex offenders, issues related to the treatment relationship (e.g., confidentiality and consent), liability for injuries inflicted by released sex offenders, among other issues. Since this is merely a portion of a much longer book concerned with treatment, the detailed coverage outlined above simply is not possible. It is possible, however, to mark out a legal framework of the area and to highlight some problems and deal more extensively with others. The coverage in this chapter is partly a matter of the author's judgment and partly reflective of questions posed by clinicians and program staff who attended several recent conferences on the treatment of the sex offender.[1]

Is There a Future for the Rehabilitative Ideal's Laws and Treatment Programs?

In some respects this is an odd time for a demonstration of heightened concern for sex offenders, certainly insofar as that concern is expressed as a need for special treatment. The rehabilitative ideal, if not dead, certainly is in extremis.[2] Ask what works in treatment and many will answer: "Nothing!" Ask again and others will say: "Some things work, sometimes, with some types of disorders."[3]

One survey suggests that the number of sex offenders has increased in more than two-thirds of our prisons.[4] This increase is not surprising since abuse-type offenses are increasingly reported and prosecuted. What may be surprising is the number of treatment programs in prison, which have been established and are pursued without any special sentencing structure.

In 1977, the Group for the Advancement of Psychiatry stated, "We see special sex offender legislation as an approach to sex psychopaths that has failed, and consequently we feel that these statutes should be repealed."[5] Indeed, the legislative trend is strongly and unequivocally following this path. In 1985, one researcher found that only 16 states and the District of Columbia had Mentally Disordered Sex Offender (MDSO) laws.[6] Another authority has claimed that involuntary treatment programs for mentally disordered sex offenders and other abnormal offenders can be "characterized by repeal and abolition."[7] This is to be differentiated from treatment programs for incarcerated sex offenders which are continuing to proliferate. Whether the Washington law on sexually violent predators discussed in Chapter 23 initiates yet another era in this saga remains to be seen.

It is not easy to identify the reasons for the current disenchantment with and abandonment of MDSO-type laws. A combination of causes including insufficient resources and the media's and the public's belief that what was expended was wasted— are responsible. In some quarters there still is concern for the infringement on civil liberties that accompanies the seemingly arbitrary and unduly extended periods of detention. However, the general mood is that harsh punishment is the only acceptable alternative, particularly for those who rape or sexually victimize children.[8]

Recently, the prevailing disfavor with MDSO-type laws gave way in the State of Washington to enactment of the highly controversial Community Protection Act of 1990. This law, which was upheld by the Washington Supreme Court in August 1993 in *In re Young*,[9] contains a provision that requires the civil commitment of so-called Sexually Violent Predators (SVP). An SVP is a person who has been convicted of or charged with a crime of sexual violence and who suffers from a mental abnormality or personality disorder that makes the person likely to engage in predatory acts of sexual violence. This unique law, which may well represent the beginning of yet another cycle in the legal treatment of sex offenders, will be treated in some detail in Chapter 23. In addition, the full text of the opinion upholding the law, *In re Young*[10] and relevant portions of the statute are reproduced as Appendices H and I , respectively.

Semantic and Conceptual Problems with the Clinical and Legal Terminology

For the purpose of legal analysis, two points alone strike a near-fatal blow to the earlier MDSO-type laws: First, it is now generally agreed that "sexual psychopathy" is neither a clinical entity nor a proper psychiatric diagnosis.[11] In addition, the clinical category of "sexually dangerous" actually is a legal term in diagnostic clothing.[12]

Second, the term "sex offender" is as imprecise and misleading as "sex psychopath" or "sexually dangerous," although for a different reason. Sex offenses may include forcible rape, a variety of homosexual practices, a variety of "fondling"-type offenses dependent on age and competency, prostitution, obscenity, obscene gestures in public, voyeurism, bigamy, adultery, and more.[13] The behavior and the proscribed harm attributable to this list of sex offenses are enormously varied. Thus, the term "sex offender" does not encompass any group of offenses or offenders with enough shared characteristics to make the term useful.[14] The term is evocative, but in the law that is a failing, not a strength. Nevertheless, the term "sex offender" will be used in this part of the book in the interest of verbal economy.

Beyond this semantic and conceptual problem is the fact that while it is colloquially acceptable to speak of "murderers," "rapists," and "burglars," it is not legally precise to do so. Persons are convicted of murder, rape, and burglary and they are then sentenced within the statutory limits of the offense.[15] What that does, however, is array and utilize factors deemed significant in sentencing for the offense. It does not convert a convicted person into a burglar. Outside of special offender laws, individuals are not convicted for being sex offenders, and, if they were, it defies the imagination to understand the uses to which the designation would be put. Again, there are simply too many different people violating too many different norms for the designation to have any significant legal meaning.

Thus, we encounter an area where many diagnostic-sounding categories are renounced as clinically improper and most legal-sounding categories are condemned as imprecise and misleading. This does not mean that there is no potential in treatment programs or in continuing research on persons who commit various sex offenses. Instead, the problem is with the flawed conceptual and policy reason for selecting one group of inaptly described offenders for inappropriate legal and clinical responses. In other words, it makes perfectly good sense to pursue treatment or research based on sound diagnostic principles and more specific categories. It is also supportable penal philosophy to enhance punishment for unlawful sexual conduct that involves force, a minor child, where the home is invaded, or where there is a gang assault.[16]

Brief History of State Statutes Dealing with Sex Offenders

The first sex psychopath statute was enacted by Michigan in 1937 and soon adopted by many other states.[17] These statutes are traceable to the earlier but less popular Defective Delinquent Laws. In some states (such as Vermont) these early laws were incorporated into the sex psychopath laws.[18] Defective delinquents were viewed as feeble-minded and antisocial; persons whose chronicity and defective genes called for indeterminate confinement in special institutions. In the period 1900-1921, "Bolsheviks" and immigrants were frequent targets of the Defective Delinquent Laws. Mental testing and the eugenics movement converged in a type of "medical model" whereby the "genetically impaired" were civilly confined in lieu of criminal prosecution and imprisonment. This is an early example of a crime control movement in the guise of therapeutic intervention.

It is interesting to note that New York's MDSO-type law did not evolve quite the same way. New York's sex offender legislation of 1950 resembled its Defective Delinquent Law, but it also grew out of a campaign led by the Prison Association.[19]

Various states have now lined up to repeal their MDSO-type laws, just as they once lined up to pass them. Sutherland's classic study of the diffusion of these laws revealed this pattern: highly publicized, often terrifying sex offenses led to community agitation. Committees, often dominated by psychiatrists, are then created. The result is the formulation and passage of sex psychopath legislation.[20] Misguided scientism and an inappropriate medical model serve to temporarily allay community fears. Although these laws often promise treatment, they more often failed to deliver.

The Supreme Court's Involvement in the Evolution of Sex Offender Laws

Court Confronts Due Process and Equal Protection Challenges. In *Minnesota ex rel. Pearson v. Probation Court*[21] the Supreme Court upheld a constitutional challenge to the Minnesota sex psychopath law, providing the judicial imprimatur for the earlier legislation and easing the way for other jurisdictions to follow. The Court was confronted with a due process/vagueness challenge and an equal protection/under-inclusion challenge; it upheld the Minnesota law on both counts. The portion of the statute challenged as vague defines the term "psychopathic personality" as meaning

the existence in any person of such conditions of emotional instability, or impulsiveness of behavior, or lack of customary standards of good judgment, or failure to appreciate the consequences of his acts, or a combination of any such conditions, as to render such person irresponsible for his conduct with respect to sexual matters and thereby dangerous to other persons.[22]

The Minnesota Supreme Court previously interpreted this statute so that it was:

to include those persons who, by a habitual course of misconduct in sexual matters, have evidenced an utter lack of power to control their sexual impulses and who, as a result, are likely to attack or otherwise inflict injury, loss, pain or other evil on the objects of their uncontrolled and uncontrollable desire. It would not be reasonable to apply the provisions of the statute to every person guilty of sexual misconduct nor even to persons having strong sexual propensities. Such a definition would not only make the act impracticable of enforcement and, perhaps, unconstitutional in its application, but would also be an unwarranted departure from the accepted meaning of the words defined.[23]

The Supreme Court accepted this interpretation as binding and simply found that these underlying conditions, calling for evidence of past conduct pointing to probable consequences, are as clear and susceptible to proof as criteria frequently applied in criminal prosecutions.[24] Parenthetically, while this language might still pass muster today, the vagueness challenge would be aimed not only at the ease with which those who are the objects of the law might understand the statute, but also—and perhaps more important—at the amount of discretion afforded those who must administer and apply the law.

The equal protection/under-inclusion claim, equally unavailing, argued that the statute selected one group (sex psychopaths) from a larger group (all psychopaths), thereby unconstitutionally singling out the smaller group. In rejecting this claim, the Court stated that the test is whether the line-drawing had any rational basis to it and not whether a larger group might reasonably have been included:

The class it did select is identified by the state court in terms which clearly show that the persons within that class constitute a dangerous element in the community which the legislature in its discretion could put under appropriate control. As we have often said, the legislature is free to recognize degrees of harm, and it may confine its restrictions to those classes of cases where the need is deemed to be clearest.[25]

Court Confronts Procedural Challenge. In *Specht v. Patterson*,[26] the Supreme Court decided a procedural challenge aimed at the Colorado Sex Offenders Act (the Act). This time the law did not survive the challenge. Petitioner was convicted of "indecent liberties," an offense with a 10-year maximum. He was not sentenced as a felon but subjected to an indeterminate term of one day to life (as a sex offender). This was done without notice or a full hearing.[27]

The trial judge, based on an ex parte decision, sent the petitioner to a mental hospital for examination. On completion of this examination, a psychiatric report was prepared and given to the judge prior to the sentencing. The critical determination that the petitioner met the Act's criteria was made without confrontation and cross-examination of adverse witnesses, without the presentation of his own evidence by use of compulsory process, and on the basis of the hearsay report to which he had no access.

Justice Douglas, for a unanimous Court, determined that the Act required new findings of fact (e.g., threat of bodily harm) as a prelude to greatly enhanced criminal punishment. However, the Court stated that before such a radically new result could be reached, due process "requires that he be present with counsel, have an opportunity to be heard, be confronted with witnesses against him, have the right to cross-examine, and to offer evidence of his own. And there must be findings adequate to make meaningful any appeal that is allowed."[28]

At first reading, S*pecht* seems procedurally protective of persons facing the application of a sex psychopath-type law. It must be emphasized, however, that Justice Douglas stated that "the invocation of the Sex Offenders Act means the making of a new charge leading to criminal punishment."[29] Thus, the Justice, without fully exposing the basis for his reasoning, characterized the Colorado law as more nearly criminal than civil.

If the Act had been characterized as more nearly a civil commitment law, with the criminal event—either a charge or conviction—serving as a trigger for civil commitment, then the *Specht* ruling would not apply,[30] and the seemingly less demanding procedural format of civil commitment law would have been invoked. Also, if Colorado had simply determined that a conviction for "indecent liberties" might subject the offender to a term of life imprisonment, then the far less demanding procedural format of criminal sentencing would apply.[31] A challenge that such a law violates the Eighth Amendment's proscription of cruel and unusual punishment in that the punishment is wholly disproportionate to the offense also would likely fail.[32]

Court Has Not Considered Whether Sex Offenders Have a Right to Treatment.
Neither *Pearson* nor *Specht* dealt with the substantive issue of a sex offender's possible right to treatment. In *Humphrey v. Cady*[33] the petitioner argued that his confinement under a Sex Crimes Act led to commitment to the state prison with no treatment, whereas a commitment to a mental hospital would have increased the likelihood of treatment. The Court decided that this was not an argument that could be dismissed out of hand, but the petitioner was released before a final determination could be made, the issue never was resolved.[34]

Court Weighs Issue of Compulsory Self-Incrimination Versus Fifth Amendment Rights. The Supreme Court's most recent encounter with sex psychopath-type laws came in *Allen v. Illinois*,[35] a fascinating case involving the question of whether the proceedings under Illinois' Sexually Dangerous Persons Act (SDPA) are criminal within the meaning of the Fifth Amendment's protection against compulsory self-incrimination. The Court, in a 5 to 4 ruling, held against the petitioner. It also answered, although obliquely, some other questions about sex offender laws.

In *Allen*, the petitioner was charged with unlawful restraint and deviate sexual intercourse. He was not tried on those charges, however. Instead, a petition was filed under the SDPA and the petitioner was ordered to submit to two psychiatric examinations.

Allen apparently acknowledged during the examination that he had been involved in deviant sexual behavior since the age of 10 and that he had, in fact, forced a woman into his car where he forced her to perform fellatio.[36] The state trial court ruled that the petitioner's statements were not of themselves admissible but that the psychiatrists could give their clinical opinions based on the petitioner's statements.[37] Illinois courts had ruled previously that no statements compelled under the SDPA could be used in any subsequent criminal proceeding.

Thus, the claim before the Supreme Court came down to the sharply defined issue of whether the SDPA itself is sufficiently criminal-like to invoke the Fifth

Amendment.[38] If this amendment had been found applicable then the examining psychiatrists would have been required to provide a clinical-type of *Miranda* warning, touching on the uses and potential consequences of the answers.

The petitioner's strongest arguments were that (1) the SPDA requires that a criminal charge be brought, with at least one proven act or attempted sexual assault, and (2) he, the petitioner, was housed at Menard Psychiatric Center with other SDP's and prisoners from other institutions in need of psychiatric care.[39]

Majority Opinion Answers Some Questions, But None That Specify What Treatment Is Required. Speaking for the majority, Justice Rehnquist stated that Illinois need not apply the SPDA to the specific class of mentally ill persons who might also be sexually dangerous. Because Illinois imposed the requirement of proof of a criminal act—a discretionary legislative judgment—on itself, the state retained its right to view the SDPA as a civil procedure and avoided the strictures of the Fifth Amendment.[40]

The petitioner also failed to convince a majority that he was, in reality, serving penal time in a maximum security prison as a result of a procedure denominated civil. On this issue, the Court held that:

> The State serves its purpose of treating rather than punishing sexually dangerous persons by committing them to an institution expressly designed to provide psychiatric care and treatment. That the [facility] houses not only sexually dangerous persons but also prisoners from other institutions who are in need of psychiatric treatment does not transform the State's intent to treat into an intent to punish.... Petitioner has not demonstrated, and the record does not suggest, that "sexually dangerous persons" in Illinois are confined under conditions incompatible with the State's asserted interest in treatment. Had petitioner shown, for example, that the confinement of such persons imposes on them a regimen which is essentially identical to that imposed upon felons with no need for psychiatric care, this might well be a different case.[41]

While upholding the SDPA as a civil proceeding, the Court also strongly suggested that a statutory treatment scheme of this sort actually does create a right to treatment. The Court laid to rest any lingering questions about whether unconvicted persons may constitutionally be required to co-mingle with convicted persons, assuming a common base of psychiatric needs and care. However the questions of just what treatment may—or must be—offered and issues associated with the possible untreatability of certain sexually related disorders remain unanswered.

Dissent Argued That Criminal Law Occupies a Central Role in SDPA Proceedings. The four dissenters in *Allen*, with Justice Stevens writing the opinion, assailed the logic and the result reached by the majority. Justice Stevens found that the criminal law occupies a central role in an SDPA proceeding. After a review of the various points of involvement Justice Stevens summarized the dissents' position stating:

> The Illinois "sexually dangerous person" proceeding may only be triggered by a criminal incident; may only be initiated by the sovereign state's prosecuting

authorities; may only be established with the burden of proof applicable to the
criminal law; may only proceed if a criminal offense is established; and has the
consequence of incarceration in the State's prison system—in this case, Illinois'
maximum security prison at Menard. It seems quite clear to me ... that the proceeding must be considered "criminal" for purposes of the Fifth Amendment.[42]

Focusing on the majority's acceptance of the goal of treatment as a primary reason for accepting the civil label applied to the SDPA, Justice Stevens argued:

> A goal of treatment is not sufficient, in and of itself, to render inapplica-
> ble the Fifth Amendment, or to prevent a characterization of proceedings
> as "criminal." ... If this were not the case, moreover, nothing would pre-
> vent a State from creating an entire corpus of "dangerous person" statutes
> to shadow its criminal code ... The goal would be "treatment;" the result
> would be evisceration of criminal law and its accompanying protections.[43]

What is fascinating is that Illinois expressly protects a civil committee's right to
silence.[44] It is only the SDP who may be compelled to give evidence on which a
deprivation of liberty may be based and to wear the stigmatic label of sex offender,
thereby subjecting himself to possible treatment.[45]

Actually Justice Stevens does not face the full implications of his own argument.
That is, if the only choices available are labeling the SDPA civil or criminal, and he
opts for criminal, then the entire package of criminal law and procedure would seem
to apply in one fell swoop. That may or may not be desirable. It seems preferable to
analyze the proceeding as criminal-like—in the tradition of Gault for juvenile proceedings—and make protection-by-protection decisions based on a functional analysis of the particular proceedings.

Allen Focuses on the Nature of the Process Instead of the Stigmatic Consequences.
If we summarize the views of the majority and the dissent, we see that the four dissenters appear to be arguing that if it looks, feels, and sounds like criminal law, then it
is criminal law. The majority is content to accept Illinois' terminology and to continue
a general policy of deference to the states' approaches to a variety of deviance.

In almost casual fashion, _Allen_ discarded some of the more sweeping language used by
the Court in the earlier _In re Gault_,[46] which has been described by some as the judicial Bill
of Rights for children. That is, _Gault_ seemed to usher in an era of functional, as opposed
to formal, decision-making. _Gault_ looked at the juvenile justice system and found it more
criminal-like than civil for the purpose of several basic constitutional procedures.

In _Allen_, the Court appears to have reverted to its pre-_Gault_ posture of battling
over labels instead of the more difficult debate over the reality of a particular proceeding. Indeed, Justice Rehnquist simply gives the back of his hand to _Gault_, writing, "First, _Gault's_ sweeping statement that 'our Constitution guarantees that no person shall be "compelled" to be a witness against himself when he is threatened with
deprivation of liberty' is plainly not good law."[47]

If _Gault's_ analytical premise had survived, the concerns in _Allen_ would focus on
the stigmatic consequences, including the precise losses associated with the overall

deprivation of liberty; the reality and potentiality of the promised treatment, the likely and potential duration of confinement, and so on. Such an analysis is far more likely to result in procedural safeguards for the individual than a one-dimensional, formalistic struggle to decide whether a given process is civil or criminal in nature. As we shall see in the next chapter, these issues are central to supporting or condemning Washington's Sexually Violent Predator Law.

Impact of Moral Preferences on Legislative Judgments. Finally, we should consider *Bowers v. Hardwick*,[48] a decision involving a challenge to Georgia's statute criminalizes consensual oral or anal sexual contact, which is referred to as sodomy. The facts of the case are as followings: A police officer entered the respondent's home in connection with an unrelated matter. When he saw two adult males engaged in sodomy he reported the incident. The prosecutor declined to proceed—as would be true virtually anywhere under the circumstances—but the respondent elected to challenge the constitutionality of the Georgia law. The Court of Appeals for the Eleventh Circuit held that the law violated the respondent's fundamental rights "because his homosexual activity is a private and intimate association that is beyond state regulation by reason of the Ninth Amendment and the Due Process Clause of the Fourteenth Amendment."[49]

Georgia appealed this holding to the Supreme Court, and a badly splintered Supreme Court reversed the court of appeals and upheld this statute. Justice White, for the majority, reasoned that whatever privacy rights have been recognized by the Court revolve around the traditional family and procreation within the marriage relationship. The majority strongly believed that homosexual sodomy simply is not a fundamental right that is so deeply rooted in our history or tradition as to deserve constitutional protection.[50]

Justice White was very conscious of the role of the Court in the discovery and enforcement of provocative new fundamental rights. "The Court is most vulnerable and comes nearest to illegitimacy when it deals with judge-made constitutional law having little or no cognizable roots in the language or design of the Constitution."[51] This is a paradigmatic statement of the judicial conservatism which now prevails on the Court and a majority of the lower federal courts.

Indeed, when the respondents urged that this sodomy law be stricken as irrational; as resting on some unproved belief that the Georgia electorate somehow finds homosexual sodomy immoral, Justice White replied that law is constantly based on morality. Moral preferences are an acceptable basis for legislative judgments and the same judgment made by Georgia has been made by some 25 states.[52]

Bowers does not deal directly with laws aimed at the commitment of sex psychopaths or SVP's. Nor does it deal with procedural issues of the sort encountered in *Specht*. What *Bowers* does make plain is that this conservative Court is in no mood to constitutionally block states from adopting or retaining laws that criminalize private, consensual sexual conduct between adults.

Criminal prosecution under the above circumstances is rare.[53] What is not rare is the prosecution of adults for the imposition of their sexual desires on children or for certain forms of public indecency.[54] Sexual imposition by an adult on a young person obviously is a primary candidate for the penal law. Public indecency, however, may well be condemned but hardly seems to be the sort of offense that might lead to prison. Nevertheless, *Bowers* is an important Supreme Court decision.

Footnotes

[1] These conferences were conducted at the NIC National Academy of Corrections in Boulder, Colorado. The author was involved in four such conferences, lecturing on the topic of this chapter and learning a great deal from the participants. In addition, the author's prison consultation work has developed additional questions and, hopefully, insight.

[2] See generally F. Allen, *The Decline of the Rehabilitative Ideal* (1981).

[3] Martinson, What works? Questions and answers about prison reform, Pub. Int., Spring 1974, at 22. Compare Martinson's "nothing works" with a slightly more hopeful view of sex offender treatment by D.J. West, Sexual Crimes and Confrontations, Ch. 10 (1987).

[4] See *Corrections Compendium* 5 (May 1987). Regrettably, the survey report does not indicate which offenses are included in the survey, and, since it is a self-report survey with various states using different criteria, we must be cautious about the data. However, the increase does seem quite authentic.

[5] Psychiatry and Sex Psychopath Legislation: The '30s to the '80s, 839 G.A.P., Pub. No. 98, April 1977 (hereinafter referred to as GAP Report).

[6] Weiner, Legal Issues Raised in Treating Sex Offenders, 3 *Behavioral Science & Law* 325, 326 (1985).

[7] G.E. Dix, "Special Dispositional Alternatives for Abnormal Offenders: Developments in the Laws," *Mentally Disordered Offenders* (1983) at 133, 136.

[8] See e.g., H.N. Pontell, *A Capacity to Punishment*, Ch. 1 (1984).

[9] See Chapter 23, supra, for a full citation to the law and an extended discussion thereof.

[10] 857 P.2d 989 (Wash. 1993).

[11] GAP Report, Chapter 16, note 5 at 840. Also see D.J. West, *Sexual Crimes and Confrontations,* 242 (1987).

[12] GAP Report, Chapter 1, note 5 at 859.

[13] In Bowers v. Hardwick, 478 U.S. 1039 (1986), the Supreme Court upheld the constitutionality of Georgia's sodomy law at least as applied to adult males, even when the conduct is in private. The Court noted that some 24 states and the District of Columbia criminalize such activity although the Model Penal Code Sec. 213.2 (P.O.D. 1962) urges decriminalization.

The point is that while such conduct remains subject to the criminal law and is characterized as a sex offense, it would be unthinkable to view those engaged in this behavior as the equivalent of violent rapists, child molesters, or even exhibitionists.

[14] However, sexually violent crimes can be spelled out. Forcible rape, forcible oral or anal copulation, any sexual contact with a child under a specified age are examples of specific sexual crimes of violence or coercion. This is a clear improvement over the general term "sex offense."

[15] It is acceptable in most sentencing schemes to take into account certain individual characteristics of the defendant.

[16] The crucial sentence values in the text are derived from U.S. Sentencing Guidelines, Sec. A 231, 232, 233, Commentary (Revised Draft, Feb. 5, 1987). The points in the text are offered only as examples of the type of consensus on values that should be sought and made explicit as opposed to simply condemning "sex offenses."

[17] G.E. Dix, "Special Dispositional Alternatives for Abnormal Offenders: Developments in the Laws," *Mentally Disordered Offenders* (1983) at 134-137.

[18] See N.F. Hahn, The Defective Delinquency Movement: A History of the Born Criminal in New York State, 1850-1966 (Ph.D. Thesis, May 1978, SUNY at Albany, School of Criminal Justice) (hereinafter, Hahn, "Defective Delinquency Thesis").

[19] Id.

[20] Sutherland, "The Diffusion of Sexual Psychopath Laws," 56 *American Journal of Society* 142 (1950).

[21] 309 U.S. 270 (1940).

[22] Id., at 272.

[23] Id., at 273.

[24] Id., at 274.

[25] Id., at 275. We should note that the Minnesota law upheld did not require conviction. In a more recent decision, Allen v. Illinois, 106 S. Ct. 2988 (1986), the Court upheld the propriety of confining together unconvicted sex psychopaths and convicted but psychiatrically disturbed prisoners.

[26] 386 U.S. 605 (1967).

[27] Id. at 608.

[28] Id. at 610. Justice Douglas also noted that the Minnesota Act upheld in Pearson contained the procedural safeguards now mandated in Specht.

[29] Id.

[30] This is not the occasion to elaborate on procedural due process and civil commitment. It is sufficient to say that civil commitments are within the ambit of the liberty protected by due process, but the procedural requirements are not as rigorous as those of the criminal law. For the leading case in this area, see Lessard v. Schmidt, 349 F. Supp. 10789 (E.D. Wisc. 1972). This case wound its way through a number of federal courts until being reaffirmed at 413 F. Supp. 1318 (E.D. Wisc. 1976). The case as first cited, however, is the one to read.

See Addington v. Texas, 441 U.S. 418 (1979), holding that "clear and convincing" is the constitutionally permissible evidentiary standard for civil commitments. See also Humphrey v. Cady, 405 U.S. 504, 511 (1972).

[31] Basically, that is a right to be present, with counsel, and make a statement (allocution). See Mempa v. Rhay, 389 U.S. 128 (1967).

[32] Cf. Rummel v. Estelle, 445 U.S. 262 (1980) with Solem v. Helm, 463 U.S. 277 (1983).

[33] 405 U.S. 504, 514 (1972).

[34] See also O'Connor v. Donaldson, 422 U.S. 263 (1980), where the Court also avoided the right to treatment issue.

[35] 106 S.Ct. 2988 (1986). The full text of this opinion appears infra as Appendix G.

[36] Ibid., at 2999, n. 18 (Stevens, J., dissenting).

[37] Ibid., at 2991.

[38] Ibid., at 2992.

[39] Ibid., at 2993-2994.

[40] Ibid., at 2993. Note how this issue resembles the equal protection claim raised in *Pearson* and also there decided in the state's favor.

[41] Ibid., at 2994.

[42] Ibid., at 2997 (Stevens, J., dissenting).

[43] Ibid., at 2998 (Stevens, J., dissenting).

[44] Id. (Stevens, J., dissenting) referring to Ill. Rev. Stat., Ch. 91 1/2, Sec. 3-208 (1985) which requires that the examiner inform the prospective patient that he need not talk to the examiner; that any statements he makes may be disclosed at a court hearing on the issue of involuntary admission; and if the subject is not so informed then the examiner may not testify to any admission.

[45] Id. (Stevens, J., dissenting).

[46] 387 U.S. 1 (1966).

[47] 106 S.Ct., at 2994.

[48] 478 U.S. 186 (1986).

[49] 478 U.S. at 189.

[50] 478 U.S. at 191.

[51] 478 U.S. at 194.

[52] 478 U.S. at 193-194.

[53] See Perkins v. North Carolina, 234 F. Supp. 333 (W.D.N.C. 1964) and discussion in F. Cohen, The *Law of Deprivation of Liberty* 89-94 (1991).

[54] See D.J. West, *Sexual Crimes and Confrontations* 266 et seq. (1987).

Chapter 23

Washington's Sexually Violent Predator Act

by Fred Cohen, D.J.P.

Overview

This chapter reviews the content and legal challenges associated with Washington's Sexually Violent Predator Act. The law, which this author finds is not very good as a matter of policy, is constitutionally suspect and likely to be reviewed by the U.S. Supreme Court. Still, it remains to be seen whether this law will trigger a number of "copycat" laws.

Background of Washington's Law

As indicated in Chapter 22, the State of Washington, in a significant reversal of the trend to repeal or ignore special civil commitment laws for sex offenders, adopted the Sexually Violent Predator Act of 1990 (the SVPA).[1] The Washington Supreme Court upheld the law in the face of a broad-based and broadly supported constitutional challenge.[2] As of August 10, 1993, twelve men had been committed under the Act and nine were being detained at the "Special Commitment Center," a designated facility at a state prison near Monroe, Washington.[3] By August 1994 the population had doubled.

Like many of its sexual psychopath law predecessors, the SVPA was passed in the heat of understandable community outrage over several particularly barbarous sex offenses involving children and offenders with prior sex offense records.[4] The SVPA coexists with other Washington laws, namely a law permitting civil commitment of the mentally ill and a variety of criminal sentencing laws that permit extended prison terms for a variety of sex offenses.[5]

It is too early to tell whether other jurisdictions will follow Washington's example or whether the SVPA will have any discernible impact either in reducing sexually-motivated crimes or in enhancing treatment of offenders. Still, the law has enough unique features to make it important enough to warrant separate attention.

Legal Challenges to the SVPA

The legal challenges brought to the SVPA can be summarized as follows:

Challenge 1: The law, while dressed in civil clothing, is in reality a criminal law that lacks the procedural and substantive protections of traditional criminal law.

Arguments:
If the law is characterized as criminal then it is unconstitutional as an ex post facto law and as imposing double jeopardy. Both points turn exclusively on the state's authority to rely on conduct engaged in prior to passage of the SVPA for commitment.

Challenge 2: The SVP law violates substantive due process.

Arguments:
1. It does not serve a valid state purpose;

2. People committed under the law need not be mentally ill (nor presently convicted of an offense) and conditions of confinement may actually preclude mandated treatment, and are subject to unconstitutional preventive detention; and

3. A finding of dangerousness without a recent overt act is permitted.

Challenge 3: The SVP law arguably violates procedural due process.

Arguments:
1. An ex parte finding of probable cause denies meaningful pre-deprivation due process;

2. Consideration of less restrictive alternatives to incarceration is not mandated but is constitutionally required;

3. The jury need not be unanimous and this dilutes the beyond a reasonable doubt burden of proof;

4. The SVPA is void for vagueness (i.e., persons of common understanding would not likely agree on, or understand, the meaning of certain key terms); and

5. There is a denial of the constitutional right to remain silent.

Challenge 4: A variety of evidentiary issues are raised.

Arguments:
Examples of these issues include the use of evidence from victims of prior crimes, evidence of prior convictions, and expert witnesses arguably offered baseless conclusions.

Washington Supreme Court's View of These Challenges. We will now examine how these issues were handled (or not handled) by the Washington Supreme Court. Predictably, a majority of the Washington Supreme Court upheld the basic components of the SVPA. As was the case in *Allen v. Illinois*,[6] the critical initial decision was whether this law should be characterized as civil or criminal. Due largely to its rehabilitative purpose and indeterminate commitment the law was found to be civil. If it had been deemed a criminal statute, the full array of substantive and procedural safeguards available to one who is criminally accused would have been triggered. This conclusion automatically disposes of the ex post facto and double jeopardy challenges.

The Washington Supreme Court also concluded that while a detainee must be permitted to appear in court for a probable cause hearing within 72 hours of detention, failure to do so was harmless (i.e., not reversible) error. The terms of the law were found to be sufficiently precise to not be void for vagueness, and neither the Fifth Amendment nor due process was found to guarantee SVP detainees a right to remain silent.

Victim testimony, prior offense testimony (including juvenile offenses), and expert witness testimony (utilized by both sides) was found to be properly employed.

The court accepted the necessity of proof of a recent overt act to prove dangerousness, but only imposed this requirement on alleged SVPs who are found in the community. That is, a requirement of a recent overt act for those alleged SVPs who are confined when commitment is sought would, states the majority, impose an impossible burden on the state. Thus, proof of an overt act to establish dangerousness was limited to non-incarcerated persons. Justice Johnson, in dissent, vigorously disagreed with this point. Indeed, he found this incarcerated/non-incarcerated distinction to be a violation of equal protection of the laws.[7]

Differences from Earlier Laws. Professor John Q. LaFond, the SVPA's most eloquent and persistent critic, pointed out that the Washington law differed from earlier sexual psychopath laws in two major ways: (1) a person subject to SVP commitment must serve his full prison term before he can be committed; and (2) the law did not require any allegation or proof of recent criminal wrongdoing, dangerous behavior, deteriorating mental state, or even inappropriate conduct before the state might seek commitment.[8]

The court's decision in *In re Young* did nothing to alter LaFond's first point and was only partially responsive to his second point. That is, the court stated:

> For incarcerated individuals, a requirement of a recent overt act under the Statute would create a standard which would be impossible to meet. Other jurisdictions have rejected the precise argument made by petitioners because it creates an impossible condition for those currently incarcerated. See People

v. Martin, 107 Cal. App.3d 714, 725, 165 Cal. Rptr. 773 (1980). We agree that "[d]ue process does not require that the absurd be done before a compelling state interest can be vindicated." Indeed, in drafting the Statute, the Legislature expressly noted that the involuntary commitment statute, RCW 71.05, was an inadequate remedy because confinement prevented any overt act. RCW 71.09.010. We conclude that where the individual is currently incarcerated no evidence of a recent overt act is required.

However, where an individual has been released from confinement on a sex offense. . . and lives in the community immediately prior to the initiation of sex predator proceedings, the above rationale does not apply. Under Harris,[9] proof of a recent overt act is necessary to satisfy due process concerns when an individual has been released into the community. When an individual has been in the community, the State has the opportunity to prove dangerousness through evidence of a recent overt act. We construe statutes to render them constitutional. Therefore, we hold that the State must provide evidence of a recent overt act in accord with Harris whenever an individual is not incarcerated at the time the petition is filed. For non-incarcerated individuals, a sex predator petition under RCW 71.09.030 must include an allegation of a recent overt act sufficient to establish probable cause when considered in conjunction with the other factors listed in RCW 71.09.040.[10]

The court did not clearly indicate the details of the required overt act. Instead, it referred to an earlier state court decision[11] in which the court reviewed Washington's civil commitment of the mentally ill law and held that involuntary commitment required a showing of a substantial risk of physical harm as evidenced by a recent act that either caused harm or created a reasonable apprehension of dangerousness.

The requisite harm need not be imminent either for commitment as mentally ill or, presumably, as an SVP.[12] Apparently, for a nonconfined person, the overt act must speak to the required "mental abnormality or personality disorder which makes the person likely to engage in predatory acts of sexual violence."[13]

Some of the specific objections to the SVPA which were briefly noted earlier are discussed in the following text. The objections are embellished with problems related to the point under discussion.

Political and Social History of the SVPA

The political and social history of the SVPA provides important clues to why this law was enacted and why it was invested with its unique characteristics. First, in 1984 the Washington legislature abolished the existing sexual psychopath law and adopted a determinate sentencing scheme that even LaFond characterized as providing "unconscionably short prison terms for serious repeat sex offenders."[14] Second, repeat sex offender Earl Shriner raped and mutilated a young boy two years after his release from prison. Earlier, Shriner had been the subject of civil commitment but the petition was denied because there was no showing of the recent overt act needed to establish dangerousness. It was Shriner's horrifying sexual misconduct, along with the usual scapegoating and jockeying for political advantage which accompanies such events, that served as the catalyst for enactment of the SVPA.

Thus, prior to the SVPA, Washington had a civil commitment of the mentally ill law which required a finding of mental illness and a recent overt act to prove dangerousness (and which had a short-term, intensive care outlook) and a presumptive sentencing statute that provided relatively short determinate sentences even for repeat sex offenders. An offender such as Earl Shriner could not have had his prison term extended due to the strictures of ex post facto law, and he could not be civilly committed without proof of an overt act, which proof apparently was lacking.

The SVPA included the following "remedies": (1) to at least formally avoid the strictures of the criminal process with its ex post facto (and double jeopardy) hurdles; (2) to avoid the existing civil commitment hurdles by relaxing the need for mental illness (requiring instead personality disorders or mental abnormality); (3) to abandon the overt act requirement; and (4) to tack the indefinite SVP commitment onto the end of a prison term.

If we stipulate that there are certain sex offenders—and Earl Shriner may well be one of them—who are deserving of extended terms of confinement, then plainly the "easiest"[15] and most honest solution is to apply the criminal law and impose extended terms of imprisonment.[16] For example, a life sentence, for a violent recidivist sex offender, would easily escape an Eighth Amendment, cruel and unusual punishment challenge—the only realistic constitutional basis for a challenge to the nature and duration of a criminal sentence.[17]

Conversely, persons who are mentally ill and engage in proscribed sexual activity may be made subject to involuntary civil commitment laws. While the Supreme Court may well have constitutionalized "dangerousness" as a component of civil commitment of the mentally ill, it has not constitutionalized a "recent, overt act" requirement.[18]

Previously, the Washington Supreme Court interpreted a state commitment law requiring evidence of threats or attempts at suicide, assault and battery, and property damage as requiring proof of a recent overt act.[19] Other jurisdictions might opt for a "straight" civil commitment law stipulating that recent acts are but one type of evidence acceptable as proof of dangerousness. Envision, for example, a situation where a prior sex offender is recorded talking about his plans for sexual violence; or one in which someone uncovers written plans involving a particular sex victim. While these events might not qualify as overt acts, they seem admissible and relevant to the dangerousness question. Of course, this is not to say that such evidence alone should establish a basis for commitment.

The basic point is that both traditional criminal law and traditional civil commitment will accommodate legitimate social defense and treatment concerns in the vast majority of these cases. Therefore, the SVPA need not be viewed as a model by other jurisdictions.

Some Problems Inherent in Civil Commitment Laws

As previously noted, once the SVPA was accepted as a civil law, a number of challenges (e.g., ex post facto, double-jeopardy, the need for perfect parallelism with criminal procedures, and so on) were put to rest. And, a number of other, equally complex problems arose in their place.

The SVPA, like its parent sexual psychopath laws, attempts to slip in between the traditional mental illness requirement basic to civil commitment law and the criminal law's need for proof of conduct that is prohibited in advance and which causes a pro-scribed harm before criminal sentences can be imposed. This evasion—or invention, if you prefer—is accomplished initially by utilizing the terms "mental abnormality" and "personality disorder" in lieu of "mental illness." Thus, the first problem relates to the viability of substituting the language of abnormality and personality disorder for illness or disease.

The second major problem is the availability of bona fide treatment for SVPs. If treatment is not made available, or if it can be shown that SVPs are not treatable, then the law arguably is an invalid type of preventive detention.

Distinction Between Mental Illness Disease and Personality Disorder/Mental Abnormality. The distinction between mental illness, disease, and personality disor-der/mental abnormality is the subject of two well-considered essays by Professors John Q. LaFond and Alexander D. Brooks that debate the issue.[20] Professor LaFond argues that the proponents of the SVPA did not believe that sex offenders were men-tally disordered and in need of treatment.[21] As evidence, he points out that the law does not apply to a group of persons who are mentally ill in any medically recognized sense because the term "mental abnormality" simply has no medically accepted diag-nostic meaning. The term "personality disorder" does have some clinical acceptance, but in practice it appears to be shorthand for the almost limitless array of maladaptive behavior that sometimes is packaged as personality disorder.

Professor Brooks, while conceding a certain awkwardness in the terms at issue, finds that they cover the range of pathologies affecting violent sex offenders.[22] "Personality disorder," he argues, is a more acceptable term than the earlier "sexual psychopath" because the latter term falsely connotes that all sex offenders are psy-chopaths. Experts, Brooks argues, will be able to sort out which sex offenders fit the American Psychiatric Association's diagnosis of personality disorder and which do not. "Mental abnormality," he continues, is a more general term that covers a larger variety of disorders (especially the paraphilias and pathologically driven rapists) than personality disorder.[23]

There is some common ground between LaFond and Brooks. Both scholars are firm in their view that not all sex offenders are in any fashion mentally disordered and both disfavor the older sexual psychopath laws. After that, agreement is difficult to come by.

Neither approach the SVPA's categorization of mental disorder as I might have. It seems to me that the debate about whether a psychiatric-sounding term has an accepted home in the law is somewhat misplaced. Whether antisocial and often ter-ribly destructive behavior fits a medical model depends on one's theory of causation and that theory, in turn, invariably leads to a preferred measure of social control. In other words, one's theory of cause is likely to be shorthand for one's desired outcome.

Causal Factors Have Little Impact. Outside the traditional insanity defense, and a rash of "compulsive disorders" struggling to gain admittance to that defense (e.g., compulsive gambling, pre-menstrual and post-menstrual syndromes, and the like), criminal law cares very little about why someone has engaged in crime. Criminal penalties may attach if a competent adult voluntarily performs an act that causes a pro-scribed harm. Who the offender is and why the offense was committed are matters for sentencing. Even there, as "just deserts" theory now dominates and leads to fixed or presumptive sentences, the "who did it" succumbs to "what was done" and con-nects with a proportionate sentence. That an offender may be "justly" imprisoned using this approach and then found to be sufficiently mentally ill to require mental health care is another proposition.

By now it is clear that the SVPA breaks with traditional criminal law in that its operative theory is that SVPs are due to mental abnormality or personality disorder. That is, a psychiatric or psychological theory of cause applies to a certain group of offenses—and sexually violent offenses are clearly identified[24]—and a certain group of offenders, SVPs. In this case, cause is neither blame affixing nor treatment pro-ducing.

Keep in mind that the search for cause need not be a single-minded activity. For example, policymakers may look to causal theories as a guide to resource allocation, and social scientists may offer explanations for behavior. In our context, however, causal theory has only one task: to justify and evoke a response consistent with it.

Will the Debate Refocus on the Legality of Isolating SVPs Until They Are "Safe"? It is here that the SVPA begins to deteriorate, although not necessarily to the point of being unconstitutional. In its statement of legislative findings, the SVPA declares:

> [S]exually violent predators generally have antisocial personality features which are unamenable to existing mental illness treatment modalities . . . the prognosis for curing sexually violent offenders is poor, the treatment needs of this population are very different than the traditional treatment modalities for people appropriate for commitment under the involuntary treatment act.[25]

This preamble-like statement comes precariously close to stating—indeed, to trumpeting—that there is no effective treatment for SVPs. The word "unamenable" in the first sentence gives way to a sort of "there is/may be treatment but it is differ-ent than for those civilly committed as mentally ill."[26]

Causal theory begins to detach from a treatment response because there is no treatment for either sex psychopaths or SVPs. The reason: there are no such clinical entities. To the extent that the SVP category has no clinical significance, and to the extent that bona fide treatment is illusory, the law collapses on its second premise.

It may now be argued that dubious or non-existent treatment is not the only legit-imate objective of such a law; that preventive detention of "abnormal" and dangerous sex offenders is both desirable and legally supportable. Thus, the debate may refocus on whether it is legally permissible and socially desirable to isolate a population of SVPs "until such time as the person's mental abnormality or personality disorder has so changed that the person is safe to be at large."[27] If you have trouble with the dan-gerousness prediction that must precede the finding of an SVP, consider what the debate is like on when a person is safe to be at large. Understandably, the commit-ment aspect has received far more attention than retention-release decision.

Preventive detention often is reviled, but it is rarely defined.[28] In our context, we may take preventive detention to mean an extended loss of liberty imposed by government based on a prediction of future misconduct.[29] The essence of the concept of dangerousness is that dangerousness is no more and no less than a prediction. To say that a person is dangerous is not the same thing as saying, for example, that a person has tuberculosis. Dangerousness is not a present condition or status. It's only meaning is as an estimate of the future that may be an instant away or many years away.

Within our system of law, the norm for punitive confinement is conviction of a criminal offense proved beyond a reasonable doubt. Therapeutic confinement must be based on a finding of mental illness and some form of dangerousness proved by the constitutional minimum of clear and convincing evidence.[30] Other official deprivations of an adults' liberty, including pre-hearing deprivations, are subject to narrow exceptions.[31]

In *United States v. Salerno*,[32] the Supreme Court endorsed such an exception when it upheld a federal law allowing denial of pretrial bail based on a prediction of dangerousness. *Salerno*, like its juvenile justice counterpart,[33] stressed the fact that the law involved pretrial detention; a limitation to the most serious crimes; proof that no less drastic alternative to the available conditions of release would assure the safety of others; and a stringent time limitation to effectuate the right to a speedy trial. In this, and a host of other decisions,[34] the Supreme Court has demonstrated its deference to legislative decisions and its unwillingness to invalidate laws based on efforts to show the inability of clinicians and others to predict dangerousness with any certainty.

Could the SVPA withstand constitutional attack if it was dealt with as a preventive detention law? *Foucha v. Louisiana*[35] is the Supreme Court decision that is most likely to be determinative of that question.

Foucha concerned a Louisiana law allowing the automatic commitment of a defendant found not guilty by reason of insanity. In *Jones v. United States*,[36] an earlier case, the Court had upheld automatic commitment in similar circumstances. Thus, the question in *Foucha* related primarily to the state's release provisions. Justice White stated the issue as follows:

> When a defendant in a criminal case ...is found not guilty by reason of insanity, he is committed to a mental hospital unless he proves that he is not dangerous. This is so whether or not he is then insane. ... [After requisite procedures] the court must hold a hearing to determine dangerousness; the acquittee has the burden of proving he is not dangerous. If found to be dangerous, the acquittee may be returned to the mental institution whether or not he is then mentally ill.[37]

In connection with the patient's efforts to be released, two doctors gave evidence that Foucha was not then mentally ill, if, indeed, he ever had been. They also testified that Foucha had an antisocial personality, and that they would not feel comfortable certifying that he was not dangerous.

A shifting coalition of Justices ultimately held that it was unconstitutional to civilly restrain someone when one of the predicates for the original commitment no longer exists. Put somewhat differently, the government cannot deprive a person of liberty based only on a prediction of dangerousness absent both a finding, and the continuation, of mental illness.[38]

Professor LaFond finds *Foucha* particularly applicable to the SVPA. He noted that the Court rejected Louisiana's claim that it could indefinitely confine Foucha as a matter of pure (albeit crime-related), preventive detention even though Foucha was not then mentally ill.[39] In addition, LaFond states that the Court specifically rejected "personality disorder" and "anti-social personality" as mental illnesses that would justify civil commitment.[40]

LaFond, however, is something of a victim of his own enthusiasm in that the Court stated, "Here, *according to the testimony given* ... Foucha is not suffering from a mental disease or illness" (emphasis added).[41] Thus, much depends on "... according to the testimony given ..." and, as indicated earlier, whether Washington's use of "personality disorder" might be upheld as mental illness. This would take the SVPA out of the dubious category of preventive detention and into the more easily sustainable category of civil commitment.

Is the SVPA Likely to Meaningfully Contribute to Community Safety or the Treatment of Offenders?

Ultimately, the question comes down to whether the SVPA is likely to make some measurable contribution either to community safety or to the treatment of offenders. If this law is consistent with its sexual psychopath ancestors, the answer will be a resounding no.

As Norval Morris has predicted, "Very few people will be committed, and then those numbers will drop off, and they'll be forgotten until some new sensational event occurs."[42] If Professor Morris is correct, and I believe he is, the civil libertarian concerns about the wholesale roundup of persons long after they have served their prison terms and fear of the broad-based use of preventive detention simply dissipates.

Other concerns are more subtle. Consider the issue of resource allocation, for example. Apparently, 36 beds have been made available in the facility used to house the SVPs. At the same time, the Sex Offender Treatment Program at Twin Rivers, directed then by editor Barbara Schwartz, a voluntary program that has shown some promise, was reduced from 370 beds to between 170 and 200.[43] The contribution to treatment of sex offenders is negligible here, as the net effect is an actual reduction in the number of beds available to SVP's.

If the SVPA proves to be illusory, then the heat and energy generated to create and enact it, and to then debate its merits, surely siphons off creative energy that could be directed at more promising approaches to sexual violence.

In fact, the SVPA actually may be anti-therapeutic. It may discourage guilty pleas and an offender's coming to grips with the need for professional help. Inmates now in prison treatment programs may discover that prosecutors will subpoena treatment records in connection with a subsequent SVP proceeding. Indeed, this has already happened when a sex offender who had completed the Washington Department of Correction's Sex Offender Treatment Program was transferred upon his release from prison to the Special Commitment Center. This, in turn, also may discourage sincere efforts by offenders to obtain help.

Footnotes

1. Wash. Rev. Code, Pt. X (Sec. 71.09 et seq.). See Appendix I, infra.

2. In re Young, 857 P.2d 989 (Wash. 1993). A federal legal action has been threatened but no further details are available at this writing. There is a strong likelihood that this law ultimately will reach the Supreme Court. An edited version of this opinion appears as Appendix H, infra.

3. See the *Seattle Times*, p. 1 (August, 10, 1993).

4. See David Boerner, "Confronting Violence: In the Act and in the Word," 15 Univ. of Puget Sound L. Rev. 525 (1992) for a full narrative of these events as well as this author's role in the drafting of the Act.

5. See Wash. Rev. Code Sec. 9.94 A.320 (Supp. 1990-91) reflecting an increase in the presumptive sentencing range for rape, child molestation, indecent liberties, and sexual misconduct. The increase was recommended by the same task force which proposed the SVP law.

6. 106 S.Ct. 2988 (1986). See the discussion of the results of that case in Chapter 22.

7. The majority's reasoning is murky both on the legal basis for the overt act requirement and the distinction drawn between the confined and unconfined. It does appear that the overt act requirement is derived from prior Washington state case law. See In re Harris, 654 P.2d 109 (Wash. 1982)

8. John Q. LaFond, "Washington's Sexually Violent Predator Law: A Deliberate Misuse of the Therapeutic State for Social Control," 15 *Univ. of Puget Sound* L. Rev. 655, 656 (1992).

9. In re Harris, 654 P.2d 109 (Wash. 1982).

10. In re Young, note 2 supra at 857 P.2d 1008-1009.

11. In re Harris, note 9 supra. See also LaFond, note 8 supra.

12. In re Young, note 2 supra 857 P.2d 1008.

13. RCW Sec. 71.09.020(1).

14. LaFond, note 8 supra at 698.

15. By easiest, I mean the avoidance of the conceptually difficult, civil liberty threatening and expensive problems raised by the SVP law.

16. See Alexander D. Brooks, "The Constitutionality and Morality of Civilly Committing Violent Sexual Predators," 15 *Univ. of Puget Sound L. Rev.* 709, 710-711 (1992). The author finds the SVP law constitutionally and morally defensible.

17. For example, in Harmelin v. Michigan, 111 S. Ct. 2680 (1991), the Supreme Court upheld a mandatory sentence of life without parole imposed on a first offender convicted of possessing about 650 grams of cocaine and with no proof of intent to sell. The Court held, essentially, that once an offense is determined to be serious, the sentencing decision is a matter of legislative judgment.

    Special rules apply to the death penalty. The Court, however, has consistently upheld habitual offender laws and I know of no individual Justice who ever dissented from the proposition that it is constitutional to enhance criminal sentences based on prior convictions.

18. See generally Foucha v. Louisiana, 112 S.Ct. 1780 (1992)(insanity acquittee who remains dangerous but not mentally ill may not be retained in a mental hospital).

19. In re Harris, 654 P.2d 109 (1982). This interpretation was cited in several subsequent Washington cases: Spencer v. King County, 692 P.2d 874 (1984); In re LaBulle, 728 P.2d 138 (1986); In re Meistrell, 733 P.2d 1004 (1987); Washington v. Lowrimore, 841 P.2d 779 (1992); In re Pugh, 845 P.2d 1034 (1993); Northwest v. Thorslund, 851 P.2d 1259 (1993); and In re Young, 857 P.2d 989 (1993).

20. See John Q. LaFond, "Washington's Sexually Violent Predator Law: A Deliberate Misuse of the Therapeutic State for Social Control," 15 *Univ. of Puget Sound L. Rev.* 655, 656 (1992) and Alexander D. Brooks, "The Constitutionality and Morality of Civilly Committing Violent Sexual Predators," 15 *Univ. of Puget Sound L. Rev.* 709, 710-711 (1992).

21. 15 *Univ. of Puget Sound L. Rev.* at 691.

22. 15 *Univ. of Puget Sound L. Rev.* at 732-733.

[23] The American Psychiatric Association, *The Diagnostic and Statistical Manual of Mental Disorders Fourth Edition*. 1994. (DSM-IV).

[24] Wash. Rev. Code § 71.09.20(4).

[25] Id. at § 71.09.010.

[26] See Bailey v. Gardebring, 940 F.2d 1150 (8th Cir. 1991), cert. denied, 112 S. Ct. 1516 (1992).

[27] Wash. Rev. Code § 71.09.060(1).

[28] See generally, Williams, J.F., "Process and Prediction: A Return to a Fuzzy Model of Pretrial Detention," 79 *Minn. L. Rev.* 325 (1994); "Note, Foucha v. Louisiana: The Danger of Commitment Based on Dangerousness," 44 *Case W. Res. L. Rev.* 157 (1993); Tobolowsky, P.M. and Quinn, J.F., "Pretrial Release in the 1990's: Texas Takes Another Look at Non-Financial Release Conditions," 19 *New Eng. J. on Crim. & Civ. Confinement* 267 (1993); Ewing, C.P., "Preventive Detention and Execution: The Constitutionality of Punishing Future Crimes," 15 *Law & Hum. Behav.* 139 (1991); and Slobogin, C., "Dangerousness and Expertise," 133 *U. Pa. L. R.* 97 (1984).

[29] See James W. Ellis, "Limits on the State's Power to Confine 'Dangerous' Persons: Constitutional Implications of Foucha v. Louisiana," 15 *Univ. of Puget Sound L. Rev.* 635, 648 (1992).

[30] Addington v. Texas, 441 U.S. 418 (1979).

[31] See Schall v. Martin, 467 U.S. 253 (1983)(Court explicitly upheld the constitutionality of a statute requiring a reasonably brief pretrial detention of juveniles. The law's premise was to protect the young person from himself and also to protect society. The Court addressed the uniqueness of youth in that young people, it was said, are always in some form of custody and, by definition, are not assumed to have the capacity to care for themselves. The "continuing custody" and "lack of capacity" rationales are not available when analyzing the SVPA).

[32] 481 U.S. 739 (1987).

[33] See n. 28, supra.

[34] The Court in Salerno cites several cases that address detention and predictions at dangerousness, 481 U.S. 739, at 748-749: see generally, Ludecke v. Watkins, 335 U.S. 160 (1948)(war-related pretrial detention); Carlson v. Landon, 342 U.S. 524 (1952) and Wong Wing v. U.S., 163 U.S. 228 (1896)(detention of illegal aliens); Addington v. Texas, 441 U.S. 418 (1979)(detention of mentally unstable persons); Jackson v. Indiana, 406 U.S. 715 (1972) and Greenwood v. U.S., 350 U.S. 366 (1956)(detention of dangerous defendant incompetent to stand trial); Schall v. Martin, 467 U.S. 253 (1984)(detention of juvenile); Gerstein v. Pugh, 420 U.S. 103 (1975)(detention of defendant for probable cause); and Bell v. Wolfish, 441 U.S. 520 (1979)(detention of an arrestee based on risk of flight).

[35] Foucha v. Louisiana, 504 U.S. 71, 73 (1992).

[36] 463 U.S. 354 (1983).

[37] 504 U.S. 71, 79 (1992).

[38] There is something of a debate as to whether the evidence of a personality disorder given in *Foucha* might in other circumstances be considered as evidence of continuing mental illness. That is, it was the evidentiary posture of Louisiana that a personality disorder is not a mental disease and is untreatable. If other expert witnesses, or another jurisdiction by legislation, chose to characterize a personality disorder as a mental disease for the purpose of confinement, then it may be argued that *Foucha* does not apply.

[39] John Q. LaFond, "Washington's Sexually Violent Predators Statute: Law or Lottery? A Response to Professor Brooks," 15 *Univ. of Puget Sound L. Rev.* 755, 759 (1992).

[40] LaFond, note 39 supra at 761.

[41] 112 S.Ct. 1780, 1784 (1992).

[42] Norval Morris, "Keynote Address: Predators and Politics," 15 *Univ. of Puget Sound L. Rev.* 517, 519 (1992).

[43] John Q. LaFond, "Washington's Sexually Violent Predator Law: A Deliberate Misuse of the Therapeutic State for Social Control," 15 *Univ. of Puget Sound L. Rev.* 655, 701 (1992).

Chapter 24

Right to Treatment

by Fred Cohen, D.J.P.

Overview

This chapter explores the right to treatment under the United States Constitution. Basically, the right revolves around definitions of three terms: "treatment," which involves the alleviation of pain or the effecting of a cure for a disease; "rehabilitation," which refers to the restoration of an inadequately socialized person to some former level of competence; and "habilitation," which refers to a maximization of functioning, typically in reference to developmental disabilities. Constitutionally, an inmate's right to "treatment" extends only to forbidding deliberate indifference to serious medical (including psychiatric) conditions. So far, the courts have ruled that sex offenders committed under criminal laws do not as such have a constitutional right to treatment. However, an individual who is confined under a Mentally Disordered Sex Offender (MDSO) Act, may well have a state-created constitutional right to adequate treatment.

U.S. Constitution Does Not Mandate Treatment for Sex Offenders

The right to treatment is, in many respects, central to the overall set of legal issues involving sex offenders. Many issues, some of which are painfully complex, flow from a treatment relationship. They will be considered after the legal foundations for such a relationship are examined:

- When is treatment required by law?
- Is the source of any such requirement constitutional or statutory?
- What does a treatment mandate require?
- What does the term "treatment" mean in the legal context?
- Does any type of institutional "programming" qualify as treatment?

The answers to all of these questions have one fundamental thing in common: the U.S. Constitution does not mandate treatment for persons convicted of sex offenses and sentenced to prison unless the inmate also suffers from another serious medical or psychiatric disorder.[1] If an inmate who is labelled a sex offender has an enforceable legal right to treatment, that right is likely to arise from the language employed in a state-created MDSO-type statute. The statute also will include the prospect of confinement beyond the statutory norm for the underlying offense, or confinement in a setting and under conditions that are indistinguishable from regular criminal confinement.[2]

Given the foregoing, is there some legal basis for such an offender to successfully claim a right to rehabilitation? Once again, the answer is "no" at the federal constitutional level, and almost certainly "no" based on any state statute.[3]

"Treatment" and Other Helping Terms: A Legal Lexicon

Before further developing the above points, a brief excursion into the special world of legal terminology is in order. Already, readers must grapple with the term "treatment," the assertion that treatment may well have different legal sources, and the implication that such treatment may be subject to different demands depending on the source. The term "rehabilitation" also has made an appearance and needs explanation. Finally, the terms "treatment" and "rehabilitation" should be compared with and contrasted with the terms "habilitation" and "training."

Treatment. Treatment, in general, refers to a process of diagnosis, intervention, and prognosis designed to relieve pain or suffering or to effect a cure.[4] In law, the concept of treatment is superimposed on a disease (or medical) model. Whether the claim to treatment is made on behalf of a civilly committed mental patient, a convicted prisoner suffering with a psychiatric diagnosis, or a sex offender confined under an MDSO-type law, the required treatment need never be state of the art for the particular illness. More important, not every ailment will be recognized as a disease for the purpose of a legal right to treatment.[5]

The significance of this point relates to my assertion in Chapter 22: "sex psychopathy," "sexually dangerous," and "sex offender" are not clinically valid terms.[6] Thus, to the extent the Constitution requires a disease as a predicate for a duty to treat, and most certainly when it requires a serious disease as in *Estelle v. Gamble*,[7] persons in the categories noted above do not, per se, qualify.

Rehabilitation. Let us now briefly examine the term "rehabilitation." One authority views the rehabilitative ideal as concerned with changing the offender both as a means of social defense and to contribute to the welfare and satisfaction of offenders.[8] Earlier, we said that inmates have no federal constitutional claim to rehabilitation, which:

> refers to the process of restoring the individual to behaviors and values which fall within the social definition of what is acceptable. Socially acceptable behavior, and values are by definition not "illegal." Thus, it is assumed in the rehabilitative process that the individual formerly held socially acceptable values with appropriate behavior....[9]

The absence of any reference to a disease or illness as the predicate for rehabilitative efforts is conspicuous. Rehabilitation also is aimed at such statuses as alcoholism, drug addiction, and sex psychopathy. Whether these conditions also may be viewed as medical problems for other purposes (e.g., medical insurance or contracted-for medical services), they are not within the constitutional law of the disease-medical care model.

The implicit causal assumptions associated with rehabilitation seem to be that an absence of adequate socialization has somehow created a poorly socialized person who requires "restoration." The rehabilitation model carries with it implications of culpability, of a kind of personal blight that needs restoration to some former, perhaps imaginary, luster. The concept of treatment, however, requires the presence of a disease or a serious medical disorder. For reasons best left unexplored here, persons are not held responsible for the mental diseases which "invade" them.

Parenthetically, rehabilitation seems to be used both in the sense of a process and as a desired outcome. Treatment, however, clearly refers only to a process. Cure or relief, for example, are among the desired outcomes of treatment.

Habilitation Versus Rehabilitation. Now let's add the term "habilitation" and contrast it with "rehabilitation." A Wisconsin court recently dealt with this definitional task in a succinct fashion by stating, "Habilitation means the maximizing of an individual's functioning and the maintenance of the individual at that maximum level. Rehabilitation means returning an individual to a previous level of functioning."[10]

Habilitation tends to be used primarily with developmentally disabled individuals. The term focuses on a variety of activities and programs designed to achieve the maximum potential of the impaired individual.[11]

Training. The term "training" also has crept into the legal lexicon of helping terms. The Supreme Court dealt with the question of training in *Romeo v. Youngberg*.[12] The case involved a 33-year-old, profoundly retarded (IQ between 8 and 10), institutionalized person who was claiming the constitutional right to a safe environment, to freedom from undue restraint, and to training or habilitation.

Justice Powell, for the Court, almost casually recognized the claimant's right to safe conditions, reasoning that if persons convicted of crimes enjoy that right (as they do), then surely it extends as well to the wholly innocent confined in government-operated institutions.[13] Similarly, the right to avoid, what this author believes is meant to mean "undue," restraint also applies to the civilly confined.[14]

Justice Powell then grappled with the claims to habilitation or training, concluding that if all Romeo demanded was the sort of minimal training related to safety or restraint, the Court would have no trouble in providing a constitutional basis for the claim. Thus, the state is obliged to provide minimal help, or "training," to enhance a resident's safety and minimize additional restraint.[15] As an aside, it would be interesting to know whether the Court intended to carve training out of the larger concept of habilitation or, given Romeo's extremely low IQ and conceded inability to live at large, whether training and habilitation were meant to be functional equivalents.

Two Constitutional Arguments for the Right to Treatment

Two somewhat distinct arguments seem to be available on behalf of sex offenders who claim a right to treatment. The first argument, and the one that is most likely to be productive for the inmate's claims, flows from the basis for the loss of liberty. That is, it flows from being confined under a special offender law and labeled as having a mental disorder arguably creates a statutory basis for a constitutionally enforceable right to treatment.

The second argument stems from the convicted person's status as an inmate. The nature of the underlying offense, an opinion about the offender (i.e., sex offender), or even a clinical-sounding diagnosis (i.e., sex psychopath) are incidental to this argument. Prison inmates have a constitutional right to treatment based on the Eighth Amendment, which prohibits cruel and unusual punishment.[16] In *Estelle v. Gamble*,[17] the Supreme Court was confronted with a Texas inmate who sustained a back injury while in confinement and who claimed that the care provided him was inadequate. On the facts presented, the Court refused to find a violation of the inmate's rights. It did, however, for the first time establish that deliberate indifference[18] to the serious medical needs of prisoners constitutes the unnecessary and wanton infliction of pain and, thus, the infliction of cruel and unusual punishment.

The "deliberate indifference" standard does not encompass either negligence or mere medical malpractice. The quality of care provided or the standard by which to measure omissions of constitutionally required care must offend evolving notions of decency and not simply be violative of the general standard of practice in the community.

Essentially, deliberate indifference must be understood as a mental element that is a member of the same legal family as intent, recklessness, and negligence. There are only two basic techniques for uncovering the existence of a mental element.

The first possibility is the health care provider's admission of wrongdoing. Not very likely.

The only real way to prove the required mental state is by inferring from conduct, that is, from acts and omissions. Ignoring cries for help, passively observing suicidal inmates committing suicide, taking away prescribed medication for no apparent reason and providing no substitute, and failing to monitor psychotropic drugs, are but a few examples of the sort of conduct which may easily rise above negligence and settle into deliberate indifference.

Did *Estelle* Intend to Include Serious Mental Disorders? *Estelle* dealt with serious medical needs. Whether serious mental disorders were intended to be included was answered clearly and in a representative fashion in *Bowring v. Godwin* where the federal court of appeals stated:

> We see no underlying distinction between the right to medical care for physical ills and its psychological or psychiatric counterpart. ... We therefore hold that Bowring (or any other prison inmate) is entitled to psychological or psychiatric treatment if a physician or other health care provider, exercising ordinary skill and care at the time of observation, concludes with reasonable medical certainty (1) that the prisoner's symptoms evidence a serious disease or injury; (2) that such disease or injury is curable or may be substantially alleviated; and (3) that the potential for harm to the prisoner by reason of delay or the denial of care would be substantial.[19]

The rationale behind the constitutional basis for medical and mental health care is clear. Inmates are captives of the state who are not free to seek medical or psychiatric care and must look to their captors for the preservation of life and health regardless of the cause of the illness or harm.

Invariably, the courts require some sort of classification-diagnostic procedure to identify the seriously ill. Examples of such systems include an acceptable medical record system that documents the continuity of care and some type of regular interaction, based on a treatment plan, between the clinician and the inmate-patient.

The goal of constitutionally mandated treatment is simple: relief of suffering and control of the basic symptoms. In other words, it is short-term relief from acute distress. This minimal standard contrasts with forward-looking psychiatric treatment that includes efforts to achieve personal growth, insight, happiness — what some refer to as "cultivation of functioning."[20] This is not to say that mental health professionals will not and should not strive to do more, or that some prison systems do not strive to do more.

Determining When a Sex Offender Has a Disease that Qualifies Him for Treatment. As previously discussed, inmates who have been convicted of a sex offense, or informally labeled as sex offenders, have no federal constitutional claim to treatment. *Estelle*'s Eighth Amendment protection only comes into play if the inmate is independently diagnosed as seriously mentally ill. Even then, the treatment does not have to be aimed at a sexual deviance or practice. It only has to be geared toward such symptoms as withdrawal, efforts to injure or kill oneself, or acting out in an aggressive manner.[21]

Clearly, the medical profession serves as the gatekeeper for entry into the world of disease. Mental disease (or illness) is not demonstrably valid or invalid. It is closer to a logical or theoretical construct than it is to the traditional definition of disease, which is associated with tissue pathology.[22] This puts the various diagnostic categories of mental disease and disorders, as well as individual diagnosis, in the hands of doctors and other mental health professionals.[23]

It is possible to construct a logical, as well as empirical, argument that at least some sex offenders are mentally ill. This is particularly easy if the symptoms of mental illness include rule-breaking and deviance.[24] Adults who coerce children into sex, sadistic rapists, and adults who are sexually aroused by pictures of very young children seem to almost automatically qualify as "sick."

In labeling such an offender as "sick," however, one is doing little more than offering a theory about why the person engaged in that conduct and, by implication, urging a particular approach. That is, sick people should be helped or treated; bad people should be punished.

Positing a Particular Pattern of Activity as a Disease to Enhance Treatment of that Pattern. One author further illustrates this point in an article that makes a strong case for the constitutional right to treatment for imprisoned sex offenders who are diagnosed as paraphiliacs.[25] The author believes that both psychological and organic factors underlie mental disorders and, therefore, both psychotherapy and organic therapy are required for treatment.[26] This is a predicate for his argument that paraphiliacs have a constitutional right to treatment and that such treatment should (even must) be Depo-Provera™ along with psychotherapeutic intervention.[27]

In my view, the author's enthusiasm has caused him to confuse a theoretical and policy position with a position that is empirically validated and constitutionally mandated. If one seeks to enhance treatment mandates for certain inmates, then the author's approach is quite understandable: simply posit a certain pattern of activity as a disease, refer to DSM-IV as authority, argue that it is a serious disease which causes the inmate needless pain (overlooked by the cited author), and then prescribe the preferred treatment. This argument is not likely to work, however, unless there is a general consensus that (1) the behavior is indicative of a serious disease and (2) the treatment urged is the only known or acceptable way to relieve or cure the symptoms.

I agree that the Estelle deliberate indifference standard is much too restrictive and deferential to prison authorities. Evolving standards of decency—a traditional aspect of the analysis of cruel and unusual punishment—should accommodate new approaches to treatment.

Selecting the Appropriate Treatment Where There Are Alternatives. The argument is made, "Where alternative treatments are proposed, lower courts should not automatically defer to the prison physician's choice of treatment, but should instead compare the alternative treatments in light of present medical standards."[28] For example, insulin is the current treatment of choice for diabetes, so there is presently a right to insulin. Should a cure for diabetes be discovered that does not use insulin, then the "cure" would be mandated instead. The bottom line is that if the proposed treatments have shared goals and similar results, the courts ought to stay out of the business of deciding. In *State v. Reddick*, the Nebraska Supreme Court was confronted directly with the interplay of Estelle's mandate of treatment and the disease implications of being labeled an MDSO.[29] Reddick was convicted of sexual assault and was thereafter examined and found to be an MDSO who was untreatable. The "untreatable" finding meant that the trial judge had to sentence the defendant for the offense.[30]

Reddick argued that it was unconstitutional to punish him as opposed to treating him. The Nebraska Court stated that this misconstrued *Estelle* and that:

> it is the need either to alleviate pain or to effect a probable cure which triggers the State's duty to provide treatment....We now hold that a mentally disordered sex offender for whom a program of treatment will not lead to a cure is "non-treatable" (for the purposes of applying criminal sanctions). There is no evidence that Reddick's disorder causes him pain which can be alleviated.[31]

Perhaps the most important implication of this analysis, as far as corrections is concerned, is that sex offender treatment programs—like alcohol or drug treatment programs—are not constitutionally mandated. Whether such programs are created, funded, and implemented is a local policy decision.

Is an Inmate Who Is Serving a Criminal Sentence While Under Civil Commitment Entitled to Treatment? *Bailey v. Gardebring*,[32] a federal decision and more recent than *Reddick*, deals with an offender who kidnapped, sexually abused, and murdered a 13-year-old girl. He pled guilty to the criminal sexual conduct in Minnesota and then to the murder in Iowa where the actual killing occurred. Bailey received concurrent sentences of 20, 40, and 40 years.

It is here that the plot thickens and interesting issues arise concerning civil commitment and *Estelle*-like claims to treatment. After the Minnesota criminal sentencing, Bailey was judicially found to be a "psychopathic personality" and civilly committed as such to the Minnesota Security Hospital. After two fruitless years of clinical interventions and the inmate's unspecified religious objections to some programs, Bailey dropped out of the available programs and was transferred to the Minnesota Department of Corrections to begin his prison term.

Thus, Bailey is in prison under a presumptively valid sentence but he also remains under civil commitment as a "psychopath" and subject to the jurisdiction of mental health authorities on completion of his prison sentence. This raises two intruiging arguments:

1. It is unconstitutional for him to be the subject of dual penal and civil commitments.
2. Either as a civil or criminal committee, Bailey argued that he has a constitutional right to treatment that was not accorded him either in the civil or penal facilities.

Bailey's first issue was rejected rather summarily. The court found no constitutional defect in the state court's position that such dual commitments are authorized and valid.

The second issue is much more interesting from our standpoint. Bailey argued that as a sex offender his need for treatment to overcome this condition is analogous to the need for treatment of a bleeding ulcer or diabetes.

Looking first at Bailey's civil committee status claims, the court relied on *Romeo v. Youngberg*[33] for its governing law on treatment. Recall that *Romeo* recognized a limited right to training on behalf of the institutionalized retarded in order to minimize the use of restraints and to maximize personal safety. If this is treatment, then it has to be the thinnest and narrowest slice imaginable.

Nevertheless, under that finding, the court determined that Bailey was committed as a psychopathic personality and was neither in danger nor subjected to any extraordinary restraints.[34] The decision of whether to treat him was made by the psychiatrists and is presumptively valid. No showing was made to overcome this presumption created by the exercise of "professional judgment."

Civil Commitment Is a Form of Preventive Detention. Without seeming to realize the significance of what it did next, the court simply announced that since Bailey had manifested his dangerousness by his criminal acts, his continued civil confinement was justified by his continuing danger to the community in general and children in particular. In effect, the court said that civil commitment may be validated as a form of preventive detention since without even the pretense of treatment that is the correct characterization of such a commitment.

Description as "Sex Offender" Is Not Enough to Mandate Treatment. Turning to Bailey's claims to treatment as a prisoner, the court established the *Estelle* basis for the claim and held that:

The right to treatment recognized in *Estelle* has limits that Bailey's claimed right to psychiatric treatment exceeds.

That the prison administrators' failure to provide medical care must rise to the level of "deliberate indifference" presupposes the availability of a cure or at least some accepted form of treatment for the prisoner's medical needs: if there is nothing that can be done, or no accepted way of treating the condition, "deliberate indifference" is indistinguishable from steadfast vigilance. A condition for which there is no known or generally recognized method of treatment cannot serve as a predicate for the conclusion that failure to provide treatment constitutes "deliberate indifference to the serious medical needs of prisoners." Cf. City of Canton v. Harris, 489 U.S. 378, 397 (1989) (O'Connor, J., concurring) ("The lack of training [in the diagnosis of mental illness] is not the kind of omission that can be characterized, in and of itself, as a 'deliberate indifference' to constitutional rights"); Eckerhart v. Hensley, 475 F. Supp. 908, 914-15 n. 16 (W.D. Mo. 1979) ("[T]he state's inability to provide a dangerous person with a reasonable opportunity to be cured or to improve his mental condition because no effective treatment is known would not render unconstitutional his involuntary confinement for the protection of himself or others.").

Here, treatment programs in the prison are available to Bailey. None of these programs, however, is specifically directed toward psychopathic individuals who have committed sexual offenses. But there is in this record no evidence of the existence of any cure or even of any generally accepted method of treatment for sexual psychopaths like Bailey. Hence, the failure of the prison administrators to provide Bailey with the precisely tailored psychiatric treatment he seeks cannot fairly be described as "deliberate indifference."

Absent a reliable medical diagnosis of some serious mental illness that can be alleviated, at least symptomatically, by some known treatment, prisoners have no constitutional right to state-provided psychiatric treatment, and we do not understand *Estelle* to hold otherwise. On this record, we are satisfied that the District Court correctly granted summary judgment for defendants on the ground that they were not "deliberately indifferent to Bailey's serious medical needs."[35]

First, we should note that the same condition which underpins Bailey's civil commitment is the predicate for this part of the holding. Second, the court never really decides whether Bailey is seriously mentally ill and entitled to appropriate treatment. It simply accepts that treatment, either as cure or relief from symptoms, is unavailing and, thus, not required. Third, whether rightly or wrongly decided, and whether well-crafted or not, Bailey surely underscores that the description of an inmate as a sex offender—without more—is not enough to mandate treatment. Bailey fastens on the lack of effective treatment for "sex psychopaths," but comes to the same no-mandated treatment conclusion.

Optional Treatment Programs Must Consider Legal Ramifications. The fact that a particular program or treatment option is not mandated does not mean that authorities have an entirely free hand in its structure and operation. When the flawed right/privilege analysis held sway, it could be argued that since a program was not required, its creation and operation was utterly at the discretion of government. For example, if the program in question was public education, access to that program was considered a privilege.

Today, selection or rejection for a program or a service does not depend on whether that program or service was mandated. The same is true for permissible intrusiveness of treatment, the need for consent, and other similar matters. Thus, the formulation of a sex offender treatment program must include an evaluation of the legal issues that will be involved.[36]

Statutory Basis for Treatment

As noted earlier, if a sex offender or MDSO can successfully enforce a right to treatment, that right is likely to arise from the statutory provision that creates a special dispositional alternative. We will look at this issue using Professor George Dix's detailed study of MDSO laws in five states as a guide.[37]

Dix's survey showed that all of these laws included some reference to a crime. However, some of the laws stipulated that a criminal charge was sufficient to invoke the MDSO law while others required a conviction. This aspect of the law may be quite significant in determining an inmate's subsequent rights. That is, are we dealing with a convicted person turned prison inmate, a person charged with a crime turned civil patient, or someone with dual status?[38]

Criteria for Commitment. The criteria for commitment varies greatly but it always contains a reference, however inaccurate, to some form of psychological impairment. For example, mental disease defect, or disorder were the criteria in California, whereas the Washington law referred to "psychoneurosis."[39] It is important to note that most of the statutes do not even try to define the impairment requirement in clinical or diagnostic terms.[40]

Dangerousness Is Common Requirement. A finding of dangerousness is a common requirement. There is, however, a lack of clarity or consistency on the likelihood of the danger or the degree of harm required. As one would expect, the danger consistently refers to the repetition of sex offenses, but without a mention of whether the reference is to all or only similar sex offenses.

Clinical Inquiry May Be Precondition for MDSO Hearing. Invariably, the statute will require a clinical inquiry to be made as a precondition to the MDSO hearing.[41] Once again, there is wide variation on where the examination occurs, the duration of the commitment for observation,[42] and the conditions under which the court may or must proceed to the hearing.

Recognition of State-Created Right: *Ohlinger v. Watson*. *Ohlinger v. Watson*,[43] is one of the leading decisions recognizing and enforcing a state-created right to treatment based on a sex offender statute. Under the Oregon sex offender statute, since repealed, a court had the authority to issue an indeterminate life sentence on a finding that the victim was under the age of 16 and the defendant had a mental condition predisposing him to the commission of certain sex offenses to such a degree that the person was a "menace."[44]

The appellants were in the Oregon State Penitentiary, having pleaded to sodomy and having been given indeterminate life sentences in lieu of the statutory maximum of 15 years imprisonment. Ohlinger had been confined about 20 years at the time of this proceeding. The appellants' basic claim was that they were denied adequate treatment for their mental illness in violation of rights claimed under the Fourteenth Amendment's due process clause and in violation of the Eighth Amendment's proscription of cruel and unusual punishment.[45]

Court Used Misleading Standard to Measure Requisite Treatment. The Ninth Circuit Court of Appeals agreed completely with the inmates. In announcing its decision, however, the court confused the concept of treatment with the concept of rehabilitation and then used a misleading standard by which to measure the adequacy of the required treatment. On the latter point, the court said that "Constitutionally adequate treatment is not that which must be provided to the general prison population, but that which must be provided to those committed for mental incapacity."[46]

As noted previously, prisoners in general have no constitutional right to treatment or rehabilitation.[47] Seriously mentally ill prisoners have a right to treatment. Assuming that is what the court meant, *Ohlinger* tries to answer the question of whether the source of a right to treatment is determinative of the required level of care.

Court Says Lack of Treatment Is Unconstitutional as Punishment Based on Sex Offender Status. In establishing the treatment mandate, the court's approach was clear and straightforward. "Having chosen to incarcerate appellants on the basis of their mental illness, the State has determined that it no longer has any interest in punishing appellants, but rather in attempting to rehabilitate (nee treat) them."[48] Treatment, stated the court, is not only desirable but is constitutionally required. Otherwise, the state is punishing someone on the basis of their status (sex offender) and that is, per se, a cruel and unusual punishment.[49]

Indeed, the real argument between the parties was the level of treatment that had to be provided. The court held that individual treatment that will provide a realistic opportunity for improvement or cure is required.[50] The court then found overwhelmingly that appellants were not receiving adequate treatment at the prison. The group therapy that was available, was not viewed as either sufficient or effective. The court's endorsement of evidence that "indicates . . . appellants require intensive individual therapy which includes a program concentrating on development of social skills, a reconditioning process, work in sexual fantasies and dreams, and community passes to gradually integrate them into the community"[51] was interesting.

Whether *Ohlinger* was merely summarizing the evidence or imposing a particular treatment regimen is speculative. In all likelihood, requiring the appellants be transferred to the state hospital, was the court's approval of treatment. The hospital staff was asked to create an adequate treatment program.[52] Earlier, it was indicated that appellants were not asking for the best possible treatment nor demanding cure.[53]

We must emphasize that *Ohlinger* located the right to treatment in (1) the state's designation of these inmates as "sick" sex offenders, (2) the extraordinary duration of the possible confinement, and (3) the fact that the confinement was in a prison without adequate mental health services.

It is reasonably clear that the *Ohlinger* court meant to distinguish the level of care mandated by the Eighth Amendment and the level of care also constitutionally enforceable but arising specifically from state law.[54] The latter is more demanding, but it is not clear precisely how. My reading of this opinion suggests that the *Ohlinger* standard more nearly resembles the standard of care offered in the community rather than *Estelle's* standard of "deliberate indifference." However, this is not stated in the opinion.

Ohlinger Distinguished—But Not Always Followed by—Other Courts

Ohlinger was noted in several subsequent decisions. We will examine these decisions in reverse chronological order.

Ninth Circuit: *Hoptowit v. Ray.* In *Hoptowit v. Ray*,[55] an important Ninth Circuit decision involving the Washington State Penitentiary, the court indicated that *Ohlinger* stands for the proposition that persons committed for mental incapacity have a constitutional right to adequate treatment. The court went on to say that "the rationale of *Ohlinger* does not extend to those serving criminal sentences. Indeed, *Ohlinger* supported the proposition that those serving criminal sentences have no constitutional right to rehabilitation."[56]

District Court (Idaho): *Balla v. Idaho State Board of Corrections.* *Ohlinger* clearly influenced the outcome of a broad-based legal challenge to the Idaho State Correctional Institution in *Balla v. Idaho State Board of Corrections*.[57] The court determined:

> The Idaho State Legislature, in enacting Idaho Code Sec. 20-233, pre-cludes the release on parole of even a model prisoner serving a sentence for the crimes enumerated in that section, or whose history and conduct indicate that such inmate is a sexually dangerous person except upon the examination and evaluation of one or more psychiatrists or psychologists. This statutory scheme requires indeterminate incarceration of sex offend-ers absent rehabilitation. Thus, having chosen to incarcerate inmates cat-egorized as sexually dangerous persons because of their mental illness, the State of Idaho has determined that it no longer has an interest in pun-ishing the inmate, but rather in attempting to rehabilitate such categorized inmate. This rehabilitative rationale is not only desirable, but it is con-stitutionally required. (Ohlinger v. Watson). Inmates are perhaps not cry-ing out for the best possible treatment, nor are they seeming to demand a guarantee to be cured of their mental incapacity or inadequacies. They are, however, entitled to a treatment program that will address their par-ticular needs, with the reasonable objective of evaluation and rehabilita-tion, to have some history or reasonable basis worked up during their incarceration whereby a psychiatrist or psychologist could give a reason-able evaluation or opinion to the parole commission indicating whether or not such sexually dangerous person is fit to return to society. Such con-stitutionally required treatment is not that which must be provided to the general prison population, but rather, that which must be provided to those committed under any of the categories set forth in Idaho Code Sec.

20-223. Certainly due process requires that the nature and duration of commitment bear some reasonable relation to the purpose for which the individual is committed. In these cases, adequate and effective treatment is constitutionally required, for absent such treatment, a Section 20-223 categorized individual inmate could be held indefinitely.[58]

The focus of the Idaho case is a bit different than *Ohlinger's*. That is, *Balla's* express concern was with a fair opportunity for release on parole, while *Ohlinger* impliedly focused on "releasability" in general and the duration and places of confinement.

California: *People v. Sherman*. *People v. Sherman*[59] involved a defendant convicted of child molestation and committed as an MDSO for a five-year maximum. Before the original term expired, California filed for a two-year extension. The defendant challenged the extension. The defendant presented two arguments. First, he said that he was being subjected to cruel and unusual punishment in that as a pedophiliac, with no hope of successful treatment according to the two testifying psychiatrists, he likely would be confined for life. Next, he intended that his retention beyond the maximum term permitted for the underlying conviction inflicted cruel and unusual punishment.

The court distinguished *Ohlinger* on the basis that Ohlinger received no treatment for 10 years, committed offenses that did not involve force, and was demanding treatment that simply was not available in the prison.[60] Except for the last point, it is difficult to understand the relevance of these supposed distinguishing factors. The court then stated that amenability to treatment may be a prerequisite for the initial commitment, but it is not a condition precedent to retention.[61]

The *Sherman* court recognized that indefinite extensions of the commitment were possible but determined that this was not violative of any constitutional rights. In effect, the California court cloaked the California law in the garb of a civil commitment and said that so long as treatment is available and attempted (as it apparently was), then a "no cure is possible" argument fails. The outcome is a judicially sanctioned life term.

Colorado: *People v. Kibel*. In the Colorado case, *People v. Kibel*,[62] the state proceeded against the defendant under the Sex Offenders Act after his conviction on a sex offense. The defendant claimed that the state law violates equal protection because it does not afford periodic judicial review on the justification for continued confinement; it only requires annual review by the parole board. The Colorado Supreme Court held as follows:

> Such a right is afforded to involuntary civil commitments . . . criminal defendants found not guilty by reason of insanity . . . and criminal defendants found incompetent to proceed. . . . In contrast, defendants confined under the provisions of the CSOA receive no judicial review following the initial determination of dangerousness; rather, the parole board annually reviews the defendant's continued confinement. . . . The denial of equal protection inherent in these inconsistent statutory schemes, the defendants assert, is particularly acute where defendants are confined under the CSOA beyond the statutory maximum prison term they might have received for their underlying crimes.

Because the classification of sex offenders under the CSOA neither creates a suspect class nor infringes upon a fundamental right, the statutory scheme will survive an equal protection challenge if the state can demonstrate that the classification bears a rational relationship to a legitimate inmate state purpose.... The state must show, in other words, that "a distinction made has some relevance to the purpose for which the classification is made." [Citations omitted.][63]

That these individuals had been convicted of a crime, as opposed to being merely civilly committed, allowed the court to characterize the procedural distinction as rational. Review by the parole board was upheld as satisfying any procedural due process owed the offender, especially since the board initially determines whether there have been post-confinement changes, but not dangerousness.[64]

First Circuit: *Cameron v. Tomes*. Finally, we review the decision in *Cameron v. Tomes*,[65] a case involving yet another confined individual with the dual status. Cameron is a Vietnam veteran who, all the parties agree, suffers from severe psychological disorders and who had a leg amputated due to an infection that was incurred while in state (Massachusetts) custody.

Cameron challenged a variety of conditions and practices employed at the Massachusetts Treatment Center: access to outside medical care, use of armed guards and shackles when being transported, searches of his person, lack of certain space accessible to him due to his handicap, and failure to provide appropriate treatment.

The First Circuit validated most of the district court's holding, particularly since the court's order required a series of reviews of the challenged practices by a "qualified decisionmaker" who would then offer his "professional judgment" as to such practices as shackling, searches, and treatment. The court generally upheld the lower court's opinion. However, it issued an interesting caution[66] about the professional judgment standard:

Any professional judgment that decides an issue involving conditions of confinement must embrace security and administration, and not merely medical judgments.

Thus when it comes to appraising the judgments of the administrators, it does not follow that they are bound to do what the doctors say is best for Cameron even if the doctors are unanimous. The administrators are responsible to the state and to the public for making professional judgments of their own, encompassing institutional concerns as well as individual welfare. Nothing in the Constitution mechanically gives controlling weight to one set of professional judgments. Indeed, when it comes to constitutional rights, none of the professionals has the last word. Professional judgment, as the Supreme Court has explained, creates only a "presumption" of correctness; welcome or not, the final responsibility belongs to the courts. See Youngberg, 457 U.S. at 323, 102 S.Ct. at 2462.[67]

Here, the court clearly divides professional judgment on security from professional judgment on treatment. However, where there may be a conflict—for example, shackling during transportation—there is a question about whether treatment trumps security. The court stated that "in matters of security, as opposed to administrative convenience, the administrators' discretion is at its zenith and Cameron is still under criminal sentence."[68] At least until the matter is re-examined, security staff need not suspend its security measures during transportation even though these measures seem now to be excessive for an amputee.

The court found it did not have to directly resolve Cameron's right to treatment claims because most of them related to the conditions of his confinement.[69] Indeed, he was receiving substantial psychological treatment for his condition. The court then stated that "under existing state law, there is already a regulation-based right to treatment...that equals or exceeds anything that the Supreme Court would likely impose under the Due Process Clause."[70] The court did not directly hold that the state-based right to treatment created a federally enforceable claim. Apparently, it only stated that Cameron's claims actually related to the conditions of confinement, properly addressed by the district court; or if they related to treatment, he was in fact receiving (at least) adequate care flowing from state mandates and practices.

Finally, *Cameron* raised a dramatic issue although it is not announced with any particular fanfare. I would characterize this issue as a claim to avoid "dehabilitation," although that term is not used here. Recall that Cameron is under a criminal sentence that will expire in 2002, and also is committed as sexually dangerous—a potential life term.

The court found that the state's procedures and constraints may be needlessly worsening his mental condition so that he may remain confined long after 2002. This, in turn, suggests the need for professional medical judgment on whether the challenged practices (restraints, searches, and the like) are antitherapeutic, needless, and a cause of deterioration.

Is this, then, a clear, unequivocal right for treatment (or therapeutic) considerations to trump security if it can be shown that antitherapeutic (or dehabilitative) results ensue? Probably not. However, in the case of the dually committed, a showing that security practices block treatment to the extent of possibly prolonging the civil commitment then there seems to be, as the court puts it, "a claim with some bite." [71]

Footnotes

[1] Estelle v. Gamble, 451 U.S. 454 (1976)(prison officials may not display deliberate indifference to the serious medical needs of prisoners and thereby inflict unnecessary and wanton pain and suffering). This decision, and its consequences, is discussed in detail in F. Cohen, *Legal Issues and the Mentally Disordered Prisoner* 54 et seq. (N.I.C. 1988) (hereinafter referred to as F. Cohen, Legal Issues).

[2] The leading case on point is Ohlinger v. Watson, 652 F.2d 775 (9th Cir. 1980), which is discussed later in this chapter. See also Allen v. Illinois, 106 S. Ct. 298 (1986).

[3] See generally, Marshall v. United States, 419 U.S. 899 (1974).

[4] See generally, F. Cohen, *Legal Issues*, at Ch. III. Much of the following text is derived from this work cited and the sources referred to thereafter.

[5] In re Rosenfield, 157 F. Supp. 18 (D.D.C. 1957), is a well known example of a psychiatric flip-flop whereby psychopathy was not a mental disorder on Friday, but a weekend vote of the mental

hospital staff converted it to a mental disorder by Monday. This occurred within the context of determining what would be recognized as a mental disease or defect for the purposes of determining competency to be tried in People v. Francabandera, 310 N.E.2d 292 (N.Y. 1974).

[6] See the discussion in Chapter 22, notes 15 and 16.

[7] Note 1 supra.

[8] F.A. Allen, *The Decline of the Rehabilitative Ideal* 2 (1981).

[9] M.B. Santamour and B. West, *Retardation and Criminal Justice: A Training Manual for Criminal Justice Personnel* 25 (1979).

[10] Matter of Athans, 320 N.W.2d 30, 32 (Wis. Ct. App. 1982).

[11] According to K.D. Gaver, reaction comment in *The Mentally Retarded Citizen and the Law* 411, 414 (1976), active habilitation requires a written individualized plan that is (1) based on (a) a comprehensive assessment of the individual's social, psychological health, and vocational capacities and liabilities, (b) the goals of improving the individual's adaptive capability and the ability to live independently, and (c) objectives related to these goals; (2) comprised of defined services, activities, or programs related to the objectives; (3) specific as to the responsibilities for the conduct of such services or activities; (4) specific as to a means to measure the program or outcome; and (5) clear as to periodic review and revision of the plan.

See also Ellis & Luckasson, "Mentally Retarded Criminal Defendants," 53 *Geo. Wash. L. Rev.* 414, 423-425 (1985).

[12] 457 U.S. 307 (1982).

[13] 457 U.S. 315 (1982).

[14] Id. While Justice Powell used the term "undue" or "needless," the author believes that is an intended modifier.

[15] Ibid., at 2459.

[16] This section is a condensation of material earlier published by the author in *Sourcebook—Legal Issues* 48 et seq. The reader is referred to the Sourcebook for a more complete version of the material presented here.

[17] 451 U.S. 454 (1976).

[18] This was the first time the Supreme Court used the seemingly oxymoronic term "deliberate indifference." While the Court stated a few things that deliberate indifference was not, it said nothing about what it is.

[19] 551 F.2d 44, 47 (4th Cir. 1977). No post-*Estelle* case to the contrary has been found.

[20] Readers who have some familiarity with consent decrees in this area may be puzzled by the text since these decrees often have provisions for mental health services going far beyond the minima referred to here. Many settlements go beyond the constitutional minima simply because the overall conditions in the prisons are shown to be so shocking that at a certain point in the development of the proof process the state finds it expedient to "cut its losses."

[21] These behaviors are listed as merely representative of the commonly encountered symptoms of mental illness in prison.

[22] Swartz, "Mental Disease: The Groundwork for Legal Analysis and Legislative Action," 111 *U. Pa. L. Rev.* 389, 394 (1963).

[23] The American Psychiatric Association is responsible for the widely accepted Diagnostic and Statistical Manual of Mental Disorders-III (1980) (DSM-III). Psychiatric nurses, social workers, and clinical psychologists occupy the field of mental disorders in a way that has no parallel in physical medicine.

In Romeo v. Youngberg, 457 U.S. 307 (1982), the Court held that if a training (or treatment) decision is made by a professional, it is presumptively valid. Since diagnosis and prognosis are inseparable from treatment decisions, the deference to professional judgment standard is quite expansive.

[24] See e.g., T.J. Scheff, *Being Mentally Ill: A Sociological Theory* 31 (1966). See also, Robert W. Wettstein, "A Psychiatric Perspective on Washington's Sexually Violent Predators Statute," 15 *Univ. of Puget Sound L. Rev.* 597 (1992).

[25] Comment, "Medical Treatment for Imprisoned Paraphiliacs: Implementing a Modified Standard

for Deliberate Indifference," 4 *Yale Law & Policy Rev.* 251 (1985). According to DSM-IV at 522-532, the features of paraphilia are unusual or bizarre imagery or acts which are necessary for the paraphiliac's sexual excitement. Specific paraphilias include exhibitionism, fetishism, frotteurism, pedophilia, sexual masochism, sexual sadism, transvestic fetishism, and voyeurism.

[26] Ibid., at 255, n. 21.

[27] Ibid., at 258.

[28] Ibid., at 268.

[29] 376 N.W.2d 797 (Neb. 1985).

[30] Ibid., at 798.

[31] Id., at 799.

[32] 940 F.2d 1150 (8th Cir. 1991).

[33] Note 23 supra.

[34] 940 F.2d at 1154.

[35] 940 F.2d at 1155.

[36] Many of those issues will surface in the discussion in Chapter 25, and others will be identified and analyzed in Chapters 26-29.

[37] See G.E. Dix, "Special Dispositional Alternatives for Abnormal Offenders: Developments in the Laws," *Mentally Disordered Offenders* (1983) at 137-147. The states studied are Illinois, Massachusetts, Oregon, Washington, and California.

[38] In California, MDSO's are accorded the full rights of patients, while in Massachusetts, committed persons have the rights of other inmates insofar as that is compatible with treatment. Ibid., at 145.

[39] The Washington law Dix's survey refers to predates the state's Sexually Violent Predator Act discussed in Chapter 23.

[40] See Dix, note 37 supra at 139.

[41] Specht v. Patterson, 386 U.S. 605 (1967). This case is discussed in detail in Chapter 23.

[42] In McNeil v. Director, Patuxent Institution, 407 U.S. 245 (1972), the Supreme Court dealt with a person who was convicted and sentenced to five years imprisonment. The sentencing court, however, committed the defendant to Patuxent Institution to determine whether he should be committed as a defective delinquent. McNeil refused to cooperate in the examination. The Court held that Maryland lost the right to hold him after the criminal sentence expired and that he must therefore be released. A 90-day observation commitment would not raise many legal eyebrows.

[43] 652 F.2d 775 (9th Cir. 1980). See also Rouse v. Cameron, 373 F.2d 451 (D.C. Cir. 1967), a paradigmatic decision on the enforcement of a state-created right to treatment. This case involves enforcement of an act of Congress encompassing the District of Columbia—thus the "state-created" proviso. The court strongly hinted that if sanity acquittees did not have the statute to rely on, there might well be a Due Process right to treatment.

[44] Ibid., at 776.

[45] Id.

[46] Ibid., at 778.

[47] See the discussion in Chapter 25.

[48] 652 F.2d at 777. The plea and the potential criminal sentence of 15 years may be used to measure a time frame within which the state has not renounced its interest in punishment.

[49] Robinson v. California, 370 U.S. 660 (1961)(Eighth Amendment prohibits punishing an addict for his addiction; addict clearly may be punished for his conduct). See also People v. Feagley, 535 P.2d 373 (Cal. 1975) on need for treatment.

A serious debate exists concerning the lawfulness of "nonpunitive" incapacitation. In United States v. Salerno, 481 U.S. 739 (1987), the Supreme Court upheld the constitutionality of pre-trial prevention detention. While this is not the occasion to engage the debate, it must be said that involuntary confinements may have a basis other than punishment or treatment/care and the permissible occasions for "pure" custody, quarantine, public safety-types of confinements will be fought out in the near future. Bailey v. Gardebring, discussed at note 32 supra, would find no right to treatment if the illness or condition is not susceptible to positive outcomes—symptomatic relief or cure. Bailey, however, does not speak directly to a statute mandating appropriate care.

[50] 652 F.2d at 779. The question of what to do if no cure or improvement was likely or possible was not explored.

[51] Id.

[52] Oregon has a widely publicized behavior modification program for sex offenders.

[53] Id.

[54] For example, at 652 F.2d 780, the court was impressed by the fact that Oregon penitentiary does not minimize American Correctional Association Standards. Such standards are never constitutional minima.

[55] 682 F.2d 1227, 1255 n. 8 (9th Cir. 1982).

[56] Id.

[57] 595 F. Supp. 1558, 1569 (D. Idaho, 1984).

[58] Ibid., at 595 F. Supp. 1569.

[59] 212 Cal. Rptr. 861 (1985).

[60] Ibid., at 864-865.

[61] Ibid., at 865.

[62] 701 P.2d 37 (Colo. 1985).

[63] Ibid., at 41-42.

[64] Ibid., at 44.

[65] 990 F.2d 14 (1st Cir. 1993).

[66] This is what lawyers refer to as dicta; portions of an opinion not directly related to the holding or actual outcome.

[67] 990 F.2d at 20.

[68] Ibid., at 21.

[69] Ibid., at 19.

[70] Ibid., at 19. This court refused to concede that the Supreme Court determined that a general right to treatment exists for the civilly committed or whether such a right would apply to someone like Cameron, who was held under criminal sentence as well.

[71] Ibid., at 14.

Chapter 25

Treatment Modalities and Consent

by Fred Cohen, D.J.P.

Overview

Inmates who happen to have been convicted of a sex offense or who are characterized in some fashion as a sex offender are in precisely the same position as any other inmate on the question of enforced medication or the right to resist intrusive treatment interventions. The fact that certain interventions (e.g., surgical castration or the drug Depo-Provera™)[1] are encountered almost exclusively with sex offenders is an empirical, but not a doctrinal, distinction.

All inmates being treated with physically intrusive or aversive techniques should be fully informed of all possible consequences. Departments of Corrections may choose to extend this principle to a variety of treatment modalities.

Use of Castration as Punishment

Before turning to questions related to treatment and consent, we will address the matter of surgical castration or the use of certain drugs as punishment. Readers may be surprised to learn that neither the Supreme Court nor any state or federal court has ruled directly that castration as punishment constitutes cruel and unusual punishment under the Eighth Amendment. Indeed, no reported decision has ruled directly on castration as punishment.[2] There are, however, numerous judicial references to castration, along with burning at the stake, breaking on the wheel, hanging in chains, crucifixion, blinding, and cutting off of hands or ears as examples of barbaric and excessively cruel punishments.[3] Even in this era of greater acceptance of harsher punishments, the "evolving standards of decency" test for determining what is cruel and unusual would find castration to be an unconstitutional punishment.[4]

Is There a Difference Between "Cruel and Unusual Punishment" and "Cruel and Unusual Treatment"? The Constitution forbids cruel and unusual punishment, not cruel and unusual treatment. This does not mean that treatment is outside of constitutional restraint, only that the language of the Eighth Amendment is limited to punishment.[5] Simply calling something treatment does not prevent a judge from analyzing the intervention and determining that it is actually punishment.[6]

One author suggests that "once the treatment exceeds the cure, it is inappropriate to label such action as treatment. The point at which castration exceeds its function to accomplish the intended goal—the preventing of recurring illegal sexual conduct— is the same point wherein treatment becomes punishment."[7] This position, which presupposes an illness and seeks some type of cure or amelioration of suffering, faces a basic problem: the terms "sex offender" and "sex psychopath" have been deemed inaccurate as a clinical description and not useful as a discrete legal description.[8]

Surgical Castration. If we go beyond this issue and identify a group of mentally ill persons who have been convicted of crimes labeled "sex offenses," castration still must be confronted as a highly intrusive and excessive measure. While it may prevent or retard protected and unprotected sexual activity, the results are variable and unpredictable, and the procedure is irreversible.[9]

As a punishment, surgical castration should be placed on the same heap of unthinkable measures as crucifixion and amputation of the hands. Judges should not have the power to offer defendants 30 years in prison or the "voluntary" submission to removal of the testicles.[10] If castration is characterized as treatment, there is no doubt that the procedure is so invasive that if it were even to be considered, a knowing and voluntary consent undoubtedly should be required. Whether such a consent should be permitted is yet another question, and is discussed below.

Depo-Provera™. Depo-Provera™ (medroxyprogesterone)—at times referred to (inaccurately) as chemical castration—raises legal issues that are somewhat similar to those involved in surgical castration. However, the use of the drug is reversible and it can be administered at varying levels, which allows for a less restrictive alternative approach unavailable with surgery.[11]

The leading article on point supports the use of Depo-Provera™, at least with repeat sex offenders:

> There is neither such a total dearth of knowledge regarding the drug's effects, nor as yet any documented and reliable reports indicating that the drug exhibits an unacceptable degree of certainty or severity of adverse effects sufficient to cause Depo-Provera™ to be classified an unreasonable treatment for male sex offenders. Of the known potential changes . . . the most severe is elevated blood pressure (hypertension) which can be controlled with medication if necessary.[12]

The article also advocates the required use of Depo-Provera™ as a condition of parole (and presumably probation) while allowing prisoners to refuse its enforced administration.[13] The state's compelling interest in protecting its citizens is not sufficiently strong to override even the limited intrusion on the inmate's privacy while the offender is in prison.[14] When a repeat offender is in the community, however, the state's interest in protecting its citizens arguably should prevail and overcome the limited loss imposed on the offender.[15]

***State v. Gauntlett*: The Only Case on Point.** *State v. Gauntlett*[16] is the only reported decision to address the legality of imposing the use of Depo-Provera™ as a condition of probation. The case itself seems out of a soap opera in that the offender, who was charged with sexual misconduct with his stepchildren, is described as a descendant of W. E. Upjohn, the founder of the pharmaceutical company that markets Depo-Provera™.[17]

After the defendant entered a nolo plea,[18] the sentencing judge imposed a five-year probation term with the first year to be served in jail. He also ordered that the defendant submit to Depo-Provera™ treatment. Failing that submission, the judge indicated he would set aside probation and resentence.[19]

On appeal, the defendant argued that the Depo-Provera™ condition was unconstitutional and, therefore unavailable as a sanction. In a very muddled opinion, the Michigan court found it could avoid the constitutional question while voiding the challenged condition. The exact grounds for decision remain unclear, but the court appeared to focus on the failure of Depo-Provera™ to gain general medical acceptance, problems in obtaining the treatment, and problems in obtaining informed consent.[20]

Gauntlett is of limited value as a precedent and of almost no didactic value because of its murky reasoning. We must await another decision to amplify our understanding of the legality of requiring Depo-Provera™ treatment as an incident of a community disposition and to find out whether its attempted use in prison calls for a different approach.[21]

Is It the Defense Attorney's Responsibility to Consider Medication as an Option?
One article has argued forcefully that it is the responsibility of defense counsel to explore the Depo-Provera™ option with the client.[22] Careful consideration of the offense and offender are urged, and the client's informed consent is deemed an absolute necessity.[23]

This article is particularly interesting because the author is a defense attorney who views Depo-Provera™ as a sensible alternative for some of his clients. He sees this as potentially helpful, less intrusive, and less expensive than long terms of incarceration.[24]

Since *Gauntlett*, it seems that more offenders argue for Depo-Provera™ and probation. However, these demands consistently fall on judicial deaf ears. A sentencing judge's election to pursue incarceration and community probation as opposed to Depo-Provera™ as a condition of probation or another sort of intermediate sanction, is unlikely to be disturbed by a reviewing court.[25]

Consent to Treatment: A General Approach

Whether one is referring to sex offenders in prison or civil mental patients, the basic postulate of the law concerning how treatment decisions should be made is most clearly embodied in the doctrine of informed consent.[26] This section begins with the posit of a general norm of the sanctity of a competent adult's body. This, in turn, implies autonomy in decision-making by the individual whose body, life, or health is at stake.

The patient has autonomy and the healer has information and expertise. Informed consent strives for some equality concerning the information base of the treater's proficiency in an effort to allow the sick or endangered person to apply his personal value system to the alternatives presented.[27]

This approach—let us call it the traditional model—applies most comfortably to physical medicine outside the area of psychological treatment. A right to refuse treatment where mental disorder may be present raises questions about the individual's competency to make the decision or, at times, even to absorb the proffered information. The matter is even more complicated when the individual is incarcerated, given the dichotomy between a conceivably legitimate constitutional right to treatment and the inherent coercion of the institutional setting. While competence rarely is an issue in sex offender treatment programs, it is important to ascertain the inmate's ability to absorb information and to reach an informed decision.

Other chapters in this volume include complete descriptions of the various treatment modalities associated with sex offenders. In determining whether informed consent should be pursued, the reader is cautioned that the greater the degree of intrusiveness, the greater the necessity and desirability of consent. In ranking invasiveness, one must consider the extent and duration of the intervention, the amount of pain involved, the degree of intrusion into the individual's body, the risk of adverse side effects, the experimental nature of the modality, and the acceptance by the medical/treatment community.

The full dimensions of the consent to treatment problems are not likely to arise in the context of prison-based sex offender programs. Nevertheless, it appears that obtaining informed consent is the norm and that it is obtained even when not plainly required (e.g., in the various verbal therapies such as psychotherapy sessions). Written consent is preferable. In instances where psychotropic medication may be a part of these treatment programs, the more recent case law developments increasingly insist on informed consent.[28]

Psychotropic Medication and Involuntary Treatment[29]

When it decided *Washington v. Harper* in 1990,[30] the Supreme Court brought a measure of clarity—and possibly consternation—to the issues of whether a competent but mentally ill inmate could be forcibly medicated and, if so, whether a judicial hearing was required to overcome the inmate's objections. The Court held that competency was not a bar to forcible use of antipsychotic medication and that certain administrative procedures satisfied the inmate's liberty interest in remaining free of the unwanted medication. That being said, the decision actually goes far beyond the central questions in terms of issues raised and decided and issues explored but not clearly decided.

The Facts in *Washington v. Harper*. Walter Harper, who had been in and out of prison for nearly 20 years, was diagnosed as mentally ill for much of that time. He had consented to the administration of antipsychotic drugs. After several years, he refused the prescribed medications. Eventually, at a hearing, Harper said he would rather die than take the medication. He complained about the right side of his body being paralyzed and being "burned out of his life." He also was exhibiting signs of dystonia (acute muscle spasms) and akathesia (agitation).[31]

Harper served his time at Washington's Special Offender Center (SOC), a 144-bed facility utilized to diagnose and treat inmates with serious mental disorders. The fact that Harper was in a treatment environment (as compared to a security environment) is important because it lends credence to the claims of treatment objectives for the forced medication. When inmate Harper refused to continue the medication, prison officials sought to invoke Policy 600.30, which is the focal point of the decision.

Procedural Requirements. Policy 600.30 is invoked when an inmate objects to a psychiatrist's determination that drugs should be administered. Under that policy, involuntary medication may then be administered if the inmate (1) suffers from a mental disorder, and (2) is "gravely disabled" or poses a "likelihood of serious harm" to himself, others, or their property.

Nonconsenting inmates are entitled to an administrative hearing before a committee composed of a psychiatrist, psychologist, and the Associate Superintendent at the SOC. None of the committee members may be currently involved in the inmate's treatment. While a majority vote will sustain the forcible medication, the committee psychiatrist must be in the majority. We should note that, as was the case here, the committee psychiatrist may well have earlier prescribed medication or otherwise have been involved in the inmate's care.

Procedurally, the inmate must be given at least 24 hours notice of the committee's intent to convene a hearing, and he may not be medicated during that time.[32] The inmate must be informed of the diagnosis, the factual basis for it, and the reasons for the staff's position on forced medication. The inmate has a right to attend, to cross-examine staff witnesses, and to the aid of a non-involved lay advisor who has some knowledge of psychiatric issues. In this case, the advisor was a nurse practitioner from another facility. Minutes of the hearing must be kept and appeals to the super-intendent, and ultimately to the state courts, are allowed.

Finally, initial forced medication is for a seven-day period and continued medication requires periodic review of the inmate's file and minutes of the initial hearing. Long-term approval allows indefinite medication with a review and report by the treating psychiatrist every 14 days.

Different Aspects of the Supreme Court's Decision

Finding of Mental Incompetence Not Required. Perhaps most important, neither the Washington law nor the Supreme Court's decision requires a finding that the protesting inmate be mentally incompetent. In other words, assume that this decision applies to competent inmates who, for whatever reason, object to psychotropic med-ication. Thus, it is first a contest between a competent adult and a psychiatrist and then a conflict between the competent adult and an administrative tribunal.

Urgency of Situation Not a Factor. Neither the state's policy nor the Supreme Court decision is aimed at either a medical or security emergency. Another SOC policy pro-vision, not at issue here, permits 72 hours of involuntary medication on an emergency basis when an inmate is suffering from a mental disorder that presents an imminent likelihood of serious harm to himself or others.

Policy 600.30 does not require that the anticipated harm be imminent, only that it be serious. There is a distinction between the magnitude of a predicted harm (here, serious), the likelihood that it actually will occur, and, if "it" should occur, when that might be (imminent, soon, sometime in the future, and so on).[33]

Intrusiveness of Treatment Method Does Not Have to Be Considered. While the decision to forcibly medicate is ostensibly a medical decision—and the dissent debates this point—the committee is not required to consider whether less intrusive methods (e.g., tranquilizers, restraints during a violent episode) might be beneficial or less harmful. Further, it does not appear that the committee must consider the poten-tial side effects of the medication. (This was a serious problem for Harper, given the history of the medication and claimed side effects.) However, the Court may have assumed that questions of less restrictive alternatives and/or side effects will be part of the "medical" input to the hearing.

No Required Standard of Proof. No standard of proof is imposed on the committee. The Court simply rejected the Washington Supreme Court's requirement of "clear, cogent and convincing."[34]

Inmate's Right to Refuse a Particular Treatment. The decision properly focuses on an inmate's right to refuse a particular treatment. This issue must be balanced against the inmate's right to obtain treatment for serious mental disorders. One has to wonder whether some type of reasonableness test might also be brought to the area of a right to treatment. This author always has believed that in the area of a right to treatment there simply are no competing security/order claims and, therefore, the reasonableness test (which will be discussed shortly) simply had no application.

Traditional Liberty Interests Balanced by Reasonableness Test. Justice Kennedy's decision for a six Justice majority is built upon a traditional liberty interest analysis and the application of the reasonableness test first established in *Turner v. Safely*.[35]

After establishing that both state-created-[36] and Due Process-based liberty interests exist, the question turns to what type of Due Process is required before the state can interfere with that interest. Remember, a liberty interest, of course, is not inviolate.

Next we must ask how the Court assessed the constitutional validity of the policy itself. In other words, did the Court decide that this liberty interest was—or was not—valid? One approach requires the state to have a compelling or strong interest in forcibly administering the drugs and that the method of administration either is the least intrusive means available or is necessary and effective.

This type of heightened scrutiny, which is more or less what the Washington Supreme Court required, was rejected by Justice Kennedy, who insisted that the Turner test applies to all inmate constitutional rights. Thus, the test is whether the regulation is reasonably related to legitimate (not compelling) penological interests.

The majority opinion is less than crystal clear about what those interests were in *Harper*. It appears that there must be a treatment objective but, given the fact that a finding of dangerous to self or others is also involved, it appears that the needs (security and order) of the facility are also endorsed, albeit obliquely. In other words, a prison may neither forcibly medicate a mentally ill person as punishment nor forcibly medicate a mentally healthy inmate to achieve security/order objectives. A seriously mentally ill inmate, however, may be forcibly medicated for treatment if, among other possibilities, the inmate is dangerous to himself and others and the treatment is in the inmate's medical interests. The Court shows no awareness of the fact that treatment is not an objective. It is a process aimed at cure or relief of symptoms. There is no mention, then, of reviewing the possibility of cure or amelioration of suffering.

Adequacy of Procedural Safeguards. The final question addressed by the Court was whether available procedural safeguards were adequate. The Court gave a resounding yes to that question, too. As stated earlier, a judicial decision is not required by Due Process. Administrative process, with the focus on a psychiatrist's decision, is constitutionally acceptable.

There were allegations that the "real" decision to medicate was made at a pre-hearing meeting between the staff and the committee members. Accepting the fact of such meetings, the majority held that absent a showing of bias or that the decision is made before the actual hearing, procedural fairness is satisfied.

Finally, and without indicating what burden of persuasion is minimally required, the majority merely rules that "clear, cogent and convincing" is not required and that the hearing need not be conducted in accordance with rules of evidence.

Issues that Should Be Reviewed According to *Harper*'s Requirements. What meaning can be derived from this major Supreme Court decision? At the operational level, sex offender treatment programs that rely on antipsychotic (or psychotropic) medication must observe the minimal Harper procedural requirements. On a more abstract level, *Harper* continues a federal judicial trend that seeks to diminish the involvement of the federal courts in corrections. It is likely that some state courts will impose even higher standards in their states for the forcible administration of such medication.[37]

Officials of every correctional system should re-examine their policy on forcible medication, remembering that *Harper* provides a floor and not a ceiling for inmate rights. These are some of the crucial questions that should be reviewed:

1. Should an inmate first be found incompetent before forcible medication is permitted?
2. Should the prescribing physician be required to state for the record a consideration and rejection of less intrusive alternatives, potential side effects, and the like?
3. Should the definitions of the basis for a forcible medication policy parallel, as in Washington, the State's civil commitment statute?
4. If the protesting inmate is provided with a lay advocate (not counsel) should there be a special training program on point for such advocates, or at least minimum qualifications, which would assure that the advocate had sufficient knowledge of psychiatric issues?
5. How often should the medication decision be reviewed, by whom, and by what criteria?
6. Since virtually all inmates actually consent to psychotropic medication, should these consents be subject to some internal review, especially in light of the "situational (or structural) coercion" inherent in prison?[38]

Harper is the type of decision that has the potential for interesting "spill over" effects. This can be seen in *Sundby v. Fiedler*,[39] which involved Wisconsin prison-based sex offender care. The inmate in this case was found eligible to participate in a new program for sex offenders. The program, called a Deniers Education Program (DEP), is designed to be a short-term (three months) education-motivation experience and to serve as an entry into the longer-term (two to three year) actual treatment program.

The inmate did not wish to be moved to the residential unit housing the DEP. He argued that a hearing was required and, more to the point, that *Harper* gave him a liberty interest allowing his refusal to participate in DEP.[40] The court finessed the question of whether a *Vitek*[41]-type hearing might apply and focused on the claimed interest to resist forcible participation in the DEP. Parenthetically, the inmate's real grievance probably was resistance to his identification as a sex offender by virtue of the designated housing area rather than forced program participation.

After reviewing *Harper* and other decisions, the court concluded that the inmate had a limited right to refuse participation in this program. However, the court's ambiguous decision in this matter makes this limited right relatively easy to overcome because the physical restraints and bodily intrusions associated with the earlier forced treatment cases were not a factor here. The court held that:

Under Turner, plaintiff's interest can be overcome by defendants' showing that the SOTP II[42] program serves a legitimate penological interest. The undisputed facts establish that the SOTP II program was designed to help sexual offenders accept their crime, educate them and motivate them to accept treatment. This rehabilitative purpose on the part of defendants is a legitimate penological interest sufficient to overcome plaintiff's limited liberty interest in refusing treatment. See White, 897 F.2d at 112-113; see also Rutherford v. Hutto, 377 F. Supp. 268 (E.D. Ark. 1974) (prison may require inmates to participate in mandatory literacy programs for purpose of rehabilitation).[43]

This author assumes that neither a *Vitek*-like transfer hearing is required nor *Harper*-like administrative procedures are mandated for transfer and forced submission to this program are required in this case. While a *Vitek*-like stigma attaches to the transfer and housing, the treatment (or program) itself is not nearly as intrusive as the behavior modification noted in *Vitek* and dealt with in *Harper*. Had this court simply stated that the transfer into the DEP was directly analogous to a prison-to-prison transfer, no procedures would be constitutionally mandated and administrative-clinical discretion would be at its zenith.[44]

Due Process Speculations

At first glance, this topic may not fit with the rest of the chapter. However, the author's knowledge of the actual workings of prison-based, and to a certain extent community-based, programs suggests that it does. The discussion is not based on a distillation of judicial decisions. Instead, much of what is stated here is speculative and anticipatory. It considers how a given parole policy's dependence on completion of some sort of sex offender treatment program affects an inmate's liberty interests. There is no right to parole, or even a parole release hearing, absent some special statutory language that establishes a "state-created" liberty interest.[45]

Release from prison short of one's full prison term plainly is a benefit; a prize that virtually any offender desires. While no state need have a parole system nor have adopted the "shall-unless" language that evokes state-created liberty interests, the courts may be responsive to claims showing an intimate relationship between parole for sex offenders and sex offender treatment. Therefore, corrections should take advantage of the opportunity to anticipate an issue and to act proactively. The basic policy and procedure adopted to create a sex offender program may just as easily include clear rules on admission, retention, or discharge and some uncomplicated, but fair, method for dealing with grievances at each stage.

This issue has three parts: (1) arbitrary or discriminatory (e.g., as to race) admission criteria or practices; (2) wholly discretionary decisions, with no recourse, concerning retention in the program;[46] and (3) decisions to terminate treatment that do not provide notification or the opportunity to be notified or to somehow challenge the reason for termination.

Program Admission Criteria. At a minimum, the rules for admission should be based on factors such as amenability to treatment and sentence duration. Selection and rejection of certain diagnostic categories or offenses for inclusion or exclusion normally will be viewed as rational. A denial of admittance to a program based on the psychiatric diagnosis or the types of offense committed will surely survive constitutional scrutiny.

Termination of Treatment. If termination can occur for failure to attend or failure to demonstrate progress, the rules should so state, and the inmate should be so informed and should have some reasonable opportunity to "make his case."

In *Jones v. Moore*,[47] a Missouri prisoner sued in federal court claiming, inter alia, that his lack of access to Missouri prison programs for sex offenders upon which his parole release date was based denied him Due Process and Equal Protection of the law. The sex offender program he was mandated to complete as a condition of parole release was not available in the high security prison to which he was transferred after an escape attempt.

Jones concedes, as he must, that he has no federally protected liberty interest in parole. He argued that Missouri law and practice, however, establish a state-created liberty interest enforceable in federal court. The state, however, also undertook what it need not have: it made Jones's parole contingent on participation in the program but then did not provide access to the program.

Finding no mandatory language restricting official discretion, and giving no constitutional weight to actual practice, the court ruled that Jones' had no cognizable federal claim for denial of access to available sex offender programs.

Community-Based Corrections. *State v. Morrow*,[48] a Minnesota state court decision, reaches into community-based corrections. Here the trial court conditioned probation on the offender's successful completion of the Alpha residential program. The approximate cost for the 18 months of residential care was $34,500.46. The offender had no insurance nor any other source of funds and no agency of government was willing to fund this treatment.

The court reviewed the sentence and found that the individual did not have the requisite funds and that no source for such funding was otherwise available. He then revoked probation and imposed a 34-month prison term at Stillwater State Prison where the judge hoped treatment was available.

Was this a denial of Equal Protection or Due Process in that a defendant was incarcerated because he was too poor to afford a less deprivational alternative? This court held that there was not because the initial decision was that there was no satisfactory alternative to residential care. With no alternative other than incarceration available to satisfy the state's penal interest, and with finances only one factor on the proper sentencing spectrum, the offender has not been denied any federal or state constitutional rights.

Are you convinced? If, for example, a prison charges for participation in a treatment program and the program is a precondition for parole release, is the impoverished inmate who is barred from the program denied an opportunity available to those with funds? Is this not the essence of a denial of Equal Protection based on wealth factors? Of course it is, and it may only be the courts and lawyers who do not agree.

Footnotes

1   Depo-Provera™ is a tradename for a drug manufactured by the Upjohn Company. The drug is a synthetic progestogen known technically as medroxyprogesterone.

2   See Comment, "Castration of the Male Sex Offender: A Legally Impermissible Alternative," 30 *Loy. L. Rev.* 377, 394, n. 111 (1984).

3   See Wilkerson v. Utah, 99 U.S. 130 (1878); Weems v. United States, 217 U.S. 349 (1910).

    The Arizona Supreme Court ruled that absent specific statutory authority, a trial judge had no jurisdiction to order that a couple convicted of child abuse submit to sterilization as a condition of receiving a lesser sentence. Smith v. Superior Court, 39 Cr. L. 2484 (9/11/86). The court contrasted the problems in Buck v. Bell, 274 U.S. 200 (1927), where the Court upheld involuntary sterilization of institutionalized "mental defectives" as a means to prevent the birth of defective children and not as an aspect of punishment, with those of the case it was deciding. The genetic premises of Buck and its dubious position of "population purity" are not endorsed here.

4   Blackstone informs us:

    Rape was punished by the Saxon laws ... with death. ... But this was afterwards thought too hard; and in its stead another severe, but not capital, punishment was inflicted by William the Conqueror; viz, castration and loss of eyes; which continued until after Bracton wrote, in the reign of Henry the Third, "In the 3 Edw. I. [1275] by the statute Westm. 1.c.13, the punishment of rape was much mitigated: the offence [sic] itself being reduced to a trespass, if not prosecuted by the women within forty days, and subjecting the offender only to two years imprisonment, and a fine at the king's will. But, this lenity being productive of the most terrible consequences, it was in ten years afterwards, 13 Edw. I. found necessary to make the offence [sic] of rape felony, by statute Westm. 2.c.34. And by statute 18 Eliz. c.7. it is made felony without benefit of clergy."[endQ] 4 W. Blackstone, Commentaries, 211-212 (1st ed. 1769).

5   As we shall see subsequently, there are considerations of the constitutional right to privacy, the First Amendment (e.g., the ability to form and express ideas), and the fundamental Due Process rights to marry and procreate.

6   In Bell v. Wolfish, 441 U.S. 520, 537-538 (1979), the Court indicated that absent a showing of an expressed intent to punish, a particular jail condition or restriction that is reasonably related to a legitimate government purpose does not, without more, amount to punishment. Under *Bell*, to decide if a measure is punishment, one must determine (1) the government's intent, (2) the measure's purpose, and (3) the extent of any excessiveness in the measure and its announced purpose. *Bell* arose in the context of pretrial detainee claims and in the framework of a constitutional rule prohibiting the infliction of any punishment prior to trial or conviction. Whether the subjective approach announced in *Bell* is wholly apt in the "treatment versus punishment" debate (as opposed to the "security versus punishment" debate) remains speculative.

    See also Knecht v. Gillman, 488 F.2d 1136 (8th Cir. 1973).

7   Comment, note 2 supra at 30 Loy. L. Rev. 389.

8   See the discussion of this issue in Chapter 22.

9   Castration has been far more popular in Europe than in the United States. See Heim, "Sexual Behavior of Castrated Sex Offenders," 10 *Arch. Sex. Behav.* 11 (1981). See also Heim and Hursch, "Castration for Sex Offenders: Treatment or Punishment? A Review and Critique of Recent European Literature," 8 *Arch. Sex. Behav.* 281, 297 (1979)(review of the European literature on surgical castration, including some startling claims to success in the prevention of recidivism; raises major questions about methodology and actual achievements).

10 This is precisely what a South Carolina trial judge attempted in a widely publicized rape case. See *Time*, December 12, 1983, p. 70.

11 See Comment, "The Use of Depo-Provera™ for Treating Male Sex Offenders: A Review of the Constitutional and Medical Issues," 16 *U. Tol. L. Rev.* 181 (1984) (hereinafter referred to as "The use of Depo-Provera™"). The author holds a graduate degree in chemistry as well as a law degree.

[12] Ibid., at 198-199.

[13] Ibid., at 205.

[14] Id. The use of Depo-Provera™ in prison would be less concerned with short-term control than with achieving long-term cure.

[15] Id.

[16] 352 N.W.2d 310 (Mich. Ct. App. 1984). At 353 N.W.2d 463 (Mich. 1984), the Michigan Supreme Court essentially upheld the intermediate appellate court except for its handling of the resentencing, a matter which is not of concern to us in this context.

[17] 352 N.W.2d at 313.

[18] See Chapter 27 supra.

[19] Id.

[20] 352 N.W.2d at 316. Again, the grounds for holding submission to Depo-Provera™ as a probation condition illegal are far from clear. Every subsequent comment on the decision which this author has read is critical of the reasoning and result.

[21] Judge James A. Malkus of San Diego, California was reported to have sentenced a sex offender to treatment with Depo-Provera™, along with incarceration for four hours every Sunday, for a fixed number of years. The sentence allowed monitoring and insured that the weekly injection of the drug occured. See Comment, "Sexual Offenders and the Use of Depo-Provera™," 22 *San Diego L. Rev.* 565, 585, n. 161 (1985). The same article reported that between October 1982 and September 1983 about 3,000 prescriptions were written for Depo-Provera™ for the treatment of sexual deviation outside the criminal justice system. Ibid., at 570, n. 36.

[22] Uphoff, "Depo-Provera™ for the Sex Offender: A Defense Attorney's Perspective," 22 *Crim. L. Bull.* 430 (1986).

[23] Ibid., at 438-439.

[24] Ibid., at 443-444.

[25] See e.g., State v. Estes, 821 P.2d 1008 (Idaho App. 1991) (community protection especially valid when sentencing a sex offender); People v. Stephenson, 555 N.E.2d 802 (Ill. App. 1990) (declining to review sentencing court's exercise of discretion in opting for incarceration and incapacitation).

[26] A more complete discussion of this topic may be found in F. Cohen, *Legal Issues and the Mentally Disordered Prisoner* (1988), at pp. 189-207. See generally F.A. Rozovsky, Consent to Treatment: A Practical Guide (1984); "Informed Consent," 1 *Behav. Science & the Law* 1 (Autumn 1983).

[27] See Making Health Care Decisions: The Ethical and Legal Implications of Informed Consent in the Patient-Practitioner Relationship 397 (President's Commission for the Study of Ethical Problems in Medicine and Behavioral Research, 1982).

[28] See generally, White v. Napolean, 897 F.2d 103 (3d Cir. 1990); Rogers v. Evans, 792 F.2d 1052 (11th Cir. 1986); Woodland v. Angus, 820 F. Supp. 1497 (D. Utah 1993); and Cody v. Hillard, 599 F. Supp. 1025 (D.S.D. 1984).

[29] Much of this section is derived from the author's previous analysis appearing in II *Correctional L. Rptr.* 1 (1990).

[30] 110 S. Ct. 1028 (1990).

[31] Interestingly these points were not mentioned by the majority. It is generally agreed that the risk of side effects increases over time. Harper was involuntarily medicated for about a four-year period and had consented to medication for some additional years.

[32] As pointed out by the dissent, some psychotropic medications remain active for much longer than 24 hours. Such notice is constitutionally required in prison disciplinary decisions involving "serious" charges. The process followed in this case appears to be modeled after prison disciplinary proceedings.

[33] That something is said to be imminent is likely also to be a statement of the likelihood of its occurrence. Nonetheless, one can distinguish likelihood ("this may never happen") from when (but if it does, it will be very soon).

[34] "Clear and convincing" evidence is constitutionally required for civil commitment itself, a standard between preponderance and beyond a reasonable doubt. See Addington v. Texas, 441 U.S.

418 (1979).

[35] See Turner v. Safely, 482 U.S. 78 (1987)("[t]he proper standard for determining the validity of a prison regulation claimed to infringe on an inmate's constitutional rights is to ask whether the regulation is 'reasonably related to legitimate penological interests,'" at 89.

[36] The language of Policy 600.30 establishes certain predicates (e.g., mental illness, "dangerousness," etc.) must exist before medication can be forcibly administered.

[37] For example, Rivers v. Katz, 67 N.Y.2d 485, 495 N.E.2d 337 (1986), decided prior to Harper, relied exclusively on the New York Constitution, holds that a competent person in confinement cannot be forcibly medicated and that it is for the courts to make the ultimate decision in competency and to review medication decisions.

[38] The term "situational (or structural) coercion" is used to mean an environment in which a decision requiring consent is such that the disparity in power dictates special safeguards for the powerless. For example, in stationhouse-police interrogation (custody) the Miranda warnings are required due to the inherent coercion of that environment. Because it may be in the inmate-patient's interest to consent to medication that may sterilize a serious, mental condition, consent should not be ruled out as impossible. However, consent to intrusive interventions should be viewed skeptically, and a call for internal review actually is a modest proposal.

[39] See also Felce v. Fiedler, 827 F. Supp. 580 (W.D. Wis. 1993).

[40] Note 38 supra at 583.

[41] Vitek v. Jones, 455 U.S. 480 (1980). The Court found Vitek had a protected liberty interest—the involuntary transfer of a state prisoner to a mental hospital. The Court held that the following minimum procedures were required to protect that liberty interest: written notice of the transfer, a hearing, an opportunity to present testimony of witnesses and to confront and cross-examine the state's witnesses, an independent decisionmaker, a written statement by the fact finder, availability of legal counsel, and notice of the foregoing rights. 455 U.S. at 493-494.

[42] SOTP II is the earlier title for the DEP.

[43] Note 38 supra at 583.

[44] See Meachum v. Fano, 427 U.S. 215 (1976).

[45] See Greenholtz v. Inmates of Nebraska Penal & Correctional Complex, 442 U.S. 1 (1979) finding the combination of shall (be released) unless (certain findings are made) to have created a right to a hearing. Without such language, there are no hearing rights.

[46] This category includes admission-retention requirements that may affect on other constitutional rights, such as freedom of religion. In Warner v. Orange Co. Department of Probation, 827 F. Supp. 261 (S.D.N.Y. 1993) the court determined that the religious components of Alcoholics Anonymous (AA) were such that for an atheist to be forced to attend such meetings as a condition of probation is to confront a valid First Amendment objection. Retention in a program based on forced admissions that may result in further incrimination is discussed in Chapter 26. This more general discussion addresses Due Process as a minimum fairness concept and suggests, however obliquely, that Equal Protection issues lurk where even a nonmandated program uses racial or other irrational factors to determine inclusion and exclusion.

[47] 996 F.2d 943 (8th Cir. 1993).

[48] 492 N.W.2d 539 (Minn. App. 1992).

Chapter 26

Confidentiality, Privilege, and Self-Incrimination

by Fred Cohen, D.J.P.

Overview

This chapter discusses the sensitive issue of confidentiality within a prison setting. Mental health professionals working in a prison setting must balance their

patients' right to confidentiality with the security of the institution. Confidentiality should be waived where questions of danger to self or others, escape, medical care, or transfers arise; and offenders should be informed of this prior to beginning treatment. A confidentiality decision involving all mental health practitioners concerns their duty to inform when a patient makes a specific threat against another. However, there is no legal duty to report a past crime unless specified by state law.

Questions of when information gained by a mental health professional from an inmate-patient/client may or must be shared are among the most frequently asked. Such questions are very difficult to answer definitively. Prisons and secure mental hospital settings create some of the most conflicting demands on mental health specialists. Questions arise about "split agency" (e.g., court-ordered evaluation, jail, or prison screening) and there are questions of confusion of loyalties.[1] There are also questions about duties owed to identifiable others who may be in danger from an inmate-patient and questions related to the general security and order of the facility.[2]

A general solution to many of these problems will be suggested in this chapter. However, readers should remember that legally safeguarded general expectations of privacy in jail or prison are virtually nonexistent. In the context of freedom from unreasonable searches and seizures, claims that an inmate's cell is "home" and thus subject to some protections simply are not recognized.[3]

Need for Confidentiality and Privilege in a Treatment Setting

The need for confidentiality and privilege, as a matter of law and professional ethics, rests on (1) the individual's expectations of privacy and nondisclosure and (2) recognition that the need for information required to provide necessary treatment generally outweighs even compelling demands for disclosure.[4] Where the relationship with the inmate is for diagnosis/evaluation/classification, as opposed to treatment, the full impact of privilege and confidentiality does not apply. For example, mental health professionals may be bound by prison or jail consent decrees that vary from the prior statement of applicable law.

Individual Should Be Advised About Mental Health Advisor's Agency Relationship

Mental health professionals and counselors in a prison or mental hospital setting are well advised to disclose their agency to the individual before proceeding. They should also disclose the purpose of the meeting, indicating both the uses to which the information will or may be put, and a willingness to answer questions concerning the risk of disclosure as concretely as possible. If the therapist is fairly certain that other uses will be made of this information, that, too, should be volunteered. Here is an example of the appropriate language:

> Mr. Jones, I am Mr. Smith, a psychologist employed by the Department of Corrections. I have been asked to meet with you and evaluate your present mental condition in order to help decide whether you should or should not be transferred to a mental hospital. Do you have any questions about who I am and what use may be made of what you say to me?

This type of disclosure is most appropriate when the inmate-clinician contact is for treatment, but it may also apply during the course of an evaluation where certain categories of information, such as those involving the Fifth Amendment privilege against self-incrimination, are likely to be disclosed.[5] This issue will be discussed in greater detail later in this chapter.

Privilege of Professional Confidentiality

The common law did not recognize the doctor-patient privilege. It was not until 1828 that New York passed the first statute granting doctors the right to refuse to testify.[6] The late-arriving and narrow medical doctor-patient privilege generally has been extended to psychotherapists and other mental health professionals.[7]

The attorney-client relationship is vital to detainees and inmates, since they have little choice as to where to meet with counsel. Clearly the attorney-client privilege, and the necessity for privacy, attaches during attorney-client contacts in the facility. Consequently, a lawyer may reveal the expressed intention of a client to commit a crime and the information necessary to prevent the crime; and the lawyer must do so if the contemplated crime is one which would serious endanger the life or safety of any person or corrupt the processes of the courts and the lawyer believes such action on his or her part is necessary to prevent it.

Recognizing that privilege and confidentiality generally apply in institutional settings and that these privacy safeguards are most clearly implicated during a treatment relationship, it has been pointed out that:

> there is a basic conflict . . . between the authoritative or controlling aspect of imprisonment, represented, in a very general way, by the custodial and administrative staff, and the need to rehabilitate, which is largely seen as the responsibility of the professional personnel. Because of this conflict, organization problems are bound to arise in an institution which must perform custodial as well as rehabilitative functions, since confidentiality may be seen as vital to the latter, but dysfunctional to the former.[8]

The problem is that clinicians often find themselves balancing the generally applicable principle of confidentiality in a treatment relationship with the countervailing demands of security: the security of specific individuals who may be in jeopardy and the general security of the institution. Consequently, every jurisdiction is urged to adopt a clear set of rules as to when confidentiality is and is not applicable.

This author suggests that mental health personnel be required to report to correctional personnel when an inmate is identified as:

- suicidal;
- homicidal;
- presenting a reasonably clear danger of injury to self or to others by virtue of conduct or oral statements;
- presenting a reasonably clear risk of escape, or the creation of internal disorder or riot;

- receiving psychotropic medication;
- requiring movement to a special unit for observation, evaluation or treatment of acute episodes; or
- requiring transfer to a treatment facility outside the prison or jail.[9]

Not according confidentiality to the categories listed above serves various purposes. The undoubted duty to preserve the life and health of inmates underpins the need to breach apparent confidences regarding suicide, homicide, or self-inflicted harm and harm to others. In light of this, it is especially important that corrections be notified that the inmate is being given psychotropic medication which can alter behavior, or create grave risks of heatstroke when cell temperatures are excessive. Riot or escape from prison are crimes and, as a general proposition, no privilege attaches to discussions of future criminality.[10]

The *Tarasoff* Situation: Mental Health Professionals Owe a Duty of Reasonable Care to Identifiable Third Parties

What has come to be known as a *Tarasoff* situation calls for some elaboration. In *Tarasoff v. Regents of the University of California,* a mental health outpatient carried out his intention to kill his former fiancée, having previously confided his plan to his therapist. The decedent's parents sued for damages and the respected Supreme Court of California held that a psychotherapist owes a duty of reasonable care to identifiable third parties endangered by the therapist's patient. The court held:

> When a therapist determines, or pursuant to the standards of his profession should determine, that his patient presents a serious danger of violence to another, he incurs an obligation to use reasonable care to protect the intended victim against such danger. The discharge of this duty may require the therapist to take one or more various steps, depending upon the nature of the case. Thus it may call for him to warn the intended victim or others likely to apprise the victim of the danger, to notify the police, or to take whatever other steps are reasonably necessary under the circumstances.[11]

Conflict Between Professional Ethics and Individual Judgment. One authority would solve the ethical question by treating such disclosures as generally confidential to the extent that the "public" is not imperiled. She states:

> Actually this … is not discrepant with the American Psychological Association's Ethical Standards of Psychologists, Principle 6, Section a (1972:3), which reads as follows: "Such information is not communicated to others unless certain important conditions are met: (a) information received in confidence is revealed only after most careful deliberation and when there is clear and imminent danger to an individual or to society, and then only to appropriate professional workers or public authorities."[12]

On a practical level, students of this problem indicate that with the exception of the probability of harm to the clinician or others, the circumstances are far from clear-cut:

It seems to be the general practice among correctional psychologists to inform their inmate clients—and the inmates must understand—that aside from plans to escape and/or harm themselves or others, the principle of confidentiality holds. Even in these two cases, the issue is not clear-cut.

Special care must be exercised not to report just any talk about escape or violence to the security authorities. Only those threats whose probability of actual execution is reasonably high should be reported, and the only basis for that decision is historical data and the psychologist's best judgment. Unnecessary reports may harm not only the inmate client in question but also the correctional psychologist's credibility to both the inmate clientele and the administration. It is obvious that in the implementation of the principle of confidentiality many decisions will be "judgment calls," and prudence (whatever that means to the psychologist) is the guide.[13]

One authority admonishes the prison counselor or therapist to consider:

1. The role conflict in seeking to balance the therapeutic needs of the patient vis à vis the security and stability of the institution.
2. Inherent problems in accurately predicting dangerousness.
3. The impact of a breach of confidentiality on the relationship with the inmate.[14]

Tarasoff Situation Does Not Exist When There Is No Identifiable Intended Victim. A _Tarasoff_ situation does not arise unless there is an identifiable victim. For example, if a patient (or client) talks generally about murderous thoughts or hostility against authority during treatment, there is no enforceable duty to an identifiable victim. In other words, if there is no identifiable intended victim and the therapist encounters "threats in the air," the question of disclosure becomes further complicated.

Confidentiality in the treatment relationship should be the norm, with the therapist ultimately having to exercise his/her best judgment on the seriousness of the general threat. Therapists who reflexively reveal their patient's every threatening word surely compromise themselves professionally and will likely undermine their ability to help inmates.

Just how should therapists discharge the duty to warn? One authority suggests that the standard safe response is the best way to alert the would-be victim.[15] In a prison or jail, the standardized safe response calls for alerting the appropriate security personnel and allowing them to take steps to protect the would-be victim.

Reverse _Tarasoff_ Situations: Prior Offenses and the Treatment Relationship

A reverse _Tarasoff_ situation may be encountered by persons conducting sex treatment programs in institutional settings. During a group or individual treatment session an inmate-client/patient may disclose the commission of a past crime. Indeed, the inmate may be required to make such disclosure as a condition of gaining admission to or remaining in the program. Does the clinician have a duty to report such a crime to the authorities? Does the possible duty, or permissive right, to report vary with the discipline of the clinician? How much detail must there be in the offense narrative before there is a problem?

Keeping the Inmate-Client Confidences General Might Be a Solution. To avoid a reporting problem, many clinicians encourage honesty, but do not allow the individual to go into detail about victim identity, the nature of the offense, location, date, or time. If the inmate's narrative is general and has no identifiable detail, the clinician has not learned of a crime. Refusing knowledge of any details may only be a ploy, but it avoids the legal issues.

Inmate-Client Preadmission Waiver. Treatment personnel are advised to adopt some form of the following written "waiver." The waiver must be signed prior to admittance to a treatment program:

> Enrollment and continuation in the [named facility and program] requires that each individual take responsibility for their sexual misconduct, including, but not limited to, the offense for which you have been convicted.

> For the purposes of this [program/therapy/treatment] it is immaterial whether you were found guilty after a trial or any plea involving a concession of guilt.

> In addition, during the course of this [program/therapy/treatment] you are likely to be required to discuss sex offenses in which you were involved even though there may have been no arrest or prosecution. For these offenses it is not necessary that you specify names, places, or dates but it is necessary that you be complete and honest in your discussion. These requirements do not have any punitive intent but are related solely to maximizing our efforts to help you.

As a general proposition, there is no duty to report a crime unless specifically required by law.[16]

When Does a Mental Health Professional Assume a Duty to Report?

The relationship between patient and mental health professionals—psychiatrists, psychologists, psychiatric social workers, psychiatric nurses, and mental health aides—is considered a fiduciary relationship.[17] Clinicians have a duty to uphold the trust and confidence of the patient with respect to communications and to do no harm to the patient. Although these principles originate in medical ethics, they are applicable to some extent to all statutorily encompassed mental health professions.[18]

As mentioned previously, there is no duty to report a crime unless specifically required by law. While this should preclude any issue of reporting with respect to a past crime that is revealed during a therapy or counseling session, the entire nature of the therapist-patient relationship makes that assessment a bit too simplistic. While there may not be a duty to report, there is the possibility that neither confidentiality nor privilege will preclude the clinician from making the revelation.

Clearly, if the clinician states at the outset that past crimes are not considered to be confidential matters, or requires a "waiver" along the lines of that noted above, then the individual who discloses is at risk. Where a promise of confidentiality is made and where the disclosure is made within the confines of a privileged relationship, the individual who is the privilege holder may assert the privilege and conceivably prevent testimony on the disputed subject.

Privilege is a matter of statute and varies from jurisdiction to jurisdiction[19] and from one mental health profession to another.[20] The privilege affects the one-on-one relationship and may be waived in the event of group or family therapy where there are more than two people in the room sharing the potentially privileged information, or when the patient offers his mental condition as an issue at trial.[21]

The privilege belongs to the patient and may be invoked to keep the therapist from testifying against the him.[22] These rights are not absolute and must be balanced against other important rights.[23] If a past crime becomes an issue and the judge rules that there is a privilege, then the therapist will be precluded from testifying about what was learned during the course of treatment.[24]

Constitutional Privilege Against Self-Incrimination

Matters of confidentiality and privilege in general are increasingly spilling over into the domain of the Fifth Amendment privilege against self-incrimination: "...nor shall I [any person] be compelled in any criminal case to be a witness against himself. ..." As sex offender treatment programs become more popular in prisons and in the community, including residential programs, legal problems concerning self-incrimination seem to multiply.

The strong desire to participate and remain in what continue to be limited treatment opportunities give rise to legal issues related to gaining entry to the programs, the scope of the particular treatment regimen, and remaining in the program until "satisfactory completion." As treatment personnel increasingly rely on confessions of guilt both to gain admission to and to be retained in treatment, and as release or retention on probation[25] or parole become more dependent on "satisfactory completion," these confession/admission issues become more significant. In this connection three recent decisions, two federal cases and one from Montana, will be discussed here.

Offender Required to Admit to a Crime He Denies and for Which He Was Not Convicted. In *Mace v. Amestoy*[26] the petitioner challenged the revocation of his probation as a violation of his Fifth Amendment right against self-incrimination, among other issues. The petitioner was charged with sexually assaulting his 14-year-old stepdaughter and he pled guilty to an amended charge of lewd and lascivious conduct. The court placed the petitioner on probation and ordered him to "attend, participate and complete" a particular sex therapy program.

Petitioner's continued denials of having intercourse with the young victim led to a revocation hearing, the revocation of his probation, and the imposition of a jail term. The victim then denied that intercourse occurred and a doctor testified that she was still a virgin.

The district court correctly stated:

The Fifth Amendment privilege against self-incrimination not only protects the individual against being involuntarily called as a witness against himself at a criminal trial in which he is a defendant, but also privileges him not to

answer official questions put to him in any other proceeding, civil or criminal, formal or informal, where the answers might incriminate him in future
criminal proceedings...unless and until he is protected at least against the use
of his compelled answers. (citations omitted) . . . Even where a person is
imprisoned or on probation, if the state compels him to make incriminating
statements that could be used in a prosecution against him for a crime other
than for which he has been convicted, his Fifth Amendment rights have been
violated.[27]

The court went on to hold that petitioner was in the "classic penalty" situation and
the privilege became self-executing. That is, ordinarily the privilege has to be affirmatively asserted. However, if the individual is deprived of a free choice to answer
(i.e., admit or go to jail)—the privilege is automatically invoked by virtue of the individual's silence. In any event, the court found that the answers required of petitioner
placed him in jeopardy of being prosecuted for the unlawful intercourse; whether the
possibility of prosecution was realistic did not alter this fact.

Thus, in *Mace* we have an offender required to admit to a crime he denies and for
which he was not convicted. The revocation of his probation is deemed unconstitutional because the probationer cannot be punished for exercising his constitutional
right to silence.

Offender Required to Admit to Crime for Which He Was Convicted. In *State v.
Imlay*,[28] the Supreme Court of Montana reached the same result as the federal district
court in Vermont but on very different facts. The Supreme Court agreed to review
Imlay, posing the question for review as follows:

Was state probationer's Fifth Amendment privilege against self-incrimination
violated by revocation of his probation for failure to comply with condition
that he complete sex offender therapy, in view of fact that successful completion of therapy requires probationer to accept responsibility for crime of
which he was convicted, 50 CrL 3179 (Mar. 4, 1992)?

The defendant, a 56-year-old widower with an otherwise unmarred life history,
was convicted of sexual assault (i.e., fondling a young girl while she was in his grocery store). He was given a suspended prison sentence and placed on probation on
the condition that he enroll in and complete a sexual therapy program. The defendant
saw a counselor over a six-month period. Eventually, the counselor concluded that
the defendant was not amenable to outpatient treatment because he did not admit that
he had committed a sexual offense. The counselor further stated that there was no
other outpatient program in Montana that would treat a "denier" and recommended
inpatient care at the Montana State Prison. The trial court agreed and sentenced defendant
to five years imprisonment.

The critical factor here is that this offender was being asked to admit only to the
offense for which he was convicted. The Montana Supreme Court found that the
defendant retained opportunities to challenge his conviction (e.g., newly discovered
evidence) and that he might face a perjury charge since he denied the charge at his
jury trial.

To argue that the assertion of a failed defense and the discussion of the offense in treatment raises the specter of a perjury charge is akin to nonsense. Under this logic, every convicted defendant who enters an alibi defense is open to a perjury charge: a very dubious proposition.

Justice Stevens, concurring in the dismissal of the appeal, wrote a brief opinion stating, in effect, that no matter which party might prevail in the Supreme Court, the defendant's prison term (five years) would be the same. This would lead the Court to issue an advisory opinion—one which does not actually resolve a live dispute between antagonistic parties culminating in an enforceable judgment—which is forbidden by Article III of the Constitution.

Justice White, who thought the Court should hear the case, wrote:

> At oral argument, however, two further questions were raised concerning whether any live controversy persists in this case. First, counsel for respondent stated that his client had been assured by state corrections officials that he would be paroled in the very near future. If this were true, the outcome of this case could have no practical effect upon respondent's sentence. Second, counsel for petitioner stated his belief that a probationer would enjoy immunity from prosecution for incriminating statements made during court-ordered therapy. This statement calls into doubt a critical assumption underpinning the Montana Supreme Court's judgment and might suggest that there really is no disagreement about the Fifth Amendment's application to this case.

> In my view, however, neither party's representation is sufficient to deprive this case of its status as a case or controversy. First, as counsel for both parties readily acknowledged, there is nothing in the record to support the expectation of respondent's counsel that respondent will be paroled shortly without regard to his completion of the State's therapy program. As far as the record is concerned, a decision in this case would affect respondent's eligibility for parole and thus have real consequences for the litigants.[29]

Justice White, in other words, is arguing that a possible violation of the petitioner's Fifth Amendment rights might well impact on the grant or denial of parole. Even though parole is not a right, given the existence of a parole system means that it cannot be withheld for unconstitutional reasons.

The Justice's second point is perhaps more on the mark for the topic under consideration in this section:

> Nor does the State's "concession" that a defendant would have immunity from prosecution based upon incriminating statements made to a therapist moot this case or otherwise render it unsuitable for review. This "concession" appeared to rest soley on the State's assumption that this Court's decision in Minnesota v. Murphy, 465 U.S. 420 (1984)[30] mandated such a result. That reading of Murphy, however, is at least debatable. Because the State's concession appears to reflect a possible misunderstanding of its obligations under the law rather than any unequivocal and unconditional declaration of its own future prosecutorial policy, this statement does not moot this case or obviate the controversy. If its reading of Murphy were shown to be erroneous, the State might well revert to the view that a defendant could be prosecuted on

the basis of statements made during postconviction therapy. Such a qualified concession is too uncertain a basis to find that no live controversy is presented. In any event, the Montana Supreme Court evidently was of the view that no grant of immunity protected respondent or others in his position and the State continues to suffer the consequences of its constitutional holding.[31]

Asherman v. Meachum[32] followed close on the heels of *Mace* and *Imlay*. In Asherman, the question was whether prison officials violated the privilege against self-incrimination by terminating the supervised home release (SHR) of a sentenced prisoner upon notification that the prisoner, on advice of counsel, would not answer certain questions about his crime at a scheduled psychiatric examination. In brief, the facts are that Asherman was convicted of manslaughter and given a term of seven to fourteen years by a Connecticut trial court. Two years after beginning his prison term, he was granted SHR by the Commissioner of Corrections and began living in the community, eventually with his wife. Some months later, Asherman was denied parole and in the wake of the denial, the Commissioner ordered him to submit to a psychiatric evaluation to determine his mental state and continued eligibility for SHR status.

Asherman had a federal habeas corpus petition pending which challenged his conviction. This was the basis for his attorney's advice to not answer any questions about the crime of conviction. When Asherman reported for the examination, he was reimprisoned and subsequently disciplined for violating the terms of his SHR.

The Commissioner reversed the disciplinary finding but confirmed the loss of SHR status based on refusal to fully participate in the psychiatric examination. Thereafter, there were a series of legal challenges to the termination with a federal district court granting relief on the basis of a violation of the self-incrimination privilege. A panel of the present court affirmed[33] and an en banc rehearing followed.

The en banc court reversed and held, with one stinging dissent on the merits, that the action taken did not violate the Fifth Amendment. The majority makes some initial and critical stipulations: (1) they will assume, without deciding, that answers to the questions Asherman refused to answer could incriminate him; (2) that Asherman may invoke federal habeas corpus to challenge revocation of SHR status; and (3) earlier, adverse rulings are not determinative here.

After a review of Supreme Court decisions involving discharges from public employment, the majority wrote:

> What clearly emerges from these decisions is both a limit and a grant of power with respect to governmental inquiries. Public agencies may not impair the privilege against self-incrimination by compelling incriminating answers, or by requiring a waiver of immunity, or even by asking incriminating questions in conjunction with an explicit threat to use the answers in criminal proceedings. But public agencies retain the authority to ask questions relevant to their public responsibilities and to take adverse action against those whose refusal to answer impedes the discharge of those responsibilities. . . .

> [W]e conclude that the Commissioner was entitled to revoke Asherman's SHR status for his refusal to discuss his crime. The inquiry was relevant to the Commissioner's public responsibilities. He was entitled to conduct periodic reviews of Asherman's suitability for home release, and he was entitled

to assess the impact of parole denial upon Asherman's mental health. Asherman's attempt to foreclose all questions about his crime prevented the Commissioner from pursuing a relevant inquiry. In pursuing the inquiry, the Commissioner took no action to impair Asherman's self-incrimination privilege. He sought no court order compelling answers, he did not require a waiver of immunity, and he did not insist that Asherman's answers could be used against him in a criminal proceeding. He stayed well within [prior] authority . . . by conducting a relevant inquiry and then taking appropriate adverse action, not for Asherman's invocation of his constitutional rights, but for his failure to answer a relevant inquiry. ... A prisoner may be terminated from home release status for refusing to divulge to a corrections commissioner information pertinent to the administration of a home release program.

We have no occasion to consider what adverse use might have been made of Asherman's answers. We decide only that, even assuming he had a privilege to prevent being compelled to answer, his home release status could be terminated upon his refusal to answer questions about his crime.[34]

The dissent argued that the Fifth Amendment does not yield in the face of relevant inquiry, which he conceded this is. Rather, the amendment limits the government's ability to conduct the inquiry. Therefore, he argued, Asherman's SHR status could not be terminated solely because he invoked a constitutional privilege.

Asherman was concerned that the answers he gave to the psychiatrist could be used against him in any new trial that he might obtain, should the writ prove successful. Without immunity, it was argued, Asherman was given an impermissible choice: relinquish his right to silence or relinquish his SHR status.

The *Alford* Plea: Admission of Guilt Not Constitutional Prerequisite to Imposition of Criminal Sentence. Somewhere in the midst of the *Mace* and *Imlay* self-incrimination problems there is a related problem that lawyers refer shorthandedly to as an *Alford* plea. In *North Carolina v. Alford*[35] the Supreme Court held that an express admission of guilt is not a constitutional prerequisite to the imposition of a criminal sentence even on a charge as serious as murder. Indeed, even a denial of guilt, at least when coupled with the establishment of a factual basis for the plea, and when coupled with the prerequisites of competence and the right to counsel, is not a bar to a valid plea of guilty.

Thus, an *Alford* plea has come to mean the profer and acceptance of a guilty plea even though the defendant refuses to concede factual guilt or even denies it (as in, "I ain't killed no man"). Note that an *Alford* plea differs from a plea of nolo contendere in that the latter cannot be used as an admission of guilt in a subsequent legal proceeding. A nolo plea, in effect, is a plea of "no defense." The plea does not require a factual basis as seems to be the case for a valid *Alford* plea.

After judicial acceptance of an *Alford* plea and the imposition of sentence, does the offender have a Fifth Amendment claim that would somehow bar his being required to admit in treatment to the offense underlying the plea? In effect, is such an offender in jeopardy for the offense related to the *Alford* plea? This situation more nearly resembles *Imlay* than *Mace*. Thus, it seems that the presumptively valid guilty plea, not the dynamics of how the plea was determined, should be the focus of attention. Given a valid plea and a consequent conviction, the offender is not in jeopardy for that offense and, thus, has no valid Fifth Amendment claim. In this respect, the situation is analogous to the expiration of the statute of limitations on a grant of immunity.

Glimpse Into the Future

There are a host of developments and new pressures in the area of confidentiality and privilege in the treatment relationship. For example, a New York court ruled that Soon-Yi Previn's psychiatrist could not be forced to testify in Mia Farrow's fight to void Woody Allen's adoption of two of her children. Farrow's lawyer wanted to see a letter Ms. Previn had written to determine if there was information relevant to Ms. Farrow's claims of sexual molestation lodged against Allen.[36]

In Los Angeles, at the trial of the Menendez brothers, who were accused of killing their adoptive parents, a psychologist for the brothers testified that they never told him about the supposed sexual abuse and fear that supports their claim of self-defense. The same psychologist was under investigation by his state's licensing board for discussing such matters with his girlfriend and having her audiotape the brothers' therapy sessions.[37]

In Massachusetts, a series of judicial decisions, culminating with *Commonwealth v. Bishop*,[38] dealt with the circumstances under which defense counsel may gain access to a rape victim's therapeutic and other private records. These cases involved persons who may be privy to the rawest and most revealing privacies possessed by a victim, therapists, and counselors at rape crisis centers.

Bishop tightened procedures and required counsel to establish some factual basis for a good-faith belief that privileged records are likely to contain relevant evidence. Judicial review in camera is required in order to prevent "fishing expeditions" by defense counsel and a wholesale trammeling of confidentiality.[39]

In a recent work, two scholars in this area write, with classic understatement, "Notwithstanding its importance, confidentiality in the mental health setting is never absolute."[40] This statement is not made in the context of an institutional setting nor even with community treatment of offenders in mind. It is made with the relatively open, contractual relationship that characterizes the non-coerced treatment relationship.

The impaired status of a convicted offender, the security pressures inherent while in confinement, the fear factor in community-based sex offender treatment, and the "normal" intricacies of confidentiality and privilege make this a daunting area. Consequently, therapists working with sex offenders either within a prison or in the community, should disclose their agency at the outset of any treatment relationship, establish the rules for confidentiality early and clearly, and indicate where disclosure must be made (e.g. child abuse reporting laws) or may be made (e.g. when the details of a hitherto uncharged crime are learned, where a future crime is threatened). Clinicians should be certain that the rules are understood.

Footnotes

---

[1] These terms are taken from T.G. Gutheil & P.S. Applebaum, *Clinical Handbook of Psychiatry and the Law* (1982). In general, this is an excellent resource for mental health professionals involved with the criminal justice system. One writer stated that: "Those who have expressed concern about the divided loyalties of psychiatrists intimate that clarification and differentiation of the psychiatrist's professional role is most urgently required in institutional settings such as hospitals, prisons, schools, and the armed services." Merton, "Confidentiality and the 'Dangerous' Patient: Implications of Tarasoff for Psychiatrists and Lawyers," 31 *Emory L.J.* 263, 273 (1982).

[2] This refers to the duty arising from the landmark decision in Tarasoff v. Regents of the University of California, 551 P.2d 334, 131 Cal. Rptr. 14 (1976).

[3] See Hudson v. Palmer, 468 U.S. 517 (1984), Black v. Rutherford, 468 U.S. 576 (1984). The term "expectations of privacy" is a legal term of art and goes beyond the hopes, desires, or even demands of inmates or detainees. It refers to those situations where the law finds the expectation "reasonable."

In Katz v. United States, 389 U.S. 347 (1967), Justice Stewart rejected the notion of Fourth Amendment rights turning on whether or not the right is asserted in a "protected area." He noted that "the Fourth Amendment protects people, not places." Ibid., at 351. This analysis cannot be taken to mean that the place is unimportant in Fourth Amendment analysis. Indeed, it is difficult to imagine how an expectation of privacy can be judged as reasonable without some reference to the placed involved.

Although notions of privacy are at the core of the Fourth Amendment and search and seizure law, it should be plain that in the context of this discussion, the Fourth Amendment as such is peripheral.

See J.J. Gobert & N.P. Cohen, *Rights of Prisoners* 176 (1981).

[4] The nature of privileges is unique. The purpose of ordinary rules of evidence is to promote the ascertainment of the truth. Another group of rules, however, is designed to permit the exclusion of evidence for reasons wholly unconnected with the ascertainment of the truth. These reasons are found in the desire to protect an interest or relationship. The term "privilege" is used broadly to describe such rules of exclusion. For relevant communications to be excluded by operation of a privilege, as Wigmore states:

> (1) The communications must originate in a confidence that they will not be disclosed;
>
> (2) This element of confidentiality must be essential to the full and satisfactory maintenance of the relation between the parties;
>
> (3) The relation must be one which in the opinion of the community ought to be sedulously fostered;
>
> (4) The injury that would inure to the relation by the disclosure of the communications must be greater than the benefit thereby gained for the correct disposal of litigation (citation omitted).

Graham, "Evidence and Trial Advocacy Workshop: Privileges—Their Nature and Operation, 19 *Crim. L. Bull.* 442 (1983) Privilege, more accurately termed testimonial privilege, is narrower than the right of confidentiality and applies in judicial or judicial-like settings.

[5] See Estelle v. Smith, 451 U.S. 454 (1981), where the Supreme Court applied the Fifth Amendment's privilege against self-incrimination to a pretrial psychiatric evaluation of a person accused of capital murder, who was convicted and sentenced to death and who made no use of psychiatric testimony himself. The psychiatrist's failure to provide a Miranda-type warning resulted in a denial of the condemned inmate's constitutional rights. This decision strived to limit itself to the unique penalty of death, but the same factors on the fairness of the type of disclosure recommended here seem applicable.

Cf. Minnesota v. Murphy, 465 U.S. 420 (1984), upholding a probationer's confession to his probation officer absent Miranda warnings.

[6] T.G. Gutheil & P.S. Applebaum, note 1 supra, at Chapter 6, note 1, p. 1, n. 1. The authors state that nearly three-quarters of the states now have such statutes.

For an interesting general discussion of privileges, see Saltzburg, "Privileges and Professionals: Lawyers and Psychiatrists," 66 *Va. L. Rev.* 597 (1980).

[7] See e.g. Ala. Code Sec. 34-26-2; Alaska R. of Evid., Rule 504; Ariz. Rev. Stat. Ann. Sec. 32-2085; Ark. Stat. Ann. Sec. 28-1001, Rule 503; Cal. Evid. Code Sec. 1010 et seq.; Colo. Rev. Stat. Sec. 13-90-107(g); Conn. Gen. Stat. Ann. Sec. 52-146c et seq. 1987 Supp.; Delaware Uniform Rules of Evid. Rule 503; Fla. Stat. Ann. Sec. 90-503; Ga. Code Ann. 24-92; Hawaii Rev. Stat. Tit. 33, Ch. 626, Rule 504.1; Idaho Rule Evid. 503; Ill. Ann. Stat., ch. 110-8-802; Ind. Stat. Sec. 25-33-1-17; Ky. Rev. Stat. Sec. 421.215; La. Rev. Stat. Sec. 13:3734 (1987 Supp.); Me. Rules of Ev. 503; Md. Cts. & Jud. Proc. Code Sec. 9-109; Mass. Gen. Laws Ann., ch. 233, Sec. 20B; Mich. Comp. Laws Ann. Sec. 330.1750; Minn. Stat. Ann. Sec. 595-02; Miss. Code Sec. 73-31-29; Mo. Rev. Stat. Ann. Sec. 337-055 (1987 Supp.); Mont. Code Ann. Sec. 26-1-807; Neb. Rev. Stat. Sec. 27-504; Nev. Rev. Stat. Sec. 49.215 et seq.; N.H. Rev. Stat. Ann. Sec. 330-A.19; N.J. Stat. Ann. Sec. 45:14B-28; N.M. Rules of Evid. 504; N.Y. Civ. Prac. Law and Rules Sec. 4507; N.C. Gen. Stat. Sec. 8-53.3; N.D. Rules of Ev. 503; Okla. Stat. Ann. Tit. 12 Sec. 24-1-207; Utah Code Ann. Sec. 58-25-8; Vt. Stat. Ann. Tit. 12 Sec. 1612; Va. Code Sec. 8.01-400.2; Wash. Rev. Code Sec. 18.83.110; Wisc. Stat. Ann. Sec. 905.04; Wyo. Stat. Ann. Sec. 33-27-103. See also D.C. Code Sec. 14-307.

The foregoing enactments vary in scope and application and no attempt is made here to classify them or the decisions construing the provisions and their exceptions. See generally 44 A.L.R. 3d 24.

For consideration of the privilege as applied to social workers, see 50 A.L.R. 3d 563.

In New York, CPLR Sec. 4507 (McKinney Supp. 1983-84) psychologists are granted the privilege as follows: "The confidential relations and communications between a psychologist and his client are placed on the same basis as those provided by law between attorney and client, and nothing in such article shall be construed to require any such privileged communications to be disclosed."

[8] Boyle, "Confidentiality in Correctional Institutions," 26 *Canadian J. of Crim. & Corrections* 26, 27 (1976).

[9] See Draft Minimum Standards (or the Delivery of Mental Health Services in New York City Correctional Facilities Sec. 7.2[a] [N.Y.C. Bd. of Correction, 1982]).

The Standards for Health Services in Correctional Institutions promulgated by the American Public Health Association are more specific than most on this point but are still general.

Confidentiality of all information obtained in the course of treatment should be maintained at all times with the only exception being the normal legal and moral obligations to respond to a clear and present danger of grave injury to the self or others, and the single issue of escape. The mental health professional shall explain the confidential guarantee, including precise delineation of the limits. The prisoner who reveals information that falls outside the guarantee of confidentiality shall be told, prior to the disclosure, that such information will be disclosed, unless doing so will increase the likelihood of grave injury. IV(B)(3)

[10] A.B.A., Standards for Criminal Justice, The Defense Function, 4-3.7(d) (1980).

[11] 551 P.2d, 334, 340

[12] Kaslow, "Ethical Problems in Prison Psychology," 7 *Crim. Justice & Behavior* 3, 4 (1980).

[13] Quijano & Logsdon, "Some Issues in the Practice of Correctional Psychology in the Context of Security," 9 *Professional Psychology* 228, 231 (1978).

[14] P.J. Lane, *Prison Counseling and the Dilemma of Confidentiality in Conference on Corrections* (V. Fox, ed., 1978). The author concludes each decision is an individual one.

[15] See Wexler, Mental Health Law: Major Issues 158 (1981). The reference, of course, is outside the prison or jail setting.

[16] Physicians and psychotherapists, among others, must disclose information under compulsory reporting requirements in state or federal law, such as in child abuse reporting statutes that have been enacted in all 50 states and in states that require reporting of injuries that result from violent acts. In New York, N.Y. Soc. Serv. Law Sec. 413 (McKinney's Supp. 1987) requires physicians, psychologists, and mental health providers to report cases of suspected child abuse when they have reasonable cause to suspect that a child coming before them in their professional or official capacity is an abused or maltreated child, or when they have reasonable cause to suspect that a child is an abused or maltreated child when the parent, guardian, custodian or other person legally respon-

sible for such child comes before them in their professional or official capacity and states from personal knowledge or facts, conditions or circumstances which, if correct, would render the child an abused or maltreated child.

Not reporting a past crime is not considered compounding a crime in New York under N.Y. Penal Law Sec. 215.45, nor is it considered a misprision of a felony under 18 U.S.C. Sec. 4 (1969). There must be knowledge and willful concealment of the offense. See United States v. Baez, 732 F.2d 780 (10th Cir. 1984).

[17] R. Sadoff, *Legal Issues in the Care of Psychiatric Patients*, 3 (1982).

[18] Id.

[19] Ibid., at 6. See Lora v. Board of Education, 74 F.R.D. 565 (E.D.N.Y. 1977) ("Privileges for information confided to a doctor were unknown to the common law....") p. 574.

The physician-patient privilege has not been recognized in federal criminal trials. U.S. v. Meagher, 531 F.2d 752, 753 (5th Cir. 1976), cert. denied 429 U.S. 853 (1976). It is not found specifically in the Fed. R. of Crim. P. 26 nor in Fed. R. Evid. 501. Proposed Fed. R. Evid. 504, however, was adjudged an appropriate guide and standard for applying Fed. R. Evid. 501 to psychotherapist-patient privileges. 74 F.R.D., at 569.

[20] See "Recent Developments: Waiving the Physician-Patient Privilege in Involuntary Commitment Proceedings in Washington," 59 *Wash. L. Rev.* 103, 105, n. 11 (1983).

See e.g., N.Y. Civ. Prac. Law Secs. 4504 (physician-patient privilege), 4507 (psychologist-patient privilege), and 4508 (social worker-patient privilege). People v. Wilkins, 65 N.Y.2d 172 (1985) held that the psychologist-patient privilege was broader than the doctor-patient privilege and equivalent to the attorney-client privilege. See also "Developments: Privileged Communications," 98 *Harv. L. Rev.* 1451, 1540 (1985).

[21] Sadoff, note 17 supra, at Chapter 20, note 18, p. 7.

[22] d.

[23] 74 F.R.D., at 567.

[24] Sadoff, above Chapter 20, note 18, at 6-7.

[25] Self-incrimination issues abound in the community supervision arena as well. For example, in State v. Steinhour, 607 A.2d 888 (Vt. 1992) the court held that while the probationer's status as such required him to answer questions on drug use and that a refusal to answer based on self-incrimination could serve as a basis for revocation, use of these answers at revocation did not violate the Fifth Amendment. On the other hand, this court strongly implies that a new prosecution would likely lead to a successful Fifth Amendment challenge. 607 A.2d at 889.

[26] 765 F. Supp. 847 (D. Vt. 1991); III CLR 33 (1991).

[27] 765 F. Supp. at 849-850.

[28] 813 P.2d 97 (Mont. 1991). The Supreme Court granted review but then dismissed the petition as improvidently granted. 113 S.Ct. 444 (1992).

[29] 113 S.Ct. at 445.

[30] In this decision the Court found that *Miranda* warnings were not required when a probationer or parolee went voluntarily to his caseworker's office and, in response to questioning without *Miranda* warning, he admitted to an earlier murder. The Court, rather incredibly, held that the supervisee was not in custody when questioned; that the requisite coercive environment was lacking. In fact, if the supervisee did not respond to the "request" for an "interview" then he could have been revoked. Of course, that speaks primarily to pressure to attend and not necessarily to respond to questioning.

[31] 113 S.Ct. at 446.

[32] 957 F.2d 978 (2d Cir. 1992) (en banc).

[33] 932 F.2d 137 (2d Cir. 1991).

[34] 957 F.2d at 982-983.

[35] 400 U.S. 25 (1970).

[36] *Albany Times Union*, A-2 (Dec. 14, 1993).

[37] *Nat'l L.J.* 3 (Sept. 13, 1993).

[38] 617 N.E.2d 990 (Mass. 1993).

[39] See Pennsylvania v. Ritchie, 107 S.Ct. 989 (1987) holding that a defendant accused of sexual offenses against his minor daughter was entitled to have a Pennsylvania Children and Youth Services file reviewed by the trial court to determine if it contained information that if known earlier would probably have altered the outcome of the trial. There is, however, no general right possessed by counsel to simply search through a state's files hoping to find helpful material.

[40] B.A. Weiner and R.M. Wettstein, *Legal Issues in Mental Health Care* 202 (1993).

Chapter 27

Liability and Negligent Release

by Fred Cohen, D.J.P.

Overview

Community outrage and grassroots movements are powerful influences on state legislatures. The following text is based on legal analysis alone, whereas political realities create powerful pressures to resist even modestly risky offenders and especially so for certain sex offenders:

A community is understandably spurred into action when it learns of a tragic occurrence in which a victim has been attacked by an offender authorities recently have released. Residents claim that authorities should have known the offender would strike again, and are outraged that he was released without the community being told. As an angry community mobilizes around a fear of sexual abuse, a vocal and motivated group of citizens comes together with the conviction to press the legislature for change.[1]

Community outrage has spurred a number of state legislatures to act, including those in Washington and New Jersey. In Washington in early 1990, a seven-year-old boy was sexually assaulted and mutilated by a previously convicted and recently released child molester. Citizens formed the "Tennis-Shoe Brigade," so named because they sent thousands of tennis shoes, representing children, to the Governor to protest the lack of protection for their children from sexual predators. In response, the Governor appointed a task force. The task force recommended legislation, which the state legislature adopted as the Community Protection Act of 1990.[2] In response to the sexual assault and murder of Megan Kanka in New Jersey, the state legislature passed "Megan's Law," a nine-bill package. Public notification are essential elements to both statutes.[3]

Civil Liability Claims May Be Brought Under State or Federal Law

At the outset, it should be established that this evolving area of civil liability is complex and confusing. Basically, there are three lines of cases to be dealt with:

1. Lawsuits brought in state court relying on state law;
2. Lawsuits brought in federal court based on the Federal Tort Claims Act; and
3. Lawsuits brought in federal court under 42 United States Code § 1983 (hereafter cited as § 1983) which involve a claimed loss of a federal constitutional right.

It is easier to give advice on how to avoid the prospect of liability than it is to give a succinct overview of the law.

Case Law Clarifies Some Trends

As confusing and as inconsistent as the decided cases are, a few things are clear:

- Lawsuits brought on behalf of crime victims challenging either the release decision, its component parts, or the manner of supervision usually do not succeed.
- State courts have been more receptive to such lawsuits than federal courts faced with civil rights actions brought under § 1983.
- Where liability is found and upheld, simple negligence generally will not suffice. Gross negligence or recklessness (i.e, conduct involving serious risk-taking and a high probability of harm) often are required as a basis for the liability of governmental agencies, supervisors, and persons associated with the challenged decision or behavior.[4]
- The longer the time lapse between release and the complaint, the dimmer the prospects for any recovery.[5] A number of jurisdictions have enacted victim compensation legislation which is on a no-fault recovery basis but quite limited in the amount recoverable.[6]

How Decision Is Reached May Have More Impact Than Decision

The manner in which a decision to release is reached is far more likely to have legal significance than the ultimate correctness of the decision.[7] In part, this is because of the vagaries of predicting future criminality. Thus, the defendant (usually a government agency) must show it met certain minimal standards of rational decisionmaking that at least reduce the risk of error, but it need not guarantee affirmative results. The reported decisions are replete with cases that did not meet this criteria. There are instances of failure to collect and keep records and relevant information (often in violation of statute), failure to make use of or properly exchange available information, failure to engage in any diagnostic efforts, failure to consult, etc.

Some Jurisdictions More Receptive to Negligent Release Claims

Still, even these negligent omissions may not create liability in a jurisdiction that is reasonably receptive to negligent release claims. For example, in *Grimm v. Arizona Board of Pardons & Parole*,[8] a wrongful death and injury suit was brought against the defendants claiming that releasing inmate Blazak was grossly negligent and reckless. The parolee had a long record which included repeated violence and drug use. During previous hospitalization, he was found to be psychotic and dangerous. While on parole, Blazak killed one person and wounded another in a bar robbery.

The trial court dismissed the suit for damages, relying on a form of judicial immunity with which it cloaked the board and its members. In an unusual ruling, the Arizona Supreme Court reversed and held that judicial immunity was not required. The court stated that:

> We hold that members of the State Board of Pardons and Paroles owe a duty to individual members of the general public when the Board decides to release on parole a prisoner with a history of violent and dangerous conduct toward his or her fellow human beings. The standard of care owed, however, is that of avoiding grossly negligent or reckless release of a highly dangerous prisoner. If the history of an applicant for parole shows a greater danger of violence to other humans, the members of the Board are under a duty to inquire further before releasing the prisoner. With medical and psychological evaluations, plus day-to-day evaluations of the prison personnel, the Board should have access to sufficient information to make an informed decision. If the entire record of the prisoner reveals violent propensities and there is absolutely no reasonable basis for a belief that he has changed, then the decision to release the prisoner would be grossly negligent or reckless. . . . [If] all the information before the Board negates the probability of lawful conduct while on parole, the Board cannot ignore such evidence. We emphasize that no liability is to be imposed when the evidence is conflicting or contradictory, that is, when reasonable minds could differ. [9]

Readers should note some of the terms emphasized above: entire record, absolutely no reasonable basis, and no liability when evidence is conflicting. From a plaintiff's point of view *Grimm*'s liberal stance is more apparent than real. Few prison-parole records are without contradictions, and it is difficult to envision a record with absolutely no reasonable basis for taking the chances inherent in virtually every parole.

Doctrine of Judicial Immunity Is Not Total

Consequently, the issue of liability exposure needs to be taken one step further. *Grimm* deals with the question of sovereign immunity (i.e., the extent to which a governmental agency or official may be sued). This ancient doctrine goes back to the early English concept that the King could do no wrong.[10] Today, neither the federal government nor any state government has full sovereign immunity.[11]

Plaintiff Must Prove Breach of Duty

A victim who gets over any of the several immunity hurdles likely to be in place must face other formidable obstacles. *Santangelo v. New York* illustrates such an obstacle.[12] That decision grapples with a rape victim's efforts to collect damages based on a claim that her assailant was negligently placed on temporary release by New York's Department of Correctional Services. The court found that prior to the decision to confer what was virtually unsupervised release, there had been only the barest form of inquiry, with no tests or evaluations administered. The problem for the victim was that while she could prove these omissions, she could not demonstrate that more adequate procedures, for example, consultation with supervisory officers or obtaining a psychiatric evaluation, would have resulted in a different decision. There was no evidence in the record of an overt propensity to commit rape and thus no trigger for a specific inquiry into that possibility. Thus, the plaintiff's case foundered not on immunity but on her inability to show a breach of duty. Liability does not result from being wrong where, as demonstrated here, reasonable minds could differ.[13]

Looking at *Grimm* (as an example of a loosening of immunity accompanied by a strict standard of liability) and *Santangelo* (as an example of the difficulty of showing an actionable breach of duty), we begin to see that legal doctrine and evidentiary requirements present serious problems for a plaintiff. Indeed, "negligent release or supervision" is a misnomer; "reckless release or supervision" seems more accurate.

Legal Perceptions Impact on Program and Policy Implementation

The reality as well as the perception of legal requirements are likely to impact on policy and its implementation. Generally, the cases involve entirely innocent plaintiffs who have been seriously injured and a defendant (the state) with a "deep pocket" and a most unsympathetic co-defendant as a "partner." As any lawyer knows, this becomes the friendly turf for negotiated settlements. At a practical level, however, the perception of liability and recovery may outdistance reality.

This should not produce debilitating caution. Given a set of problems and offenders as complex and intractable as many sex offenses and sex offenders, action and risk-taking clearly are preferable to inaction and excessive caution. The threat of a lawsuit for informed, good-faith decisions should be neither a stop sign nor a yield sign. Rather, when the risks are high—as with the release of a chronic sex offender or the undertaking of a promising treatment program with aversive measures—risk-taking should be the preferred option. In other words, the law providing a framework for action, not a barrier.

The Supreme Court's important decision in *Martinez v. California* as well as some later cases are basic to an understanding of this topic.[14] *Martinez* arose out of a murder of a 15-year-old girl by a parolee. Earlier, the parolee had been convicted of attempted rape and committed to a state hospital under California's (then) Mentally Disordered Sex Offender Law. Not being amenable to treatment, he was sentenced to 1-20 years imprisonment with a recommendation that he not be paroled. Nonetheless, he was released five years later by parole authorities who were fully informed of his history, propensities, and the likelihood he would commit another violent crime. The parole authorities failed to observe certain unspecified formalities,[15] and the release decision was characterized as negligent, reckless, wanton, and malicious. However, relying on California's statutory grant of absolute immunity to public officials, the state trial judge, in effect, dismissed the complaint.

The Supreme Court had two problems with *Martinez*:

1. Whether the Fourteenth Amendment invalidated California's immunity statute.
2. Whether California officials were immune from suit under § 1983.[16]

The plaintiffs raised the issue of the state's failure to supervise adequately, but did not pursue it.

Supreme Court's View of Immunity Statutes. The Court determined that the California immunity statute did not deprive the decedent's survivors of either due process or property.[17] Instead, it provided a defense to liability that does not diminish the constitutional rights of possible victims:

> At most, the availability of such a defense may have encouraged members of the parole board to take somewhat greater risks of recidivism in exercising their authority to release prisoners than they otherwise might. But the basic risk that repeat offenses may occur is always present in any parole system.[18]

The Court's reaffirmed the state's strong interest in fashioning its own tort law. Such interests prevail unless the state tries to transfer liability for its irrational and arbitrary actions to its citizens. The Court held that it is entirely reasonable for the state to want parole boards to make their parole release decisions without fear of liability. From our standpoint, this is the most important aspect of *Martinez* because it upholds the constitutionality of a state law granting absolute immunity to public employees making parole-type release decisions. This, of course, does not mandate, nor directly encourage, such immunity; it merely allows it. Note that the law of each particular jurisdiction governs whether these employees have absolute or qualified immunity.

Supreme Court's View of § 1983 Claims. Having upheld California's immunity law, the Court turned to whether any federal right was taken under § 1983 and, if so, whether the taking was of a constitutional dimension.[19] The Fourteenth Amendment provides assurance that life will not be taken by the state without due process of law. This victim lost her life due to the actions of a parolee some five months after release. The parolee was not an agent of the state and the parole authority was not aware that the decedent was in any special danger. Consequently, the danger was to the general public—not a particular individual—so no § 1983 liability was created.[20] However, the Court reserved decision on whether another set of facts might create liability for a life taken in connection with a parole release decision.

In *DeShaney v. Winnebago County*,[21] a claim was made that Wisconsin was liable for the injuries a father inflicted on his four-year-old son because the social service agency involved failed to intervene in a reasonable, protective fashion. The victim's representative argued that while the state may not have a general obligation to protect individuals against private violence, there is a duty to do so when a "special relationship" exists. The Court noted that some courts had read its response to this claim as implying that once a state learns that a third party poses a special danger to an identified victim, and indicates its willingness to protect the victim, that an affirmative duty of care then arises.[22] In finding no liability in *DeShaney*, the Court rather clearly said that mere notice and noncustodial interventions do not create a basis for § 1983 liability.

The Court decided two other cases affecting § 1983 suits. In *Daniels v. Williams*[23] and *Davidson v. Cannon*,[24] the Court unambiguously removed negligence from the ambit of liability under § 1983. In *Daniels*, which involved injuries suffered by a jail inmate who slipped on a pillow negligently left on some stairs by a correctional officer, the Court held that: "Where a government official's act causing injury to life, liberty, or property is merely negligent, no procedure for compensation is constitutionally required."[25]

In *Davidson*, one inmate was seriously injured by another. The injured inmate based his claim on procedural due process, arguing that state officials were negligent in failing to protect him and by denying him an opportunity to sue in state court.[26] Despite the inmate's serious injuries, his abortive efforts to obtain protection from prison officials, and the lack of a remedy in state courts, the Court reiterated its view that negligence alone will not support a § 1983 claim.

Narrowing the Basis for Federal Tort Actions Will Either Cause More State-Based Actions or Change How Cases Are Presented

Narrowing the basis for a federal tort action will either (1) encourage more damage claims to be brought in state courts, or (2) change the way federal plaintiffs plead their cause. That is, future plaintiffs may simply embellish their complaints with terms like "recklessness," "deliberate indifference," and "wanton and malicious." Indeed, in *Daniels* such an approach would not have been frivolous.

State Court Claims of "Negligent or Reckless Release"

Litigants who go into state court with a claim for damages based on a claim of "negligent or reckless release" encounter the immunity issues raised earlier in this chapter. Where suit is permitted, the plaintiff will have to prove the injury complained of resulted from the breach of a duty owed the victim. If a given federal or state jurisdiction has waived total immunity from tort liability, several legal and practice issues must be considered. Our discussion of these issues will focus on an analysis of *Payton v. United States*,[27] which was brought under the Federal Tort Claims Act (FTCA). This case is representative of similar cases brought in state courts.[28]

In *Payton*, a parolee from federal custody raped and murdered three women and hideously mutilated the bodies. The suit on Payton's behalf alleged a number of acts of negligence by federal authorities. The district court dismissed the action solely because it believed it lacked jurisdiction under the FTCA. On appeal, the central issue was whether the alleged conduct by personnel of the United States Board of Parole and the United States Bureau of Prisons comes within the FTCA or is exempt as a discretionary function under 28 U.S.C. § 2680(a).

The FTCA authorizes suits for money damages against the United States for personal injury or death caused by the tortious actions of government employees acting within the scope of their employment and under circumstances where a private person would be liable (28 U.S.C. § 1346(b)). Claims based upon the exercise by a government agency or employee of a "discretionary function or duty" are specifically exempt from jurisdiction (28 U.S.C. § 2680(a)).

Unfortunately, the term "discretionary function" is not defined in the Act, and that has been a source of judicial consternation and confusion since the FTCA was enacted. Still, we can safely say that the FTCA exempts decisions made at the policy-planning level rather than the operational level. As a practical matter, though, liability is not likely to come from a decision to initiate a program, but from operational decisions made in its implementation.

It should be noted that this exemption is not an issue of constitutional dimension. It is strictly a matter of statutory interpretation within the framework of an act that, among other things, is a waiver of sovereign immunity.[29]

The court also said that the steps in the decision-making process cannot be ignored with impunity.[30] Before turning to a specific discussion of the court's holdings in *Payton* we will briefly review its treatment of two earlier decisions on which plaintiffs relied.

In *Fair v. United States*,[31] an FTCA suit was allowed to proceed. The case involved a seriously mentally disturbed Air Force captain who killed a student nurse he had threatened earlier. Prior to the homicide, "[a] cursory psychiatric examination was made of [the officer] and he was released."[32] This author feels that the *Fair* court allowed the FTCA suit for two reasons: (1) it determined there was inadequate diagnosis, and (2) the detective agency guarding the nurse was not notified of the release as government representatives had promised.

In *Payton*, the court stated: "Thus, the [*Fair*] court did not base its decision on the 'negligent release' of the officer, but rather on his 'negligent medical treatment' which encompassed the decision to release him from the hospital."[33]

It must be stressed that the *Payton* decision unequivocally characterizes only parole release as a discretionary decision exempted from FTCA coverage. If the release decision is based on prior negligent medical treatment, however, then the lack of adequate care may not be discretionary and liability is possible.

The other decision on which the *Payton* plaintiffs relied is *Underwood v. United States*,[34] which involved a mentally disturbed airman who killed his wife with a military weapon after being released from hospitalization. *Underwood* seems to be utilized properly in *Payton* in that the key liability factor was the initial physician's failure to provide his replacement with vital information concerning the airman's mental state. Presumably, the replacement might have made a circumspect decision if the information was available.

Thus, *Fair* and *Underwood* may be viewed as a combination of failure to adequately diagnose, failure to warn as promised (which is not based on a judicially imposed duty to warn third parties),[35] and failure to share diagnostic material. These decisional steps (or omissions) are treated as nondiscretionary and thus within the FTCA, whereas the actual release decision is treated as discretionary and exempt.

It may be easier to understand the difference between a discretionary act that is exempt from liability and a nondiscretionary (or "ministerial") act that is subject to liability if we turn to the specific claims and findings in *Payton*.

In the first count of the complaint, the United States was alleged to be liable for Payton's death because the parole board negligently released a person known to be a dangerous psychotic. The court disagreed, stating that:

> [I]f the initial request for parole, whether submitted by the prison bureaucracy or by the prisoner himself, shows a reasonable probability that the prisoner is capable of living in society without violating the laws or endangering the public welfare, then the parole board may, in its discretion, release the prisoner on parole. The decision to release the prisoner on parole must necessarily entail an evaluation by the parole board of the prisoner's records. Thus, the parole board's final decision that the prisoner is worthy to live in society as a free person is not different from the decision to release him on parole. The statute clearly describes this as a discretionary function.[36]

The court rejected the plaintiff's liability claims, which were based on a failure to supervise or to provide continued care and failure to acquire certain records showing the parolee to be homicidal. These activities, along with the release decision itself, were viewed as discretionary.

However, the court did accept claims based on a failure of the Bureau of Prisons to supply the board with records showing the parolee's dangerousness (18 U.S.C. § 4208(c)), failure to examine and report on the inmate so that a decision could be made by the Attorney General on whether to seek hospitalization for the remainder of his prison term (18 U.S.C. § 4241), and, finally, the negligent rendering of psychiatric care while the parolee was in prison. Two of these counts were based on explicit and mandatory statutory language; the third, negligent care, was based on the general proposition that while psychiatric care may not always be required for inmates, once it is undertaken it cannot be done negligently.

Drawing a Distinction Between the Decision and the Steps in the Decision Process

The upshot of a case like *Payton*, as well as its ancestors and progeny, is the judicial creation of very fine distinctions between the steps in a decision process and the decision itself. As noted earlier, the key is adhering to the legally required steps in the decision-making process as well as to one's professional norms. Clinicians do not have to be correct, but they do have to acquire and share relevant information, faithfully keep promises about warnings, and provide care in accordance with professional norms.[37] As the court stated in *Lipari v. Sears, Roebuck & Co.*:

> It may be difficult for medical professionals to predict whether a particular mental patient may pose a danger to himself or others. This factor alone, however, does not justify banning recovery in all situations. The standard of care for health professionals adequately takes into account the difficult nature of the problems facing psychotherapists. . . . Under this standard a therapist who uses the proper psychiatric procedures is not negligent even if his diagnosis may have been incorrect.[38]

Duty to Warn Faces Special Problems

In *Fair*, a failure to warn as promised formed a significant part of the court's rationale in creating a basis for liability. It was suggested that a duty to warn created by a nonmandatory promise to do so is distinguishable from the judicially created duty to warn identifiable victims.[39] *Thompson v. County of Alameda*[40] is a highly controversial decision in this area. The case involved the release of a violent youth to his mother. The county knew of the youth's violent propensities regarding children and that the youth had indicated that if he was released he would kill an unspecified youngster in his neighborhood. Within 24 hours of release, the youth assaulted and murdered the plaintiff's son. A majority of the California Supreme Court—a court then highly favorable to plaintiffs—first disposed of the easier points: as a parole decision, the release is wholly immunized under California law, and selection of a proper custodian for a minor is inherently a discretionary decision and is also exempt from liability.[41]

The most troublesome aspect of the case is a claim of liability based on the failure to warn local police and neighborhood parents. The court then drew a highly debatable conclusion. It determined that the county had no special relationship with the particular plaintiffs nor did the defendant place this particular victim into a foreseeably dangerous situation. The court contrasted *Tarasoff*,[42] which was described as involving a foreseeable victim (versus the general "neighborhood children") and a special relationship (the therapist-patient relationship extending also to known third parties).[43]

The court declined to impose liability for failure to warn police, neighbors, the mother of the assailant, or other children. Perhaps the most crucial points were the absence of specific threats to specific victims and a sense of futility in judicially calling for some sort of generalized neighborhood alarm.[44] Justice Tobriner filed a vigorous dissent based on *Tarasoff* principles and a belief that the failure to warn the custodian-mother that her son had threatened to kill a neighborhood child could be viewed as the proximate cause of the death.[45]

Special Relationships; Negligent Supervision

Using *Thompson* as a point of departure, we will now turn to a phenomenon that puts an even greater focus on liability. Consider the following two scenarios. First, suppose authorities place a youth with homicidal tendencies and a background of violence and cruelty into a foster mother's home and fail to inform the woman of these facts.[46] Next, assume that a probationer with a history of sexual abuse of children is allowed to rent a room with young children and participate in a work release program in proximity to young children, without notice to the respective parents.[47]

Liability has—and seemingly should have—attached in both situations. The first situation involved the creation of a special relationship between the ward and the foster parent, and a clear duty to warn of a foreseeable peril not readily discoverable by those at risk. The second situation may be characterized as negligent supervision with the possible addition of liability which flows from the violation of judicially imposed probation conditions which prohibited contact with children under the age of 15.

Guidelines for Clinicians and Others Who Work with Sex Offenders

The need to know and follow legally mandated steps in the decision-making process is critical. Adherence to all required information gathering-studying-sharing steps will go a long way toward insulating clinicians and others who work with sex offenders from liability if a decision turns out to be erroneous or if there is misplaced trust.

In addition, the courts will be influenced by the clinician's ability to control an inmate or a patient. In *Semler v. Psychiatric Institute*,[48] there was contravention of a court order regarding the issuance of release passes and the placement of a patient on an outpatient basis without prior judicial approval. The hospital was found to have tort liability for a death caused by the patient based on a special relationship between the hospital and the patient and the consequent duty of the hospital to maintain custody of the patient until there was a judicial order.

This type of negligence is often referred to as "negligence per se"; that is, the violation of the court's orders obviates the need to prove that release was otherwise improper. Perhaps of more interest is the fact that "the degree and manner of a therapist's control over a patient is often a key factor in negligent release cases."[49]

In a prison setting, clinical and program staff have little to do with the actual release of an inmate. It is more likely that their role will involve providing diagnosis and treatment along with release or custody recommendations. Within the facility itself, clinical and program staff are likely to play key roles in the level and nature of the confinement ordered for an inmate. As discussed earlier, a basis for liability may be found where a law mandates a report and it is not developed, or where important diagnostic material exists and is not shared as legally mandated.

Where release of a sex offender is anticipated and promises have been made concerning notification, it is imperative that those promises be kept. If, for example, a child molester is released and placed in proximity to young people, or if a rapist is offered a job in a women's dormitory, that is recklessness of the most culpable sort and a certain invitation to liability.

Generally, the duty to warn will not be confronted in the context of a prison program. If an inmate is currently making specific threats about an identifiable victim in the community, it is unlikely that any sort of discretionary release would occur.[50] However, there may be an interesting question on a possible duty to seek civil commitment where an inmate is about to "max out" and staff believes that person remains dangerous.[51]

Footnotes

[1] Note, "A Framework for Post-Sentence Sex Offender Legislation: Perspectives on Prevention, Registration, and the Public's 'Right' to Know," 48 *Vand. L. Rev.* 219, 228 (1995).

[2] Id.

[3] Ibid., at 229.

[4] R.V. del Carmen, *Potential Liabilities of Probation and Parole Officers* 89 (National Institute of Corrections, Rev'd ed., 1985) (hereinafter referred to as "Potential Liabilities").

The statement in the text is general. For example, the State of Washington may be unique in its liability exposure and consequent frequent settlements since the decision in Petersen v. State, 100 Wash. 2d 421, 429, 671 P.2d 230 (1938). Petersen allowed a motorist, who was injured by a pot-smoking former state hospital patient, to sue successfully, based on the state's duty to take reasonable precautions to protect anyone who might be endangered by the patient's drug-related mental problems. The state's duty included seeking an additional commitment.

[5] See e.g., Leverett v. State, 399 N.E.2d. 106 (Ohio Ct. App. 1978) (injury caused within three months of an alleged negligent release from a state hospital was a question for the jury whereas an earlier decision was reaffirmed holding that a two-year gap was too long as a matter of law).

[6] N.Y. Exec. Law § 631 (McKinney 1982 and Supp. 1995), which provides for awards to victims of crime in the amount of out-of-pocket expenses including indebtedness incurred as a result of the crime for medical or other services, loss of earnings not to exceed $20,000, burial expenses not to exceed $2,000, and the cost of repair or replacement or property which was lost, damaged, or destroyed in the crime. Awards are made only if the board finds that financial difficulty will result if the award is denied.

[7] See generally, Center for Studies of Crime and Delinquency (U.S.), *Dangerous Behavior: A Problem in Law and Mental Health* (Calvin Frederick, ed., 1973).

[8] 564 P.2d 1227 (Ariz. 1977).

[9] 564 P.2d at 1234. See also Ryan v. Arizona, 656 P.2d 597 (Ariz. 1982) (a suit to recover damages for injuries inflicted by a youth who escaped from custody and shot the plaintiff; court held that the state will be subject to the same tort law as private citizens with liability preferred to immunity).

[10] See C.D. Robinson, *Legal Rights, Duties, and Liabilities of Criminal Justice Personnel: History and Analysis*, Ch. 5 (1984).

[11] Potential Liabilities, note 1 supra, at p. 33.

[12] 426 N.Y.S.2d 931 (N.Y. Ct. Cl. 1980).

[13] Ibid., at 935.

[14] 444 U.S. 277 (1980).

[15] Ibid., at 556.

[16] The California courts accepted jurisdiction of the federal claim. Although it is not a common practice to bring this federal claim into state court, the court raised no objection to it although it is plain that the § 1983 claim is governed by federal law. See 44 U.S., at 282-283, ns. 6-7.

[17] Ibid., at 281.

[18] Ibid. Note that the quoted text is consistent with the author's earlier caution against excessive caution.

[19] Ibid., at 283.

[20] Ibid., at 285.

[21] 489 U.S. 189 (1989).

[22] 489 U.S. at 197-198, n. 4 (1989).

[23] 474 U.S. 327 (1986).

[24] 474 U.S. 344 (1986).

[25] 474 U.S. at 333.

[26] A New Jersey statute exempted public entities and employees from liability for injuries inflicted on one prisoner by another.

[27] 679 F.2d 475 (5th Cir. 1982), on rehearing en banc; reviewing and affirming in part, 636 F.2d 132 (5th Cir. 1981).

[28] See e.g., Lloyd v. State, 251 N.W.2d 551 (Iowa 1977).

[29] See Dalehite v. United States, 346 U.S. 15 (1953) (first important interpretation of the FTCA by the Supreme Court).

[30] 679 F.2d at 481.

[31] 234 F.2d 288 (5th Cir. 1966).

[32] Ibid., at 290.

[33] 679 F.2d, at 481. This author finds virtually no support for this reading of *Fair*, although for these purposes this is not a debate that needs to be furthered.

[34] 356 F.2d 92 (5th Cir. 1966).

[35] That is, this is not kin to Tarasoff v. Board of Regents, 551 P.2d 334 (Cal. 1976), which turned on a clinician's duty to warn identifiable third parties.

[36] 679 F.2d at 480. In Greenholtz v. Inmates of Nebraska Penal & Correctional Complex, 442 U.S. 1 (1979), the Court determined that inmates had no federal constitutional liberty interest in the parole decision for purposes of obtaining even rudimentary procedural due process. If, however, a particular state used mandatory language in its parole statute, such as "shall release...unless," then a state-created liberty interest is involved and minimal due process is mandated. Most jurisdictions escape due process obligations and minimize their liability exposure by using language similar to that in the federal statute.

[37] The latter statement should not be confused with the less demanding "deliberate indifference" standard that applies when the cruel and unusual punishment provision of the Eighth Amendment is invoked as the constitutional norm in a prison treatment situation. For example, in Sellers v. Thompson, 452 So.2d 460 (Ala. 1980), a suit was brought against the state parole board for releasing a parolee without a psychiatric report. The Alabama law on point used apparently mandatory language—"shall obtain"—concerning the missing report but the Alabama Supreme Court disagreed. The court decided that the legislature would not have intended that result and it read *Payton* as a failure to provide existing records vis a vis failure (as here) to develop one initially.

[38] 497 F. Supp. 185, 192 (D. Neb. 1980).

[39] See Tarasoff v. The Regents of the University of California, 529 P.2d 553 (1974), discussed generally in Chapter 26, infra. See also Stone, "The Tarasoff Decisions: Suing Psychotherapists to Safeguard Society," 90 *Harv. L. Rev.* 358 (1976).

[40] 614 P.2d 728 (Cal. 1980). Given the existence of absolute immunity by the state, the county became a more accessible defendant.

[41] Ibid., at 731. See also Petersen v. State, 671 P.2d 230 (1983).

[42] Note 35 supra.

[43] See Fleming & Maxiou, "The Patient or His Victim: The Therapist's Dilemma," 62 *Calif. L. Rev.* 1025, 1030-31 (1974), predating *Tarasoff* and arguing that there was even then enough authority to conclude that by entering into a doctor-patient relationship, a therapist is sufficiently involved to assume responsibility for the patient and also for the safety of any third party known to be threatened by the patient. The authors extruded this position from the then firmer base of control of dangerous persons in actual detention.

[44] See the discussion at Then Cal. Penal Code, § 290 required that certain sex offenders notify the police of their presence in the community. This section became inoperative after January 1, 1988, although there is a new duty on Youth Authority wards to register.

[45]614 P.2d, at 738-742 (Tobriner, J., dissenting).

[46]Johnson v. State, 947 P.2d 352 (Cal. 1968).

[47]Aceredo v. Pim County Adult Probation Dept., 690 P.2d 38 (1984). See Eiseman v. New York, 70 N.Y.2d. 175, 511 N.E.2d 1128, 518 N.Y.2d. 608 (1987), which concerned the duty of the state and a college when an ex-felon who had a history of drug abuse and criminal conduct was conditionally released from prison and accepted into a college program raped and murdered a fellow student. While the case has many interesting facets, of particular interest here is the conceded failure of a prison physician to accurately complete the prisoner's medical history as an aspect of the college's admission requirements. If this had been done, the prisoner-applicant's history of drug abuse and suicide attempts would have been disclosed. The court determined that the doctor's duty was to the applicant and other persons who might reasonably rely on the doctor for this service to his patient. There was no duty to the unknown students who would not know of this material in any event. The medical data was not part of the college admission criteria and was used for other post-admission purposes. Thus, there was no breach of duty to the college.

[48]538 F.2d 121 (4th Cir.), cert. denied. 429 U.S. 827 (1976). See Aceredo v. Pim County Adult Probation Dept., note 47 supra, for a similar disregard of judicial orders. There may be a problem of previously made threats or ambiguous threats. The more ancient or nonspecific the threat, however, the less basis there is for liability.

[49]Note, "Psychiatrists' Liability to Third Parties for Harmful Acts Committed by Dangerous Patients," 64 N. Car. L. Rev. 1534, 1538 (1986) analyzing Pangburn v. Saad, 326 S.E.2d 365 (N.C. App. 1985)(sustaining liability for wrongful release of a patient).

[50]A different problem exists if the threats are directed at a fellow inmate.

[51]No such case has been uncovered. For more detailed coverage of the legal issues discussed in this section, readers are advised to consult the following American Law Report Annotations wherein all reported cases within the annotation title are collected, analyzed, and updated:

1. Immunity of Public Officer from Liability for Injuries Caused by Negligently Released Individual, 5 A.L.R. 4th 773.

2. Liability of Governmental Officer or Entity for Failure to Warn or Notify of Release of Potentially Dangerous Individual from Custody, 12 A.L.R. 4th 723.

3. Governmental Tort Liability for Injuries Caused by Negligently Released Individual, 6 A.L.R. 4th 1155.

4. Probation Officers' Liability for Negligent Supervision of Probationer, 44 A.L.R. 4th 638.

Chapter 28

Duty to Protect

by Fred Cohen, D.J.P.

Overview

This chapter explores the issue of the duty to protect. It is important to distinguish the duty to protect from the duty to treat. Certain sex offenders by virtue of their offense and certain inmates virtue of their sexual preference may be said to represent high-risk categories. Prison officials should be alert to their security needs and make available safe environments. In many prisons, sex offenders are at risk from the general population due to the nature of their crime. Prison authorities have the duty to provide protection to offenders who request it and to mandate it when the authorities believe that a threat exists for a specific individual. Confidentiality must be maintained, particularly regarding sex offender treatment.

No Exemption from Incarceration on Ground of Potential for Personal Harm

It is well accepted that prison inmates have a constitutional right to be protected from the constant threat of violence and from physical assault by other inmates.[1] Nevertheless, the fact that a person convicted of crime may also be a member of a group that is particularly at risk in prison generally will not exempt such person from a prison sentence. One technique that has been used with success in some prison systems involves placing sex offenders in a closely observed dormitory setting during initial reception and classification. This allows prison officials to determine how the inmate behaves, whether he is at risk and, if so, how the risk is handled, and it is a good check on who knows what about the inmate and the offense.

In a New York case, two defendants argued that they should be exempt from incarceration because of their homosexual orientation and physical appearance.[2] They claimed they would be subject to physical and sexual abuse in prison. The court could find no cases exempting homosexuals from confinement:

> In short, there is no support in the law for defendants' contentions that an
> increased possibility of homosexual rape in prison constitutionally prohibits

incarceration. Even granting that the defendants here may be at a relative disadvantage because of their size, inexperience, youth, or sexual preference, none of these factors entitles them to such special consideration from the court. Many prisoners are younger or in worse physical condition.[3]

In a recent California case, a trial judge indicated that he was granting probation, in lieu of an otherwise likely prison term, partly because the defendant was "blonde and slender, which would make him the target of sexual abuse in a state prison." However, the state successfully sought a writ of mandate arguing that the trial judge rendered an impermissible disposition.[4] The reviewing court found that neither a showing of impermissible risk to the defendant nor that the Department of Corrections could not afford him reasonable protection.

These cases indicate that one's sexual orientation or particular crime of conviction is unlikely to be a bar to imprisonment. Both factors, however, should alert authorities to the need for special protection during confinement.

In *Zatler v. Wainwright,* a former inmate brought a civil rights action against Florida prison officials based on his having been forcibly raped by inmates on eight occasions at six different institutions.[5] As a young, white, slightly built homosexual, Zatler claimed he was obviously at risk and that inadequate protection was afforded him. Zatler's suit was not successful because he could not show that the alleged failures to adopt adequate policies for inmate protection were a breach of duty and evidenced a reckless disregard or deliberate indifference to the inmate's constitutional rights. Defendant Wainwright, however, was able to show a general policy that allowed inmates who needed protection to request it and be placed in protective custody. In addition, he showed that Zatler was placed in such custody every time he asked and was released only at his own request. The court found Wainwright not guilty of a reckless disregard of Zatler's right to be free of violence.

Judge Clark's dissenting opinion accepted Zatler's argument that prison officials discouraged such requests by maintaining harsh conditions in protective confinement. Zatler lost his case, in part, because he did not claim that the conditions themselves constituted cruel and unusual punishment.

Sex Offenders Require Special Treatment

Prison officials must be alert to sex offenders who enter the system. Special protective environments or transitional placements should be readily available for these "at-risk" inmates. Protective custody may be insisted upon when prison officials independently determine that an individual is in imminent danger of attack. In jurisdictions where protective custody space is at a premium, it is imperative that additional "safe space" be created or that an at-risk inmate be allowed to lock-in his cell as a temporary measure.

Obviously, prison officials should not act in a way to create or heighten the risk for a sex offender. In one recent case, a prison counselor apparently posted a list of sex offenders in connection with a treatment program.[6] It should have been clear that the list would get around the prison. The plaintiff was in protective custody.

Although the federal judge in this case declined to take further action, he cautioned prison officials about their duty to safeguard an inmate's personal safety.

Prison officials should be aware of the risk to certain sex offenders, and must be especially cautious about safeguarding information regarding their treatment. The affected inmates are not likely to give themselves away, so cautionary measures need to be directed at others. Many prisons now divide sex offender programs into "education" and "treatment." While the education program is generally designed as a getaway to "real" treatment and often is limited to "deniers," some inmates find it easier to enroll in a class and be designated a student than to be in treatment and be designated a client or a patient. The bottom line here is that where treatment programs exist, the programs should be offered in such a way that other inmates will not know of the nature of the group or individual treatment activity.

"Protection" Versus "Treatment"

This chapter only looks at an inmate's claim to protection due to sexual orientation or conviction on a sex offense. The special protection prisons owe at-risk inmates does not include treatment. Treatment is a type of position intervention aimed at change or symptom relief, it is not merely a form of quarantine.

Footnotes

[1] See Zatler v. Wainwright, 802 F.2d 397 (11th Cir. 1986) and cases cited therein.

[2] People v. Fellman, 405 N.Y.S.2d 210 (N.Y. Sup. Ct. 1978).

[3] Ibid., at 405 N.Y.S.2d at 212.

[4] People v. Superior Court, 230 Cal. Rptr. 890 (1986). The trial judge also indicated that he relied on a lack of a substantial prior record and the fact that the defendant's distinctive surname is the same as a local district attorney with a hard-liner reputation.

[5] Note 1 supra at 398. Except for state immunity issues, the same claim could be brought as a tort with a lower negligence burden.

[6] Hollie v. Manville, No. 485-376 (S.D. Ga., May 2, 1986).

Chapter 29

Therapeutic Uses of Sexually Explicit Material and the Plethysmograph

by Fred Cohen, D.J.P.

Overview

This chapter explores the use of sexually explicit materials in the behavioral treatment of sex offenders. The courts have ruled that such material is not obscene when used by professionals in a recognized treatment program. However, since these materials were produced as pornography involving real victims who, in the case of children, were being sexually exploited, do these victims have the right to avoid further invasion of their privacy by insisting that these materials be destroyed when they are no longer needed by the courts? Furthermore, should this be done routinely, even when the victim is never identified? These questions have never been raised in the courts. Computer-created composite pictures can now be produced. In this author's opinion, audiotapes may be more effective and avoid the issue entirely.

Legal Issues Concerning the Use of Sexually Explicit Photographs of Young Persons

Clinicians and others involved with certain aversive treatment techniques have raised two separate yet interrelated questions concerning the use of sexually explicit photographs of young persons. The first question is whether the users might be guilty of criminal conduct in the possession and "exhibition" of putatively obscene material. The second and more difficult question relates to whether the subjects in the photographs might suffer legally cognizable harm and possibly collect monetary damages for the unauthorized use of the photographs in question.

Obtaining the Material. Before turning to these two questions, let's briefly and in oversimplified fashion relate how such materials are often obtained and used. Law enforcement agencies frequently confiscate photographs depicting sexual activity by young persons. While such material quite often is destroyed when it has outlived its evidentiary life, law enforcement agencies may make this material available to persons involved in legitimate sex offender treatment programs. Some experts insist that it is highly desirable to use the most sexually explicit material available. The material may be used in classification/diagnosis, treatment, and/or evaluation of treatment.

For example, if the treatment program focuses on homosexual pedophiles, then the offender may be shown a variety of sexually explicit photographs of young males.[1] When the offender-subject's sexual arousal reaches a given point, a negative stimulus, for example, a putrid smell, will be applied to create negative reinforcement of the fantasy and ultimately, one hopes, eliminate the behavior sought to be changed.

Persons who conduct these behavior modification programs unanimously agree that the arousal factor is compromised if the photographs are obviously touched-up to hide the identity of the youth. However, newer computer techniques allow photographs to be altered so perfectly that composites can be created with no predictable loss of the power to arouse the offender.[2] Other experts argue that accurate determination of a person's sexual preference (age and gender) can be done without use of erotica or sexually explicit photographs. For example, nude photographs of children raised in a nudist environment, obtained with parental consent, are said to be effective.[3] Ultimately, these approaches may be the best solution to the second question, but the legal issues involved must be reviewed before any solutions are proposed.

Are Users Guilty of Criminal Conduct in the Possession and Exhibition of the Material? Sexually explicit material that may otherwise be obscene and which is distributed to scholars and educators for use in bona fide treatment programs should not be subject to criminal prosecution. Practically speaking, it is highly unlikely that material obtained from a local law enforcement agency is later going to be the subject of criminal prosecution. This would be especially true if the user informed the local prosecutor about how the material will be used.[4]

There simply can be no serious question of commercial exploitation where the programs involved represent a decent chance for altering deviant behavior. Then any conceivable state interest in prosecuting is outweighed by the value of the programs.[5]

A different set of considerations arises where nude pictures of children are used with parental consent and with a comprehensive set of contractual limitations as to therapeutic or educational uses. A debate was touched off in late 1993 as to the Justice Department's prosecutorial position on child pornography. The defendant was charged with violating federal law prohibiting the distribution or possession of tapes or pictures of minors involved in sexually explicit conduct (i.e., "lascivious exhibition of the genital or pubic area"). The material involved was a videotape in which the camera zoomed in on the genital areas of young girls who were fully clothed. The Justice Department first took the position that possession of this tape could not be prosecuted because the girls were fully clothed and did not act lasciviously. However, a political firestorm ensued and federal officials raced for cover.[6]

This issue involves the question of interpreting and applying special laws to child pornography, laws which need not reach the level of the obscene to be constitutionally valid. In our discussion, the use of nude photographs simply bears no relationship to pornography or obscenity, particularly since sexually provocative positions or poses need not be required.[7]

Sexual Performance. In *New York v. Ferber*, the Supreme Court upheld a New York law criminalizing the use of children in a sexual performance.[8] The term "sexual performance" includes films and is not limited to obscene material. In the face of a strong First Amendment challenge, the Court reasoned that a state's interest in safeguarding minors is compelling:

> The value of permitting live performances and photographic reproductions of children engaged in lewd sexual conduct is exceedingly modest if not de minimis. We consider it unlikely that visual depictions of children performing sexual acts or lewdly exhibiting genitals would often constitute an important and necessary part of a literary performance or scientific or educational work.[9]

Justice O'Connor, concurring, wrote to emphasize that the Court did not hold that New York (and the 20 or so states with similar laws) must except material with serious literary, scientific, or education value from the statute.[10] The Justice also wrote that clinical pictures of adolescent sexuality might not involve the type of exploitive abuse targeted by the New York law.[11]

Impact of Public Perception. Let's assume the worse case analysis where some irate citizen learns of the arrangement and publicly denounces such a program. The courts began dealing with this issue as early as 1957. In *United States v. 31 Photographs*,[12] the government attempted to block the importation of obscene material to be used for scholarly purposes by the Kinsey Institute. The federal court was able to avoid the First Amendment constitutional question by finding that, where otherwise obscene material is imported for the sole use of qualified staff or scholars and held under secu-rity conditions, then there is lacking in the material an appeal to prurient interest, a sine qua non for a finding of obscenity.[13]

In effect, the court determined that material is variably obscene, and when other-wise obscene material is used for legitimate scholarly or educational purposes, it loses its obscene quality while retaining its sexual explicitness.

A case that is closer to the problem at issue arose in California in 1962. *People v. Marler*[14] involved the use of admittedly obscene films for experimental treatment purposes on hospitalized sex offenders. On appeal, the case presented somewhat sub-tle legal questions concerning the trial judge's instructions. The appellate court, how-ever, pointed out that admittedly obscene material may lawfully be distributed, in good faith, when (1) it is to be used exclusively within a professional group pursuing legitimate professional purposes, (2) the material is germane to those purposes, and (3) it is not likely to fall into the hands of others. Clearly, a bona fide sex offender treatment program, created and staffed by professional persons who are pursuing a generally recognized form of treatment, meets these criteria.

The only remote caveat to this position is when the photographs used to create arousal also involve the community's protective interests concerning the young. The photographs of concern are of value only to the extent that, in a controlled situation, the offender experiences pleasure followed by something painful or disgusting. This is somewhat different than a historical study of erotica or the depiction of masturba-tory techniques in a medical textbook. The basic rationale, however, of exempting from criminal punishment the legitimate and controlled use of sexually explicit mate-rial remains intact.

Use of Materials May Be Deemed an Invasion of Privacy

The second question posed at the beginning of this chapter—possible violation of as-yet-undefined rights of unconsenting juveniles depicted in such materials—is more difficult to assess because the issues are more tentative and the conclusions more speculative. We are assuming that the materials we are referring to do not have parental consent or any of the agreed upon contractual limitations noted for the nude pho-tographs discussed earlier.

No precise civil or criminal case on point has been uncovered. In addition, experts we sought guidance from, including the legal advisor for the National Institutes of Health, thought the question was novel.[15] It is not clear whether a law enforcement agency must destroy pornographic or obscene pictures that have been confiscated.[16] If we assume that there are no statutory requirements that the police destroy such photographs (and therefore do not establish a reference point for the creation of a tort of behalf of the subject), we must look to the tort of invasion of privacy for an answer.

Invasion of Privacy Statutes Do Not Protect Photographs of Juveniles Used in Bona Fide Treatment Programs. The relatively new tort of invasion of privacy, first enunciated in 1890, is recognized in almost every U.S. jurisdiction that has considered it.[17] Comment A to § 651A of the Restatement (Second) of Torts, sets forth four gen-eral principles that focus on the revelation of private matters (including photographs) to the public. These rules do not seem to apply to the use of photographs in a bona fide treatment program. However, Comment C to the same section indicates that "nothing in this Chapter is intended to exclude the possibility of future developments in the tort law of privacy."

State Statutes Protect Only Unauthorized Commercial Use of Name, Portrait, or Photograph. Most states have codified the right to privacy.[18] However, these statutes provide protection only in instances where a person's name, portrait, or picture is used without consent for advertising or for trade purposes.[19] Consequently, they do not provide relief for the juveniles in the photographs under this analysis simply because there is no publication of their photograph in an advertising or commercial sense.

Return of Photographs and Fingerprints to Acquitted Criminal Defendants. Many states require that photographs and fingerprints be returned to an accused person if criminal actions end in their favor.[20] There appears to be no analogous requirement to provide for the destruction of obscene materials depicting juveniles that were confiscated by police.[21] If there were, this could create a type of privacy interest for those pictured in the photographs.

Juveniles Depicted as Victims of Sex Crimes

Looking at the problem from another angle, if one views the minors depicted in the photographs as victims of a sex crime, they may well be covered under the statutory provisions of some states which seek to protect the privacy of sex crime victims. We will use New York law to illustrate this issue.[22] New York's penal law describes the sexual conduct involved in child pornography.[23] Therefore, it may be said that these minors, if such acts are involved in the photographs, are the victims of a sex offense in New York and that these identifying photographs are private and should not be disclosed to anyone unless such action satisfies certain statutory elements not relevant here. Clearly, there is no issue of the subject having consented to the photographs and therefore somehow waiving future objections. Even if the youth is old enough to give valid consent, that would not be a defense to the offense (and would not be valid either as a civil waiver).

Unfortunately, a circuitous method of analysis must be utilized in order to arrive at any present statutory protection. For example, under New York Civil Rights Law, § 50-b, the identity of any sex offense victim under the age of 18 is kept confidential unless otherwise specified by the statute. The designated sex offenses are described in Article 130 of the New York Penal Law and include, among others, sodomy. Obscenity is defined in Penal Law § 235.00. It states in § 235.00(1)(b): "...any material or performance is obscene if it depicts or describes in a patently offensive manner, actual or simulated: sexual intercourse, sodomy, sexual beastiality, masturbation, sadism, masochism, excretion or lewd exhibitions of the genitals. ..." Furthermore, § 235.00(7) states that sodomy means any of the types of sexual conduct defined in Penal Law § 130.00, under which sodomy is defined as a sex offense. Therefore, it may be concluded that a child photographed while engaging in sodomy, actual or simulated, is a victim of a sex offense under Penal Law § 130.00, and such a photograph identifying that child is warranted protection under Civil Rights Law, § 50-b.

If one were to consider the applicability of the Federal Civil Rights Act, 42 U.S.C. § 1983.25, the requisite state action would be present in the manner in which the photographs were obtained and most certainly in their use in state facilities by state employees. The question, however, for any prospective litigant would be the establishment of the deprivation of "rights, privileges, or immunities secured by the Constitution and laws of the United States."[24]

Supreme Court's View of Privacy Issue. Although the U.S. Supreme Court has recognized a constitutional right to privacy, that right has been narrowly confined to the protection of a woman's right to choose between pregnancy and abortion.[25] Indeed, the Court has clearly signaled its reluctance to expand constitutional notions of privacy.[26]

Professional Ethics and Privacy Issues. Aside from possible legal sources of protection of privacy or the vindication of invasions thereof, the ethical codes of the medical and psychological professions indicate that the privacy of these children should be protected.[27] Indeed, some therapists have strong religious or moral objections to the use of such photographs. For them, the prospect of litigation is not the issue.

For those without such objections, we are led to conclude that there is no clear answer to the question. Obtaining a written release hardly seems feasible since the users will rarely, if ever, know the subject's identity. Nevertheless, the likelihood is slight that a parent or child will actually learn of the use, or in any direct way be harmed by such use. One problem was raised at the NIC special issue seminars. Suppose an offender in a treatment program is released and either stalks or stumbles upon a youngster whose picture was used in treatment and suppose further that the offender sexually molests the youngster. Could it be said that the use of the picture caused the new offense? Is the state liable if only simple negligence is made out? A successful lawsuit on these facts would be improbable but not impossible.

Returning to a theme raised earlier, the simplest, most economic solution protective of the youngsters and still consonant with treatment needs is either to alter the photographs or use the pictures described by Bill Farrall as diagnostically or therapeutically effective. Computers can scan original photographs, translate the images into a pattern of binary numbers, and then produce precisely the composite picture desired by the treatment specialists. Apparently, the majority of images seen in advertising today are not "real." They are computer composites which are completely undetectable as such. The author urges the investigation and adoption of this technique instead of running the risk, however slight, of causing further injury to a young person who already has been victimized.

The Plethysmograph

The penile plethysmograph is an individually applied physiological test that measures to flow of blood to and from the genital area. Use of this device to measure penile arousal has evolved to the point where it is one of the most important tests in the assessment, treatment, and treatment evaluation of sex offenders.[28] While it is by no means the only possible satisfactory technique for measuring sexual arousal (e.g., EEG and pupillary dilation have some validity) it is the more popular and among the most intrusive.

The plethysmograph is a device that involves placing a gauge on the penis which, in turn, measures change in penile circumference in response to certain visual and auditory erotic stimuli. A baseline is first established and calibration adjusted to establish degrees of tumescence.[29]

> Barker and Howell, in their summary of the research on the plethysmograph state: Misuse of the plethysmograph is a major concern. Using [it] to predict innocence, guilt, or likelihood of reoffending is beyond the scope of the test's validity... [P]redicting who is at risk to commit a sexual crime and who is likely to recidivate cannot be predicted with even a moderate level of confidence.[30]

Use of Plethysmograph as Condition of Employment. A federal court recently described the device and the procedure for its use as "a highly intrusive physical test of sexual arousal."[31] This case concerned a police officer who, along with about 20 other persons, had been charged by two children with sexual abuse. The officer was suspended from his job. No criminal charges were brought against the officer, but he was required to submit to plethysmograph testing as a condition of reemployment. When the officer refused, the local prosecutor stated that he would not prosecute any cases where this officer made the arrest. Ultimately, the officer sued prosecution and executive officials. Summary judgment was entered for the defendants.

The reviewing court found that given the seriousness of the allegations of sexual misconduct, the officer had no protected privacy interest in the material sought to be developed by the psychological examination, including the plethysmograph.[32] The issue then became one of technique: given the right of access to such information (sexual profile), are the means to be employed here too intrusive? In overturning the summary judgment and remanding the case for trial, the court stated that:

> A reasonable finder of fact could conclude that requiring the plethysmograph involves a substantive due process violation. The procedure, from all that appears, is hardly routine. One does not have to cultivate particularly delicate sensibilities to believe degrading the process of having a strain gauge strapped to an individual's genitals while sexually explicit pictures are displayed in an effort to determine his sexual arousal patterns. The procedure involves bodily manipulation of the most intimate sort. There has been no showing regarding the procedure's reliability and, in light of other psychological evaluative tools available, there has been no demonstration that other less intrusive means of obtaining the relevant information are not sufficient.[33]

Thus, the court found that there may indeed be an invasion of protected privacy given the means employed. Even more interesting is a challenge to produce evidence of reliability and that less drastic means ought not to be employed.

In this instance, the device would not be used as a part of a treatment program. Its use would be for assessment and, perhaps, a judgment on guilt as to the earlier charges and a prediction of future criminality.

Use of Plethysmograph as Condition of Parole. In another recent decision, a federal district court upheld a requirement that a convicted child molester submit to penile plethysmograph evaluation as a condition of his parole.[34] The Seventh Circuit's test to determine whether a challenged probation or parole condition violates the Fourth Amendment was whether there was a reasonable relationship between the condition and the purposes of the supervised release.[35]

The court identified rehabilitation and public safety as the relevant governmental purposes. Given the fact that the defendant was a convicted child molester who could be required to enroll in a mental health program, his submission to a plethysmograph was reasonable.[36]

Informed Consent Should Be Obtained for Use of Plethysmograph. There is little doubt that it would be prudent to obtain informed consent when the plethysmograph is used in an aversive conditioning program.[37] Use of the device is intrusive although there is no evidence of the sort of side-effects associated with some psychotropic drugs. There is no invasion of the body, in the sense of surgery, nor is there any effort to alter the brain's chemical structure.

Courts that uphold a requirement that a parolee submit to the plethysmograph, and that submission may be mandated for a community-based or facility-based program, are not also stating that it may be forcibly imposed. Parenthetically, that is the case with psychotropic medication, as discussed earlier in Chapter 25.

However, denial of supervised release, revocation, or denial of access to a facility-based treatment program for failure to comply would likely be upheld. Nonetheless, informed consent still makes good sense as a desirable practice; it shows respect for the dignity of the person; it provides a base of information of technique, uses, and consequences; and it would seem to enhance the potential for effective treatment.

Footnotes

---

[1] See, e.g., G.G. Abel & E.B. Blanchard, "The Measurement and Generation of Sexual Arousal in Male Sexual Deviates," 2 *Prog. Behav. Modif.* 99 (1976).

[2] See Ditlea, "Digital Disinformation—Artificial Intelligence," 9 *Omni* 26 (Feb. 1987), which describes exactly how this process is completed. This issue will be discussed again later in this chapter.

[3] *Assessment News Letter* 1, 2 (Farrall Inst., 1993).

[4] On February 8, 1994, members of the Association for the Treatment of Sexual Abusers were informed by letter that the Attorney General of Nebraska took the position that the pictures of nude children used and disseminated by Dr. William Farrall, an expert in this area, suggested the "significant danger of exploitation or abuse to children." Although Dr. Farrall had, indeed, obtained approval from two county attorneys, he agreed to the January 17, 1999 destruction of videos, slides, and photographs in the presence of a local police officer. As of this writing, no further detail is available. Nevertheless, an unexpected flag of caution was raised for therapists about the stimuli but not about the device itself.

[5] It is true that one of the evils of child pornography is that the pictures are a permanent record of the earlier exploitation. There is no doubt in this author's mind that the pictures can be, and in most instances should be, destroyed. However, that is not the problem addressed in the text.

See also People v. Wrench, 371 N.Y.S.2d 833 (Dist. Ct. Suff. Co. 1975); State v. Piepenburg, 602 P.2d 702 (Utah 1979), both involving statutory defenses to a charge of possession of obscene materials. The statutes in question are derived from the Model Penal Code, § 251.4(3) providing for the "scientific" exception. Readers should consult the statutes in their jurisdiction before using a similar defense.

[6] See *N.Y. Times* 11 (Dec. 13, 1993), where President Clinton rebuked Attorney General Reno while stating he was not doing so.

[7] See I *Assessment Newsletter* 3 (Farrall Inst. 1993), which states that if provocative images are used, then, in the interest of treatment efficacy, all images used as stimuli must show these characteristics. Apparently, Texas, Colorado, and Illinois have specific statutory exemptions in their child pornography laws for use of such pictures by therapists.

[8] 458 U.S. 747 (1982).

[9] Ibid., at 762.

[10] Ibid., at 774.

[11] Ibid.

[12] 156 F. Supp. 350 (S.D.N.Y. 1957).

[13] Ibid., at 358.

[14] 18 Cal. Rptr. 923 (Cal. App. 1962).

[15] Robert Lanman has indicated that the definition of research on human subjects in the Health and Human Service Regulations, at 45 C.F.R. § 46.102(f), does not include a child in a photograph.

[16] For example, New York's Penal Law § 400.05 (McKinney's 1980) provides for the destruction of weapons and dangerous instruments, appliances, and substances, but there is no specific statute regarding the destruction of pornographic materials. However, New York State Police internal practices regulate the destruction and preservation of confiscated pornographic materials. Other states handle this issue differently, see e.g., Conn. Gen. Stat. Ann. § 53a-205 (West 1985) (specifically discusses destruction of obscene materials); Mass. Ann. Laws Ch 276 § Michie/Law. Co-op. 1980) (disposition of all property seized); N.J. Stat. Ann. § 2C:64-1, 6 (West 1982) (disposition of any illegal property). State law must be consulted in this matter.

[17] Restatement (Second) of Torts, § 652A, Comment A (1965) sets forth the following principles:

    1. One who invades the right of privacy of another is subject to liability for the resulting harm to the interests of the other.

    2. The right of privacy is invaded by:

        a. unreasonable intrusion upon the seclusion of another, or

        b. appropriation of the other's name or likeness, or

        c. unreasonable publicity given to the other's private life, or

        d. publicity that unreasonably places the other in a false light before the public.

[18] See Chapter 30.

[19] See, e.g., N.Y. Civil Rights Law §§ 50, 51 (McKinney's 1976).

[20] See, e.g., N.Y. Crim. Proc. Law § 160.50 (McKinney's Supp. 1987); Eddy v. Moore, 487 P.2d 211 (Wash. 1971).

[21] See Chapter 30.

[22] See, e.g., N.Y. Civ. Rights Law § 50-b (McKinney's Supp. 1987).

[23] While child pornography is not one of the four sex offenses defined in N.Y. Penal Law § 130, it is described in N.Y. Penal Law § 263.00. Specifically, § 263.00(3) describes the sexual conduct which may be involved in the photographs or other materials. Some are identical to the acts and offenses described in N.Y. Penal Law § 130.

[24] See C.D. Robinson, *Legal Rights, Duties, and Liabilities of Criminal Justice Personnel: History and Analysis* 97 (1984).

[25] See Griswold v. Connecticut, 381 U.S. 479 (1965); Roe v. Wade, 410 U.S. 113 (1973). See also Note, "Developments in the Law—The Constitution and the Family," 93 *Harv. L. Rev.* 1156 (1980).

[26] See Bowers v. Hardwick, 106 S.Ct. 2841 (1986).

[27] Even when preparing a training videotape on psychotherapy, clinicians are urged to protect the identity of persons other than the patient under American Medical Association Principles of Ethics, Section 4. Therefore, one may ask, why should they not attempt to protect the privacy and identity of the juvenile in the photograph that the clinician may be using. See *American Psychiatric Association, Opinions of the Ethics Committee on the Principles of Medical Ethics* 21-22 (1983).

[28] See J.G. Barker & R.J. Howell, "The Plethysmograph: A Review of Recent Literature," 20 *Bull. Am. Acad. Psychiatry Law* 13 (1992).

[29] Ibid., at 16.

[30] Barker & Howell, n. 29 supra at 22. Other students of the device strongly believe that as an evaluative device, it is best limited to judgments on potential treatment.

See also Moon v. State, 856 S.W.2d 276, 280 (Ct. App. Ft. Worth, Tex. 1993), where an expert testified to using plethysmograph results to form only 1% of his opinion because he found the device somewhat unreliable. It was held to be permissible to allow cross-examination on this point and to allow a state's expert to testify in rebuttal to the results of the plethysmograph tests even though this would not have been allowed in the state's case in chief. Rebuttal evidence is "offered by a party after he has rested his case and after the opponent has rested in order to contradict the opponent's evidence." *Black's Law Dictionary* 1267 (6th Ed.).

[31] Harrington v. Almy, 977 F.2d 37, 38 (1st Cir. 1992).

[32] Ibid., at 44.

[33] Ibid., at 46.

[34] Walrath v. U.S., 830 F. Supp. 444 (N.D. Ill. 1993).

[35] See e.g., U.S. v. Williams, 787 F.2d 1182 (7th Cir. 1986).

[36] 830 F. Supp. at 447.

[37] See generally M. Perlin, 2 *Mental Disability Law: Civil and Criminal* § 5.59 (1989).

Chapter 30

Registration and Scarlet Letter Conditions

by Fred Cohen, D.J.P.

Overview

This chapter examines the ways that state legislatures and courts have responded to public outrage over a perceived increase in violent crime, specifically rape and murder. Well publicized, sickeningly detailed, sexually driven rapes and murders as well as brutal exploitation, particularly of children, have become daily fare for the media. Priests are exposed as pedophiles preying on choir boys. Parents stand accused of almost unbelievable sexual abuse of their own children. Does requiring registration of sex offenders or stipulating so-called "scarlet letter" probation conditions protect the public without violating individual rights? Both responses are likely to survive constitutional challenges.

Examples of Scarlet Letter Probation Conditions

Not knowing exactly what to do about these grievous events but believing we must do something has caused the legal landscape to become littered with reflexive reactions. In Oregon, an offender was convicted of sexual abuse, placed on probation, ordered into treatment, and also required to post signs reading: "DANGEROUS SEX OFFENDER—NO CHILDREN ALLOWED," in three inch lettering on the door to his residence and on both doors of any vehicle he operates.[1] Other offenders have been required to publish apologies in a local newspaper;[2] attend church weekly;[3] limit sexual intercourse to their spouse;[4] wear taps on the soles and heels of their shoes to alert possible victims;[5] and wear a T-shirt in public announcing the nature of the offender's offense and sentence.[6]

Conditions' Objectives Not Clear

The objectives of these scarlet letter conditions of supervised release or sex offender registration laws are not clear. Some questions about there purpose come to mind:

- Are they designed to protect the public?
- Are they intended to impose additional punishment and stigma?
- Are they supposed to deter the offender or aid in his or her rehabilitation?
- Are they intended to assist law enforcement in keeping track of potential offenders and aid in criminal investigations when offenses occur?
- Are they designed to simply make the public feel a bit safer? Take revenge? Take precautions?
- Are they designed to give judges and legislators an inexpensive yet publicity generating answer to "Why don't you do something? Anything?"
- Do we have any studies or data on the effectiveness of these sanctions, whether measured by crime reduction or simply a feeling of enhanced security?

The smorgasbord of possible objectives (and motives) implied by this series of questions is probably broad enough to satisfy anyone's crime fighting appetite. Whether legitimate law enforcement-deterrence objectives are served by any of these measures remains dubious. There are, however, few legal barriers either to registration laws or the various conditions described earlier.

Examples of State Registration Laws

Thirty-four states have enacted some form of sex offender registration law,[7] none more demanding of the offender than the State of Washington.[8] In Washington any juvenile or adult convicted of a sex offense in Washington must register with the sheriff in the county in which he or she intends to reside within 24 hours of release from confinement.

The duration of the duty to register depends on the seriousness of the underlying offense but relief from the duty requires court action. Law enforcement departments decide what registration information to release to which segments of the population. Some departments simply allow the public to browse through its directory, while others take affirmative steps to release names, addresses, and mug shots to the media. Press conferences to announce the release of sex offenders are not uncommon.[9]

Legal Challenges to Aspects of Registration Laws

Probationer Must Be Notified of Duty to Register. In *Lambert v. California*[10] the Supreme Court voided the application of a general criminal registration law because there had been no showing that the probationer knew or should have known of the duty. To punish someone for a failure to act (register) when all the probationer did was simply reside in a place, was found to violate the principle of notice which is at the core of the Due Process Clause.[11]

Lambert in no way impinged on the essential legality of registration laws. It spoke only to a duty to provide notice and that may be provided by the judge, probation and parole conditions, and in some jurisdictions by signs posted at transportation hubs or on major highways.

Washington State's Registration Law Not Unconstitutional Ex Post Facto Law. The Washington sexual offender registration law has been unsuccessfully challenged as an unconstitutional ex post facto law. The argument is that the law reaches persons whose convictions predate the registration law and imposes disadvantages relating to invasions of privacy and limitations on freedom of movement.

A law is an ex post facto law if it:

1. aggravates a crime or makes it greater than it was when committed; 2. permits imposition of a different or more severe punishment than when the crime was committed; 3. changes the legal rules to permit less or different testimony to convict the offender than was required when the crime was committed; or 4. is made retroactive and disadvantages the offender.[12]

The fourth claim, that of "disadvantage," is the one most likely to succeed for one challenging the retroactive application of Washington's law. However, the state courts determined that the requisite "disadvantage" must be punitive and, "Since the purpose of the registration requirement is not to impose punishment, but to protect the public, and the effect of the requirement is not punitive, the registration requirement does not constitute an ex post facto law."[13]

In *State v. Taylor*[14] a similar challenge was rejected over the vigorous dissent of Judge Agid who argued that the registration law does, in fact, promote the traditional aims of punishment—retribution and deterrence. The registration information is available to anyone; it enhances the likelihood of rearrest on marginal cause; and it plainly impedes travel.[15]

The dissenter believes the law should not be allowed retroactive application, but this author takes it that he sees no constitutional impediments to such a law if it were prospective only.

Privacy Claims. Persons convicted of crime—whether it be a sex offense or not—retain only a small residuum of privacy while under the strictures of a criminal sentence. This is true whether the offender is incarcerated or in the community under some form of supervision.[16] Whatever privacy claims survive conviction and sentence relate to the most intrusive forms of searching the person (e.g., body cavity probes).[17]

Publication of such public records as police reports and official court records open to public inspection may not be negatively sanctioned.[18] Plaintiffs find it exceedingly difficult to prevail in a tort action for damages based on invasion of privacy due to publication of even older court records.[19]

Thus, sex offender registration laws, including the posting of warning signs, will likely withstand any legal challenge. They will have to be dealt with as a matter of public policy and gauged for effectiveness.

Some sex offenders will be tracked down and harassed. There are reports of residents arming themselves, building fences, pelting the offender's home with eggs, posting of the offender's picture in grocery stores, telephone networks tracing an offender's movements, and more.[20] This, indeed, may be viewed favorably, as additional "just deserts," and as reasonably related to achieving security. However, such actions may increase the chances for recidivism. In making it difficult to obtain a residence or employment, the community may, indeed, reap the opposite of what it seeks.

Legal Challenges to Scarlet Letter Conditions

Few scarlet letter conditions are successfully challenged. In *People v. Hackler*,[21] where the probationer was required to wear a T-shirt stating his crime and the sentence he received, the condition was found to be unreasonably broad and as having an adverse effect on the individual's employment prospects. The condition was struck down as a matter of state law.[22]

However, the courts generally will uphold the conditions where they are found to be reasonably related to the offense, the offender's demonstrated personal characteristics, and the potential for deterring future criminality.[23] In truth, the discretion of a judge (or parole authority) is so broad in the determination of conditions that it can become the vehicle for the decision-maker's wisdom or foolishness. The validity or invalidity of scarlet letter conditions, as well as other conditions designed to publicly humiliate or strip a person of the most basic aspects of dignity, will continue to be determined in an ad hoc fashion. We lack a clear vision of the legal identity of the person under community supervision. An important contribution from legal scholarship would be a clear statement of principles to bind decision-makers in the invention and imposition of scarlet letter-like conditions.[24]

Footnotes

[1] See State v. Bateman, 765 P.2d 249 (Ore. 1987).

[2] See Alternative Sentencing, A.B.A. J., November 1, 1987, at 32; See also Drunk Driver Penalty, *Newsday*, March 29, 1989, at 14(1) Suffolk ed.

[3] Commonwealth v. Kuhn, 327 Pa. Super. 72, 83, 475 A.2d 103, 108 (1984).

[4] Wiggins v. State, 386 So.2d 46 (Fla. Dist. Ct. App. 1980).

[5] People v. McDowell, 59 Cal. App.3d 807, 130 Cal. Rptr. 839 (1976).

[6] People v. Hackler, 16 Cal. Rptr.2d 681 (Cal. App. 1993)(voiding a probation condition that the probationer never appear in public without a T-shirt emblazoned with "My record plus two six packs equals four years" on the front and "I am on felony probation for theft" on the back.

[7] A recent computer search on Westlaw disclosed the following states as having enacted some form of sex offender registration statute: Alabama, Alaska, Arizona, Arkansas, California, Colorado, Delaware, Florida, Georgia, Idaho, Illinois, Indiana, Kansas, Kentucky, Louisiana, Maine, Michigan, Minnesota, Missouri, Montana, Nevada, New Hampshire, New Jersey, New York, Ohio, Oklahoma, Rhode Island, South Dakota, Utah, Virginia, Washington, West Virginia, Wisconsin, and Wyoming. Other states are contemplating similar legislation.

[8] Wash. Rev. Code Ann. § 9A.44.130.

[9] See Note, "Registration of Sexual Offenders: Would Washington's Scarlet Letter Approach Benefit Minnesota?," 13 *Hamline J. of Pub. Law & Policy* 163, 172 (1992).

[10] 355 U.S. 225 (1957).

[11] This decision is sui generis and has not been expanded to create an ignorance of the law defense

based on constitutional principles. Persons who own rental property or simply engage in business, for example, are duty bound to discover and observe relevant legal requirements. The nature of those undertakings is a form of notice to inquire.

[12] State v. Estavillo, 848 P.2d 1335 (Wash. App. 1993). Although the quotation in the text is from an intermediate court of appeals, it represents an accurate distillation of federal law and, in any event, is the framework for analysis used by Washington courts.

[13] Ibid., at 1337.

[14] 835 P.2d 245 (Wash. App. 1992).

[15] Ibid., at 250 (dissenting opinion).

[16] Hudson v. Palmer, 768 U.S. 517 (1984)(inmates have no privacy claims to their possessions or living quarters); Griffin v. Wisconsin, 483 U.S. 868 (1987)(search of probationers' or parolees' home allowed without a warrant or probable cause).

[17] Bell v. Wolfish, 441 U.S. 5201 (1979)(allowed for the body cavity inspection of a pretrial detainee without articulable suspicion or cause other than a body contact visit).

[18] Cox Broadcasting v. Cohen, 420 U.S. 469 (1975); Florida Star v. B.J.F., 491 U.S. 524 (1989). Once such material is available, the First Amendment is a powerful inhibitor against any governmental efforts to censor or suppress such material.

[19] Dresbach v. Doubleday & Co., 518 F. Supp. 1285 (D.D.C. 1981), involving a book published 19 years after a crime.

[20] Accounts from the *Seattle Times* reported in Note, Registration of Sexual Offenders: Would Washington's Scarlet Letter Approach Benefit Minnesota?, 13 *Hamline J. Pub. Law & Policy* 163, 171-72 (1992). In Paul v. Davis, 424 U.S. 693 (1976) the Court held that where a person had been arrested on shoplifting charges, and the local chief of police circulated hundreds of flyers designating the arrestee as an "active shoplifter," any reputational harm suffered is not protected by the Fourteenth Amendment.

But see Wisconsin v. Constantineau, 400 U.S. 433 (1971) invalidating on procedural due process grounds a state posting law allowing without notice or hearing, the posting of a notice in retail liquor stores identifying an "excessive drinker" and forbidding sales or gifts of liquor to such person for a year. This law deprived the person of a state-created right to obtain and consume liquor and, thus, some form of notice and a hearing was required.

There is obviously a thin line between Davis and Constantineau but the registration laws discussed in the text involve convictions, often apply to a supervisee, and are found not to unduly infringe on privacy or reputational interests even with the expiration of time.

[21] 116 Cal. Rptr.2d 681 (Cal. App. 1993).

[22] The court distinguished Hackler from People v. McDowell, 130 Cal. Rptr. 839 (Cal. App. 1976) where a probationer was required to put taps on leather soled shoes in that such shoes are relatively common and did not label the probationer as a thief. However, the court did not also argue that to publicly brand a thief as a thief was impermissible.

[23] See N.P. Cohen & J.J. Gobert, *The Law of Probation and Parole* §§ 5.02, 5.03 (1983, 1992 Supp.).

[24] F. Cohen, "Legal Issues in Community Corrections: An Overview," I *Community Corrections Rpt.* 1, 14 (1993).

Appendices

Appendix A

Psychological Evaluation

Name: Mr. A   **Age:** 36

Referral Source: Veterans Administration Hospital

Reason for Referral: Psychological evaluation relevant for the assessment of sexual deviance

Assessment Procedure: Psychological interviews, administration of Minnesota Multiphasic Personality Inventory (MMPI) and Thematic Apperception Test (TAT), psychophysiological assessment of sexual responsivity

Background Information: Mr. A, a 36-year-old service-connected veteran, was referred by the Veterans Administration Hospital to the Sex Offender Research and Treatment (S.O.R.T.) Program. Mr. A was referred to the S.O.R.T. Program for psychological evaluation relevant for the assessment of sexual deviance. Mr. A apparently reported deviant sexual urges and insinuated deviant sexual behavior to the psychiatric staff at the VA Hospital.

Mr. A presented himself in a well-groomed, neat, casual fashion for each interview and testing session involved in the assessment procedure. He was generally cooperative during the assessment procedure, but he also appeared to be quite suspicious. He raised some concerns at the outset of the assessment procedure. He wanted to know what the limits of confidentiality were. These limits were explained to him. Also, he wanted a copy of the state laws regarding the release of information. These requests were granted him.

After having his initial concerns about confidentiality and the release of information addressed, Mr. A said he was seeking treatment for deviant sexual urges. Mr. A reported deviant sexual urges directed toward his 2-year-old daughter and 4-year-old son. He stated that he's watched these urges evolve and that he's seeking treatment to prevent himself from acting on these urges. When asked outright by the examiner whether he currently was sexually molesting his children, Mr. A replied that admitting to this would be tantamount to turning himself in and that "the logical answer is 'no'."

Overall, Mr. A manifested a rather restricted range of affective expression during the assessment procedure. From his verbal behavior during the assessment procedure, it appeared that Mr. A uses a very intellectualized coping style. At points during the assessment procedure when Mr. A related some of the more painful, difficult events of his life, however, he appeared to be on the verge of crying. Other impressions concerning Mr. A's behavior during the assessment procedure were that his speech tends to be circumstantial, he rather easily loses his train of thought, he sometimes uses rather peculiar, idiosyncratic expressions, and his style of thinking sometimes appears very unusual.

Brief History: Mr. A was born on June 15, 1948. He is part Choctaw Indian. His father died when he was two; his mother, a teacher, lives in Oklahoma. Mr. A has two older brothers. As a child, Mr. A said he was a quiet, introverted loner. He described his home environment as disciplined but noted that he was not physically abused as a child.

Mr. A said that he was an average student throughout his school years. He attended college on and off between 1967 and 1983; during this interval, he changed his major area of study several times. He received a bachelor's degree in computer science from Southeastern Oklahoma State University in 1983.

Mr. A served in the Army from 1967 until 1972. He said that he considered himself a conscientious objector at the time he was drafted. While in the Army, Mr. A worked as a finance clerk. Though he was stationed in Vietnam for a portion of his time in the Army, he said he experienced no frontline or combat duty.

Concerning his marital history, Mr. A has been married twice to the same woman. Their first marriage began in 1973 and ended in divorce in 1977. Mr. A noted the following factors as contributing to their divorce in 1977. He said his wife was unready and unprepared for marriage; there was frequent interference by his mother-in-law; he was often experiencing considerable physical pain; and he was very independent. During this first marriage, Mr. A and his wife lived in Albuquerque. After their divorce in 1977, Mr. A moved back to MacAllister, Oklahoma to live with his mother. While they were divorced, however, Mr. A and his wife maintained contact. In 1978, they were remarried and lived in Oklahoma. In 1980, Mr. A and his wife had a son. This same year, Mr. A faced accusations raised by the State of Oklahoma of child neglect and/or physical abuse. These accusations apparently stemmed from an incident during which Mr. A slapped his young son in public.

Perhaps contributing to these accusations were some unusual childrearing practices mentioned by Mr. A. For example, he said that his infant son seemed to be disturbed by bright lights, so Mr. A kept the infant blindfolded or covered up. Eventually, after a period during which Mr. A's son was placed in the custody of Mr. A's mother, the accusations were dropped. Around 1981, Mr. A said his wife overdosed on Dilantin, which she was apparently taking because of a history of epileptic seizures. Though Mr. A said his wife has a history of suicidal ideation, it is not clear whether this overdose was intentional. Mr. A said his wife hasn't been the same since the overdose; she experiences loss of equilibrium, her eyes flutter up and down; and her handwriting is poor. Mr. A noted, however, that his wife apparently didn't suffer any intellectual deterioration as a result of the overdose. In 1982, Mr. A and his wife had their second child, a daughter. After Mr.

A received his college degree in 1983, he and his family moved back to Albuquerque, where he obtained employment as a computer programmer and is still employed.

Mr. A briefly discussed his current marital situation, which sounded rather unpleasant. He and his wife are presently experiencing financial problems, which Mr. A seemingly attributes to his wife's spending habits. He said his household is often untidy because his wife fails to keep up with the housework. The sexual aspect of their marriage is apparently poor, with Mr. A and his wife having sexual intercourse approximately once per month. Mr. A noted that he sometimes seeks sexual relationships with other women because he isn't satisfied sexually by his wife. Concerning the children, Mr. A said his wife has difficulty managing them while he is away. He attributed this to his wife's failure to use discipline. Mr. A described himself as the disciplinarian of the family and said that he sometimes gets "too aggressive" when disciplining his children. As a sort of summary statement about his marital/home situation, Mr. A said he felt like he just lived there.

Mr. A related several things about his medical history and current physical condition. At the age of four, he was struck by an automobile and lost consciousness. He additionally reported a history of duodenal ulcers and prostatitis. Mr. A reported several unusual current physical complaints. He said he is frequently in pain and that the pain is related to weather conditions. Specifically, he reported feeling generally uncomfortable, light-sensitive, and "sunburned" all over when there is a local high-pressure system. Mr. A's comments about how the weather determines his physical condition led the present examiner to suspect that Mr. A suffers from somatic delusions and possibly somatic hallucinations. It should be noted here that Mr. A said he has been previously diagnosed by VA psychiatrists as having neurotic disorder with hypochondriacal features. This diagnosis is apparently the basis for his service-connected disability compensation.

In regard to his psychological history, Mr. A reported the following information. He described himself as introverted and introspective. He said he experiences some social anxiety, but in a special sense—Mr. A said he feels his actions are often at odds with the rest of society and that this gets him into trouble. Mr. A reported that he experienced "nervous breakdowns" between 1972 and 1977, which he ascribed to difficulties he had in dealing with the Veterans Administration. Mr. A said he felt the VA had twisted regulations and improperly treated him when he was seeking help for his physical and psychological complaints in the 1970s. Mr. A said he withdrew socially and felt irritable, tense, depressed, and demoralized during these nervous breakdowns. Additionally, Mr. A mentioned that he'd been diagnosed as having paranoid schizophrenia around 1976. The circumstances around this diagnosis are unclear, but it appears that he received the diagnosis from a psychiatrist at the VA Hospital in Albuquerque. Mr. A said he was placed on some medications, which he believed were minor tranquilizers, around the time this diagnosis was made. However, he said he discontinued these medications because they were ineffective in alleviating his physical complaints. Mr. A reported that in 1977, he sought psychological treatment at a mental health agency in Oklahoma. He said the personnel at this facility told him he was a "threat" and insisted that he take medications, apparently major tranquilizers. Mr. A took these medications for a time but discontinued them because he felt they were interfering with his functioning. Finally, it should be noted that Mr. A reported no history of suicidal ideation or attempts. Mr. A noted no current suicidal ideation or plans.

Mr. A mentioned several significant facts regarding his sexual history. He reported being sexually molested around the age of 16 by a dentist. Also, around this age he became involved in homosexual activity. He said there were several isolated episodes of homosexual activity and one relatively prolonged homosexual relationship with a neighbor two years younger than he. Mr. A said that around 1972 he began to feel deviant sexual urges, which he apparently believes were the result of a "brainwashing" process he underwent in Army basic training. At that time, he had urges to rape adult women. He described how he had made plans to rape women on the

university campus, but he indicated that he's never taken action on these plans. In 1976, Mr. A was charged with indecent exposure by a female neighbor. The charges were later dropped, but Mr. A admitted to the present examiner that he, in fact, had exposed himself and masturbated while visible to the neighbor woman. Significantly, Mr. A also reported a history of pedophilic activity. Several years ago, he said, on two separate occasions he had fondled 6- to 9-year-old girls while bus riding. Additionally, he noted two other incidents in which he had fondled or engaged in mutual masturbation with an 11-year-old girl and a 12-year-old girl. About his pedophilic activity, Mr. A said he felt it was precipitated by stress and an inability to satisfy his sexual drive. He also said that his deviant sexual urges seem to be worse in the spring because spring is the "mating season for people."

Test Results:

TAT. Mr. A's TAT responses included several elements which may be indicative of serious psychological difficulty. Some of his TAT responses were loosely and vaguely constructed; some contained peculiar, idiosyncratic expressions. Mr. A seemed to try approaching the TAT stimuli in a very intellectualized manner. He was occasionally confused by affect-laden TAT stimuli and sometimes he would not speculate about the emotions portrayed in the TAT stimuli. Prominent themes in Mr. A's TAT responses were psychological distress, grief, hostility and interpersonal conflict, and sex.

MMPI. Mr. A's MMPI suggested that he responded frankly to the test items. Furthermore, his MMPI profile was a valid one. Mr. A's MMPI was indicative of an anxious, depressed individual whose coping resources are limited. Individuals with MMPI profiles like Mr. A's are typically described as being impulsive, unpredictable, nonconforming, socially isolated, marginally adjusted, resentful of authority, and distrustful. Furthermore, MMPI profiles like Mr. A's are fairly typical among individuals manifesting sexually deviant behavior as well as paranoid schizophrenia, schizoid personality disorder, paranoid disorders, or antisocial personality disorder. Given the particular configuration of Mr. A's MMPI profile, the likelihood of psychosis and bizarre symptomatology, including paranoid suspiciousness, is relatively high.

Psychophysiological Assessment of Sexual Responsivity:

The psychophysiological assessment of sexual responsivity, conducted with a penile plethysmograph, consisted of the following: (1) measurement of Mr. A's erection responses to heterosexual, homosexual, female pedophilic, and male pedophilic slides, and (2) measurement of Mr. A's erection responses to audiotapes describing heterosexual, nonviolent female pedophilic, and violent female pedophilic activities. Mr. A was given instructions either to enhance or suppress sexual arousal during the slide and audiotape presentations. Additionally, he was asked to give a verbal rating of his degree of full erection after each stimulus presentation.

The results of the first part of the assessment indicated that Mr. A became moderately to strongly aroused by heterosexual slides; moderately sexually aroused to homosexual and female pedophilic slides; and only slightly sexually aroused to the male pedophilic slides. Mr. A's ratings of degree of erection correlated highly with the actual measured values. Finally, Mr. A appeared to have some capability, though sporadic, to suppress his sexual arousal during the slide presentations.

The results of the second part of the assessment indicated that Mr. A became strongly sexually aroused to audiotapes describing both nonviolent and violent pedophilic activity. He manifested moderate sexual arousal to the audiotape describing heterosexual activity. Again, Mr. A's ratings of degree of full erection correlated highly with the actual measured values and he manifested a sporadic capability to suppress his sexual arousal.

Summary and Conclusions:

Mr. A, though presently functioning at a marginal level, seems to be having increasing difficulty coping.

At the moment, it appears as if he is keeping himself relatively psychologically intact through his intellect.

Mr. A reported the following: (1) a history of deviant rape and pedophilic urges; (2) a history of pedophilic behavior with young females; (3) previous exhibitionistic sexually deviant behavior; and (4) current deviant sexual urges directed toward his 2-year-old daughter and 4-year-old son. The interview material and test results suggest that Mr. A may be psychotic, perhaps paranoid schizophrenic. Mr. A appears to manifest somatic delusions and possibly somatic hallucinations, suspiciousness, unusual thinking, circumstantial speech, and easy distractibility. The psychophysiological assessment indicates that Mr. A becomes sexually aroused by deviant female pedophilic stimuli and that his ability to suppress his sexual arousal is sporadic. Given the previous information and lacking any form of therapeutic intervention, Mr. A is at high risk for engaging in deviant pedophilic behavior.

Several factors suggest that Mr. A's children may be currently experiencing neglect and/or physical and sexual abuse. First, Mr. A was reluctant to discuss his current situation until the limits of confidentiality were clearly demarcated. While he has apparently insinuated that he may be engaging in deviant sexual behavior, he realizes that an admission of this would be tantamount to turning himself in. Second, Mr. A said he has previously faced accusations of neglect and physical abuse; he also admitted to being "too aggressive" sometimes when he disciplines his children. Third, neither Mr. A nor his wife appear to be emotionally stable. Fourth, from the way Mr. A described his home, the home environment of his children may be inadequate. Fifth, Mr. A described some very peculiar childrearing practices, and the likelihood exists that he may be currently using some unusual practices in raising his children.

The recommendations that can be made regarding treatment for Mr. A include the following. Mr. A is seen as being at very high risk for sexual acting-out and probably should be hospitalized and placed on antipsychotic medications. We consider him too disturbed to be seen on an outpatient basis. Behavior modification techniques can be implemented to attempt to reduce his deviant sexual arousal. One anticipated difficulty in treating Mr. A is that he may not comply with a therapeutic regimen.

Appendix B

Minnesota's Transitional Sex Offenders Program (TSOP)

TSOP Orientation

The TSOP Orientation Phase is an intensive, four-week therapeutic-educational approach to working with sex offenders. The aim is to open them up, get them talking about and beginning treatment of their sexually abusive behavior. Educational material is presented in a variety of mediums on five basic topics.

The model is adaptable to an inpatient or outpatient setting, in a prison, in the community, in a mental hospital or in a day or evening treatment program. The basic idea is to present the material to known sexual offenders, discuss it, and have them apply it to themselves, their crimes and their life situation. The discussion is best accomplished in a small group of seven to nine sex offenders with one or two skilled therapists who are able to deal with the sexual abuse realistically and yet in a way that is supportive to the offender's growth and change.

During the four weeks, the offender will write a 30-page autobiography and complete several written assignments. The counselor will review the assignments with him either individually or in a small group discussion. Some group discussions will intensely focus on the offender's known sexual assaults. Specific use is made in group of the victim's statements about the assaults as they come from the Pre-Sentence Investigation or Police Reports. Attention in these groups is directed towards labeling the emotional state of the offender and his reasoning that allowed him to justify the assaults at the time he did them.

The groups should also be supportive of the man taking full responsibility and openly saying what he did in his sexual assault.

Overcoming denial is unquestionably the hardest and most important part of the treatment process so most of the materials and approaches are aimed at this problem.

There are also a number of written exercises that the offender completes on the reading material. This is in the form of short essay-type answers to written questions. Some of these questions are attached. The questions are designed to focus the man's attention on important points in the written articles and to get him to think about and apply these ideas to himself. The major topics and materials used are listed and described below:

Sexual Addiction

The main material used here is a book by Pat Carnes entitled *Out of the Shadows* (formerly *The Sexual Addiction*) published by CompCare Publications, Minneapolis, MN.

The men read chapters 1, 2, 3, 5, and 6:

Chapter 1	The Addiction Cycle
Chapter 2	Levels of Addiction
Chapter 3	The Family and the Addict's World
Chapter 5	The Belief System
Chapter 6	Twelve Steps to Recovery

This material describes in simple terms from the offender's perspective the feelings, impulses, and behaviors involved in a sexual

A-7

addiction cycle. The material is applicable to both child molesters and rapists, although it often angers rapists, who are more likely to deny the sexual problems in their behavior.

It gives specific examples of how a preoccupation with sexuality manifests itself in seemingly benign activities, such as pornography, prostitutes, fetishes, peeping or promiscuity. The book shows how these preoccupations can progress to more serious sexual assaults which then bring people into trouble with the law. It also touches on the impact the sexual addiction has on the family and on the steps to recovery which are similar to the AA Steps of Recovery. This is helpful in laying down a philosophy of treatment which involves a lifetime of involvement, if necessary, in a support group after "formal treatment" is completed. Support groups for sexual addicts and/or sex offenders are becoming more and more common in all parts of the country. They are free, run by the men who have finished treatment themselves, and often are a valuable adjunct to the therapy process.

We also use a videotape of "The Phil Donahue Show" in which an addict, his wife, and Pat Carnes discuss sexual addiction and treatment of the problem.

The book and the videotapes present examples of other men and women who have had sexual addiction problems and have learned to control them and stay out of trouble. It gives a hopeful message about the possibilities of being honest with yourself and learning to trust other people.

It is important to review with a counselor written answers the offenders put together. This can be done in a small group discussion, two chapters at a time, by having each man read his answers to the group and in some cases discuss their ideas. This helps them to see similarities between themselves and others, and they do not feel so strange or so alone with their problems. For some settings it is helpful to put this material on video- or audiotape and have the men listen to it. Many men who are illiterate are able to understand the ideas and concepts and apply them to themselves. They can audiotape their answers if they can't write or someone else can write for them.

Typology of Offenders

Sexual Assault of Children and Adolescents, by Ann Wolbert Burgess and A. Nicholas Groth, published in 1978 by Lexington Books, D.C. Heath and Company, Lexington, MA. Chapter 1.

Men Who Rape, the Psychology of the Offender, by A. Nicholas Groth. Plenum Press, New York, 1979. They read Chapters 1, 2, and 3.

Film: "Acquaintance Rape," from MTI Teleprograms, 108 Wilmot Road, Deerfield, IL 60015; 800-323-5776.

"Incest: The Hidden Crime"—The Media Guild, 118 South Acacia Avenue, Box 881, Solano Beach, CA 92075; 714-755-9191.

These readings describe the typology of offenders who assault children and the typology of rapists. It gives case histories and examples and explains the difference between a fixated and a regressed child molester. The chapter talks about the characteristics, problems and feelings of men involved in these kinds of assaults and some of the incidents that preceded or triggered assaults on children, as well as background factors in their lives which predisposed them to develop patterns of assault against children.

The readings on the rapists describe the typology of anger, power, and sadistic rapists. The patterns in these types are different and the men usually are able to see themselves in these patterns and case histories. Again questions are answered in writing and then discussed in a group with a counselor. We have found it useful in our therapy groups to mix child offenders and adult sexual offenders. The groups which are heterogeneous as to types of sex offenders function better. It is valuable then to have the men understand all of the different types of sex offenders and the different backgrounds they come from.

"The Acquaintance Rape" films are four eight-minute films dealing with sex role stereotypes, teenage sexuality, and miscommunication in dating situations which then lead to sexual assault. These films are excellent for viewing and then group discussion on: What is a rape? Why does it happen? Where are the misunderstandings?

The film, "Incest: The Hidden Crime," shows interviews with family members, how each person felt and what was done once the veil of secrecy was lifted. This gives a good overview of the impact of incest on a family and opens the men up for discussion of their own families and their situation.

These films and others we use carry a heavy emotional impact. They do open the men up, and their ideas and feelings need to be discussed and talked about within a safe and supportive group following the viewing of the films. It teaches the clients to talk about issues and feelings they have long kept hidden. Offenders model the people in the films and books who are talking about sexual abuse, and they experience great relief when they can disclose things they have never told anyone before. The advantage of a group is that they also find out others have hidden similar or worse problems and others feel terrible about their behavior. The shared feelings bond the groups together and prepare them to work in treatment together.

Victimization

Films: "The Last Taboo"—MTI Teleprograms

"Shattered"—MTI Teleprograms

"Incest: The Victim Nobody Believes"—MTI Teleprograms

"Not Only Strangers"—Centron Films, 1621 W. 9th, Box 687, Lawrence, KS 66044; 914-843-0400.

Anyone working with this population knows that it is easy for offenders to minimize their actions or the impact their anger has on others or how afraid their families are of them. Rapists fail to understand the long-range impact of a rape on the victim and others.

The films listed above and others are available to help the offenders better understand and feel the impact of their actions on others. These were originally used to sensitize offenders to the feelings of their victims.

We have found the more powerful impact of these films is that the offenders, often for the first time, open up on and identify victimization in their own lives. These are the most powerful and sensitive films we use, and it is important to have a good therapeutic experience following the showing of these films. Like any victim of physical or sexual assault, they need to talk through their experiences of victimization and express anger at their offenders and then resolve or let go of their bitterness. For some we have found this to be a fairly lengthy process. Very often there is obvious connection between what they did in their crimes and what happened to them as victims.

Sexual Information

Films: "A Family Talks About Sex," "The Masturbatory Story." (Unfortunately, these films are no longer available.)

Article: "Orgasmic Reconditioning: Changing Sexual Object Choice Through Controlling Masturbation Fantasies," by John N. Marquis in *J. Behavioral Therapy and Exp. Psychiat.*, Vol. 1, pp. 263-271, Peragmon Press, 1970.

Just talking about sexual issues, ideas, and feelings is a large barrier for most sex offenders and many counselors, as far as that goes. Using the explicit words: intercourse, oral sex, anal sex, masturbation, penis, or vagina, is not easy at first. We have found movies again to be helpful in starting this process and opening the clients up for discussion. In this section, we try to present sexuality in a positive or at least neutral light. The movies and readings are meant to openly acknowledge the existence and power of sexuality in their lives and the need to come to terms with it within themselves. Many of the preceding sections have emphasized the harmful aspects of sexuality, and this needs to be moderated. Neither of these movies are explicit. They do not show nudity or sexual acts.

The movie, "A Family Talks About Sex," shows scenes of families with children from pre-school years through college age discussing sexual questions and issues with their parents. Most of the offenders will, in discussion, reflect on their own childhood and what they were taught about sexuality and how this has influenced them as adults. Most express great concern that they were never able to talk about their sexuality with their parents. In doing this, they open themselves up to discuss their sexuality now in treatment.

The one topic that has proved hardest to approach and talk about with clients and other helping professionals is that of masturbation. It is easier to discuss rape or incest than masturbation. "The Masturbatory Story" deals with the topic in a light, humorous sort of way. It tells of how a young man discovers that earlier injunctions about "blindness" and "insanity" are not true and that masturbation can be a good thing. Especially for a restricted or incarcerated population, it is important to recognize from the start that masturbation is going on regularly and it makes a great deal of difference as to what they are masturbating to.

The article, "Orgasmic Reconditioning," is a bit technical in the beginning and hard for most of them to follow, but it eventually describes a method for changing deviant sexual fantasies to more appropriate sexual fantasies. Many hardened sex offenders are unable to be aroused or ejaculate except to deviant fantasies. Although they may know that this is unhealthy and amounts to practicing for their next crime, they do not know what to do to change their fantasies and arousal pattern. The article explains clearly a process for changing it and gives 11 case histories of clients who applied the method and changed their sexual patterns into a healthier direction. This article should be read, questions answered in a written form and then discussed in a group. Men in our treatment program have said repeatedly that they wish they had known of this when they first came to prison; it would have saved them years of unhealthy practices. It is likely that a large range of men, not just sex offenders, would appreciate knowing more about this and would use the information on reconditioning constructively, with or without help from a counselor.

Psychological Tests

1. CAQII
2. 16PF, FORM C
3. MAT
   Available from IPAT, Inc., P.O. Box 188, Champaign, IL 61820; 800-225-4728
4. MSI
   Available from Multiphasic Sex

Inventory, Nichols and Molinder, 437 Bowes Drive, Tacoma, WA 98466; 206-565-4539

5. Hostility-Guilt

Available from Hostility-Guilt Inventory, A.H. Buss and A. Durkee, "An Inventory for Assessing Different Kinds of Hostility," *J. of Consulting Psychology*, 21, 1957, 343-349.

These five psychological tests are used at entrance to the program and after 10 months of treatment, when they are getting ready to leave the program. At intake they are taken one-a-day so as not to tire the man out or diminish their effectiveness. Psychological tests should not be used except under the supervision of a trained psychologist but, with this consultation, they can be a useful tool to motivate and direct the client in treatment. Before he takes the test, he is told that a counselor will go over the results with him. He will be shown how he scored in comparison to others, the norms. Sometimes, review of testing is just as effective in a small group as individually. Especially if he lives with others who have begun to learn what his behavior is like, they can point out to him what they see socially, in his behavior and how this relates to what the test is indicating.

This kind of open approach to psychological testing decreases the mysticism and paranoia about the tests and increases their cooperativeness and interest in the tests. We have had men ask to take the tests at various points to see how they are doing as a check on their progress in therapy. If the counselors or therapists review the testing with their clients, the counselors make better use of the tests also.

The 16PF is a factor analytically derived test which shows how the individual scores on 16 personality variables which are named in straightforward, understandable language. The variables are presented as continuums from shy and inhibited to venturesome and socially bold, or introverted versus extroverted. The continuums are presented as ten scores, from 1 to 10, indicating where the individual falls compared to the sample which standardized the test. This is an easily understandable way to present and discuss normal personality factors. Reviewing testing often helps crystallize needed changes that can become goals for treatment.

Form C of the 16PF is used because the language is at a simpler 10th grade level, which more offenders are better able to understand. This is a well standardized and developed test. More information on it is available from the IPAT Company.

The CAQ Part II is an extension of the 16PF to cover clinical or psychiatric problems. It also reports scales on a continuum of 1 to 10, measuring depression, psychosis, schizophrenia, and neurotic symptoms. It is helpful for detecting mental illness when this is also present and may point to a need for psychotropic medications which would help control psychiatric symptoms to the point where the man can participate in treatment.

The Multiphasic Sex Inventory is a 300-item true/false test developed on sex offenders. It covers all kinds of sexual behaviors such as homosexuality, voyeurism, fetishes, sexual functioning problems, cruising, child abuse, and rape. It is only as accurate as the man makes it. There are several validity scales which compare his answers with his known criminal history. The main advantage of the test is that it systematically asks about areas a counselor might not think of or might be unaware of. It is helpful to go over specific items with the man and ask about new information which he may choose to disclose on the test.

The Motivational Analysis Test is given every three months in the program, and the results are reviewed with the offender in his therapy group. This is a very fluid test which measures changing emotional states in ten areas of motivational drive. Is he more interested in a career or materialistic things? Or living up to his conscience or sexual drive? How are these motivational patterns changing during treatment? The test taps both conscious and unconscious drive states and shows where there might be a conflict between them. The fear scale is particularly useful in indicating a potential for violence. More information is available through the IPAT Corporation.

The Hostility-Guilt Inventory measures the way in which the man expresses his anger; is it verbal or physical? Is it direct or passive, as in sarcasm or ridicule? It is useful in pointing out areas that need to change in treatment.

Summary

Some samples of questions on the reading assignments are attached, as well as an outline for an autobiography. The life story should be started a week or two into the Orientation Phase. There will be more depth and more disclosure if the men have first seen some films and done some discussing of the material. They need to know they are in an environment that is safe for disclosing painful, shameful material and that they will be supported for doing this.

Real change in behavior takes more than 30 days and more than just opening up and discussing sexual abuse. The Orientation Phase should be followed by therapy, group or individual, once to three times a week for a year or so. This material is only meant as a beginning for change. It should help pinpoint the specific areas of behavior that need to change to stop the sexual assaults.

Out of the Shadows

Read Introduction and Chapter 1

1. Give an example of a "dramatic moment" for a sexual addict. Was it for you?

2. What are some of the myths which allow the addict to repeat his/her behavior?

3. Name and describe four parts of the addictive cycle. Use yourself as an example. How did you experience each of these stages?

4. Is it possible to have more than one addiction? How do they reinforce each other? What other related addictions have you had?

5. "Recovery from addiction is the reversal of alienation." What is meant by that? What are you doing today to reverse the alienation?

Read Chapter 2

1. When is sexual behavior a binge? How do you know when it crosses the line and becomes a compulsive addiction?

2. Give examples of sexual behavior at each of the three levels of addiction.

3. What is Corollary I? Do you believe it is true? Why?

4. How does sexual behavior between the levels reinforce one another? Give an example.

5. The driving force from each cycle of addiction comes from what?

Read Chapter 3

1. Do you think the Cermak family is very different from most families where incest has occurred? Why or why not?

2. Why has it been helpful to include family members in treatment? In what other fields of treatment has this shown positive results?

3. How do families teach the core belief: "I am basically a bad and unworthy person?" What is the worst threat for a child?

4. How and why do addicts learn not to count on other relationships?

5. How is the fusion between sex and nurturing cemented?

6. Fill out the abuse checklist for yourself.

Read Chapter 5

1. What is the key factor in our socialization process that trains men to be rapists?

2. The most effective therapists were those who were able to help their clients do what?

3. How do these beliefs contribute to sex offenses: I must have sex and I am powerless to influence my relationships? Are these beliefs true?

4. What are the beliefs you have had about women and sex? Share these in your group. What others can you think of in your group?

5. What beliefs did the children have about sexuality? How did they learn them?

6. What is the task for the addict in the recovery process?

Rape: Myths and Realities

1. Give several reasons why the public stereotypes men who rape. Do you consider this true today? Why?

2. What is the common misconception in the stereotypes and popular notions in viewing the sexual offender? What, in fact, do clinical studies reveal concerning this misconception?

3. There are three basic ways in which a person gains sexual access to another individual.

Name them and give a definition of each. Which ways are familiar to your experience?

4. Why does the author state some offenders are very likely to become repetitive offenders? What do you feel can be done to avoid this happening?

5. State two examples of myths that persist concerning victims. What do you feel should be done to change this situation?

6. What does the author mean by "external objects"? and what does this have to do with the behavior of the offender?

Psychodynamics of Rape (Questionnaire)

1. What are the main parts of rape? Is rape the first thought of your sexual desire?

2. Describe the two main approaches used by the anger rapist. What is anger rape?

3. Describe what happens in the development of anger rape. Of the many upsetting events that were pointed out in the articles as to what happens before most assaults, which if any can you relate to your offense? Explain.

4. Why is it important when working with the victim of an anger rape to help them understand and know the underlying reasons of such an offense?

5. The power rapist aim is to capture and control his victim. Describe the three ways the author suggests he may do this. Do any of these fit your offense? Explain.

6. Is the power rapist offense done with a desire for sexual gratification? In this type of rape, is this the offender's first or only offense?

Clinical Aspects of Rape (Questionnaire)

1. What is primary impotency? What is secondary impotency? Which is common during rape?

2. Explain the difference between premature ejaculation and spontaneous ejaculation. What is ejaculatory incompetence?

Article by Marquis

1. What is the physical sign during masturbation that occurs four seconds before ejaculation that means an orgasm is inevitable? Will switching fantasies at this point stop ejaculation?

2. In the method of treating deviant arousal, what is the first step?

3. Would you consider it important with Case One that he learn through masturbation to couple sexuality and tenderness and respect? Why? How had sex conditioned to a "bad girl" messed up his life?

4. Which of these cases did you find most interesting? Why?

Autobiography Outline

A. Early Childhood (0-6 Years)

1. Where did you live? What kind of work did your mother and father do? How did they feel about their work?

2. What was the religious and ethnic background of your family?

3. Who named you? Why was your name chosen?

4. What is your earliest memory? What are the feelings connected to it?

5. What was it like being a small child in your home? Who was special to you, you cared the most about you?

6. Give the names and birthdates of other children in the family in which you grew up:

   a. How did you get along with them?

   b. What was your place in the family?

   c. How did the parents treat each of the children?

7. Who disciplined you?

   a. How did they do it?

   b. Why did they do it?

   c. How did you feel about the discipline you received?

8. Were there any health problems in your family? Any deaths?

9. Did you family attend church or Sunday School? How often? Did parents attend? What church? How important was religion in the family?

10. How did your family show feelings toward each other?

    a. Anger?

    b. Love?

    c. Closeness?

    d. Fear?

11. How did your parents get along with each other? What did they enjoy together? What did they fight about? How did they fight? What effect did their relationship have on you then and now?

B. School Activities (6-19 Years)

1. How did you feel when you started school? What was good about school? What was bad about it?

2. Who were your friends at school? What did you do with them? What games or hobbies did you enjoy with other children during grade school years?

3. How did the teachers treat you?

4. Did you enjoy schoolwork? Was any of it hard for you? What subjects?

5. What did your parents want for you in school? Did they want you to do well in sports, schoolwork, or religion?

6. Were there changes in your living arrangements or family during high school years? Financial changes? Deaths? Moves?

7. Did your feelings about school or achievements in school change in your high school years?

8. What friends and/or activities were you involved with during high school years?

9. What kind of future job dreams or plans did you think about in your high school years? What were your goals?

C. Sexual Development

1. When you were very young, what did your parents teach you about sex?

2. When did you start to masturbate? What did your parents tell you about it? What were your feelings about masturbating?

3. Did you have sexual contact with other family members? Who? When?

4. What was your first sexual experience you remember as a child? What were your feelings then?

Adolescence

5. How did you feel about the changes in your body as a teenager?

6. How often did you have sexual feelings and thoughts about sex as a teenager?

7. When did you start to date?

8. When did you start to have sexual contact with others? Male or female?

9. What did you think was the expected sexual behavior of men during your teenage years?

10. What did you think was the expected sexual behavior of women during your teenage years?

11. Who scared or humiliated you sexually? How? When?

12. What was your father's sexual behavior like? How did you feel about it?

13. What was your mother's sexual behavior like? How did you feel about it?

14. What has your sexual behavior been as an adult? When and why have you been involved in sexual relations with other people?

15. How often do you masturbate now? To what thoughts or fantasies do you usually masturbate?

16. Do you sometimes have different kinds of fantasies that you masturbate to? When and what kinds of thoughts or fantasies?

D. Adulthood

1. What schooling or training were you involved in beyond high school? How did you like it and how did you do in it?

2. What kinds of jobs have you had? For how long? How did you like them?

3. When did you get romantically involved with someone for the first time? How did you meet? What was attractive about the person to you? How long did it last? When and how did it end?

4. How many serious relationships did you have before you married? How long did they last? When did they break up?

5. What first attracted you to your wife? Why did you decide to marry? How did the relationship change after you were married?

6. What were the good parts of your marriage? What were the troubles in the marriage?

7. When did you have children? How many? (Names and ages) How did they affect the marriage?

8. Did you or your wife have other sexual relationships? Why? When?

9. Did the marriage end? When? Why?

E. Behavior That Brought You Into Trouble With the Law

1. When and how did you first get involved with the law? What happened?

2. What other things have you been arrested for? When? What happened?

3. Have you served time in other institutions? How long? Where? For what?

4. What was the situation leading up to your most recent sex offense? What was going on in your life? How were you feeling?

5. What was the specific incident that seemed to trigger your sexually assaultive behavior?

6. What did you say and do to your victim? How did you feel about him/her at the time?

7. What did you feel about the victim and yourself after the crime? What did you say to them?

8. What other similar crimes have you been involved with and for how long?

9. Which drugs or chemicals have you abused? For how long? Do you still use or plan on using?

F. Treatment

1. What other treatment have you or your family members been involved in? For what kinds of problems?

2. What helps you the most in treatment?

3. What do you wish you had done differently? How could you have gotten more from the treatment?

4. What is the most important thing you need now in treatment? How can we help you get it?

List on a separate piece of paper a minimum of four (4) specific goals that you want to work on in treatment. Consider which part of yourself you need to change that caused your crime. Consider your own goals for the future.

Appendix C

Evaluation Schemes

Evaluation Variables	Types of Measures
I. Pre-Treatment Characteristics	General Demographic Data
	Offense Characteristics
	Victim Characteristics
	Criminal History
	Attitude to Treatment
	Education
	Vocational
	Substance Abuse
	Intellectual Measure
	Social Skill/Adjustment
	Psychiatric Diagnosis
	Predictor Equation Questionnaire (Laws, 1984)
II. Service Delivery System	A. Survey of Identification/ Engagement into Treatment Efforts for Sex Offenders in General Population
	B. 1. Client Interview
	2. Moos Environmental Scales
	3. Staff Interview
III. In-Treatment Change	Pre/Post Tests each Module
	Situational Competency Test
	Sex Knowledge Inventory
	Bem Sex Role Inventory
	Interpersonal Behavior Survey
	Attitude to Women Scale
	Novaco Anger Inventory
	Mosher Sex Guilt Scale
	Becker Cognition Scale
	Goal Attainment Scale
	MMPI
	CPI
	Sexual Arousal Patterns

Evaluation Variables	Types of Measures
IV. Follow-Up Outcome	General Demographic Data
	Type of Discharge from Treatment
	Level of Supervision
	Type of Legal Contact
	Type of Arrest
	Type of Conviction
	Relative Adjustment Scale (Seiter)
	Self-Report: Crime
	Self-Report: Fantasy Activity

Appendix D

Suggested Sentencing Conditions for Sex Offenders

General Conditions for All Sex Offenders

1. Individual assumes responsibility for paying counseling costs for victims.

2. All sex offenders classified as Level 2 supervision, no less than one time per month contact with parole and probation officer.

3. Individual must successfully enroll, participate in and complete a treatment program for sex offenders approved by parole and probation officer.

4. Not possess any type of deadly weapon.

5. Submit to polygraph examination to determine involvement in sexual criminal activity or compliance with parole and probation conditions. These examinations would be periodic, upon parole and probation officer's request.

6. Maintain full-time school and/or employment, as approved by parole and probation officer.

7. Individual should not associate with ex-felons.

Community

1. Not driving alone at night or key times when he would offend. Keep detailed driving log, including time, place, and miles.

2. Drive at night only with parole and probation officer's permission and specific destination.

3. No picking up hitchhikers.

4. Not driving with single female unless for a specific reason, e.g., pre-arranged date (usually for rapist).

5. Use of curfew when necessary.

Contact with Children

1. (a) No socialization with individuals under the age of 16 in work or social situations unless accompanied by an approved, responsible adult who is aware of the individual's sexual deviancy; or

   (b) No contact with males or females under the age of 18.

2. No contact with victim unless approved by victim's therapist and offender's therapist and visits are supervised.

3. Individual will not frequent places where children congregate, i.e., parks, playgrounds, schools, etc.

4. Not live in an apartment complex which allows children or neighborhoods with large numbers of children or neighborhoods near schools, parks, playgrounds, etc. Parole and probation officer must approve residence.

5. No involvement with women who have children without approval of parole and probation officer and therapist.

**Conditions Addressing Possible
Pre-Assault Behaviors**

1. Individual should not view TV shows or motion pictures which are geared towards offender's modus operandi, act as stimulus for offender's deviant cycle, or act as stimulus to arouse offender in deviant fashion, e.g., pedophiles not viewing shows whose primary character is a child.

2. Individual not engage in use of pornography, erotica, or frequent adult book stores, sex shops, topless bars, massage parlors, etc.

3. Individual should not use illegal substances; individual with known alcohol problems not to use alcoholic beverages.

4. Individuals with history of alcohol problems not to frequent bars, taverns, and businesses whose primary function is to serve alcoholic beverages.

5. Individual not to associate with alcohol and drug users/abusers.

6. Individual maintain use of prescribed medications.

7. Any offender with a substance abuse problem will attend and successfully complete a drug and/or alcohol treatment program.

**Conditions for Low-Functioning
Offenders**

1. Attend once a week a verifiable social activity (club, church, etc.)

2. Attend counseling (especially important is relationship counseling).

3. Keep budget of money earned and spent.

4. Keep log of daily activities.

Appendix E

Treatment Level Descriptions: CFFPP Sex Offender Treatment Program

Level 1:

1. You are maintaining good personal hygiene. This means:

   a. Shower, using soap, and shampoo hair at least five times weekly.

   b. Brush teeth daily.

   c. Comb and brush hair daily and get a trim when barber comes, as needed.

   d. Change clothes, top to bottom, after shower; wear socks and slippers or shoes at all times.

   e. Wash clothes after two changes of dirty clothes have accumulated.

   f. Change linen weekly.

   These are responsibilities to yourself and to others, and you may be reminded one time before this is seen as a problem behavior.

2. You are dressing appropriately for all situations. This includes clean pants, shirt, socks, and shoes. A coat is to be worn if the weather warrants it. You are to be sleeping in proper sleeping attire.

3. You are keeping your room clean. This includes:

   a. Bed neatly made with fresh linen weekly (more often if necessary).

   b. Nothing under your bed (this is part of the fire code).

   c. Locker cleaned inside and out. Top neatly arranged (not cluttered).

   d. Window sills clean and dusted.

   e. Floors swept daily; mopped weekly.

4. You are assisting in ward clean-up with willingness, without complaining, and doing a thorough job.

5. You are to attend all assigned ward programs and activities (this includes group) without being disruptive. You are expected to be on time, attend group consistently, listen to discussion and express opinions if called on. Schedules are posted on the Bulletin Board. You are to be clean and dressed appropriately for group.

6. Complete first draft of the sexual acting-out scenario on one of each type of sexual crimes. This is to be a complete, specific description of the offense, including, but not limited to:

   a. What were you doing before the offense?

   b. What happened during the offense?

   c. What were you thinking before, during, and after the offense?

   d. What were you feeling before, during, and after the offense? and,

   e. What did the victim do or say?

7. Regardless of the type of crime, complete the first draft of your clarification letter to the victim(s). (This is to be done even if there is no intent to send the letter.)

8. When the first drafts of the acting-out scenarios and the clarification letter have been completed and approved, you will begin attending Sex Offender Group (SOG). You are to discuss with the group your crime relative to:

   a. Your feelings towards the person/persons involved then and now.

   b. Your attitude and thinking at the time of the crime and any changes since.

   c. How your behavior led to the crime.

   d. Demonstrate insight into the impact on the victim.

9. Read and report on at least one library book. (The book and the report must be approved by the Case Monitor. The report must apply the information in the book to your own personal situation.)

10. Complete mini-module on Thinking Errors.

11. If there are significant others (spouse, girlfriend, parents, etc.) involved in your life, set up a time for an initial interview with staff.

12. Each month, identify a behavior you need to change. (This could include one of the general treatment level requirements or specific ones designed for you.) With your Case Monitor, Behavioral Therapist, or Group Leader, develop a contract for change. Present contract to Family Group. You should review your progress each week with your Case Monitor, Behavioral Therapist, or group.

13. Participate meaningfully in assigned Activity Therapy assignments, groups, modules, and activities. This includes being prepared and on time, actively participating and accepting and giving feedback on behaviors and attitudes.

14. You are completing on time and accepting feedback on any additional assignments given you from your groups. Case Monitor, Behavioral Therapist, Activity Therapist, educational module facilitators, or other staff members.

During Levels 1, 2, and 3, you must read either *Father-Daughter Incest* or *Hidden Victims* or *Men Who Rape*, in addition to *Inner Child of the Past*.

Level 2:

1. You are to participate meaningfully in prescribed treatment programs. You are expected to pay attention, interact appropriately, contribute appropriate comments voluntarily twice each group meeting, follow directions and clean up after groups without reminders.

2. Begin writing the first draft of your autobiography.

3. You are accepting the responsibility of group wake-up person or assume other responsibility as assigned.

4. Sign in and out each time you leave the ward for groups or walks. Show your name, destination, time left.

5. You are to be on time for medication without reminders.

6. Complete the clarification letter to the satisfaction of the SOG.

7. Begin keeping a daily thinking, feeling and/or fantasy log as assigned. Turn the log in to the Case Monitor or Behavioral Therapist as requested, on time and without reminders.

8. Read and report on at least one more book per Case Monitor or Behavioral Technician.

9. Complete sexual acting-out scenarios per Behavior Therapist.

10. Participate satisfactorily in any behavioral treatment per Behavior Therapist.

11. Successfully complete module on difference between assertiveness and aggressiveness, and giving and receiving feedback.

12. Hold first session between staff and significant other(s).

13. You are to maintain all Level 1 responsibilities without reminders from staff or group members.

Level 3:

1. You are to sponsor a new resident into your group. You need to be available to help new people prepare for group (remind of grooming, time, dress, etc.).

You are demonstrating your awareness of routine in group activities and are actively involved.

2. You are to serve on the Ward Council as elected or assume other responsibilities as assigned or elected.

3. You are demonstrating realistic improvement in giving and receiving feedback. You are showing yourself to be an increasingly responsible and mature human being. In group, you share your feelings and thoughts on topics being discussed. You accept responsibility for your own behavior without excuses and appropriately assist others through support and confrontation. Give and receive feedback in group; contribute several times each meeting.

4. You are expected to know security procedures for your ward and all areas which you travel in. You are expected to demonstrate a positive attitude towards security at all times.

5. You are showing self-direction concerning leisure time.

6. Successfully complete Thinking Errors and Anger Management modules when offered.

7. Begin to identify and write out danger cycle thinking and behavior patterns per Case Monitor and Behavior Therapist.

8. You are presenting the first draft of your autobiography to SOG and are accepting feedback regarding more details needed.

9. Read and report on at least two more books per Case Monitor or Behavior Therapist.

10. Interview with staff and significant other(s) dealing with past responsibility of all parties.

11. You are aware of your fiscal responsibilities and are demonstrating mature money management.

12. You are maintaining all responsibilities from previous levels without reminders from staff or group members.

Level 4:

1. In group, you are continuing to play a leadership role and are available to facilitate group members having difficulty. This includes sharing yourself honestly and openly, participating in nearly all discussions in group, model assertiveness in group and bring up relevant issues in group without prompting.

2. You are to present the final draft of your autobiography to group and accept feedback on it.

3. You are continuing to assume leadership roles on the ward. This includes appropriate role-modeling behavior and a positive attitude toward treatment.

4. Complete and present to SOG your danger cycle thinking and behavior patterns.

5. Successfully complete Problem-Solving Module.

6. If substance abuse or dependency has played a part in your antisocial behavior, you will begin attending a community-based AA or NA group.

7. Read and report on at least two books per Case Monitor or Behavior Therapist.

8. At least one more session between staff and significant other(s) is to be held.

9. You are maintaining all responsibilities from previous levels without reminders from staff or group members.

Level 5:

1. You continue to participate openly and actively in group. Take a leadership role in group, giving and receiving feedback, supporting and confronting, facilitating discussion. Lead group when assigned.

2. You will begin attending Transition Group and openly and honestly discuss fears, frustrations, and problems dealing with community transition and living.

3. You are developing a transition plan. Your very detailed plans should involve the following:

   a. Housing.

b. Household budget.

c. Mental health, medical and dental aftercare.

d. Probation/parole supervision

e. Employment.

f. Relationship with family.

g. Leisure time activities.

h. Support groups, both therapeutic and recreational.

i. In the transition planning, thoroughly list all danger cycle thinking and behaviors, and specifically what you intend to do to identify and stop that cycle. Include a specific, continuing self-administered behavioral treatment plan when in the community.

4. Participate in Victim Awareness Program (as available).

5. Participate in a structured empathy assignment.

6. Demonstrate less than 20% arousal to all deviant material in two successive assessments.

7. Demonstrate consistent, adequate response to stress, pressure, and frustration.

8. Demonstrate appropriate assertiveness behavior with persons in authority.

9. At least two more sessions with staff and significant other(s) dealing with danger cycle thinking and behavior patterns.

10. Read and report on at least two more books per Case Monitor.

11. You are demonstrating effective time management, prioritizing and problem-solving skills in most aspects of ward and community behavior.

12. You are maintaining all responsibilities from previous levels without reminders from staff or group members.

Level 6:

1. You are continuing to participate in group and are acting as a proper role model.

2. You are now participating appropriately and responsibly in all relevant aspects of community transition.

3. At least one session with the staff and significant other(s) dealing with responsibilities of all parties upon discharge.

4. Complete discharge evaluation, including final Minnesota Multiphasic Personality Inventory (MMPI).

5. You are maintaining all responsibilities from previous levels without reminders from staff or group members.

Appendix F

Pastoral Assessment

Interview Format

1. Religious background of client and family. What did you like most about it? What did you like least?

2. Have there been changes in your religious activity and/or affiliation? What precipitated these changes?

3. What has most influenced the way you feel about religion? What people? What experiences?

4. What do your parents think about God and about religion?

5. What is your earliest memory of a religious experience or belief?

6. What does religion mean to you?

7. What is the most important thing that God does?

8. What is the most important thing that religion teaches?

9. What is your favorite Bible verse? Why?

10. What is your favorite Bible story? Why?

11. Who is your favorite Bible character? Why?

12. What Bible character are you most like? How are you like this character?

13. How does God function in your personal life?

14. When in your life did God feel closest?

15. When did God feel furthest away?

16. How do you think God feels about you right now?

17. What does prayer mean to you?

18. If you pray, what kinds of things do you pray about or for?

19. What is the worst sin that a person could commit?

20. What is the most religious thing that a person could do?

21. What do you think about bad things that happen in the world?

22. What are your ideas of an afterlife, what do you think happens after you die?

23. If God would grant you any three wishes, what would you want?

24. What do you see as your number one goal in life?

25. Do you feel like God approves of this goal?

26. What do you think about this story?

27. Who would you be in the story?

28. How do you think this man felt about being forgiven?

29. Who would carry you the way that the four friends carried their paralyzed buddy?

30. Who would you be willing to carry this way?

31. If you were to sum up what you want from God in a short prayer, what would that Life Prayer be?

32. The Old Testament put a lot of emphasis on the idea of "covenant." This was the idea that persons would act in a certain way, and in response Yehweh would be

their God. As you think about the work we've just done, and your life, how would you describe your covenant with God? What would it sound like if you finished this sentence, "God, I am your person...."?

33. Were there any questions that made you particularly anxious or that raised other questions that we didn't talk about? Is there anything else that you think it is important to say about your faith or your religious experience?

Appendix G

Illinois v. Allen,
478 U.S. 364 (1986)

Justice REHNQUIST delivered the opinion of the Court.

The question presented by this case is whether the proceedings under the Illinois Sexually Dangerous Persons Act (Act), Ill.Rev.Stat., ch. 38, para. 105-1.01 *et seq.* (1985), are "criminal" within the meaning of the Fifth Amendment's guarantee against compulsory self-incrimination.

Petitioner Terry B. Allen was charged by information in the Circuit Court of Peoria County with committing the crimes of unlawful restraint and deviate sexual assault. Shortly thereafter the State filed a petition to have petitioner declared a sexually dangerous person within the meaning of the Act.[1]

After a preliminary hearing on the information, the criminal charges were dismissed for lack of probable cause, and the petition was apparently dismissed as well. Petitioner was then recharged by indictment, and the petition to declare him sexually dangerous was reinstated.

Pursuant to the Act, with petitioner and counsel present, the trial court ordered petitioner to submit to two psychiatric examinations; the court explained the procedure as well as petitioner's rights under the Act, and petitioner indicated that he understood the nature of the proceedings. At the bench trial on the petition, the State presented the testimony of the two examining psychiatrists, over petitioner's objection that they had elicited information from him in violation of his privilege against self-incrimination. The trial court ruled that petitioner's statements to the psychiatrists were not themselves admissible, but allowed each psychiatrist to give his opinion based upon his interview with petitioner. Both psychiatrists expressed the view that petitioner was mentally ill and had criminal propensities to commit sexual assaults. Petitioner did not testify or offer other evidence at the trial. Based upon the testimony of the psychiatrists, as well as that of the victim of the sexual assault for which petitioner had been indicted, the trial court found petitioner to be a sexually dangerous person under the Act. Consistent with the requirements of Illinois case law, the court made three specific findings: that at the time of trial petitioner had been suffering from a mental disorder for not less than one year; that he had propensities to commit sex offenses; and that by his actions he had demonstrated such propensities.

* * *

The Self-Incrimination Clause of the Fifth Amendment, which applies to the States through the Fourteenth Amendment, *Malloy v. Hogan*, 378 U.S. 1 (1964), provides that no person "shall be compelled in any criminal case to be a witness against himself." This Court has long held that the privilege against self-incrimination "not only permits a person to refuse to testify against himself at a criminal trial in which he is a defendant, but also 'privileges him not to answer official questions put to him in any other proceedings, civil or criminal, formal or informal, where the answers might incriminate him in future criminal proceedings.'" In this case the Illinois Supreme Court ruled that a person whom the State attempts to commit under the Act is protected from use of his compelled answers in any subsequent criminal case in which he is the defendant. What we have here, then, is not a claim that petitioner's statements to the psychiatrists might be used to incriminate him in some future criminal proceeding, but instead his claim that because the sexually-dangerous-person proceeding is itself "criminal," he was entitled to refuse to answer any questions at all.

The question of whether a particular proceeding is criminal for the purposes of the Self-Incrimination Clause is first of all a question of statutory construction. Here, Illinois has expressly provided that proceedings under the Act "shall be civil in nature," Para. 105-3.01, indicating that when it files a petition against a person under the Act it intends to proceed in a nonpunitive, noncriminal manner, "without regard to the procedural protections and restrictions available in criminal prosecutions." As petitioner correctly points out, however, the civil label is not always dispositive. Where a defendant has provided "the clearest proof" that "the statutory scheme [is] so punitive either in purpose or effect as to negate [the State's] intention" that the proceeding be civil, it must be considered criminal and the privilege against self-incrimination must be applied. We think that petitioner has failed to provide such proof in this case.

The Illinois Supreme Court reviewed the Act and its own case law and concluded that these proceedings, while similar to criminal proceedings in that they are accompanied by strict procedural safeguards, are essentially civil in nature. We are unpersuaded by petitioner's efforts to challenge this conclusion. Under the Act, the State has a statutory obligation to provide "care and treatment for [persons adjudged sexually dangerous] designed to effect recovery," Para. 105-8, in a facility set aside to provide psychiatric care. And "[i]f the patient is found to be no longer dangerous, the court shall order that he be discharged." Para. 105-9. While the committed person has the burden of showing that he is no longer dangerous,[2] he may apply for release at any time.[3] In short, the State has disavowed any interest in punishment, provided for the treatment of those it commits, and established a system under which committed persons may be released after the briefest time in confine-

ment. The Act thus does not appear to promote either of "the traditional aims of punishment-retribution and deterrence." *Kennedy v. Mendoza-Martinez*, 372 U.S. 144 (1963). Cf. *Addington v. Texas*, 441 U.S. 418 (1979) (in Texas "civil commitment state power is not exercised in a punitive sense").

Petitioner offers several arguments in support of his claim that despite the apparently nonpunitive purposes of the Act, it should be considered criminal as far as the privilege against self-incrimination is concerned. He first notes that the State cannot file a sexually-dangerous-person petition unless it has already brought criminal charges against the person in question. Para. 105-3. In addition, the State must prove that the person it seeks to commit perpetrated "at least one act of or attempt at sexual assault or sexual molestation." To petitioner, these factors serve to distinguish the Act from other civil commitments, which typically are not tied to any criminal charge and which petitioner apparently concedes are not "criminal" under the Self-Incrimination Clause. We disagree. That the State has chosen not to apply the Act to the larger class of mentally ill persons who might be found sexually dangerous does not somehow transform a civil proceeding into a criminal one. And as the State points out, it must prove more than just the commission of a sexual assault; the Illinois Supreme Court, as we noted above, has construed the Act to require proof of the existence of a mental disorder for more than one year and a propensity to commit sexual assaults, in addition to demonstration of that propensity through sexual assault.

The discussion of civil commitment in *Addington*, in which this Court concluded that the Texas involuntary-commitment scheme is not criminal insofar as the requirement of proof beyond a reasonable doubt is concerned, fully supports our conclusion here:

[T]he initial inquiry in a civil commitment proceeding is very different from the central issue in either a delinquency proceeding or a criminal prosecution. In the latter cases the basic issue is a straightforward factual question—did the accused commit the act alleged? There may be factual issues to resolve in a commitment proceeding, but the factual aspects represent only the beginning of the inquiry. Whether the individual is mentally ill and dangerous to either himself or others and is in need of confined therapy turns on the *meaning* of the facts which must be interpreted by expert psychiatrists and psychologists. *Id.*, 441 U.S., at 429 (emphasis in original).

While here the State must prove at least one act of sexual assault, that antecedent conduct is received not to punish past misdeeds, but primarily to show the accused's mental condition and to predict future behavior.

In his attempt to distinguish this case from other civil commitments, petitioner places great reliance on the fact that proceedings under the Act are accompanied by procedural safeguards usually found in criminal trials. In particular, he observes that the Act provides an accused with the right to counsel, Para. 105-5, the right to demand a jury trial, *ibid.*, and the right to confront and cross-examine witnesses. At the conclusion of the hearing, the trier of fact must determine whether the prosecution has proved the person's sexual dangerousness beyond a reasonable doubt. Para. 105-3.01. But as we noted above, the State has indicated quite clearly its intent that these commitment proceedings be civil in nature; its decision nevertheless to provide some of the safeguards applicable in criminal trials cannot itself turn these proceedings into criminal prosecutions requiring the full panoply of rights applicable there.

Relying chiefly on *In re Gault*, 387 U.S. (1967), petitioner also urges that the proceedings in question are "criminal" because a person adjudged sexually dangerous under the Act is committed for an indeterminate period to the Menard Psychiatric Center, a maximum-security institution that is run by the Illinois Department of Corrections and that houses convicts needing psychiatric care as well as sexually dangerous persons. Whatever its label and whatever the State's alleged purpose, petitioner argues, such commitment is the sort of punishment—total deprivation of liberty in a criminal setting—that *Gault* teaches cannot be imposed absent application of the privilege against self-incrimination. We believe that *Gault* is readily distinguishable.

First, *Gault*'s sweeping statement that "our Constitution guarantees that no person shall

be 'compelled' to be a witness against himself when he is threatened with deprivation of liberty," *id.*, at 50, is plainly not good law. Although the fact that incarceration may result is relevant to the question whether the privilege against self-incrimination applies, *Addington* demonstrates that involuntary commitment does not itself trigger the entire range of criminal procedural protections. Indeed, petitioner apparently concedes that traditional civil commitment does not require application of the privilege. Only two Terms ago, in *Minnesota v. Murphy*, 465 U.S. at 435, n. 7, this Court stated that a person may not claim the privilege merely because his answer might result in revocation of his probationary status. Cf. *Middendorf v. Henry*, 425 U.S. 25, 37 (1976). ("[F]act that a proceeding will result in loss of liberty does not *ipso facto* mean that the proceeding is a 'criminal prosecution' for purposes of the Sixth Amendment").

The Court in *Gault* was obviously persuaded that the State intended to *punish* its juvenile offenders, observing that in many States juveniles may be placed in "adult penal institutions" for conduct that if committed by an adult would be a crime. Here, by contrast, the State serves its purpose of *treating* rather than punishing sexually dangerous persons by committing them to an institution expressly designed to provide psychiatric care and treatment. That the Menard Psychiatric Center houses not only sexually dangerous persons but also prisoners from other institutions who are in need of psychiatric treatment does not transform the State's intent to treat into an intent to punish. Nor does the fact that Menard is apparently a maximum-security facility affect our analysis:

> The state has a legitimate interest under its *parens patriae* powers in providing care to its citizens who are unable because of emotional disorders to care for themselves; the state also has authority under its police power to protect the community from the dangerous tendencies of some who are mentally ill. *Addington*, 441 U.S., at 426.

Illinois' decision to supplement its *parens patriae* concerns with measures to protect the welfare and safety of other citizens does not render the Act punitive.

Petitioner has not demonstrated, and the record does not suggest, that "sexually dangerous persons" in Illinois are confined under conditions incompatible with the State's asserted interest in treatment. Had petitioner shown, for example, that the confinement of such persons imposes on them a regimen which is essentially identical to that imposed upon felons with no need for psychiatric care, this might well be a different case. But the record here tells us little or nothing about the regimen at the psychiatric center, and it certainly does not show that there are no relevant differences between confinement there and confinement in other parts of the maximum-security prison complex. Indeed, counsel for the State assures us that under Illinois law sexually dangerous persons must not be treated like ordinary prisoners. We therefore cannot say that the conditions of petitioner's confinement themselves amount to "punishment" and thus render "criminal" the proceedings which led to confinement.

* * *

For the reasons stated, we conclude that the Illinois proceedings here considered were not "criminal" within the meaning of the Fifth Amendment to the United States Constitution, and that due process does not independently require application of the privilege. Here, as in *Addington*, "[t]he essence of federalism is that states must be free to develop a variety of solutions to problems and not be forced into a common, uniform mold" of the sort urged by petitioner. 441 U.S., at 431. The judgment of the Supreme Court of Illinois is therefore

Affirmed.

Justice STEVENS, with whom Justice BRENNAN, Justice MARSHALL, and Justice BLACKMUN join, dissenting.

* * *

A goal of treatment is not sufficient, in and of itself, to render inapplicable the Fifth Amendment, or to prevent a characterization of proceedings as "criminal." With respect to a conventional criminal statute, if a State declared that its goal was "treatment" and "rehabilitation," it is obvious that the Fifth Amendment would still apply. The sexually-

dangerous-person proceeding similarly may not escape a characterization as "criminal" simply because a goal is "treatment." If this were not the case, moreover, nothing would prevent a State from creating an entire corpus of "dangerous person" statutes to shadow its criminal code. Indeterminate commitment would derive from proven violations of criminal statutes, combined with findings of mental disorders and "criminal propensities," and constitutional protections for criminal defendants would be simply inapplicable. The goal would be "treatment"; the result would be evisceration of criminal law and its accompanying protections.

The Illinois Attorney General nevertheless argues that the importance of treatment in the Act has a special significance. The State contends that recognizing a right to silence would make it impossible to reach a correct diagnosis concerning the existence of a mental disorder and the need for treatment. However, the Illinois General Assembly has squarely rejected this argument in other civil commitment proceedings. Illinois' civil commitment procedure expressly protects the individual's right to silence.[14]

* * *

The Attorney General's emphasis on the interference with treatment that the right of silence would create thus indeed has a significance, but not the one he suggests. For, not only would a characterization of the proceeding as "criminal" lead to a right to silence under the Fifth Amendment, but a characterization of the proceeding as "civil" would also lead to a right to silence under state law. It is only in the "sexually dangerous person" proceeding that the individual may be compelled to give evidence that will be used to deprive him of his liberty. The fact that this proceeding is unique—neither wholly criminal nor civil—surely cannot justify the unique deprivation of a constitutional protection.

It is, of course, true that "the State has a substantial interest in ... protecting the public from sexually dangerous persons." But the fact that an individual accused of being a "sexually dangerous person" is also considered a danger to the community cannot justify the denial of the Fifth Amendment privilege; if so, the privilege would never be available for any person accused of a violent crime. The fact that it may be more difficult for the State to obtain evidence that will lead to incarceration similarly cannot prevent the applicability of the Fifth Amendment; if so, the right would never be justified, for it could always be said to have that effect. Nor can the fact that proof of sexual dangerousness requires evidence of noncriminal elements—the continuing requirement that a future criminal "propensity" be proved, for instance—prevent the applicability of the Fifth Amendment; if anything, that requirement should be the subject of greater, rather than lesser, concern.

In the end, this case requires a consideration of the role and value of the Fifth Amendment. The privilege sometimes does serve the interest in making the truth-seeking function of a trial more reliable. Indeed, a review of the psychiatrists' reports in this very case suggests the propriety of that concern.[5]

* * *

For the Court, these concerns are not implicated today because the prosecution-initiated and prison-destined, sexually-dangerous-person proceeding is not "criminal" in nature. In my opinion, permitting a State to create a shadow criminal law without the fundamental protection of the Fifth Amendment conflicts with the respect for liberty and individual dignity that has long characterized, and that continues to characterize, our free society.

I respectfully dissent.

NOTES

[1]The Act defines sexually dangerous persons as follows:

All persons suffering from a mental disorder, which mental disorder has existed for a period of not less than one year, immediately prior to the filing of the petition hereinafter provided for, coupled with criminal propensities to the commission of sex offenses, and who have demonstrated propensities toward acts of sexual assault or acts of sexual molestation of children, are hereby declared sexually dangerous persons. [Para. 105-1.01].

[2] Even if he fails to meet his burden the committed person may nonetheless be conditionally released:

If the court finds that the patient appears no longer to be dangerous but that it is impossible to determine with certainty under conditions of institutional care that such person has fully recovered, the court shall enter an order permitting such person to go at large subject to such conditions and such supervision by the Director as in the opinion of the court will adequately protect the public. [Para. 105-9].

[3]The Act further provides that "[u]pon an order of discharge every outstanding information and indictment, the basis of which was the reason for the present detention, shall be quashed." *Ibid.*

[4]See Ill.Rev.Stat., ch 91 1/2, Para. 3-208 (1985) ("Whenever a petition has been executed pursuant to Section 3-507, 3-601, or 3-701, and prior to this examination for the purpose of certification of a person 12 or over, the person conducting this examination shall inform the person being examined in a simple comprehensible manner of the purpose of the examination; that he does not have to talk to the examiner; and that any statements he makes may be disclosed at a court hearing on the issue of whether he is subject to involuntary admission. If the person being examined has not been so informed, the examiner shall not be permitted to testify at any subsequent court hearing concerning the respondent's admission").

[5]One of the psychiatrist's reports stated, in part:

The defendant wanted to be found sexually dangerous and did so because he felt that it was a better alternative than a trial trying to be found not guilty.... I have the definite impression that he is unreliable and that sometimes he is not telling the truth. App. 36-37.

That doctor reported that the defendant admitted that he had "sexual intercourse" with the victim—a fact that she denied. None of the other incidents described in the doctor's report (the first of which occurred when the defendant was 10 years old) had any corroboration or involved an identified partner or victim.

Appendix H

In re Young, 857 P.2d 989 (Wash. 1993)[*]

DURHAM, Judge.

In this case, the sexually violent predator provisions of the Community Protection Act of 1990 are challenged by two people who have been civilly committed under its authority. Important constitutional and technical issues are raised by this unique legislation, which seeks to protect our citizens by incapacitating and attempting to treat those whose mental abnormalities create a grave risk of future harm. Although the ultimate goal of the statute is to treat, and someday cure those whose mental condition cause them to commit acts of sexual violence, its immediate purpose is to ensure the commitment of these persons in order to protect the community. In this sense, it is similar to any other civil commitment. However, the Legislature has found that the exceptional risks posed by sexual predators, and the seemingly intractable nature of their illness, necessitates a specially tailored civil commitment approach. After exhaustive review of the numerous challenges raised by petitioners, we conclude that the sex predator provisions of the Community Protection Act of 1990 are constitutional. However, for reasons stated below, we reverse petitioner Cunningham's commitment, and remand petitioner Young's case for consideration of less restrictive alternatives.

The numerous issues raised by Young and Cunningham can be categorized as follows:

---

[*] This is such a significant opinion that it is reproduced here in its entirety, including all citations and the dissenting opinion. Note that this decision is binding only in Washington although it may be persuasive elsewhere.

First, petitioners claim that the act violates the ex post facto clause and the prohibition against double jeopardy. Resolution of those issues depends on whether the law is civil or criminal in nature. Second, petitioners raise several substantive due process arguments. They claim that the State lacks sufficient justification to deprive them of their liberty, and that the sex predator statute amounts to unconstitutional preventive detention. They also contend, as a substantive matter, that dangerousness must be proved by evidence of a recent overt act, and that they are entitled to less restrictive conditions of confinement. Third, petitioners argue that there are several procedural deficiencies. They claim that the probable cause hearing should not be held ex parte, that the jury verdict should be unanimous, that the selection of the juries was flawed, that the act is void for vagueness, and that they were unconstitutionally denied a right to remain silent. Finally, several evidentiary issues are raised.

I. Background

1. *The Act*

The Community Protection Act of 1990 (the Act) was passed in response to citizens' concerns about the State's laws and procedures regarding sexually violent offenders. *See* Governor's Task Force on Comm'ty Protec., *Final Report* I-1 (1989) (hereinafter *Report*). The impetus for convening the task force was the commission of two violent crimes: the murder of a Seattle woman by an offender on work release, and the violent sexual attack on a young Tacoma boy. *Report*, at I-1. The Act contains 14 separate sections, dealing with such topics as registration of sex offenders, crime victims' compensation, background checks, and increased penalties for sex offenders. Laws of 1990, ch. 3, p. 12.

Part X of the Act is entitled "Civil Commitment" and is codified at RCW 71.09 (hereinafter Statute). Under the Statute, those defendants who are determined to be "sexually violent predators" can be involuntarily committed after they have served their sentences. The Legislature enacted extensive findings. Among those, the Legislature stated:

In contrast to persons appropriate for civil commitment under chapter 71.05 RCW, sexually violent predators generally have antisocial personality features which are unamenable to existing mental illness treatment modalities and those features render them likely to engage in sexually violent behavior. ... The legislature further finds that the prognosis for curing sexually violent offenders is poor, the treatment needs of this population are very long term, and the treatment modalities for this population are very different than the traditional treatment modalities. ... RCW 71.09.010.

A "sexually violent predator" is someone "who has been convicted of or charged with a crime of sexual violence and who suffers from a mental abnormality or personality disorder which makes the person likely to engage in predatory acts of sexual violence." RCW 71.09.020(1). Crimes of sexual violence are enumerated in the Statute, and include crimes not usually considered sex offenses if they are determined beyond a reasonable doubt to have been "sexually motivated." RCW 71.09.020(4)(c). The term "personality disorder" is not defined by the Statute, but the term "mental abnormality" is defined as "a congenital or acquired condition affecting the emotional or volitional capacity which predisposes the person to the commission of criminal sexual acts." RCW 71.09.020(2). "Predatory" acts are those directed at strangers, or individuals groomed by the offender for the purpose of victimization. RCW 71.09.020(3).

Under the Statute, when a person's sentence for a sexually violent offense has expired or is about to expire, the State is authorized to file a petition alleging the per-

son to be a sexually violent predator. RCW 71.09.030; see also RCW 71.09.025. When the petition is filed, a judge must determine ex parte if "probable cause exists to believe that the person named in the petition is a sexually violent predator." RCW 71.09.040. When probable cause is found, the person is taken into custody and transferred to a facility for evaluation, pursuant to rules developed by the Department of Social and Health Services (DSHS). Within 45 days, the court shall conduct a trial to determine if the person is a sexually violent predator. RCW 71.09.050. Either party, or the court, may demand a jury trial.

The detainee has a statutory right to counsel. In addition, the detainee may be examined by a qualified expert of his or her choice. Both services will be provided if the person is indigent. RCW 71.09.050. The burden is on the State to prove, beyond a reasonable doubt, that the detainee is a sexually violent predator. RCW 71.09.060(1). If so, then he or she shall be committed to a facility "for control, care, and treatment" until "safe to be at large." RCW 71.09.060(1). The Statute limits treatment centers to mental health facilities located within correctional institutions. RCW 71.09.060(3); RCW 10.77.220.

The detainee must be examined annually to determine his or her mental condition, and the results must be provided to the trial court. RCW 71.09.070. In addition, the person may obtain an additional examination at state expense, if necessary. RCW 71.09.070. If it appears that the person is no longer a sexually violent predator then the secretary of DSHS shall authorize the detainee to petition the court for release. RCW 71.09.090. When such a petition is filed, the court must order a hearing within 45 days. At the hearing, a jury may be demanded by either party, and the burden is on the State to prove, beyond a reasonable doubt, that the detainee is not safe to be at large. RCW 71.09.090(1).

A detainee may also petition the court directly without the approval of the secretary. RCW 71.09.090(2). Upon filing such a petition, a show cause hearing is held, at which time the petitioner has the right to be represented by appointed counsel, but not the right to be present. If the court finds probable

cause that the detainee is no longer dangerous, then a full hearing is held with the same
procedures as above. The court will not hold
any further hearings unless the detainee can
show a change of circumstance. RCW
71.09.100.

2. *Andre Brigham Young*

The petition in Andre Brigham Young's
case was filed on October 24, 1990, 1 day
prior to his release from prison for his most
recent rape conviction. The certification for
determination of probable cause (certificate)
references two psychological evaluations of
Young and describes his criminal history,
which includes six violent felony rapes of
adult female strangers. These rapes, which the
record suggests may be only a partial account-
ing of Young's sexual assaults, occurred over
the past 31 years during the intermittent periods when Young was not in custody.

Young's first series of known rapes
occurred in the fall of 1962, when he broke
into the respective homes of four different
women, forcing them to engage in sexual
intercourse. On at least two of these occasions, Young threatened his victims with a
knife. In another incident, he raped a young
mother with a 5-week old infant nearby.
Young was convicted in October 1963 on four
counts of first degree rape, with two deadly
weapon findings.

Less than a year later, while free on an
appeal bond for his 1963 convictions, Young
entered the home of another woman. With
her child present, he exposed himself, threatened to hurt the child, and threatened to rape
and kill the woman. Fortunately, he was
frightened away. Young was charged with
attempted rape, but was never tried for this
offense because he was found incompetent.

Young was released on parole in January of
1972. After roughly 5 years of freedom,
Young was again convicted of rape. As with
the previously known offenses, he raped this
woman after illegally entering her home in
the early morning hours. Young pleaded
guilty to third degree rape.

He was released from prison in 1980. In
1985, he raped another woman, again forcing
his way into her apartment. Three small children were present. Young was convicted of
first degree rape.

After reviewing the petition and supporting
certificate, Judge Johnson issued an ex parte
order which found probable cause, and directed the clerk to issue a no-bail arrest warrant
and to transfer Young to the Special
Commitment Center at Monroe. Following
Young's detention at Monroe, counsel for
Young brought motions seeking transportation back to King County, a probable cause
hearing to challenge the ex parte ruling, and
bail—all of which were denied by Judge
Johnson. On November 14, 1990, over
Young's assertion of a right to remain silent,
Judge Johnson ordered him to participate in
psychiatric evaluations. Young refused to
participate in the evaluations. A pretrial hearing was held in mid-January where the
Superior Court rejected constitutional challenges to the Statute. Young was not allowed
to attend this hearing.

Trial began on February 12, 1991, in front
of Judge Bever. Both sides presented testimony by expert witnesses. Young called Dr.
Nancy M. Steele, a psychologist who works
with sex offenders in Minnesota. She testified that there is no particular mental disorder
that makes a person likely to re-offend. In
addition, Dr. G. Christian Harris testified that
rape is a behavior, not a diagnostic category,
and that he could not accurately predict that
any particular person would re-offend. Young
also called Dr. Fred Wise, who questioned the
legitimacy of the diagnostic impressions
made by the State's expert witness.

The State called Dr. Irwin Dreiblatt, a
licensed clinical psychologist who has evaluated some 1,400 sexual offenders and treated
approximately 700 in his 25 years of practice.
Based upon a records review, Dr. Dreiblatt
testified to a reasonable psychological certainty that it was his diagnostic impression
that Young suffered from: (1) a severe personality disorder not otherwise specified,
with primarily paranoid and anti-social features, (2) a severe paraphilia, which would be
classified as either paraphilia sexual sadism
or paraphilia not otherwise specified (rape).
Dr. Dreiblatt stated that the severe paraphilia
constituted a "mental abnormality" under the
sex predator commitment Statute. Dr.
Dreiblatt further concluded that the severe
paraphilia—in combination with the person-

ality disorder, the length of time spanning Young's crimes, his recidivism record, his use of weapons, his persistent denial of the crimes and his lack of empathy or remorse for his victims—made it more likely than not that Young "would commit further sexually violent acts." Report of Proceedings Young (RPY) (Feb. 27, 1991), at 166.

The victims of Young's previous rape convictions testified regarding the circumstances of their assaults. Evidence was introduced pertaining to a 1972 conviction for a bomb threat. Defense motions for jury instructions regarding the presumption of innocence, the appropriate inference from Young's failure to testify, and others were denied by the court. At the request of the State, the jury was instructed that a unanimous verdict was required. On March 8, the jury concluded that Young was a "sexually violent predator."

3. *Vance Russell Cunningham*

The petition in Vance Russell Cunningham's case was filed on December 21, 1990, about 4½ months after Cunningham had completed his most recent prison sentence for rape. As with Young, the certificate for determination of probable cause references two psychological evaluations of Cunningham and describes his extensive history of sexual crimes. Although Cunningham was only 26 when the petition was filed, his criminal history spans the prior 10 years and includes three convictions for raping adult female strangers.

Cunningham's first felony occurred in 1980 when he was 15 years old. A woman was walking through a Seattle-area park with her three young children, when Cunningham, armed with a knife, jumped out of some bushes and commanded, "nobody move." After the woman screamed, Cunningham fled. When he was apprehended, Cunningham confessed to the assault and admitted that his purpose was to force the woman to commit oral sex upon him. For this juvenile assault, he received a short sentence and some unspecified counseling.

In 1984, Cunningham raped a woman hitchhiker to whom he had offered a ride. Cunningham threatened to kill his victim, struck her several times, forced her to the ground, and then raped her. Cunningham

pleaded guilty to second degree rape, and was sentenced to 31 months in prison.

Only 3 months after his release in November 1986, Cunningham committed his next rape. He grabbed the victim around the throat, and then forced her to have anal intercourse with him. Two months later, in April 1987, Cunningham assaulted another woman in a similar manner, forcing her to engage in additional acts of intercourse. For these actions, a jury found him guilty on two counts of second degree rape.

In an ex parte proceeding, after reviewing the petition and supporting affidavit, Judge Johnson found probable cause and ordered the clerk to issue a no-bail arrest warrant, and transfer Cunningham to the Special Commitment Center at Monroe. Judge Johnson also ruled that Cunningham "has no blanket Fifth Amendment privilege to refuse to answer any and all questions" put to him during the evaluation. Clerk's Papers, at 1183. On January 2, defense counsel brought motions to vacate the ex parte order and to allow Cunningham's participation in pretrial proceedings. The motions were denied. Cunningham was allowed to be present at his March 15, 1991, pretrial hearing.

Following jury selection, trial commenced on May 21, 1991, in front of Judge McCullough. The jury heard extensive testimony from expert witnesses for both sides. Cunningham called Dr. Steele to testify on his behalf. Based upon a records review, Dr. Steele stated that Cunningham was not suffering from a mental abnormality which would make him dangerous to women.

The State's expert was Dr. Leslie Rawlings, a licensed clinical psychologist who specializes in the assessment and treatment of sexual offenders. After reviewing Cunningham's records, Dr. Rawlings stated his diagnostic impression to a reasonable psychological certainty that Cunningham suffered from a severe paraphilia, not otherwise specified (rape). Dr. Rawlings further testified that paraphilia qualifies as a "mental abnormality" under the sex predator commitment Statute. Citing the paraphilia and several other factors, Dr. Rawlings concluded that "[i]t's my professional opinion that Mr. Cunningham is more likely than not to engage in predatory acts of sexual violence if out in the community." Report of Proceedings Cunningham (RPC) (May 21, 1991), at 39.

The jury also heard testimony from the victims involved in Cunningham's previous rape convictions. Cunningham testified on his own behalf. Over defense objections, the jury was instructed that a unanimous verdict was not required. On May 31, 1991, the jury returned a 11-to-1 verdict which found Cunningham to be a "sexually violent predator."

Both Young and Cunningham brought personal restraint petitions and motions for immediate release, which were heard by this court in January 1991. The motions for release were denied, and the court accepted jurisdiction over the petitions. The petitioners were consolidated with the direct appeals from the trials.

II. Ex Post Facto Law and Double Jeopardy

Petitioners argue that the Statute is unconstitutional, because it violates the double jeopardy clause and the prohibition against ex post facto laws. Generally, these clauses apply to criminal matters. Thus, if the Statute is civil rather than criminal in nature, the Statute survives this challenge. We conclude that the Statute is civil, and hold that it does not violate either double jeopardy or the ex post facto clause.

The categorization of a particular statute as civil or criminal is largely a matter of statutory construction. *Allen v. Illinois*, 478 U.S. 364, 368, 106 S.Ct. 2988, 2991, 92 L.Ed.2d 296 (1986); *United States v. Ward*, 448 U.S. 242, 248, 100 S.Ct. 2636, 2641, 65 L.Ed.2d 742 (1980). The Supreme Court has adopted a 2-part analysis.

> First, we have set out to determine whether Congress, in establishing the penalizing mechanism, indicated either expressly or impliedly a preference for one label or the other. Second, where Congress has indicated an intention to establish a civil penalty, we have inquired further whether the statutory scheme was so punitive either in purpose or effect as to negate that intention. (Citations omitted.) *Ward*, 448 U.S. at 248-49, 100 S.Ct. at 2641.

Thus, we look first to the language of the Statute and the legislative history, then turn to an analysis of the purpose and effect of the statutory scheme.

Both the language of the Statute and the legislative history evidence a clear intent to create a civil scheme. The section of the law as enacted by the Legislature is entitled "Civil Commitment," Laws of 1990, ch. 3, part X, and is codified at RCW Title 71, Mental Illness.[1] Persons committed are placed in the custody of the DSHS and housed at a DSHS treatment facility. RCW 71.09.060(1); WAC 275-155. The Department of Corrections has no role in caring for committed sex predators. In addition, the provisions at issue here are compared in the text of the Statute to RCW 71.05, the civil involuntary commitment act. RCW 71.09.010.

An examination of the Act's legislative history further supports a civil intent. The Legislature's final report refers to the section as "Civil Commitment," and reports that "[a] new civil commitment procedure is created for 'sexually violent predators.'" *1990 Final Legislative Report*, 2nd SSB 6259, at 144. Moreover, the Legislature enacted a bill substantially similar to that proposed by the Governor's Task Force on Community Protection. In its report, the Task Force quite plainly recommended a civil law, because neither the criminal system nor the existing civil system could accommodate the special needs of sex predators. Report, at II-20 to II-23. In light of the Statute's language and legislative history, then, it is clear that the Legislature intended a civil statutory scheme.

This does not end our inquiry, however. We next consider whether the actual impact of the Statute is civil or criminal:

> [T]he civil label is not always dispositive. *Where a defendant has provided "the clearest proof"* that "the statutory scheme [is] so punitive either in purpose or effect as to negate [the State's] intention" that the proceeding be civil, it must be considered criminal. ... (Italics ours.) *Allen*, 478 U.S. at 369, 106 S. Ct. at 2992 (quoting *Ward*, 448 U.S. at 248-49, 100 S.Ct. at 2641-42).

In performing this inquiry, we take particular notice of the high level of proof petitioners must satisfy in order to overcome the presumption favoring the Legislature's civil designation. *Allen*, 478 U.S. at 369, 106 S. Ct. at 2992.

In *Allen*, a Fifth Amendment self-incrimination case, the Supreme Court held that an Illinois statute which provided for civil commitment of sexually dangerous persons was properly categorized as civil, not criminal. *Allen*, at 369, 106 S.Ct. at 2992. Under the Illinois statute, a "sexually dangerous person" was one who suffered from "a mental disorder ... coupled with criminal propensities to the commission of sex offenses." *Allen*, 478 U.S. at 366 n. 1, 106 S.Ct. at 2990 n. 1. In holding the statute civil, the Court found several factors significant: the Illinois Supreme Court had determined that the statute was civil in nature; the State had a statutory obligation to provide care and treatment designed to effect recovery for those committed; detainees were discharged when no longer dangerous; and, conditional release was also available. *Allen*, at 369, 106 S.Ct. at 2992. The Court summarized:

> In short, the State has disavowed any interest in punishment, provided for the treatment of those it commits, and established a system under which committed persons may be released after the briefest time in confinement. *Allen*, at 370, 106 S.Ct. at 2992.

The provisions of our sexually violent predator Statute are remarkably similar to those of the Illinois statute upheld in *Allen*. Most notably, the Statute's definition of "sexually violent predator" is almost identical to Illinois' definition of "sexually dangerous person"—both require a mental disorder which leads to the commission of violent sex offenses. *Compare* RCW 71.09.020(1) *with* Ill.Ann.Stat. ch. 38, Sec. 105-1.01 (Smith-Hurd 1980). Similarly, both the Illinois statute and RCW 71.09 require care and treatment for the committed individual, and provide this care in a psychiatric facility. *Compare* RCW 71.09.060(1) *and* RCW 71.09.080 *with* Ill.Ann.Stat. ch. 38, Sec. 105-8 (Smith-Hurd 1980). In addition, under both schemes, committed persons must be released as soon as they are no longer dangerous. *Compare* RCW 71.09.090(1) *with* Ill.Ann.Stat. ch. 38, Sec. 105-9 (Smith-Hurd 1980).

Petitioners argue that the Court's holding in *Allen* is distinguishable because the Illinois statute provides for commitment in lieu of serving a criminal sentence. While this is a distinguishing factor, it is by no means a contradictory one. That the State of Illinois chose to forego criminal liability for the offender's initial actions does not require Washington to do so. *See, e.g., Bailey v. Gardebring*, 940 F.2d 1150 (8th Cir. 1991) (constitutional to both civilly commit and imprison sexually dangerous individual), *cert. denied*, — U.S. —, 112 S.Ct. 1516, 117 L.Ed.2d 652 (1992). As we discuss below, the goals of civil and criminal confinement are quite different; the former is concerned with incapacitation and treatment, while the latter is directed to retribution and deterrence. The sexually violent predator Statute is not concerned with the criminal culpability of petitioners' past actions. Instead, it is focused on treating petitioners for a current mental abnormality, and protecting society from the sexually violent acts associated with that abnormality. Additional guidance for the determination of whether a statute is criminal was set forth by the Supreme Court in *Kennedy v. Mendoza-Martinez*, 372 U.S. 144, 168-69, 83 S.Ct. 554, 567-68, 9 L.Ed.2d 644 (1963). The court should consider:

> Whether the sanction involves an affirmative disability or restraint, whether it has historically been regarded as a punishment, whether it comes into play only on a finding of *scienter*, whether its operation will promote the traditional aims of punishment—retribution and deterrence, whether the behavior to which it applies is already a crime, whether an alternative purpose to which it may rationally be connected is assignable for it, and whether it appears excessive in relation to the alternative purpose assigned.... (Footnotes omitted.)

These factors weigh heavily on the side of a finding that this Statute is civil. Although the scheme here does involve an affirmative restraint, the civil commitment goals of incapacitation and treatment are distinct from punishment, and have been so regarded historically. Moreover, no finding of scienter is required to commit an individual who is a sexually violent predator; the determination is made based on a mental abnormality or personality disorder rather than on one's culpability. Furthermore, the Statute is necessary to serve the legitimate and vital purpose of protecting innocent potential victims.[2]

Finally, we also inquire into the purposes of the legislation. Our construction of the Statute should be that which best advances the legislative purpose. *Wichert v. Cardwell*, 117 Wash.2d 148, 151, 812 P.2d 858 (1991). The Statute promotes civil ends rather than criminal ones. The Statute before us is primarily concerned with incapacitation and treatment. Incapacitation has often been recognized as a legitimate civil goal. *See Addington v. Texas*, 441 U.S. 418, 99 S.Ct. 1804, 60 L.Ed.2d 323 (1979). Treatment is also a proper aim of civil legislation. As one commentator has remarked:

the Sexually Violent Predator civil commitment scheme is not a method of punishment. Washington is undertaking to treat the offender pursuant to its parens patriae power and to protect the public "from the dangerous tendencies of some who are mentally ill" pursuant to the state's police power. Marie A. Bochnewich, Comment, *Prediction of Dangerousness and Washington's Sexually Violent Predator Statute*, 29 Cal. W. L. Rev. 277, 278 (1992).

In contrast, the Supreme Court has said repeatedly that retribution and deterrence are punitive, and thus are the goals of criminal law. *United States v. Halper*, 490 U.S. 435, 448, 109 S.Ct. 1892, 1901-02, 104 L.Ed.2d 487 (1989); *Mendoza-Martinez*, 372 U.S. at 168, 83 S.Ct. at 567-68; *Bell v. Wolfish*, 441 U.S. 520, 539 n. 20, 99 S.Ct. 1861, 1874 n. 20, L.Ed.2d 447 (1979). Thus, the Court reasoned:

[A] civil sanction that cannot fairly be said solely to serve a remedial purpose, but rather can only be explained as also serving either retributive or deterrent purposes, is punishment, as we have come to understand the term. *Halper*, at 448, 109 S.Ct. at 1902; *accord Austin v. United States*, — U.S. —, —, 113 S.Ct. 2801, 2805-07, 125 L.Ed.2d 488 (1993).

This court has applied similar reasoning:

[T]he determinative factors for resolving a double jeopardy claim are whether [the sanction] has a rational connection to some purpose other than retribution or deterrence, and whether the sanction appears

excessive in relation to the alternative purpose. *O'Day v. King Cy.*, 109 Wash.2d 796, 817, 749 P.2d 142 (1988), (citing *Mendoza-Martinez*, 372 U.S. at 168-69, 83 S.Ct. at 567-68).

Absent any indication that a criminal purpose was intended, or actually served by the statute, the stated civil goals of the Legislature are controlling. *See Mendoza-Martinez*, 372 U.S. at 168-69, 83 S.Ct. at 567-68.

In sum, we conclude that the sexually violent predator Statute is civil, not criminal, in nature. The language and history of the Statute so indicate, as do its purposes and effect. Petitioners have failed "to provide the clearest proof" to the contrary.

Turning to the specific challenges made here, petitioners argue that RCW 71.09 violates the ex post facto clause. The prohibition against ex post facto laws is expressly leveled against states in U.S. Const. art. 1, Sec. 10.

A law violates the ex post facto prohibition if it aggravates a crime or makes it greater than it was when committed; permits imposition of a different or more severe punishment than was permissible when the crime was committed; or, changes the legal rules to permit less or different testimony to convict the offender than was required when the crime was committed. *State v. Edwards*, 104 Wash.2d 63, 70-71, 701 P.2d 508 (1985) (citing *Calder v. Bull*, 3 U.S. (3 Dall.) 386, 1 L.Ed. 648 (1798)).

The purposes of the prohibition are to give individuals fair warning of the effect of legislative acts, and to restrict the power of the State to impose arbitrary or vindictive legislation. *Weaver v. Graham*, 450 U.S. 24, 28-29, 101 S.Ct. 960, 963-65, 67 L.Ed.2d 17 (1981).

The ex post facto clause has been interpreted to apply only to criminal matters. *Calder v. Bull, supra; see* William W. Crosskey, *The True Meaning of the Constitutional Prohibition of Ex-Post-Facto Laws*, 14 U. Chi. L. Rev. 539 (1946-1947), cited in 1 Wayne R. LaFave & Austin W. Scott, Jr., *Substantive Criminal Law* Sec. 2.4 n. 9 (1986). In addition, at least one court has held that sexual psychopath proceedings did not involve the ex post facto prohibition because it was not a criminal remedy. *State ex rel. Sweezer v. Green*, 360 Mo. 1249, 1253,

, S.W.2d 897, 24 A.L.R.2d 340 (1950). cause the Statute is civil, therefore, the ex ɔst facto prohibition does not apply.

Petitioners argue further that the prohibition against double jeopardy is violated by the Act. The Fifth Amendment provides, in part: "[N]or shall any person be subject for the same offense to be twice put in jeopardy of life or limb." The double jeopardy clause prohibits multiple punishment for the same offense. *Halper*, 490 U.S. at 440, 109 S.Ct. at 1897; *O'Day*, 109 Wash.2d at 816, 749 P.2d 142. This prohibition "has deep roots in our history and jurisprudence." *Halper*, at 440, 109 S.Ct. at 1897.

In general, the prohibition against double jeopardy applies only to criminal measures: "[a] double jeopardy violation does not occur simply because two adverse consequences stem from the same act." *In re Mayner*, [107 Wash.2d 512, 730 P.2d 1321 (1986)] [107 Wash.2d] at 521 [730 P.2d 1321]. Double jeopardy does not apply "unless the sanction sought to be imposed in the second proceeding is punitive in nature so that the proceeding is essentially criminal." *Beckett v. Department of Social & Health Servs.*, 87 Wash.2d 184, 188, 550 P.2d 529 (1976) [*overruled on other grounds by Dunner v. McLaughlin*, 100 Wash.2d 832, 676 P.2d 444 (1984)]; see *Emory v. Texas Bd. of Med. Examiners*, 748 F.2d 1023, 1026 (5th Cir. 1984). *O'Day*, 109 Wash.2d at 816-17, 749 P.2d 142. The prohibition has, however, been found to be implicated in some circumstances by "civil" penalties as well as "criminal." In *Halper*, the Supreme Court found that a civil fine imposed in a Medicare fraud case after a criminal sentence had been served violated double jeopardy. *Halper*, at 452, 109 S.Ct. at 1903-04. The Supreme Court focused on whether the sanction was remedial or punitive in nature, noting that the purpose actually served by the sanction, rather than the underlying nature of the proceeding, determined the issue. *Halper*, at 447 n. 7, 109 S.Ct. at 1901, n. 7. The court held that a "civil as well as a criminal sanction constitutes punishment when the sanction as applied in the individual case serves the goals of punishment." *Halper*, at 448, 109 S.Ct. at 1901-02.

Here, as noted above, the statutory scheme has not been shown to serve any punitive

goal; indeed, it does not. Moreover, in *Halper*, the Court inquired as to the remedial function of the civil penalties, and questioned if the Government could impose a monetary penalty after a criminal sentence had been exacted. Essentially, *Halper* ruled that the State may not bring a separate civil action based on criminal conduct that is not rationally related to a legitimate civil goal. *Halper*, at 449, 109 S.Ct. at 1902. Incapacitation and treatment, though, are legitimate civil goals, as evidenced by the ordinary civil commitment law. See *Addington v. Texas*, 441 U.S. 418, 99 S.Ct. 1804, 60 L.Ed.2d 323 (1979). Therefore, enforcement of the Act does not violate double jeopardy.

III. Substantive Due Process

Petitioners argue that substantive constitutional requirements are violated by the Statute, and that it should be overturned. The propriety of the statutory scheme here is a matter of first impression. Although somewhat different from our sex predator Statute, the United States Supreme Court has upheld statutory schemes where sexual offenders were committed in lieu of serving their criminal sentences. Until 1984, and the passage of sentencing reform, Washington utilized such a scheme. Former RCW 71.06. In *Minnesota ex rel. Pearson v. Probate Court*, 309 U.S. 270, 60 S.Ct. 523, 84 L.Ed.2d 744, 126 A.L.R. 530 (19400, the Court refused to invalidate a "psychopathic personality" proceeding. As noted earlier, the Court has upheld confinement under the Illinois Sexually Dangerous Persons Act. *Allen v. Illinois*, 478 U.S. 364, 106 S.Ct. 2988, 2994-95, 92 L.Ed.2d 296 (1986).

In their substantive challenges to the Statute, petitioners argue that it does not serve a valid state purpose. They further argue that the Statute violates due process because petitioners are not mentally ill and that constitutionally required treatment is precluded due to the conditions of confinement. As such, they argue that the Statute authorizes unconstitutional preventive detention. Finally, petitioners argue that evidence of a recent overt act which proves dangerousness is mandated. Although we agree that evidence of an overt act may be required in *limited* circumstances, we conclude that there are no substantive constitutional impediments to the sexually violent predator scheme.

1. *Strict Scrutiny*

The constitution requires that a person shall not be deprived of life, liberty, or property without due process of law. U.S. Const. amends. 5, 14; Const. art. 1, Sec. 3. An individual's liberty interest is important and fundamental. *United States v. Salerno*, 481 U.S. 739, 750, 107 S.Ct. 2095, 2103, 95 L.Ed.2d 697 (1987). When a state's laws impinge on fundamental rights, such as liberty, they are constitutional only if they further compelling state interests, and are narrowly drawn to serve those interests. *State v. Farmer*, 116 Wash.2d 414, 429, 805 P.2d 200, 812 P.2d 858 (1991); *In re Schuoler*, 106 Wash.2d 500, 508, 723 P.2d 1103 (1986).

Applying the strict scrutiny test to the Statute as a whole, it is irrefutable that the State has a compelling interest both in treating sex predators and protecting society from their actions. *Addington v. Texas*, 441 U.S. 418, 426, 99 S.Ct. 1804, 1809-10, 60 L.Ed.2d 323 (1979); *Vitek v. Jones*, 445 U.S. 480, 495, 100 S.Ct. 1254, 1264-65, 63 L.Ed.2d 552 (1980). The Supreme Court has stated that:

The state has a legitimate interest under its parens patriae powers in providing care to its citizens who are unable because of emotional disorders to care for themselves; the state also has authority under its police power to protect the community from the dangerous tendencies of some who are mentally ill. *Addington*, 441 U.S. at 426, 99 S.Ct. at 1809; *see also Salerno*, 481 U.S. at 748-49, 107 S.Ct. at 2102 ("the government may detain mentally unstable individuals who present a danger to the public").

Here, petitioners Young and Cunningham were diagnosed with a mental disorder and share a lengthy criminal history of violent rape. Other individuals encompassed under the commitment law share similar profiles. In such circumstances, the Court has consistently upheld civil commitment schemes. *See Addington v. Texas*, *supra*; John Q. LaFond, An Examination of Purposes of Involuntary Civil Commitment, 30 Buff. L. Rev. 499, 513 (1981).

Any criticism of the Statute, then, would have to be based on the requirement that it be narrowly drawn. We will address petitioners' various "least restrictive alternative" arguments in subsequent sections of this opinion.

2. *Mentally Ill and Dangerous*

Petitioners argue that the Statute allows the State to hold individuals without proving that the person is both mentally ill and dangerous. In *Addington*, the Supreme Court held that a person must be both mentally ill[3] and dangerous for a civil commitment to be permissible under the due process clause of the constitution. *Accord, e.g., Foucha v. Louisiana*, — U.S. — , 112 S.Ct. 1780, 118 L.Ed.2d 437 (1992). The sexually violent predator Statute satisfies this due process standard.

The Statute clearly requires proof of a "mental abnormality or personality disorder" for civil commitment. RCW 71.09.020(1). Although "mental abnormality" is not defined in the American Psychiatric Ass'n, *Diagnostic and Statistical Manual of Mental Disorders* (3d rev. ed. 1987) (DSM-III-R),[4] the Legislature has given it a meaning which incorporates a number of recognized mental pathologies:

In using the concept of "mental abnormality" the legislature has invoked a more generalized terminology that can cover a much larger variety of disorders. Some, such as the paraphilias, are covered in the DSM-III-R; others are not. The fact that pathologically driven rape, for example, is not yet listed in the DSM-III-R does not invalidate such a diagnosis. The DSM is, after all, an evolving and imperfect document. Nor is it sacrosanct. Furthermore, it is in some areas a political document whose diagnoses are based, in some cases, on what American Psychiatric Association ("APA") leaders consider to be practical realities. *What is critical for our purposes is that psychiatric and psychological clinicians who testify in good faith as to mental abnormality are able to identify sexual pathologies that are as real and meaningful as other pathologies already listed in the DSM.* (Italics ours.) Alexander D. Brooks, *The Constitutionality and Morality of Civilly Committing Violent Sexual Predators*, 15 U. Puget Sound L. Rev. 709, 733 (1992).

In both Young's and Cunningham's respective trials, expert witnesses for petitioners and

State were competent and able to offer .imony on the mental pathologies underlyg the sex predator condition. These same xperts testified that the statutory term "menial abnormality" was nearly identical to the notion of "mental disorder" as defined in the DSM-III-R.[5]

Both Young and Cunningham were primarily diagnosed with a mental disorder known as "paraphilia." Classified as a sexual disorder, the essential features of a paraphilic mental illness are "recurrent intense sexual urges and sexually arousing fantasies generally involving either (1) non-human objects, (2) the suffering or humiliation of oneself or one's partner (not merely simulated), or (3) children or other non-consenting persons." DSM-III-R, at 279. The DSM-III-R contains an extensive discussion of paraphilia; none of the experts at Young's and Cunningham's commitment trials challenged the acceptance of this diagnostic category.

The specific diagnosis offered by the State's experts at each commitment trial was "paraphilia not otherwise specified." This is a residual category in the DSM-III-R which encompasses both less commonly encountered paraphilias and those not yet sufficiently described to merit formal inclusion in the DSM-III-R. DSM-III-R, at 280. As the testimony reflected, paraphilias are classified as either mild, moderate or severe. Young and Cunningham were both diagnosed with a severe paraphilia; i.e., "[t]he person has repeatedly acted on the paraphilic urge." DSM-III-R, at 281.

The expert testimony further reflected that both Young and Cunningham could be classified within the "paraphilia not otherwise specified" category as suffering from "rape as paraphilia." According to the seminal article on this mental disorder, portions of which were read into testimony at both trials, certain patterns of rape fall into this diagnosis:

Clinical interviews of rapists, however, provide support for the classification of rape as a paraphilia, because many individuals report having recurrent, repetitive, and compulsive urges and fantasies to commit rapes. These offenders attempt to control their urges, but the urges eventually become so strong that they act upon them, commit rapes, and then feel guilty afterwards with a temporary reduction or urges, only to have the cycle repeat again. This cycle of ongoing urges, attempts to control them, breakdown of those attempts, and recurrence of the sex crime is similar to the clinical picture presented by exhibitionists, pedophiles, and other traditionally recognized categories of paraphiliacs. Gene G. Abel & Joanne-L. Rouleau, *The Nature and Extent of Sexual Assault, in Handbook of Sexual Assault: Issues, Theories and Treatment of the Offender* 9, 18 (W.L. Marshall, et al. eds., 1990) (hereinafter *Handbook of Sexual Assault*).[6]

The article goes on to state that "[s]uch a categorization raises the issue of the offender's need for psychiatric and psychological treatment before he can gain control over his sexual assaultiveness." *Handbook of Sexual Assault*, at 20. It recognizes that "[i]n our culture, this has meant that not only must the individual so categorized serve his time for his illegal act of sexual assault, but he must also serve time receiving psychiatric and psychological treatment for his paraphilia." *Handbook of Sexual Assault*, at 20.

In Young's trial, the State's expert testified that Young also suffered from an "anti-social personality disorder." Like paraphilia, antisocial personality disorder is classified as a mental disorder in the DSM-III-R. In general, a personality disorder diagnosis is appropriate "only when *personality traits* are inflexible and maladaptive and cause either significant functional impairment or subjective distress." DSM-III-R, at 335. Antisocial personality disorder is characterized by a long-term pattern of irresponsible and antisocial behavior. DSM-III-R, at 342.

Petitioners nonetheless argue that the Statute does not address a mental disorder because treatment of sex offenders is impossible. Indeed, the Legislature adopted specific findings that "sexually violent predators ... have antisocial personality features which are unamenable to existing mental illness treatment," and that "the prognosis for curing sexually violent offenders is poor." RCW 71.09.010. Moreover, as argued by amicus, it is commonly believed that violent sex offenders cannot be successfully treated, especially involuntarily. Brief of Amicus Curiae Washington State Psychiatric Association, at 10; *see also* ABA *Criminal Justice Mental Health Standards*, at 7-8.1 n. 16 (1989).

There are two flaws in this line of argument. First, the mere fact that an illness is difficult to treat does not mean that it is not an illness.[7] For example, some forms of schizophrenia cannot be treated, but the diagnosis nonetheless remains a valid one. The Legislature should not be admonished for its honest recognition of the difficulties inherent in treating those afflicted with the mental abnormalities causing the sex predator condition.

Second, petitioners have failed to show that the *specific* conditions of confinement are incompatible with treatment. As the Supreme Court noted in *Allen*:

> Petitioner has not demonstrated, and the record does not suggest, that "sexually dangerous persons" in Illinois are confined under conditions incompatible with the State's asserted interest in treatment. Had petitioner shown, for example, that the confinement of such persons imposes on them a regimen with is essentially identical to that imposed upon felons with no need for psychiatric care, this might well be a different case. *Allen*, 478 U.S. at 373, 106 S.Ct. at 2994.

Similarly, the Washington Statute provides for treatment, and petitioners have failed to prove that this goal cannot be effectuated under the Statute's terms.

Due process concerns are similarly satisfied because the sexually violent predator Statute requires dangerousness as a condition for civil commitment. RCW 71.09.020(1). The Court has said that mental illness is insufficient, standing alone, to justify confinement. *O'Connor v. Donaldson*, 442 U.S. 563, 575, 95 S.Ct. at 2497-98 (Burger, C.J., concurring). Similarly, this court has often said that "the only basis for involuntary commitment is dangerousness." *In re Patterson*, 90 Wash.2d 144, 153, 579 P.2d 1335 (1978), *overruled on other grounds by Dunner v. McLaughlin*, 100 Wash.2d 832, 676 P.2d 444 (1984); *In re Levias*, 83 Wash.2d 253, 257, 517 P.2d 588 (1973), *overruled on other grounds by Dunner v. McLaughlin*, 100 Wash.2d 832, 676 P.2d 444 (1984).

Here, the Statute inherently applies only to dangerous offenders. Under the very definitions of the Statute, only "sexually violent offenders"—those "likely to engage in predatory acts of sexual violence"—are subject to its provisions. RCW 71.09.020(1). Individuals involuntarily committed under the Statute possess a proven history of rape and sexually motivated violence. Their likelihood of re-offense is extremely high. According to supplemental authority submitted by petitioners themselves and specific to the sex predator program, "[u]sing theoretically relevant and empirically tested predictors, predictive accuracy [of sexual recidivism] can realistically be expected to be in the 80% range." Dr. Vernon Quinsey, *Review of the Washington State Special Commitment Center Program for Sexually Violent Predators*, at 9 (appended to Wash. State Inst. for Pub. Policy, *Review of Sexual Predator Program: Community Protection Research Project*, (Feb. 1992)); *see also Heller v. Doe*, — U.S. — , —, 113 S.Ct. 2637, 2644 (1993) ("Previous instances of violent behavior are an important indicator of future violent tendencies.").[8] Thus, there is no doubt that commitment is predicated on dangerousness under the Statute.[9]

In short, the Statute satisfies the due process concerns outlined in *Addington v. Texas*, 441 U.S. 418, 99 S.Ct. 1804. Expert testimony in both the Young and Cunningham trials diagnosed petitioners with a mental disorder, and informed the jury of the dangerousness arising out of that disorder.[10]

3. *Nature and Duration*

In a related issue, the Supreme Court has stated that due process "requires that the nature and duration of commitment bear some reasonable relation to the purpose for which the individual is committed." *Jones v. United States*, 463 U.S. 354, 368, 103 S.Ct. 3043, 3051, 77 L.Ed.2d 694 (1983) (quoting *Jackson v. Indiana*, 406 U.S. 715, 738, 92 S.Ct. 1845, 1858, 32 L.Ed.2d 435 (1972)). Thus, an inquiry into the purposes of the Statute is required.

Two underlying purposes for commitment are often advanced — treatment and incapacitation. See La Fond, *supra*. The Statute at issue here serves both purposes. The Statute requires that constitutionally mandated care

, treatment be provided, RCW 71.09.080, d charges DSHS with the responsibility of roviding "control, care, and treatment until such time as the person's mental abnormality or personality disorder has so changed that the person is safe to be at large." RCW 71.09.060(1). DSHS has promulgated regulations to effect this purpose. An individualized treatment plan is developed and maintained for each person committed under the Statute, including:

(a) A description of a person's specific treatment needs;
(b) An outline of intermediate and long-range treatment goals, with a projected timetable for reaching the goals;
(c) The treatment strategies for achieving the treatment goals;
(d) A description of [sexual predator program] staff persons' responsibility; and
(e) Criteria for recommending to the court whether a person should be released from the [sexual predator program]. WAC 275-155-040(1)

The regulations governing the program make it clear that committed individuals shall "[r]eceive adequate care and individualized treatment." WAC 275-155-050(3)(a).

The purpose of incapacitation is also well served by this Statute. The task force responsible for drafting the legislation initially noted that an additional goal of the program was to "confine repeat violent offenders who present an extreme safety risk." *Report*, at I-1. Sexually violent predators, those who are adjudged likely to engage in acts of violence, are housed in a special commitment center which must be located within a correctional institution. The record reflects that the current facility is rated maximum security. Given the nature of sexually violent predators, it would not be safe to house them in a less secure setting. Thus, it appears that the commitment is related to the purpose of the Statute.

Finally, petitioners argue that they are constitutionally entitled to the least restrictive alternatives to confinement available.[11] It is true that those who are civilly committed must be treated differently than criminals. The Supreme Court has said this explicitly:

Persons who have been involuntarily committed are entitled to more considerate

treatment and conditions of confinement than criminals whose conditions of confinement are designed to punish. *Youngberg v. Romeo*, 457 U.S. 307, 321-22, 102 S.Ct. 2452, 2461, 73 L.Ed.2d 28 (1982).

Nevertheless, we need not place undue limitations on the administration of state institutions. *Romeo*, at 322, 102 S.Ct. at 2461-62.

In light of these considerations, giving the presumption of correctness to "decisions made by the appropriate professional" (here, DSHS), individuals who have been involuntarily committed have the right to "conditions of reasonable care and safety, reasonably nonrestrictive confinement conditions, and such training as may be required by these interests." *Romeo*, at 324, 102 S.Ct. at 2462. Here, the dangerousness of committed sex predators justifies a secure confinement facility. Moreover, the regulations governing the commitment facility specifically provide for a wider range of privileges than those associated with a prison setting:

(3) A person the court commits to the SPP [sexual predator program] *shall*:

(a) Receive adequate care and individualized treatment;
(b) Be permitted to wear the committed person's own clothes and keep and use the person's personal possessions, except when deprivation of possessions is necessary for the person's protection and safety, the protection and safety of others, or the protection of property within the SPP;
(c) Be permitted to accumulate and spend a reasonable amount of money in the person's SPP account;
(d) Have access to reasonable personal storage space within SPP limitations;
(e) Be permitted to have approved visitors within reasonable limitations;
(f) Have reasonable access to a telephone to make and receive confidential calls within SPP limitations; and
(g) Have reasonable access to letter writing material and to:
(i) Receive and send correspondence through the mail within SPP limitations; and
(ii) Send written communication regarding the fact of the person's

commitment. (Italics ours.) WAC 275-155-050.

There is no evidence in the record addressing either the actual conditions of confinement, or the quality of treatment. These issues are not currently before the court. Facially, the Statute and associated regulations suggest that the nature and duration of commitment is compatible with the purposes of the commitment.

4. *Foucha v. Louisiana*

Petitioners next argue that the Supreme Court's recent decision in *Foucha v. Louisiana*, — U.S. —, 112 S.Ct. 1780, 118 L.Ed.2d 437 (1992) forbids the civil commitment of sexually violent predators because it constitutes unconstitutional preventive detention. As is patently obvious, however, both the facts and the statute in *Foucha* differ significantly from those presented here. Contrary to petitioner's claim, our holding is consistent with and supportive of *Foucha*.

In *Foucha*, the Court overturned a Louisiana statute dealing with insanity acquittees because the release procedures were inadequate. The Court described the statute as follows:

> When a defendant in a criminal case pending in Louisiana is found not guilty by reason of insanity, he is committed to a psychiatric hospital unless he proves that he is not dangerous. This is so whether or not he is then insane. After commitment, if the acquittee or the superintendent begins release proceedings, a review panel at the hospital makes a written report on the patient's mental condition and whether he can be released without danger to himself or others. If release is recommended, the court must hold a hearing to determine dangerousness; the acquittee has the burden of proving that he is not dangerous. If found to be dangerous, the acquittee may be returned to the mental institution whether or not he is then mentally ill. *Foucha*, — U.S. — - —, 112 S.Ct. at 1781-82.

Four years after Terry Foucha had been committed, following an acquittal by reason of insanity of aggravated burglary and illegal discharge of a firearm, the superintendent of the facility where he was held recommended that he be released. The review panel reported that "there had been no evidence of mental illness since admission." *Foucha*, — U.S. at —, 112 S.Ct. at 1782.

The trial court heard medical testimony that Foucha was probably in remission from what had been a temporary condition—likely a drug induced psychosis. The court heard further testimony that Foucha had an "antisocial personality," that such condition was not a mental illness, and that he had no other mental disorders. However, an ultimate medical determination about his dangerousness could not be made. Instead, a doctor testified only that he could not "certify that [Foucha] would not constitute a menace to himself or others if released." *Foucha*, — U.S. at —, 112 S.Ct. at 1782. Based solely on this equivocal testimony, the trial court returned him to the mental institution.

The United States Supreme Court reversed, holding that absent a determination of current mental illness and dangerousness, continued confinement under the Louisiana scheme was impermissible. *Foucha*, — U.S. at — - —, 112 S.Ct. at 1788-89. The Court relied on three reasons to overturn the confinement and the underlying statute. First, the statute did not meet the minimal due process requirement "that the nature of commitment bear some reasonable relation to the purpose for which the individual is committed." *Foucha*, — U.S. at —, 112 S.Ct. at 1785. The State of Louisiana was continuing to confine Foucha in a psychiatric facility even though he was not suffering from a mental disease or illness. Second, the statute did not provide constitutionally adequate procedures. *Foucha*, — U.S. —, 112 S.Ct. at 1785. Finally, the Court determined that Foucha was not confined under any previously recognized authority of the State. It recognized three ways in which an individual could be confined: by the criminal justice system; pursuant to civil commitment law; or under the narrow circumstances set forth in *United States v. Salerno, supra. Foucha*, — U.S. at — - —, 112 S.Ct. at 1785-86.

The Statute here withstands the scrutiny required in *Foucha*. As explained above, the sexually violent predator Statute is narrowly tailored to serve a compelling state interest. Also, before a person can be civilly committed, the State must prove that the individual is ally ill[12] and dangerous—a condition that satisfied in Young's and Cunningham's pective trials. As such, the sexually violent edator commitment scheme falls squarely within Foucha's definition of constitutionally permissible civil commitment. See Foucha, — U.S. at — - —, 112 S.Ct. at 1784-86. "The State may also confine a mentally ill person if it shows 'by clear and convincing evidence that the individual is mentally ill and dangerous.'" Foucha, — U.S. at —, 112 S.Ct. at 1786 (quoting Jones, 463 U.S. at 362, 103 S.Ct. at 3048).

In addition, the sex predator Statute does not suffer from the procedural infirmities that rendered Louisiana's insanity acquittee scheme unconstitutional. Under the Washington law, the State must satisfy the highest burden of proof to civilly commit a sex predator. A higher burden of proof "tends to equalize the risks of an erroneous determination that the subject of a commitment proceeding has the condition in question." Heller, — U.S. at —, 113 S.Ct. at 2644. Whereas Louisiana attempted to continue Foucha's confinement without claiming that he suffered from a mental illness, the Washington Statute makes proof of a current mental disorder a condition of commitment. Also, in regard to dangerousness, Louisiana placed the burden on Foucha, while the Washington Statute places the burden on the State. In contrast to the Louisiana statute, the sexually violent predator Statute is the type of "sharply focused scheme" which the Supreme Court called for in Foucha. — U.S. at —, 112 S.Ct. at 1786.

Our interpretation of the holding in Foucha finds support in Justice O'Connor's crucial concurring opinion. In providing the necessary fifth vote which formed the majority, Justice O'Connor carefully pointed out the limitations of that holding:

I write separately, however, to emphasize that the Court's opinion addresses only the specific statutory scheme before us, which broadly permits indefinite confinement of sane insanity acquittees in psychiatric facilities. Foucha, — U.S. at —, 112 S.Ct. at 1789 (O'Connor, J., concurring).

Where the incapacitation is more closely tailored to "reflect pressing public safety concerns related to the acquittee's continuing dangerousness," continued confinement may be permitted. Foucha, — U.S. at —, 112 S.Ct. at 1789 (O'Connor, J., concurring).

The dissent claims that the sex predator program constitutes "preventative detention" because the statute is not "civil commitment" and sex predators are "detained" for an indefinite period of time. We reject this characterization. First, the sex predator statute does not rely upon the Salerno line of cases. It falls comfortably within the "civil commitment" category discussed in Foucha because the State must prove both a mental illness and dangerousness. Second, civil commitments are not subject to any rigid time limit. Rather, the commitment is tailored to the nature and duration of the mental illness. Finally, unlike pretrial detainees, those committed under the sex predator statute have been through a full trial with a complete range of procedural protections. In short, despite the dissent's protests to the contrary, the sex predator statute does not create any ominous "dangerousness court," but rather follows traditional civil commitment norms.

Even though petitioners potentially face a long period of civil commitment, the sexually violent predator Statute is wholly sustainable. Those committed under the sex predator Statute have been through a full trial with a complete range of procedural protections. From this trial, a jury has determined that the State has met the highest burden possible—beyond a reasonable doubt—in proving that the committed individual suffers from a mental abnormality which renders him a danger to the community. Although the period of confinement is not predetermined, the Statute's release provisions provide the opportunity for periodic review of the committed individual's current mental condition and continuing dangerousness to the community.

In sum, the circumstances of the Foucha case clearly dictated the result reached by the United States Supreme Court. The case before us deals with vastly different facts and law, and is wholly consistent with the principles enunciated in Foucha.

5. Overt Act

Petitioners next argue that the constitution requires evidence of a recent overt act to prove dangerousness, relying on In re Harris, 98 Wash.2d 276, 654 P.2d 109 (1982). Harris had been detained under RCW 71.05.150(1)(a), which provides for short-term detention for evaluation and treatment if "a person, as a result of a mental disorder, presents a likelihood of serious harm to others or himself." *Harris*, at 279, 654 P.2d 109. The phrase "likelihood of serious harm" is defined explicitly in RCW 71.05.020(3), as follows:

(a) A substantial risk that physical harm will be inflicted by an individual upon his own person, as evidenced by threats or attempts to commit suicide or inflict physical harm on one's self, (b) a substantial risk that physical harm will be inflicted by an individual upon another, as evidenced by behavior which has caused such harm or which places another person or persons in reasonable fear of sustaining such harm, or (c) a substantial risk that physical harm will be inflicted by an individual upon the property of others, as evidenced by behavior which has caused substantial loss or damage to the property of others[.]

The definition contains the inference that the harm at issue be evidenced by some act or behavior. The court noted that "such evidence must be recent to be meaningful." *Harris*, at 284, 654 P.2d 109. Thus, interpreting RCW 71.05, this court held that involuntary commitment was only permitted upon:

a showing of a substantial risk of physical harm as evidenced by a recent overt act. This act may be one which has caused harm or creates a reasonable apprehension of dangerousness. *Harris*, at 284-85, 654 P.2d 109.

However, the court rejected an additional requirement of "imminent danger," relying primarily on statutory interpretation. *Harris*, at 283-84, 654 P.2d 109. We compared the emergency detention provisions contained in RCW 71.05.150(2)—which *do* require that the likelihood of serious harm be imminent, with the remaining procedures contained in RCW 71.05—which do *not* impose the condition of imminence. *Harris*, at 282, 654 P.2d 109. We concluded that the omission expressed the Legislature's intent not to impose the condition of imminence. *Harris*, at 282, 654 P.2d 109. In addition, the court noted:

the practical effect of being placed in the hospital will usually eliminate the "immi-

nence" of one's dangerousness. If we were to require "imminent danger" as a requirement of continued commitment, we would be creating a standard that (in many cases) would invalidate commitment as soon as it occurs.... A standard of "imminent danger" for all commitments would be impracticable. *Harris*, at 284, 654 P.2d 109.

In many cases, sexually violent predators are incarcerated prior to commitment. *Cf. In re LaBelle*, 107 Wash.2d 196, 204, 728 P.2d 138 (1986). For incarcerated individuals, a requirement of a recent overt act under the Statute would create a standard which would be impossible to meet. Other jurisdictions have rejected the precise argument made by petitioners because it creates an impossible condition for those currently incarcerated. *See People v. Martin*, 107 Cal.App.3d 714, 725, 165 Cal.Rptr. 773 (1980). We agree that "[d]ue process does not require that the absurd be done before a compelling state interest can be vindicated." *Martin*, 107 Cal.App.3d at 725, 165 Cal.Rptr. 773. Indeed, in drafting the Statute, the Legislature expressly noted that the involuntary commitment statute, RCW 71.05, was an inadequate remedy because confinement prevented any overt act. RCW 71.09.010. We conclude that where the individual is currently incarcerated no evidence of a recent overt act is required.

However, where an individual has been released from confinement on a sex offense (as referenced in RCW 71.09.030) and lives in the community immediately prior to the initiation of sex predator proceedings, the above rationale does not apply. Under *Harris*, proof of a recent overt act is necessary to satisfy due process concerns when an individual has been released into the community. 98 Wash.2d 284, 654 P.2d 109. When an individual has been in the community, the State has the opportunity to prove dangerousness through evidence of a recent overt act. We construe statutes to render them constitutional. Therefore, we hold that the State must provide evidence of a recent overt act in accord with *Harris* whenever an individual is not incarcerated at the time the petition is filed. For non-incarcerated individuals, a sex predator petition under RCW 71.09.030 must include an allegation of a recent overt act suf-

it to establish probable cause when con-
red in conjunction with the other factors
d in RCW 71.09.040.

Petitioner Cunningham was released from
ison and living in the community for some
½ months before the State filed a sex preda-
.or petition. He was gainfully employed as an
assistant engineer on a ship and was planning
to go to sea for a period of time. The State did
not allege a recent overt act in its petition, nor
did the State offer such evidence at
Cunningham's trial. We find, therefore, that
the proof presented at trial was insufficient
and Cunningham's commitment as a sex
predator is hereby reversed.

In sum, the Statute does not violate substantive due process. The State's interest in
preventing the sort of harm exacted by sexually violent predators is clearly compelling.
The Statute complies with due process
because it conditions civil commitment on a
finding of both a mental disorder and dangerousness. The Supreme Court's opinion in
Foucha does not alter this long-established
law, nor forbid Washington's efforts to ameliorate an important societal problem. As
noted by the chair of the task force when he
transmitted the *Report* to the Governor, the
Statute is "a serious response commensurate
with the harm caused." *Report*, Letter of
transmittal from Norm Maleng to The Hon.
Booth Gardner (Nov. 28, 1989).

IV. Procedural Due Process

Petitioners contend that the Statute must be
overturned because it deprives them of their
liberty without adequate procedural protections and denies them equal protection.
Several procedural infirmities are alleged:
that the ex parte finding of probable cause
denies meaningful predeprivation due
process, that consideration of less restrictive
alternatives to confinement is necessary, that
the burden of proof at trial is inadequate
because the jury need not be unanimous, that
the Statute is void for vagueness, and that
petitioners were unconstitutionally denied a
right to remain silent.[13]

1. *Probable cause hearing*

Petitioners argue that an adversarial probable cause hearing is required by due process

considerations. During the 45-day period
prior to trial, despite repeated requests, petitioners were denied the opportunity to appear
personally in court. Although this detention
is preceded by a judicial determination that
probable cause exists, RCW 71.09.040, the
decision is made ex parte and without prior
notice to the detainee.

In contrast, under RCW 71.05 (involuntary
commitment), an individual is subject first to
a 72-hour detention for evaluation and treatment. RCW 71.05.150(1)(b). That statute
also requires a psychological evaluation within the first 24 hours of detention. RCW
71.05.210. A probable cause hearing, at
which the individual may be present, is then
held to determine if an additional 14-day
detention is warranted. RCW 71.05.200.

The standard for determining the appropriate level of procedure that is due prior to
depriving an individual of his right to life, liberty or property is well established:

[T]he specific dictates of due process generally requires consideration of three distinct factors: First, the private interest that
will be affected by the official action; second, the risk of an erroneous deprivation of
such interest through the procedures used,
and the probable value, if any, of additional or substitute procedural safeguards; and
finally, the Government's interest, including the function involved and the fiscal and
administrative burdens that the additional
or substitute procedural requirement would
entail. *Mathews v. Eldridge*, 424 U.S. 319,
335, 96 S.Ct. 893, 903, 47 L.Ed.2d 18
(1976).

We have said that this is "[t]he appropriate
test for reviewing the constitutional adequacy
of involuntary commitment procedures." *In
re LaBelle*, 107 Wash.2d 196, 221, 728 P.2d
138 (1986) (citing *Dunner v. McLaughlin*,
100 Wash.2d 832, 839, 676 P.2d 444 (1984));
see also In re Schuoler, 106 Wash.2d 500,
510, 723 P.2d 1103 (1986); *In re Harris*, 98
Wash.2d 276, 285, 654 P.2d 109 (1982).
Thus, the court must balance the extent of the
individual's interest against the interests of
the State.

In addition, equal protection principles of the
Fourteenth Amendment and article 1, section
12 of our constitution require that we examine

the protections contained in the Statute in light of protections afforded those who are committed under the involuntary commitment statute. The equal protection clause requires that "persons similarly situated with respect to the legitimate purposes of the laws receive like treatment."[14] *In re Knapp*, 102 Wash.2d 466, 473, 687 P.2d 1145 (1984). To determine if equal protection has been violated, we examine the purpose of the Statute—incapacitation and treatment of violent offenders.

It is important to note at the outset that there are good reasons to treat mentally ill people differently than violent sex offenders. *See People v. Pembrock*, 62 Ill.2d 217, 322, 342 N.E.2d 28 (1976) (A sexually dangerous person "creates different societal problems, and his past conduct is different in degree and kind from the conduct of persons in the larger, more inclusive class defined under the Mental Health Code."). Sexually violent predators are generally considerably more dangerous to others than the mentally ill. Treatment methods are also markedly different for the two populations. *See* RCW 71.09.010. Nevertheless, these distinctions between the two groups must be related to any differences in treatment under the respective statutes. That is, "[e]qual protection does not require that all persons be dealt with identically, but it does require that a distinction made have some relevance to the purpose for which the classification is made." Baxstrom v. Herold, 383 U.S. 107, 111, 86 S.Ct. 760, 763, 15 L.Ed.2d 620 (1966). The Supreme Court has said that the dangerousness of the detainee "may be a reasonable distinction for purposes of determining the type of *custodial or medical care* to be given, but it has *no relevance whatever* in the context of the opportunity to show whether a person is mentally ill *at all*." (Some italics ours.) *Baxstrom*, at 111, 86 S.Ct. at 763.

All individuals who are involuntarily committed are entitled to procedural and substantive protections. *Jackson v. Indiana*, 406 U.S. 715, 724, 92 S.Ct. 1845, 1851, 32 L.Ed.2d 435 (1972). Thus, the Court in *Jackson* held:

> that by subjecting Jackson to a more lenient commitment standard of release than those generally applicable to all others not charged with offenses, and by thus condemning him in effect to permanent institu-

tionalization without the showing required for commitment or the opportunity for release ... Indiana deprived petitioner of equal protection of the laws under the Fourteenth Amendment. *Jackson*, 406 U.S. at 730, 92 S.Ct. at 1854.

A person cannot be deprived of procedural protections afforded other individuals merely because the State makes the decision to seek commitment under one statute rather than another statute. *Humphrey v. Cady*, 405 U.S. 504, 512, 92 S.Ct. 1048, 1053-54, 31 L.Ed.2d 394 (1972). Thus, in regard to the initial determination of whether there is probable cause for detention, an individual is entitled to the same opportunity to appear before the court to contest detention in any civil commitment proceeding.

Application of the due process and equal protection principles discussed above requires that detainees under the Statute be afforded an opportunity to appear in person to contest probable cause. Petitioners' liberty interests are substantially infringed during the 45-day period leading up to trial. Absent an opportunity to appear and respond to the petition for commitment, we believe that the risk of wrongful detention is too great.

In contrast, the burden of providing notice and an opportunity for a detainee to appear is not too onerous. The breadth of such a hearing would remain within the discretion of the trial court. Insofar as this hearing is limited to verification of the detainee's identity and the determination of probable cause to believe that he or she is a sexually violent predator, we do not anticipate a lengthy proceeding. Because many of the individuals affected will be imprisoned prior to commitment, *see* RCW 71.09.030, notification of the proceedings is simple.

In *Harris*, we imposed such requirements as a function of "inherent judicial power." *In re Harris*, 98 Wash.2d 276, 287, 654 P.2d 109 (1982). "[D]ue process is flexible and calls for such procedural protections as the particular situation demands." *Morrissey v. Brewer*, 408 U.S. 471, 481, 92 S.Ct. 2593, 2600, 33 L.Ed.2d 484 (1972). On several prior occasions, we have supplemented the commitment procedures of RCW 71.05 to bring that statute into compliance with procedural due process guaranties [sic]. *In re Schuoler*, 106 Wash.2d 500, 510, 723 P.2d 1103 (1986); *In re Cross*, 99 Wash.2d 373, 662 P.2d 828 (1983); *In re Harris*, *supra*. In addition, we often interpret statutes in a manner which renders them constitutional. *State v. Browet, Inc.*, 103 Wash.2d 215, 219, 691 P.2d 571 (1984). Here, too, additional procedures are needed to ensure that the Statute is enforced fairly.

Therefore, we hold that a 72-hour hearing is required by the constitutional guaranty [sic] to due process, and must be available to detainees under the Statute. While this requirement was not complied with here, it had no bearing on the ultimate outcome of petitioner's trials; thus the omission in this instance does not require reversal.

2. *Less restrictive alternative*

Petitioners argue that the Statute violates equal protection because it does not require consideration of such alternatives as a precursor to confinement. *See* RCW 71.05.240, .320.

We agree. The State cannot provide different procedural protections for those confined under the sex predator statute unless there is a valid reason for doing so. Here, the State offers no jurisdiction for not considering less restrictive alternatives under 71.05, and denying the same under RCW 71.09. Not all sex predators present the same level of danger, nor do they require identical treatment conditions. Similar to those committed under RCW 71.05, it is necessary to account for these differences by considering alternatives to total confinement. We therefore hold that equal protection requires the State to comply with provisions of RCW 71.05 as related to the consideration of less restrictive alternatives.

Less restrictive alternatives were not considered in either Young's or Cunningham's respective trials. Given our resolution in Cunningham's case, we are concerned only with the effect of this holding in regard to Young. We remand Young's case for consideration of alternatives to confinement. Because the sex predator determination has already been made, the finder of fact need only consider if the less restrictive alternatives are appropriate.

3. *Jury verdict and selection*

Petitioners claim that the Statute provides an inadequate burden of proof by failing to require a unanimous verdict. The Statute is silent on the issue, but we believe that it must be construed to afford an individual the right to a unanimous 12-person verdict.

Our primary goal in interpreting statutes is to carry out the intent of the Legislature. *Anderson v. O'Brien*, 84 Wash.2d 64, 67, 524 P.2d 390 (1974). The sexually violent predator Statute requires the State to prove beyond a reasonable doubt that the person is a sexually violent predator. RCW 71.09.060(1). The Legislature's use of the "beyond a reasonable doubt" standard suggests an acute awareness of the need for heightened procedural protections in these proceedings. Moreover, in Washington, the beyond a reasonable doubt standard generally requires a unanimous verdict. *See State v. Petrich*, 101 Wash.2d 566, 569, 683 P.2d 173 (1984). Considering the context normally associated with this high burden of proof, *State v. Elgin*, 118 Wash.2d 551, 556, 825 P.2d 314 (1992), we find that the Legislature included the need for a unanimous verdict when it required "proof beyond a reasonable doubt" in the statutory scheme.

Here, over defense objections, the jury in Cunningham's trial was not instructed that unanimity was required, and an 11-to-1 verdict was returned—at least one person on the jury felt that the State failed to meet its burden. Under the standards announced here, the verdict was insufficient. In Young's case, the verdict was unanimous, and the jury's finding is affirmed.

Petitioners also contend that they are entitled to 12 peremptory challenges at trial. Young requested the additional challenges at a pretrial hearing. The trial court refused, and apparently gave three challenges to each side, plus an additional challenge to be used for the alternate seat. Cunningham also requested additional challenges. The trial court granted six challenges per side plus one for each alternate. Neither petitioner claims that he was prejudiced by the allegedly insufficient number of challenges; indeed, neither petitioner even submits the record of voir dire.

Petitioners argue that because the Statute subjects them to indefinite incarceration, they should be afforded the same number of peremptory challenges as defendants in capital cases under CrR 6.4. We disagree. The proceedings here are civil, not criminal, in nature. Thus, the appropriate number of challenges is found in RCW 4.44.130, which deals with civil juries: "Each party shall be entitled to three peremptory challenges." *See also* 14 Lewis H. Orland & Karl B. Tegland, Wash. Prac., *Trial Practice Civil* Sec. 206, at 334 (4th ed. 1986). This is the same number of peremptory challenges allowed in RCW 71.05 civil commitment proceedings. *See* MPR 3.4(a). Therefore, three peremptory challenges are sufficient.

4. *Vagueness*

Petitioners and amicus American Civil Liberties Union argue that various terms in the Statute—such as "comparable," "sexually motivated," "safe to be at large," "mental abnormality," and "likely"—are unconstitutionally vague.

The issue of vagueness involves the procedural due process requirements of fair notice of the conduct warranting detention and clear standards to prevent arbitrary enforcement by those charged with administering the applicable statutes. *In re LaBelle*, 107 Wash.2d 196, 201, 728 P.2d 138 (1986) (citing Hontz v. State, 105 Wash.2d 302, 308, 714 P.2d 1176 (1986); *see also Clyde Hill v. Roisen*, 111 Wash.2d 912, 916, 767 P.2d 1375 (1989).

Exact specificity is not required; rather, the language used must be susceptible to understanding by persons of ordinary intelligence. *Seattle v. Eze*, 111 Wash.2d 22, 26-27, 759 P.2d 366, 78 A.L.R. 4th 1115 (1988). We do not find the Statute to be so vague as to deny due process.

Ample standards are present to guide the exercise of discretion and to provide notice to potential detainees of prohibited conduct. The Statute is quite specific and explicit. It requires that a person "who suffers from a mental abnormality or personality disorder which makes the person likely to engage in predatory acts of sexual violence," RCW 71.09.020(1), as determined at a jury trial if so requested, RCW 71.09.050, be committed to the custody of DSHS for care and treatment. RCW 71.09.060. The definitional section sets out precise standards, and defines "mental abnormality." RCW 71.09.020(2). As the record indicates, the experts who testified at the commitment trials adequately explained and gave meaning to this term within a psychological context. E.g., CPY, (Feb. 2, 1991), at 159-60; CPC (May 5, 1991), at 54-65. Likewise, the term "personality disorder" has a well-accepted psychological meaning. *See* DSM-III-R at 335-58. The application of these standards to a particular set of facts is, of course, a determination for the factfinder, but the definitions provide sufficient guidance to do so properly.

Similar challenges based on vagueness have been rejected. The United States Supreme Court, in analyzing a sexual psychopath statute, held that the statute was not vague because it could be applied only to a narrowly defined group of offenders. *Minnesota ex rel. Pearson v. Probate Court*, 309 U.S. 270, 274-75, 60 S.Ct. 523, 525-26, 126 A.L.R. 530 91940). The statute there turned on "underlying conditions, calling for evidence of past conduct pointing to probable consequences ... as susceptible proof as many of the criteria constantly applied in prosecutions for crime." *Pearson*, at 274, 60 S.Ct. at 526. Similarly, our Statute calls for particular evidence of past conduct and a propensity toward violence. *See also People v. Pembrock*, 62 Ill.2d 317, 342 N.E.2d 28 (1976). The sex predator Statute is not so vague that it denies due process.

5. *Right to remain silent*

Petitioners argue that they were denied their right to remain silent. Both were ordered by the trial court to speak to the State's psychologists. In addition, testimony was allowed at trial that Young refused to abide by the court's order. First, petitioners claim that the Fifth Amendment privilege against self-incrimination should apply to them. Second, they argue that because persons committed under the involuntary commitment act, RCW 71.05, have a right to remain silent, application of equal protection to the Statute compels this court to find that sexually violent predators possess that same right.

Under the Fifth Amendment, no person "shall be compelled in any criminal case to be a witness against himself." The Supreme Court has not entirely limited application of the Fifth Amendment privilege to criminal cases. *See, e.g., Boyd v. United States*, 116 U.S. 616, 6 S.Ct. 524, 29 L.Ed. 746 (1886). However, the Court has refused to apply the privilege to civil cases unless it has been shown conclusively that the penalty imposed is punishment tantamount to a criminal sanction. *United States v. Ward*, 448 U.S. 242, 254, 100 S.Ct. 2636, 2644, 65 L.Ed.2d 742 (1980). More to the point, in assessing the Illinois statute, found above to be significantly similar to RCW 71.09, the Supreme Court held that the Fifth Amendment does not apply, *Allen v. Illinois*, 478 u.S. 364, 375, 106 S.Ct. 2988, 2995, 92 L.Ed.2d 296 (1986). Where, as here, "the State serves its purpose of *treating* rather than punishing sexually dangerous persons by committing them to an institution expressly designed to provide psychiatric care and treatment," the action is not a "criminal case" for purposes of the privilege against compulsory self-incrimination." *Allen*, at 373-74, 106 S.Ct. at 2994.[15]

Furthermore, we see good reasons to refuse the statutory right to remain silent to sexually violent predators even though the Legislature has granted such a right to the mentally ill. Equal protection requires that similarly situated persons be treated alike. *In re Knapp*, 102 Wash.2d 466, 473, 687 P.2d 1145 (19840. However, sexually violent predators are not similarly situated to the mentally ill in regard to the treatment methods employed, or the information necessary to ensure that they receive proper diagnosis and treatment. The Legislature made specific findings which are pertinent to this distinction:

> [A] small but extremely dangerous group of sexually violent predators exist who do not have a mental disease or defect that renders them appropriate for the existing involuntary treatment act, chapter 71.05 RCW.... [S]exually violent predators generally have antisocial personality features which are unamenable to existing mental illness treatment modalities and those features render them likely to engage in sexually violent behavior.... The legislature further finds that the prognosis for curing sexually violent offenders is poor,... and the treatment modalities for this population are very different than the traditional treatment modalities for people appropriate for commitment under the involuntary treatment act. RCW 71.09.010.

The problems associated with the treatment of sex offenders are well documented, and have continued to confound mental health professionals and legislators. The mental abnormalities or personality disorders involved with predatory behavior may not be immediately apparent. Thus, their cooperation with the diagnosis and treatment procedures is essential.[16] *See also Heller*, — U.S. at —, 113 S.Ct. at 2645 ("the different treatment to which a committed individual is subjected provides a rational basis"); *Bailey v. Gardebring*, 940 F.2d 1150, 1153 (8th Cir. 1991) (no constitutional right is violated when persons who suffer from severe mental disorders are treated differently from persons with less serious disorders), *cert. denied*, — U.S. —, 112 S.Ct. 1516, 117 L.Ed.2d 652 (1992); *People v. Parrott*, 244 Ill.App.3d 424, 184 Ill.Dec. 278, 283, 613 N.E.2d 305, 310 (1993) (When individual is committed using "beyond a reasonable doubt" standard, "he was not more harshly treated than other persons whose commitment rests upon a finding of mental illness by clear and convincing evidence.").

V. Evidentiary Issues

1. *Prior crimes*

Petitioners contend that several of the State's witnesses should not have been allowed to testify, and that other testimony was admitted in error. They claim that all the testimony of the victims of their prior crimes should have been excluded, as it was irrelevant and unfairly prejudicial. In addition, they argue that the victims' testimony pertaining to their emotional state at the time of the crimes should have been excluded as unfairly prejudicial. Cunningham argues separately that evidence relating to his juvenile conviction should have been excluded. Young claims that testimony about his 1972 bomb threat conviction was inadmissible.

Generally, all relevant evidence is admissible and all irrelevant evidence is inadmissible. ER 402. Relevant evidence is any "evidence having the tendency to make the existence of any fact that is of consequence to the determination of the action more probable or less probable than it would be without the evidence." ER 401. Even relevant evidence will be excluded "if its probative value is substantially outweighed by the danger of unfair prejudice." ER 403. The determination of relevance is within the broad discretion of the trial court, and will not be disturbed absent manifest abuse of that discretion. *State v. Swan*, 114 Wash.2d 613, 658, 790 P.2d 610 (1990), *cert. denied*, 498 U.S. 1046, 111 S.Ct. 752, 112 L.Ed.2d 772 (1991).

The evidence here was properly admitted. The manner in which the previous crimes were committed has some bearing on the motivations and mental states of the petitioners, and is pertinent to the ultimate question here. Moreover, the likelihood of continued violence on the part of petitioners is central to the determination of whether they are sexually violent predators under the terms of the Statute. Thus, we cannot say that the trial court abused its discretion in admitting the victims' testimony. Although we agree that the testimony presented by the victims was compelling, and, therefore, had a substantial effect on the jury, we do not believe that its prejudicial effect outweighed its probative value. In assessing whether an individual is a sexually violent predator, prior sexual history is highly probative of his or her propensity for future violence.

In a similar vein, the trial court acted within its discretion when it admitted evidence of Cunningham's sexually motivated juvenile conviction. A person's history of sexually violent offenses is relevant to the sex predator determination. RCW 71.09.020(1). By using the word "offense," the Legislature indicated an intent to include prior juvenile adjudications within the scope of permissible proof at sex predator proceedings. *See In re A, B, C, D, E*, 121 Wash.2d 80, 87, 847 P.2d 455 (1993).

We do not, however, perceive any relevance to the testimony presented about Young's 1972 conviction for a bomb threat. The threat was made on a college campus where Young was a student. No sexual motivation was alleged for this crime. On the other hand, it is hard to conceive of any juror attaching much significance to the conviction in light of Young's prior history of violent sex offenses, which includes at least six felony rapes. The jury instructions make it clear that only sex offenses or sexually motivated felonies are considered in making the sex

predator determination. Any error was harmless.

2. *Validity of prior convictions*

Young contends that all evidence relating to his conviction in 1963 for four rapes should have been excluded because the jury instructions given there were in error. We disagree. The trial court properly held that the convictions were admissible.[17]

We have previously held that the State may use prior convictions without proving their constitutional validity in appropriate circumstances. *State v. Ammons*, 105 Wash.2d 175, 187, 713 P.2d 719, 718 P.2d 796, *cert. denied*, 479 U.S. 930, 107 S.Ct. 398, 93 L.Ed.2d 351 (1986). Because an individual subject to civil commitment would have no greater constitutional protections in this regard, we apply the *Ammons* case by analogy. In sentencing proceedings, the court has established the following rule:

> [A] prior conviction which has been previously determined to have been unconstitutionally obtained or which is constitutionally invalid on its face may not be considered. Constitutionally invalid on its face means a conviction which without further elaboration evidences infirmities of a constitutional magnitude. (Citations omitted.) *Ammons*, at 187-88, 713 P.2d 719.

> To hold otherwise would require appellate review of all prior convictions, which would "unduly and unjustifiably overburden the [trial] court." *Ammons*, at 188, 713 P.2d 719.

Finally, Young contends that the testimony of interrogating officers concerning his confessions to the rapes was wrongly admitted. He argues that because tape recordings were made (but not offered into evidence) the testimony must be excluded. Furthermore, he asserts that he should have been permitted to offer impeachment evidence of a criminal trespass charge and disciplinary history against the officers. These arguments are patently meritless.

3. *Expert testimony*

Petitioners argue that the testimony of the State's expert witnesses, Dr. Dreiblatt and Dr. Rawlings, should have been excluded because they testified as to theories which are not generally accepted in the scientific community. They contend that the experts had no basis for their testimony that any particular mental abnormality or personality disorder exists which makes a person likely to rape, or that Young or Cunningham was in fact likely to re-offend. They are supported in this claim by amicus, the Washington State Psychiatric Association. We conclude that the testimony was properly admitted.

Petitioners point to testimony offered by their own experts that rape is not necessarily caused by mental illness or disease. At trial, the jury heard a broad spectrum of evidence pertaining to the petitioners' condition. In addition to the State's expert testimony presenting the diagnoses of petitioners, the jury heard testimony from experts presenting the contrary view. From this evidence relating both to the accuracy of the diagnosis in general, and the specific criticism of the diagnoses made in Young's and Cunningham's cases, the jury was able to return a verdict that petitioners were sexually violent predators.

Initially, we must determine "if the evidence in question has a valid, scientific basis." *State v. Cauthron*, 120 Wash.2d 879, 887, 846 P.2d 502 (1993). The standard for determining if evidence based on novel scientific procedures is admissible is that set forth in *Frye v. United States*, 293 F. 1013, 1014, 34 A.L.R. 145 (D.C. Cir. 1923) (rejecting precursor to the modern polygraph test). The rule is well-established:

> [E]vidence deriving from a scientific theory or principle is admissible only if that theory or principle has achieved general acceptance in the relevant scientific community. *State v. Martin*, 101 Wash.2d 713, 719, 684 P.2d 651 (1984) (rejecting hypnotically induced testimony).

Under *Frye*, "[t]he core concern...is only whether the evidence being offered is based on established scientific methodology." *Cauthron*, 120 Wash.2d at 889, 846 P.2d 502.

We have previously held that predictions of future dangerousness do not violate due process, despite the inherent uncertainties of psychiatric predictions. *In re Harris*, 98 Wash.2d 276, 280, 654 P.2d 109 (1982). Our reasoning there is convincing in this context as well:

> Petitioner's argument would eviscerate the entire law of involuntary commitment as well as render dubious the numerous other

areas where psychiatry and the law intersect. There is no question the prediction of dangerousness has its attendant problems. ...But we are not prepared to abandon the possibility of conforming the law of involuntary civil commitment to the requirements of the constitution. *Harris*, at 280-81, 654 P.2d 109.

In addition, we have held that a finding of future dangerousness provides an appropriate reason to impose an exceptional sentence on a sex offender. *State v. Pryor*, 115 Wash.2d 445, 454, 799 P.2d 244 (1990). Our holding in *Pryor* implies that predictions of future dangerousness are sufficiently accurate and reliable. We see no reason to reconsider that holding here. *See State v. Janes*, 121 Wash.2d 220, 235, 850 P.2d 495 (1993) (independent *Frye* determination unnecessary when an analogous proposition has already been deemed admissible).

We are also not persuaded that the trial court erred in allowing the remainder of the experts' testimony. The sciences of psychology and psychiatry are not novel; they have been an integral part of the American legal system since its inception. Although testimony relating to mental illnesses and disorders is not amenable to the types of precise and verifiable cause and effect relation petitioners seek, the level of acceptance is sufficient to merit consideration at trial. As Justice White pointed out in *Foucha*, "such opinion is reliable enough to permit the courts to base civil commitments on clear and convincing medical evidence that a person is mentally ill and dangerous." — U.S. — n. 3, 112 S.Ct. at 1783, n. 3.

Our position is supported by the Legislature's determination, following numerous hearings, that the sexually violent predator condition is not only recognized, but treatable *and* capable of diagnosis. *See* RCW 71.09. As Justice O'Connor pointed out in *Foucha v. Louisiana*, — U.S. —, —, 112 S.Ct. 1780, 1789, 118 L.Ed.2d 437 (1992), the inherent uncertainty involved in making psychological judgments requires courts to "'... pay particular deference to reasonable legislative judgements' about the relationship between dangerous behavior and mental illness." (O'Connor, J., concurring) (quoting *Jones v. United States*, 463 U.S. 354, 365, n.

13, 103 S.Ct. 3043, 3050 n. 13, 77 L.Ed.2d 694 (1983).

Next, we must determine if expert testimony was properly admitted. ER 702 provides as follows:

> If scientific, technical, or other specialized knowledge will assist the trier of fact to understand the evidence or to determine a fact in issue, a witness qualified as an expert by knowledge, skill, experience, training, or education, may testify thereto in the form of an opinion or otherwise.

The determination of whether expert testimony is admissible is within the discretion of the trial court. *State v. Ortiz*, 119 Wash.2d 294, 310, 831 P.2d 1060 (1992). Unless there has been an abuse of discretion, this court will not disturb the trial court's decision.

The 2-part test we apply for ER 702 matters is whether: "(1) the witness qualifies as an expert and (2) the expert testimony would be helpful to the trier of fact." *Cauthron*, 120 Wash.2d at 890, 846 P.2d 502. Here, there is no dispute as to either of the State's experts' qualifications. Moreover, the expert testimony was certainly helpful to the trier of fact— psychiatric testimony is central to the ultimate question here: whether petitioners suffer from a mental abnormality or personality disorder.

In a related argument, Young claims that Dr. Dreiblatt's testimony that Young suffers from a *combination* of mental abnormality and personality disorder was insufficient to meet the definition of sexually violent predator. We disagree. The definition is phrased in the alternative and states that a sexually violent predator is someone who suffers from a mental abnormality *or* a personality disorder. RCW 71.09.020(1). We must construe it, however, in a manner which effectuates its purpose. *Wichert v. Cardwell*, 117 Wash.2d 148, 151, 812 P.2d 858 (1991). The Legislature intended that all dangerous sex offenders be incapacitated and treated. Frequently, as Young's case amply demonstrates, an individual will suffer from multiple mental abnormalities and personality disorders which make violent rape likely. It would thwart the legislative purpose if the Statute only allowed the commitment of those who suffer from one or the other, while prohibiting the commitment of more seriously afflicted sexually violent predators. Thus,

the showing that Young suffers both a mental abnormality *and* a personality disorder meets the requirements of the Statute.

Petitioners also claim that the expert testimony should be excluded because it was based on hearsay. Under ER 703, an expert's opinion may be heard on materials "of a type reasonably relied upon by experts in the particular field." Both experts for the State here relied on psychological reports and criminal history of petitioners. They testified that these are the types of materials reasonably relied on to diagnose future dangerousness of sex offenders. Indeed, in the face of petitioners' refusals to cooperate, no other course was open to the State's experts.

Finally, it must be pointed out that petitioners each presented expert testimony of their own. The juries were urged by defense experts to reject the opinions of the State's experts, and had ample opportunity to weigh the testimony of both sides. The ultimate decision of whether or not petitioners were sexually violent predators was made by the factfinder only after a thorough presentation of the experts' views.

VI. Conclusion

In sum, we conclude that the overall statutory scheme presented in the sexually violent predator portions of the Act is constitutional. We hold that RCW 71.09 is civil rather than criminal, and does not violate either the prohibition against ex post facto laws or the double jeopardy clause. We further hold, after a searching inquiry, that the basic statutory scheme implicates no substantive due process concerns. Although we conclude that a detainee must be permitted to appear in court within 72 hours to contest probable cause, the failure to accord petitioners this right was harmless error.

We conclude that the Statute is not void for vagueness; the terms are sufficiently specific and explicit. Further, due process does not operate to guarantee petitioners a right to remain silent; there are ample reasons to treat these detainees differently than others involuntarily committed. As to the remaining evidentiary issues, in most instances the trial courts acted properly within their discretion. The testimony of the victims of previous sexual crimes, including any juvenile offenses, is relevant and may be admitted. The expert testimony was also properly admitted. We hold that the evidence pertaining to a bomb threat conviction in Young's case was inadmissible, but that error was harmless. Finally, we have given ample consideration to all of the remaining arguments raised in the personal restraint petitions and on appeal, as well as those advanced by amici, and conclude that they lack merit.

Turning to the specific disposition in petitioners' cases, we reverse Cunningham's commitment due to the State's failure to prove dangerousness through evidence of a recent overt act. Also, the commitment was in error because the jury was not unanimous. We affirm the sex predator determination in petitioner Young's case, but remand solely for a consideration of less restrictive alternatives.

ANDERSEN, C.J., and BRACHTENBACH, GUY, MADSEN and DOLLIVER, JJ., concur.

JOHNSON, Justice (dissenting).

I dissent.

[I]ncarceration of persons is ... one of the most feared instruments of state oppression and ... freedom from this restraint is essential to the basic definition of liberty in the Fifth and Fourteenth Amendments....[18]

The sexually violent predator statute, RCW 71.09 (hereinafter Statute), is a well-intentioned attempt by the Legislature to keep sex predators off the streets. However, by authorizing the indefinite confinement in mental facilities of persons who are not mentally ill, the Statute threatens not only the liberty of certain sex offenders, but the liberty of us all. By committing individuals based solely on perceived dangerousness, the Statute in effect sets up an Orwellian "dangerousness court," a technique of social control fundamentally incompatible with our system of ordered liberty guaranteed by the constitution and contrary to the recent United States Supreme Court decision in *Foucha v. Louisiana*, — U.S. —, 112 S.Ct. 1780, 118 L.Ed.2d 437 (1992).

History has proven the grave error in creating special classes of individuals for whom constitutional rights are diminished. Today the majority condones the Legislature's creation of such a special class, trampling these individuals' rights. I cannot agree. The Statute is nothing more or less than a preventive detention scheme based on allegations of future dangerousness. Once a person has committed a sexually motivated crime, no matter how remote in time or place, the State is authorized to hold that person forever for the "good of the community." Our community would be better served by steadfast adherence to constitutional principles.

The majority concedes the unconstitutionality of the Statute and attempts to salvage it by reading in requirements not included by the Legislature. Unfortunately, the majority's pen stops short. Under *Foucha*, the State must prove an individual is *both* mentally ill and dangerous before the person can be involuntarily committed; however, the Statute still fails to meet the mental illness requirement. Thus, the Statute offends the due process clause by subjecting individuals to lifetime confinement based not on any crime committed, but instead on fears of future crimes, and it offends the prohibitions against ex post facto laws and double jeopardy by masquerading as a civil commitment law when its purpose is penal.

I. *Substantive Due Process*

The sexual predator Statute violates substantive due process. Under the Fifth and Fourteenth Amendments, no person shall be deprived of life, liberty, or property without due process of law. U.S. Const. amend. 5; U.S. Const. amend. 14, Sec. 1. "[T]he Due Process Clause contains a substantive component that bars certain arbitrary, wrongful government actions 'regardless of the fairness of the procedures used to implement them.'" *Zinermon v. Burch*, 494 U.S. 113, 125, 110 S.Ct. 975, 983, 108 L.Ed.2d 100 (1990) (quoting *Daniels v. Williams*, 474 U.S. 327, 331, 106 S.Ct. 662, 664-65, 88 L.Ed.2d 662 106 S.Ct. 677, 88 L.Ed.2d 662 (1986)). The test to be applied in determining the constitutionality of a statute under substantive due process depends upon whether a fundamental right is at stake.

An individual's liberty interest is fundamental in nature. *See United States v. Salerno*, 481 U.S. 739, 750, 107 S.Ct. 2095, 2103, 95 L.Ed.2d 697 (1987). "Freedom from bodily restraint has always been at the core of the liberty protected by the Due

Process Clause from arbitrary governmental action." *Foucha v. Louisiana*, — U.S. —, —, 112 S.Ct. 1780, 1785 (1992); *Reno v. Flores*, — U.S. —, —, 113 S.Ct. 1439, 1454, 123 L.Ed.2d 1 (1993) (O'Connor, J., concurring). Physical confinement in a mental institution entails a "massive curtailment of liberty." *Vitek v. Jones*, 445 U.S. 480, 491-92, 100 S.Ct. 1254, 1262-63, 63 L.Ed.2d 552 (1980).

When a statute implicates a fundamental right such as a person's liberty, the test for whether the statute passes constitutional muster is one of strict scrutiny. For the statute to be constitutional, it must further a compelling state interest and must be narrowly tailored to achieve that interest. *State v. Farmer*, 116 Wash.2d 414, 429, 805 P.2d 200, 812 P.2d 858, 13 A.L.R.5th 1070 (1991); *In re Schuoler*, 106 Wash.2d 500, 508, 723 P.2d 1103 (1986).

Although the majority acknowledges the Statute must pass strict scrutiny, it fails to adequately analyze whether the Statute is narrowly tailored to achieve the State's interest. The most recent statement of the Supreme Court's requirements for narrowly tailoring an involuntary commitment statute is *Foucha v. Louisiana*, — U.S. —, 112 S.Ct. 1780, 118 L.Ed.2d 437 (1992). The majority has failed to see or has chosen to ignore that *Foucha* recognizes only three situations in which the State has such a compelling interest in public safety that a complete deprivation of an individual's liberty interest is justified: criminal conviction, civil commitment, and limited detention of persons shown to be dangerous to the community. *Foucha*, — U.S. at — - —, 112 S.Ct. at 1785-86.

Even in these three situations, however, the State is required to narrowly tailor its statutes. For example, the requirement that a person be both mentally ill and dangerous is a way to constitutionally tailor civil commitment statutes. In addition, strict time limits for pretrial detention are another specific way to narrow the conditions under which an individual may be confined.

In contrast, the sexual predator Statute is not narrowly tailored to achieve its compelling interest. In order to be narrowly drawn, the Statute must satisfy certain requirements set out by the United States Supreme Court for either civil commitment or preventive detention statutes. The sex predator Statute fails on both counts.

Under civil commitment, substantive due process requires that an individual be both mentally ill and dangerous before he or she may be involuntarily committed. *Foucha*, — U.S. at —, 112 S.Ct. at 1784. In *Foucha*, an insanity acquittee who had regained his sanity sought release from a mental institution. Foucha was found to be no longer mentally ill, but still dangerous to others because of his "antisocial personality, a condition that is not a mental disease and ... is untreatable." *Foucha*, — U.S. at —, 112 S.Ct. at 1782. The Court held that Foucha's continued confinement based on dangerousness alone violated due process. *Foucha*, — U.S. at —, 112 S.Ct. at 1784.

Like the statute in *Foucha*, RCW 71.09 violates substantive due process because it requires only dangerousness and not mental illness as a prerequisite to commitment. The Statute, by its own terms, applies specifically to individuals who "do not have a mental disease or defect that renders them appropriate for the existing involuntary treatment act." RCW 71.09.010.

The Statute provides for the indefinite commitment of any person deemed to be a "sexually violent predator," but the Statute's definition of this term does not apply to a group of individuals who are mentally ill in any medically recognized sense. *See* LaFond, *Washington's Sexually Violent Predator Law: A Deliberate Misuse of the Therapeutic State for Social Control*, 15 U. Puget Sound L. Rev. 655, 691-92 (1992-1992); Comment, *Sexual Violence, Sanity & Safety: Constitutional Parameters for Involuntary Civil Commitment of Sex Offenders*, 15 U. Puget Sound L. Rev. 879, 898-900 (1991-1992).

The Statute defines "sexually violent predator" as any person who meets the following two criteria: (1) the person must at any time in his or her life been either charged with or convicted of a sexually violent crime; and (2) the person must suffer from "a *mental abnormality* or *personality disorder* which makes the person likely to engage in predatory acts of sexual violence." (Italics mine.) RCW 71.09.020(1). The second criterion involves a prediction of dangerousness based on a "mental abnormality" or "personality disorder," but these two terms do not involve any medically recognized mental illness.

Amicus, the Washington State Psychiatric Association, points out the term "mental abnormality" has no clinically significant meaning and no recognized diagnostic use; the term "abnormality" has long been in disuse because it can have a variety of different meanings. The Statute defines the term "mental abnormality" as:

a congenital or acquired condition affecting the emotional or volitional capacity which predisposes the person to the commission of criminal sexual acts in a degree constituting such person a menace to the health and safety of others. RCW 71.09.020(2).

A "mental abnormality" which makes a person "likely to engage in predatory acts of sexual violence" is thus defined by the Statute as a mental condition that may predispose a person to commit a sex crime. RCW 71.09.020(1), (2). This definition is merely circular, and, as one commentator has observed, allows a "mental abnormality" to be established in a circular manner: the "abnormality" will be derived from the person's past sexual behavior, and this in turn will be used to establish the person's predisposition to future dangerous sexual behavior. Wettstein, *A Psychiatric Perspective on Washington's Sexually Violent Predators Statute*, 15 U. Puget Sound L. Rev. 597, 602, 633 (1991-1992) (concluding the Statute's definition of "sexually violent predator" fails to coincide with clinical or empirical knowledge regarding sex offenders). *See also* Rideout, *So What's in a Name? A Rhetorical Reading of Washington's Sexually Violent Predators Act*, 15 U. Puget Sound L. Rev. 781, 793 (1991-1992) (discussing the tautology "in the statement that sexually violent predators have features that lead to sexually violent behavior").

The Statute also does not provide a definition for the term "personality disorder." Amicus points out this term has a clinically recognized meaning, but there is no "personality disorder" specific to sex offenders. Because of this problem, the task of determining whether a causal relationship exists between a "personality disorder" and the person's potential dangerousness is nothing more

than "a matter of speculation or meaningless circularity." Wettstein, 15 U. Puget Sound L. Rev. at 603; *see also* Comment, *Washington's Sexually Violent Predator Law: The Need to Bar Unreliable Psychiatric Predictions of Dangerousness From Civil Commitment Proceedings*, 39 U.C.L.A. L. Rev. 213 (1991-1992).[19]

Despite some psychiatric incantations, therefore, the sexual predator Statute deals with potentially dangerous people, but not mentally ill people. Because under *Foucha* a prediction of dangerousness alone is an unconstitutional basis for indefinite confinement in a mental institution, the Statute violates due process.

Even if a personality disorder or mental abnormality is a mental illness, this court has previously required proof of a recent overt act as evidence of dangerousness before a person can be detained to assess whether he or she is mentally ill. *See* In re Harris, 98 Wash.2d 276, 654 P.2d 109 (1982). The plain language of the sex predator Statute contains no such requirement.[20] The majority attempts to salvage the Statute's constitutionality by reading in a requirement of a recent overt act, but *only* for individuals who have been released into the community. For individuals currently incarcerated, no evidence of a recent overt act is required.

This judicial rewriting of the Statute is unprincipled decisionmaking at its worst. Although the majority is correct that a court must construe a statute to render it constitutional, majority at 1009, *a court cannot rewrite a statute by reading into it language that simply is not there*. Addleman v. Board of Prison Terms & Paroles, 107 Wash.2d 503, 509, 730 P.2d 1327 (1986) (stating if language of a statute is clear, a court may not "read things into it which are not there"). Such judicial rewriting is not only unprincipled, but also unfair. The parties could not have anticipated this new construction and have not had an opportunity to brief or argue the constitutionality of the majority's new version of the Statute.

The court's wholesale reading in of an overt act requirement also runs counter to the Legislature's intent. The Statute was enacted in response to intense public outcry over two brutal sex crimes: the rape and mutilation of a Tacoma boy, and the rape and murder of a Seattle woman. *See* Boerner, *Confronting Violence: In the Act & in the Word*, 15 U. Puget Sound L. Rev. 525 (1991-1992). The individuals who committed the crimes had recently been released after serving time for previous sex crimes. To the extent that the majority now requires evidence of a recent overt act by such released individuals, the majority paves the way for a repeat of the above brutal crimes, which is exactly what the legislation was enacted to avoid! This is an absurd result.

Finally, the majority's rewriting of the Statute raises new equal protection concerns. By reading in this new requirement, the court creates two classes of persons under the same statute: those incarcerated versus those who are not. This is a distinction without a difference. Immediately upon release, an individual must now commit an overt act to be incarcerated under the Statute, whereas the day before release, the same individual could be committed without proof of an overt act. This new distinction is arbitrary, violating even a rational basis review.

Equal protection requires that "persons similarly situated with respect to the legitimate purposes of the laws receive like treatment." *In re Knapp*, 102 Wash.2d 466, 473, 687 P.2d 1145 (1984). The purpose of the Statute is to prevent sexual predators from reoffending and thereby protect the community. It is difficult to see the difference between an individual the day before he or she leaves prison versus an individual the day after departing from jail. The only rationale offered by the majority is that an incarcerated individual does not have the opportunity to commit a recent overt act. I disagree. Evidence amounting to a "recent overt act" is often present even while in jail. Such evidence could be based on prison activities or conduct, such as inappropriate drawings of sexual encounters with children.

The court cannot choose to have two standards for commitment: one of those presently incarcerated and another for everybody else.[21] The United States Supreme Court has been careful to harmonize the constitutional requirements for *civil* commitment in the ordinary situation with those arising when there has been a finding of insanity at a *criminal* trial. *See Jones v. United States*, 463 U.S. 354, 103 S.Ct. 3043, 77 L.Ed.2d 694 (1983). Although the majority's requirement of a recent overt act by released individuals harmonizes RCW 71.09 with the State's short-term detention statute, RCW 71.05,[22] this requirement does not render the Statute constitutional. Under the majority's interpretation, incarcerated individuals still face the potential for lifetime detention based only on the possibility of future dangerousness. Because incarceration under the Statute can follow a long prison term and because the majority does not require a recent overt act for these individuals, the determination that they are "dangerous" is not even based on the same standard used for others who are civilly committed. If an individual once committed a sex crime and someone thinks that individual is still dangerous, the Statute authorizes a lifetime term in a mental facility. This is pure preventive detention.

The United States Supreme Court has permitted preventive detention only in the pretrial context and only if the duration of confinement is *strictly limited*, not indefinite as in this case. *See, e.g., United States v. Salerno*, 481 U.S. 739, 747-51, 107 S.Ct. 2095, 2101-04, 95 L.Ed.2d 697 (1987); *Schall v. Martin*, 467 U.S. 253, 264-71, 104 S.Ct. 2403, 2409-14, 81 L.Ed.2d 207 (1984); *Jackson v. Indiana*, 406 U.S. 715, 738, 92 S.Ct. 1845, 1858, 32 L.Ed.2d 435 (1972).

In *Salerno*, the Supreme Court upheld a federal act authorizing pretrial detention of defendants deemed dangerous. The Court noted that preventive detention under the act was "limited by the stringent time limitations of the Speedy Trial Act." *Salerno*, 481 U.S. at 747, 107 S.Ct. at 2101-02. In *Schall*, the Court upheld a state statute authorizing the preventive pretrial detention of juveniles accused of crimes who were deemed dangerous, and the Court noted the maximum possible detention under the act was only 17 days. *Schall*, 467 U.S. at 269-70, 104 S.Ct. at 2412-13. Finally, in *Jackson*, the Court held that a criminal defendant who was incapable of proceeding to trial could be detained only for the reasonable period of time necessary to determine whether a substantial probability existed the defendant would ever become capable to proceed to trial. *Jackson*, 406 U.S. at 738, 92 S.Ct. at 1858. Under this standard, the Court in *Jackson* found the defendant's 3½ year confinement excessive because the defendant, a deaf mute, was not expected to ever gain the competency to stand trial.

The Supreme Court has never upheld a lifetime preventive detention scheme for those who are feared dangerous. It was asked to do precisely that in *Foucha*. The State of Louisiana argued that *Salerno* authorized preventive detention for persons who pose a danger to the community. *Foucha*, — U.S. at —, 112 S.Ct. at 1786. The Court disagreed and distinguished *Salerno* on three grounds. First, the Court noted the statute at issue in *Salerno* was narrowly focused on the most serious of crimes and required a finding that no conditions of release could reasonably assure the safety of the community. *Foucha*, — U.S. at —, 112 S.Ct. at 1786. Second, the Court contrasted the time limits for pretrial detention with indefinite commitment authorized by the Louisiana law. *Foucha*, — U.S. — at — - — , 112 S.Ct. at 1786-87. Finally, the Court pointed out that less restrictive alternatives were available to deal with persistent criminal behavior, including enhanced sentences for recidivists. *Foucha*, — U.S. at — - —, 112 S.Ct. at 1786-87.

Like the statute in *Foucha*, the sexual predator Statute is fundamentally flawed. Its scope is broad, covering everything from murder-rape to attempted sexually motivated burglary. Its duration is indefinite. Unlike *Salerno*, *Schall* and *Jackson*, the Statute in this case produces lifetime preventive detention. The Legislature found that "sexually violent predators" are "unamenable to existing mental illness treatment modalities" and that the prognosis for curing them is "poor." RCW 71.09.010. The Statute thus creates a class of persons who, by definition, are not likely to be "cured," and thus not likely to ever be released.

As a result, the Statute does precisely what *Foucha* expressly says the government may not do: confine someone indefinitely as dangerous who is not mentally ill but simply has a personality disorder or antisocial personality. As the Supreme Court noted:

[T]he State asserts that because Foucha once committed a criminal act and now has an antisocial personality that sometimes leads to aggressive conduct, a disorder for which there is no effective treatment, he may be held indefinitely. This rationale would permit the State to hold indefinitely any other insanity acquittee not mentally ill who could be shown to have a personality disorder that may lead to criminal conduct. *The same would be true of any convicted criminal, even though he has completed his prison term.* (Italics mine.) *Foucha*, — U.S. at —, 112 S.Ct. at 1787.

The Legislature has other options for dealing with sex offenders. Enhanced sentences for repeat offenders and supervised release are but two of the most obvious.

The sexual predator Statute has each of the constitutional weaknesses of the statute in *Foucha*, weaknesses that caused the Supreme Court to consider the *Foucha* statute

only a step away from substituting confinements for dangerousness for our present system which, with only narrow exceptions...incarcerates only those who are proved beyond a reasonable doubt to have violated a criminal law. (Italics mine.) *Foucha*, — U.S. at —, 112 S.Ct. 1787.

I would hold the sexual predator Statute is an unconstitutional violation of substantive due process.

II Ex Post Facto and Double Jeopardy

In addition to violating substantive due process, the Statute's commitment provisions violate the constitutional prohibition against ex post facto laws. U.S. Const. art. 1, Sec. 10. A law violates this prohibition if it "makes more burdensome the punishment for a crime, after its commission." *Collins v. Youngblood*, 497 U.S. 37, 42, 110 S.Ct. 2715, 2719, 111 L.Ed.2d 30 (1990) (quoting *Beazell v. Ohio*, 269 U.S. 167, 159, 46 S.Ct. 68, 68, 70 L.Ed. 216 (1925)). The purpose of the ex post facto prohibition is to give individuals fair warning of the effect of legislative acts and to restrict the power of the State to impose arbitrary or vindictive legislation. *Weaver v. Graham*, 450 U.S. 24, 101 S.Ct. 960, 67 L.Ed.2d 17 (1981).

The commitment provisions also violate the prohibition on double jeopardy. U.S.

Const. amend. 5. The double jeopardy clause protects against multiple punishments for the same offense. *North Carolina v. Pearce*, 395 U.S. 711, 717, 89 S.Ct. 2072, 2076-77, 23 L.Ed.2d 656, 89 S.Ct. 2089, 23 L.Ed.2d 656 (1969). When the government has already imposed a criminal penalty, the double jeopardy clause precludes the government from seeking additional punishment in a second proceeding if it is dissatisfied with the sanction obtained in the first. *United States v. Halper*, 490 U.S. 435, 449-50, 109 S.Ct. 1892, 1902-03, 104 L.Ed.2d 487 (1989).

Because RCW 71.09 authorizes retroactive extension of a criminal sentence if the State is dissatisfied with the original length, it violates both of these provisions. The majority argues that these provisions do not apply because the Statute is civil rather than criminal in nature. However, a statute must be deemed criminal in nature when the statute is "so punitive either in purpose or effect" as to negate a legislature's intent to establish a civil statute, *United States v. Ward*, 448 U.S. 242, 248, 100 S.Ct. 2636, 2641, 65 L.Ed.2d 742 (1980).

The factors to be considered deciding whether a statute has criminal or civil purpose include whether the act disavows all interest in punishment, whether it provides treatment, and whether release is possible at any time. *Allen v. Illinois*, 478 U.S. 364, 106 S.Ct. 2988, 92 L.Ed.2d 296 (1986).

The statute in *Allen* allowed the State to divert persons charged with crimes from the criminal system to the civil system for treatment of mental illness. In contrast, the sexually violent predator Statute is not an alternative to criminal imprisonment. It allows the State to seek a criminal conviction against an individual, and only after the individual has completed his or her sentence does the Statute purportedly seek to provide specialized "care and treatment" for the individual. *See* RCW 71.09.030, .060. Far from disavowing criminal punishment, such punishment is an essential component of the Statute's commitment provisions.

Although the Statute provides for treatment, this goal is completely subordinated to punishment. An individual's need for diagnosis and treatment is *never* sufficiently compelling under the Statute until the individual is nearing the end of his or her criminal sentence. The timing alone is a strong indication that the Legislature was less interested in treatment than in confinement.

While both the Illinois statute in *Allen* and the Washington Statute provide for an indefinite period of confinement, there are important procedural differences. In Illinois, an individual may file a petition for release at any time and is entitled to a case review every 6 months. The court is required to hear all petitions. Here a petition for release normally must be authorized by the Department of Social and Health Services. Although an individual may petition over the Department's objection, he or she must then prevail at a show cause hearing in order to obtain a real trial. Once a person has petitioned over the Department's objection and been denied, the court is mandated to deny subsequent petitions unless the person can make a showing of changed circumstances in the petition itself. Case reviews are conducted only once a year.

Based on a comparison of these factors, RCW 71.09 is punitive in purpose and effect. Therefore, the prohibitions against ex post facto laws and double jeopardy apply here, and the Statute is unconstitutional.

In conclusion, I would hold that Washington's sexually violent predator Statute, RCW 71.09, violates petitioners' rights to substantive due process and violates the constitutional prohibition against ex post facto laws and double jeopardy.

UTTER and SMITH, JJ., concur.

NOTES

[1] The title "Civil Commitment" is not properly a part of the law. Laws of 1990, ch. 3, Sec. 1404. However, it provides evidence of the legislative intent to treat this Statute as civil.

[2] The mere fact that the State chose to establish a special commitment procedure for sex predators has no bearing on the question of whether the law is civil or criminal. As the Supreme Court stated in *Allen*, "[t]hat the State has chosen not to apply the Act to the larger class of mentally ill persons who might be found sexually dangerous does not somehow transform a civil proceeding into a crim-

inal one." *Allen*, 478 U.S. at 3709, 106 S.Ct. at 2993.

[3]Although the Supreme Court in *Foucha v. Louisiana*, — U.S. —, 112 S.Ct. 1780, 118 L.Ed.2d 437 (1992) used the term "mentally ill" almost exclusively, the Court has always used the term "mentally ill" interchangeably with "mentally disordered." *See, e.g., Allen v. Illinois*, 478 U.S. 364, 106 S.Ct. 2988 (upholding an Illinois statute requiring both a "mental disorder" and dangerousness); *Addington v. Texas*, 441 U.S. 418, 99 S.Ct. 1804 (using both terms). Indeed, the terms are largely synonyms. Longman Dictionary of Psychology and Psychiatry 451 (1984).

[4]The DSM-III-R is a document frequently relied upon by courts in determining the acceptance of psychiatric diagnosis. *E.g., Heller v. Doe*, — U.S. —, —, 113 S.Ct. 2637, 2642-44, 125 L.Ed.2d 257 (1993); *State v. Hutsell*, 120 Wash.2d 913, 917, 845 P.2d 1325 (1993); *In re Rice*, 118 Wash.2d 876, 890-91, 828 P.2d 1086, *cert. denied*, — U.S. —, 113 S.Ct. 421, 121 L.Ed.2d 344 (1992).

[5]Despite the testimony at trial, petitioners suggest that a "mental abnormality" is not a true mental illness because it is a term coined by the Legislature, rather than the psychiatric and psychological community. This argument is meritless. Over the years, the law has developed many specialized terms to describe mental health concepts. For example, the legal definitions of "insanity" and "commitment" vary substantially from their psychological and psychiatric counterparts. The DSM-III-R explicitly recognizes this fact, noting that the scientific categorization of a mental disorder may not be "wholly relevant to legal judgments." DSM-III-R, at xxix.

[6]According to expert testimony, rape as paraphilia falls within the DSM-III-R category of "paraphilia, not otherwise specified." CPY (Feb. 27, 1991), at 132. Dr. Steele, an expert for petitioners who testified at both trials agreed that rape is a paraphilia. CPY (Mar. 1, 1991), at 148; CPC (May 23, 1991), at 66. The article by Doctors Abel and Rouleau reviews the pertinent scientific literature and concludes that "[t]he weight of scientific evidence, therefore, supports rape of adults as a specific category of paraphilia." *Handbook of Sexual*

Assault, at 19. Moreover, the DSM-III-R specifies violent rape as a symptom of "paraphilia sexual sadism." DSM-III-R, at 287-88.

[7]It is by no means clear that the mental abnormalities and personality disorders underlying the sex predator condition are "untreatable." Of the experts who testified at trial, many reported that a significant portion of their practices were devoted to treating sex offenders. Also, the *Handbook of Sexual Assault* contains six chapters discussing the treatment of sex offenders. *See Handbook of Sexual Assault*, at 279-382.

[8]Although predictions of future dangerousness are certainly less than perfect, this court has previously decided that predictions of dangerousness do not violate due process. *In re Harris*, 98 Wash.2d 276, 280-81, 654 P.2d 109 (1982).

[9]The dissent seriously underplays the quantum of proof necessary to meet the dangerousness prong of the sex predator statute. The State must do far more than merely reprove a past criminal act, or present testimony from someone who thinks that individual is still dangerous. *See* dissent, at 1020-1021. Instead, the statute requires *proof beyond a reasonable doubt* that the person has been convicted or charged with a crime of sexual violence, and suffers from a mental abnormality or personality disorder "which makes the person likely to engage in predatory acts of sexual violence." RCW 71.09.020(1). In the current cases, testimony came from licensed mental health professionals familiar with petitioners' past conduct and current mental profiles.

[10]Citing a handful of law review articles, the dissent claims that RCW 71.09 is unrelated to any known mental illness. In making this claim, however, the dissent does not respond to the extensive expert testimony presented at both Young's and Cunningham's respective trials.

[11] A related argument is advanced that petitioners have a right to treatment. The Statute provides that any constitutional requirements concerning care and treatment must be met. RCW 71.09.080.

[12] Petitioners raise the issue that, under *Foucha*, it is impermissible to civilly commit

someone who has an "antisocial personality," because that condition is not a mental disorder. According to petitioners, the sex predator Statute violates this holding. This argument belies a careless reading of the *Foucha* facts. First, the condition in *Foucha* was an "antisocial personality." This condition falls within the DSM-III-R section entitled "V Codes for Conditions Not Attributable to a Mental Disorder" and is formally designated "antisocial behavior"; it is not a mental disorder. As such, anti-social behavior cannot form the basis for civil commitment. *Foucha v. Louisiana*, — U.S. —, 112 S.Ct. 1780. The sex predator Statute, however, requires proof of a "personality *disorder*" as one of the alternative means of commitment. (Italics ours.) RCW 71.09.020. Unlike "antisocial behavior," an "antisocial personality disorder" is a recognized mental disorder which is defined in the DSM-III-R, at 342. Second, petitioners ignore the limitations inherent in the Court's discussion of this issue. *Foucha* came before the Court on a limited trial record. As such, the Court pointed out several times that its discussion on the status of Foucha's condition as a mental illness was "according to the testimony given at the hearing in the trial court." *Foucha*, — U.S. —, 112 S.Ct. 1t 1785.

[13]Petitioners argue additionally that the Statute is facially invalid because of defects in the procedures for release. The release provisions of the two civil commitment statutes differ. The maximum period of commitment under RCW 71.05 is 180-day intervals. At the expiration of each period, the detainee is entitled to the full range of procedural protections, including jury trial. RCW 71.05.310, .320(2). The confinement interval for sex predators is 1 year, and after one petition has been rejected, the burden shifts to the detainee to show he or she is safe to be at large. RCW 71.09.090.100. Because neither petitioner here has applied for release, the record before the court is insufficient to decide if the Statute contains adequate release provisions. We decline to decide the matter on the limited information before us.

[14]Both this court and the United States Supreme Court have repeatedly applied this provision to a comparison of different commitment schemes. Thus, commitment of the mentally retarded has been compared to involuntary civil commitment. *Heller v. Doe*, — U.S. —, 113 S.Ct. 2637, 125 L.Ed.2d 257 (1993); court-ordered treatment has been compared to the sexual psychopathy statute, *In re Knapp*, 102 Wash.2d 466, 687 P.2d 1145 (1984); commitment for incompetency to stand trial has been compared to civil commitment under RCW 71.05, *In re Patterson*, 90 Wash.2d 144, 579 P.2d 1335 (1978); commitment of the criminally insane has been compared to civil commitment of the mentally ill, *Baxstrom v. Herold*, 383 U.S. 107, 86 S.Ct. 760, 15 L.Ed.2d 620 (1966); commitment in lieu of sentence under the Wisconsin sex crimes law has been compared to commitment for treatment under the mental health act, *Humphrey v. Cady*, 405 U.S. 504, 92 S.Ct. 1048, 31 L.Ed.2d 394 (1972); and, commitment for incompetency to stand trial has been compared with all other civil commitments, *Jackson v. Indiana*, 406 U.S. 715, 92 S.Ct. 1845, 32 L.Ed.2d 435 (1972).

[15]Of course, detainees could not be compelled to incriminate themselves by answering questions about prior uncharged or unconvicted criminal behavior. *See State v. Post*, 118 Wash.2d 596, 610-11, 826 P.2d 172, 837 P.2d 599 (1992).

[16]Our rejection of petitioners' claim to a right to remain silent resolves several additional issues. First, petitioners claim that expert opinion testimony was based on statements obtained in violation of petitioners' right to remain silent. Second, petitioners assert that they have the unequivocal right to testify without notifying the State in advance. Because these proceedings are civil in nature, and because petitioners have no absolute right to remain silent, these contentions are without merit. Moreover, since we reverse the verdict against Cunningham, we need not consider the State's argument made on cross appeal, that the admission of his testimony despite discovery violations was in error.

[17]Although a habeas corpus petition is currently being considered on its merits, the judgment and sentence are facially valid, see ER 803(a)(22), and have been affirmed on appeal. *State v. Young*, 65 Wash.2d 938, 400 P.2d 374, *cert. denied*, 382 U.S. 963, 86 S.Ct. 446, 15 L.Ed.2d 365 (1965).

[18][1] *Foucha v. Louisiana*, — U.S. —, —, 112 S.Ct. 1780, 1791, 118 L.Ed.2d 437 (1992) (Kennedy, J., dissenting.).

[19][2] The majority chides the dissent for relying on a handful of law review articles in support for the claim that a "mental abnormality" or "personality disorder" does not constitute "mental illness" as required by *Foucha*. Majority, at 1004 n. 10. It is curious that the majority also relies on a law review article in support of its proposition that the Statute's terms do constitute "a number of recognized mental pathologies," i.e., mental illness. *See* majority, at 1001. It is also curious that, after concluding the statute requires a showing of mental illness, the majority states in its equal protection analysis, "there are good reasons to treat *mentally ill people* differently than *violent sex offenders*." (Italics mine.) Majority, at 1010. The majority cannot have it both ways.

[20][3] To commit a person under the Statute, the State is required to reprove the defendant committed a prior crime and to present an evaluation by a psychologist establishing the person is likely to reoffend. However, this "evaluation" is often based merely on a review of the police reports and prior psychological evaluations rather than on a personal interview with the defendant.

[21][4] The majority implies that *Heller v. Doe*, — U.S. —, 113 S.Ct. 2637, 125 L.Ed.2d (1993) authorizes a 2-tier civil commitment process. Majority, at 1010. *Heller* is inapt, however, for two reasons: first, the Court did not review the statute under a heightened scrutiny standard, and second, it deals with mentally retarded, not mentally ill, persons.

[22][5]The majority also reads into RCW 71.09 a requirement from RCW 71.05, which requires the State to consider less restrictive alternatives as a precursor to confinement. Majority, at 1012. Although perhaps a good idea, the majority's rewriting of the Statute is still inappropriate for the same reasons discussed above. By reading in these new requirements, the court transforms RCW 71.09 into a statute that looks more like RCW 71.05, and thereby frustrates the Legislature's manifest intent to create a *new* statutory scheme since RCW 71.05 was deemed to be inadequate. *See* RCW 71.09.010.

Moreover, the majority's treatment of the equal protection question is inconsistent with its treatment of due process. In explaining why the incarceration of sexual predators within correctional institutions comports with due process, the majority implies that no less restrictive alternatives would effectively address the problem of preventing sex offenders from committing further crimes. The majority states:

Given the nature of sexually violent predators, it would not be safe to house them in a less secure setting. ...

...Here the dangerousness of committed sex predators justifies a secure confinement facility. Majority, at 1005.

Yet with respect to equal protection, the majority concludes that the State has proffered no "valid reason" for treating sexually violent predators differently from persons committed under RCW 71.05. Majority, at 1012.

It is also incorrect to aver that the State has put forth no justification for the disparate treatment of sexually violent predators under RCW 71.09. In this regard, the majority again flaunts the express intent of the Legislature, which found that:

[T]he treatment modalities for [sexually violent predators] are very different than the traditional treatment modalities for people appropriate for commitment under the involuntary treatment act. RCW 71.09.010.

Appendix I

Revised Code of Washington*

71.09.010. Findings

The legislature finds that a small but extremely dangerous group of sexually violent predators exist who do not have a mental disease or defect that renders them appropriate for the existing involuntary treatment act, chapter 71.05 RCW, which is intended to be a short-term civil commitment system that is primarily designed to provide short-term treatment to individuals with serious mental disorders and then return them to the community. In contrast to persons appropriate for civil commitment under chapter 71.05 RCW, sexually violent predators generally have antisocial personality features which are unamenable to existing mental illness treatment modalities and those features render them likely to engage in sexually violent behavior. The legislature further finds that sex offenders' likelihood of engaging in repeat acts of predatory sexual violence is high. The existing involuntary commitment act, chapter 71.05 RCW, is inadequate to address the risk to reoffend because during confinement these offenders do not have access to potential victims and therefore they will not engage in an overt act during confinement as required by the involuntary treatment act for continued confinement. The legislature further finds that the prognosis for curing sexually violent offenders is poor, the

---

* This is Part X of the Community Protection Act of 1990 and is commonly referred to as the "Sexually Violent Predators Law." Appendix H included the 1992 amendments to this Act.

treatment needs of this population are very long term, and the treatment modalities for this population are very different than the traditional treatment modalities for people appropriate for commitment under the involuntary treatment act.

71.09.020. Definitions

Unless the context clearly requires otherwise, the definitions in this section apply throughout this chapter.

(1) "Sexually violent predator" means any person who has been convicted of or charged with a crime of sexual violence and who suffers from a mental abnormality or personality disorder which makes the person likely to engage in predatory acts of sexual violence.

(2) "Mental abnormality" means a congenital or acquired condition affecting the emotional or volitional capacity which predisposes the person to the commission of criminal sexual acts in a degree constituting such person a menace to the health and safety of others.

(3) "Predatory" means acts directed towards strangers or individuals with whom a relationship has been established or promoted for the primary purpose of victimization.

(4) "Sexually violent offense" means an act committed on, before, or after July 1, 1990, that is: (a) An act defined in Title 9A RCW as rape in the first degree, rape in the second degree by forcible compulsion, rape of a child in the first or second degree, statutory rape in the first or second degree, indecent liberties by forcible compulsion, indecent liberties against a child under age fourteen, incest against a child under age four-

teen, or child molestation in the first or second degree; (b) a felony offense in effect at
any time prior to July 1, 1990, that is comparable to a sexually violent offense as defined
in (a) of this subsection, or any federal or out-
of-state conviction for a felony offense as
defined in this subsection; (c) an act of murder in the first or second degree, assault in the
first or second degree, assault of a child in the
first or second degree, kidnapping in the first
or second degree, burglary in the first degree,
residential burglary, or unlawful imprisonment, which act, either at the time of sentencing for the offense or subsequently during civil commitment proceedings pursuant
to chapter 71.09 RCW, has been determined
beyond a reasonable doubt to have been sexually motivated, as that term is defined in
RCW 9.94A.030; or (d) an act as described in
chapter 9A.28 RCW, that is an attempt, criminal solicitation, or criminal conspiracy to
commit one of the felonies designated in (a),
(b), or (c) of this subsection.

**71.09.025. Notice to prosecuting attorney
prior to release**

(1)(a) When it appears that a person may
meet the criteria of a sexually violent predator as defined in RCW 71.09.020(1), the
agency with jurisdiction shall refer the person in writing to the prosecuting attorney of
the county where that person was charged,
three months prior to:

(i) The anticipated release from total confinement of a person who has been convicted
of a sexually violent offense;

(ii) The anticipated release from total
confinement of a person found to have committed a sexually violent offense as a juvenile;

(iii) Release of a person who has been
charged with a sexually violent offense and
who has been determined to be incompetent
to stand trial pursuant to RCW 10.77.090(3);
or

(iv) Release of a person who has been
found not guilty by reason of insanity of a
sexually violent offense pursuant to RCW
10.77.020(3).

(b) The agency shall inform the prosecutor of the following:

(i) The person's name, identifying fac-

tors, anticipated future residence, and offense
history; and

(ii) Documentation of institutional adjustment and any treatment received.

(2) This section applies to acts committed
before, on, or after March 26, 1992.

(3) The agency, its employees, and officials shall be immune from liability for any
good-faith conduct under this section.

(4) As used in this section, "agency with
jurisdiction" means that agency with the
authority to direct the release of a person
serving a sentence or term of confinement
and includes the department of corrections,
the indeterminate sentence review board, and
the department of social and health services.

**71.09.030. Sexually violent predator
petition—Filing**

When it appears that: (1) The term of
total confinement of a person who has been
convicted of a sexually violent offense is
about to expire, or has expired on, before, or
after July 1, 1990; (2) the term of total confinement of a person found to have committed a sexually violent offense as a juvenile is
about to expire, or has expired on, before, or
after July 1, 1990; (3) a person who has been
charged with a sexually violent offense and
who has been determined to be incompetent
to stand trial is about to be released, or has
been released on, before, or after July 1,
1990, pursuant to RCW 10.77.090(3); or (4)
a person who has been found not guilty by
reason of insanity of a sexually violent
offense is about to be released, or has been
released on, before, or after July 1, 1990, pursuant to RCW 10.77.020(3); and it appears
that the person may be a sexually violent
predator, the prosecuting attorney of the
county where the person was convicted or
charged or the attorney general if requested
by the prosecuting attorney may file a petition alleging that the person is a "sexually
violent predator" and stating sufficient facts
to support such allegation.

**71.09.040. Sexually violent predator peti-
tion—Judicial determination—Transfer
for evaluation**

Upon the filing of a petition under RCW
71.09.030, the judge shall determine whether

probable cause exists to believe that the person named in the petition is a sexually violent predator. If such determination is made the judge shall direct that the person be taken into custody and the person shall be transferred to an appropriate facility for an evaluation as to whether the person is a sexually violent predator. The evaluation shall be conducted by a person deemed to be professionally qualified to conduct such an examination pursuant to rules developed by the department of social and health services. In adopting such rules, the department of social and health services shall consult with the department of health and the department of corrections.

71.09.050. Trial—Rights of parties

Within forty-five days after the filing of a petition pursuant to RCW 71.09.030, the court shall conduct a trial to determine whether the person is a sexually violent predator. At all stages of the proceedings under this chapter, any person subject to this chapter shall be entitled to the assistance of counsel, and if the person is indigent, the court shall appoint counsel to assist him or her. Whenever any person is subjected to an examination under this chapter, he or she may retain experts or professional persons to perform an examination on their behalf. When the person wishes to be examined by a qualified expert or professional person of his or her own choice, such examiner shall be permitted to have reasonable access to the person for the purpose of such examination, as well as to all relevant medical and psychologist records and reports. In the case of a person who is indigent, the court shall, upon the person's request, assist the person in obtaining an expert or professional person to perform an examination or participate in the trial on the person's behalf. The person, the prosecuting attorney or attorney general, or the judge shall have the right to demand that the trial be before a jury. If no demand is made, the trial shall be before the court.

71.09.060. Trial—Determination—Commitment procedures

(1) The court or jury shall determine whether, beyond a reasonable doubt, the person is a sexually violent predator. If the state alleges that the prior sexually violent offense that forms the basis for the petition for commitment was an act that was sexually motivated as provided in RCW 71.09.020(4)(c), the state must prove beyond a reasonable doubt that the alleged sexually violent act was sexually motivated as defined in RCW 9.94A.030. If the court or jury determines that the person is a sexually violent predator, the person shall be committed to the custody of the department of social and health services in a secure facility for control, care, and treatment until such time as the person's mental abnormality or personality disorder has so changed that the person is safe to be at large. Such control, care, and treatment shall be provided at a facility operated by the department of social and health services. If the court or jury is not satisfied beyond a reasonable doubt that the person is a sexually violent predator, the court shall direct the person's release.

(2) If the person charged with a sexually violent offense has been found incompetent to stand trial, and is about to or has been released pursuant to RCW 10.77.090(3), and his or her commitment is sought pursuant to subsection (1) of this section, the court shall first hear evidence and determine whether the person did commit the act or acts charged if the court did not enter a finding prior to dismissal under RCW 10.77.090(3) that the person committed the act or acts charged. The hearing on this issue must comply with all the procedures specified in this section. In addition, the rules of evidence applicable in criminal cases shall apply, and all constitutional rights available to defendants at criminal trials, other than the right not to be tried while incompetent, shall apply. After hearing evidence on this issue, the court shall make specific findings on whether the person did commit the act or acts charged, the extent to which the person's incompetence or developmental disability affected the outcome of the hearing, including its effect on the person's ability to consult with and assist counsel and to testify on his or her own behalf, the extent to which the evidence could be reconstructed without the assistance of the person, and the strength of the prosecution's case. If, after

the conclusion of the hearing on this issue, the court finds, beyond a reasonable doubt, that the person did commit the act or acts charged, it shall enter a final order, appealable by the person, on that issue, and may proceed to consider whether the person should be committed pursuant to this section.

(3) The state shall comply with RCW 10.77.220 while confining the person pursuant to this chapter. The facility shall not be located on the grounds of any state mental facility or regional habilitation center because these institutions are insufficiently secure for this population.

71.09.070. Annual examinations

Each person committed under this chapter shall have a current examination of his or her mental condition made at least once every year. The person may retain, or if he or she is indigent and so requests, the court may appoint a qualified expert or professional person to examine him or her, and such expert or professional person shall have access to all records concerning the person. The periodic report shall be provided to the court that committed the person under this chapter.

71.09.080. Detention and commitment to conform to constitutional requirements

The involuntary detention or commitment of persons under this chapter shall conform to constitutional requirements for care and treatment.

71.09.090. Petition for release— Procedures

(1) If the secretary of the department of social and health services determines that the person's mental abnormality or personality disorder has so changed that the person is not likely to engage in predatory acts of sexual violence if released, the secretary shall authorize the person to petition the court for release. The petition shall be served upon the court and the prosecuting attorney. The court, upon receipt of the petition for release, shall within forty-five days order a hearing. The prosecuting attorney or attorney general, if requested by the county, shall represent the state, and shall have the right to have the peti-

tioner examined by an expert or professional person of his or her choice. The hearing shall be before a jury if demanded by either the petitioner or the prosecuting attorney or attorney general. The burden of proof shall be upon the prosecuting attorney or attorney general to show beyond a reasonable doubt that the petitioner's mental abnormality or personality disorder remains such that the petitioner is not safe to be at large and that if discharged is likely to engage in predatory acts of sexual violence.

(2) Nothing contained in this chapter shall prohibit the person from otherwise petitioning the court for discharge without the secretary's approval. The secretary shall provide the committed person with an annual written notice of the person's right to petition the court for release over the secretary's objection. The notice shall contain a waiver of rights. The secretary shall forward the notice and waiver form to the court with the annual report. If the person does not affirmatively waive the right to petition, the court shall set a show cause hearing to determine whether facts exist that warrant a hearing on whether the person's condition has so changed that he or she is safe to be at large. The committed person shall have a right to have an attorney represent him or her at the show cause hearing but the person is not entitled to be present at the show cause hearing. If the court at the show cause hearing determines that probable cause exists to believe that the person's mental abnormality or personality disorder has so changed that the person is safe to be at large and is not likely to engage in predatory acts of sexual violence if discharged, then the court shall set a hearing on the issue. At the hearing, the committed person shall be entitled to be present and to the benefit of all constitutional protections that were afforded to the person at the initial commitment proceeding. The prosecuting attorney or the attorney general if requested by the county shall represent the state and shall have a right to a jury trial and to have the committed person evaluated by experts chosen by the state. The committed person shall also have the right to have experts evaluate him or her on his or her behalf and the court shall appoint an expert if the person is

indigent and requests an appointment. The burden of proof at the hearing shall be upon the state to prove beyond a reasonable doubt that the committed person's mental abnormality or personality disorder remains such that the person is not safe to be at large and if released is likely to engage in predatory acts of sexual violence.

71.09.100. Subsequent petitions

Nothing in this chapter shall prohibit a person from filing a petition for discharge pursuant to this chapter. However, if a person has previously filed a petition for discharge without the secretary's approval and the court determined, either upon review of the petition or following a hearing, that the petitioner's petition was frivolous or that the petitioner's condition had not so changed that he or she was safe to be at large, then the court shall deny the subsequent petition unless the petition contains facts upon which a court could find that the condition of the petitioner had so changed that a hearing was warranted. Upon receipt of a first or subsequent petition from committed persons without the secretary's approval, the court shall endeavor whenever possible to review the petition and determine if the petition is based upon frivolous grounds and if so shall deny the petition without a hearing.

71.09.110. Department of social and health services—Duties—Reimbursement

The department of social and health services shall be responsible for all costs relating to the evaluation and treatment of persons committed to their custody under any provision of this chapter. Reimbursement may be obtained by the department for the cost of care and treatment of persons committed to its custody pursuant to RCW 43.20B.330 through 43.20B.370.

Appendix J

Annotated Bibliography

Abel, G.G., Blanchard, E. B., and Becker, J.V. (1978). An integrated treatment program for rapists. In R. Rada (Ed.), *Clinical aspects of the rapist.* New York: Grune & Stratton.

A good rationale for the use of behavioral techniques to alter sexual arousal patterns. Also argues for a comprehensive approach to treatment with attention given to social skills and anger management.

Able, G.G., Becker, J.V., Murphy, W.D., and Flanagan, B. (1981). Identifying dangerous child molesters. In R. Stuart (Ed.) *Violent behaviors: Social learning approaches to prediction, management and treatment.* New York: Brunner/Mazel.

A practical and clear article on performing and analyzing physiological assessments.

Allen, C.M. (1991) *Women and men who sexually assault children: A comparative study.* Brandon, VT: The Safer Society Press.

An excellent research study using a highly representative sample which reveals interesting data about both male and female sex offenders.

Amir, M. (1971). *Patterns in forcible rape.* Chicago: University of Chicago Press.

An interesting sociological and criminological analysis of sexual assault. Statistics are now out of date, but analysis of "culture of violence" represents a relevant perspective.

Barbaree, H.E., Marshall, W.L., and Hudson, S.M. (Eds.) (1993) *The Juvenile Sex Offender.* New York: Guilford Press.

A highly useful guide to the treatment of this population.

The Revised Report from the National Task Force on Juvenile Sexual Offending, 1993 of the National Adolescent Perpetrators Network (1993). *Juvenile and Family Court Journal,* 44(4).

An invaluable resource that delineates standards for the care of juvenile sex offenders.

Barnard, G.W., Fuller, A.K., Robbins, L., and Shaw, T. (1989). *The child molester: An integrated approach to evaluation and treatment.* New York: Brunner/Mazel.

A comprehensive description of a Florida-based program which integrates a wide variety of treatments.

Barlow, D.H. (1974). The treatment of sexual deviation: Toward a comprehensive behavioral approach. In K.S. Calhoun, H.E. Adams and K.M. Mitchell (Eds.), *Innovative treatment methods in psychopathology.* New York: Wiley.

Introduces the idea that simply modifying sexual arousal is insufficient as a treatment approach to sexual aggression and diversity and stresses that other skill deficits, such as social skills deficits or impulse and anger control problems, must also be addressed.

Barlow, D.H., and Abel, G.G. (1981). Outlines developments in assessment and treatment of paraphilias and gender identity disorder. In W.E. Craighead, A.E. Kazdin and M.J. Mahoney (Eds.), *Behavior modification: Principles, issues and applications* (2d ed.). Boston: Houghton Mifflin.

Another rationale for and overview of behavioral assessment and treatment procedures.

Brownell, K.D., Hayes, S.C., and Barlow, D.H. (1977). Patterns of appropriate and deviant sexual arousal: The behavioral treatment of multiple sexual deviations. *Journal of Consulting and Clinical Psychology*, 45, 1144-1155.

A case study of the use of behavioral procedures to modify multiple sexual deviations in a single individual.

Brownmiller, S. (1975). *Against our will: Men, women and rape*. New York: Simon and Schuster.

A provocative view of sexual assault based on a radical feminist perspective.

Burgess, A., and Holmstrom, L. (1974). *Rape: Victims of crisis*. Bowie, MD: Robert J. Brady Co.

Summation of views of authors who were among the first to focus professional attention on the rape victim and her treatment.

Carnes, P. (1983). *Out of the shadows*. Minneapolis, MN: CompCare Publications.

A compelling description of the phenomenology of the sexual offender. Men who have sexually abused others consider the depiction of the compulsive aspect of sexual offenses contained in this book to be an accurate portrayal of their experience.

Chaney, E.F., O'Leary, M.R., and Marlatt, G.A. (1978). Skill training with alcoholics. *J. Consulting and Clinical Psychology*, 46:1092-1104.

This publication introduces an assessment technique known as the Situational Competency Test, initially used to evaluate coping skills of substance abusers. It has been revised for use with sex offenders, and it appears to those using the Relapse Prevention theory that response latency, blocking, and elaboration details may be related to an increased likelihood of relapse.

Conrad, S.R., and Wincze, J.P. (1976). Orgasmic reconditioning: A controlled study of its effect upon the sexual arousal of adult male homosexuals. *Behavior Therapy*, 7, 155-166.

A well controlled outcome study of the effects of orgasmic reconditioning in which the authors conclude that, by itself, the procedure is suspect.

Cook, M., and Howell, K. (1981). *Adult sexual interests in children*. London: Academic Press.

Interesting overview of pedophilia which includes articles on theory, treatment and sociological implications.

Finkelhor, D. (1984). *Child sexual abuse: New theory and research*. New York: The Free Press, a division of MacMillan, Inc.

Highly readable report of his theory.

Foote, W.E., and Laws, D. R. (1981). A daily alteration procedure for orgasmic reconditioning with a pedophile. *Journal of Behavioral Therapy and Experimental Psychiatry*, 12, 267-273.

A good description of the fantasy alteration procedure for altering sexual arousal.

Fortune, M. (1983). *Sexual violence*. New York: Pilgrims.

An outstanding analysis from a pastoral counseling perspective. Includes theory and suggestions for counseling victims, families and offenders.

Freeman-Longo, R., and Wall, R. (1986). Changing a lifetime of sexual crime. *Psychology Today*. 20:58-62.

Describes therapeutic interventions that are employed in a sex offender treatment program at Oregon State Hospital. The efficacy of therapy in diminishing the relapse rates of sexual offenders is discussed.

Freud, S. (1919). A child is being beaten: A contribution to the study of the origin of sexual perversions. In S. Freud (Ed.) *Collected papers, Vol.2*. London: International Universities Press.

Historically interesting psychoanalytic study.

Gebhard, P., Gangnon, J., Pomeroy, W., and Christenson, C. (1964). *Sex offenders: An analysis of types*. New York: Harper & Row.

Historically interesting analysis of typologies.

Gil, E. (1983). *Outgrowing the pain*. Walnut Creek, CA: Launch Press.

A book for and about adults abused as children. Easy reading materials, appropriate for offenders to read.

Greer, J. (1983). *The sexual aggressor*. New York: Van Nostrand & Rhinehold.

Extremely interesting collection of articles focused on therapeutic interventions with highly specific directions on setting up and conducting physiological assessments.

Groth, A.N. (1979). *Men who rape: The psychology of an offender*. New York:Plenum Press.

The classic refutation of rape as a purely sexual crime.

Guttmacher, M.S. (1951). *Sexual offenses: Problem, causes and prevention*. New York: Norton.

Historically interesting text.

Haaven, J., Little, R., and Petre-Miller, D. (1990) *Treating Intellectually Disabled Sex Offenders: A Model Residential Program*. Brandon, VT.: The Safer Society Press.

A concise description of the exceptionally creative treatment program for developmentally disabled sex offenders at the Oregon State Hospital.

Karpman, B. (1954). *The sexual offender and his offenses: Etiology, pathology and treatment*. New York: Julian Press.

A radical book for its time in terms of advocating treatment. Includes a useful, lengthy social history interview.

Kelly, R.J. (1982). Behavioral reorientation of pedophiliacs: Can it be done? *Clinical Psychology Review*, 2(3), 287-408.

A review of 32 studies since 1960 using a variety of behavioral procedures to alter sexual arousal in pedophiles which concludes that, despite some methodological issues, behavioral procedures seem to be effective.

Kilman, P.R., Sabalis, R.F., Gearing, M.L., Bukstel, L.H., and Scovern, A.W. (1982). The treatment of paraphilias: *A review of the outcome research. Journal of Sex Research*, 18(3), 193-252.

A methodological evaluation of studies involving the treatment of multiple and singular sexual paraphilias in which issues in treatment planning are discussed.

Knopp, F.H. (1984). *Retraining adult sex offenders: Models and methods*. Syracuse: Safer Society Press.

An extremely useful review of model treatment programs. The index contains a collection of forms and treatment suggestions which are invaluable to the clinician.

Langevin, R. (1983). *Sexual strands: Understanding and treating sexual anomalies in men*. Hillsdale, NJ: Lawrence Erlbaum Associates.

Highly documented analysis of the men who engage in sexual abuse, and excellent reference for anyone who wishes to gain greater understanding of men who abuse.

Lanyon, R.I. (1986). Theory and treatment in child molestation. *Journal of Consulting and Clinical Psychology*, 54(2), 176-182.

Review of theory and treatment in child molestation that revises Groth's fixated-regressed typology.

Laws, D.R., and O'Neal, J.A. (1981). Variations on masturbatory conditioning. *Behavioral Psychotherapy*, 9, 111-136.

Reviews orgasmic reconditioning literature and suggests alternatives, including the daily fantasy alteration method.

Laws, D.R., Meyer, J., and Holmen, M.L. (1978). Reduction of sadistic sexual arousal by olfactory aversion: A case study. *Behavior Research and Therapy*, 16, 281-285.

A case study showing the effects of olfactory aversion to reduce sadistic sexual fantasies.

Laws, D.R. (1989). *Relapse prevention for sex offenders*. New York: Guilford Press.

A basic handbook in the area of relapse prevention.

Maletzsky, B.M. (1974). "Assisted" covert sensitization in the treatment of exhibitionism. *Journal of Consulting and Clinical Psychology, 42*, 34-40.

Introduces the rationale and procedures of assisted covert sensitization.

Maletzky, B. (1991). *Treating the sexual offender*. Newbury Park, CA: Sage Publications.

An excellent work on behavioral techniques.

Marlatt, G.A., and Gordon, J. (1980). Determinants of relapse: Implications for the maintenance of change. In P.O. Davidson and S.M. Davidson (Eds.) *Behavioral medicine: Changing health lifestyles*. New York: Brunner/Mazel.

Discussion of factors that precipitate re-offenses in a variety of compulsive behavioral disorders. On the basis of the identified risk factors, appropriate treatment interventions are proposed.

Marlatt, G.A. and Gordon, J.R. (1985). *Relapse Prevention*. New York: Guilford Press.

This comprehensive work concerning Relapse Prevention presents the theoretical basis of Marlatt and Gordon's model for maintaining behavioral change. Assessment and treatment techniques are covered generally, and specific chapters are dedicated to behavioral disorders such as alcohol, overeating, and gambling.

Marshall, W.L., Laws, D.R., and Barbaree, H.E. (Eds) (1990). *Handbook of sexual assault: Issues, theories, and treatment of the offender*. New York: Plenum Press.

Excellent overview of the cognitive behavioral model.

Marshall, W.L. (1979). Satiation therapy: A procedure for reducing deviant sexual arousal. *Journal of Applied Behavior Analysis*, 12, 10-22.

Introduces and describes the rationale and procedures for masturbatory satiation therapy.

Mathews, R., Matthews, J.K., and Speltz, K. (1989) *Female sexual offenders*. Brandon, VT: The Safer Society Press.

A pioneering work on female sex offenders written be therapist who have researched their patient population.

Ostrow, M. (1974). *Sexual deviation: Psychoanalytic insights*. New York: New York Times Book Co.

Theoretically interesting work which updates the psychoanalytic approach.

Paitich, D., Langevin, R., Freeman, R., Mann, K., and Handy, L. (1977). The Clarke SHQ: A clinical sex history questionnaire for males. *Archives of Sexual Behavior*. 6:421-436.

Announces the creation of a questionnaire intended to assist clinicians and researchers in gaining comprehensive histories of men who have engaged in sexual abuse. The complete Clarke Sexual History Questionnaire is contained in Langevin (1983), cited previously.

Pithers, W.D., Marques, J.K., Gibat, C.C., and Marlatt, G.A. (1983) Relapse Prevention with sexual aggressives: A self-control model of treatment and maintenance of change. In J.G. Greer and I.R. Stuart (Eds.), *The sexual aggressor: Current perspectives on treatment*. New York: Van Nostrand Reinhold.

Presents the first comprehensive coverage of the modification of Relapse Prevention for sexual offenders.

Prendergast, W.E. (1991) *Treating sex offenders in correctional institutions and outpatient clinics: A guide to clinical practice*. New York: The Haworth Press.

Interesting description of the work and treatment techniques developed by a pioneering sex offender specialist.

Prentky, R.A. and Burgess, A.W. (1991). Hypothetical biological substrates of a fantasy-based drive mechanism for repetitive sexual aggression. In A.W. Burgess (Ed.) *Rape and sexual assault III* (pp. 235-256). New york: Garland.

Article presents an interesting theory of the interplay between physiological correlates and sexual assault.

Prentky, R.A. and Quinsey, V.L. (1988) *Human sexual aggression: Current perspectives.* New York: The New York Academy of Sciences.

Overview of the outstanding research on typologies conducted at the Massachusetts Treatment Center.

Quinsey, V.L., and Marshall, W.L. (1983). Procedures for reducing inappropriate sexual arousal. In J.G. Geer and I.R. Stuart (Eds), *The sexual aggressor: Current perspectives on treatment.* New York: Van Nostrand Reinhold.

An excellent review of a variety of procedures for treating the sex offender. Deals with the issues in practical as well as theoretical terms.

Salter, A.C. (1988). *Treating child sex offenders and victims: A practical guide.* Newbury Park, CA: Sage Publications.

An interesting review of sex offender treatment techniques. Appendix includes a wide variety of reproducible tests.

Schrenck-Notzing, A. (1895) *The use of hypnosis in psychopathia sexualis.* New York: Institute for Research in Hypnosis Publication Society and Julian Press.

Probably the first article published on treating the paraphiliac.

Stoller, R.J. (1975). *Perversion: The erotic form of hatred.* New York: Random House.

An interesting Jungian analysis of the problem.

Yochelson, S., and Samenow, S. (1976). *The criminal personality. Vol. 1: A profile for change.* New York: Jason Aronson.

Introduces an approach to the treatment of individuals who engage in repetitive criminal acts. Rather than blaming sociological or familial factors, authors propose that criminals engage in "thinking errors" that enable them to justify abuse of others. Primary thinking errors of criminals are then delineated. Methods for assisting offenders in altering their thinking patterns are briefly discussed.

Index

[References are to pages.]

[References are to pages.]

[References are to pages.]

[References are to pages.]

[References are to pages.]

[References are to pages.]

[References are to pages.]

[References are to pages.]

[References are to pages.]

[References are to pages.]

[References are to pages.]

[References are to pages.]